Quantitative Business Methods using Lotus 1-2-3

Quantitative Business Methods using Lotus 1-2-3

David Whigham
Glasgow Polytechnic

Prentice Hall
New York   London   Toronto   Sydney   Tokyo   Singapore

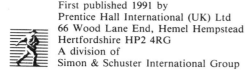

First published 1991 by
Prentice Hall International (UK) Ltd
66 Wood Lane End, Hemel Hempstead
Hertfordshire HP2 4RG
A division of
Simon & Schuster International Group

© Prentice Hall International (UK) Ltd, 1991

All rights reserved. No part of this publication may be
reproduced, stored in a retrieval system, or transmitted,
in any form, or by any means, electronic, mechanical,
photocopying, recording or otherwise, without prior
permission, in writing, from the publisher.
For permission within the United States of America
contact Prentice Hall Inc., Englewood Cliffs, NJ 07632.

Printed and bound in Great Britain
by Page Bros, Norwich

Library of Congress Cataloging-in-Publication Data

Whigham, David, 1949–
   Quantitative business methods using Lotus 1-2-3 / David Whigham.
     p. cm.
   Includes bibliographical references and index.
   ISBN 0-13-747288-9
    1. Business mathematics – Computer programs. 2. Lotus 1-2-3
(Computer program) I. Title.
HF5691.W47   1991
650'.0285'5369 – dc20   90-22081

British Library Cataloguing in Publication Data

Whigham, David *1949–*
   Quantitative business methods using Lotus 1-2-3.
   1. Microcomputer systems. Spreadsheet packages : Lotus 123
   I. Title
   005.369

   ISBN 0–13–747288–9

1 2 3 4 5   95 94 93 92 91

'Lotus' and '1-2-3' are registered trademarks of the Lotus Development
Corporation.

Contents

Preface   xi

Introduction: How to use this text   xiii

1   **The Lotus 1-2-3 Spreadsheet**   1

     1.1   Introduction   1
     1.2   Preliminaries   2
     1.3   The initial screen   4
     1.4   Data entry   6
     1.5   Function keys   8
     1.6   Using formulae   9
     1.7   Menu commands   12
         1.7.1   Relative copying
         1.7.2   Absolute copying
         1.7.3   Erasing the contents of cells
         1.7.4   Altering the column width
         1.7.5   Inserting rows or columns
         1.7.6   Deleting rows or columns
         1.7.7   Naming a range
     1.8   The Lotus @ functions   20
         1.8.1   Functions that take numerical or single-cell address arguments
         1.8.2   Functions that take a range of cell address arguments
         1.8.3   Functions that take more than one argument
         1.8.4   Using more than one function at a time
     1.9   Quitting, saving and retrieving   23
         1.9.1   Saving a worksheet file
         1.9.2   Erasing and then retrieving the current worksheet
     1.10   The Lotus graphics facility   24
     1.11   Exercises   28

2 Principles of Algebraic Modelling — 31

- 2.1 The need for algebra — 31
- 2.2 Elements of spreadsheet modelling — 32
- 2.3 The algebra of indices — 40
- 2.4 Functions and equations — 46
  - 2.4.1 Functional notation and operations
  - 2.4.2 Solution of equations
- 2.5 Linear functions — 60
- 2.6 Quadratic functions — 74
- 2.7 Hyperbolic functions — 81
- 2.8 Logarithmic functions — 86
- 2.9 Exponential functions — 90
- 2.10 Algebraic series — 95
  - 2.10.1 Arithmetic series
  - 2.10.2 Geometric series
  - 2.10.3 Infinite geometric series
- 2.11 Exercises — 116
- 2.12 Solutions to the exercises — 119

3 Financial Mathematics — 130

- 3.1 Introduction — 130
- 3.2 Simple interest — 132
- 3.3 Compound interest — 136
- 3.4 Fractional years — 142
- 3.5 Annuities — 144
- 3.6 Sinking funds — 148
- 3.7 Reducing balance debts — 155
- 3.8 Variations in the compounding period — 160
- 3.9 Continuous compounding — 164
- 3.10 The equivalent annual rate — 166
- 3.11 Growth rate calculations — 167
- 3.12 Exercises — 171
- 3.13 Solutions to the exercises — 173

4 Discounting Techniques — 181

- 4.1 Present value — 181
- 4.2 Discounting multiple receipts — 185
- 4.3 Variations in the discounting period — 190
- 4.4 Asset depreciation — 193
- 4.5 Investment appraisal — 195
- 4.6 The internal rate of return — 201
- 4.7 The annual percentage rate — 203

	4.8	Financial security appraisal	206
	4.9	The financial arithmetic of inflation	209
	4.10	Exercises	211
	4.11	Solutions to the exercises	215
5	**Linear Programming I**		**226**
	5.1	Principles of linear programming	226
	5.2	Graphical solution methods	231
	5.3	Using Lotus to solve linear programs	236
	5.4	Changes in the coefficients of the objective function	240
	5.5	Minimization	246
	5.6	Duality	250
	5.7	Linear programming with a choice of production techniques	253
	5.8	Exercises	261
	5.9	Solutions to the exercises	263
6	**Matrix Algebra**		**278**
	6.1	Preliminaries	278
	6.2	Special types of matrix	280
		6.2.1 The identity matrix	
		6.2.2 The null matrix	
	6.3	Matrix addition and subtraction	281
	6.4	Matrix multiplication	283
	6.5	Inverting a matrix	288
	6.6	Using matrix algebra to solve sets of linear equations	289
	6.7	Input–output analysis	290
	6.8	Exercises	294
	6.9	Solutions to the exercises	296
7	**Linear Programming II**		**303**
	7.1	The simplex algorithm	303
	7.2	The LINPRO program	305
	7.3	The final tableau used for sensitivity analysis	311
	7.4	Changes in the coefficients of the objective function	314
	7.5	Exercises	316
	7.6	Solutions to the exercises	321
8	**Principles of Differential Calculus**		**338**
	8.1	Differential rates of change	338
	8.2	The derivative as a measure of the gradient of a function	346
	8.3	Identifying stationary points in a function	350

	8.4	Some further rules of differentiation	364
		8.4.1 The chain rule	
		8.4.2 The product rule	
	8.5	The derivative of the exponential function	372
	8.6	Inventory control	380
	8.7	Exercises	383
	8.8	Solutions to the exercises	386
9	**Introductory Statistical Analysis**		**397**
	9.1	Preliminaries	397
		9.1.1 Data collection	
		9.1.2 Data collation	
		9.1.3 Visual portrayal of the data	
		9.1.4 Summary characterizations	
		9.1.5 Drawing conclusions	
	9.2	Collating the data	399
	9.3	Pictorial representation of data sets	408
	9.4	Measures of central tendency in simple data sets	412
		9.4.1 The arithmetic mean	
		9.4.2 The mode	
		9.4.3 The median	
		9.4.4 The geometric mean	
		9.4.5 The harmonic mean	
	9.5	Measures of central tendency in collated data sets	420
	9.6	Measures of dispersion in simple data sets	424
	9.7	Z scores	429
	9.8	Measures of dispersion in collated data sets	433
	9.9	Index numbers	435
	9.10	Exercises	439
	9.11	Solutions to the exercises	443
10	**Linear Regression and Business Forecasting**		**456**
	10.1	Introduction	456
	10.2	The problem	456
	10.3	The model	457
	10.4	The data	459
	10.5	The scatter diagram	461
	10.6	The 'least squares' regression equation	462
	10.7	Linear regression using Lotus 1-2-3	465
	10.8	Understanding the results	468
	10.9	Sampling variation in the values of the regression coefficients	472
	10.10	Association versus causation	480
	10.11	Nonlinear models transformed into linear ones	480

	10.12	Rank correlation	485
	10.13	Time series analysis	488
	10.14	A case example	496
	10.15	Discussion and solutions	497
	10.16	Exercises	505
	10.17	Solutions to the exercises	509
11	**Principles of Probability and Decision Making**		**518**
	11.1	Uncertainty and probability	518
	11.2	Principles of probability analysis	518
	11.3	Probabilities for more complex events	521
	11.4	Expected values	533
	11.5	Conditional probabilities	537
	11.6	Simulating random behaviour on Lotus	546
	11.7	Markov chains	558
	11.8	The binomial distribution	566
	11.9	The Poisson distribution	571
	11.10	The normal distribution	577
	11.11	Exercises	586
	11.12	Solutions to the exercises	588

Appendix 595

Index 599

*To Kate, Lisa and Sara,
for being there.*

Preface

The purpose of this text is to provide first- and second-year students in the general area of business studies and accountancy with an approach to quantitative analysis that uses the Lotus 1-2-3 spreadsheet as the predominant teaching vehicle. It is hoped that the logic of such a spreadsheet approach to quantitative problems will allow various aspects of business analysis to be presented in a manner that does not require as much formal mathematical training as would otherwise be the case.

In the light of this objective, the text is designed to be easily accessible to those increasing numbers of students who possess the minimum amount of numerical skills required for entry to business studies/accountancy degree or HND qualifications.

As a result of this moderate level of access requirement, the text contains a corresponding emphasis on directing the explanation of the topics considered towards those students who have always found quantitative analysis difficult, when presented in the formal manner.

The spreadsheet medium is invaluable here, since some of the required formality can be derived from the spreadsheet structure itself. In this sense, it acts as a useful template in assisting the design, presentation and analysis of various business problems.

All of the topics that normally constitute the quantitative techniques modules of the first year on a BA or HND in business studies or accountancy are included in the text. In addition, however, it will be found that many topics contained in several related courses, such as business analysis, business economics or computer information technology applications, are also covered to a varying degree. For this reason, it is expected that there will be a number of courses, at a variety of levels, which can benefit from the instruction provided.

At base, however, this book is designed for those students who found school mathematics unintelligible, abstract and without any clearly identified purpose, yet who now find themselves on 'business' courses containing curricula that require a considerable amount of numerical analysis. By using the spreadsheet to explain and clarify those mathematical and statistical concepts that frequently cause difficulties, and by continually relating these concepts to business problem solving, it is hoped that these students will achieve a level of quantitative skill which would otherwise be unattainable with more conventional approaches.

In short, the approach adopted by this book is that with their ever-increasing availability and user friendliness, spreadsheets are being used by more and more business practitioners to solve their quantitative problems. As a result, in much the same way as the electronic calculator has become a standard aid to calculation, the spreadsheet medium must become an integral part of the means by which elementary quantitative analysis is explained and learned.

David Whigham
Glasgow Polytechnic
1991

Introduction: How to use this text

Since the essential approach of this book uses a spreadsheet to explain quantitative business methods, this clearly means that to obtain the greatest benefit from some of the instruction you will have to gain access to a computer on which Lotus 1-2-3 or one of its many clones has been installed.

However, since most of the spreadsheet output has also been reproduced in the text, the learning process need not be exclusively computer based. You can read and digest the ideas and principles explained without a computer, and then apply them once you are seated in front of one.

You will also find that in the first instance it is a good idea to make up the exhibited worksheets for yourself, especially if you are a spreadsheet novice. But as the size and complexity of these worksheets increases it will sometimes become wasteful of valuable computer access time to continue to do this.

For this reason a disk containing many of the more difficult exhibited worksheets and exercise solutions is available from the author (at a nominal charge of £1 to cover disk and distribution costs).

To receive this disc contact:

David Whigham
Department of Economics
Glasgow Polytechnic
Glasgow G4 0BA
Tel: (041) 331 3307

and remember to state the required size of disk (3.5 or 5.25 in.).

This disk will allow you to proceed through the text at a much faster pace, and to make changes that result from tutorial discussion, etc.

You should always attempt the exercises on your own at first (after deciding whether one of the prepared worksheets is appropriate to the question posed) and then consult the solutions which accompany each set of exercises. These solutions are fully documented and some also contain additional instructions, so you should always consult them even if you feel confident that your own solution is correct.

Finally, although every effort has been made to ensure that solutions and cell references, etc., are correct, in a text of this size and complexity there are bound to be arithmetic slips which have escaped the correction process. The author feels confident that none of these will affect the principles and methods being explained, but would nevertheless welcome any information about their nature and occurrence.

1
The Lotus 1-2-3 Spreadsheet

1.1 Introduction

With the demand for personal computing facilities continuing to rise, there has been a corresponding increase in the demand for software programs to run on these personal computers. As a result, along with wordprocessing and database facilities, spreadsheet packages have become more and more widespread in all types of business endeavour. This means that any student of business must become familiar with spreadsheet capabilities as early as possible. Indeed, knowledge of a spreadsheet package can be likened in importance to the required familiarity with electronic calculators that is taken as given by most employers.

However, although in one sense a spreadsheet is no more than an extremely sophisticated calculator, there is another sense in which it is much more than that. This is because all spreadsheet packages have the ability to perform algebraic as well as arithmetic calculations.

By this we mean that, although, for example, a spreadsheet can easily tell you the result of multiplying 6 by 8 (as can a calculator), the spreadsheet can also be instructed to tell you the result of multiplying whatever the first number is by whatever the second number is.

The ability to specify the mathematical operation to be performed, in advance, and only once, and then obtain the correct result regardless of the values adopted by the numbers is one of the most important distinguishing characteristics of all spreadsheet packages. It is a *programming* facility which uses algebraic rather than arithmetic principles, since the latter require that the numbers be specified (1, 3, 5, etc.), while the former allow numbers to be represented *abstractly* by symbols, and then defines what is to be done to the numbers in terms of these symbols.

The traditional symbols employed by algebra are, of course, x and y, a, b and c, etc., but there is no reason to adhere religiously to these. The crucial notion is 'whatever the first number is', 'whatever the second number is', etc., and, although, as you will soon see, a spreadsheet does not use x and y to represent these numbers, it does not deviate from this crucial notion in any way.

Another distinguishing feature of all spreadsheet packages is the ability to replicate text, numbers and algebraic formulae. By this we mean that a formula, for example, that is to apply to a certain set of numbers need not be retyped in order to apply to a different set of numbers somewhere else in the spreadsheet. It can be replicated, i.e. copied, electronically, so that the formula can relate to all those parts of the spreadsheet that require to make use of it. More will be said on this at a later stage in the discussion, but it should already be apparent that, in conjunction with its algebraic capability, this replicating facility puts a spreadsheet on a different computational plane from even the most sophisticated of calculators. In short, a spreadsheet can be (under)used as a calculator, but a calculator cannot be used as a spreadsheet.

The spreadsheet that we will be using in this text is Lotus 1-2-3, since it is by far the most widely available package. If you do not have access to Lotus 1-2-3, then you can also use the spreadsheet component of the package known as Integrated Seven (I7). This is what is known as a 'Lotus clone', meaning that all of the subsequent documentation can be used interchangeably between the two packages.

If you only have access to another spreadsheet package (Supercalc, Multiplan or Expresscalc, for example), then you can still benefit from many aspects of this text, since much of the discussion of quantitative methods is not package specific. However, where Lotus 1-2-3 is used to enhance and develop this discussion you will have to translate the instructions into a form that is germane to your own spreadsheet package. This obviously requires that you already possess an understanding of that package, since only Lotus 1-2-3 commands are explained in this text, but this being the case you can then use your own spreadsheet to follow the text.

Before we proceed however, it should be made absolutely clear that this text is in no way to be regarded as a Lotus 1-2-3 reference manual. Although some instruction will be provided, and many commands and special functions will be explained, only those elements of Lotus that are relevant to the quantitative methods component of the text will be fully documented. If you require further instruction, then there are lots of Lotus manuals available, and there is also a sophisticated 'help' facility contained within Lotus itself.

1.2 Preliminaries

The Lotus spreadsheet is simply a table or matrix consisting of identifiable cells into which data and/or text entries can be made. Conventionally, the columns of the spreadsheet are identified by letters:

$$(A, B, C, \ldots Z, AA, AB, \ldots AZ, BA, BB \ldots \text{etc.})$$

while the rows are numbered:

$$(1, 2, 3, 4, \text{etc.})$$

Using this notation, it therefore follows that the cell in the 5th column and the 8th row of the spreadsheet would be addressed as E8. This letter–number coordinate is known as the *cell address* and provides a unique identity for every cell in the spreadsheet.

However, if a spreadsheet could only refer to a single cell then it would be little more than a sophisticated calculator. It is the ability to refer to a range of cells that gives a spreadsheet its real computational power. Under Lotus a range of cells can be referred to by visualizing the range as a block and then typing the top left cell address in the block followed by two full stops and then the bottom right cell address in the block. This means that a range can be any one of the following:

1. A single cell (e.g. A1..A1).
2. A portion of a single row (e.g. A1..G1).
3. A portion of a single column (e.g. A1..A50).
4. A block of cells spanning both rows and columns (e.g. A1..G50).
5. Any of the above that have been *named* by you as a named range. For example, it is an easy matter to name the range of cells between, say, A1 and A50 as DATA. Once this has been done, Lotus understands that every time, thereafter, when you refer it to the range called DATA it is to read the contents of the cells between A1 and A50. As you will see later, naming a range is a very useful and powerful device that can reduce considerably the amount of time required to process information.

To see for yourself the way these ideas work you should now load the Lotus spreadsheet into your computer. This can be done in a variety of ways depending upon the computing facilities you are using, but normally you will select Lotus (or I7) from the menu provided on most computers of the teaching institutions.

Once you have done this you will find yourself either in the spreadsheet itself or in what is known as the Lotus Access System. In the former case you are ready to begin, but in the latter you must select 1-2-3 from the menu that has appeared at the top of the screen. This menu will always have the first option highlighted and will have a brief explanation of its function in the line below.

To move between the various options use the cursor keys, i.e. the arrow keys located on the righthand side of your keyboard, and you will see that the highlight will move to the next option. Notice also that the menu line effectively wraps around the screen, i.e. if you highlight '1-2-3' and then press left arrow you will be taken to 'Exit', which is the last option in the menu list. This 'wraparound' feature is common to all of the Lotus menus, and can frequently save a considerable amount of time.

Once you have decided which option you want to be carried out there are two ways of telling Lotus to do this. Either you can point to the desired option so that it is highlighted and then press the return key (↵), or you can press the key corresponding to the first letter of the menu option required. In both cases the desired option will be invoked, i.e. carried out. Like the wraparound feature mentioned above, these two methods of invoking a menu option are also common to all Lotus menus.

Using whichever method you prefer you should now select the '1-2-3' option, and locate yourself in the spreadsheet.

Are you in the Lotus spreadsheet? If so, proceed. If not, repeat the steps outlined above and/or check that Lotus or I7 is installed on the machine that you are using.

1.3 The initial screen

The screen now displayed is the worksheet of the Lotus spreadsheet which is defined by, and is operational within, the border of numbers and letters. The top lefthand cell of the worksheet (A1) will be highlighted and this is known as the *cursor location*. Above the worksheet area is a control panel area that provides important status information, and you will see that the current cell address (i.e. the cell in which the cursor is currently located) is displayed there.

Below the worksheet additional useful information will be displayed, but at this stage it is enough to note that the current date and time are displayed in the bottom lefthand corner of the screen.

You will also see that 'READY' is displayed in an indicator panel at the top righthand corner, thereby informing you that the worksheet is ready to accept information from you via the keyboard. For that reason this situation is often referred to as INPUT MODE. *Only* if 'READY' is displayed can information be typed into the worksheet.

There are, however, a number of other forms that this indicator can adopt. The most important of these are the following:

1. MENU – when one of the Lotus menus has been invoked.
2. HELP – when a help screen has been requested.
3. WAIT – when Lotus is in the process of calculation and cannot accept any further instructions. Do not touch the keyboard if this indicator is showing.
4. EDIT – when the contents of a cell are being altered (edited).
5. ERROR – when an error has occurred. Usually this will have occurred because you tried to enter an illegal formula or function.
6. VALUE – when a number or formula is being entered.
7. LABEL – when text (known by Lotus as a label) is being entered.
8. POINT – when a range of cells in the worksheet is being pointed to with the cursor keys.

Some of these indicators refer to later stages of this text, so at the moment you should merely bear them in mind for future reference.

Making sure that you are still located in the worksheet and that READY is displayed, you are now in a position to start moving the cursor around the worksheet. This is done via the cursor keys, which cause the highlighted cell to move one column to the left (right) every time the left (right) arrow is pressed; or one row up (down) every time the up (down) arrow is pressed. As long as READY is still showing, anything that is typed at the keyboard will be returned to whatever cell is highlighted after you press the return (↵) key. This is the standard method of data entry.

However, as you can easily imagine, moving around such a large worksheet one row or column at a time can become very tedious. For this reason there are a number of 'large' movement keys which make life a lot easier. Each time one of these keys is pressed, the following cursor movement takes place:

1. PgUp – moves up one screen page at a time.
2. PgDn – moves down one screen page at a time.
3. Tab (⇆) – moves one screen page to the right at a time.
4. Shift (↑) and Tab together – moves one screen page to the left at a time.
5. Home – moves the cursor to A1.

Have you still got the worksheet on the screen and are you still in READY mode? If so, practise using these keys to move around the worksheet.

If not, keep pressing the Escape key (Esc) until you return to the worksheet and then practise using these movement keys.

In addition to these movement keys, there are a few further keys that require explanation at this stage:

1. Return (↵) This is probably the key that you will use most often, since it is the only method of sending information from the keyboard to the spreadsheet. Remember that anything you type from the keyboard is in 'limbo' (i.e. not received by the computer) until you press the return key. Furthermore, as you have seen above, the return key is struck to invoke whatever menu option is currently highlighted.
2. Escape (Esc) Almost as important as the return key, the Escape key 'undoes' whatever was done previously and thereby allows you to rectify mistakes. It is also used to take you from the main menu to the worksheet, or from a submenu to the main menu. Basically, you press it as many times as is needed to take you back to where you started (i.e. in the worksheet with READY showing).
3. Backslash (/) This key is the method of leaving input mode and entering menu mode whereby the first of Lotus's many menus can be used. Remember that any spreadsheet has two basic modes – input and menu. The first is used to enter information to the worksheet while the second is used to allow you to take advantage of the many preprogrammed facilities (commands) that the

spreadsheet possesses. Backslash takes you from input mode to the first command menu, while Escape takes you from the first command menu back to input mode. Bear these two modes in mind and you will never get lost.

Have you still got the worksheet on the screen and are you still in READY mode? If so, practice using these keys to move between input mode and menu mode. You will see the main command menu appear in the control panel at the top of the screen, i.e. (Worksheet Range Copy Move File Print Graph Data System Quit).

If not, keep pressing the Escape key (Esc) until you return to the worksheet with READY showing and then practice using these keys.

1.4 Data entry

We will now show you how to enter information into any specified cell of the worksheet. The procedure (after ensuring that you are in input mode with READY showing) is simply to use the cursor keys to position the cursor over the cell into which you want to make an entry. Now type the desired entry (it will appear at the top of the screen as you are typing), and when you have finished press the return key. The entry will be made in the appropriate cell.

If you now find that you have made a mistake in your typing then you can correct it by using the EDIT function key. These function keys (F1, F2, ..., F10) are located either on the lefthand side or at the top of the keyboard, and each one performs a special function. The EDIT function key in Lotus is F2, and after pressing it you will find that the contents of the cell *that is currently highlighted* will appear at the top of the screen along with a cursor. You are now in EDIT mode and can use the arrow keys to position the cursor over the characters that are to be altered. Once you have done this there are three further keys that allow alterations to be made:

1. Backspace (← Del)   This key deletes whatever character is *immediately prior* to the cursor when you are entering or editing data.
2. Delete (Del)   This key (on the numeric keypad) is similar to backspace except that it deletes whatever character is *directly below* the cursor. Once again it only works when you are entering or editing data.
3. INSERT (Ins)   Also located on the numeric pad, this key allows you to insert a character *immediately prior* to the cursor location.

Are you still in input mode with READY showing? If not, press the Escape key until you are.

Now type the following into the specified cells:

in A1	INKOMF	
in A2	1000	
in B1	SPUNDING	
in B2	800	
in C1	SLURLPUS	
in C2	1000−800	

Now use the edit key to correct the spelling mistakes and to change your spending to 805.

Once you have done this does your edited spreadsheet look all right? Probably not, since it still shows a surplus of 200 instead of 195 as it should do. The reason for this is that you have put an *arithmetic* expression in C2 which will always produce 200 regardless of the values in A2 and B2. Obviously we require some algebraic formula that will always produce the correct result no matter what is contained in the A2 and B2 cells. But how do we do this? Keep your worksheet as it is and read on.

The way that Lotus works is that depending upon what you have returned from the keyboard, either the entry *itself* will be made in the appropriate cell, or the *result of the calculation requested* will be placed there.

To understand this last point you must realize that as far as Lotus is concerned, a cell entry can either be textual (such as INCOME) in which case LABEL is indicated, or numerical (in which case VALUE is indicated).

These numerical entries can be any of the following:

1. A number (such as 1000 or 800).
2. An arithmetic calculation (such as 1000−800).
3. An algebraic formula defining the result of some numerical calculation (such as the contents of cell A2 minus the contents of the cell B2).

Since any letter can therefore have either a textual meaning (as in the 'I' of INCOME), or a numerical meaning (as in a reference to the data contained in the cell I5), we obviously require some method of distinguishing between 'textual' and 'numerical' letters. This is always done by putting a plus sign (+), or a minus sign (−), or a bracket (() in front of numerical formula entries.

If Lotus does not encounter any one of these symbols in front of a letter, then it assumes that the entry is textual and regards it as a label. It indicates this to you both by displaying LABEL in the indicator panel and by placing an apostrophe in front of the entry when it is displayed on the control panel. For example:

A is a label (Lotus shows 'A).
+ A2 is a cell reference (Lotus shows + A2).
A2 − B2 is a textual label − even although it says very little (Lotus shows 'A2 − B2).
500 is a number (Lotus shows 500).
+ A2 − B2 is a formula for subtracting the contents of cell B2 from the contents of cell A2 (Lotus shows + A2 − B2).

Now change your worksheet so that the cell C2 contains the appropriate formula. You should type the following:

$$+A2-B2$$

Can you see that the calculation in C2 is now correct, and, more importantly will remain correct regardless of what numbers you place in the cells A2 and B2? Try changing these numbers now, and observe what happens.

You should also note that any formula that is contained in a particular cell can be inspected when the cursor is placed over that cell, since the cell contents will then be displayed at the top of the screen.

Sometimes, however, we might like to use a 'numerical' letter, as for example, in '2nd September'. If you simply type 2nd September as an entry, then an error message will appear since the system thinks you are trying to combine letters and numbers in an inconsistent way. You will then automatically be taken to EDIT mode in order to correct the mistake.

To deal with this, if we precede any number with an apostrophe (or a space), then Lotus will interpret it as text. Try it for yourself by typing, in A2:

$$'1000$$

Make sure to keep a careful eye on the variable identification that the system provides in the indicator panel at the top of the screen.

You will also notice that ERR has appeared in C2. Can you work out why?

The answer is that you have not entered 1000 as a *number* but rather as a *label*, and the spreadsheet is trying to subtract the number in B2 from the textual label that is now in A2. It is exactly the same as if you wrote:

$$\text{thousand} - 805 \quad \text{or} \quad \text{fish} - 20$$

In short, text entries and numerical entries cannot be combined in arithmetic operations.

Now change the entry in A2 back to a number (1000 say).

1.5 Function keys

We saw above that the F2 key invokes the edit facility, but you may well be wondering what the other function keys do. For our purposes the most important are the following:

F1 This key calls up the Lotus HELP facility on to the screen. Use it freely if you forget anything or want to do something not explained in this text. Press Esc to return to wherever you were.

F2 This, as we have seen, is the EDIT key.

F3 This is the NAME key, which as we will see later (section 1.7.7) provides a list of all those range names that have been created in the current spreadsheet.

Using formulae 9

F5 This is the GOTO key and will move the cursor to whatever cell address you type and return.

F9 This key recalculates the spreadsheet and is known as CALC. As you may have noticed Lotus automatically recalculates the spreadsheet after any changes have been returned, but you can stop this happening if you wish; in which case you must press F9 every time you want a recalculation of the worksheet.

F10 This key will display any graph that has been created on the screen. If no graph is current, then an error message will appear.

1.6 Using formulae

Writing formulae such as the one we created in the last example ($+A2-B2$) is one of the most important aspects of spreadsheet usage. Before you can do this effectively, however, the rules of the 'game' must be understood. To write a formula you must refer to one or more cells by their cell address(es), and then include an arithmetic *operator* which defines what arithmetic operations are to be carried out on the specified cell or cells. In our last example the cell addresses were A2 and B2 and the operators were the plus and minus signs (with the plus sign being used to tell Lotus that a formula was to be expected).

Bearing this in mind, Lotus uses the following arithmetic operator symbols:

+ Addition.
− Subtraction.
∗ Multiplication.
/ Division.
^ Exponentiation, i.e. raising one number to the power of another number.

Lotus also employs the standard mathematical priority system whereby certain arithmetic operations are carried out before others. These priorities are as follows:

1. Exponentiation.
2. Multiplication and division.
3. Addition and subtraction.

What this means is that an expression such as 3∗4^2 would be evaluated as 48 since first of all the 4 would be squared and then the result (16) would be multiplied by 3, giving 48.

Suppose, however, that what we actually wanted was to multiply the 3 by the 4 and then raise the result to the power of 2 (producing 144). How can we override the priority system that Lotus uses? The answer in a spreadsheet is the same as in conventional algebra, and involves making use of parentheses. What these do is to force any calculation to take place inside the brackets first of all, regardless of the normal priority rules, and then continue evaluation outside the brackets.

Now we can see how to achieve our stated objective, since the following expression will force Lotus to evaluate as required:

$$(3*4)^2 = 12^2 = 144$$

Bearing all of these ideas in mind, we can now proceed to write some formula that will perform a variety of algebraic tasks. However, as we have said before, conventional algebra uses x and y to represent variables, yet Lotus would treat an expression such as

$$x + y$$

as a text label, and would not be able to perform any arithmetic operations upon it. Lotus does, however, understand an expression such as

$$+A1 + A2$$

and takes it to mean 'add whatever the contents of A1 are, to whatever the contents of A2 are.' This means that the contents of A1 are being regarded by Lotus as the first variable (x), and the contents of A2 as the second variable (y). Furthermore, since the contents of both A1 and A2 can be whatever we choose them to be (or the result of some specified calculation), they can truly be regarded as variables in the algebraic sense of the word. The only difference is that we refer to these variables by their cell addresses in Lotus, whereas we would call them x and y in normal written algebra.

Now it is time to put these ideas together and at the same time illustrate two of the most powerful aspects of spreadsheet operations.

Make sure that you are still in the worksheet and that READY is displayed. Now move the cursor to A10 and read on.

In this illustration we are going to create a simple spreadsheet that will take an opening balance, add monthly income to it, subtract monthly expenditure from it, and then calculate the monthly closing balance. We will, however, do this in two ways, so that you can appreciate the full mathematical capabilities of the spreadsheet.

First of all enter the monthly labels JAN, FEB, MARCH and APRIL into the cells B10, C10, D10 and E10. Move to A11 and type: OB (Opening Balance). In A12 type: SALINC (Salary Income); in A13 type: EXP (Expenditure); and in A14 type: CB (Closing Balance). These are the *labels* to identify the data that we are going to enter in the spreadsheet.

Now enter a figure of 1000 in B11 (January, Opening Balance), 800 in B12 (January's Salary), and 600 in B13 (January's Expenditure).

In B14 (containing the Closing Balance) we obviously require a formula to carry out the calculations implied by the problem. This would be the Opening Balance plus the Salary minus the Expenditure in that month. In terms of a Lotus formula this would be:

$$+B11+B12-B13$$

Making sure that you understand how this was derived, type it now into the B14 cell.

You will notice that although a formula was entered, it is the *result* of the specified calculation (1200) that appears in B14. If this is not the case (if, for example, the formula appears in B14), then this is because you have entered it as a label and not as an operational formula (you have probably forgotten the plus sign in front of the first cell address). Type it in again if this is the case.

This closing balance of 1200 in January is obviously the opening balance for February. Accordingly, type 1200 in C11, and then complete the spreadsheet for the remaining months as follows:

in C12	900	
in C13	700	
in C14	+C11+C12−C13	(1400 will be returned)
in D11	1400	
in D12	750	
in D13	850	
in D14	+D11+D12−D13	(1300 will be returned)
in E11	1300	
in E12	800	
in E13	500	
in E14	+E11+E12−E13	(1600 will be returned)

Your spreadsheet should look like Worksheet 1.1.

There are two things to notice here. Firstly, it is needlessly laborious to perform the transfer of one month's closing balance to the next month's opening balance *manually* as we have done above. This is because it can be done by an appropriate formula. To see this, instead of typing 1200 in C11, type +B14. Although the result will still be 1200, the fact that a formula has been used will mean that if, for example, January expenditure were to change, the entry in C11 would still remain correct. This is because the formula in B14 has been carried over to C11 by the

```
WORKSHEET 1.1
              A         B         C         D         E
      8
      9
     10                JAN       FEB       MARCH     APRIL
     11    OB         1000      1200      1400      1300
     12    SALINC      800       900       750       800
     13    EXP         600       700       850       500
     14    CB         1200      1400      1300      1600
     15
```

reference +B14, which is entered to C11. *Now* if the value for EXP in B13 is changed, not only does the value in B14 change but that changed value is carried over to C11 by the fact that C11 has been set equal to *whatever* value is contained in B14. This, in turn, creates a further ripple effect so that C14 changes appropriately, which means that D11 must change and so on.

Secondly, if we had to perform these calculations for a large number of months, it would become extremely tedious to type each formula individually into each cell that required it. Yet, as you can see, there is a pattern to the required formulae in the sense that the row addresses remain the same, but that each column address goes up a letter at a time. In other words +B11+B12−B13, +C11+C12−C13, etc., and +B14, +C14, etc.

Now, provided a pattern such as this can be observed, Lotus has the ability to *replicate* any one formula in such a way that not only is it entered in all appropriate cells, but also that the column references are modified as required. This is done via the COPY command, which is accessed from the main menu.

1.7 Menu commands

> Make sure that you are in input mode, that READY is showing, and that the cursor is positioned in C14.

Bearing our recent remarks about replication in mind, we would like to take the formula in B14 and replicate it appropriately into the cells C14, D14 and E14. Since the correct formulae are already there, to appreciate whether the replicating process has been successful, we need to erase the formulae in these last three cells. To do this, simply place the cursor over the cell whose contents are to be erased, press the spacebar once, and then press return. A 'blank' character will be sent to the cell. Do this for all three cells (i.e. C14, D14 and E14). (*Note:* There is a more efficient way of erasing cell contents than this, which will be explained shortly.)

> Now position the cursor in B14 and bring up the main command menu by pressing the backslash key (/) once.

The main command menu should have appeared. There are a number of features contained in this menu that we will need to use at various junctures, but at the moment we will concentrate on the most important commands.

1.7.1 Relative copying

With the cursor still in B14, select copy from the main menu (i.e. point to copy and press return, or type c).

You will then be prompted:

> Enter the range to copy from:

and the control panel will be displaying the current cell address in the form B14..B14. Since you are currently located in copy mode, this is indicating to you that the contents of the B14 cell are now ready to be copied. If this is what you want, press return (if not, press Escape, position the cursor properly and repeat the process above).

After pressing the return key, a second prompt will appear:

> Enter the range to copy to:

and the control panel will still display B14..B14 since this is where the cursor is still located.

If we consider what we are attempting to do, it should be obvious that what we want is to take the formula in B14 and apply it to the cells C14 to E14 inclusive. Consequently, point with the cursor to the first cell that you want to copy to (C14). Now press the full stop key once, and then move the cursor to the last cell that you want to copy to (E14). You will see that the range that is to receive the copied formula has been highlighted.

If everything looks in order, press return and you will see the values that you previously erased reappear in the cells C14 to E14, and that you are returned to input mode. You will also see that if you move the cursor through the range C14 to E14, then the appropriate formula is contained in each cell.

If this is not the case, then repeat the steps outlined above until you obtain the desired result.

Copying is a crucial spreadsheet technique, so if you had difficulty with the last section, do it again until you are happy that you have mastered it.

The copying process illustrated above is just one of the many ways that Lotus can replicate the contents of one or more cells. In all of these ways, however, a few basic points remain constant.

1. Unless you tell Lotus otherwise, the copying from this menu is always done 'relatively', i.e. columns and/or rows are increased by a letter and/or a number throughout the range that is copied to. This of course is only effective if it is formulae that are being copied, since a number such as 100 cannot be copied relatively. The copied number will still be placed in the cells that are copied to, but there is no aspect of column and/or row adjustment involved since there is no formula to adjust.
2. Instead of pointing to the cell to be copied from, and then pointing to the cell(s) to be copied to, you can type in the cell address(es) after the 'copy from:' and

WORKSHEET 1.2

	A	B	C	D	E
8					
9					
10		JAN	FEB	MARCH	APRIL
11	OB	1000	1200	1400	1300
12	SALINC	800	900	750	800
13	EXP	600	700	850	500
14	CB	1200	1400	1300	1600
15		200	200	300	-300

'copy to:' prompts. For our example above this would require that you type C14..E14 after the second copy prompt. Try it this way for yourself.

3. In our illustration above the contents of one cell were copied to a range of cells, but Lotus is just as capable of copying from one range of cells to another range. To do this you simply point to the range to be copied from (it will be highlighted as you continue pointing), then press return, and then point to the range of cells to be copied to. This latter range must, of course, be at least the same size as the range being copied from.

To practise this last point, copy the range of cells B14..E14 to the range of cells B15..E15. You will see that although the copying process itself is performed correctly, the formulae that result in B15..E15 do not make much sense in this case (they might do in other problems of course).

Your worksheet should now look like Worksheet 1.2.

The result of the copying process will have placed the following formula in B15:

$$+B12+B13-B14$$

and this will also be present (with the appropriate column letter adjustment) in columns C, D and E. Although this makes no accounting sense, it nevertheless illustrates the nature of the Lotus copying facility.

WORKSHEET 1.3

	A	B	C	D	E
8					
9					
10		JAN	FEB	MARCH	APRIL
11	OB	1000	1200	1400	1300
12	SALINC	800	900	750	800
13	EXP	600	700	850	500
14	CB	1200	1400	1300	1600
15		200	200	300	-300
16		1600	1900	1850	2400

```
WORKSHEET 1.4
         A              B                C                 D
  8
  9
 10                     JAN              FEB              MARCH
 11     OB             1000              +B14             +C14
 12     SALINC          800              900               750
 13     EXP             600              700               850
 14     CB        +B11+B12-B13      +C11+C12-C13      +D11+D12-D13
 15               +B12+B13-B14      +C12+C13-C14      +D12+D13-D14
 16               +B13+B14-B15      +C13+C14-C15      +D13+D14-D15
```

Finally, copy the range B14..E14 into the block of cells defined by the range B15..E16. Once again, confirm that the formulae are copied relatively, and as a result do not make much sense. You should obtain something like Worksheet 1.3.

The copied entry in B16 will be:

$$+B13+B14-B15$$

Furthermore, if the *formulae* contained in the cells of Worksheet 1.3 were displayed we would obtain Worksheet 1.4.

The ability to display the formulae of a worksheet as they have been written (rather than as the numerical result that the formulae produce) is often a useful device. You can make Lotus do it by selecting Range from the main command menu and then selecting Format from the next menu that appears. This will produce a third menu which offers a number of options governing how the contents of the cells of the worksheet are to appear. To reproduce Worksheet 1.4 you should select text from this third menu. Lotus will then ask you to tell it the range of cells that are to be displayed in this format, so you should respond with B14..E16. Now you will find that part of the formula in each cell will be displayed (since the columns are not currently wide enough to display the entire formula). Do not worry about this, since you will find out how to rectify it shortly.

To convert the entries back to numbers, you simply reverse the procedure outlined above, but from the third menu you should select 'Fixed'. This will display numbers in a form in which the number of decimal places is fixed by the response that you make to the prompt which Lotus immediately displays. You should then enter (as a number) the desired number of decimal places to be displayed (2 is the default).

1.7.2 Absolute copying

Although the ability to make a relative copy of one or more formulae is an extremely useful asset, as we saw above it can sometimes produce meaningless results. Furthermore, there may well be circumstances when you want to copy a formula but you do not want the columns or the rows (or both) to adjust.

To deal with this, Lotus allows you to exercise complete control over the *extent* to which copying is done on a relative basis.

As we have already said, Lotus assumes that you want to copy relatively unless you tell it otherwise. To do this (i.e. tell it otherwise), you must precede the column letter in the cell address(es) of the cell(s) to be copied with a dollar sign ($). This will then ensure that the copying process will *not* adjust the columns as it copies.

Similarly, if you precede the row number in the cell address(es) of the cell(s) to be copied with a dollar sign, then the copying process will *not* adjust the rows as it copies.

Finally, if you precede both the column letter and the row number in the cell address(es) of the cell(s) to be copied with a dollar sign, then the copying process will *not* adjust the columns or the rows as it copies. The cell address will be fixed absolutely.

To see how this facility can be used, first of all enter the average closing balance in F14. The formula to do this would be:

$$(B14+C14+D14+E14)/4$$

and will return a value of 1375.

Now suppose that we want to calculate the difference between each month's closing balance, and the average closing balance for the four months. We would first of all enter ABOVE AV. (i.e. Above Average) in A20, and then in B20 enter the following formula:

$$+B14-F14$$

Do this now and confirm that the B20 cell now contains the required figure for the month of January (-175).

To obtain the remaining months' figures, copy the formula in B20 into the range C20..E20, in the same manner as you have done before.

Since this copying has been done relatively, you will find that the formulae produced in C20, D20 and E20 are $+C14-G14$, $+D14-H14$ and $+E14-I14$. These three replicated formulae are obviously not appropriate since they make references to three cells (G14, H14 and I14) that are all blank.

Clearly we require that the F14 cell reference containing the average is 'fixed' in the copying process so that it always pertains to each month's closing balance figure. In other words we want to produce $+C14-F14$, $+D14-F14$ and $+F14-F14$. To do this we must change the formula to be copied (i.e. $+B14-F14$ in B20) to incorporate a dollar sign which fixes the column address of the average balance.

Consequently, change the entry in B20 to:

$$+B14-\$F14$$

Notice that since we are only copying along one row (row 20) there is no need to fix the row reference in this new formulation (although there may be in other circumstances).

Now copy the contents of B20 into the range C20..E20, and you will find that correct results are obtained.

Practice this process by repeating the exercise above for the opening balance figures.

1.7.3 Erasing the contents of cells

The Lotus spreadsheet understands that you want to use its menu system to perform certain operations on the worksheet. It also understands, however, that these operations can be done in either of two ways:

1. To the whole spreadsheet (*globally*).
2. Only to a *range* of designated cells.

For this reason its menu structure keeps these two options separate from one another so that the likelihood of errors is reduced. Once again it is important that you appreciate this distinction since as we shall see there are a number of options that influence the general appearance of the worksheet and can be done in either of these two ways. At the moment, however, we are concerned with erasure.

To erase the *entire* worksheet you must select the Worksheet option from the main menu and then select Erase from the submenu which then appears. Consequently, to erase the entire contents of the current worksheet the command sequence would be as follows:

/ (Menu) W (Worksheet) E (Erase)

You will then be asked whether you really want to erase the entire worksheet, and if this is the case then you must select 'Yes' and press the return key. If you select 'No', then you will be returned to input mode (READY showing).

If you are following these instructions on you own worksheet, select 'No' at the moment since we do not want the entire worksheet erased just yet.

If, on the other hand, it is only a section of the worksheet that you want to erase, then this is done via the Range option on the main menu. The command sequence is as follows:

/ (Menu) R (Range) E (Erase)

You will then be prompted for the range to be erased and you can either type in the coordinates, or point as you did in copying.

Now erase the superfluous lines of calculations that you have built up in the range B15..E16.

1.7.4 Altering the column width

It will frequently be the case that the number of characters you want to use in a label will exceed the available column width which Lotus sets automatically (nine characters). However, you can alter this setting in either of two ways: globally or only for one column.

To alter the column width globally, select Worksheet from the main menu and then choose Global from the submenu which appears. Now select Column-Width from next menu, and you will then be prompted by Lotus to enter the desired width as a number (representing the number of characters).

Change all the column widths from 9 to 15 and then back to 9 again.

It will more frequently be the case, however, that only one or two columns require expansion (to accommodate labels usually). To do this, place the cursor in the cell that you wish to widen (while you are still in input mode) and then call up the main menu (/). This time, however, select Range instead of Worksheet, and from the submenu that appears choose Column, and then Set Width.

Once again the current column width setting will be displayed and you are prompted to enter the new setting to apply to the column in which the cursor is located.

Notice that once any one column has had its width altered from its default setting, then global column widening will no longer apply to that column.

Change the width of column A from 9 to 16 and then from 16 to 12.

1.7.5 Inserting rows or columns

The Insert facility allows new rows or columns to be inserted at any desired location. Furthermore, it has the very powerful feature that if this insertion causes any formulae in subsequent cells to become inappropriate then these formulae will be *logically updated* to take account of the effects of the insertion.

For example, suppose that we wanted to enter another item of income between rows 12 and 13. To do this, place the cursor in any column of the row that is to have a row inserted before it (A12 itself will do).

Now invoke the menu (/), select Worksheet and then select Insert. You will now be prompted as to whether it is a column or row that is to be inserted; select row in this case.

The next prompt will be 'Enter range:' and the range A12..A12 will be showing (since this is where the cursor is located). If this is the desired location (as it is in our case), press return and the new row will be inserted.

You can insert more than one row (or column) by widening the range that you return. For example, if in response to the prompt you had entered the range A12..A14, then three rows would have been placed before the first row address. For illustration purposes you should confine the insertion procedure to one row only (at A12).

As you can see, what was previously A12 (with SALINC in it) has now become A13, and so on throughout the entire worksheet. What is more important, however, is the fact that all of the formulae that have been written have been adjusted so that their logic remains correct.

For example, the following formula was previously in B14:

$$+B11+B12-B13$$

However, as a result of the insertion it *should* now read (in B15):

$$+B12+B13-B14$$

As you can see, this is precisely what has happened, since the necessary adjustment is carried out *automatically* by the Insert command, so that appropriate formulae are maintained.

Finally, as was indicated above, the Insert command can also be used to create new columns with the obvious difference that row references are replaced with column references and that 'column' instead of 'row' is selected.

1.7.6 Deleting rows or columns

Unlike the Erase command, the Delete command removes the actual row or column as well as their contents from the spreadsheet.

Like the Insert command, however, it adjusts all formulae to take account of any subsequent implications that the deletion may have upon the logic of the spreadsheet.

Be careful, however, that you do not attempt to delete a row or column that contains information (formulae or numbers) that other formulae in later sections of the worksheet require to use. No amount of automatic adjustment can cope with this and an error entry in all affected cells will result.

The command sequence is similar to the Insert command with the exception that Delete is selected from the Worksheet menu:

/ W(Worksheet) D(Delete) R(Row) or C(Column) range.

Practise the Delete command by removing the row that you inserted in the last section.

1.7.7 Naming a range

This is a very useful feature if you are dealing with large spreadsheets since 'Naming a Range' enables you to replace cell coordinates by the range name in a variety of circumstances. For example, in our simple model we might want to call the cells B11..E11 'OPBAL'. To get Lotus to do this, invoke the menu (/), Range (R), Name (N), Create (C) and when prompted 'Enter Name:' type OPBAL; and when prompted 'Enter Range:' use any of the methods you now know, to specify it as B11..E11. Then press return.

You should repeat this process for the ranges representing Salary Income, Expenditure and Closing Balance, using names such as SALINC, EXP and CLOBAL.

Notice that these range names that you have created are much more than mere labels, since they are data ranges which Lotus can access, and perform certain operations upon, whenever you tell it the relevant name. Furthermore, there is an extremely powerful property that only named ranges possess and which we will be explaining and using shortly.

For this reason you should make every effort to use range names as much as possible.

Also note that you can invoke any range name that you have created whenever you want by pressing the function key F3 at any time when you are being prompted by Lotus for a range of worksheet cells.

1.8 The Lotus @ functions

Lotus contains a number of preprogrammed functions which can reduce keyboard time considerably, and which are all characterized by the feature that they must be preceded by the @ symbol. Lotus then expects to encounter a *keyname* which defines the function to be used (SUM or COUNT for example), which must then be followed by a set of brackets in which the *argument* to which the function is to apply is contained. The general construction of these functions can therefore be viewed as:

@KEYNAME(ARGUMENT)

The Lotus @ functions 21

The argument that each function requires varies depending upon its type, but will usually be a number, or a cell address, or a range of cell addresses (named or otherwise). Furthermore, some functions require more than one argument, in which case each argument must be separated by commas.

The following list of functions is by no means exhaustive but will lay sufficient foundation for the discussion that is to follow. Further functions will be explained and used as and when they are required.

Notice that no spaces are allowed between the constituent terms of the function, and that you may use either upper- or lowercase characters, or a mixture of both.

1.8.1 Functions that take numerical or single-cell address arguments

Practise the following functions in a vacant part of the worksheet and notice that they all refer to the average closing balance that we calculated in F14:

1. @ABS(F14)   Returns the absolute value of the number in F14 (i.e. ignoring the algebraic sign if it is negative).
2. @INT(F14)   Returns the predecimal point portion of the number in F14.
3. @SQRT(F14)   Returns the square root of the number in F14.

1.8.2 Functions that take a range of cell address arguments

These functions can be used to perform a number of calculations on a range of the worksheet. For illustrative purposes we will apply them to the range B14..E14 which contains the closing balance figures for our example. Practise them for yourself in any vacant part of the worksheet.

1. @MAX(B14..E14)   Returns the maximum value of the values contained in the range of cells B14 to E14.
2. @MIN(B14..E14)   As for MAX except the minimum value is returned.
3. @SUM(B14..E14)   Returns the sum of the values in the cells B14 to E14.
4. @COUNT(B14..E14)   Returns the number of observations in the range of cells B14 to E14. Notice that a zero entry in a cell counts as an observation but that a blank does not.
5. @AVG(B14..E14).   Returns the arithmetic mean (i.e. average) value of the entries in the cells B14 to E14.

1.8.3 Functions that take more than one argument

The most important of these is what is known as the LOGICAL IF function, whereby the spreadsheet can be instructed to perform a 'test' on the contents of any cell, and, depending upon the result of that test, carry out a specified task. The general idea of the LOGICAL IF function is that the spreadsheet is instructed to determine IF something is true, and THEN do something if it is, or ELSE do something different if it is not.

The general syntax of these so-called *conditional statements* is therefore:

@IF(TEST,ACTION IF TRUE,ACTION IF FALSE)

As you can see, there are three arguments required by the @IF function.

For example, suppose we want to increase a given data element (contained in A20, say) by 10 if it is less than 100, but reduce it by 20 if it is 100 or more. The following conditional statement will do this if we enter the value to be tested in A20 (enter 50 say), and the statement itself in A21:

@IF(A20<100,A20+10,A20−20)
(THEN) (ELSE)

Try it now, remembering to separate each argument of the function with a comma.

You should find that because the value that you entered in A20 (50) was less than 100, this has caused a value of 50 + 10 = 60 to be returned to the cell containing the conditional statement (i.e. A21).

Now change the entry in A20 to a number that exceeds 100 (150 will do), and you will see that Lotus automatically recalculates the conditional statement and now returns a value of 150 − 20 = 130 to A21.

Conditional statements can contain all of the available mathematical operators in their arguments, and in addition employ a set of *conditional operators*. These are as follows:

<   less than
≤   less than or equal to
=   equal to
>   greater than
≥   greater than or equal to
< >   not equal to

Finally, *conditional statements* can be used to return textual rather than numeric test results. To see this try replacing the arithmetic operations in the statement above with the responses LARGE if the number exceeds 100, and SMALL if it does not. To do this you must enclose these responses in inverted commas as follows:

@IF(A20>100,"LARGE","SMALL")

(Do not forget that any textual response required by the statement must always be enclosed in inverted commas.)

Two further functions that require more than one argument should be mentioned at this stage. @ROUND(F14,N) will round the number in F14 to N decimal places. You must of course specify the number of decimal places in your actual application. For example @ROUND(0.859,2) will round the contents of F14 *up* (because N is positive) to two decimal places (producing 0.86); while

@ROUND(8.4569, −3) would round *down* to three decimal places (producing 8.456).

The function @MOD(X,Y) returns the remainder of the first number (X) divided by the second number (Y). Once again, either numbers or cell references containing numbers must be used in the actual application. Hence @MOD(6,3) would return a value of 0 (since 6/3 = 2 with no remainder), while @MOD(9,5) would return a value of 4 (since 9/5 = 1 with a remainder of 4).

1.8.4 Using more than one function at a time

Any of the functions above can themselves be used as arguments in another function, provided that they are separated with parentheses. Frequently the resulting 'combination' will not make any mathematical sense, but in other cases useful calculations can be performed.

For example, the following composite function would produce the integer portion of the maximum number in the range B14..E14.

@INT(@MAX(B14..E14))

Notice how the brackets are used: one pair to 'isolate' the MAX function itself (so that it is an argument of the INT function), and another pair to isolate the argument of the MAX function (i.e. the range B14..E14). This use of brackets is referred to as 'nesting', as one function is nested inside the argument brackets of another, and is a crucial concept in various areas of spreadsheet usage.

Similarly, the following conditional statement performs a test upon the mean value of the range B14..E14, and then returns the maximum value in this range if the mean is greater than 0, or the minimum value in the range otherwise:

@IF(@AVG(B14..E14)<0,@MAX(B14..E14),@MIN(B14..E14))

Study this expression carefully until you are sure that you understand it.

1.9 Quitting, saving and retrieving

You can *quit* the worksheet at any time by selecting Quit from the main menu and then responding 'Yes' to the prompt that appears. However, Lotus also provides you with a useful reminder to save the current worksheet. If you have not done this, then all your work will be lost, so it is important to make sure that you know how to save and then retrieve your worksheet.

1.9.1 Saving a worksheet file

To start with, you must choose the option 'File' from the main menu.

From the new menu that appears, the first thing that we need to do (and this only has to be done once in each session of work) is to set the default Directory. To do this we choose the option 'Directory' (D). You will now be prompted to 'Enter the current directory'. If a current default is showing (C:\ for example), this should be deleted first.

As you will usually save your work onto disks in drive A, you should now type A:\ and then press return. Now while using the spreadsheet it will always access the A drive, thus saving you time.

Make sure that you have a data disk in Drive A.

You will now be back at the worksheet, so again invoke the menu (/), choose File (F), but this time the option we require is Save (S). You will now be prompted 'Enter save file name A:\'. Type in the name of the file as TEST and press return. The top right indicator will flash the word 'WAIT' while the file is being saved and a suffix of .WK1 will be added automatically to the file's name (this suffix identifies a file as a Lotus 1-2-3 worksheet file).

We can check that the file has been saved by invoking the menu (/), choosing File (F), this time choosing the List (L) option, and finally the Worksheet (W) option. The screen will change and a list of all current worksheet files will appear. Notice that the date, time created and size of each file will be shown at the top of the screen. To return to the worksheet simply press the Escape key the requisite number of times.

1.9.2 Erasing and then retrieving the current worksheet

If you have successfully saved TEST.WK1, and you have identified it on your disk using the List command, you can move on (if not, repeat the Saving procedure outlined above). Invoke the menu (/), choose Worksheet (W), then choose Erase (E) and then the 'Yes' option. The current worksheet will now be blanked and we can retrieve the file we saved. Invoke the menu (/), choose File (F), Retrieve (R). This time you will find the file TEST.WK1 will be listed on the screen, highlight this and press return and the worksheet you had previously saved will return to the screen. We now have a routine for saving, listing and retrieving files – remember it well otherwise calamities can occur.

1.10 The Lotus graphics facility

Lotus supports a highly effective yet easy-to-use graphing capability, which is best illustrated in terms of Worksheet 1.5.

The data in columns A and B represent the results of an experiment aimed at

WORKSHEET 1.5

	A	B
1	Speed (mph)	Fuel use (mpg)
2	0	0
3	10	17
4	20	24
5	25	29
6	30	34
7	35	39
8	40	42
9	45	45
10	50	52
11	55	56
12	60	48
13	65	40
14	70	31
15	75	26
16	80	19

investigating the relationship between the fuel consumption and the road speed of a 1-litre car.

To graph these data on Lotus you must first of all select Graph from the main menu. This will cause the main Graph menu to appear, which, as you can see, contains a number of options.

From this menu the first step will usually be to select the Type of graph to be constructed. There are five choices: Line, Bar, XY, Stacked Bar and Pie. So, select Type and then choose Line.

Lotus needs to know the range where the data that are to be placed on the X axis is located. This is referred to as the *independent variable*, and for our illustration is speed (since it would seem clear that fuel consumption is *dependent* upon speed).

Accordingly, select X from the menu on the screen and in response to the resulting prompt for the range, tell Lotus that the data representing speed are contained in the range A2..A16. The horizontal axis will now represent speed.

Next you must inform Lotus where the data to be placed on the vertical axis are located. This can be in any of six predetermined graph ranges defined as A–F. For this illustration we shall select the first of these, so choose A from the menu and then respond to the subsequent prompt with the range containing the data for fuel consumption, i.e. B2..B16.

All you have to do now is select View from the Graph menu and the diagram will be drawn. Press the Escape key when you have finished viewing and you will be returned to the main graph menu, where if you select Quit you can then return to the worksheet.

WORKSHEET 1.6

	A	B	C
1	Speed (mph)	One litre (mpg)	Two litre (mpg)
2	0	0	0
3	10	17	13
4	20	24	20
5	25	29	22
6	30	34	27
7	35	39	30
8	40	42	33
9	45	45	38
10	50	52	40
11	55	56	44
12	60	48	40
13	65	40	36
14	70	31	32
15	75	26	29
16	80	19	25

Now suppose that the same experiment as above was also carried out for a 2-litre car and the fuel usage results recorded in column C, as shown in Worksheet 1.6.

You can obtain a comparative graph if you define graph range B as the contents of the range C2..C16, since when you select View both graphs will be displayed on the same axes.

If you want to change the Type of graph then simply select Type from the main Graph menu, and make your new choice, while if you want to alter the range containing the data, select Reset from the Graph menu. This will allow you to alter the cell addresses of any or all of the six graph ranges (A–F).

Finally, you will usually want to annotate your axes with some indicator of what each variable represents and what the graph is displaying. To do this you must select Options from the main Graph menu and then select Titles from the submenu which then appears. As you can see, you can have up to two titles (first and second) which will be placed at the top of the graph, and one title for each axis (X and Y). Now you can enter titles such as 'Fuel consumption survey' (as first), 'January 1990' (as second), 'mph' (as X) and 'mpg' (as Y).

Furthermore, when you elect to display more than one graph on the screen at once (as in our last example) it will also be desirable to have each graph identified (1-litre car, 2-litre car, etc.). To do this, select Options once again, but this time choose Legend from the submenu. Now you can enter a title for any or all of the graph ranges, so A would be 1 litre and B would be 2 litre.

If, in addition, you want each plotted point labelled on the graph, then select options and this time choose Data Labels. You will then be prompted to choose the graph range (A–F) that you want labelled and which observations in that range are to be labelled. You can tell Lotus to label all the observations or just some of them.

Lastly, if you want to use more than one graph at once, then you should name the graphs as you create them. This is done from the main Graph menu by selecting 'Name'. You can then Use an existing named graph, Create a new named graph (any name less than eight characters will do), or Delete an existing named graph.

Printing the graph requires that you understand some of the intricacies of the Print Graph menu, and this exceeds the remit of this text. However, in most cases, and with most printers, a satisfactory print can be obtained by using Print Screen. This will, however, require that the MS-DOS command GRAPHICS has been loaded before you start your Lotus session.

Taking all of these modifications into account, our final graph would look something like Figure 1.1.

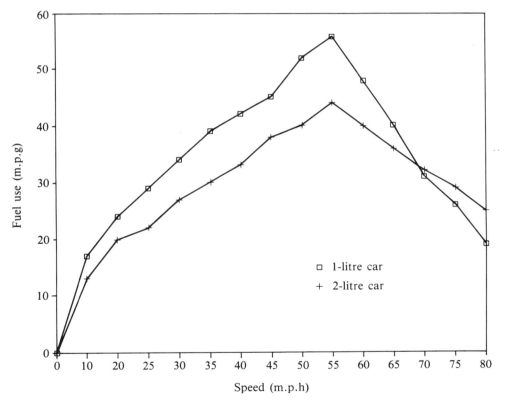

Figure 1.1 Speed versus fuel use

1.11 Exercises

1.1

The data we will use in this exercise refer to the four-monthly sales volumes and sales prices of a firm's product. This would produce the initial worksheet shown as Worksheet 1.7.

Reproduce this worksheet for yourself.
(a) Add the label 'SALES REVENUE' in column D.
(b) Write an appropriate formula in D3 that will calculate the firm's revenue.
(c) Copy this formula into the cells D4..D6.
(d) Make an absolute value copy of the data in D1..D6 into the range E1..E6.
(e) Name the numerical data in this new range (i.e. E3..E6) as REV.
(f) Calculate the total, average, minimum and maximum sales revenues by using formulae that refer to the named range, i.e. @SUM(REV), etc.
(g) Insert a row at the appropriate place to accommodate the inclusion of data for January.
(h) Enter data for January of 7000 for sales volume and £4.20 for sales price. Check that your calculations are still correct.
(i) Now name the data for sales volume and sales price in the same way as you did for sales revenue.

Your final worksheet should look something like Worksheet 1.8.
Furthermore, a 'formula dump' of the worksheet would produce Worksheet 1.9.

(j) Now suppose that the firm's monthly overhead costs were £32 000. Devise five logical formulae that will return 'OHCOV' (i.e. Overhead Covered) or 'OHNOTCOV' (Overhead Not Covered), depending upon whether the monthly revenue exceeds £32 000 or not.
(k) Prepare a graph that displays the behaviour of Sales Revenue in terms of Sales Volume.

```
WORKSHEET 1.7
                    A          B          C
            1     MONTH      SALES      SALES
            2                VOLUME     PRICE
            3     FEB        7800       4.50
            4     MARCH      6400       4.90
            5     APRIL      8900       4.90
            6     MAY        6500       5.00
            7
```

WORKSHEET 1.8

	A	B	C	D	E
1	MONTH	SALES	SALES	SALES	SALES
2		VOLUME	PRICE	REVENUE	REVENUE
3	JAN	7000	4.20	29400	29400
4	FEB	7800	4.50	35100	35100
5	MARCH	6400	4.90	31360	31360
6	APRIL	8900	4.90	43610	43610
7	MAY	6500	5.00	32500	32500
8	TOTAL	36600	23.5	171970	171970
9	AVERAGE	7320	4.7	34394	34394
10	MAX	8900	5	43610	43610
11	MIN	6400	4.2	29400	29400
12					

WORKSHEET 1.9

	A	B	C	D	E
1	MONTH	SALES	SALES	SALES	SALES
2		VOLUME	PRICE	REVENUE	REVENUE
3	JAN	7000	4.2	+B3*C3	29400
4	FEB	7800	4.5	+B4*C4	35100
5	MARCH	6400	4.9	+B5*C5	31360
6	APRIL	8900	4.9	+B6*C6	43610
7	MAY	6500	5	+B7*C7	32500
8	TOTAL	@SUM(B3..B7)	@SUM(C3..C7)	@SUM(D3..D7)	@SUM(REV)
9	AVERAGE	@AVG(B3..B7)	@AVG(C3..C7)	@AVG(D3..D7)	@AVG(REV)
10	MAX	@MAX(B3..B7)	@MAX(C3..C7)	@MAX(D3..D7)	@MAX(REV)
11	MIN	@MIN(B3..B7)	@MIN(C3..C7)	@MIN(D3..D7)	@MIN(REV)

1.2

(a) A firm sells its product to six clients whose annual order quantities are 4550, 8970, 4730, 6500, 2900 and 9000.

Prepare a spreadsheet that will calculate the annual invoice to be sent to the customer if the price of the product is £25 per unit and if VAT is charged at 15 per cent.

(b) Modify the spreadsheet above to take account of the fact that the firm allows a discount of 10 per cent of the unit price to all customers whose annual orders exceed 4000 units.

The solution is provided in Worksheet 1.10 where the crucial formula in C7 is displayed at the top of the worksheet. Notice how the dollar signs attached to the B1 and D1 cell addresses allow it to be copied consistently into C8..C12.

WORKSHEET 1.10

```
C7: [W14] @IF(B7>=B$1,D$1,0)

            A              B           C           D           E
    1    Threshold       4000      Discount       0.1
    2                    8000
    3    Price             25      VAT rate       0.15
    4
    5    Client        Purchase    Discount     Value of    Invoice +VAT
    6                  Quantity    Applicable   Order
    7    Anderson        4550         0.1       102375       117731.25
    8    Cummings        8970         0.1       201825       232098.75
    9    Dodds           4730         0.1       106425       122388.75
   10    Masterson       6500         0.1       146250       168187.5
   11    Williams        2900         0           72500        83375
   12    Young           9000         0.1       202500       232875
```

Once the discount rate to be applied has been determined, all that remains is to write formulae that will calculate the value of the order (including any discount applicable), and from this, the invoice with VAT included.

The formulae to do this are:

        in D7   +B7*B$3*(1−C7)   copied into D8..D12
        in E7   +D7*(1+D$3)   copied into E8..E12

Once again, the dollar signs are essential to ensure that the given data elements (price in B3, and VAT rate in D3) do not update in the copying process.

Formulated in this way, the worksheet can easily accommodate any changes that take place in the environment of the problem, and therefore provides an important introduction to the art of worksheet design (a continuing theme throughout the entirety of this text).

2
Principles of Algebraic Modelling

2.1 The need for algebra

Few people would deny the need for numerical calculations in the everyday running of their lives, since many activities that we frequently take for granted are fundamentally based upon our inherent knowledge of the rules of arithmetic. Yet those same people will often be the first to deny the need to know anything about mathematics.

On closer examination, however, this denial is frequently based upon a dislike of a particular type of mathematics that is known as algebra. Furthermore, it is arguable that this disinclination is symptomatic of a deeper aversion that is typified by the reluctance to move from the specific (numeric) to the general (algebraic) approach to quantitative problems.

Yet, while it is not the purpose of algebra to decry arithmetic, it is surely the case that the former is a more powerful analytical tool. This power stems from algebra's ability to use a symbol (x or y) to represent a range of numerical values, so that a statement involving x or y can refer to a large number of arithmetic values and yet still behave as if it is *only one single value*.

Consequently, the statement:

Let $x =$ the price of a pint of beer

makes a *general* statement about the global price of beer, rather than a *specific* statement about the price of beer in a particular hostelry.

In this sense, x represents a variable that by definition is capable of *changing* its value in such a way that it remains relevant to whatever situation is being considered.

Clearly it is this idea of using a symbol to represent the range of values that a variable can adopt that forms the cornerstone of algebraic analysis.

It is, of course, important to be aware of the legitimate values that the variable can adopt, and in the context of business studies it will usually be the case that we constrain most of our operational variables to be zero or positive. (This will not always be the case, since a negative rate of return or a negative profit are clearly permissible, but it is a reasonable expectation in the majority of cases.)

The final requirement in the correct definition of any algebraic variable is a clear statement of what is being measured and in what units. Consequently, if we are analyzing the price of beer in the United Kingdom, then the units of measurement will clearly be pounds sterling per pint.

Taking all of these points together means that our previous statement should really have been written as:

$$\text{Let } x = \text{the price in £s of a pint of beer } (x \geqslant 0)$$

Armed with these fundamental ideas governing the specification of algebraic variables, we are now ready to see how they can be employed in the context of modelling various types of business problems.

2.2 Elements of spreadsheet modelling

As has already been suggested in the previous chapter, the full modelling capability of a spreadsheet is difficult to appreciate and employ without a sound grasp of various principles of algebra.

In this respect, the key word is *generality*, and should be understood in terms of developing worksheets that have a high degree of *modelling flexibility* as a result of their general algebraic structure.

By this we mean that the construction of your spreadsheet should allow you to take account of any changes that may occur in the arithmetic assumptions on which the model was initially based.

Before you can do this, it is important to distinguish clearly between four types of numerical term that your model may contain.

Universal constants These terms have the feature that regardless of the environment which the model is attempting to simulate, their value is always the same. Some examples would be: $\pi = 22/7$; $e = 2.71829$; free-fall acceleration $= 32.6$ feet per second per second.

Endogenous variables These are the operational terms of your model, and will usually have been defined by you during its construction. Their fundamental feature is that they vary their values in accordance with changes in other data values of the model. For example, if you define the cell C3 to be the sum of cells C1 and C2, then the contents of C3 is an endogenous variable whose value is determined by whatever the values in C1 and C2 happen to be. Any change in the value of the data in these two cells, will *automatically* cause the value of C3 to vary in response. (This is because Lotus uses automatic recalculation by default.)

In this sense, the value adopted by any endogenous variable is entirely determined within the confines of the worksheet model, and is therefore *dependent* upon the values of those other variables to which it has been related.

Exogenous variables These are variables that are *not determined* within the model that we are currently using, and must therefore be taken as given by the analysis. For example, the value of gross national product, or the exchange rate are instances of variables that may well be crucial parts of a spreadsheet model, but do not adopt a value that can be determined *by that model*.

Of course, as the size, complexity and degree of aggregation of your model increases, it may well be the case that variables which were previously regarded as exogenous become endogenous. For example, the value of the exchange rate would certainly be an exogenous variable for the model being used by a firm's accountant, but would not be so for the model employed by the Bank of England.

Parameters In many ways these are terms that are very similar to exogenous variables, in the sense that in the first instance they will be fixed coefficients (constants), and will be used to calculate the values of the endogenous variables of the model. Their long-term constancy, however, depends upon any changes that may take place in the external environment that the model is attempting to mirror.

Perhaps one of the best examples would be the current rate of income taxation, which is obviously a constant for any worksheet created today, but not necessarily the *same* constant in a year's time. The value of the constant has varied. (If this seems like a contradiction in terms, take heart, because it is. This is why the term parameter is frequently used since it implies neither constancy nor variability.)

The crucial distinction between a parameter and an exogenous variable lies in the frequency of variation and in the extent to which the variable is under control. Once again, the income tax rate or the national insurance contribution, are good examples of parameters, since they are policy instruments that (subject to certain constraints) can be altered by the government in order to achieve its objectives. On the other hand, the rate of inflation or the volume of imports are exogenous variables for most of us, but (to the extent that economic policy influences them at all) would be endogenous variables in the Treasury Department's economic model. Finally, the price of gold, or the rate of growth in world trade, will be exogenous variables, even for the Treasury's model, while the EC regulations on maximum permissible exhaust emissions are more properly regarded as a parameter in that model.

Clearly it is these exogenous variables and parameters that must be specified properly if your worksheet model is to be truly flexible.

To do this we must allow each of them to *occupy its own unique cell* and then refer to them thereafter by their cell address (and not by their actual arithmetic value) in all formulae that require use of that variable.

For example, suppose the rate of income taxation was 20 per cent at the moment and that an individual's taxable income was £12 000. The tax payable could be defined as follows:

$$\text{tax payable} = (\text{tax rate}) \times (\text{taxable income})$$

Now it should be clear that in this simple example, tax payable is the endogenous variable, the tax rate is a parameter, and taxable income is an exogenous variable.

You could rewrite the expression above as:

$$\text{tax payable} = 0.25 \times (12\ 000)$$

but this would only be accurate *as long as the tax rate remained at 25 per cent and taxable income remained at £12 000.*

A much better way is to enter the tax rate and taxable income as cell values (in B3 and B4 say), and with tax payable in cell B5, write:

$$+ B3*B4$$

in the B5 cell.

Written in this way, if the tax rate should change to 27 per cent, for example, then all you have to do is enter 0.27 in B3 (overwriting the 0.25 that previously was there) and the new result will be produced in B5. This follows from the fact that the general equation in B5 is still correct, which would not be the case if you had written:

$$0.25*B4$$

in the B5 cell.

The procedure illustrated above is of crucial importance if a large number of equations in a model make reference to particular parameters or exogenous variables. If you do not follow an equivalent procedure, then every single equation that makes such a reference would have to be rewritten to accommodate whatever change has taken place in the value adopted by that parameter. This is not only time consuming but also potentially error creating, since certain references to the parameter may be overlooked and not altered appropriately.

In short, if it seems possible that at any stage in the future the value of a parameter can change, then include it in your model in its own cell, and refer to it thereafter by its cell address in all equations that need to make use of it.

As a more concrete example of these ideas, look at the following example.

EXAMPLE 2.1

A simple income tax system consists of a fixed allowance of £5000 on which no tax is paid, a superannuation payment of 7 per cent of gross income on which no tax is paid, and a tax rate of 25 per cent on all taxable income.

(a) Prepare a worksheet that will calculate the tax payable and the net income of an employee who earns at least £8000 per annum.
(b) Repeat these calculations if the superannuation rate rises to 8 per cent, the tax rate to 30 per cent, and the fixed allowance to £5500.
(c) Calculate the net income of an employee who earns £5000 per annum. Are you happy with your result?

SOLUTION 2.1

(a) Before constructing the worksheet model it is often a good idea to obtain an algebraic picture of the relationships to be modelled. Consequently let

y = gross income
a = the fixed allowance
s = the superannuation rate
t = the tax rate
x = taxable income
p = tax payable
z = net income.

Now we can write:
$$x = (y - a - sy)$$
$$p = tx = t(y - a - sy)$$
$$z = y - p - sy$$

These simple relationships allow us to prepare the worksheet as shown in Worksheet 2.1.

In terms of Lotus formulae, the entries in B5, B6 and B7 are the key to the problem. These are as follows:

In B5 $+B1 - B2 - B1*B3$

Notice how similar this is to our expression for x, with the only difference

WORKSHEET 2.1

B5: +B1-B2-B1*B3

	A	B
1	Gross Income	10000
2	Fixed Allowance	5000
3	Superann. Rate	0.07
4	Tax rate	0.25
5	Taxable Income	4300
6	Tax Payable	1075
7	Net Income	8225

being that the cell references of the variables and parameters are used to replace their symbols (B1 is y, B2 is a, B3 is s).

In B6   +B4*B5

Once taxable income has been calculated in B5, it can then be used to calculate the tax payable by multiplying it by the tax rate. This is equivalent to our expression for p when you remember that B5 is the same as x, and B4 is the equivalent of t.

In B7   +B1−B6−B1*B3

Once again this is equivalent to our expression for z, when you appreciate that B6 will contain the tax payable (p), and that B1*B3 represents the superannuation payment.

In our worksheet we have entered a value of £10 000 for gross income, and as you can see this produces a tax bill of £1075 and a net income of £8225.

(b) All you have to do is make the appropriate changes to the B2, B3 and B4 cells and Lotus will do the rest for you. Now you should fully appreciate the importance of using a general model.

(c) If you enter a value of £5000 in B1, then the taxable income in B5 will become negative (−350), and so too will the tax payable in B6 (−87.5).

Unfortunately, however, few tax systems allow for negative taxation and so we really need to modify the worksheet so that a tax bill of 0 is the *lowest* that can occur.

To do this we should use a *conditional statement* in B6 which will prevent Lotus from calculating a negative value for tax payable. This is easily done if you change the entry in B6 to:

@IF(B5>0, B4*B5, 0)

What this does is to test the value in B5 (taxable income) to see whether (IF) it is positive, and if it is (THEN) apply the tax rate to it, but if it is not (ELSE), return a value of 0.

Make sure you understand the construction of conditional statements like this, since we will be using them extensively throughout this text.

Now that you have made this modification you should find that the worksheet will give the correct answer regardless of the value for gross income that is entered.

EXAMPLE 2.2

Now suppose that with the data from part (a) of Example 2.1 there was a higher rate of taxation on all taxable incomes in excess of £30 000.

Prepare a spreadsheet that will calculate the tax payable and the net income of an employee who earns £50 000 per annum.

SOLUTION 2.2

It should be clear that the introduction of this added complication requires that we write another conditional statement to test whether the employee's taxable income exceeds the threshold for the higher rate of tax. Unfortunately it is not quite as simple as this, since if you think about it carefully you will see that there are in fact two conditional statements required.

This is because we must first of all test whether the taxable income is positive, and *then* if it is, whether it is less than 30 000.

You can see this more clearly if you consider the following possibilities:

Taxable income	*Tax paid*
0	0
10 000	2500
20 000	5000
30 000	7500
40 000	7500 + 0.4(40 000 − 30 000) = 11 500

The crucial point to recognize is that the higher rate of tax is only paid on that part of taxable income that exceeds 30 000, so that once this threshold is exceeded the tax payable is a constant 7500 (25 per cent of 30 000) plus 40 per cent of the difference between the actual taxable income and the threshold.

Bearing this in mind, and remembering that we require two conditional statements, we can proceed to deal with the problem by using a process that is known as *nesting* the conditional statements.

To see how this works, you should appreciate that the Lotus conditional statement is logically constructed as follows:

IF THEN ELSE

However, the THEN part of the statement can in turn contain another IF THEN ELSE statement provided it is contained in brackets (nested), and thereby separated from the main statement. This means that we would obtain something like:

@IF(TEST1, (THEN), ELSE)

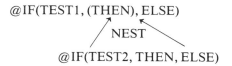

@IF(TEST2, THEN, ELSE)

The nest is seen to be a totally included part of the first THEN part of the conditional statement (and you could nest a third test inside the second THEN if you wanted).

But how does this allow us to perform the required test upon the value of taxable income? First of all we require to make a few modifications to Worksheet 2.1. These are shown in Worksheet 2.2.

WORKSHEET 2.2

B8: @IF(B7>0,(@IF(B7<=B6,B4*B7,B4*B6+B5*(B7-B6))),0)

	A	B
1	Gross Income	50000
2	Fixed Allowance	5000
3	Superann. Rate	0.07
4	Tax Rate 1	0.25
5	Tax Rate 2	0.4
6	Threshold	30000
7	Taxable Income	41500
8	Tax Payable	12100
9	Net Income	34400

As you can see, we have added two new rows to contain the higher tax rate and the threshold for this higher rate. (Once again, you should appreciate that this will allow us to accommodate any subsequent changes to either of these parameters.)

Consequently, remembering that taxable income is now contained in B7 and calculated from:

$$+B1 - B2 - B3*B1$$

we require that the test be directed to that cell. Hence we could start by writing, in B8:

$$@IF(B7>0,(TEST2, THEN, ELSE), 0)$$

This means that if B7 is greater than 0, then further testing inside the nest is to be carried out, but otherwise (i.e. if B7 is negative or 0) the tax payable is 0.

As you can see, we have written our (as yet unknown) nested conditional as (TEST2, THEN, ELSE). This will not work as an actual Lotus formula of course, but it should help you to see how the one that will work is derived.

All we have to do now is work out the structure of the test inside the nest. Thus, as long as B7 is not negative, we want to distinguish between values that are less than or equal to 30 000, and those that are greater. Consequently, we could perhaps try:

$$@IF(B7<=30000, B4*B7, B4*30000+B5*(B7-30000))$$

This means that if B7 (taxable income) is less than or equal to 30 000, then the tax payable is B4 (the lower tax rate) times B7 (taxable income). But otherwise (if B7 exceeds 30 000), then the tax payable is B4 (the lower tax rate) times the threshold (30 000), plus B5 (the higher tax rate) times the difference between taxable income and the threshold (B7 − 30000).

Now all we have to do is replace TEST2, THEN, ELSE in our original statement with this extra conditional statement. However, before we do this, it should be remembered that we have allocated the threshold its own cell reference (B6), and that there is no sense in having done this if we keep on referring to 30 000 in our conditional formula. Consequently, every occurrence of 30 000 in the last formula above should now be replaced with the cell reference B6. After substituting for TEST2, THEN, ELSE as well, this will produce the following expression in B8:

```
@IF(B7)>0,(@IF(B7<=B6,B4*B7,B4*B6+B5*(B7-B6))),0)
```

Try it for yourself and you should find that the correct answer is always produced. Also notice that the entry in B9 is now:

```
+B1-B8-B3*B1
```

For example, what tax would be paid by an employee who earns £60 000 per annum? If you have prepared the last worksheet correctly you should find that the answer is £15 820, because

$$\text{taxable income} = 60\,000 - 5000 - 0.07(60\,000) = £50\,800$$

The first £30 000 of taxable income is taxed at 25 per cent, giving a payment of £7500, and the remaining 20 800 is taxed at 40 per cent giving an additional payment of £8320. The total tax due is therefore £15 820.

However, if gross income was only £10 000 then the same tax as before is due. Confirm this for yourself on your own worksheet.

EXAMPLE 2.3

The price of electricity is determined by a multipart tariff whereby monthly usage rates of 20 000 kWh or less are charged at a standard rate of £0.1 per kWh.

For usage rates in excess of 20 000 kWh, however, the charge is £0.07 per kWh, for those units (and only those units) that are in excess of 20 000 kWh.

Prepare a worksheet that will calculate the electricity bill for any entered usage level.

SOLUTION 2.3

You should form Worksheet 2.3.

The crucial element of the analysis is the entry in B5. This is:

$$@IF(B1 < B4, B3*B1, B3*B4 + B2*(B1 - B4))$$

The logic of this statement is identical to that of the last example, with the exception that there is no need for a nested conditional in this case.

If you work you way through the statement then you can see that if the usage level (B1) is less than the threshold (B4), then the charge is simply the higher tariff (B3) times the usage level. If this is not the case, however, then the threshold number of units (B4) are all charged at the higher tariff (B3), but the extra units

WORKSHEET 2.3
```
B5: @IF(B1<B4, B3*B1, B3*B4*(B1-B4))

                    A                    B
            1   Usage Rate (KWH)      40000
            2   Lower Rate               0.07
            3   Standard Rate            0.1
            4   Threshold            20000
            5   Invoice               3400
```

(B1 − B4) are charged at the lower tariff (B2). The total charge is therefore the sum of these two elements.

2.3 The algebra of indices

In algebra, the process of multiplying a number of identical terms together is known as *exponentiation*, with the value of any one of the identical terms being known as the base, and the number of these terms that are to be multiplied being known as the *exponent* or *power* or *index*.

This means, for example, that multiplying 6 terms of 2 together is to be thought of as raising 2 to the power of 6, with 2 being the base and 6 being the index or exponent of that base.

If the terms are numerically unspecified, then it is common to let the base be denoted by x and the exponent by n, so that x^n defines the process of raising x to the power of n.

Clearly this terminology is a useful abbreviating technique for expressing what could otherwise be cumbersome expressions, but it should also be understood that these abbreviated expressions can be used as operational algebraic terms, provided the necessary rules have been understood.

For example, suppose that we were required to square a number and then multiply this square by the cube of the same number. Using our index terminology, we could let the number be represented by x and then write:

$$(x^2)(x^3)$$

However, you should be able to see that this is equivalent to multiplying 5 terms in x together, and that the required product could be written more succinctly as x^5.

This idea gives us our first rule of index operations since it clearly implies that if two or more identical indexed bases are to be multiplied together, then the required product will be given by the base to the power of the *sum of the indices*. That is:

$$(x^n)(x^m) = x^{n+m}$$

WORKSHEET 2.4

	A	B
1	x	10
2	n	2
3	m	3
4	x^n	100
5	x^m	1000
6	(x^n)(x^m)	100000
7	n+m	5
8	x^(n+m)	100000

You can confirm this rule quite easily if you prepare Worksheet 2.4. All you have to do is enter any three positive numbers in B1..B3 and then the following formulae in B4..B8:

in B4   +B1^B2
in B5   +B1^B3
in B6   +B4*B5
in B7   +B2+B3
in B8   +B1^B7

As you can see, the same result is returned to B8 as to B4, thereby confirming that:

$$(x^n)(x^m) = x^{n+m}$$

Try a few more examples for yourself until you feel happy that you have understood the point.

Now suppose that we were required to divide x^5 by x^3, how would the rules of indices allow us to do this? We could, for instance, proceed as follows:

$$x^5/x^3 = (x^3)(x^2)/x^3$$

All we have done is to rewrite the numerator of the expression as a product that contains the denominator of the expression (x^3) as one of its terms. However, written in this form, it should be clear that since $x^3/x^3 = 1$, this quotient reduces to x^2.

We therefore conclude that:

$$x^5/x^3 = x^2$$

It is no coincidence that the answer has an index that is equal to the difference between the index of the numerator and the index of the denominator, since this is our second rule of index operations. That is:

$$x^n/x^m = x^{n-m}$$

Once again you can confirm this on Worksheet 2.4, since all you have to do is enter a negative value in B3 (for the index) and the implied quotient will be evaluated in both B4 and B8.

An important point emerges from this procedure, since if the entry in B3 is negative, then the entry in B5 will be evaluated as B1 to a negative power. Furthermore, although B6 still instructs Lotus to *multiply* B4 by B5, yet, since a division process has clearly been performed, you should be suspecting that in the algebra of indices a negative index implies a division process (as opposed to a multiplication process when the indices are positive).

This is exactly the case, since a negative index is simply another way of writing the reciprocal of a term with a positive index. That is:

$$1/x^n = x^{-n}$$

This should allow you to see that since multiplying any term by a reciprocal term is identical to *dividing* that term by the denominator of the second term, the algebra of indices uses this fact to allow any division process to be expressed as an equivalent product. In other words:

$$x^n/x^m = x^n(1/x^m) = (x^n)(x^{-m})$$

It is precisely this logic which meant that in Worksheet 2.4 we did not need to change the entry in B6 from B4*B5 to B4/B5, to move from a multiplication to a division process. Lotus knew that when the negative index in B3 was encountered, a division process was being instructed (even although the formula in B6 still contained the multiplication instruction).

Having explained positive and negative indices, you may be wondering what sort of process is implied by an index of 0.

In fact, the answer is quite simple since if we multiply x^n by x^0, then the first rule of index operations tells us that the product will be given by $x^{n+0} = x^n$. This implies that x^n has had its value *unaltered* as a result of being multiplied by x^0, and since the only value of x^0 that will do this is 1, we conclude that:

$$x^0 = 1$$

You may have noticed that all the indices employed so far have been whole numbers. This meant that they could easily be interpreted as multiplying a given number of base terms together.

But what sort of arithmetic process would an index term of 0.5 or 1.5 imply?

To see this, you must understand that whereas x^n means multiply n identical x terms together, $x^{1/n}$ means calculate the number that, *if n of them were multiplied together* would give the value of x. In other words, $x^{1/n}$ means take the nth root of x.

For example, since x^2 means square the value of x, it follows that $x^{1/2}$ means take the square root of x. Or, since x^3 means cube the value of x, $x^{1/3}$ means take the cube root of x.

From these examples it should be clear that taking the reciprocal of an integer index implies the process of finding the specified root of the base.

WORKSHEET 2.5

	A	B
1	x	64
2	n	2
3	1/n	0.5
4	m	3
5	1/m	0.333333
6	x^(1/n)	8
7	x^(1/m)	4
8	(x^1/n)(x^1/m)	32
9	1/n+1/m	0.833333
10	x^(1/n+1/m)	32

You can see this in Worksheet 2.5 where integer indices have had their reciprocals calculated and then applied to a base value.

The entries in B3 and B5 are now 1/B2 and 1/B4; B6 and B7 now contain +B1^B3 and +B1^B5; B8 and B9 contain +B6*B7 and +B3+B5; while B10 contains +B1^B9.

As you can see, the basic rule of multiplying and dividing index expressions still apply, even when reciprocal indices are employed. In other words:

$$[x^{1/n}][x^{1/m}] = x^{1/n + 1/m}$$

and

$$[x^{1/n}]/[x^{1/m}] = x^{1/n - 1/m}$$

This means that if $x = 64$ and $n = 2$, then:

$$x^{1/n} = x^{0.5} = 8$$

Also, if $m = 3$ then:

$$x^{1/m} = x^{0.333\,33} = 4$$

and so:

$$[x^{1/n}][x^{1/m}] = (8)(4) = x^{1/n + 1/m} = x^{0.8333} = 32$$

Now you should practise a few of these operations in your own worksheet so that you become quite confident with the processes involved.

However, although integer indices and their reciprocals represent mathematical processes that are easily visualized (power and root), the same cannot be said for an expression such as $x^{m/n}$. For example, what is the value of $8^{2/3}$? The answer is 4, and can be understood in terms of raising 8 to the power of 2 (giving 64) and then taking the cube root of this result (giving 4).

In general, therefore $x^{m/n}$ is to be viewed as the *n*th root of *x* to the power of *m*.

This is a useful idea since it allows us to separate the two processes involved in such a way that another rule of index operations becomes clear. Namely, if we are required to evaluate:

$$(x^m)^{1/n}$$

then since we are looking for the nth root of x to the power of m, and since we already know this to be $x^{m/n}$, we can conclude that to raise one indexed expression to the power of another index we simply have to multiply the indices together. That is:

$$(x^m)^n = x^{mn}$$

and

$$(x^m)^{1/n} = x^{m/n}$$

You can confirm these ideas in Worksheet 2.6.
The entries of importance are:

in B5 (B1^B2)^B4, i.e. $(x^2)^3$
in B6 (B1^B4)^B3, i.e. $(x^3)^{0.5}$
in B7 +B2*B3
in B8 +B4*B3

Now use your worksheet to experiment with different index expressions and to confirm that raising x to the power of n and then raising the result to the power of m is identical to raising x to the power of n times m.

The result of these discussions is that we have four basic rules that govern operations on indexed terms:

1. $(x^n)(x^m) = x^{n+m}$
2. $1/x^n = x^{-n}$
3. $x^n/x^m = x^{n-m}$
4. $(x^n)^m = x^{nm}$

WORKSHEET 2.6

	A	B
1	x	8
2	n	2
3	1/n	0.5
4	m	3
5	(x^n)^m	262144
6	(x^m)^(1/n)	22.62741
7	nm	6
8	m(1/n)	1.5
9	x^(nm)	262144
10	x^(m(1/n))	22.62741

The algebra of indices

EXAMPLE 2.4

A country's population (p) at time t is given by:

$$p = 1.2t^{0.25}$$

where p is measured in millions.

(a) Calculate the country's population when $t = 6$.
(b) Calculate the percentage increase in the population between $t = 3$ and $t = 8$.

SOLUTION 2.4

(a) When $t = 6$ we have:

$$p = 1.2(6^{0.25}) = 1.2(1.565\ 08) = 1.8781 \text{ million.}$$

(b) When $t = 3$:

$$p = 1.2(3^{0.25}) = 1.645\ 09 \text{ million.}$$

While when $t = 8$:

$$p = 1.2(8^{0.25}) = 2.018\ 15 \text{ million.}$$

Therefore between $t = 3$ and $t = 8$ the population has increased by

$$(2.01815 - 1.645\ 09)/1.645\ 09 = 22.68 \text{ per cent.}$$

EXAMPLE 2.5

The relationship between a firm's output (z) and its usage of labour and capital is given by:

$$z = (x^{0.3})(y^{0.5})$$

where x is the number of labour units employed, and y is the number of capital units employed.

(a) Calculate the output obtainable from employing 100 units of labour and 60 units of capital.
(b) If either the usage level of labour or the usage level of capital could be doubled from their values in part (a) above, which would have the greatest effect upon the output obtainable?
(c) If both the usage levels of labour and capital could be increased by a factor of k (a constant), what would be the effect upon the output obtainable?

SOLUTION 2.5

(a) When $x = 100$ and $y = 60$, we have:
$$z = (100^{0.3})(60^{0.5}) = (3.9811)(7.7459) = 30.84 \text{ units}.$$

(b) If the labour input is doubled (to 200) then:
$$z = (200^{0.3})(60^{0.5}) = 37.96 \text{ units}.$$

If the capital input is doubled (to 120) then:
$$z = (100^{0.3})(120^{0.5}) = 43.61$$

With these conditions of production, doubling the capital employed will have a greater effect upon output than doubling the labour input.

(c) If both inputs are increased by a factor of k, then we have:
$$z = [(kx)^{0.3}][(ky)^{0.5}] = [(k^{0.3})(x^{0.3})(k^{0.5})(y^{0.5})]$$

Therefore:
$$z = k^{0.3+0.5}[(x^{0.3})(y^{0.5})] = k^{0.8}(z)$$

As you can see, the effect of increasing both input usage levels by a factor of k has been to increase the output obtainable by a factor of $k^{0.8}$. This means, for example, that if both input usage levels were doubled ($k = 2$) then output would increase by a factor of $2^{0.8} = 1.741$.

2.4 Functions and equations

The fundamental characteristic of a function is the idea that the relationship between two variables (which we will call y and x) can be expressed in a particular mathematical form.

If we say, for example, that y is a function of x, then we are simply stating that the association between y and x is such that it can be expressed by a functional relationship. This relationship can be quantitatively *indeterminate* in the sense that the *exact* nature of the association between y and x is unknown, or it can be quantitatively *precise* in the sense that the function provides a specific rule that will always convert any given x value into a unique value for y.

In either case, the fact that y is regarded as a function of x is the starting point for the construction of any model.

As a simple example of this idea, we might argue that the fuel consumption per mile travelled by a car (m.p.g.) was a function of the engine size measured in cubic centimetres (c.c.). Accordingly, we would write:

$$\text{m.p.g. is a function of engine size (c.c.)}$$

As such, this is a fairly 'safe' statement as it does not say what the exact nature of the relationship is, though we would expect that as engine size increases, so too does fuel consumption. This means that we are expecting what is known as a *direct* relationship between y and x (as opposed to an *indirect* one when one variable decreases as the other increases).

Notice that we still do not know the exact nature of the function, since in most cases exact specification of functional forms will be obtained on the basis of observation, experimentation and statistical analysis. But before this can be understood, a working knowledge of the types of function that can be estimated will have to be obtained.

2.4.1 Functional notation and operations

In notational terms the general functional relationship is usually represented as:

$$y = f(x)$$

where the brackets do not imply a multiplication procedure, and the 'f' symbol does not represent a numerical quantity that can be subjected to algebraic or arithmetic operations. In short, when the above expression is encountered, it is to be read as 'y is a function of x' and the 'f' is to be regarded as a symbol that represents the (perhaps unknown) rule for obtaining the value of y from any given value of x.

This means for example, that:

$$y = f(3)$$

is simply another way of saying 'the value of y that results from the functional rule when x adopts a value of 3'.

Now, if $y = f(x)$ is the general functional form (from which no calculations can be derived), the specific functional form requires a more determinate statement of the relationship between y and x.

For example, if:

$$y = f(x) = 4x$$

then we have a functional form of x that relates y to x in a specific and unique manner. To see this we note that for any given value of x there is *one and only one* associated value of $f(x)$. This value is of course determined by the rule:

$$y = 4x$$

and implies that if x can be any real number, then the value of y is given by the rule:

$$f(x) = 4x$$

So:

$$y = f(3) = 4(3) = 12$$

and
$$y = f(-5) = 4(-5) = -20$$

More will be said at a later stage about the properties possessed by various types of functional forms, but at the moment we should consider some of the less obvious implications of making functional statements.

When we consider the statement $y = f(x)$, it is the mathematical convention to denote y as the *dependent* variable and x as the *independent* variable. However, the apparent implication of this — that the value of y *depends* upon the value of x — has to be interpreted with care. Stated as above, the implication is valid, since the value of y does indeed depend upon the value of x, but this cannot necessarily be construed to imply a *causal* relationship between the variables.

This is because when we write $y = f(x)$ we are merely stating that y is the value obtained when x is operated on by the functional rule, and while this obviously implies that there is a systematic association between y and x, this implication cannot necessarily be extended to a direct causal link between y and x.

This reservation derives from the fact that the systematic association between the variables can stem from a number of sources:

x influences y.
y influences x.
x and y are both systematically related to some third variable.
x and y are associated by chance.

Only the first of these possibilities can be interpreted as x having a *causal effect* upon y.

These ideas mean that the difficulty of identifying the exact nature of any causal relationship between two or more variables is a perpetual source of confusion in business and economics.

For example, it is a fundamental tenet of elementary economic theory that the quantity demanded of a product by an individual depends (amongst other things) in an indirect manner upon its price.

Letting q represent an individual's demand quantity, and letting p represent the market price of the product, we could write:

$$q = f(p)$$

The direction of causation in this case is unambiguous since any one individual's demand is unlikely to be able to influence the market price, thereby precluding the possibility that the value of p is 'caused' by the value of q.

So, in the case of individual demand, we can invest $q = f(p)$ with a causal direction which implies that changes in price cause changes in the quantity demanded, but not vice versa.

However, suppose we aggregated all individual demands to obtain the overall demand for this product and call this Q. We can presumably still write Q as an indirect function of p:

$$Q = g(p)$$

but can we still invest this function with a one-way causal link from p to Q?

The answer is 'surely not', since it is now equally likely that changes in the overall market demand for the product will cause changes in the market price. The causal relationship between p and Q is now ambiguous and the functional statement $Q = g(p)$ cannot have a unique causal inference attributed to it.

The importance of this discussion justifies further illustration by means of another example.

Consider a thermostatically controlled heating system which is used to heat a building. Given the setting on the thermostat, the amount of fuel that the system consumes (y) is obviously dependent in an *indirect* manner upon the outside temperature (x). We can therefore write:

$$y = f(x)$$

Given any value of x (outside temperature), and the thermostat setting, we could calculate the fuel usage (i.e. the value of y) if we know the functional rule. However, it is equally true that given any value of y, and the thermostat setting, we could also calculate the associated value of x. Mathematically, it makes no difference whether we know x or y, since as long as we know one we can determine the other. Yet it is apparent that changes in y are caused by changes in x rather than vice versa.

There is, however, another point to be noted. This is the fact that we were careful to specify that the thermostat setting had to be given. If we denote this setting by the symbol s, then we can see that the simple model above is in fact specified in terms of *two* independent variables: x and s.

That is, instead of confining ourselves to $y = f(x)$, *given a value of s*, we could explicitly recognize the thermostat setting as a variable and write:

$$y = f(x, s)$$

This expression states that y is a function of *both* x and s, and that the value of y is jointly determined by the values of x, s and the functional rule.

Once again x and s are regarded as the independent variables but in the context of this example, while it remains valid to argue that x has a causal effect upon y, we cannot be so sure about any causal link between s and y. At first sight it would seem that a change in the setting would cause y to change in the *same* direction, but there is also the possibility that an increase in y will cause the setting to be reduced in order to save on energy use. The causal link between y and s is therefore ambiguous, with y being a direct function of s, but s perhaps depending in an indirect manner upon y.

Furthermore, as regards this example it might also be thought that x and s themselves could be functionally related to one another, since a drastic change in the outside temperature might induce a change in the thermostat setting. But this is to misunderstand the purpose of a thermostat. If, for example, it is wished to keep the building at a temperature of 19°C, and the thermostat is set accordingly, then the heating will operate whether the outside temperature is 18.9°C or −5°C, but it will obviously operate longer and more intensively in the latter case than in the former.

This means that variations in the outside temperature do not provide a logical reason for altering the thermostat setting, and that we should not anticipate a causal relationship between x and s.

However, this need not be the case in other circumstances when different variables are being considered, and the possibility exists that there are cross-effects between one independent variable and another.

Three final points have to be made about functions of more than one independent variable. Firstly, there is a distinction to be made between controlled and uncontrolled variables. In the context of the last example it should be clear that x is uncontrollable, while s is subject to control. This idea of a controlled variable is of considerable importance in decision- and policy-making contexts as some element of control is an essential component of any attempt to use particular variables as means of achieving identified objectives.

Secondly, if a specific form of $y = f(x, s)$ was to be graphed, it would require a three-dimensional construction, in which any given y value is related to a *pair* of x and s values.

If there is a somewhat natural reluctance to become embroiled in three-dimensional geometry, then the only alternative is to adopt a piecemeal approach in which s is fixed at several representative values and y is then graphed in terms of x. This will create what is known as a *level curve*, in which each level represents the relationship between y and x for *different* chosen values of s. You can see how this could be done later on in this chapter in Example 2.12.

Thirdly, we should recognize that there is no need to restrict ourselves to two independent variables, since the functional notation is perfectly capable of accommodating as many variables as we care to choose.

Returning to our previous example we could recognize that the efficiency of the boiler (e) and the effectiveness of any insulation (i) are two further variables that will influence fuel consumption, and consequently we could write:

$$y = f(x, s, e, i)$$

Obviously there may be a tendency to run out of letters of the alphabet before we run out of variables, and so we can conclude by stating the most general formulation:

$$y = f(x_1, x_2, x_3, \ldots, x_n)$$

where y is now to be regarded as a function of the n independent variables $x_1, x_2, x_3, \ldots, x_n$.

Finally, as another application of these ideas, we could argue that in terms of the elementary theory of demand the quantity demanded (Q) could be represented as:

$$Q = f(p, y, u_1, u_2, ..., u_n, v, t)$$

where p is the price of the product itself, y is an index of consumers' income levels, $u_1, u_2, ..., u_n$ are the prices of other relevant products, v is a variable representing tastes, and t is a time variable representing the influence of the passage of time upon the quantity demanded.

2.4.2 Solution of equations

Closely related to the idea of function is the notion of an equation, and finding the solution to an equation or set of equations is arguably one of the most important aspects of elementary mathematical analysis.

In its simplest form an equation is merely a statement that relates a term or terms on the lefthand side of an equality sign to a term or terms on the righthand side. The equality sign implies that the lefthand side must equal the righthand side, and the 'solution' to the equation is that value (or those values) of the variable (or variables) which satisfies the equality requirement. It is, however, important to recognize that while some equations may have only one solution, there are others that have a large number or even none.

Consider, for example, the following equation:

$$2 + 4 = 6$$

Although it is by definition true that the lefthand side equals the righthand side, it will be noticed that there is no variable term in the equation and consequently that it cannot be 'solved' as such.

For this reason it is frequently referred to as an identity and the triple equality symbol used:

$$2 + 4 \equiv 6$$

Nevertheless, the expression $2 + 4 \equiv 6$ could be thought of as representing the result of solving the following equation:

$$2x + 4 = 6$$

This is because when $x = 1$ the lefthand side becomes $2(1) + 4 = 2 + 4 = 6$.

However, it could also represent the solution to:

$$2 + 4x = 6$$

or

$$2 + 4 = 6x$$

since in each case when $x = 1$ the equation is 'solved' in the sense that only when $x = 1$ do the two sides balance.

Many types of simple equation are easily solved by algebraic transformation in which variables and/or constant terms are transferred from one side of the equality sign to the other in order to make the solution more obvious. Hence if:

$$6x + 2 - 6 = 0$$

we could rewrite this as:

$$6x - 4 = 0$$

Implying that

$$6x = 4$$

and that

$$x = 4/6 = 2/3$$

Although the student often finds it easier to deal with equations involving only variables and numbers, it is perfectly feasible to apply the logic above to equations containing only variables and undefined constant terms. Hence:

$$ax + b - c = 0$$

is a perfectly valid equation even though the constant terms a, b and c do not have numerical definition. The solution is obtained as before:

$$ax + b - c = 0$$

Implying that

$$ax = c - b$$

and that

$$x = (c - b)/a$$

This discussion also highlights an important source of confusion between the concepts of 'unknowns' and variables. In the equation:

$$ax + b - c = 0$$

there are four *unknown* terms, but only one of these is a variable, which, by convention we have denoted as x. It is this term that varies in the arithmetic value it adopts in order to satisfy the equation and hence provide a solution.

An equation need not, of course, contain only one variable, but if more than one variable is present, then it cannot be solved on the basis of one equation alone. Hence if the constant term b in the last equation was to be regarded as a variable, and denoted by y, the equation would become:

$$ax + by - c = 0$$

Implying that

$$ax = c - by$$

and that
$$x = (c - by)/a$$
You should be able to see that this is not really a solution to the equation, since the value that x adopts cannot be obtained without knowing the value of y and vice versa.

To clarify this point consider the equation:
$$x/y = 2$$
Transposition yields $y = 2x$ but this is *all* that can be achieved, since the equation has no unique solution unless a specific value of y or x is known (effectively making it a constant). That is, $x = 2y$ is satisfied by the following (x, y) values (and a lot more too tedious to mention):
$$(1, 2); \ (2, 1); \ (1, 0.5); \ (0, 0); \ (-0.5, -0.25); \ (-1, -0.5)$$
Clearly, the single equation $x = 2y$ contains only *one* piece of information about the relationship between x and y, and since there are *two* variables whose values must be obtained, a *unique* solution cannot be found.

If, however, we had *another* equation (such as $x + y = 6$), as well as $x = 2y$, then these two equations would convey two pieces of information about the relationship between x and y, and could then be taken *together* (i.e. simultaneously) to provide a unique solution. So:
$$x = 2y$$
implies that
$$x + y = 6$$
can be rewritten as
$$2y + y = 6$$
and that
$$3y = 6$$
whereby
$$y = 2$$
Furthermore, when $y = 2$ it follows that $x = 2y$ gives $x = 4$ and that the unique solution of the two equations is:
$$y = 2 \quad \text{and} \quad x = 4$$
Since this unique solution was obtained by taking the information contained in both equations simultaneously, it is sometimes referred to as the *simultaneous solution*.

More will be said about simultaneous equations and their solution at a later stage, but for the moment it is sufficient to appreciate that as the number of variables increases, then the number of equations necessary to provide a unique solution must increase accordingly i.e. *n* variables require *n* independent equations before a unique solution can be obtained.

Returning to simpler equations, you should appreciate that the rules of indices discussed in the previous section provide an important method for solving equations that contain variables whose index is not equal to 1.

Consider, for example:

$$x^2 = 4$$

Common sense suggests that if $x^2 = 4$ then x must equal the square root of 4, i.e. ± 2. This is indeed correct, but such common sense is frequently abandoned when equations such as:

$$(x^{5/3}) = 32$$

are encountered.

Yet the rules of indices provide a simple method for obtaining a solution, which is to raise both sides of the equation to the power of the reciprocal of the exponent (3/5) and then obtain:

$$(x^{5/3})^{3/5} = 32^{3/5}$$

but, by the rules of indices, the lefthand side is equivalent to x to the power of 1 since:

$$x^{[(5/3)(3/5)]} = x^1 = x$$

Therefore:

$$x = 32^{3/5} = 8$$

More generally, if n is any constant index, and c is any positive constant, then the equation

$$x^n = c$$

can be solved as follows:

$$(x^n)^{1/n} = c^{1/n}$$

Therefore

$$x^{n(1/n)} = x^{n/n} = x = c^{1/n}$$

EXAMPLE 2.6

The value of a company's assets (v) over a given period was known to be given by:

$$v = 1000t^{3/2}$$

where v is measured in pounds sterling and t represents time such that $t = 1, ..., 11$.

(a) Obtain the value of the company's assets at the end of: (i) the first time period; (ii) the fifth time period.
(b) After how many periods did the value of the company's assets reach £4000?
(c) After how many periods was the value of the assets double its value at the end of the third period?

SOLUTION 2.6

(a) (i) With $t = 1$, we have:
$$v = 1000(1^{3/2}) = £1000$$
(ii) With $t = 5$, we have:
$$v = 1000(5^{3/2}) = 1000(11.180\,339) = £11\,180.34.$$

(b) We require t such that
$$4000 = 1000 t^{3/2}$$

Therefore
$$t^{3/2} = 4000/1000 = 4$$

So
$$(t^{3/2})^{2/3} = 4^{2/3}$$

and
$$t = 4^{2/3} = 2.519 \text{ years}$$

Assuming that the value of the assets increased continuously over the period, then a value of £4000 was achieved after 2.52 time periods.

(c) The value at the end of the third period will be given by
$$v(3) = 1000(3^{3/2}) = £5196.15$$

Double this value is £10 392.30, and we therefore require t such that
$$10\,392.3 = 1000(t^{3/2})$$

Implying that
$$t^{3/2} = 10.392$$

and that
$$t = 10.392^{2/3} = 4.762$$

It will take 4.762 time periods before the value of the assets is double its value at the end of the third time period.

EXAMPLE 2.7

In a particular month the price of a unit of electricity was 1.5 times the price of a unit of gas.

In that month, a customer used 1000 units of gas and 700 units of electricity, and received a *combined* bill of £1025.

What were the respective prices of units of gas and electricity in that month?

SOLUTION 2.7

Let x = the price of gas per unit; let y = the price of electricity per unit.
From the first sentence we therefore have

$$y = 1.5x$$

From the second sentence we know that

$$\text{total gas expenditure} = 1000x$$
$$\text{total electricity expenditure} = 700y$$

Therefore

$$\text{total fuel expenditure} = 1000x + 700y$$

which we know to have been £1025. Consequently

$$1000x + 700y = 1025$$

However, since $y = 1.5x$, we can rewrite this as

$$1000x + 700(1.5x) = 1025$$

Implying that

$$1000x + 1050x = 1025$$

and that

$$2050x = 1025$$

Therefore

$$x = £0.5 \text{ and } y = 1.5(0.5) = £0.75$$

EXAMPLE 2.8

The total cost (c) of producing a firm's product is given in terms of the number of units produced per time period (x) by

$$c = 8x^{0.9}$$

If each item is sold at a constant price of £4, how many units will have to be sold if the firm is to break even in a particular time period?

SOLUTION 2.8

The firm will break even when its total costs of production are equal to its total revenue from sales. So, since each unit is sold at a constant price of £4 its revenue (r) will be given by

$$r = 4x$$

We therefore require

$$r = c$$

Implying that

$$4x = 8x^{0.9}$$

If we now divide both sides of this equation by x, then by the rules of indices we obtain

$$4 = 8x^{0.9}/x = 8x^{-0.1}$$

Implying that

$$4 = 8/x^{0.1}$$

Therefore

$$4x^{0.1} = 8 \text{ (after cross-multiplication)}$$

and

$$x^{0.1} = 8/4 = 2$$

Consequently

$$x = 2^{1/0.1} = 2^{10} = 1024 \text{ units.}$$

EXAMPLE 2.9

(a) Using the information from parts (a) and (b) of Example 2.1, can you find the increase in the fixed allowance that would be necessary to leave the tax bill of an employee who earns £10 000 unchanged in the face of the increased tax and superannuation rates?
(b) Using the same information as above, can you find the increase in the fixed allowance that would be necessary to leave the employee's net income unchanged in the face of the increased tax and superannuation rates? (Once again assume that the employee earns £10 000.)

SOLUTION 2.9

(a) The easiest way to deal with this problem is to modify Worksheet 2.1 so that column B contains the 'before' information, and column C contains the 'after' information. (All you have to do is copy the range B1..B7 into C1..C7.) This has been done in Worksheet 2.7.

As you can see, with a gross income £10 000, the effect of the changed rates and allowances is to increase the tax payable to £1110 and reduce net income to £8090.

What we require is that the allowance be changed in such a way that the same tax (on the same income) is payable as before (£1075). Therefore, we require $p = 1075$. But

$$p = t(y - a - sy)$$

and

$$t = 0.3, \ y = 10\,000, \ s = 0.08$$

So we require

$$0.3[10\,000 - a - 0.08(10\,000)] = 1075$$

Implying that

$$3000 - 0.3a - 240 = 1075$$

and that

$$0.3a = 3000 - 240 - 1075 = 1685$$

WORKSHEET 2.7

```
C10: +B1-C3*B1-B6/C4
```

	A	B	C
1	Gross Income	10000	10000
2	Fixed Allowance	5000	5500
3	Superann. Rate	0.07	0.08
4	Tax Rate	0.25	0.3
5	Taxable Income	4300	3700
6	Tax Payable	1075	1110
7	Net Income	8225	8090
8			
9			
10			5616.666
11			
12			
13			
14			5950

Therefore
$$a = 1685/0.3 = 5616.66$$

Now check that this is correct by entering 5616.66 into C2. You will find that the tax due is the same as before.

More generally, however, we can obtain an expression for the required value of a in terms of y, s, p and t by reasoning as follows:
$$p = t(y - a - sy) = ty - ta - tsy$$

Therefore
$$ta = ty - tsy - p$$

and
$$a = (ty - tsy - p)/t$$

or
$$a = y - sy - p/t$$

You can enter this as a Lotus formula in any vacant cell of the worksheet, in which case you will always obtain the change in the fixed allowance that is needed to make the other changes 'neutral' in their impact upon the tax that is due.

This has been done in the C10 cell of Worksheet 2.7 from the formula:
$$+B1 - C3*B1 - B6/C4$$

As you can see, the same result is returned as previously calculated, but this expression will also provide the required value of a for different changes in the superannuation and/or tax rates. Try it.

(b) The logic for finding the change in the fixed allowance that will leave an employee's net income unchanged is similar to that of the last problem, with the exception that we must remember that net income will also be reduced directly by the changed superannuation rate as well as the direct and indirect effects of the changed tax rate. Consequently, since
$$z = y - t(y - a - sy) - sy$$

then when $t = 0.3$, $y = 10\,000$ and $s = 0.08$ the value of z must remain at 8225.

We therefore require
$$10\,000 - 0.3[10\,000 - a - 0.08(10\,000)] - 0.08(10\,000) = £8225$$

Implying by the same logic as before, that
$$0.3a = 8225 - 10\,000 + 3000 - 240 + 800 = £1785$$

Therefore
$$a = £5950$$

Once again you can enter this as a Lotus formula in any vacant cell of the worksheet, in which case you will always obtain the change in the fixed allowance that is needed to make the other changes 'neutral' in terms of their effect upon net income.

This has been done in the C14 cell of Worksheet 2.7 from the formula

$$(B7 - B1 + C4*B1 - C4*C3*B1 + C3*B1)/C4$$

It is left as an exercise for you to deduce how this formula has been derived from the general algebraic expression for the required value of a. The procedure is identical to that employed in the previous part of the question.

These examples conclude our introductory discussion on functions and equations, but as you might imagine some functional forms are used more often than others, and consequently have names given to them. The simplest of these is known as the linear function and requires further examination.

2.5 Linear functions

If any of you have ever cooked a chicken or a turkey then you will know that to avoid the dangers of food poisoning the bird must be cooked for a period of time that depends upon its weight. You will probably know as well that it is also recommended to allow a certain cooking time over and above the time required by the weight. In other words the cooking instructions would be something like:

50 minutes per kilogram of weight and 20 minutes over.

What you perhaps do not know is that these instructions are simply the result of a linear function that has been derived to model the required cooking time for poultry.

This function would have the form

$$y = f(x) = 20 + 50x$$

where y is the required cooking time in minutes, and x is the weight of the bird in kilograms. This means, for example, that a 6 kilogram turkey would require a total of $6(50) = 300$ minutes plus 20 minutes = 320 minutes in all.

Now there is a slight peculiarity about this formulation, since if you think about it, the implication is that you require 20 minutes cooking time even to cook a nonexistent (weightless) turkey. This follows from the fact that when $x = 0$ the value of $f(x) = f(0)$ is 20 (minutes). Clearly this is nonsense, but it can be made more sensible if you think of the 20 minutes as being the minimum cooking time required if you are going to cook *at all*.

On the other hand, there can be circumstances in which the value of the function when x adopts a value of 0 have a more obvious meaning. For example, telephone bills are usually composed of two elements: a standing charge for the rental of the equipment which has to be paid regardless of whether any calls are made; and a charge per metered unit that is used. In this case, any customer's telephone bill (y) will be described by the following linear function of the number of metered units used (x):

$$y = a + bx$$

where a represents the standing charge, and b represents the charge per unit.

This means, of course, that if no calls are made (i.e. $x = 0$) then $f(x) = f(0) = a + bx = a + b(0) = a$. (You will still get a bill even if you make no calls at all.)

More generally, we can say that a function of the form

$$y = f(x) = a + bx$$

is known as a *linear function*, since if it were plotted, the resulting graph would be a straight line.

In the context of this function a and b are constant terms and are respectively known as the intercept and gradient of the graph of the function.

The intercept term is defined as the value of $f(x)$ when $x = 0$ and is therefore the y coordinate associated with the intersection between the line and the y axis.

The term b represents the gradient of the associated line, in the sense that it measures the change in the value of y resulting from a given change in the value of x. Hence $b = 2$ implies that for every unit change in the value of x, the value of y changes by 2 units, and that, in general, for every unit change in the value of x the value of y changes by b units.

This can be more clearly understood if we consider a specific example.

EXAMPLE 2.10

A firm's total annual costs of production (c) depend upon the rent and rates for its factory, and upon the number of units of output produced (x). If the annual rent and rates are £15 000, and if each unit of output costs £10 to produce, derive the firm's total cost function, and graph its behaviour for output levels not exceeding 18 000 units.

SOLUTION 2.10

Clearly the firm's total costs will be given by the following function of output.

$$c = 15\ 000 + 10x$$

Given this function you can tell Lotus to graph it for you from Worksheet 2.8. Notice that once again, we have prepared a flexible worksheet in the sense that you can easily change the values adopted by the intercept and gradient terms (a and b).

WORKSHEET 2.8

	A	B	C	D
1	Intercept	15000	x (output)	y (cost)
2	Gradient	10	0.00	15000
3			1000.00	25000
4			2000.00	35000
5			3000.00	45000
6			4000.00	55000
7			5000.00	65000
8			6000.00	75000
9			7000.00	85000
10			8000.00	95000
11			9000.00	105000
12			10000.00	115000
13			11000.00	125000
14			12000.00	135000
15			13000.00	145000
16			14000.00	155000
17			15000.00	165000
18			16000.00	175000
19			17000.00	185000
20			18000.00	195000

The entries in C2..C20 are the values of x and were obtained from the Data Fill command with a start value of 0 and a step value of 1000. The command sequence is as follows:.

/ Data Fill C2..C20 (fill range) 0 (start value) 1000 (step value) 18000 (stop value)

In D2 we have written the equation of the straight line to be graphed in terms of the intercept term in B1, and the gradient term in B2. The entry is

$$+ B\$1 + B\$2*C2$$

where the $ signs in the formula ensure that the copying process (from D2 into D3..D20) always refers to the cells B1 and B2.

With the X range being defined as C1..C20, and the A range as D2..D20, the graph shown in Figure 2.1 is then produced. As we predicted the graph is linear and, since b is positive, displays total cost as a direct function of output.

However, indirect relationships in which y and x move in opposite directions can also be represented by the general form

$$y = f(x) = a + bx$$

provided, of course, that b is made to adopt a negative value.

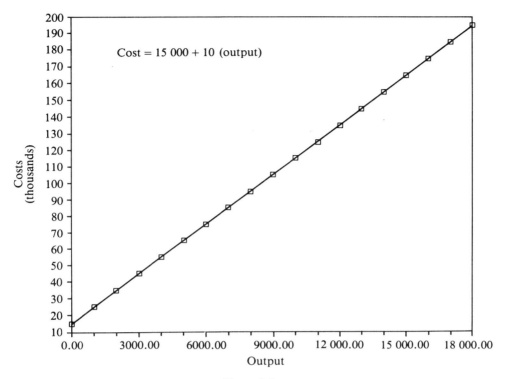

Figure 2.1

EXAMPLE 2.11

The quantity demanded (y) of a firm's product is known to depend upon the price charged (x) in such a way that if a price of 0 is charged 17 000 units are sold, and for every £1 increase in the price the quantity demanded decreases by 1000 units.

Graph the firm's demand function in the form

$$y = f(x) = a + bx$$

SOLUTION 2.11

Since we know that when $x = 0$, $y = 17\,000$, then the intercept must be 17 000. Furthermore, since each £1 increase in the price causes the demand to fall by 1000 units, we can conclude that the gradient of the required function must be -1000. Consequently

$$y = 17\,000 - 1000x$$

WORKSHEET 2.9

	A	B	C	D
1	Intercept	17000	x (price)	y (demand)
2	Gradient	-1000	0.00	17000
3			1.00	16000
4			2.00	15000
5			3.00	14000
6			4.00	13000
7			5.00	12000
8			6.00	11000
9			7.00	10000
10			8.00	9000
11			9.00	8000
12			10.00	7000
13			11.00	6000
14			12.00	5000
15			13.00	4000
16			14.00	3000
17			15.00	2000
18			16.00	1000
19			17.00	0

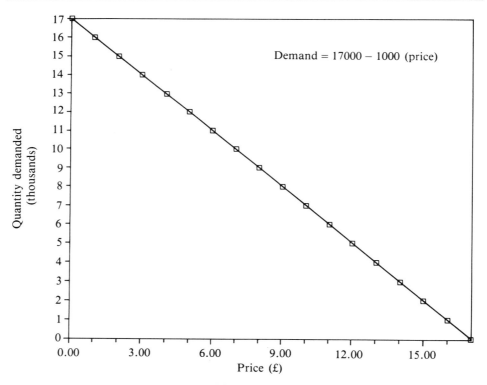

Demand = 17000 − 1000 (price)

Figure 2.2

All you have to do now is replace the values in B1 and B2 of your last worksheet with 15 000 and -1000 respectively, alter the values of x to 0–19, and then the Worksheet 2.9 and the graph (suitably relabelled) shown in Figure 2.2 can be obtained. (You will notice that we have curtailed the values in the X range and the A range so that negative sales are not displayed.)

EXAMPLE 2.12

A thermostatically controlled building is heated by a central heating system that always uses 10 units of fuel to raise the inside ambient temperature by $1°C$.

The insulation of the building is such that *in the absence of any heating* the inside ambient temperature is always $2°C$ higher than the outside temperature.

(a) Assuming that the thermostat is set at $16°C$, obtain an expression for the fuel usage (y) of the system as a function of the outside temperature (x).
(b) Prepare a worksheet that will display the fuel usage of the system for any outside temperature between $-2°C$ and $16°C$, and any chosen thermostat setting, and graph this relationship for temperature ranges between $16°C$ and $-2°C$.

SOLUTION 2.12

(a) In the absence of any heating we know that because of the insulation, the inside temperature will be given by $x + 2$. So if $x = 0$, then the system will have to raise the inside temperature by $16 - 2 = 14$ degrees until the thermostat switches the heating off, and this will use a total of $10(14) = 140$ units of fuel.

This logic means that we can write

$$y = 10[16 - (x + 2)]$$

or equivalently

$$y = 10(16 - 2 - x) = 10(14 - x)$$

as our functional form.

Although this is not written in the standard linear form ($a + bx$), it is an easy matter to make it adopt this form by collecting terms to produce

$$y = 10(14 - x) = 140 - 10x$$

You should notice of course, that this equation is only valid for x values that are less than or equal to 14, since otherwise it implies a *negative* fuel usage.

However, although it is perfectly valid to rewrite the function as we have done above, the original form is much more appropriate for answering the second part of the question.

(b) Written in the form

$$y = 10(16 - 2 - x)$$

you should be able to see that the thermostat setting of $16°C$ can easily be replaced by the variable s to allow for different settings. This means that

$$y = 10(s - 2 - x)$$

is the most general form of the function, and can be used in your worksheet as shown in Worksheet 2.10. Notice that we have entered the thermostat setting, the fuel usage rate *and* the insulation factor in their own cells. This allows the entry in B1 to calculate the intercept term from

$$(B3 - B4)*(-B2)$$

That is, when $x = 0$, the fuel usage is the difference between the thermostat setting and the insulation factor times the amount of fuel required to raise the temperature by $1°C$ (10 units in this case). For example, if $s = 16°C$ and the insulation factor is $3°C$, then the system has to raise the temperature from $0°C$ to $16 - 3 = 13°C$, and this will take $13(10) = 130$ units of fuel.

More generally, since

$$y = 10(s - 2 - x)$$

WORKSHEET 2.10

D2: -B$2*(B$3-B$4-C2)

	A	B	C	D
1	Intercept	140	x (temperature)	y (fuel use)
2	Gradient	-10	-2.00	160
3	Thermostat setting	16	-1.00	150
4	Insulation	2	0.00	140
5			1.00	130
6			2.00	120
7			3.00	110
8			4.00	100
9			5.00	90
10			6.00	80
11			7.00	70
12			8.00	60
13			9.00	50
14			10.00	40
15			11.00	30
16			12.00	20
17			13.00	10
18			14.00	0
19			15.00	-10
20			16.00	-20

can be re-written as

$$y = 10(s - 2) - 10x$$

this implies that the intercept of the equation is given by

$$10(s - 2)$$

When the outside temperature is not 0, however, the fuel usage will be given by $10(16 - 2 - \text{temperature})$, which in Lotus terms is equivalent to $-\text{B\$2}*(\text{B\$3} - \text{B\$4} - \text{C2})$ (copied from D2 into D3..D20). This allows the graph shown in Figure 2.3 to be produced for the parameter values used in Worksheet 2.10.

However, it is an easy matter to get the worksheet to produce the appropriate graph for different thermostat settings, since all you have to do is alter the value in B1 and, if necessary, the range of x and y values to be plotted. Try it for yourself with a thermostat setting of 14°C and then 15°C. This will produce the level curves (lines) that we spoke of earlier, since each time you change the thermostat setting, the new fuel usage will be calculated for that thermostat setting.

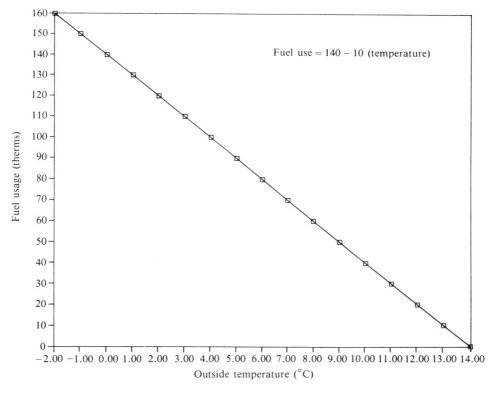

Figure 2.3

Furthermore, with the insulation factor also included in its own cell (as a variable), this means that the function could be written more generally as

$$y = 10(s - i - x)$$

where i represents the insulation factor of the building.

Formulated like this, you can easily consider variations of the problem such as the following.

EXAMPLE 2.13

For an outlay of £10 000 on improved insulation, the difference between the outside and inside temperatures when no heating is used can be increased to a constant amount of 4°C. This expenditure is deemed to be justifiable only if it produces a reduction in fuel usage of at least 10 per cent for all temperature levels between $-2°C$ and when the heating switches off, and for all thermostat settings between 20°C and 16°C.

Is the outlay justifiable?

SOLUTION 2.13

You can modify the last worksheet to perform the calculations for you.

Once again we should adopt a 'before' and 'after' approach so the new parameter values are entered in B7..B10.

The 'old' values of y are calculated from the old parameter values in B1..B4 as before, while the 'new' values are calculated from the new parameter values in B7..B10 from the formula in E2

```
-B$8*(B$9-B$10-C2)
```

which was then copied into E3..E20.

Finally, the percentage reduction in fuel usage is calculated in F2..F20 from the formula in F2

```
(D2-E2)/D2
```

i.e. (old usage − new usage)/(old usage) and this was then copied into F3..F20.

These alterations produce Worksheet 2.11. As you can see, with a thermostat setting of 16°C and the new insulation factor of 4°C, then the heating system will now switch off at an outside temperature of 12°C as opposed to 14°C previously (when the thermostat was set at 16°C and the insulation factor was 2°C). Also for all temperature values until the heating switches off the percentage reduction in fuel usage is at least 10 per cent.

Now you can systematically consider different thermostat settings in the specified

WORKSHEET 2.11

	A	B	C	D	E	F
1	Intercept	140	x (temp)	old y	new y	Reduction %
2	Gradient	-10	-2.00	160	140	0.125
3	Thermostat	16	-1.00	150	130	0.133333
4	Insulation	2	0.00	140	120	0.142857
5			1.00	130	110	0.153846
6	After		2.00	120	100	0.166666
7	Intercept	120	3.00	110	90	0.181818
8	Gradient	-10	4.00	100	80	0.2
9	Thermostat	16	5.00	90	70	0.222222
10	Insulation	4	6.00	80	60	0.25
11			7.00	70	50	0.285714
12			8.00	60	40	0.333333
13			9.00	50	30	0.4
14			10.00	40	20	0.5
15			11.00	30	10	0.666666
16			12.00	20	0	1
17			13.00	10	-10	2
18			14.00	0	-20	ERR
19			15.00	-10	-30	-2
20			16.00	-20	-40	-1

range, and you will find that this result is repeated and that as a consequence, the insulation is a worthwhile investment given the evaluation criterion.

There is in fact an alternative way of answering this question if we reason as follows.

With an insulation factor of $2°C$ the equation for fuel usage is

$$10[s - (x + 2)] = 10s - 10x - 20$$

While with the improved insulation this becomes

$$10[s - (x + 4)] = 10s - 10x - 40$$

The effect has been to reduce the fuel usage by a constant amount of 20 units at all thermostat settings and at all temperatures. However, whether this represents the required percentage reduction will depend on the setting and the outside temperature.

So, if $s = 20$ (and taking $x = -2$), the old usage will be $10(20) - 10(-2) - 20 = 200$ and the new usage will be 180, which represents a $20/200 = 10$ per cent reduction.

At the other extreme, (and still with a thermostat setting of 20), with an outside temperature of 16 the old usage would be $10(20) - 10(16) - 20 = 20$ and the new usage would be 0, which represents a reduction of 100 per cent.

Now taking the lowest thermostat setting to be considered (16) a similar logic would show that when $x = -2$.

$$\text{old usage} = 160$$
$$\text{new usage} = 140$$
$$\text{percentage reduction} = 12.5 \text{ per cent}$$

While when $x = 12$ (when the heating switches off)

$$\text{old usage} = 20$$
$$\text{new usage} = 0$$
$$\text{percentage reduction} = 100 \text{ per cent}$$

We conclude that for all thermostat settings between $20°C$ and $16°C$ inclusive, and for all temperatures between $-2°C$ and when the heating switches off, the effect is to produce at least the required 10 per cent reduction.

Sometimes it will be the case that we need to use *two* linear equations to model the problem being considered. Under these circumstances, as we explained earlier, it will be necessary to consider the information contained in both of them together (i.e. simultaneously).

EXAMPLE 2.14

The quarterly bill for domestic gas users is made up of a £15 standing charge and a variable charge of £0.4 per therm consumed, while the quarterly bill for electricity consists of a standing charge of £20 and a variable charge of £0.3 per kWh consumed.

For the first quarter of a particular year a customer's combined gas and electricity bill was £155, and a total of 350 units of both kinds of fuel was used.

How many therms and how many kWh were used by this customer?

SOLUTION 2.14

The information provided suggests that if x represents the number of therms used, and y represents the number of kWh used, then

$$x + y = 350$$

and

$$15 + 0.4x + 20 + 0.3y = 155$$

Collecting terms in this last equation then produces

$$35 + 0.4x + 0.3y = 155$$

Implying that

$$0.4x + 0.3y = 120$$

Linear functions

Clearly we should take the information contained in the first equation and incorporate it into the second. This yields

$$x + y = 350$$

Implying that

$$x = (350 - y)$$

This means that the second equation can be written *entirely in terms of y* as

$$0.4(350 - y) + 0.3y = 120$$

So

$$140 - 0.4y + 0.3y = 120$$

and

$$-0.1y = -20$$

Whereby

$$y = 200 \quad \text{and} \quad x = 350 - 200 = 150$$

Another way of solving these two equations would be to get Lotus to graph them for us and then observe where they intersect.

WORKSHEET 2.12

	A	B	C
1	x value	y<1>	y<2>
2	0	350	400.00
3	10	340	386.67
4	20	330	373.33
5	30	320	360.00
6	40	310	346.67
7	50	300	333.33
8	60	290	320.00
9	70	280	306.67
10	80	270	293.33
11	90	260	280.00
12	100	250	266.67
13	110	240	253.33
14	120	230	240.00
15	130	220	226.67
16	140	210	213.33
17	150	200	200.00
18	160	190	186.67
19	170	180	173.33
20	180	170	160.00

To do this we will have to rewrite each equation in the following form:

$$y_1 = 350 - x$$
$$0.3y_2 = 120 - 0.4x$$

implying that (after multiplying all terms by 10/3)

$$y_2 = 400 - 1.3333x$$

Now we can enter the values of x in column A and the two associated values of y (y_1 and y_2) in columns B and C. This produces Worksheet 2.12. The formulae in B2 and C2 are

$$350 - A2 \text{ in B2 and } 400 - 1.3333*A2 \text{ in C2,}$$

and these have been copied into B3..C20.

In fact, in this case you do not even have to ask Lotus to graph the sets of y values against x in order to see that only when $x = 150$ is the value of y the same

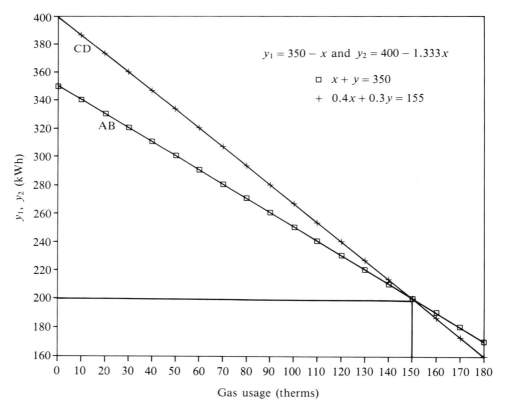

Figure 2.4

Linear functions 73

in both cases (200). However, since it will not always be as clear as this you should define the X range as A2..A20, and the A and B ranges as B2..B20 and C2..C20 respectively. Then, after appropriate labelling, the graph shown in figure 2.4 can be produced. As you can see, the values of x and y that simultaneously satisfy both equations are $x = 150$ and $y = 200$. For all other combinations of x and y values there are three possible situations:

1. The first equation is satisfied but not the second, (all values of x and y lying *on* the line labelled AB).
2. The second is satisfied but not the first (all values of x and y lying *on* the line labelled CD),
3. Neither equation is satisfied (all values of x and y *not* lying on either AB or CD).

EXAMPLE 2.15

In order to conform to health regulations, the fat content of a litre of milk must be exactly 10 per cent.

A large creamery uses two types of milk, the first of which contains 13 per cent fat, and the second of which contains 8 per cent fat.

What blend of the two types of milk must be made if the regulations are to be satisfied?

SOLUTION 2.15

We know that the blend must supply 1 litre of milk, so letting $x =$ the amount of the first type of milk used in the blend, and $y =$ the amount of the second type used, we have

$$x + y = 1$$

But we also know that each litre of the first type provides 13 per cent fat, and each litre of the second type supplies 8 per cent fat. Consequently

$$0.13x + 0.08y = 0.1(x + y)$$

Taking both of these pieces of information together, we can replace x with $(1 - y)$ in the last equation to produce

$$0.13(1 - y) + 0.08y = 0.1(1 - y) + 0.1y$$

Expanding and transposing terms produces

$$0.13 - 0.13y + 0.08y - 0.1 + 0.1y - 0.1y = 0$$

Implying that

$$0.03 = 0.05y$$

and that
$$y = 0.6 \text{ litres} \quad \text{and} \quad x = 0.4 \text{ litres}$$

2.6 Quadratic functions

A quadratic function is fundamentally distinguished from a linear function by the introduction of a term containing x^2, and can be written in the following form:

$$y = f(x) = ax^2 + bx + c$$

where a, b and c are constant terms (often known as coefficients).

In its most general form a quadratic function can be represented by a 'U' or inverted 'U' shaped curve, but the specific nature of such curves is ultimately determined by the values of the coefficients, a, b and c.

To see how these influence the shape that the curve adopts you should prepare Worksheet 2.13.

The entry in D2 is

$$+ B\$3*C2^2 + B\$2*C2 + B\$1 \quad \text{(copied into D3..D20)}$$

WORKSHEET 2.13

```
D2: +B$3*C2^2+B$2*C2+B$1
```

	A	B	C	D
1	Intercept (c)	400	x	y
2	Coeff of x	50	0.00	400
3	Coeff of x^2	-1	5.00	625
4	discriminant	4100	10.00	800
5			15.00	925
6			20.00	1000
7			25.00	1025
8			30.00	1000
9			35.00	925
10			40.00	800
11			45.00	625
12			50.00	400
13			55.00	125
14			60.00	-200
15			65.00	-575
16			70.00	-1000
17			75.00	-1475
18			80.00	-2000
19			85.00	-2575
20			90.00	-3200

Quadratic functions

Now you can use this worksheet to investigate the respective properties of the various types of quadratic function, since these are entirely determined by the values adopted by a, b and c.

In this respect, there are three key aspects that should be appreciated.

1. The value adopted by c determines where the graph of the function intersects the vertical axis [since when $x = 0$, $y = f(x) = f(0) = c$], and therefore influences the general *position* but not the *shape* of the graph.

You can see this if you first of all let $c = 100$ (say) and then with any chosen values for a and b, increase c to 150. The two graphs that can then be produced will have the same shape, but the value of the second one will always be 50 more than the value of the first. Try it.

2. If the value adopted by a is negative, then the graph of the function will rise and then fall, while if a is positive then the opposite is the case. (If $a = 0$ then the graph becomes linear of course.)

Confirm this for yourself, by graphing any quadratic function with the value of

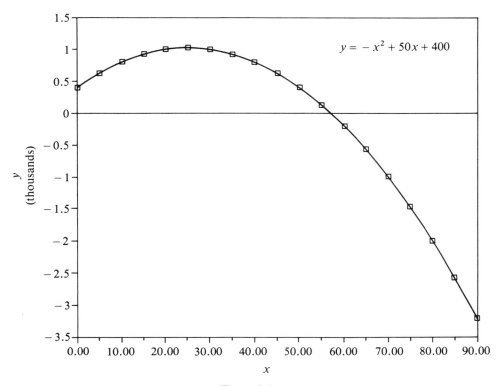

Figure 2.5

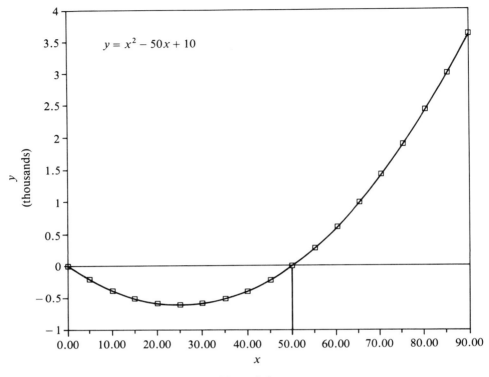

Figure 2.6

a being first of all negative, and then positive. You should obtain graphs with the general shape shown in Figures 2.5 and 2.6.

3. Whether the graph of any quadratic function intersects the horizontal axis is determined by the algebraic sign of what is known as the *discriminant* of the function. This is defined by the following expression:

$$b^2 - 4ac \text{ [when } f(x) = ax^2 + bx + c]$$

and has been entered in the B4 cell of the last worksheet by the following formula:

$$+B2^2-4*B1*B3$$

If the discriminant is negative, then you will find that there is no intersection between the graph of the function and the horizontal axis.

On the other hand, if the discriminant is greater than 0 then the *x* axis will be intersected twice, while if it is exactly equal to 0, then the graph of the function will *just* touch the *x* axis at *one* value of *x*.

Quadratic functions

You can generate each of these possibilities for yourself if you enter values for a, b and c such as $a = 0.1$, $b = 0.1$, $c = 100$; $a = 1$, $b = -100$, $c = 2100$; $a = 1$, $b = -80$, $c = 1600$.

Try it, and you should obtain graphs similar to those shown in Figures 2.7–2.9.

Now, the last two circumstances (discriminant ≥ 0) will often be of interest to us, since you should be able to see that if the x axis is intersected at all, then this implies that the value of the function is 0, and that the *intersection* value(s) of x represent the *solution* value(s) of the following quadratic equation:

$$ax^2 + bx + c = 0$$

For example, if you enter values of $a = 1$, $b = -13$ and $c = 36$, then you should find that the graph of the function intersects the x axis at values of $x = 4$ and $x = 9$. Try it.

These two values ($x = 4$ and $x = 9$) are known as the characteristic roots of the quadratic equation, and can be thought of as the values of x that solve the equation formed by setting the functional expression equal to 0.

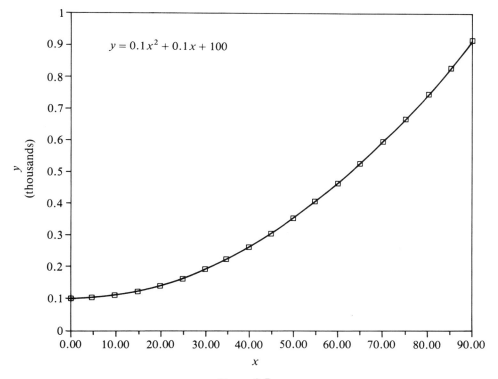

Figure 2.7

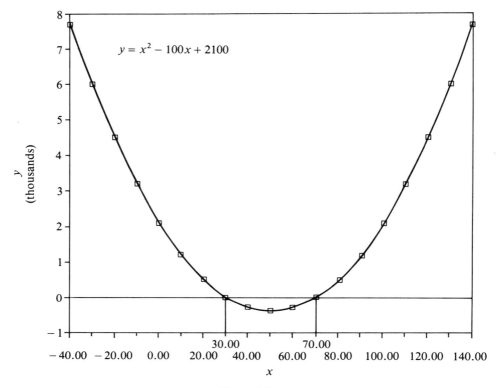

Figure 2.8

Of course you will not always have Lotus available to do this graphing process for you, so you might be wondering whether there is another way of obtaining the characteristic roots of any given quadratic function.

The answer is that they can be obtained from what is known as the quadratic formula. This states that the characteristic roots (x_1 and x_2) of the equation

$$ax^2 + bx + c = 0$$

are given by

$$x_1, x_2 = [-b \pm (b^2 - 4ac)^{0.5}]/2a$$

Accordingly, if we apply this formula to our last illustration, then we obtain

$$x_1, x_2 = [-(-13) \pm (169 - 4(1)(36))^{0.5}]/2$$
$$x_1, x_2 = [13 \pm (25)^{0.5}]/2$$
$$x_1 = (13 + 5)/2 = 9$$
$$x_2 = (13 - 5)/2 = 4$$

which confirms our previous result.

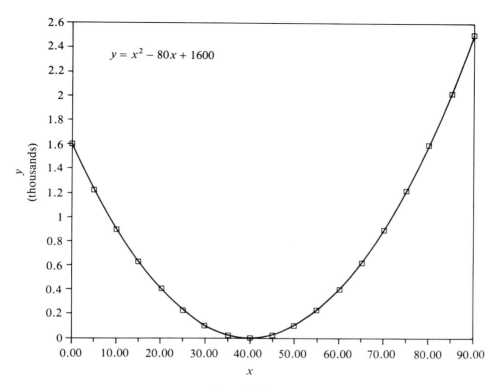

Figure 2.9

```
WORKSHEET 2.14
              A              B         C         D
      1  Intercept (c)     1600         x         y
      2  Coeff of x         -80      0.00      1600
      3  Coeff of x^2         1      5.00      1225
      4  discriminant         0     10.00       900
      5  First root          40     15.00       625
      6  Second root         40     20.00       400
      7                            25.00       225
      8                            30.00       100
      9                            35.00        25
     10                            40.00         0
     11                            45.00        25
     12                            50.00       100
     13                            55.00       225
     14                            60.00       400
     15                            65.00       625
     16                            70.00       900
     17                            75.00      1225
     18                            80.00      1600
     19                            85.00      2025
     20                            90.00      2500
```

Sometimes the calculations involved in evaluating the quadratic formula can be tedious, so we should get Lotus to do them for us. This has been done in B5 and B6 of the worksheet shown in Worksheet 2.14, where (remembering that B4 contains the discriminant) the formulae are $(-B2+B4^{\wedge}0.5)/2*B3$ (in B5) and $(-B2-B4^{\wedge}0.5)/2*B3$ (in B6). As you can see, because the discriminant is 0, there is only one solution value of x ($x_1 = x_2 = 40$).

As an application of quadratic functions, consider the following.

EXAMPLE 2.16

The total cost (c) of producing a company's product is given in terms of the output (x) per time period by

$$c = x^2 + 30x + 3600$$

If each item of output was sold at a constant price of £160, what output levels are associated with the firm breaking even?

SOLUTION 2.16

In order to break even the firm's total revenue (r) must equal its total costs. So $c = r$ implies that

$$x^2 + 30x + 3600 = 160x$$

Therefore

$$x^2 - 130x + 3600 = 0$$

And, entering values of $a = 1$, $b = -130$ and $c = 3600$ to the last worksheet, you should find that

$$x_1 = 90 \quad \text{and} \quad x_2 = 40$$

The firm will break even if either 40 units or 90 units of output are produced.

EXAMPLE 2.17

A firm sells its product in a market where the demand is given by

$$p = 1000 - 2x$$

where p represents the price charged, and x represents the annual quantity demanded of the product, expressed in appropriate units.

The firm also receives income from the lease of a property which produces an annual income of £1 million.

(a) Calculate the level of sales associated with the total revenue being £1.125 million.

The firm's total costs of production (c) are known to be given by

$$c = x^2 + 500x + 750\,000$$

(b) Calculate the output levels that should be produced in order to break even.

SOLUTION 2.17

(a) The firm's revenue (r) will be given by:

$$r = (1000 - 2x)x + 1\,000\,000$$

and this will equal 1 125 000 when

$$1000x - 2x^2 + 1\,000\,000 = 1\,125\,000$$

Implying that

$$1000x - 2x^2 - 125\,000 = 0$$

which, after rearrangement, implies that

$$a = -2, \ b = 1000 \ \text{and} \ c = -125\,000$$

If we enter these values into the worksheet containing the quadratic formula, then (since the discriminant is 0), the single solution value is found to be

$$x_1 = x_2 = 250$$

(b) Once again, break even requires that total revenue equals total costs. So

$$1000x - 2x^2 + 1\,000\,000 = x^2 + 500x + 750\,000$$

Collecting terms produces:

$$-3x^2 - 500x + 250\,000 = 0$$

This equation has only one positive solution which you should find to be:

$$x_1 = 217.12 \ \text{units}$$

which therefore represents the break-even level of production.

2.7 Hyperbolic functions

You may well have heard of a figure of speech known as hyperbole, which is used to describe a tendency to excessive exaggeration. Correspondingly, as this name should now suggest, a hyperbolic function is simply one that behaves 'excessively' for certain values of x and/or y.

Principles of Algebraic Modelling

The easiest way to understand this misbehaviour is to remember that dividing any quantity by zero produces an indeterminate (infinite) result, and so any function that requires division by a zero value of x can be thought of as hyperbolic.

Hyperbolic functions are frequently created when some *average* quantity is being modelled, since this will usually involve dividing the total function $[f(x)]$ by x and will create difficulties if any constant term in $f(x)$ has to be divided by an x value of 0.

You can see this quite clearly in the following example.

EXAMPLE 2.18

The quarterly bill for domestic gas is made up of two components, a standing charge of £15 per quarter and a variable charge of £0.4 per therm consumed.

Obtain an expression for the average cost per therm consumed, and graph the implied function.

SOLUTION 2.18

The total bill (y) will clearly be given in terms of therms consumed (x) by the

WORKSHEET 2.15

B3: 15/A3+0.4

	A	B
1	x (therms)	c (cost per therm)
2	0	ERR
3	10	1.9
4	20	1.15
5	30	0.9
6	40	0.775
7	50	0.7
8	70	0.614285
9	100	0.55
10	200	0.475
11	400	0.4375
12	500	0.43
13	1000	0.415
14	3000	0.405
15	4000	0.40375
16	5000	0.403
17	6000	0.4025
18	8000	0.401875
19	9000	0.401666
20	10 000	0.4015

following linear function:

$$y = 15 + 0.4x$$

From this, it follows that the *cost per therm consumed* (c) will be given by:

$$c = (15 + 0.4x)/x = 15/x + 0.4$$

If you observe this expression carefully, you should be able to see that when 0 therms are consumed the cost per therm is infinite (since $15/0 = \infty$), but that as the number of therms consumed increases, the term $15/x$ gets smaller and smaller, so that c will get closer and closer to a value of £0.4.

You can see this in Worksheet 2.15, where values of c for various x values between 0 and 10 000 have been evaluated, and these values have been graphed in figure 2.10.

Clearly the value of c is approaching a value of £0.4, and is therefore said to be *asymptotic* to a value of $c = 0.4$ on the x axis (and asymptotic to a value of $x = 0$ on the y axis). In other words, as x tends to infinity, c tends towards 0.4, and when $x = 0$, $c = \infty$.

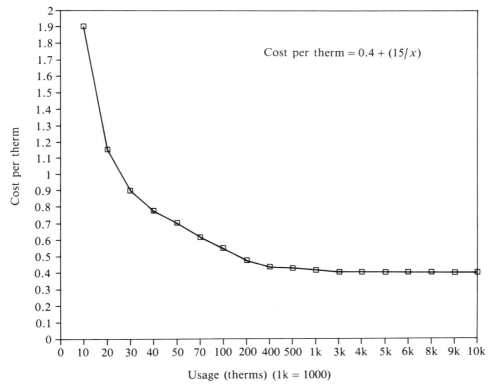

Figure 2.10

Furthermore, the hyperbolic nature of the function is indicated by the ERR message which Lotus has returned to the C2 cell when it was instructed to try to divide by 0.

EXAMPLE 2.19

A firm's capital equipment has a value of £0.5 million just now, and depreciates in such a way that its eventual scrap value is never less than £0.05 million.

Derive a hyperbolic function that will describe the behaviour of the value (v) of the firm's assets over time (x).

SOLUTION 2.19

We require our function to do two things:

(a) Adopt a value of 0.5 when $x = 0$, i.e. $v = f(x)$ such that $f(0) = 0.5$.
(b) Asymptotically approach a value of 0.05, i.e. $v = f(x)$ such that $f(\infty) = 0.05$.

WORKSHEET 2.16

C2: 0.45/B1+0.05

	A x (time)	B (x+1)	C v (value)
1			
2	0	1	0.50
3	1	2	0.30
4	2	3	0.22
5	3	4	0.18
6	4	5	0.15
7	5	6	0.13
8	6	7	0.12
9	7	8	0.11
10	8	9	0.11
11	9	10	0.10
12	10	11	0.10
13	12	13	0.09
14	14	15	0.08
15	16	17	0.08
16	20	21	0.07
17	25	26	0.07
18	35	36	0.06
19	70	71	0.06
20	100	101	0.05

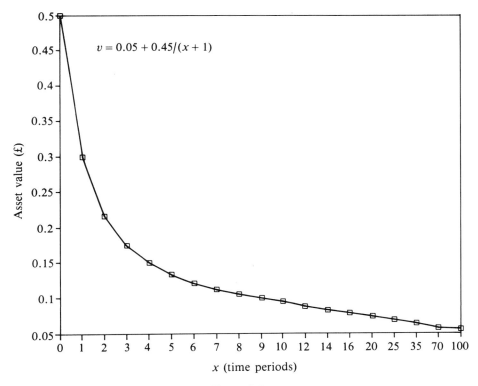

Figure 2.11

The simplest form for v would be

$$v = f(x) = 0.5/x$$

But this has a value of ∞ when $x = 0$ (not 0.5 as required) and asymptotically approaches a value of 0 when x becomes infinitely large (not 0.05 as required).

However, if we write

$$v = f(x) = 0.45/(x + 1) + 0.05$$

then both of these objections are answered.

You can see this in Worksheet 2.16 and Figure 2.11, where this last function has been evaluated and then graphed. Notice how the use of the term $(x + 1)$ allowed evaluation to take place when $x = 0$, and allowed v to adopt a value of 0.5 when this was the case.

2.8 Logarithmic functions

It is now time to turn our attention to a class of function known as logarithmic functions, which play an important role in many areas of quantitative analysis.

In its simplest form a logarithm is no more than an index or exponent, defining the result of a particular mathematical calculation. This is because a logarithmic function is defined in terms of its base (b) and its variable (x) in such a way that the logarithm of x to the base b, ($\log_b x$), is the power to which b must be raised in order to equal x.

Consequently

$$\log_2 8 = 3 \quad \text{since} \quad 2^3 = 8$$

or

$$\log_5 625 = 4 \quad \text{since} \quad 5^4 = 625$$

Historically, most calculators and spreadsheets can calculate logarithms to two special bases: 10 (common logarithms) and e = 2.718 28 (natural logarithms).

The rationale for the latter of these bases is not straightforward and will be explained later, but the logic involved in the former is easy enough to appreciate since the number 10 is the basis of our decimal number system.

Consequently

$$\log_{10} 100 = 2 \quad \text{since} \quad 10^2 = 100$$

But what would be the value of $\log_{10} 80$? You can see the answer and its rationale in Worksheet 2.17. As you can see, Lotus will evaluate any common logarithm for you from the following formula in B2:

```
@LOG(B1)
```

Furthermore, the reason that the entry in B2 represents the logarithm of whatever number is in B1 can be seen from the formula in B3

```
+10^B2
```

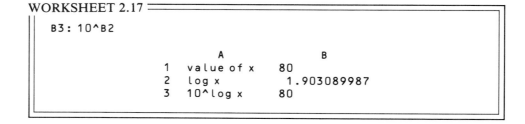

```
WORKSHEET 2.17
  B3: 10^B2
                    A              B
            1   value of x       80
            2   log x            1.903089987
            3   10^log x         80
```

i.e. 10 to the power of the logarithm of the number in B1 will reproduce the number in B1.

Now enter a value of 1 in the B1 cell, and you will find that Lotus evaluates the logarithm to be 0. This is because any number to the power of 0 is 1, and so the logarithm of 1 to any base is 0. That is

$$\log_b 1 = 0 \quad \text{since} \quad b^0 = 1$$

Furthermore, if you now enter a value of 0 in B1, then you will find that Lotus returns an error message (ERR), since there is no mechanism whereby raising a positive base to any given power can produce a result that is 0 or negative. For this reason the logarithm of 0 and all negative numbers is undefined.

This does not mean, however, that a logarithm itself cannot adopt a negative value (it is the logarithm of a negative number that is undefined). In fact, since the logarithm of 1 is always 0, you should suspect that the logarithm of any number lying between 0 and 1 will be negative. This is indeed the case as you can confirm if you enter a value of 0.6 in B1, whereupon a value of -0.2218 will be returned to B2.

What this means is that the required *index* is negative, and that as a result a reciprocal has been formed. Consequently

$$\log_{10} 0.6 = -0.2218$$

because

$$10^{-0.2218} = 1/10^{0.2218} = 0.6$$

Or, as another example

$$\log_{10} 0.1 = -1$$

because

$$10^{-1} = 1/10 = 0.1$$

```
WORKSHEET 2.18
                  A                          B
    1    value of x              5
    2    log x                   0.698970004
    3    value of y              20
    4    log y                   1.301029995
    5    log x + log y           2
    6    10^(log x + log y)      100 = (value of x)(value of y)
```

You can see some of the further implications of logarithms if you prepare Worksheet 2.18. The entries in B2 and B4 are @LOG(B1) and @LOG(B3) respectively, while the entries in B5 and B6 are +B2+B4 and 10^B5.

Now enter a value of 5 in B1 and a value of 20 in B3, and you will find that the result in B5 is 2, and that B6 contains 100. But what is the significance of these results?

Surely they suggest that the product of 5 and 20 is 100, and that the logarithm of 100 to the base 10 is 2. This should explain the entry in B5, and also suggest that adding the logarithms of any two numbers is performing a process that is equivalent to multiplying the two numbers together (in the same way as adding the index terms of any two expressions of the same variable performs a multiplication process).

It should also suggest that when the resulting sum of the two logarithms is used as the index to which 10 is raised, then the product of the two numbers is obtained.

In other words, if x and y are any two positive numbers then:

$$xy = 10^{\log_{10} x + \log_{10} y}$$

The reason for this is easy to understand, since all the process does is to express each number in index form as a power of 10, and then, using the rules of indices, adds their exponents.

For example, suppose you want to multiply 100 by 1000. The answer is clearly 100 000. But, using indices we can express (100)(1000) as

$$(10^2)(10^3)$$

which is equal to

$$10^{2+3} = 10^5 = 100\ 000$$

Furthermore, as you should now expect, the common logarithms of 100 and 1000 are 2 and 3 respectively, and so their sum is 5. Consequently

$$10^{\log_{10} 100 + \log_{10} 1000} = 10^{2+3} = 10^5 = 100\ 000$$

This discussion can be summarized by one of the first rules of logarithmic operations. Namely

$$\text{if } z = xy \text{ where } x \text{ and } y \text{ are both } > 0$$

then

$$\log z = \log x + \log y$$

You will notice that we have not defined a base for these logarithms in this case, and this is because it is a general statement that is true regardless of the base employed.

Logarithmic functions

By a similar logic we would also argue that if

$$z = x/y \text{ where } x \text{ and } y \text{ are both } > 0$$

then, since this could be rewritten as

$$z = x(y^{-1})$$

it follows that

$$\log z = \log x - \log y$$

Now suppose that two numbers of the same magnitude are to be multiplied together. In other words we require

$$z = (x)(x) \text{ where } x > 0$$

By your basic rule of logarithms we can write

$$\log z = \log x + \log x = 2(\log x)$$

In other words, the logarithm of the square of any number is twice the logarithm of that number.

This should give us an idea for a more general rule, since, following the previous logic, we would expect that:

$$\log(x^3) = 3(\log x)$$
$$\log(x^5) = 5(\log x)$$
$$\log(x^n) = n(\log x)$$

This last line means that if, for example, we have an equation such as

$$y = x^n$$

then

$$\log_b y = n(\log_b x)$$

and

$$\log_b x = (\log_b y)/n$$

whereby

$$x = b^{(\log_b y)/n}$$

For example, if

$$y = x^{3.5}$$

then by the rules of indices

$$x = y^{1/3.5} = y^{0.285\,7142}$$

So, if $y = 45$, then $x = 2.967\,19$.

Alternatively, taking logarithms to the base 10

$$x = 10^{(\log_{10} 45)/3.5}$$
$$x = 10^{1.653\ 212\ 5/3.5} = 10^{0.472\ 346\ 4} = 2.967\ 19$$

Once again, you can see that the logarithmic operations are no more than a modification of the rules of indices.

This being the case, you may then be wondering why we have spent time explaining what is apparently no more than an alternative to the rules of indices.

The answer is that there are circumstances that arise from certain types of equation which require that logarithms be used in order to provide a solution. Knowledge of index operations will not be enough in these cases.

These equations derive from what is known as the exponential class of function, and it is to these that we now turn our attention.

2.9 Exponential functions

As the name should now suggest, exponential functions are characterized by the fact that the independent variable (x) appears as the index (exponent) of the function, rather than as the base to which a constant exponent is applied.

This means that a constant base is being raised to a variable power, rather than a variable base being raised to a constant power.

For example, one of the simplest types of exponential function would be

$$y = f(x) = 2^x$$

The behaviour of this function can then be investigated in the usual way, by preparing a worksheet similar to Worksheet 2.19 and then graphing the results, as shown in Figure 2.12.

As you can see, the fact that the variable appears as the exponent means that $f(0) = 2^0 = 1$, and that thereafter the graph rises rapidly with increases in the value of x.

More generally, the exponential class of function is given by

$$y = f(x) = a(b^{rx})$$

where a, b and r are all constants.

As you might expect, the general behaviour of this class of function is more complex than those we have previously discussed. However, as a general rule it is the sign of r and the magnitude of b that exercise the greatest influence on the overall appearance of the graph of the function.

To understand this you should appreciate three things:

1. For positive values of x, the value of b^{rx} will increase as x increases if b is greater than 1, and decrease if b is less than 1.
2. If r and b are both positive, then $f(x)$ will increase as x increases if b is greater than 1 and decrease if b is less than 1.

WORKSHEET 2.19

	A	B
1	x	y = 2^x
2	0	1
3	0.25	1.189207115
4	0.5	1.414213562
5	0.75	1.681792830
6	1	2
7	1.25	2.37841423
8	1.5	2.828427124
9	1.75	3.363585661
10	2	4
11	2.25	4.75682846
12	2.5	5.656854249
13	2.75	6.727171322
14	3	8
15	3.25	9.51365692
16	3.5	11.31370849
17	3.75	13.45434264
18	4	16
19	4.25	19.02731384
20	4.5	22.62741699

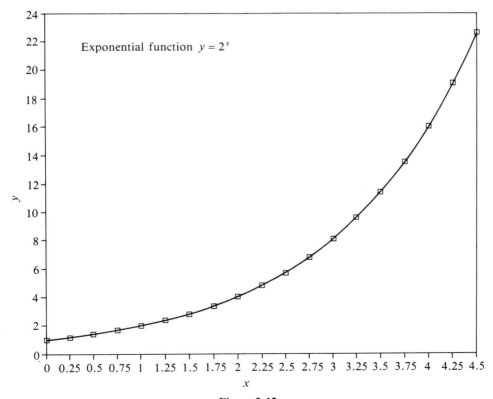

Exponential function $y = 2^x$

Figure 2.12

3. If r is negative and b is positive, then since the negative value of r means that the function becomes

$$f(x) = a/b^{rx}$$

this implies that if b is less than 1, $f(x)$ will increase as x increases, but will decrease if b is greater than 1.

These points can be seen more clearly below, where the symbols i, d and c are used as follows:

$i = f(x)$ increases as x increases
$d = f(x)$ decreases as x increases
$c = f(x)$ is constant as x increases

Value of b:	<1	1	>1
Value of r			
<0	i	c	d
=0	c	c	c
>0	d	c	i

You can also see this if you construct Worksheet 2.20 and then graph the function for each of these nine possibilities. Try it for yourself, and confirm that

WORKSHEET 2.20

```
D2: +B$3*(B$4^(B$5*C2))

                A                   B           C               D
1   Function is: y = a(b^rx)                    x               y
2                                               0.00            4
3   Value of a                      4           0.75            3.704952794
4   Value of b                      0.6         1.50            3.431668801
5   Value of r                      0.2         2.25            3.178542729
6                                               3.00            2.944087691
7                                               3.75            2.726926479
8                                               4.50            2.52578347
9                                               5.25            2.339477131
10                                              6.00            2.166913083
11                                              6.75            2.007077670
12                                              7.50            1.859032006
13                                              8.25            1.721906456
14                                              9.00            1.594895534
15                                              9.75            1.477253166
16                                              10.50           1.368288311
17                                              11.25           1.267360901
18                                              12.00           1.173878077
19                                              12.75           1.087290716
20                                              13.50           1.007090194
```

Exponential functions

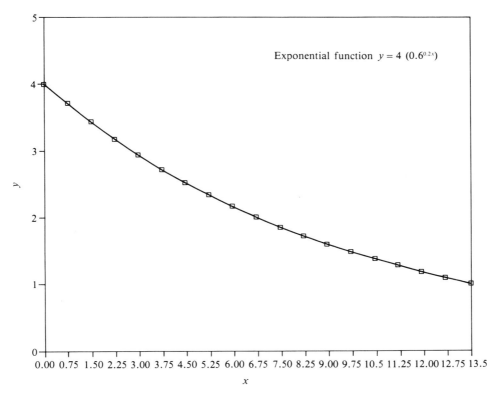

Figure 2.13

for example, if b is <1 and r is >0, then a diagram such as the one shown in Figure 2.13 is produced.

Notice the form of the entry in D2:

$$+B\$3*(B\$4\char`\^(B\$5*C2))$$

The two sets of brackets are essential otherwise Lotus will raise the entry in B4 to the power of the entry in B5 and then multiply this by the entry in C2. This is clearly not want we want, so the brackets are used to tell Lotus to multiply B5 by C2 and then use this product as the power to which B4 is raised.

Exponential functions (with $r < 0$), can be useful in a number of modelling circumstances. This is because they approach the x axis in a way that is a much more realistic description of many types of business variable. Asset value as a function of time, or sales or market share as a function of price are just a few examples of this.

EXAMPLE 2.20

A firm's sales (y) are believed to depend upon the price charged (x) as follows:

$$y = 25\,000(1.25^{-0.9p})$$

Calculate the firm's sales if a price of £10 is charged.

SOLUTION 2.20

When $p = 10$ we have:

$$y = 25\,000(1.25^{-9}) = 3355.44 \text{ units}$$

You should remember that in our discussion of logarithms we said that there were two bases that most calculators and spreadsheets can evaluate. The first of these was 10 and the second was $e = 2.71828$.

You should now appreciate that logarithms to the base e are entirely derived from a special kind of exponential function that takes e as its base. That is if $b = e$ then the general expression for the exponential class of function becomes

$$y = f(x) = ae^{rx}$$

Since this is no more than a special case of the exponential function, the previous comments we have made about this class of function's general behaviour remain valid. However, as you might expect, the reason for choosing such an obscure number for the base must lie in some peculiar properties that this number possesses. A full appreciation of what these properties are must wait until later in the text, but at the moment there is nothing to prevent you from getting Lotus to graph the function for you.

All you have to do is replace the value for the base (b) in the last worksheet with @EXP(1) in B4 and Lotus will evaluate this expression to be 2.718 28. Try it now.

To calculate $e^{0.6}$, the Lotus expression would be @EXP(0.6), and it can even adopt the syntax @EXP(A1), in which case e will be raised to the power of whatever the contents of A1 are.

You should also appreciate that if e is used as the base of an exponential function, then logarithms to the base e (known as natural logarithms and given the symbol ln) will be the most appropriate logarithm to use in any analysis of such a function.

For example, if

$$y = a(e^x)$$

then

$$\ln y = \ln a + x(\ln e) = \ln a + x(1) = \ln a + x$$

2.10 Algebraic series

Any algebraic series is simply a collection of numerical terms in which each term is related to the previous one by a known relationship, and it is the fact that there is such a known relationship which distinguishes a series from any other haphazard collection of terms.

The nature of the relationship between each term and the previous one can adopt a variety of forms, but as long as it can be identified, then order is brought to the terms and more general investigation can be carried out.

2.10.1 Arithmetic series

One of the simplest series identifiable is known as an arithmetic series (or progression), and is characterized by the fact that each term is different from the previous term by a constant amount.

You have already encountered an arithmetic series when you employed the Lotus Data Fill command, since this took a start value and then added or subtracted a constant step value to the start value and each subsequent term thereafter.

Viewed in this way the numbers 4, 7, 10, 13 are the first four terms of an arithmetic series in which the first term (start value) is 4, and in which the common difference (step value) is 3.

As we have said, this common difference can be positive or negative and is often denoted by the symbol d.

Furthermore, the first term in the series is usually denoted by a, the number of terms in the series by n and the nth term in the series by u_n.

In this notation u_n is a subscripted variable, with the subscript defining any particular term in the series. So, for example, u_1 is the first term of the series (a), u_4 is the fourth term, and u_n is the nth term.

Using this notation means that any arithmetic series can be represented generally by the following statement:

$$u_n = u_{n-1} + d \quad \text{or} \quad u_n - u_{n-1} = d$$

EXAMPLE 2.21

Use the Lotus Data Fill command to generate the first 13 terms of an arithmetic series in which the first term is 60, and the common difference is 6.6.

SOLUTION 2.21

All you have to do is select Data and then Fill, and then define the fill range as A1..A13. Now tell Lotus that the start value is 60 and that the step value is 6.6 and press the return key in response to the prompt for the stop value. The first 13 terms will be entered in A1..A13.

Although the Data Fill command is preprogrammed for you, it will still be useful if you could write some Lotus formulae for yourself that will generate an arithmetic series. This is because the method of doing this is instructive and will allow you to generate other series which Lotus is not programmed to produce.

Consequently, you should now prepare Worksheet 2.21. As you can see, the required first term and common difference are entered in E1 and E2 respectively.

The cells A2..A20 contain the individual term numbers, and the cells B2..B19 contain the actual terms of the series, which are generated from +E1 in B2 and +B2+E$2 in B3, which was then copied into the range B3..B19.

The first 19 terms of any arithmetic series can now be generated by making the appropriate changes to E1 and/or E2.

Look at any term (other than the first) that you have generated. The question we would like to answer is whether there is a general algebraic method for obtaining the value of any chosen term, and to answer this we could proceed as follows:

the first term is a
the second term is $a + d$
the third term is $a + d + d = a + 2d$
the fourth term is $a + d + d + d = a + 3d$

WORKSHEET 2.21

	A	B	C	D	E
1	Term no.	Term Value		First term	3
2	1	3		common diff.	5
3	2	8			
4	3	13			
5	4	18			
6	5	23			
7	6	28			
8	7	33			
9	8	38			
10	9	43			
11	10	48			
12	11	53			
13	12	58			
14	13	63			
15	14	68			
16	15	73			
17	16	78			
18	17	83			
19	18	88			
20	19	93			

Therefore, if we extend this logic it surely follows that the *n*th term will be

$$u_n = a + (n-1)d$$

You can confirm this expression if you let *n* equal any term number that you have generated in your worksheet, and then substitute whatever first term and common difference you have used in your worksheet into this last expression. You should find that the value of the chosen term is reproduced by the formula. Try it now.

Having established an analytical method for calculating any term in an arithmetic series, the next question that arises is whether an equivalent expression can be derived for the *sum* of the first *n* terms that are in arithmetic progression.

Clearly we could modify Worksheet 2.21 so that the sum of the terms is generated at each stage (a running total). This has been done in Worksheet 2.22 for a series with $a = 22$, $d = 5$ and a total of 19 terms.

Column C has been used to calculate the running total, with the formula in C2 being +B2 and the formula in C3 being +C2+B3. This last entry was then copied into the range C4..C20 so that each previous total has the next term added to it.

As you can see, the sum of the first 12 terms, for example, is 594, but once again we should wonder whether there is an analytic method of obtaining the same result.

The answer is that the sum of the first *n* terms in an arithmetic series (S_n) is

```
WORKSHEET 2.22
         A            B          C         D            E
 1    Term no.    Term Value    Sum     First term     22
 2       1           22          22     common diff.    5
 3       2           27          49
 4       3           32          81
 5       4           37         118
 6       5           42         160
 7       6           47         207
 8       7           52         259
 9       8           57         316
10       9           62         378
11      10           67         445
12      11           72         517
13      12           77         594
14      13           82         676
15      14           87         763
16      15           92         855
17      16           97         952
18      17          102        1054
19      18          107        1161
20      19          112        1273
```

always given by
$$S_n = n/2[2a + (n-1)d]$$

Now although we have not derived this result formally, it is an easy matter to confirm its accuracy, since all we have to do is substitute our parameter values into this last expression. This would produce

$$S_{12} = 12/2[2(22) + (12-1)(5)] = 6(99) = 594$$

thereby confirming the result that we obtained in our worksheet.

We can summarize these results as follows. For any arithmetic series in which the first term is represented by a, the common difference by d and the number of terms by n, then the nth term (u_n) and the sum of the first n terms (S_n) are given by

$$u_n = a + (n-1)d$$
$$S_n = n/2[2a + (n-1)d]$$

EXAMPLE 2.22

An occupation's salary scale starts at £9000 and rises in equal annual increments of £500 to a maximum of £15 000

(a) How many 'points' are there in the salary scale?
(b) How much would an individual be earning on salary point 8?
(c) What would be the total earnings of an individual who progressed from point 1 to the maximum point and then remained at the maximum for 11 years?

SOLUTION 2.22

(a) This problem can be modelled by an arithmetic progression in which $a = £2000$, $d = £500$ and n is initially unknown.

Since the nth term of an arithmetic series is given by

$$u_n = a + (n-1)d$$

we can write

$$u_n = 9000 + (n-1)(500)$$

and then note that this must equal 15 000 (the maximum point).
Therefore

$$9000 + (n-1)(500) = 15\,000$$

Implying that

$$500(n-1) = 15\,000 - 9000 = 6000$$

Algebraic series 99

and that
$$(n-1) = 6000/500 = 12$$

Consequently
$$n = 13$$

The salary scale therefore has 13 'points'.

(b) With n now equal to 8 and a and d as before, we have
$$u_8 = 9000 + (8-1)(500) = £12\,500$$

(c) The progression from point 1 to point 13 on the salary scale produces 13 annual salaries of 9000, 9500, ..., 15 000, which have a sum given by
$$S_{13} = 13/2\,[2(9000) + 12(500)] = £156\,000$$

However, since this individual stays at the maximum for 11 years there are a *further* 10 maximum salaries to be added on. The total accumulated income is therefore
$$156\,000 + 10(15\,000) = £306\,000$$

EXAMPLE 2.23

The salary earned by an executive of a large company starts at £35 000 and increases annually by equal annual amounts to a maximum of £70 000.

A newly appointed executive calculates that by the end of his first year of earning the maximum salary he will have earned a total of £420 000.

Determine the annual increase in salary and the length of time needed to progress from the bottom to the top of the salary scale.

SOLUTION 2.23

This problem represents an arithmetic progression in which the first term is given by $a = £35\,000$ and the common difference d, and number of terms n are unknown.

We know, however, that after n years the annual salary will be £70 000 and so we have
$$u_n = 70\,000$$

But
$$u_n = a + (n-1)d$$

So
$$35\,000 + (n-1)d = 70\,000$$

Therefore
$$(n-1)d = 35\,000$$

We also know that the total accumulated income over the n years is £420 000, so it follows that
$$S_n = 420\,000$$

But
$$S_n = n/2\,[2a + (n-1)d]$$

So
$$n/2\,[2(35\,000) + (n-1)d] = 420\,000$$

These two pieces of information are enough to allow us to solve for both n and d, since we can replace the term $(n-1)d$ in the last expression with 35 000 [remembering that we deduced earlier that $(n-1)d = 35\,000$]. Therefore
$$S_n = n/2\,[2(35\,000) + 35\,000] = 420\,000$$

And
$$n/2\,(105\,000) = 420\,000$$

Consequently
$$n/2 = 4$$

and thus
$$n = 8$$

There are therefore eight points on the salary scale, which means that
$$(n-1)d = 35\,000$$
$$d = 35\,000/7 = £5000$$

2.10.2 Geometric series

The next important series is known as a geometric progression and is characterized by a constant common ratio (or factor) as opposed to a common difference.

This means that each term in a geometric series is a constant multiple of the previous term. For example, the series

$$10, 20, 30, 80, 160, \ldots$$

is characterized by the fact that each term is exactly twice the previous term, while the series

$$100, 50, 25, 12.5, \ldots$$

has each term exactly half the previous term.

Algebraic series

They can both therefore be thought of as geometric series in which the first terms are respectively 10 and 100, and in which the common factors are 2 and 0.5 respectively.

More generally, if we denote this common factor by *m*, then we can define any geometric series by the following statement:

$$u_n = m(u_{n-1}) \quad \text{or} \quad u_n/u_{n-1} = m$$

You should be able to see that if *m* is greater than 1, then the terms in the series are increasing in magnitude, but if *m* is less than 1, the terms are decreasing in magnitude, while if *m* is equal to 1 the terms are all identical and equal to the first term.

A geometric series can be an extremely useful modelling device, if, for example, we were required to force some base value (*a*) to increase at a rate of (say) 10 per cent per period. Under these circumstances the behaviour of the base value could represented by a geometric series in which the common factor was 1.1.

Alternatively, if the base value was required to *decrease* at a rate of 10 per cent per time period, then we could use a geometric series in which the common factor was 0.9.

In general, if some base value (*a*) is required to grow at a rate of *g* per cent per period (or decline at *g* per cent per period), then the behaviour of the variable can be modelled by a geometric series in which the common factor (*m*) is (1 + *g*) for positive growth, or (1 − *g*) for negative growth (decline).

WORKSHEET 2.23

	A	B	C	D	E
1	Term no.	Term Value		First term	22
2	1	22.00		common ratio	1.2
3	2	26.40			
4	3	31.68			
5	4	38.02			
6	5	45.62			
7	6	54.74			
8	7	65.69			
9	8	78.83			
10	9	94.60			
11	10	113.52			
12	11	136.22			
13	12	163.46			
14	13	196.15			
15	14	235.39			
16	15	282.46			
17	16	338.95			
18	17	406.75			
19	18	488.09			
20	19	585.71			

You can see this idea operating in the Worksheet 2.23 where the necessary formulae to create any geometric series have been derived.

Once again, the parameters (a and m) of your series are entered as cell values in E1 and E2, and the term numbers in A2..A20.

The actual terms of the series are calculated in B2..B20 from the formulae +E1 in B2 and +B6*E$2 in B3, which is then copied into the range B4..B20.

As you can see, each term is evaluated as the previous term times the common factor, with the result that the ratio between any two consecutive terms will always be equal to the common factor.

EXAMPLE 2.24

A firm's profits at the end of 1980 were £1.2 million, and increased at a constant rate of 3.6 per cent per annum.

Calculate the firm's profits at the end of 1990.

SOLUTION 2.24

You can do this in a worksheet similar to Worksheet 2.24.

Since 1980 represents the first term of the series, we can deduce that the 11th

WORKSHEET 2.24

	A	B	C	D	E
1	Term no.	Term Value		First term	1.2
2	1	1.20		common ratio	1.036
3	2	1.24			
4	3	1.29			
5	4	1.33			
6	5	1.38			
7	6	1.43			
8	7	1.48			
9	8	1.54			
10	9	1.59			
11	10	1.65			
12	11	1.71			
13	12	1.77			
14	13	1.83			
15	14	1.90			
16	15	1.97			
17	16	2.04			
18	17	2.11			
19	18	2.19			
20	19	2.27			

Algebraic series

term will represent the firm's profits at the end of 1990. Consequently

$$u_{11} = 1.71 \text{ million}$$

Now it should also be clear that the sixth term of this series is 1.43, but can we obtain a general expression which will produce this result? The answer is to reason as follows:

the first term is a
the second term is am
the third term is $am(m) = am^2$
the fourth term is $(am^2)(m) = am^3$

Therefore the nth term will be am^{n-1}.

This means that the nth term in a geometric series in which the first term is a, and the common factor is m, will be given by

$$u_n = am^{n-1}$$

You should now confirm this for the values used in the last example. This would be done as follows:

$$a = £1.2 \text{ million}$$
$$m = 1.036$$
$$n = 11$$

WORKSHEET 2.25

	A	B	C	D	E
1	Term no.	Term Value	Sum	First term	1.2
2	1	1.20	1.2	common ratio	1.036
3	2	1.24	2.443		
4	3	1.29	3.731		
5	4	1.33	5.065		
6	5	1.38	6.448		
7	6	1.43	7.880		
8	7	1.48	9.364		
9	8	1.54	10.901		
10	9	1.59	12.493		
11	10	1.65	14.143		
12	11	1.71	15.852		
13	12	1.77	17.623		
14	13	1.83	19.457		
15	14	1.90	21.358		
16	15	1.97	23.326		
17	16	2.04	25.366		
18	17	2.11	27.479		
19	18	2.19	29.669		
20	19	2.27	31.937		

Therefore

$$u_{11} = 1.2(1.036)^{10} = 1.709$$

which confirms the result obtained in Worksheet 2.24.

By a similar logic

$$u_6 = 1.2(1.036)^5 = 1.43$$

But suppose we now ask what is the total *accumulated* profits over the 11 years being considered?

It is an easy matter to modify Worksheet 2.24 (in the same way as we did for the arithmetic series) to obtain the sum of the first n terms. This has been done in Worksheet 2.25.

The running total in column C is calculated from $+B2$ in C2 and $+C2+B3$ in C3 (copied into C4..C20).

The total accumulated profit for the 11 years is therefore £15.852 million.

But is there an equivalent algebraic formula for the sum of the first n terms?

The answer is that there is, but that it is different for circumstances when the common factor is less than 1 than when m exceeds 1.

When $m > 1$

$$S_n = a[(m^n) - 1]/(m - 1)$$

When $m < 1$

$$S_n = a[1 - (m^n)]/(1 - m)$$

If you want to confirm that these formulae give the correct results, then with $a = 1.2$ and $m = 1.036$ (which exceeds 1) we have

$$S_{11} = 1.2[(1.036^{11}) - 1]/(1.036 - 1) = 15.852$$

Alternatively, if you change the entry in E2 to 0.9, then the worksheet will calculate S_{11} to be 8.234, which is identical to

$$S_{11} = 1.2[1 - (0.9^{11})]/(1 - 0.9) = 8.234$$

EXAMPLE 2.25

A manager's annual salary was £10 000 for the year 1980 and was increased by m per cent per annum in each of the subsequent five years.

After his salary for 1981 had been included, his total accumulated income for these two years was £22 000.

(a) Find the manager's salary in 1985.
(b) Find the manager's total accumulated salary after the inclusion of his 1985 salary.

Algebraic series

SOLUTION 2.25

(a) To model this problem by a geometric series, we must first of all find m. Accordingly, since we know that $a = 10\,000$, his salary in 1981 will be $10\,000(m)$. Consequently, his total accumulated income for 1980 and 1981 will be given by

$$10\,000 + 10\,000m$$

which we know is £22 000. Therefore

$$10\,000m = 22\,000 - 10\,000$$

Implying that

$$m = 1.2$$

His salary in 1985 is therefore the sixth term of a geometric series with $a = 10\,000$ and $m = 1.2$, and since

$$u_n = am^{n-1}$$

we have

$$u_6 = 10\,000(1.2)^5 = £24\,883.2$$

(b) To find the total accumulated income for the years 1980–1985 inclusive we require the sum of the first six terms of the geometric series with

$$a = 10\,000, \ m = 1.2 \text{ and } n = 6$$

That is

$$S_6 = 10\,000[(1.2^6) - 1]/(1.2 - 1) = £99\,299.2$$

Now check this result on your last worksheet.

EXAMPLE 2.26

A firm's sales of its product was 100 000 units in 1986 and increased by a constant 10 per cent per annum in the years 1987–1992 inclusive.

The price at which the product was sold was £15 in 1986 and was increased by a constant 7 per cent per annum over the period 1987–1992.

(a) Find the firm's sales in 1992.
(b) Find the price of the product in 1992.
(c) Find the firm's total revenue from sales in 1992.
(d) Find the total accumulated revenue over the period 1986–1992 inclusive.

SOLUTION 2.26

(a) The firm's sales can be represented by a geometric series in which $a = 100\,000$ and $m = 1.1$.

The period 1986–1992 inclusive represents seven years, and so $n = 7$. Therefore

$$u_7 \text{ (sales)} = 100\,000(1.1^6) = 177\,156.1$$

(b) The behaviour of product price is modelled by a geometric series with $a = £15$, $m = 1.07$ and $n = 7$, giving

$$u_7 \text{ (price)} = 15(1.07^6) = £22.51$$

(c) Revenue in 1992 is therefore $(177\,156.1)(22.51) = £3\,987\,953$.

(d) This is a more difficult question to answer since it requires that we find the sum of seven annual revenue terms.

In other words, letting $R_1, R_2, ..., R_7$ denote the revenue in each of the years 1986, 1987, ..., 1992, we require

$$R_1 + R_2 + \cdots + R_7$$

Now since the revenue in each year will be that year's price times that year's sales, we can let S_1 to S_7 and P_1 to P_7 represent sales and price respectively in the years 1986–1992.

This allows us to rewrite the revenue expression above as

$$R_1 + R_2 + \cdots + R_7 = S_1 P_1 + S_2 P_2 + \cdots + S_7 P_7$$

We could of course evaluate each of these terms individually and then sum to obtain the required result, but the issue posed here is whether our knowledge of geometric progressions can be used to simplify this task.

The answer is that it can, but that we must be careful how we do it. The problem can be solved as follows.

Sales are in geometric progression with $m = 1.1$, $a = 100\,000$ and $n = 7$.
Price is in geometric progression with $m = 1.07$, $a = 15$ and $n = 7$.
Therefore revenue = (sales)(price) is in geometric progression with

$$a = (15)(100\,000) = 1.5 \text{ million}$$
$$m = (1.1)(1.07) = 1.177$$
$$n = 7$$

That this is an accurate formulation can be confirmed by calculating R_7 (which we already know to be £3 987 953) on the basis of this composite geometric series for R. That is

$$R_7 = (1.5 \text{ million})(1.177^6) = £3\,987\,953$$

This confirms that our formulation is correct, and so we can use these figures in

Algebraic series

our expression for the sum to n terms of a geometric series. This produces

$$S_7 = 1.5 \text{ million}[(1.177^7) - 1]/(1.77 - 1) = £18\,044\,184$$

Consequently, the total accumulated revenue is £18 044 184.

The logic outlined above allows us to produce a general result. Namely, if the series A is in geometric progression with first term a and common ratio m, and if the series B is in geometric progression with first term b and common ratio r, then the following generalizations can be made:

1. The series $(A)(B)$ is in geometric progression with first term ab and common ratio mr.
2. The series (A/B) is in geometric progression with first term a/b and common ratio m/r.

You must not conclude, however, that a similar logic applies for the series $(A + B)$ which we encounter in the next example.

EXAMPLE 2.27

In January 1980 a firm's monthly production level was 1000 units, and this was increased by a constant rate of 8 per cent per month from February 1980 to August 1980 inclusive.

In January 1980 the firm's monthly sales were 900 units, and these increased by a constant rate of 7 per cent per month from February 1980 to August 1980 inclusive.

Any output that is produced but not sold is added to stock. The firm estimates that the monthly cost (c) of holding a unit of stock is given by $c = 2x$, where x is the *maximum* monthly stock holding.

(a) Find the firm's total accumulated stock level at the end of August 1980.
(b) What are the stockholding costs incurred by the firm in the month of June 1980?
(c) What are the total stockholding costs *between* January and August 1980 inclusive?

SOLUTION 2.27

(a) Letting P stand for production and S for sales we have

P is a geometric series with $a = 1000$, $m = 1.08$ and $n = 8$ (months)
S is a geometric series with $a = 900$, $m = 1.07$ and $n = 8$ (months)

Total accumulated production is therefore the sum of the first eight terms of the series P. That is

$$S_8(P) = 1000[(1.08^8 - 1)]/(1.08 - 1) = 10\,636.628$$

By a similar logic, total accumulated sales for the period is the sum to eight terms of the series S.

$$S_8(S) = 900[(1.07^8) - 1]/(1.07 - 1) = 9233.822$$

The total accumulated stock is therefore

$$S_8(P) - S_8(S) = 10\,636.63 - 9233.82 = 1402.81 \text{ units}$$

It should be noted that although P and S are *each* in geometric progression, $(P-S)$ is not, although the sum of the terms in $(P-S)$ can be obtained by summing both P and S and then taking the difference of these two totals.

(b) To determine the stockholding costs for June 1980 we must first obtain the maximum stock held in that month. This is obviously obtained by summing the stocks held in the months January to June inclusive and since this involves six months we require

$$\begin{aligned}S_6(P) &- S_6(S) \\ &= 1000[(1.08^6) - 1]/(1.08 - 1) - 900[(1.07^6) - 1)]/(1.07 - 1) \\ &= 7335.92 - 6437.96 = 898 \text{ units}\end{aligned}$$

That is, the maximum amount of stock held in the month of June is 898 units, and the stockholding costs for June are therefore given by C, where $C = 2x$ and where $x = 898$. Therefore

$$C = £1796$$

These results, and the method by which they were obtained, are frequently more easily understood if the problem is tabulated in a worksheet. So look at Worksheet 2.26. The production and sales series are generated in B3..B10 and C3..C10 from the following:

in B3
  +B12 (which contains the first term of the production series)
in C3
  +B15 (which contains the first term of the sales series)
in B4
  +B3*B$13 (generating the production series on the basis of the production common ratio in B13)
in C4
  +C3*B$16 (generating the sales series on the basis of the sales common ratio in B16)

These entries in B4 and C4 are then copied into B5..C10.

The daily addition to stock is calculated from the following:

in D3   +B3−C3 (copied into D4..D10)

and the accumulated stock is calculated from

in E3   +D3
in E4   +E3+D4 (copied into E4..E10).

Finally, the monthly stockholding cost is calculated from the following:

in F3   +E3*B$20 (copied into F4..F10)

and the total accumulated stockholding cost

in G3   +F3
in G4   +G3+F4 (copied into G4..G10).

(c) As you can see, this worksheet confirms our previous results (1402 and £1796) and also allows us to conclude that the total stockholding costs between January and August inclusive are £10 612.

2.10.3 Infinite geometric series

You will certainly have noticed that when m is less than 1, each subsequent term in the geometric progression is less than the previous one, and that as a result, the sum of the first n terms is being increased by less and less as each extra term is added on.

Under such circumstances it will eventually be the case that additional terms add such an inconsequential amount to the total that the sum of the terms is effectively unchanged, and is said to have reached a limit.

But what is the value of this limit?

If you examine the formula for the sum to n terms when m is less than 1, you should see that since $m < 1$, m^n decreases as n increases, meaning that as n becomes infinitely large, m^n is effectively 0, and so

$$S_n = a(1 - m^n)/(1 - m)$$

becomes equivalent to

$$S_n = a(1 - 0)/(1 - m) = a/(1 - m)$$

Now since we have let n become infinitely large, it would seem logical to regard S_n as the sum to infinity and give it the symbol S_∞. Consequently

$$S_\infty = a/(1 - m)$$

Examples of sums to infinity are not difficult to find as you can see below.

WORKSHEET 2.26

	A Month	B Production	C Sales	D Stock	E Sum stock	F Cost per month	G Total cost
1							
2							
3	January	1000.00	900	100.000	100	200	200
4	February	1080.00	963.000	117.000	217	434	634
5	March	1166.40	1030.410	135.990	352.99	705.98	1339.98
6	April	1259.71	1102.539	157.173	510.1633	1020.326	2360.306
7	May	1360.49	1179.716	180.773	690.9358	1381.871	3742.178
8	June	1469.33	1262.297	207.032	897.9673	1795.934	5538.113
9	July	1586.87	1350.657	236.217	1134.184	2268.368	7806.481
10	August	1713.82	1445.203	268.621	1402.805	2805.610	10612.09
11							
12	a (prod)	1000.00					
13	m (prod)	1.08					
14							
15	a (sales)	900.00					
16	m (sales)	1.07					
17	stock						
18	holding						
19	cost						
20	per unit	2.00					

Algebraic series

EXAMPLE 2.28

In an effort to stop smoking a man decides to halve the daily number of cigarettes that he smokes.

On the first day of this regime he smoked 40 cigarettes.

(a) What is the total number of cigarettes smoked before he has given up smoking entirely?
(b) The brand that he smokes is 10 cm long, but cannot be lit for parts of cigarettes that are less than 0.5 cm long. How many days will it now take before he has stopped smoking, and how many cigarettes will he have smoked?

SOLUTION 2.28

(a) We have $m = 0.5$ and $a = 40$. Thus

$$S_\infty = 40/(1 - 0.5) = 80 \text{ cigarettes}$$

(b) We require the nth term of the series to be equal to $0.5/10 = 0.05$ of the length of a cigarette. Therefore, since

$$am^{n-1} = u_n$$

We require

$$40(0.5^{n-1}) = 0.05$$

Implying that

$$0.5^{n-1} = 0.00125$$

and that

$$(n-1)\log_{10} 0.5 = \log_{10} 0.00125$$

Therefore

$$(n - 1) = 9.64$$

hence

$$n = 10.64$$

The portion of a cigarette available will be equal to 0.5 cm after 10.6 days, so he will be able to smoke up to and including the 10th day but will be stopped on the 11th.

The total number of cigarettes smoked will be given by

$$S_{10} = 40(1 - 0.5^{10})/(1 - 0.5) = 79.92 \text{ cigarettes}$$

As you can see, this is only 0.08 of a cigarette less than the sum to infinity, and indicates that the greatest part of any sum to infinity is achieved after remarkably few terms.

A more important example of an infinite summing process can be seen in the process of modelling a simple economic system.

Consider an economy that produces an annual national income of £Y.

From the point of view of the demands upon this economy's income, assume that these derive entirely from two sources, consumption demands (C) and investment demands (I). In other words, the output of the economy is entirely used by a combination of consumption and investment needs. In symbols we can write

$$Y = C + I$$

However, since this national income will be received by the companies and individuals who comprise the economy, it will also be the case that the income received can be allocated between consumption expenditure and savings (S).

In other words (in this simple model) income received is either consumed or saved, and we can write

$$Y = C + S$$

Now since it should be clear that collectively, and in the absence of foreign trade, an economy cannot use more of its output than it produces, we can use this fact to define the notion of balance or equilibrium in terms of

$$C + I = C + S$$

Implying that

$$I = S$$

What this means is that an economy cannot carry out more investment activity than its residents have decided to save (i.e. not consume).

As such, however, this says very little since at this stage we do not have any behavioural equations in the model that will allow us to analyze how much of the national income will be saved, and how much will be required for investment purposes.

But suppose we take the level of investment expenditure to be given for the current time period (an exogenous variable), and at the same time argue that consumption is a linear function of income. That is

$$C = a + bY$$

where a and b are constants. Then since

$$Y = C + I$$

we can rewrite this as

$$Y = a + bY + I$$

Implying that
$$Y - bY = a + I$$
and that
$$Y(1 - b) = a + I$$
Therefore
$$Y = (a + I)/(1 - b)$$

Now this last equation is more than a simple identity, since you should be able to see that it defines the value that Y must adopt if, given the values of a, b and I, the economic system is to be in equilibrium.

For example, if we have $I = 10$, $a = 20$ and $b = 0.7$, then
$$Y = (10 + 20)/(1 - 0.7) = 100$$

What this means is that only with an income level of 100 will the investment demands of the economy be matched by the economy's provision of savings. This is because, with an income of 100, consumption will be
$$C = 20 + 0.7(100) = 90$$
leaving exactly enough savings $(100 - 90 = 10)$ to finance the investment demands of 10.

Now suppose that in the next time period the desire to invest increases by 6 (to 16). Assuming that credit is available to allow this investment level to be achieved, what will happen to the level of national income?

Clearly, if our equilibrium equation is correct, the new level of income will have to be
$$Y = (16 + 20)/(1 - 0.7) = 120$$

Only if this happens will the level of consumption $[20 + 0.7(120) = 104]$, leave enough savings $(120 - 104 = 16)$ to match the new level of investment. However, this raises the question of how such an adjustment takes place, and how long it will take.

To answer this we should recognize that in the first instance, the increased investment (6) represents an increase in income of 6 for the recipients of the investment expenditure. In other words, the construction workers who build a new power station, for example, and the firms that supply the materials will find that their income has increased by 6.

But, since we know that out of every *extra* pound of income that is received, 70 per cent will be consumed, this means that $0.7(6) = 4.2$ further units of income will be created when the construction workers spend their salaries and the firms pay their suppliers and their workers.

Clearly the recipients of this 4.2 extra income units will also spend 70 per cent of it and will therefore create a further $0.7(4.2) = 2.94$ units of income for the recipients of this expenditure.

By now it should be clear that we are dealing with a geometric series in which each round of expenditure creates further income, which is always 70 per cent of that expenditure. In other words we have a geometric series in which the first term is 6 and the common factor 0.7.

It is the total income generated by this process that concerns us here, and since there is no obvious mechanism to stop the process, we should suspect that we require the sum to infinity of the series. This would be given by

$$S_\infty = 6/(1 - 0.7) = 20$$

which is exactly the amount of extra income that the equilibrium equation predicted would be created.

Of course since it is derived on the basis of an infinite series, this means that it will never actually be achieved. However, as Worksheet 2.27 indicates, approximately 95 per cent of the extra income and the extra savings will have been generated after the first eight rounds of the process.

The intercept and gradient values for the consumption function (20 and 0.7) are entered in B1 and B2 and the current level of investment in B7. This allows the equilibrium level of income to be calculated in B4 from $(B1 + B7)/(1 - B2)$, i.e. $(a + I)/(1 - b)$. Given this equilibrium value, the associated consumption and savings are calculated from $+B1 + B2*B4$ (in B5), i.e. $a + bY$, and $+B4 - B5$ (in B6), i.e. $Y - C$.

Finally, the difference between savings and investment is calculated in B8 from $+B6 - B7$. This will always be 0, of course, in equilibrium.

With any change in investment entered in B9, then since this causes income to change by an equal amount, the entry in B10 is $+B9$.

The implied change in consumption is therefore $+B10*B2$, i.e. bY, and the change in savings is $+B10 - B11$, i.e. (change in income) − (change in consumption).

In the first round the cumulative change in income is simply $+B10$ and the cumulative change in savings is $+B12$. However, this will increase as the number of rounds of the process increases. We deal with this in column C.

The new income is $+B6 + B14$, i.e. the old income plus the extra income. The new savings are $+B4 + B16$, i.e. the old savings plus the extra savings.

The new difference between savings and investment will therefore be $+B18 - \$B7 - \$B9$, i.e. the new savings level minus the initial level of investment minus the change in investment. Notice that the dollar signs allow this expression to be copied appropriately into subsequent periods.

The secret of simulating the income generating process over subsequent periods is to recognize now that for period 2 the change in income will be given by the change in consumption in the previous period. Thus, the entry in C10 is $+B11$ and the change in consumption in C11 will be $+C10*\$B2$, giving a change in savings in C12 of $+C10 - C11$.

Clearly the total change in income is the change in the first round plus the change in the second round, so the entry in C14 is $+B14 + C10$.

WORKSHEET 2.27

	A	B	C	D	E	F	G	H	I
1	intercept (a)	20							
2	gradient (b)	0.7							
3	Period	1	2	3	4	5	6	7	8
4	Income	100.0							
5	Consumption	90.0							
6	Savings	10.0							
7	Investment	10.0							
8	Sav. - Invest.	0.0							
9	Change in Inv.	6.0							
10	Change in Income	6.0	4.2	2.9	2.1	1.4	1.0	0.7	0.5
11	Change in Cons.	4.2	2.9	2.1	1.4	1.0	0.7	0.5	0.3
12	Change in Sav.	1.8	1.3	0.9	0.6	0.4	0.3	0.2	0.1
13	Cumulative								
14	Change in Income	6.0	10.2	13.1	15.2	16.6	17.6	18.4	18.8
15	Cumulative								
16	Change in Sav.	1.8	3.1	3.9	4.6	5.0	5.3	5.5	5.7
17	New Income	106.0	110.2	113.1	115.2	116.6	117.6	118.4	118.8
18	New Saving.	11.8	13.1	13.9	14.6	15.0	15.3	15.5	15.7
19	Sav. - Invest.	-4.2	-2.9	-2.1	-1.4	-1.0	-0.7	-0.5	-0.3
20									

A similar logic applies to the cumulative change in savings, so the entry in C16 is $+B16+C12$.

The new income is the last period's income level, plus any change in income in this period, so C17 contains $+B17+C10$, and the new savings level will be given in C18 by $+B18+C12$.

Finally, the difference between savings and investment will be given by the previous period's difference (B19) plus the extra savings generated in the current period (C12) minus any change in investment which takes place in the current period ($C9 = 0$ in this simple case). So the entry in C19 should be $+B19+C12-C9$.

Set up in this way, the formulae in column C can now be copied into as many further columns as the desired number of periods require.

Now use this worksheet to observe what the effects of the extra 6 units of investment would have been if 80 per cent of every extra unit of income was consumed. You should find that more income has to be generated in order to compensate for the fact that less of every extra unit of income is saved. Try it.

Up until now we have assumed that there was a single 'one-off' increase in the level of investment, but the last worksheet has been constructed in such a way that increases (or decreases) in each of the time periods can be accommodated. The secret of this is to remember that in any given period, the increase in income will be given by the change in consumption in the previous period plus the change in investment in that current period.

This means that all you have to do is change the entry in C10 to $+B11+C9$ and copy this into all subsequent columns. (Of course if the entry in C9 is 0 then the results are unchanged.)

The worksheet can now deal with periodic increases and decreases in the level of investment activity, and will indicate the amount of income generated in each of the subsequent periods. If you experiment with various patterns of investment expenditure over the periods of your model, then some interesting results can be obtained.

2.11 Exercises

2.1

A television rental firm rents sets to customers for a monthly rental of £20. However, in the case of large orders, it employs a discount policy such that the *total bill* to the customer is reduced by 5 per cent for *each and every* set in excess of 10 that is rented.

Design a spreadsheet that will calculate the invoice to be sent to a customer when the number of sets rented is entered.

The design of you spreadsheet should allow easy alteration of the discount rate, the monthly rental and the threshold number of sets that must be rented for the discount to apply. This is because you should now prepare an invoice if the discount rate is 7 per cent, the monthly rental is £25 and the threshold number of sets is 8.

2.2

On the first day of a production run of 15 days an output of 5000 units was produced. This output was increased by 4 per cent per day for each day of the production run.

The demand for the output was 4200 on the first day and was expected to increase at a rate of 3.5 per cent per day for each day of the production run.

Any output that is not sold is added to stock and imposes a stockholding cost of 2p per unit *per day that it is held in stock* including its day of production.

Create a spreadsheet that will calculate the following:

(a) The stockholding cost for the day that the production run ends.
(b) The total stockholding costs incurred between the start of the production run and the day that it finished.

If production was limited to 5000 units for the first five days of the run, then increased to 7000 units for the next five days and then increased to 9000 units for the last five days, would this strategy reduce the total stock holding costs for the period calculated above?

2.3

The total cost (c) of producing a firm's product is known to vary in relation to the output produced (x) as follows:

$$c = 100x^{0.75}$$

If an output of 1200 units is produced, calculate the total and the average cost of production.

2.4

The sales (s) of a firm's product have changed over time (t) as follows:

$$s = 10t^{1.5}$$

Calculate the length of time required for the firm's sales to reach 1000 units.

2.5

The relationship between a firm's output (q) and its usage level of two resources is known to be given by

$$q = 100(x^{0.2})(y^{0.6})$$

where x is the quantity of the first resource employed and y is the quantity of the second resource employed.

(a) Assuming that the firm uses 100 units of the first resource, and wishes to produce an output of 1500 units, find the amount of the second resource that must be employed in order to do this.

(b) If the firm produces an output that imposes total production costs of £900, and uses 150 units of the first resource to do so, find the output level produced, if it is also known that units of the first and second resource cost £4 and £10 respectively.

2.6

For particular groups of income earners, the quantity of beer demanded per week (q) is know to be a linear function of weekly household income (x).

It is also known that when household income is £120, the demand for beer is 1000 units, while when household income is £80, the demand for beer is 800 units.

Find the equation of the 'demand for beer' function, and use this to estimate the weekly demand if household income were £95.

2.7

A local authority has just taken delivery of a new bridge at a total cost £10 million.

(a) Assuming that there are no maintenance costs, what price (p) should be charged per crossing if the local authority needs to recover 5 per cent of the total cost in the first year, and if the annual number of crossings depends upon the price as follows:

$$x = 1 - 0.01p \text{ (where } x \text{ is measured in millions)}$$

(b) If, in addition to the fixed cost of £1 million, there were maintenance costs of £0.03 per crossing, what price would now have to be charged if 5 per cent of the fixed cost and all of the annual maintenance costs had to be recovered in the first year?

2.8

The value of a firm's capital equipment depreciates in such a way that from its current value of £100 000 it has a value of £50 000 after five years.

If the scrap value of the equipment is never less than 10 000, derive an appropriate hyperbolic function that will model this depreciation pattern.

2.9

A company's profits (p) grow continuously over time (t) in such a way that

$$p = 10\ 000(e^{0.1t})$$

(a) After how many years will the profits be double their initial value?
(b) After how many years will the profits be 15 000?

2.10

The quantity demanded (q) of a particular product is thought to depend upon its

price (p) as follows:
$$q = 1000(2^{-0.5p})$$
(a) Calculate the quantity demanded when a price of £10 is charged.
(b) What price would have to be charged in order to ensure a demand of 500 units?

2.11

The price (P) per kWh of industrial electricity is known to be equal to its average cost of production plus 15 per cent profit mark-up.

The daily demand in kWh (Q) is known to depend upon the price as follows:
$$Q = 5000 - 80P$$
The total daily cost of production (C) is given by:
$$C = 10\,000 + 30Q \text{ (where } C \text{ is measured in £s)}$$

Determine the equilibrium price and quantity of industrial electricity and the associated profit made.

2.12

An organization's salary structure for a particular grade of employee starts at £10 000 in the first year of employment and rises in annual increments of £750 in each of the next nine years of employment. Thereafter the employee's salary is increased at an annual compound rate of 10 per cent for all subsequent years of employment.

(a) Calculate the salary earned by an employee who is in the 18th year of employment.
(b) Calculate the total earnings to date of an employee who has completed exactly 20 years of employment.

After an employee has been with the company for a minimum of 20 years, early retirement can be taken with an annual pension which is calculated on the basis of 2 per cent of the final salary earned for each year of employment.

(c) An employee has been with the company for 25 years. Calculate the pension entitlement.

2.12 Solutions to the exercises

2.1

Before you attempt to construct your worksheet, you should obtain a clear idea of the relationships involved in the problem. Consequently, if we let $x =$ the number of sets rented, then by the nature of the agreement we know that if $x \leqslant 10$, then the discount rate (d) is 0 per cent.

WORKSHEET 2.28

```
B6: @IF(B1>B3,B2*(B1-B3),0)
```

	A	B
1	No. of sets rented	16
2	Discount rate	0.05
3	No. of sets for discount	10
4	Rental	20
5	Invoice without discount	320
6	Discount %	0.3
7	Total discount	96
8	Net Invoice	224

On the other hand, if $x > 10$, then the discount rate is 5 per cent for *every* set in excess of 10 that is rented.

This means that if 12 sets were rented, then the total bill would be discounted by $(12 - 10)(5$ per cent$) = 10$ per cent.

Now since the number of sets in excess of 10 will be given by $(x - 10)$, it follows that the discount will be given by $0.05(x - 10)$.

This discount must be applied to the total bill (b), which, since the sets are rented at £20 per month, will be given by $b = 20x$, implying that the amount of the discount will be given by $0.05(x - 10)(20x)$.

Consequently the net invoice (n) will be the difference between the total bill and the amount of the discount. That is

$$n = 20x - 0.05(x - 10)(20x)$$

Having established this relationship, it is now an easy matter to write a conditional statement that will test whether the discount is to apply, and if it is, to calculate the net invoice to be sent to the customer.

You can see this operating in Worksheet 2.28. The entries are as follows:

in B5	+B1*B4
in B6	@IF(B1 > B3, B2*(B1 − B3), 0)
in B7	+B6*B5
in B8	+B5 − B7

With this worksheet operational you can now make the necessary changes in B2, B4 and B3 to find the new net invoice. You should also appreciate that the discount strategy is not very sensible since eventually the sets will be rented out for nothing.

2.2

Worksheet 2.29 models the information supplied in this problem.

The entries in B6 and C6 are +B5*1.04 and +C5*1.035 (copied into B6..C19).

WORKSHEET 2.29

	A Day	B Production	C Demand	D Daily addition to stock	E Total stock held	F Stock holding cost (£)	G Total stock holding cost (£)
1							
2							
3							
4							
5	1	5000	4200	800	800	16.00	16
6	2	5200	4347	853	1653.00	33.06	49.06
7	3	5408	4499.145	908.855	2561.86	51.24	100.30
8	4	5624.3	4656.615	967.7049	3529.56	70.59	170.89
9	5	5849.2	4819.596	1029.696	4559.26	91.19	262.07
10	6	6083.2	4988.282	1094.982	5654.24	113.08	375.16
11	7	6326.5	5162.872	1163.722	6817.96	136.36	511.52
12	8	6579.6	5343.572	1236.085	8054.05	161.08	672.60
13	9	6842.8	5530.597	1312.247	9366.29	187.33	859.92
14	10	7116.5	5724.168	1392.390	10758.68	215.17	1075.10
15	11	7401.2	5924.514	1476.706	12235.39	244.71	1319.81
16	12	7697.2	6131.872	1565.397	13800.79	276.02	1595.82
17	13	8005.1	6346.488	1658.672	15459.46	309.19	1905.01
18	14	8325.3	6568.615	1756.752	17216.21	344.32	2249.33
19	15	8658.3	6798.516	1859.865	19076.08	381.52	2630.86

This allows the daily addition to stock to be calculated in D5 from +B5 − C5 (copied into D6..D19).

The total stock held is the sum of each daily addition to stock. The entry in E5 is therefore +D5 and that in E6 is +E5+D6 (copied into E7..E19).

Since each unit of stock imposes a cost of £0.02 per day that it is held, the daily stockholding cost is £0.02 times the number of units of stock held on that day. So the entry in F5 is 0.02*E5 (copied into F6..F19).

Finally the total stockholding cost for the period is the sum of each day's stockholding cost and is calculated in G5..G19 by the now familiar method for obtaining a running total.

The worksheet indicates that the answers are as follows:

(a) £381.52 for the 15th day.
(b) £2630.86 for the whole period.
(c) You can replace the entries in B5..B9, B10..B14 and B15..B19, with 5000, 7000 and 9000 respectively, whereupon you should find that the total stockholding costs for the period have declined.

2.3

We have

$$c = 100x^{0.75}$$

Therefore, when $x = 1200$

$$c = 100(1200^{0.75}) = 100(203.8853) = £20\,388.53$$

The average cost of production (avc) will be given by the total cost divided by the output level. Therefore:

$$(avc) = c/x = 100x^{-0.25} = 100(0.1699)$$
$$= £16.99 \text{ when } x = 1200$$

2.4

Since $s = 10t^{1.5}$, and we require to find t such that $s = 1000$ we can write

$$1000 = 10t^{1.5}$$

Implying that

$$t^{1.5} = 100$$

and that

$$t = 100^{1/1.5} = 100^{0.666\,66} = 21.54 \text{ time periods}$$

2.5

(a) We have
$$q = 100(x^{0.2})(y^{0.6})$$
So, with $x = 100$ and the requirement that $q = 1500$, we can write
$$1500 = 100(100^{0.2})(y^{0.6}) = 251.188(y^{0.6})$$
Implying that
$$y^{0.6} = 1500/251.188 = 5.972$$
and that
$$y = 5.972(1/0.6) = 19.655 \text{ units}$$

(b) The cost of production (c) will be given by
$$c = 4x + 10y$$
and we know that this was equal to £900 when $x = 150$. Therefore
$$900 = 4x + 10y$$
Implying that
$$10y = 900 - 4x$$
and that
$$y = 90 - 0.4x$$
Substituting this information into the equation for q then produces
$$q = 100(x^{0.2})[(90 - 0.4x)^{0.6}]$$
which when $x = 150$ evaluates to
$$q = 100(100^{0.2})(50^{0.6}) = 2626.52 \text{ units}$$

2.6

Since we know that the quantity demanded (q) is a linear function of income (x), we can write
$$q = a + bx$$
Also, since we know that when $x = 120$, $q = 1000$, we can use this information to obtain
$$1000 = a + 120b$$
By a similar logic, since $q = 800$ when $x = 80$, we can write
$$800 = a + 80b$$

These two pieces of information need to be taken together in order to calculate the values of a and b. So, from the first equation we have

$$a = 1000 - 120b$$

which can then be substituted into the second equation to produce:

$$800 = (1000 - 120b) + 80b$$

Implying that

$$40b = 200$$

and that

$$b = 5$$

This information then allows us to find the value of a, since

$$a = 1000 - 120b = 1000 - 120(5) = 400$$

The demand for beer function is therefore given by

$$q = 400 + 5x$$

(We should treat this equation with extreme suspicion, since the implication is that 400 units will be consumed even when income is 0.)

2.7

(a) The cost in millions (c) of the bridge is given by $c = £10$, and since 5 per cent must be recovered in the first year, an income of £0.5 million must be generated.

The income (r) will depend upon the price charged (p) and the number of crossings (x) that take place at that price. So

$$r = (1 - 0.01p)p = p - 0.01p^2$$

Consequently, since we require $r = 0.5$, this implies that

$$-0.01p^2 + p - 0.5 = 0$$

If you now use the quadratic formula to find the roots of this equation, then you will find that

$$p_1 = £0.50 \quad \text{and} \quad p_2 = £99.50$$

This implies that the local authority has got a choice of prices to charge, since in either case the required £0.5 million will be raised. (Check this for yourself by evaluating the expression for revenue when each of the prices is charged.)

(b) The introduction of maintenance costs at £0.03 per crossing means that the income must recover

$$c = 500\,000 + 0.03x$$

Therefore
$$(1\,000\,000 - 10\,000p)p = 500\,000 + 0.03x$$
But since we know that
$$x = 1\,000\,000 - 10\,000p$$
we can rewrite the previous expression as
$$1\,000\,000p - 10\,000p^2 = 500\,000 + 0.03(1\,000\,000 - 10\,000p)$$
Implying that
$$1\,000\,000p - 10\,000p^2 = 500\,000 + 30\,000 - 30p$$
Collecting terms and rearranging then produces
$$-10\,000p^2 + 1\,000\,030p - 530\,000 = 0$$
Solution by the quadratic formula then produces
$$p_1 = 0.53 \quad \text{and} \quad p_2 = 99.47$$

Notice the implication of this result, since it would appear to be the case that the lower price should be increased and that the higher price should be decreased. This has a logical interpretation if you remember that the introduction of maintenance costs that depend upon the number of crossings will have a greater effect when the price is low and the number of crossings in high, than when the price is high and the number of crossings is low. (Of course, not all maintenance costs depend upon the number of crossings and a more detailed analysis would have to include such factors as weathering effects as well.)

2.8

The information suggests that
$$v(0) = 100$$
$$v(\infty) = 10$$
$$v(5) = 50$$

Now we can try to relate this knowledge to a general form of the hyperbolic function such as
$$v = a/(x + c) + b$$
where x represents time, and a, b and c are constants.

Taking $v(\infty)$ first of all, then the term $a/(x + c)$ tends to 0 as x becomes infinite, and so the function becomes
$$v(\infty) = b$$
Clearly implying that $b = 10$ [since $v(\infty) = 10$].

Incorporating this deduction means that we can write
$$v = a/(x+c) + 10$$
Now using our knowledge of $v(0) = 100$, we can also write
$$v = a/c + 10 = 100$$
Implying that
$$a/c = 90$$
and that
$$a = 90c$$
Finally, we know that $v(5) = 50$, so
$$v = a/(5+c) + 10 = 50$$
Implying that
$$a/(5+c) = 40$$
and that
$$a = 40(5+c) = 200 + 40c$$
But, we already have
$$a = 90c$$
Therefore
$$90c = 200 + 40c$$
Implying that
$$c = 4$$
$$a = 360$$
Our function is therefore given by
$$v = 360/(x+4) + 10$$

2.9

We have
$$p = 10\,000 e^{0.1t}$$
Therefore, if we take *natural* logarithms of both sides of this equation, we obtain:
$$\ln p = \ln 10\,000 + 0.1t(\ln e)$$
But $\ln e = 1$ (since $e^1 = e$). So
$$\ln p = \ln 10\,000 + 0.1t$$

Implying that

$$t = 10(\ln p) - 10(\ln 10\,000)$$

(a) When $t = 0$, $p = 10\,000$, so for a doubling of the initial value we require $p = 20\,000$. Consequently

$$t = 10(\ln 20\,000) - 10(\ln 10\,000) = 6.93 \text{ years}$$

(b) We require $p = 15\,000$, so

$$t = 10(\ln 15\,000) - 10(\ln 10\,000) = 4.05 \text{ years}$$

2.10

(a) When $p = 10$ we have

$$q = 1000(2^{(-0.5)(10)}) = 1000(2^{-5}) = 31.25 \text{ units}$$

(b) To obtain $q = 500$, we require p such that

$$500 = 1000(2^{-0.5p})$$

Implying that

$$2^{-0.5p} = 0.5$$

Taking logarithms of both sides then produces

$$-0.5p(\log 2) = \log 0.5$$

Implying that

$$-0.5p = \log 0.5 / \log 2 = -1$$

Therefore

$$p = 2$$

A price of £2 must be charged in order to ensure a demand of 500 units, as you can easily confirm if you substitute a value of $p = 2$ into the expression for q.

2.11

Since the total daily cost of production is given by

$$C = 10\,000 + 30Q$$

it follows that the average daily cost of production will be given by

$$C/Q = 10\,000/Q + 30$$

The price charged is therefore

$$P = 1.15(10\,000/Q + 30) = 12\,500/Q + 37.5$$

The demand is given in terms of the price charged by

$$Q = 5000 - 80P$$

Implying that

$$P = 62.5 - Q/80$$

Since equilibrium requires that the same quantity be demanded as is supplied, we then have

$$62.5 - Q/80 = 12\,500/Q + 37.5$$

Implying that

$$12\,500/Q + Q/80 - 25 = 0$$

Multiplying throughout by Q then produces

$$12\,500 + Q^2/80 - 25Q = 0$$

Implying that

$$0.0125Q^2 - 25Q + 12\,500 = 0$$

The quadratic formula only produces one positive solution, and you can confirm that this is $Q = 1000$ units. Consequently the price charged is

$$P = 62.5 - 1000/80 = 50$$

and the profit made is

$$50(1000) - [10\,000 + 30(1000)] = 10\,000$$

2.12

Although you can solve this problem by using algebraic series, making up a worksheet like Worksheet 2.30 is probably more efficient.

The entry in B4 is +B3+750 and this is copied into B5..B12 to give the first 10 terms of the arithmetic series. Thereafter, since growth is geometric the entries in column B are +B12*1.1 (in B13) and this is copied into B14..B27.

The earnings to date are calculated from the running total formulae that we have used frequently before, and the pension in the 20th and all subsequent years is calculated from +B22*A22*0.02, i.e. 2 per cent of salary times number of years of employment.

So the answers to the questions are as follows:

(a) £35 905.11 = the salary of an employee in the 18th year of employment.
(b) £427 397.05 = the total earnings of an employee who has been employed for exactly 20 years.
(c) £34 984.45 = the annual pension of an employee who retires after 25 years of service.

WORKSHEET 2.30

	A	B	C	D
1	Year	Salary	Earnings	Pension
2			to date	
3	1	10000	10000.00	
4	2	10750	20750.00	
5	3	11500	32250.00	
6	4	12250	44500.00	
7	5	13000	57500.00	
8	6	13750	71250.00	
9	7	14500	85750.00	
10	8	15250	101000.00	
11	9	16000	117000.00	
12	10	16750	133750.00	
13	11	18425.00	152175.00	
14	12	20267.50	172442.50	
15	13	22294.25	194736.75	
16	14	24523.68	219260.43	
17	15	26976.04	246236.47	
18	16	29673.65	275910.11	
19	17	32641.01	308551.13	
20	18	35905.11	344456.24	
21	19	39495.62	383951.86	
22	20	43445.19	427397.05	17378.07
23	21	47789.70	475186.75	20071.67
24	22	52568.68	527755.43	23130.21
25	23	57825.54	585580.97	26599.74
26	24	63608.10	649189.07	30531.88
27	25	69968.91	719157.98	34984.45

3
Financial Mathematics

3.1 Introduction

In this chapter we will consider the effect that the passage of time, and the consequent payment of interest, exercises upon the nominal value of any given sum of money.

The simplest starting point is the notion that if any sum of money (which we will call the Principal) bears interest at a rate of r per cent per annum, then after one year has passed this Principal has earned interest equal to the Principal times $(r/100)$.

When this interest is added to the Principal, then the value of the account becomes:

$$(\text{Principal}) + [(\text{Principal}) \times (r/100)]$$

For example, a Principal of £200 deposited at an interest rate of 10 per cent per annum would bear an annual interest payment of £200(10/100) = £20.

Furthermore, the value of the deposit when the annual interest has been included is easily seen to have increased from £200 to £200 + the annual interest payment, i.e. £200 + £20 = £220.

In general, then, we can state the following:

$$\text{amount after one year} = [\text{Principal}] + [(\text{Principal})(r/100)]$$

Although we have referred to the interest rate as a percentage rate per annum, it will usually be more convenient to convert it to a decimal expression (which will be denoted as i). This means that an interest rate of 15 per cent per annum, for example, can be re-expressed as $15/100 = 0.15$.

In general, of course, we could say that an interest rate of r per cent per annum could be written in decimal form (i) as:

$$i = r \text{ per cent}/100$$

This means that the expression above for the amount after one year can now be rewritten as:

$$\text{amount after one year} = [\text{Principal}] + [(\text{Principal})(i)]$$

Introduction

Furthermore, since the righthand side of the last expression above can have P factorized out of it, we can rewrite it as:

$$\text{amount after one year} = (\text{Principal})(1 + i)$$

Obviously it becomes extremely tedious to write out lengthy expressions like the ones above, and so we shall use the following symbols as abbreviations:

t = the number of years for which the principal is deposited
i = the interest rate expressed as a decimal
P = the principal
A_t = a subscripted variable representing the amount after t years have passed

Taking these last two definitions together you should be able to see that we can also write

$$P = A_0$$

That is, the Principal is by definition the same as the amount after 0 years have passed.

Furthermore, using these symbols more extensively, we can state that the amount after one year (A_1) is given by:

$$A_1 = P(1 + i) = A_0(1 + i)$$

EXAMPLE 3.1

Find the amount after one year of a Principal of £1500, if interest is paid at a rate of 6 per cent per annum.

SOLUTION 3.1

We have

$$P = A_0 = £1500$$
$$i = r/100 = 6/100 = 0.06$$
$$t = 1$$

Therefore

$$A_1 = 1500(1 + 0.06) = 1500(1.06) = £1590$$

The procedure illustrated above is perfectly adequate if only one year's interest is to be calculated, but it is easy to envisage circumstances in which we need to find the value of a deposit after two, or three, or more years have passed.

In this case we must identify from the outset whether the annual interest rate is being applied on a *simple* or on a *compound* basis, since the calculation methods are significantly different in these two cases.

3.2 Simple interest

If interest is calculated on a simple basis, then what this means is that at the end of *each* year for which the Principal was deposited, a constant interest payment of £iP is paid. This means that the annual interest received is the *same* regardless of the length of time for which the Principal has been deposited.

Viewed in this way it is easy to see that simple interest can be represented in terms of an arithmetic progression in which the first term is the Principal, and the common difference is iP. We therefore have

$$A_0 = P$$
$$A_1 = P + iP$$
$$A_2 = P + iP + iP \quad\quad = P + 2iP$$
$$A_3 = P + iP + iP + iP = P + 3iP$$

Following this sequence through, you should be able to see that the amount after t years, which we will denote by A_t, will be given by

$$A_t = P + iP + iP + \cdots + iP = P + tiP$$

and that this can then be rewritten as

$$A_t = P(1 + ti) \tag{3.1}$$

EXAMPLE 3.2

FInd the amount after five years of a deposit of £2500, if the annual simple interest rate for the period is 13 per cent per annum.

SOLUTION 3.2

We have

$$P = A_0 = £2500$$
$$i = r/100 = 13/100 = 0.13$$
$$t = 5$$

Therefore

$$A_5 = 2500[1 + (5)(0.13)] = 2500(1.65) = £4125$$

Simple interest

This solution can be confirmed as follows:

$$A_0 = 2500$$
$$A_1 = A_0 + (0.13)(2500) = 2500 + 325 = 2825$$
$$A_2 = A_1 + (0.13)(2500) = 2825 + 325 = 3150$$
$$A_3 = A_2 + (0.13)(2500) = 3150 + 325 = 3475$$
$$A_4 = A_3 + (0.13)(2500) = 3475 + 325 = 3800$$
$$A_5 = A_4 + (0.13)(2500) = 3800 + 325 = 4125$$

You should notice that in this last explanation we have made use of what is known as a recursive relationship. That is, that each term in the series is related to the previous term in a constant, known fashion. Hence, for example A_2 is always equal to A_1 plus the interest accruing during the second year.

Bearing this in mind, you should be able to see that the general form of the recursive relationship for this problem can be stated as:

$$\text{any term} = [\text{previous term}] + [(i)(\text{first term})]$$

Identifying any recursive relationships that exists in a problem can often aid understanding and modelling, but on their own they are relatively weak computational aids. This is because before any chosen term can be evaluated, all previous terms must have been calculated.

Nevertheless, as we saw above, inspection of the recursive relationship often displays an expression that can be applied to any particular term which has to be evaluated. This was obviously the case in our simple example, since we were easily able to derive, from the recursive relationship, an expression for A_t. Namely that

$$A_t = P(1 + ti)$$

Lotus can also use recursive relationships to facilitate the modelling of problems. In this case since an arithmetic series has been identified we can use the Data Fill command sequence.

For example, to reproduce Solution 3.2 above you should proceed as follows:
Select 'Data' from the main menu, and then 'Fill' from the next menu.

You are now prompted to enter the 'Fill Range', i.e. the first and last cell references of the range of the worksheet that is to be filled with data. Since there are six terms in this problem, enter A10..A15.

Now you are asked to enter the value at which the data set is to start, so reply with 2500.

The step in which the data set is to ascend or descend (i.e. the common difference of the arithmetic progression) is now requested, so respond with 325.

If a value at which the data is to stop is required, you can now enter it at the next prompt, otherwise just press return and the data set will be entered in the range that you specified earlier (A10..A15 in this case).

Try it for yourself now.

WORKSHEET 3.1

```
B3: (T) +B1*B2

         A                           B
  1  Principal                    2500
  2  Interest Rate                  0.13
  3  Annual Interest Payment     +B1*B2
  4
  5
  6
  7
  8
  9                   Amount      Year
 10                    2500         0
 11                    2825         1
 12                    3150         2
 13                    3475         3
 14                    3800         4
 15                    4125         5
```

Of course, the simple procedure illustrated above can be made more flexible if you prepare a spreadsheet similar to Worksheet 3.1.

Now access the Data command and then the Fill option. Enter the data range as before, i.e. A10..A15. In response to the prompt for the start value you can now enter B1, and this will ensure that whatever value is contained in that cell will be entered in A10 as the first value of the series.

The step value can now be entered as the annual interest payment by typing B3 after the prompt.

No stop value is required in this case, so just press return and you will find that the required terms of the series are entered in the range A10..A15. Try it.

In all of the previous examples we were required to find the amount after a specified number of years, i.e. A_t, but this need not always be the problem posed. Nevertheless, simple transposition of equation (3.1) will always be sufficient to determine the value of any specified argument in the equation. To see this, consider the following example.

EXAMPLE 3.3

What annual simple interest rate would be required, if applied to the whole period, to cause a Principal of £2000 to amount to £3260 after seven years?

SOLUTION 3.3

We have
$$P = 2000$$
$$t = 7$$
$$A_7 = 3260$$
$$i = \text{unknown}$$

Therefore, since $A_t = P(1 + ti)$, we can write

$$A_7 = P(1 + 7i)$$

and

$$3260 = 2000(1 + 7i)$$

Therefore

$$3260/2000 = (1 + 7i)$$
$$1.63 = 1 + 7i$$
$$1.63 - 1 = 7i$$
$$0.63/7 = i$$
$$i = 0.09$$

The required interest rate is 9 per cent per annum.

EXAMPLE 3.4

How many years will it take for a Principal of £4000 to amount to £6400 if the annual simple interest rate for the period is 12 per cent?

SOLUTION 3.4

We have
$$P = A_0 = 4000$$
$$i = r/100 = 12/100 = 0.12$$
$$A_t = 6400$$
$$t = \text{unknown}$$

Therefore

$$6400 = 4000[1 + t(0.12)]$$

Transposition produces

$$[1 + t(0.12)] = 6400/4000 = 1.6$$

Therefore

$$t(0.12) = 1.6 - 1$$

and

$$t = 0.6/0.12 = 5$$

We can conclude that a deposit of £4000 will amount to £6400 after five years if the annual simple interest rate is 12 per cent for the entire period.

3.3 Compound interest

It will have been noticed in the previous discussion that because simple interest was being paid, the Principal did not increase in magnitude as each subsequent year's interest was paid. This is contrary to our normal expectation that if a Principal of £500 was deposited at a simple interest rate of 10 per cent per annum, then after one year had passed the interest payment due would be £50, and that this payment should then be added to the account. The value of the account *upon which the next year's interest is calculated* would then become £550.

This would once again attract interest at an annual rate of 10 per cent, and would mean that the second year's interest payment would be £55 (as opposed to £50 under simple interest). When this payment is added to the account, then the value of the account at the start of the next period becomes £605, and the interest due at the end of the third year becomes £60.5.

This steady increase in the size of the interest payment that results from the previous period's interest payment being added to the account and being left on deposit to gain further interest is the crucial feature of compound interest.

Furthermore, since compound interest is by far the most prevalent practice among financial institutions, it is crucial that its logic is fully understood.

This logic can be more generally appreciated as follows.

For the first year the situation is identical to simple interest. Hence

$$A_1 = P + P(i) = P(1 + i)$$

After two years, however, it should be apparent that the amount accumulated is equal to the amount after one year plus i times the amount after one year. That is

$$A_2 = A_1 + A_1(i)$$

However, since we already know that $A_1 = P(1 + i)$, we can rewrite this last expression as

$$A_2 = P(1 + i) + [P(1 + i)](i)$$

which upon factorization becomes

$$A_2 = P(1 + i)[1 + i] = P(1 + i)^2$$

By a similar logic we could find the amount after three years to be

$$A_3 = A_2 + A_2(i)$$

Once again using our knowledge that $A_2 = P(1+i)^2$, we can write

$$A_3 = P(1+i)^2 + [P(1+i)^2](i)$$

Upon factorizing the term in $P(1+i)^2$, this then produces

$$A_3 = [P(1+i)^2](1+i) = P(1+i)^3$$

Careful inspection of the relationships that we have built up here should provide an obvious expression for the amount after t years. That is

$$A_t = P(1+i)^t \tag{3.2}$$

To confirm this expression consider the following example.

EXAMPLE 3.5

Find the compounded amount after three years of an initial deposit of £1000 if interest is compounded at a rate of 8 per cent per annum for the period.

SOLUTION 3.5

We have
$$P = A_0 = 1000$$
$$i = 8/100 = 0.08$$
$$t = 3$$

Therefore
$$A_1 = 1000 + 1000(0.08) \quad = 1080$$
$$A_2 = 1080 + 1080(0.08) \quad = 1166.4$$
$$A_3 = 1166.4 + 1164.4(0.08) = £1259.71$$

This result could have been obtained more easily from equation (3.2) which we derived above. If we substitute the values for our problem into this equation, we obtain

$$A_3 = 1000(1 + 0.08)^3 = 1000(1.259\ 71) = £1259.71$$

EXAMPLE 3.6

Find the amount accumulated after eight years in an account in which £1000 was deposited at an annual compound interest rate of 6 per cent for the period.

SOLUTION 3.6

We have

$$P = 1000$$
$$i = 6/100 = 0.06$$
$$t = 8$$

Therefore $A_t = P(1 + i)^t$ becomes

$$A_8 = 1000(1 + 0.06)^8 = 1000(1.593\ 85) = £1593.85$$

Lotus can readily produce all of the results above, so to see this take a blank worksheet and reproduce Worksheet 3.2.

Notice two things about this formulation:

1. A recursive relationship has been set up in the cells C4, D4 and E4, so that the amount after any year can be calculated from the previous year's amount plus the interest rate times the previous year's amount.
2. This recursive relationship can be copied relatively for as many columns as the number of years in the problem require. To do this, however, requires that the interest rate cell reference (B3) be fixed in the copying process. This is done by the $B$3 expression.

WORKSHEET 3.2

C2: [W15]

	A	B	C	D	E
1	Year	0	1	2	3
2	Principal	1000			
3	Interest Rate	0.05			
4	Amount	+B2	+B4+B4*$B$3	+C4+C4*$B$3	+D4+D4*$B$3
5					

WORKSHEET 3.3

E4: (F2) [W15] +D4+D4*$B$3

	A	B	C	D	E
1	Year	0	1	2	3
2	Principal	1000			
3	Interest Rate	0.05			
4	Amount	1000.00	1050.00	1102.50	1157.63
5					

WORKSHEET 3.4

```
B4: +B1*(1+B2)^B3
```

	A	B
1	Principal	1000
2	Interest Rate	0.05
3	Number of Years	5
4	Amount	1276.281
5		

Of course, when these formulae are evaluated by Lotus, then your worksheet should look something like Worksheet 3.3.

In the formulation above you should notice that you obtain the value of the account at the end of *each* of the years of the period. However, if you only require the amount at the *end* of the period, then Lotus can also accept the expression for the amount after t years which we derived above.

Write it for yourself as a formula so that you end up with something similar to Worksheet 3.4.

Notice that the entry in B4 is simply the Lotus formulation of equation (3.2); since B1 contains the Principal, B2 contains the interest rate, and B3 contains the number of years.

EXAMPLE 3.7

A sum of £1000 was placed in an account for nine years at a constant rate of interest of r per cent per annum. At the end of this period the value of the account was £2171.89. Find the interest rate that was being paid on this account.

SOLUTION 3.7

Assuming that no interest has been withdrawn, we have

$$P = 1000$$
$$t = 9$$
$$A_9 = 2171.89$$
$$i = r/100 = \text{unknown}$$

Therefore

$$1000(1 + i)^9 = 2171.89$$

and
$$(1 + i)^9 = 2.171\ 89$$
Whence
$$(1 + i) = (2.171\ 89)^{1/9} = 1.09$$
Therefore
$$i = 1.09 - 1 = 0.09$$
and
$$r = 9 \text{ per cent}$$

As has already been demonstrated, sometimes the nature of the problem requires a transposition of the basic expression in order to alter the variable appearing on the lefthand side. As a further example of this consider the following example.

EXAMPLE 3.8

How many years will it take before a Principal of £10 000 amounts to £14 641 if the interest rate is 10 per cent per annum?

SOLUTION 3.8

Clearly we require to solve for t in equation (3.2) above.
  Therefore since
$$A_t = P(1 + i)^t$$
Taking logarithms of both sides produces
$$\log(A_t) = \log(P) + t[\log(1 + i)]$$
Therefore
$$t = [\log(A_t) - \log(P)]/\log(1 + i)$$
Substituting the values for our problem, we obtain
$$t = [\log(14\ 641) - \log(10\ 000)]/\log(1.1)$$
$$t = (4.1656 - 4.0000)/0.0414$$
Therefore
$$t = 4$$

Fortunately, however, Lotus possesses an in-built function known as Compound Term (@CTERM) which will perform the above calculations for you. The syntax of this function is:

@CTERM(Interest Rate, Eventual Amount, Principal)

Definition The Lotus Compound Term function @CTERM(i,A,P), calculates the number of years required for a Principal of £P to amount to £A, when the interest rate is i ($= r$ per cent/100) per annum.

You can therefore confirm the above calculation by typing the following in a vacant cell of your worksheet:

@CTERM(0.1,14 641,10 000).

You should find a value of 4 returned to the cell containing this formula.

In all of the previous examples it will have been noticed that the interest rate was constant over the entire period under consideration. However, it is not hard to envisage circumstances in which the rate changes from time to time. To deal with this additional complication we must approach the problem as follows.

Let i_1, i_2, i_3, etc., be the interest rates received respectively for periods of t_1, t_2, t_3, etc., years. It then follows that the amount after t_1 years (A_{t_1}) is given by

$$A_{t_1} = P(1 + i_1)^{t_1}$$

This amount can then be regarded as the Principal to which the next period's interest rate (i_2) will apply for the whole of the next period (t_2). Consequently the amount after $t_1 + t_2$ years will be given by

$$A_{t_1 + t_2} = [P(1 + i_1)^{t_1}][(1 + i_2)^{t_2}]$$

By a similar logic the amount after $t_1 + t_2 + t_3$ years will be given by

$$A_{t_1 + t_2 + t_3} = [P(1 + i_1)^{t_1}][1 + i_2)^{t_2}][(1 + i_3)^{t_3}]$$

EXAMPLE 3.9

Over a period of ten years the annual compound interest rate was 7 per cent for the first five years, 9 per cent for the next three years, and 11 per cent for the next two years. At the start of the period a deposit of £1500 was made and no withdrawals were made over the ten-year period. Find the value of the account after ten years.

SOLUTION 3.9

We have

$$A_5 = 1500(1 + 0.07)^5 = 2103.83$$

```
WORKSHEET 3.5
                    A                          B
   1   Principal                             1500
   2   1st Interest Rate                     0.07
   3   1st Period                            5
   4   2nd Interest Rate                     0.09
   5   2nd Period                            2
   6   3rd Interest Rate                     0.11
   7   3rd Period                            3
   8   Amount after Period 1                 +B1*(1+B2)^B3
   9   Amount after Period 1+2               +B8*(1+B4)^B5
  10   Amount after Period 1+2+3             +B9*(1+B6)^B7
```

Then

$$A_7 = 2103.83(1 + 0.09)^2 = 2499.56$$

and

$$A_{10} = 2499.56(1 + 0.11)^3 = 3418.47$$

The value of the account after ten years is £3418.47.

To produce a similar result on Lotus you should take a blank worksheet and then reproduce Worksheet 3.5. You should be able to see that you can now change the interest rates and/or the periods to accommodate any change in the specifications of the problem being considered.

For example, if the Principal changed to £3000 and the interest rates to 6.5 per cent for three years, 8.9 per cent for two years, and 9.75 per cent for five years, modify your spreadsheet to produce the new amount after ten years. (You should obtain an answer of £6843.03.)

3.4 Fractional years

In all of the previous discussion the number of years for which the Principal was deposited was always an integer. But you may well be wondering what happens if a deposit is made for 2.5 or 3.6 years or some other non-whole number of years.

In this respect it would be reasonable to expect equation (3.2) to still apply, with the obvious difference that t no longer adopts an integer value.

In fact, this is not the case, since most financial institutions evaluate interest payments on what is known as a daily basis. What this means is that interest is compounded for the integer number of years for which the money has been deposited, and any extra non-integer number of years is then treated on a 'pro rata' basis in relation to the annual interest rate.

Fractional years

For example, suppose £1000 was deposited at an annual compound interest rate of 7 per cent for two years and 100 days. The amount after two years is easily calculated to be

$$A_2 = 1000(1.07)^2 = £1144.9$$

This amount then attracts that proportion of the interest rate that corresponds to the proportion of 365 days for which the funds have been deposited. Consequently, since the interest rate is 7 per cent, and the funds have been on deposit for 100/365 of a year; the additional interest payment due is given by

$$1144.9(100/365)(0.07) = £21.96$$

When this interest payment is added to the previous value of the account, we then obtain

$$£1144.9 + £21.96 = £1166.86$$

The same result could, of course, have been obtained by the following expression:

$$A_{2,100} = [P(1.07)^2][1 + (100/365)(0.07)] = £1166.85$$

where $A_{2,100}$ represents the amount after two years and 100 days.

In general, then, if funds are deposited for t years and d days, at an annual compound rate of i per annum, then the accumulated amount at the end of this period ($A_{t,d}$) is given by

$$A_{t,d} = [P(1+i)^t][1 + (d/365)(i)] \qquad (3.3)$$

Notice that if the £1000 was deposited for two years and 365 days (i.e. three years), then the formula above remains correct since

$$A_{t,d} = 1000[(1.07)^2][1 + (365/365)(0.07)]$$
$$= (1144.9)(1.07) = 1225.04$$

which is identical to

$$A_3 = 1000(1.07)^3$$

as you can confirm for yourself.

EXAMPLE 3.10

Find the amount accruing to a Principal of £5000 which is deposited at an annual interest rate of 8 per cent per annum, for a period of five years and 234 days.

SOLUTION 3.10

We have

$$A_{5,234} = [5000(1.08)^5][1 + (234/365)(0.08)]$$
$$= (7346.64)[1 + 0.05129] = £7723.43$$

On Lotus you can obtain the same result as shown in Worksheet 3.6. The entry in B6 should be 7723.43 when evaluated.

WORKSHEET 3.6

	A	B
1	Principal	5000
2	Interest Rate	0.08
3	Years	5
4	Days	234
5	Amount after Integer years	+B1*(1+B2)^B3
6	Amount after extra days	+B5*(1+B4/365*B2)
7		

3.5 Annuities

So far we have only considered the future value of a single Principal that has been placed on deposit. However, many popular savings schemes allow for a number of equal Principals to be deposited at periodic (usually annual) intervals.

Such schemes are known as *annuities*, and to calculate their terminal value (i.e. immediately after the last deposit has been made) requires that we take account of *all* of the deposits and *all* of the interest payments that each of these deposits attracts. The method of doing this is illustrated in the following example.

EXAMPLE 3.11

Starting today, four annual deposits of £2000 are made to an account that bears interest at an annual rate of 11 per cent per annum over the entire period during which the deposits are made. Calculate the terminal value of the account immediately after the fourth deposit has been made.

SOLUTION 3.11

The first deposit will attract interest at the prevailing rate for three years, and consequently will have a terminal value given by

$$A_3 = 2000(1.11)^3 = £2735.26$$

Similarly, the second deposit will attract interest for a period of two years, and will therefore have a terminal value of

$$A_2 = 2000(1.11)^2 = £2464.20$$

The third deposit will only bear interest for one year, and therefore has a terminal value of

$$A_1 = (1.1)^1 = £2200.00$$

Finally, since we are required to calculate the value of the account immediately after the fourth deposit has been made, we must include this fourth deposit in the calculations without any interest added to it. Hence

$$A_0 = 2000(1.1)^0 = £2000.00$$

Clearly the total terminal value of the account can be obtained by adding each of these individual terminal values together, to produce

$$£2735.26 + £2464.20 + £2200 + £2000 = £9419.46$$

Viewed in this methodical way the calculation of the terminal value of an annuity is easily understood. However, such an approach is needlessly laborious, since to identify a short-cut we can approach the problem as follows.

We know that the terminal value of this annuity can be calculated from

$$A_0 + A_1 + A_2 + A_3$$

and we also know that this can be written as

$$2000(1.11)^3 + 2000(1.11)^2 + 2000(1.11) + 2000$$

Viewed in this way (but in reverse order) it should now be easy to observe that we are effectively searching for the sum of the first four terms (S_4) of a geometric progression in which the first term is 2000 and the common factor is 1.11.

This can be calculated from the standard formula to be

$$S_4 = 2000[(1.11^4 - 1]/(1.11 - 1)$$
$$S_4 = 2000(1.5181 - 1)/(0.11)$$
$$S_4 = 2000(4.709\,731) = 9419.46.$$

Thereby confirming the result obtained above.

In general, then, we can conclude that the terminal value of an annuity of n deposits of £P which receive an interest rate of i ($= r$ per cent/100) per annum, is given by

$$P + P(1 + i) + P(1 + i)^2 + \cdots + P(1 + i)^{n-1}$$

When this is factorized we obtain
$$P[1 + (1+i) + (1+i)^2 + \cdots + (1+i)^{n-1}]$$
where $i = r$ per cent/100, as usual.

The sum of the first n terms in this geometric series is therefore given by
$$S_n = P\{[(1+i)^n] - 1\}/[(1+i) - 1]$$
Which, since $(1+i) - 1 = i$, becomes
$$S_n = P\{[(1+i)^n] - 1\}/(i) \tag{3.4}$$

EXAMPLE 3.12

Find the terminal value of an annuity of 20 annual deposits of £500 made to an account that bears interest at an annual interest rate of 12.5 per cent.

SOLUTION 3.12

We have
$$P = 500$$
$$i = 0.125$$
$$n = 20$$

Therefore
$$S_{20} = 500[(1.125^{20}) - 1]/(0.125) = £38\,180.37$$

As you should expect by now, Lotus can perform many of these calculations for you, as Worksheet 3.7 demonstrates. Reproduce it for yourself. When Lotus evaluates these expressions, you should find that a value of 9419.46 is returned to the B7 cell.

Although this method works, there is in fact an easier way to obtain the same result. This is to use the Lotus Future Value function (@FV), which has the

WORKSHEET 3.7

	A	B	C	D	E
1	Year	0	1	2	3
2	Interest Rate	0.11			
3	Principal	2000			
4	Amnt after 1 yr	+B3*(1+B2)	+B3		
5	Amnt after 2 yrs	+B3*(1+B2)^2	+C4*(1+B2)	+B3	
6	Amnt after 3 yrs	+B3*(1+B2)^3	+C4*(1+B2)^2	+D5*(1+B2)	+B3
7	Account value	@SUM(B6..E6)			

following syntax:

@FV(Principal, Interest rate, Number of deposits)

Definition The Lotus Future Value function @FV(P,i,n) calculates the terminal value of n annually deposited Principals of £P when the interest rate is i ($=r$ per cent/100) per annum for the duration of the period. The function therefore gives the value of the account $(n-1)$ years from now, since it assumes that the first deposit is made just now (year 0) and that the last (nth) deposit is made $(n-1)$ years from now. This last deposit is deemed to attract no interest and therefore is included in the calculations simply at its face value of £P.

As an example of its use, you can replicate the solution to Example 3.11 above by typing the following in cell A8 of Worksheet 3.7:

@FV(2000,0.11,4)

Try it, and confirm that this will produce the required result of 9149.46.

Similarly, you could obtain the solution to Example 3.12 by entering the following expression in any vacant cell of your worksheet:

@FV(500,0.125,20)

which gives 38 180.37 when evaluated.

You can also use cell references in the Future Value formula. For example (and continuing to use the figures from Example 3.12), if you place the Principal of £500 in A20, the interest rate of 12.5 per cent (expressed as a decimal, of course) in A21, and the number of deposits of 20 in A22, then the same result as above can be obtained by typing (in A23 say)

@FV(A20,A21,A22)

This method has the advantage that if the specifications of your problem change, then all you have to do is make the appropriate alterations to the contents of cells A20 to A22, and the new solution will be produced in A23. Try it.

WARNING! You will obtain nonsensical results if you enter the interest rate as a percentage (12.5) as opposed to its decimal equivalent (0.125).

Although Lotus is well endowed with financial functions (as you will continue to see) the question arises of what to do when the problem posed is not immediately capable of being fitted into the format of one of the available functions. If this is the case, then it is important to remember the principles of financial mathematics that we have been developing from the beginning of this chapter.

For example, suppose ten annual deposits of £800 were made to an account that bore interest at an annual rate of 9 per cent. After the tenth deposit was made, however, suppose that all the deposited funds received a 'premium' rate of 11 per cent per annum for the next five years, whereupon the account is closed and its terminal value calculated. What is this terminal value?

You should be able to see that the first part of the problem requires that we obtain the value of the account immediately after the tenth deposit has been made. On Lotus this is easily obtained by entering (in B1 say)

@FV(800,0.09,10) = 12 154.34

This sum then receives interest for a further five years at the premium rate of 11 per cent per annum, and consequently has a terminal value that Lotus can calculate (in B2, say) from +B1*(1.11)^5 as 20 480.78

3.6 Sinking funds

We have already seen that simple transposition of the basic formulae of financial mathematics is often necessary to deal with problems that are not in a 'standard' form. As a further example of this process reconsider equation (3.4) which we derived above for the terminal value of an annuity of n payments:

$$S_n = P\{[(1+i)^n] - 1\}/(i)$$

Bearing this is mind, consider the following example.

EXAMPLE 3.13

In order to pay for her daughter's education a mother decides that a lump sum of £20 000 is required in 12 years time. She therefore decides to start paying equal annual amounts into an account that guarantees an interest rate of 15 per cent per annum. If she makes the first payment today, and the last payment in 12 years time (i.e. a total of 13 payments), how much must she deposit each year in order to secure the required sum of £20 000 after 12 years?

SOLUTION 3.13

In this problem you should be able to see that the (required) terminal value is known, but that the 13 annual deposits needed to achieve this terminal value are unknown.

Such a process of making several equal annual deposits in order to secure some eventual terminal amount is known as establishing a sinking fund, and first received public prominence when William Pitt the Younger set one up in order to pay for the increased National Debt that the Napoleonic Wars required. However, the fact that his fund eventually proved inadequate to cover the magnitude of the debt was in no way due to Pitt's inability to transpose equation (3.4) above in order to solve for P. When this is done it is easy to obtain the solution to the mother's problem.

Sinking funds

To do this we note that from equation (3.4)

$$S_n = P\{[(1+i)^n] - 1\}/(i)$$

Transposing P to the lefthand side then produces

$$P = [S_n(i)]/\{[(1+i)^n] - 1\} \tag{3.5}$$

Therefore, since

$$S_n = 20\,000$$
$$i = 15/100 = 0.15$$
$$n = 13$$

it follows that

$$P = [(20\,000)(0.15)]/[(1.15^{13})^{-1}]$$
$$= (3000)/(6.1528 - 1)$$
$$= £582.21.$$

The mother should make 13 annual payments of £582.21, and this will ensure that after the 13th payment has been made a terminal amount of £20 000 will be available. The fact that the cost of her daughter's education could easily be double the initial estimate is no fault of the calculation, as Pitt the Younger would confirm were he still alive.

It is unfortunate, however, that Lotus does not possess a 'built-in' sinking fund formula, but you can write it for yourself as shown in Worksheet 3.8.

You should now confirm that the formula in B5 is the Lotus equivalent of equation (3.5) above, and that when this is evaluated by Lotus the required solution of £582.21 will be contained there.

Now suppose that the mother still requires an eventual amount of £20 000, that the interest rate is still 15 per cent, but that annual payments of £500 are the most she can afford.

How many annual payments of £500 are required to ensure the eventual terminal value of £20 000?

You should be able to see that you can solve this problem by transposing either one of equations (3.4) or (3.5) above, so that the number of payments (n) appears

```
WORKSHEET 3.8
                A                                          B
    1   Required Terminal Amount                       20000
    2   Number of Years from now when Required            12
    3   Number of Sinking Fund Payments                   13
    4   Sinking Fund Interest Rate for period            0.15
    5   Annual Sinking Fund Payment              (B1*B4)/((1+B4)^B3-1)
    6
```

on the lefthand side. This is done as follows:

$$(S_n)(i)/P = [(1+i)^n] - 1$$

Therefore

$$[(S_n/P)(i) + 1] = [(1+i)^n]$$

Taking logarithms of both sides produces

$$\log[(S_n/P)(i) + 1] = n[\log(1+i)]$$

Therefore

$$n = \log[(S_n/P)(i) + 1]/[\log(1+i)]$$

Using the values from our problem this produces

$$\begin{aligned}n &= \log[(20\,000/500)(0.15) + 1]/[\log(1.15)] \\ &= \log(6+1)/\log(1.15) \\ &= 13.92\end{aligned}$$

However, since a non-integer number of payments makes no sense, we conclude that 14 annual payments of £500 will be required, and that these will supply slightly more than the required terminal amount (£20 252.35 to be exact).

Once again, Lotus has a predefined function that can perform these calculations for us. It is called the Term function (@TERM) and has the following syntax:

@TERM(Payment, Interest Rate, Terminal Amount)

Definition The Lotus Term function @TERM(P,i,A) calculates the number of annual payments of £P necessary to produce a terminal amount of £A when the interest rate is i (= r per cent/100) per annum for the duration of the period.

To replicate the result obtained above the required expression would be

@TERM(500,0.15,20000)

Try it for yourself in a vacant cell of your worksheet, and then alter the Term function values so that you can confirm that 13 annual payments of £582.21 are needed to ensure a terminal amount of £20 000 when the sinking fund interest rate is 15 per cent per annum for the duration of the period.

Now consider a further variation upon this basic type of problem.

EXAMPLE 3.14

In order to buy a house, a family borrows £100 000 today from a bank which charges an interest rate of 13 per cent per annum for the next ten years. After this length of time the debt and all accumulated interest must be repaid in one payment.

To do this, the family decides to set up a sinking fund consisting of 11 equal

Sinking funds

annual payments to an account that guarantees to pay an annual compound rate of 12 per cent.

Calculate the size of the required sinking fund payments.

SOLUTION 3.14

The variation in this problem is obviously created by the fact that a debt is incurred just now rather than a required amount being needed at some time in the future. Nevertheless it is an easy matter to convert the problem into this form, since it should be apparent that after ten years the family will have to repay an amount that is given by

$$100\,000(1.13)^{10} = £339\,456.74$$

Knowing this then allows you to solve for the value of P in the standard manner, although you will have to remember that the interest rate that the sinking fund attracts is only 12 per cent. Hence using equation (3.5)

$$P = [(339\,456.74)(0.12)] / [(1.12^{11}) - 1]$$
$$= (50\,918.51) / (3.478\,55 - 1)$$
$$= 20\,543.67$$

This means that 11 annual payments of £20 543.67 will be sufficient to repay the debt plus interest after ten years.

Now since these payments are not insignificant amounts, and since the first payment has to be made just now, the family will almost certainly have to borrow this first payment and incur interest at the current borrowing rate of 13 per cent. Accordingly, they may well set up a second sinking fund in order to pay for the first payment. This means that a terminal amount of

$$20\,543.67(1.13)^{10} = £69\,736.87$$

will be required in 10 years time.

Clearly the 11 payments required to ensure this terminal sum can be obtained in the same way as before

$$P = [(69\,736.87)(0.12)] / [(1.12^{11}) - 1]$$
$$= £3376.34$$

An immediate payment of £3376.34 will therefore secure a loan of £20 543.67 for ten years and will allow the family to make the first payment to the large sinking fund.

Thereafter they must make a further ten payments of

$$£3376.34 + £20\,543.67 = £23\,920$$

at the end of each year.

You can use a variation of Worksheet 3.8 to confirm these results if you make the necessary changes to the required terminal sum and the interest rate. At the same time you can also confirm that your calculations are correct by entering the appropriate @FV function in a vacant cell (B8 will do), as follows:

$$@FV(B7,B6,B5)$$

This will confirm that 11 annual payments of £20 543.67 to an account that bears interest at a rate of 12 per cent per annum will produce a terminal amount of £339 456.74 after ten years, and will therefore pay off the incurred debt.

Your spreadsheet formulae should look something like Worksheet 3.9. The results in this worksheet can be generalized, if, for the sake of simplicity, we assume that the lending rate on the debt and the borrowing rate on the sinking fund are the same, and denoted by i.

Then, from the last example, you should be able to see that if a debt of £D is undertaken today, then a terminal amount after t years of

$$S_n = D(1 + i)^t$$

is required.

Accordingly, using equation (3.5) the n payments of £P to the sinking fund needed to secure this terminal amount will be given by

$$P = [S_n(i)] / \{[(1 + i)^n - 1\}$$

which, upon substituting for S_n becomes

$$P = \{[D(1 + i)^t](i)\} / \{[(1 + i)^n] - 1\} \tag{3.6}$$

Since we know that n is always one more than t (i.e. the number of payments is always one more than the term of the debt), we can write

$$n = t + 1$$

or

$$t = n - 1$$

WORKSHEET 3.9

	A	B
1	Debt Incurred just now	100000
2	Borrowing Rate	0.13
3	Number of Years of Debt	10
4	Terminal Value of Debt	+B1*(1+B2)^B3
5	Number of Sinking Fund Payments	+B3+1
6	Sinking Fund Interest Rate	0.12
7	Annual Sinking Fund Payment	(B4*B6)/((1+B6)^B5-1)
8	Future Value of Payments	@FV(B7,B6,B5)
9		

Sinking funds

Substituting this last equation into equation (3.6) then produces

$$P = \{[D(1+i)^{n-1}](i)\}/\{[(1+i)^n] - 1\} \tag{3.7}$$

For example, if a debt of £D is to be paid off in three payments to a sinking fund (i.e. after two years), then the payments are given by

$$P = [D(1+i)^2](i)/\{[(1+i)^3] - 1\} \tag{3.8}$$

Furthermore, if the debt incurred is £3000 and if the interest rate is 10 per cent, for example, then we obtain

$$P = £1096.68$$

Study these last two expressions carefully, since we will make reference to them again shortly.

Of course, if the borrowing and lending rates are different: b, say, for the (family's) borrowing rate on its debt, and s, say, for the (family's) lending rate to the sinking fund, then the last expression above becomes

$$P = [D(1+b)^2](s)/\{[(1+s)^3] - 1\}$$

or, more generally

$$P = [D(1+b)^{n-1}](s)/\{[(1+s)^n] - 1\} \tag{3.9}$$

Now suppose that the family in our example feel that the necessary annual repayments on the debt (£20 543.67) are too large in relation to their income over the next few years. As a result, they contract to make an initial six annual payments of £10 000 to the sinking fund, and ask the loan company to calculate the required size of the remaining five payments. What is the size of these last five payments?

Clearly, the terminal value of the debt is the same as previously, so an eventual terminal amount of

$$100\,000(1.13)^{10} = £339\,456.74$$

is required.

Furthermore, the first six payments of £10 000 to the sinking fund will have a terminal value after five years that is given by

```
@FV(10000,0.12,6)=£81 151.89
```

(Confirm this figure for yourself either on Lotus or from the appropriate formula.)

These funds must remain on deposit at the prevailing rate of 12 per cent for the next five years and will therefore produce an eventual amount of

```
@FV(10000,0.12,6)*(1.12^5)=£143 017.36.
```

The shortfall in relation to the required terminal amount is therefore

$$£339\,456.74 - £143\,017.36 = £196\,439.38.$$

This means that a second sinking fund consisting of five payments must be set up

WORKSHEET 3.10

	A	B
1	Debt Incurred just now	1000000
2	Borrowing Rate	0.14
3	Number of Years of Debt	7
4	Terminal Value of Debt	+B1*(1+B2)^B3
5	Sinking Fund Interest Rate	0.12
6	Total Number of Sinking Fund Payments	+B3+1
7	Initial Number of Payments	4
8	Value of Initial Payments	150000.00
9	Value of 1st Sinking Fund after last Payment	716899.20
10	Terminal Value of 1st Sinking Fund	1128054.77
11	Shortfall on Required Amount	1374214.02
12	Number of Payments to 2nd Sinking Fund	4.00
13	Required Size of 2nd set of Payments	287532.90
14	Terminal Value of 2nd Sinking Fund	1374214.02
15	Overall Shortfall	0.00

(the first payment being made six years from now), and that this must provide a terminal value of £196 439.38 after a further four years (i.e. ten years from now). Using equation (3.5) the size of these payments is therefore given by

$$P = [(196\,439.38)(0.12)] / [(1.12^5) - 1] = £30\,921.47$$

Consequently, an initial set of six annual payments of £10 000, followed by a further five annual payments of £30 921.47 will pay off the debt after ten years.

You can confirm this result on Lotus by typing the following formula in a vacant cell:

`(@FV(10000,0.12,6))*(1.12^5)+@FV(30921.47,0.12,5)`

You should then obtain the required terminal amount of £339 456.74.

Of course it is much more efficient to set up a general Lotus model which can deal with all possible variations in the numerical values of the problem. Consider Worksheet 3.10 and notice how its logic has been constructed.

When the formulae in this model are evaluated you should find that the results of the last illustration (i.e. five extra payments of £30 921.47) are reproduced, and that the eventual shortfall should be 0.

Now use this model to solve the following example.

EXAMPLE 3.15

A company borrows £1 million for seven years at an interest rate of 14 per cent, and agrees to make eight annual payments to a sinking fund that guarantees to pay interest at an annual rate of 12 per cent. The size of the first four payments is agreed to be £150 000. Calculate the required size of the remaining four payments to the sinking fund if the debt is to be cleared after seven years.

SOLUTION 3.15

From the model constructed above you should find that the company has to make a final four payments of £287 532.89.

This process of making a number of payments to a sinking fund, the terminal value of which is then used to pay off an incurred debt is often referred to as an *endowment*. Its most salient feature is that the debt itself and the repayments to the sinking fund are separated from one another. In other words the debt grows *independently* of the provisions for its eventual repayment.

By contrast, however, many debts are serviced on what is known as a reducing balance basis, whereby each repayment reduces the size (balance) of the outstanding debt as soon as it is made.

As we will see, there are circumstances in which this produces exactly the same stream of repayments as in the sinking fund method, but before this can be appreciated an understanding of how a reducing balance debt operates must be obtained.

3.7 Reducing balance debts

Suppose that a loan of £D is secured at an interest rate of i. This debt is to be repaid in three equal annual instalments of £X, with the first repayment being made immediately.

If the debt is administered on a reducing balance basis calculate the size of the three repayments.

Since the first repayment is to be made immediately, this means that the size of the debt on which interest is charged is given by

$$(D - X)$$

This outstanding debt then attracts interest charges so that at the end of the first year the outstanding debt becomes

$$(D - X)(1 + i)$$

When the second payment of £X is made, this outstanding debt reduces to

$$[(D - X)(1 + i) - X]$$

which then attracts interest charges so that at the end of the second year the outstanding debt is

$$[(D - X)(1 + i) - X](1 + i)$$

When the third and final repayment of £X is made, then the debt must be cleared (i.e. outstanding debt = 0). We can therefore derive the following equation:

$$[(D - X)(1 + i) - X](1 + i) - X = 0$$

Collecting terms and simplifying, we then obtain

$$(D - X)(1 + i)^2 - X(1 + i) - X = 0$$

Therefore

$$D(1 + i)^2 - X(1 + i)^2 - X(1 + i) - X = 0$$

and

$$D(1 + i)^2 = X[(1 + i)^2 + (1 + i) + 1]$$

Since the terms inside the square brackets above represent the sum of the first three terms in a geometric progression with first term = 1 and common ratio = $(1 + i)$, we can rewrite the last expression as

$$D(1 + i)^2 = X[(1 + i)^3 - 1]/[(1 + i) - 1]$$

Simplification produces

$$D(1 + i)^2 = (X/i)[(1 + i)^3 - 1]$$

Finally, cross-multiplication produces a solution for X

$$X = [D(1 + i)^2](i)/\{[(1 + i)^3] - 1\}$$

Comparison of this last expression with equation (3.8) above reveals that the two are identical; and when values of $D = 3000$ and $i = 0.1$ are inserted we obtain $X = £1096.68$.

In other words, the size and number of the necessary payments to repay any given debt of £D, at any given interest rate, over any given period of time are the same *regardless* of whether n payments of £P are made to a sinking fund or whether n reducing balance repayments of £X are made. This result is valid as long as the first repayment is made just now in both cases.

In general, then, if a debt of £D is secured for t years and is to be repaid in n annual instalments of £X, then since $t = n - 1$ the value of X is given by

$$X = [D(1 + i)^{n-1}](i)/\{[(1 + i)^n] - 1\} \tag{3.10}$$

This expression can be seen to be identical to equation (3.7) which we derived earlier.

Using Lotus you can confirm these calculations in Worksheet 3.11.

When evaluated, you should find that the outstanding debt is reduced to zero as soon as the third payment of £1096.68 is made. This payment is, of course, calculated by Lotus from the formula in B4, which is the equivalent of equation (3.10).

However, many reducing balance debts allow the debtor to have one (or more) year's delay before the first payment has to be made. This being the case, then for

WORKSHEET 3.11

	A	B
1	Size of Debt	3000
2	Interest Rate on Debt	0.1
3	Number of Repayments	3
4	Size of Repayments	+B1*(1+B2)^(B3-1)*B2/((1+B2)^B3-1)
5		
6	Year	0
7	Debt	+B1
8	Repayment Number	1
9	Repayment Amount	+B4
10	Outstanding Debt	+B7-B9
11	Year	1
12	Debt	+B10*(1+B2)
13	Repayment Number	2
14	Repayment Amount	+B4
15	Outstanding Debt	+B12-B14
16	Year	2
17	Debt	+B15*(1+B2)
18	Repayment Number	3
19	Repayment Amount	+B4
20	Outstanding Debt	+B17-B19

the last example (with one year's delay) we have the following formulae:

Initial debt	$= D$
debt after one year	$= D(1 + i)$
debt after first payment	$= D(1 + i) - X$
debt after two years	$= [D(1 + i) - X](1 + i)$
debt after second payment	$= [D(1 + i) - X](1 + i) - X$
debt after three years	$= \{[D(1 + i) - X](1 + i) - X\}(1 + i)$
debt after third payment	$= \{[D(1 + i) - X](1 + i) - X\}(1 + i) - X$

Setting this last term equal to zero, collecting terms and solving for X as before produces

$$X = [D(1 + i)^3](i)/\{[(1 + i)^3] - 1\} \qquad (3.11)$$

We can modify Worksheet 3.11 as follows to accommodate this variation, and, more importantly use the Lotus Payment function (@PMT) to calculate the size of the required repayments. This function has the following syntax:

$$\text{@PMT(Debt, Interest Rate, Number of repayments)}$$

Definition The Lotus Payment function @PMT(D, i, n) calculates the size of the n repayments needed to repay a debt of £D after $(n - 1)$ years if the interest rate is i per annum, and if the first repayment is made *in one year's time*. Worksheet 3.12 gives an example of the use of this function.

WORKSHEET 3.12

	A	B
1	Size of Debt	3000
2	Interest Rate on Debt	0.1
3	Number of Repayments	3
4	Size of Repayments	@PMT(B1,B2,B3)
5		
6	Year	0
7	Debt	+B1
8	Repayment Number	0
9	Repayment Amount	0
10	Outstanding Debt	+B7−B9
11	Year	1
12	Debt	+B10*(1+B2)
13	Repayment Number	1
14	Repayment Amount	+B4
15	Outstanding Debt	+B12−B14
16	Year	2
17	Debt	+B15*(1+B2)
18	Repayment Number	2
19	Repayment Amount	+B4
20	Outstanding Debt	+B17−B19
21	Year	3
22	Debt	+B20*(1+B2)
23	Repayment Number	3
24	Repayment Amount	+B4
25	Outstanding Debt	+B22−B24

In this case you should once again find that the outstanding debt has been reduced to zero after the third payment of £1206.34 is made, but that this time this does not take place until three, as opposed to two, years have elapsed.

As you can see by comparing equations (3.10) and (3.11), the effect of the one year's delay has been to increase the value of the exponent in the numerator from 2 to 3. This fact should give us a clue as to how a more general expression can be obtained, since if a debt of £D is to be paid off in n annual instalments of £X with the first payment being made in m years' time, then the debt will be fully repaid after $t = n - 1 + m$ years. Furthermore, if the interest rate for the period is represented by i, then the value of X can be obtained from

$$X = [D(1+i)^{n-1+m}] (i)/\{[(1+i)^n] - 1\} \qquad (3.12)$$

For example, in our previous two illustrations the first payments were to be made just now and in one year's time (i.e. $m = 0$ and $m = 1$ respectively).

Taking $m = 0$ first of all (and $n = 3$ in both cases) we have

$$X = [3000(1.1)^2] (0.1)/[(1.1^3) - 1] = £1096.68$$

which replicates the result obtained earlier.

Reducing balance debts 159

WORKSHEET 3.13

```
          A                              B
1  Size of Debt                                            3000
2  Interest Rate on Debt                                    0.1
3  Number of Repayments                                       3
4  Years till 1st Repayment                                   1
5  Value of Repayments    (B1*B2)*((1+B2)^(B3-1+B4))/((1+B2)^B3-1)
6
```

Now taking $m = 1$ we have

$$X = [3000(1.1)^3](0.1)/[(1.1^3) - 1] = £1206.34$$

again reproducing the previous result.

As you can see, the effect of the one-year delay has been to increase the three annual repayments from £1096.68 if the first repayment is made just now, to £1206.68 if the first repayment is to be made after one year.

You can write the necessary formulae to allow Lotus to do these calculations for you as shown in Worksheet 3.13.

As you should confirm for yourself, the formula in B5 above is the Lotus version of equation (3.12), and will produce a value of £1206.34 for the required repayments. This is the same result as would be produced by the appropriate @PMT function since the first payment is delayed by exactly one year. However, if the delay before the first payment has to be more than one year, then the formulation above has the advantage that it can easily deal with this modification.

EXAMPLE 3.16

A loan of £6500, secured at a rate of 11.5 per cent per annum, is to be repaid in ten equal annual instalments with the first repayment to be made in four years' time. Calculate the value of the necessary repayments.

SOLUTION 3.16

You can use the model developed in Worksheet 3.13 to solve this problem, since we have the following:

in B1   6500
in B2   0.115
in B3   10
in B4   4

Which yields the required repayments (in B5) as £1562.17.

3.8 Variations in the compounding period

All of the analysis so far has assumed that interest is compounded on an annual basis (i.e. once a year). However, many financial organizations offer savings schemes (or loans) on which interest is compounded on a half-yearly, quarterly or even daily basis. Such variations in what is known as the compounding period exercise a considerable effect upon the eventual value of any given Principal even when the annual interest rate and the length of time of the investment are the same.

To see this effect, consider a Principal of £500 that is deposited for two years at an interest rate of 12 per cent per annum.

If interest is compounded annually, then it is an easy matter to calculate the amount after two years to be

$$A_2 = 500(1.12)^2 = £627.2$$

Suppose now, however, that interest was compounded semi-annually (i.e. twice a year). What this means is that after six months, half a year's interest is credited to the account, which therefore increases in value accordingly. This larger value then forms the base upon which the next six months' interest is calculated, and so on.

Now since the annual interest rate is 12 per cent, this surely implies that the appropriate rate for the half-year will be 12 per cent/2 = 6 per cent. Furthermore, since the funds are deposited for two years this means that the problem can be viewed in terms of four half-year periods in each of which the appropriate interest rate is 6 per cent.

Bearing these points in mind you should be able to see that the amount after two years can be calculated from

$$A_2 = 500(1.06)^4 = £631.24$$

The fact that this amount is £4.04 greater than under annual compounding is entirely due to the greater number of compounding periods (since all other factors are the same).

Continuing this line of reasoning, it should be clear that if interest was compounded quarterly, then the amount after two years could be derived from viewing the problem in terms of eight periods of three months, in each of which the effective interest rate was 3 per cent. Therefore

$$A_2 = 500(1.03)^8 = £633.38$$

Once again, the effect of increasing the number of compounding periods in the year (from two to four) is seen to increase the amount after two years from £631.24 to £633.38.

Now suppose that interest is compounded on a monthly basis. Clearly, the amount after two years can be calculated by evaluating the following expression:

$$A_2 = 500(1.01)^{24} = £634.86$$

(Since there are 24 periods in which the interest rate for the period is 1 per cent.)

Variations in the compounding period

We should now be able to generalize this result to deal with any number of compounding periods in the year. To do this it is simply necessary to recognize that if interest is compounded m times per annum, then any period of t years contains m times $t = mt$ compounding periods. Furthermore, if the annual interest rate is represented, as usual, by i, then the relevant interest rate for the period must be given by

$$i/m$$

This means that the amount after t years will be given by

$$A_t = P(1 + i/m)^{mt} \qquad (3.12)$$

For example, if interest was compounded weekly, then there would be 52 compounding periods in one year, and therefore $m = 52$. Consequently

$$A_t = P(1 + i/52)^{52t}$$

In order to keep our symbols consistent, however, we really should recognize the effect exercised by variations in the compounding period by including it in our expression for A_t. Consequently, we should define $A_{t,m}$ to be the amount after t years when interest is compounded m times per annum.

Of course, if interest is compounded on an annual basis, then $m = 1$ and the expression above becomes

$$A_{t,1} = P(1 + i)^t$$

which produces our basic compound interest formula.

EXAMPLE 3.17

Find the value after one year of £3000 deposited in an account that bears interest at a rate of 10 per cent per annum, compounded quarterly.

SOLUTION 3.17

We have

$$P = 3000$$
$$i = 0.1$$
$$m = 4$$
$$t = 1$$

Therefore

$$i/m = 0.025$$
$$mt = 4$$

and

$$A_{1,4} = 3000(1.025)^4 = £3311.44$$

EXAMPLE 3.18

Find the value after four years of £5000 deposited in an account that bears interest at a rate of 9 per cent per annum, compounded semi-annually.

SOLUTION 3.18

We have

$$P = 5000$$
$$i = 0.09$$
$$m = 2$$
$$t = 4$$

Therefore:

$$i/m = 0.045$$
$$mt = 8$$

and

$$A_{4,2} = 5000(1.045)^8 = £7110.5$$

You can see the effect of variations in the compounding period on Lotus if you set up Worksheet 3.14.

When evaluated, this should produce a value in B7 of 7110.5, since the formula there is the Lotus equivalent of equation (3.12).

An important result emerges if we choose certain values for P, i, m and t in equation (3.12). To see this, consider the following example.

WORKSHEET 3.14

	A	B
1	Principal	5000
2	Annual Interest Rate	0.09
3	Number of Years	4
4	Number of Compounding Periods per annum	2
5	Total Number of Compounding Periods	+B3*B4
6	Interest Rate per Compounding Period	+B2/B4
7	Eventual Amount	+B1*(1+B6)^B5

EXAMPLE 3.19

Find the value after one year of £1 deposited in an account that bears interest at a rate of 100 per cent per annum, compounded annually.

Variations in the compounding period

SOLUTION 3.19

Use the Lotus model of Worksheet 3.14 with the following values:

$$B1 = 1.00$$
$$B2 = 1.00$$
$$B3 = 1.00$$
$$B4 = 1.00$$

You should obtain a result of 2 in B7 since equation (3.12) would be evaluated as

$$A_t = 1(1 + 1/1)^1 = 2$$

Now modify Example 3.19 so that interest is compounded semi-annually. This means that the entry in B4 should become 2 and the result in B7 will become 2.25.

Now suppose that we let the number of compounding periods in the year go through a steadily increasing sequence, and that we calculate the associated value of equation (3.12). Worksheet 3.15 performs the necessary calculations.

When these formulae are evaluated by Lotus you should obtain Worksheet 3.16.

Clearly what is happening is that the value of A_t at first increases quite dramatically, but that as the number of compounding periods increases, A_t starts to increase less rapidly. In fact, it can be shown by more advanced techniques that the value of A_t tends towards a definite limit, which mathematicians denote by e. This happens as the number of compounding periods in the year (i.e. the value of m) becomes infinitely large, and consequently, as the time between compounding periods becomes infinitesimally small.

In symbols we can say that the *limit* of $1(1 + 1/m)^m$ as m tends to infinity is e ($= 2.7183$).

WORKSHEET 3.15

	A	B	C
1	Principal	1	
2	Annual Interest Rate	1.00	
3	Number of Years	1	
4			
5	Interest Compounded	Annual Number	
6	Every:	of Compounding	Amount
7		Periods	
8	Year	1.00	+B$1*(1+B$2/B8)^(B8*B$3)
9	Half-Year	2.00	+B$1*(1+B$2/B9)^(B9*B$3)
10	Quarter	4.00	+B$1*(1+B$2/B10)^(B10*B$3)
11	Month	12	+B$1*(1+B$2/B11)^(B11*B$3)
12	Week	52	+B$1*(1+B$2/B12)^(B12*B$3)
13	Day	365	+B$1*(1+B$2/B13)^(B13*B$3)
14	Hour	8760	+B$1*(1+B$2/B14)^(B14*B$3)
15	Minute	525600.00	+B$1*(1+B$2/B15)^(B15*B$3)
16	Second	31536000.00	+B$1*(1+B$2/B16)^(B16*B$3)

WORKSHEET 3.16

	A	B	C
1	Principal	1	
2	Annual Interest Rate	1.00	
3	Number of Years	1	
4			
5	Interest Compounded	Annual Number	
6	Every:	of Compounding	Amount
7		Periods	
8	Year	1.00	2.000000
9	Half-Year	2.00	2.250000
10	Quarter	4.00	2.441406
11	Month	12	2.613035
12	Week	52	2.692597
13	Day	365	2.714567
14	Hour	8760	2.718127
15	Minute	525600.00	2.718279
16	Second	31536000.00	2.718282

3.9 Continuous compounding

As we have previously said, when m becomes infinitely large, the time between compounding periods becomes infinitesimally small, and effectively can be regarded as zero. When this happens we refer to such a situation as continuous compounding, since instead of there being a countable period of time between compounding periods, there is so little time that the process can be regarded as continuous. It is almost as if the interest for a millisecond is added to the Principal in the instant of its passing and hence forms an infinitesimally larger base upon which the interest for the next millisecond is calculated.

The sceptical reader will no doubt argue that few financial institutions would ever offer terms as beneficial to the lender as continuous compounding implies; and on this there is no dispute. However, many natural phenomena do not recognize the accounting habits of banks and building societies and insist on growing in a fashion that is most appropriately modelled by continuous compounding and the use of e.

To see how this can be done, we should now relax some of the restrictive values that we imposed upon P, i and t terms in the previous illustration.

First of all we should allow the value of the interest rate to be i as usual, instead of 100 per cent. When this is done you should be able to see that equation (3.12) can be written as

$$A_1 = 1(1 + i/m)^m$$

Now we have already seen that if $i = 1$, then the limit of this expression as m tends to infinity is 2.7183 = e.

The question therefore arises of what happens when i adopts some value other than 1. In particular, does this expression also reach a definite limit, and if so, what is it?

The answer is 'yes', although the algebra to prove it is beyond the scope of this text. Nevertheless it can be taken on trust that the limit of $A_1 = 1(1 + i/m)^m$ as m tends to infinity is given by e^i.

This can be confirmed by an appropriate modification of the model in Worksheet 3.15. All you have to do is enter a value of 0.1 (for example) in B2, whereupon you will find that a value of 1.105 171 will be returned to the C16 cell.

At the same time you should make the following entries in A17 and B17.

	A	B
17	Exponential function	@EXP(B2)

This Lotus function simply takes the value of e (2.7183) and raises it to whatever power is contained in the bracketed argument.

Used in this way you should find that the entries in C16 and B17 are identical, thereby confirming that $A_1 = 1(1 + i/m)^m$ tends towards e^i as m tends to infinity.

EXAMPLE 3.20

Confirm that a sum of £1 compounded by the hour at an annual rate of 16 per cent will amount to $e^{0.16}$ after one year.

SOLUTION 3.20

Use the modified version of Worksheet 3.15 to confirm that

$$A_1 = 1(1 + 0.16/8760)^{8760} = 1.1735$$

and that

$$@EXP(0.16) = 1.1735$$

Now suppose that the Principal of £1 is deposited for more than one year and continuously compounded at an annual rate of i. The expression for A_t becomes

$$A_t = 1(1 + i/m)^{mt}$$

If we rewrite this as

$$A_t = [1(1 + i/m)^m]^t$$

we can see that since the limit of the expression inside square brackets has been shown to be e^i, we can write

$$A_t = (e^i)^t = e^{it}$$

In other words, the limit of $1(1 + i/m)^{mt}$ as m tends to infinity is given by e^{it}.

Keeping the same figures as you used in the last example (i.e. $i = 0.16$, $P = 1$), you can again confirm this on Worksheet 3.15 by making the following modifications.

In B3 enter

$$5$$

i.e. 5 years.

In B16 enter

$$@EXP(B2*B3)$$

You should now find that with hourly compounding the entries in C14 and B16 are identical and equal to 2.2254.

This, of course, is because

$$1(1 + i/m)^{mt} = 1(1 + 0.16/8760)^{(5)(8760)} = 2.2254$$

whereas

$$e^{(5)(0.16)} = e^{0.8} = 2.2254$$

Finally, if a Principal of £P is deposited, then we have

$$A_t = P(1 + i/m)^{mt}$$

It is left as an exercise for you to confirm that the limit of this expression as m tends to infinity is given by

$$P(e^{it}) \tag{3.13}$$

Notice that this last expression is the continuous compounding equivalent of equation (3.12).

You should also modify Worksheet 3.15 appropriately so that you can find the value of a Principal of £2500 that is continuously compounded at an annual rate of 11.5 per cent for a period of seven years. The answer is £5591.74, as opposed to £5356.29 under annual compounding.

3.10 The equivalent annual rate

The discussion in the previous section has produced the important implication that the effective rate of interest being paid on deposited funds not only depends upon the quoted nominal rate but also upon the frequency with which interest is compounded. In other words, with any nominal rate of interest, a given Principal will amount to more if that interest is compounded monthly than if it is compounded annually. Clearly this implies that the effective rate on the monthly compounded funds exceeds that on the annually compounded funds. The notion of the equivalent annual rate (EAR) allows you to express any nominal annual rate (NAR) in terms that take account of the frequency with which interest is compounded. To do this we simply note that if interest is compounded m times per annum at the quoted NAR, then the amount after t years is given by

$$A_t = P[1 + (NAR/m)]^{mt}$$

However, in the simplest case of annual compounding this expression reduces to

$$A_t = P(1 + NAR)^t$$

It should be clear that only under annual compounding will the nominal and the equivalent rates be the same, and using this knowledge allows us to rewrite the last expression as

$$A_t = P(1 + EAR)^t$$

If we now equate the righthand sides of these expressions we obtain

$$P(1 + EAR)^t = P[1 + (NAR/m)]^{mt}$$

Eliminating P from both sides and then raising both sides to the power of $1/t$ produces

$$(1 + EAR) = [1 + (NAR/m)]^m$$

Therefore

$$EAR = \{[1 + (NAR/m)]^m\} - 1$$

For example, if a savings scheme offers quarterly compounding at a nominal annual rate of 12 per cent, then the last expression above would become (with NAR = 0.12 and $m = 4$)

$$EAR = (1.03^4) - 1 = 0.1255$$

The effect of quarterly compounding has been to make the nominal annual rate of 12 per cent become equivalent to an annually compounded rate of 12.55 per cent.

Furthermore, if the compounding process was continuous, then you should be able to see that our expression for the EAR becomes

$$EAR = (e^{NAR}) - 1$$

which, if NAR = 0.15 for example, implies that the annual equivalent rate of a nominal rate of 15 per cent compounded continuously is given by

$$(e^{0.15}) - 1 = 0.1618, \text{ i.e. } 16.18 \text{ per cent}$$

This is clearly the highest value, *for any given nominal rate*, that the equivalent annual rate can adopt.

3.11 Growth rate calculations

We have already suggested that although financial institutions do not offer continuously compounded interest rates, there are a number of naturally occurring processes in which the growth in the variable's value is of a continuous nature. Population growth, the rate of inflation, gross national product, and the appreciation/depreciation of company assets, are all examples of such continuous growth processes. In each of these cases the most important feature is that although accountants may measure the value of the variable at one point in time and then measure it again at some later date, the variable is in fact changing continuously throughout the duration of the measurement period. In other words, it does not remain constant for 99.99 per cent of the measurement period and then suddenly change its value at the time of the second measurement.

What this means is that the arbitrary choice of the length of the measurement period will influence how the growth in the value of the variable is perceived and calculated. Of course, continuous monitoring of the variable's value is the only way to remove this problem completely, yet this would be a time-consuming and expensive practice.

Nevertheless, knowledge of the process of continuous compounding and its relationship with the exponential function allows us to calculate the appropriate growth rate as if it had been subject to continuous monitoring.

To see this consider the following example.

EXAMPLE 3.21

An accountant estimates the 'book' value of a company's assets to be £1.64 million on 1 January 1988, and to be £2.14 million two years later. Calculate the rate of growth of the company's assets.

SOLUTION 3.21

To deal with this problem we must decide whether the growth process is to be regarded as simple or compound, and, if it is compound, we must then decide upon the number of compounding periods per annum.

We can consider these alternatives as follows:

Simple growth In this case we can calculate the value of i from the appropriate transposition of equation (3.1).
Since
$$A_2 = P(1 + ti)$$
it follows that
$$i = [(A_2/P) - 1]/t$$

therefore
$$i = [(2.14/1.64) - 1]/2 = 0.1524$$
The simple growth rate is 15.24 per cent per annum.

Annual compound growth In this case equation (3.12) applies, and this can be transposed to produce an expression for i as follows:
$$A_t = P(1 + i/m)^{mt}$$
$$(A_t/P) = (1 + i/m)^{mt}$$
$$(A_t/P)^{1/mt} = (1 + i/m)$$
$$(A_t/P)^{1/mt} - 1 = i/m$$
$$[(A_t/P)^{1/mt}] - 1](m) = i$$

Now since for annual compounding we have $m = 1$, we can write
$$[(2.14/1.64)^{1/2} - 1](1) = i$$
implying that $i = 0.1423$.

The annually compounded growth rate is 14.23 per cent per annum.

Quarterly compound growth In this case we have $m = 4$, and so
$$i = [(2.14/1.64)^{1/8} - 1](4) = 0.1353$$
The quarterly compounded growth rate is 13.53 per cent per annum.

Monthly compound growth For this case we have $m = 12$, and so
$$i = [(2.14/1.64)^{1/24} - 1](12) = 0.1337$$
The monthly compounded growth rate is 13.37 per cent per annum.

Continuous compound growth In this case we must make use of equation (3.13) as follows:
$$A_t = P(e^{it})$$
Therefore
$$e^{it} = A_t/P$$
$$it(\ln e) = \ln(A_t/P)$$
$$i = [\ln(A_t/P)]/t$$

For the figures of our example this produces
$$i = [\ln(2.14/1.64)]/2$$
$$i = 0.1330$$
The continuous compound growth rate is 13.3 per cent per annum.

As you can clearly see from the illustrations above, the calculated growth rate is highly sensitive to the number of compounding periods used. Nevertheless, as you might expect, it approaches a limit that is provided by the continuous compound rate.

EXAMPLE 3.22

Calculate the continuous compound annual rate of inflation if the index of retail prices was 134.67 on 1 January 1985, and had risen to 204.78 by 1 January 1990.

SOLUTION 3.22

We have

$$P = 134.67$$
$$t = 5$$
$$A(5) = 204.78$$
$$i = \text{unknown}$$

Therefore

$$i = [\ln(204.78/134.67)]/5$$
$$i = 0.0838$$

The continuously compounded inflation rate for the period was 8.38 per cent per annum.

This concludes our discussion on the principles of financial mathematics as applied to the compounding process. However, in the next chapter you will find that all of these ideas are used and developed in relation to the process of investment appraisal.

Finally, since the syntax and meaning of the various Lotus financial functions is not always easy to remember, we conclude with a summarizing list of those functions whose purpose has been explained.

1. @CTERM(i, A, P) This function calculates the number of years required for a given Principal (P) to accumulate to a given amount (A) at the prevailing interest rate (i).

    It therefore solves for t in the basic compounding equation

    $$A = P(1 + i)^t$$

    If interest is compounded in periods that are less than annual (quarterly, say) then @CTERM($i/4, A, P$) will give the number of (quarterly) periods required to achieve the required terminal amount.

2. @RATE(A, P, t) This function calculates the rate of interest required to turn a given Principal (P) into a terminal amount of A after t years.

It therefore solves for i in the compounding equation

$$A + P(1+i)^t$$

If t is meant to represent periods (quarters or months, for example), then the calculated interest rate will be a quarterly or monthly rate, and you must multiply this rate by the number of annual periods to obtain the annual rate. This will, however, be the annual rate compounded quarterly or monthly, etc., and so you may want to convert it into an equivalent annual rate by the method outlined earlier.

3. @TERM(P, i, A) This function only applies to annuity calculations, where a *series* of payments of £P are made to an account bearing a given annual interest rate (i), and are required to amount to a given terminal sum (A).

The @TERM function will provide the *number* of payments required to achieve this objective, on the assumption that the first payment is made immediately.

The function therefore solves for t in the equation

$$P + P(1+i) + P(1+i)^2 + \cdots + P(1+i)^t$$

and then adds 1 to give the number of annual payments required.

4. @FV(P, i, n) This is also an annuity function and gives the eventual value, after $n-1$ years, of a series of n deposits at the prevailing interest rate (i). The first deposit is assumed to be made immediately.

For example, three payments of £100 to an account bearing interest at an annual rate of 10 per cent would have a terminal value after two years of

$$100 + 100(1.1) + 100(1.1)^2 = £331$$

Consequently @FV(100, 0.1, 3) would return a value of 331. Because of this it will also be the case that @TERM(100, 0.1, 331) will return a value of three (payments).

5. @PMT(D, i, n) This function calculates the size of the n annual payments required to repay a debt of £D at the given borrowing rate (i). The first payment is assumed to be made after one year. Consequently, to repay a debt of £1000 in two equal annual instalments at a borrowing rate of 10 per cent per annum, there would have to be two payments of @PMT(1000, 0.1, 2). This can be confirmed to evaluate to £576.19.

3.12 Exercises

3.1

A Principal of £2000 is deposited in an account that bears interest at a rate of 11 per cent per annum compounded annually. Calculate the value of the account at the end of each of the next ten years.

3.2

Repeat Exercise 3.1 if the interest rate changes to 11 per cent per annum compounded quarterly.

3.3

After how many years will a Principal of £10 000 amount to £60 000, if the interest rate for the period is 20 per cent per annum: (a) compounded annually, (b) compounded monthly and (c) compounded continuously?

3.4

What quarterly compounded rate of interest is being paid if a Principal of £1500 amounts to £3000 after five years?

3.5

A sum of £25 000 is borrowed just now and is to be repaid in 25 years' time. The interest rate on this debt is 16 per cent per annum compounded monthly.
   What is the size of the debt at the end of the 25-year period?

3.6

In order to repay the debt incurred in Exercise 3.5 above a sinking fund is established which guarantees to pay an annually compounded rate of 14 per cent per annum. If 26 equal annual payments of £5000 are made to the sinking fund, and if the first payment is made just now, what proportion of the terminal value of the debt will be supplied after last payment has been made?

3.7

What is the size of the 26 equal annual payments that must be made to the sinking fund in Exercise 3.6 if the debt is to be exactly repaid?

3.8

A shipping company has just taken delivery of an £8 million cargo vessel. The payment terms imposed by the shipyard are that 25 per cent of the amount due must be paid immediately, but that the outstanding balance can be repaid in five equal annual instalments. The shipyard will, however, charge an annual flat rate interest charge of 10 per cent of the incurred debt for each year that there is any debt outstanding.

(a) If the first instalment is to be made one year from now, calculate the size of the five equal payments that will have to be made by the shipping company.
(b) Funds are also available from the shipping company's bankers at a rate of 10.5 per cent per annum compounded semi-annually. This would mean that the

outstanding debt to the builders could be borrowed from the bank and cleared off immediately.

Which of the two loan arrangements should the shipping company use, assuming that it can also lend funds at a market rate of 10 per cent per annum compounded annually?

3.9

Rank the following savings schemes in terms of their effective rates of return.

Scheme A   9.0 per cent per annum compounded quarterly.
Scheme B   9.5 per cent per annum compounded annually.
Scheme C   8.8 per cent per annum compounded monthly.
Scheme D   7.5 per cent per annum compounded daily.
Scheme E   7.0 per cent per annum compounded continuously.

3.10

Calculate the size of the 15 equal annual payments required to pay off a debt of £7000 incurred at an interest rate of 17 per cent per annum if the first repayment is to be made: (a) one year from now, (b) immediately and (c) two years from now.

3.11

How many equal annual payments of £200 will be required to pay off a debt of £3000 incurred at an annually compounded interest rate of 8 per cent?

3.12

Assuming that the first payment is to be made just now, what is the terminal value of eight equal annual payments of £200 made to an account that bears interest at a rate of 12 per cent per annum (a) compounded annually or (b) compounded quarterly?

3.13 Solutions to the exercises

3.1

Worksheet 3.3 can be used directly to solve this problem although for reasons of space we have transposed rows and columns in Worksheet 3.17. However, the principles involved in formulating the worksheet formulae remain the same as for Worksheet 3.3.

WORKSHEET 3.17

```
B6: +B$1*(1+B$2)^A6
```

	A	B
1	Principal	2000
2	Interest Rate	0.11
3		
4		
5	Years	Amount
6	0	2000.00
7	1	2220.00
8	2	2464.20
9	3	2735.26
10	4	3036.14
11	5	3370.12
12	6	3740.83
13	7	4152.32
14	8	4609.08
15	9	5116.07
16	10	5678.84

3.2

You should use a combination of Worksheets 3.17 and 3.14 to produce the required Lotus worksheet as shown in Worksheet 3.18.

WORKSHEET 3.18

```
B6: +B$1*(1+B$2/B$3)^(A6*B$3)
```

	A	B
1	Principal	2000
2	Interest rate	0.11
3	Comp. Periods	4
4		
5	Years	Amount
6	0	2000.00
7	1	2229.24
8	2	2484.76
9	3	2769.57
10	4	3087.02
11	5	3440.86
12	6	3835.25
13	7	4274.85
14	8	4764.84
15	9	5311.00
16	10	5919.75

3.3

Lotus can solve part (a) for you with its @CTERM function. The formulation would be

$$@CTERM(0.2, 60000, 10000) = 9.82 \text{ years}$$

For part (b) you have to force @CTERM to deal with monthly as opposed to annual compounding and so you should write

$$@CTERM(0.12/12, 60000, 10000)$$

This will produce an answer of 108.3989 *months*.
Consequently

$$@CTERM(0.12/12, 60000, 10000)/12$$

will produce the answer in years to be 9.0332, i.e. 9 years and 1 month to the nearest month.

This approach should provide us with a useful method. Namely, take a blank worksheet and make the following entries:

in B1   the principal
in B2   the required terminal Amount
in B3   the annual interest rate
in B4   the number of compounding periods in the year

Then, in B5 we could write

$$@CTERM(B3/B4, B2, B1)/B4$$

This will calculate the number of *periods* required for the terminal sum to be achieved on the basis of the entered data parameters.

Alternatively, you could proceed manually as follows.

$$A_t = P(1 + i/m)^{mt} \tag{3.12}$$

Therefore

$$mt[\log(1 + i/m)] = \log(A_t/P)$$

and

$$t = [\log(A_t/P)]/(m)[\log(1 + i/m)]$$

So, for both parts (a) and (b) we have

$$A_t = 60\,000$$
$$P = 10\,000$$
$$i = 0.2$$
$$t = \text{unknown}$$

For part (b) we have $m = 12$ and therefore

$$t = (\log 6)/(12)[\log(1.016\,66)] = 9.03 \text{ years}$$

For part (c) we should remember that the expression $(1 + i/m)^{mt}$ tends towards e^{it} as m becomes infinitely large. Therefore

$$A_t = P(e^{0.2t})$$

and

$$t = [\ln(A_t/P)]/0.2 = \ln(6)/0.2 = 8.958 \text{ years}$$

3.4

Once again we should employ equation (3.12), only this time transpose it in such a way that the interest rate appears as the only argument on the lefthand side. That is

$$A_t = P(1 + i/m)^{mt}$$

Therefore

$$(1 + i/m)^{mt} = A_t/P$$

and

$$(1 + i/m) = (A_t/P)^{1/mt}$$

With $m = 4$, $A_5 = 3000$, $t = 5$ and $P = 1500$, this produces

$$1 + 0.25i = 2^{1/20}$$

Therefore

$$i = 4[(2^{1/20}) - 1] = 0.1410$$

This means that a quarterly compounded interest rate of 14.1 per cent per annum will cause the Principal to double after five years. Alternatively, @RATE(3000, 1500, 20)*4 will give the same answer.

3.5

After 25 years, and using equation (3.12) again, the size of the debt will be given by

$$25\,000(1 + 0.16/12)^{(12)(25)} = £1\,329\,348$$

3.6

The 26 annual payments of £5000 to the sinking fund will have a terminal value that can be obtained directly from the Lotus @FV function (or from equation 3.5). Using the Lotus function we have

$$@FV(5000, 0.14, 26) = £1\,041\,663.71$$

Therefore, the proportion of the debt which can be repaid is

$$1\,041\,663/1\,329\,348 = 78.35 \text{ per cent}$$

Solutions to the exercises 177

This may seem quite surprising, since you would think that 26 payments of £5000 would easily clear the debt. But you have to remember that monthly compounding at an annual rate of 16 per cent is an extremely fast growing process, especially in comparison to annual compounding at 14 per cent.

3.7

To obtain the correct answer you must solve for P in equation (3.5):

$$P = [S_n(i)]/\{[(1+i)^n] - 1\}$$

Of course, the required value of S_n is the terminal value of the debt (£1 329 348) and so we have

$$P = (1\,329\,348)(0.14)/[(1.14^{26}) - 1] = £6380.89$$

You can confirm on Lotus that this is correct, since the future value of these 26 payments would be

$$@FV(6380.89, 0.14, 26) = 1\,329\,348$$

3.8

(a) The first part of the problem is straightforward since the debt of £6 million will attract five annual interest payments of £0.6 million, which, in conjunction with the repayment of the initial loan means that the five annual payments that must be made will be

$$[6.0 + (5)(0.6)]/5 = £1.8 \text{ million}$$

(b) This part of the question is more complicated since we have to work out what the debt to the bank will be after five years and then compare this with the amount that the 'saved' payments to the builders would have accumulated to, also after five years.

You can visualize the problem more clearly in Worksheet 3.19.
The debt to the bank will accumulate after five years to

$$6(1.0525)^{10} = £10.0085 \text{ million}$$

On the other hand the five saved payments of £1.8 million can be placed on deposit at the available rate of 10 per cent, and would have a terminal value after five years of

$$@FV(1.8, 0.1, 5) = £10.989\,18 \text{ million}$$

You might think that there is a problem here since we have stressed that the @FV function calculates the value after $(n - 1)$ years of n deposits on the assumption that the first deposit is made immediately. Clearly, however, the first saved interest payment to the builders will not be due until one year has passed, and so you might think that the @FV function would be inappropriate. This is not the case, however,

WORKSHEET 3.19

```
B18: @FV(1.8,0.1,5)
```

	A	B	C	D
1	LOAN FROM BUILDERS		LOAN FROM BANK	
2	Flat rate	0.1	Compound rate	0.105
3	Cost	8	Comp. Periods	2
4	Deposit	2	Debt incurred	6
5	Debt incurred	6		
6	Interest	0.6		
7	Term of debt	5		
8	Annual Payment	1.80		
9				
10	Years	Debt Payments	Years	Size of Debt
11	0		0	6.00
12	1	1.80	1	6.65
13	2	1.80	2	7.36
14	3	1.80	3	8.16
15	4	1.80	4	9.03
16	5	1.80	5	10.01
17	Value of saved			
18	Debt payments	10.99		

The entry in D11 is +D$4*(1+D$2/D$3)^(C11*D$3) and has been copied into D12..D16.

since if the first deposit is delayed by one year the @FV function gives the terminal value after n years of n deposits as opposed to the terminal value after $(n-1)$ years of n deposits when the first deposit is made immediately.

Now it is exactly this figure that we require (i.e. the terminal value after five years of five deposits of £1.8 million) and so the integrity of the @FV function is retained.

Clearly the bank's loan terms are a better prospect than those offered by the builders since the 'saved' interest payments to the builders accumulate to an amount (£10.989 18 million) that is more than sufficient to repay the debt to the bank (£10.0085 million).

3.9

You can use Lotus to calculate the equivalent annual rates of return of the various schemes as follows. After each value has been calculated in the A4 cell do a Range Value copy of the result into the cell associated with the appropriate scheme. Then order the results in descending order as shown in Worksheet 3.20.

3.10

Part (a) can be solved directly from the Lotus @PMT function as

$$@PMT(7000, 0.17, 15) = £1314.75$$

Solutions to the exercises 179

```
WORKSHEET 3.20
  B4: (1+B1/B2)^B2-1
                        A                    B
       1    Nominal Rate                  0.07
       2    Comp. Periods         100000000000
       3    Scheme                            E
       4    Equiv. Annual Rate          0.0725
       5
       6
       7    Scheme B                    0.0950
       8    Scheme A                    0.0931
       9    Scheme C                    0.0916
      10    Scheme D                    0.0779
      11    Scheme E                    0.0725
```

For parts (b) and (c), however, you will have to use the logic outlined in Worksheet 3.13 or equation (3.12). This will produce the following results:

(b) Since $m = 0$ we have
$$7000(1.17^{14})(0.17)/[(1.17^{15}) - 1] = £1123.72$$

(c) Since $m = 2$ we have
$$7000(1.17^{16})(0.17)/[(1.17^{15}) - 1] = £1538.26$$

As you can see, our general expectation that the size of the required payments increases as the delay before the first repayment increases has been confirmed.

3.11

The answer can be obtained from the Lotus @TERM function as follows:
$$@TERM(200, 0.08, 3000) = 10.245 \text{ payments}$$

Notice that it is @TERM and *not* @CTERM.

3.12

Part (a) is easily solved from the @FV function and would be
$$@FV(200, 0.12, 8) = £2459.94$$

However, Lotus cannot deal with part (b) so you will have to treat it as a geometric progression (with first term 200 and common factor 1.03^4) and then sum the first eight terms. This gives

$$\underset{200\ +}{\text{1st term}} \quad \underset{200(1.03^4)\ +\ \cdots\ +\ 200(1.03^{24})\ +\ 200(1.03^{28})}{\text{2nd term}\ \ldots \quad\quad\quad\quad\quad\quad \text{7th term}\quad\quad\quad \text{8th term}}$$

The eighth term is the value of the first deposit after seven years, the seventh term is the value of the second deposit after six years, ..., the second term is the value of the seventh deposit after one year, and the first term is the value of the last deposit after zero years.

We therefore require:

$$S_8 = 200[(1.03^4)^8 - 1]/[(1.03^4) - 1] = £2509.91$$

You might have though that you could have addressed part (b) of this problem by using

@FV(200, 0.12/4, 32)

but this would give the Future Value of *32 quarterly* deposits of £200 compounded quarterly, and not eight annual deposits of £200 as we require. This amount will clearly be much larger than it should be, since four times as many deposits of the same magnitude are made. Furthermore

@CTERM(200/4, 0.12/4, 32)

will still not give the correct answer, since this supplies the Future Value of 32 quarterly deposits of £50 compounded quarterly.

In this case you will just have to accept that Lotus cannot always do everything for you.

4

Discounting Techniques

4.1 Present value

The ideas of compounding outlined in the previous chapter have an important extension in an area known as discounting. To understand the issues involved ask yourself the following question:

'When is a pound not a pound?'

One answer would be:

'When it is received at some future date rather than at the present.'

What this means is that £1 (or any other amount) that is to be received ten years from now, is worth less than £1 that is to be received five years from now, which is worth less than £1 that is to be received one year from now. Only if the funds are received just now is their *current* worth the same as their nominal worth.

This idea can be stated more formally as follows. Any two or more nominally equal monetary sums must be regarded as unequal in *current* magnitude unless they are received at exactly the same time. Furthermore, the current magnitude of these monetary sums is only equal to their nominal magnitude if the funds are received just now.

Diagrammatically, we can illustrate these two statements as shown in Figure 4.1.

This explicit introduction of the time dimension to the calculation of the current worth of funds that are to be received at some future date means that any future sum must have its nominal value modified downwards in order to take account of the reduction in current value caused by the time lapse that exists before the funds are received.

This reduction stems entirely from the fact that the recipient of the funds must wait for a finite period of time before the money is received and can then be spent or reinvested; and the reduction in real value compared to nominal value therefore represents the cost to the individual of having to wait.

The procedure of modifying nominal values into current values is known as discounting, and there are two things that must be clearly understood about it.

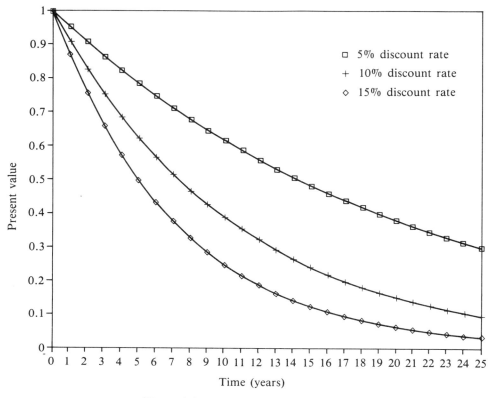

Figure 4.1 Present value versus time

Firstly, the word discount is not used in the popular sense of the word to mean a reduction in the price paid for an article expressed as a percentage of the higher price. Discounting as used here means a systematic reduction in the nominal value of monetary sums, but as we will see it is not done in a simple percentage manner.

Secondly, the cost of having to wait mentioned above has got nothing to do with the existence of a positive inflation rate. It is true that if inflation exists, then the penalty of having to wait becomes higher, but this penalty exists whether there is inflation or not, and is to be understood in terms of the interest payments that have to be forgone as a result of having to wait for the funds to be received.

As in the case of some of our previous analysis, a simple transposition of a basic equation is sufficient to illustrate the basic idea. This is because it will be remembered that equation (3.2) stated that

$$A_t = P(1 + i)^t$$

If a Principal of £P amounts to A_t after t years when the interest rate is given by i, it surely follows that if a sum of £A is to be received after t years then this is equivalent to a Principal just now of

$$P = (A_t)/(1 + i)^t$$

When this transposition is made, the term P is usually referred to as the present value (PV) of the future amount A_t, and the i term is known as the discount rate (i.e. the interest rate used for discounting purposes). We therefore have

$$PV = (A_t)/(1 + i)^t \qquad (4.1)$$

EXAMPLE 4.1

Find the present value of £1000 that is to be received in ten years' time if the interest rate for the period is 10 per cent per annum.

SOLUTION 4.1

Using equation (4.1) we can write

$$PV = (1000)/(1 + 0.1)^{10} = £385.54$$

The implication of this is that an individual would be indifferent between the choice of £1000 to be received in ten years' time, and £385.54 to be received just now. This is because the 'present' sum of £385.54 could be placed on deposit for ten years and would eventually amount to

$$385.54(1.1)^{10} = £1000$$

As we have already said, the further into the future a given sum is to be received, then the less is its present value, as you can confirm if you prepare a worksheet similar to Worksheet 4.1. For reasons of space only two years have been reproduced, but on your own actual worksheet you can do it for as many years as you want. This is because if the formula in the B4 cell is specified correctly, then it can be copied into all relevant cells of the worksheet. This correct specification has three aspects:

1. The Future Amount in the B1 cell must be absolutely fixed ($B$1) so that it will remain as B1 when copied along rows and down columns.
2. The different interest rates in A4..A8 must be allowed to vary as copying is done down any column, but must be fixed as copying is performed along any row. This means that the formula in B4 must contain the term $A4 (always column A but the row addresses varying in the sequence 4, 5, 6, etc.).
3. The different years in B2, C2, etc. must be allowed to vary along any given row, but must be fixed for any given column. This means that the cell reference must be B$2 (always row 2 but the column address varying in the sequence B, C, etc.).

WORKSHEET 4.1

	A	B	C	D
1	Future Amount	1000		
2	Number of Years	0	1	2
3	Discount Rate			
4	0	+$B$1/(1+$A4)^B$2	+$B$1/(1+$A4)^C$2	+$B$1/(1+$A4)^D$2
5	0.05	+$B$1/(1+$A5)^B$2	+$B$1/(1+$A5)^C$2	+$B$1/(1+$A5)^D$2
6	0.1	+$B$1/(1+$A6)^B$2	+$B$1/(1+$A6)^C$2	+$B$1/(1+$A6)^D$2
7	0.15	+$B$1/(1+$A7)^B$2	+$B$1/(1+$A7)^C$2	+$B$1/(1+$A7)^D$2
8	0.2	+$B$1/(1+$A8)^B$2	+$B$1/(1+$A8)^C$2	+$B$1/(1+$A8)^D$2

When Lotus evaluates these formulae, you should find that the present value declines both as you move down any given column (increasing the interest rate), and as you move to the right along any given row (increasing the time before the funds are received).

It will also be noticed from the table that there is in fact another answer to our original question 'when is a pound not a pound?', since you should see that the response 'when the interest rate is zero' is also correct. This answer should be intuitively obvious since if no interest is paid on funds borrowed, then there is no penalty in having to wait before the funds are received.

You can, of course, graph any or all of these calculated present values in the standard manner. The cells containing the different years (B2..M2 say) will be the X variable on the horizontal axis, while the present values for any given interest rate will be the A, B, C, etc. ranges. For example, if you select a line graph, and then enter B2..M2 for the X range, and B5..M5 for the A range, then you will obtain a graph similar to Figure 4.1, indicating how the present value varies with time for an interest rate of 5 per cent. Try this for yourself.

4.2 Discounting multiple receipts

The ideas involved in the basic notion of discounting can of course be extended to situations in which there is more than one single payment. In this respect consider the following example.

EXAMPLE 4.2

Imagine a situation in which a sum of £1000 was to be received just now, and after one year, and after two years and after three years. Also assume that the interest rate is 14 per cent per annum compounded annually. What is the present value of this *stream* of income receipts?

SOLUTION 4.2

Clearly the £1000 that is received just now has a present value of £1000, while the receipt of £1000 that is to be received in one year's time has a present value of £1000/(1.14) = £877.19. By a similar logic the final two receipts will have present values of £1000/$(1.14)^2$ = £769.47 (for the receipt after two years) and £1000/$(1.14)^3$ = £674.97 (for the receipt after three years).

Consequently, the combined present value of all four income receipts (i.e. the present value of the entire income stream) must be given by

$$£1000 + £877.19 + £769.47 + £674.97 = £3321.63$$

What this means is that with an annual interest rate of 14 per cent a lump sum payment just now of £3321.63 is equivalent to an income stream of four annual receipts of £1000 with the first receipt being received immediately.

A moment's consideration should reveal that there are a number of savings and pension schemes available which use exactly this notion.

EXAMPLE 4.3

Suppose that in exchange for a specified lump sum payment just now, a savings scheme guaranteed to pay £5000 immediately, and then a further five payments of £5000 after one year, two years, three years and four years. What must be the size of this lump sum payment if the interest rate over the period is 12.5 per cent?

SOLUTION 4.3

Clearly the answer to this question can be obtained by finding the present value of the guaranteed income stream since no rational saver would agree to pay *more* than this present value as the initial lump sum payment. Similarly, no rational borrower would be willing to accept *less* than the present value of the income stream as the initial payment. In either case the size of the initial payment would be different from the present value of the income stream that the initial payment was designed to secure.

This initial lump sum payment must therefore be at least equal to the present value of the secured income stream, which, for our example is given by

$$5000 + 5000/(1.125) + 5000/(1.125)^2 + 5000/(1.125)^3 + 5000/(1.125)^4 = £20\,028.20$$

From what we have done it should be clear that we can derive a general expression for the present value of any given income stream (of £R per annum), receivable for each of t years, when the interest rate is i ($= r/100$) per cent per annum. Assuming that the first income receipt is received just now this would be

$$\text{PV} = R + R/(1+i) + R/(1+i)^2 + \cdots + R/(1+i)^{t-1} \quad (4.2)$$

Notice that the maximum power in this series is $(t-1)$ and not t, since although there are a total of t receipts, the fact that the first receipt is received just now means that the power of the denominator in the first term is zero. This is often a source of confusion, but it should be eradicated if you view the problem as shown in Table 4.1.

Of course, it is entirely conceivable that the first receipt in schemes such as these is not received until the end of the first year (as opposed to immediately). In this case equation (4.2) above becomes

$$\text{PV} = R/(1+i) + R/(1+i)^2 + \cdots + R/(1+i)^{t-1} + R/(1+i)^t \quad (4.2\text{a})$$

Table 4.1

Term	1	2	3	4	t
Year	0	1	2	3	$(t-1)$
PV	R	$R/(1+i)$	$R/(1+i)^2$	$R/(1+i)^3$	$R/(1+i)^{t-1}$

Clearly, if several years are involved, then these calculations become extremely tedious; however, as you might expect by now Lotus can perform them for you. Once again you could write the required formulae yourself, but for this example Lotus has a dedicated function know as Present Value (@PV), which has the following syntax:

@PV(Receipt, Discount Rate, Number of Receipts)

Definition The Lotus Present Value function @PV(R, i, n) calculates the present value of *n equal* annual receipts of £R when the discount rate is i (= r per cent/100) per annum. It assumes that the first receipt *is to be received one year from now*, and is therefore exactly equivalent to equation (4.2a) above.

Now take a blank worksheet and prepare Worksheet 4.2 as the solution to Example 4.3.

Notice how we have used a conditional expression in B5 above so that if the first receipt is received after one year (B4 = 1) the standard Lotus @PV function applies. On the other hand, if the first receipt is received immediately, then the @PV function is modified in two ways.

Firstly, the number of receipts in the @PV function is reduced by one (5 becomes 4); and secondly, the first payment is added to the value of @PV *at its nominal value*.

The logic for these two modifications should be clarified by the following illustration.

Lotus @PV with $n = 3$ calculates the present value of the following stream:

$$R/(1+i) + R/(1+i)^2 + R/(1+i)^3$$

Now if the first receipt is actually received just now, then we require the present value of

$$R + R/(1+i) + R/(1+i)^2$$

This is clearly the Lotus @PV function with a value of $n = 2$, i.e. $[R/(1+i) + R/(1+i)^2]$ *plus R*.

Confirm for yourself that this amendment produces the result obtained manually (£20 028.20).

WORKSHEET 4.2

	A	B
1	Receipt	5000
2	Discount Rate	0.125
3	Number of Receipts	5
4	Year of 1st Receipt (0 or 1)	1
5	Present Value	@IF(B4=1,@PV(B1,B2,B3),@PV(B1,B2,B3-1)+B1
6		

EXAMPLE 4.4

Find the present value of 25 equal annual payments of £50, if the first payment is to made just now, and if the interest rate for the period is 8 per cent compounded annually.

SOLUTION 4.4

We can use Worksheet 4.2 to provide the solution if we amend the entry in B1 to 50, the entry in B2 to 0.08, and the entry in B3 to 25. With B4 entered as 0 this will provide a solution of £576.44 in the B5 cell.

EXAMPLE 4.5

Find the present value of the following stream of income if the interest rate for the period is 13 per cent per annum compounded annually.

Year	Income
0	1000
1	2000
2	2500
3	1500
4	1000
5 and after	0

SOLUTION 4.5

We will have to be careful here, since the Lotus @PV function is *only* valid if the annual receipts are of *equal* magnitude. This is clearly *not* the case in this instance. Consequently, we should write the relevant formulae for ourselves. This is moderately easy, however, if we take full advantage of Lotus's copying facility. To do this set up a worksheet in which the first two lines are similar to Worksheet 4.3.

Once you have done this then you can use the Data Fill command (with a step of 1) to produce the required year entries in A3..A6.

Next, you will have no alternative but to type in the actual income values, and then enter the interest rate in C2 and the present value formula in D2. This last cell (D2) can then be copied into the range D3..D6.

Finally, you should enter, in C10 say

Total Present Value

```
WORKSHEET 4.3
D2: [W15] +B2/(1+C$2)^A2

        A         B           C              D
    1  Year     Income    Discount Rate   Present Value
    2   0        1000         0.13           1000
    3
```

```
WORKSHEET 4.4
D3: [W15] +B3/(1+C$2)^A3

        A         B           C              D
    1  Year     Income    Discount Rate   Present Value
    2   0        1000         0.13           1000
    3   1        2000                     1769.9115044
    4   2        2500                     1957.8667084
    5   3        1500                     1039.5752434
    6   4        1000                      613.31872768
    7
    8
    9
   10                      Total Present Value  6380.672184
   11
```

and in D10 the formula

@SUM(D2..D6)

Using this last method would produce Worksheet 4.4.

When Lotus evaluates this you will obtain the correct result of £6380.67, although it should be mentioned that there is a related Lotus function which can help us here. It is called @NPV and will be explained shortly in the section on investment appraisal.

4.3 Variations in the discounting period

It will have been noticed that the foregoing discussion has only considered situations in which interest is discounted on an annual basis. Yet, as was the case with compounding, account should be taken of situations in which interest is discounted more frequently than once per year.

For example, consider an amount of £2000 that is to be received five years from now. If the current interest rate is 7 per cent compounded annually, then the present value of this amount is easily obtained from

$$PV_5 = 2000/(1.07^5) = £1425.97$$

Now suppose that the interest rate of 7 per cent per annum was compounded half-yearly. Then, in the same way that any sum deposited just now would be worth *more* after a given number of years than under annual compounding, any sum received in the same given number of years will be worth *less* than if annual discounting prevailed. To be exact (and using the same notation as in the compounding case)

$$PV_{5,2} = 2000/(1.035^{10}) = £1417.83$$

The figure above results from the fact that there are now 10 discounting periods in each of which the interest rate is 3.5 per cent.

By a similar logic, if interest was compounded quarterly, monthly, weekly or daily; then the present values would be given by:

Quarterly: $PV_{5,4} = 2000/(1.008\ 75^{20}) = £1413.65$
Monthly: $PV_{5,12} = 2000/(1.005\ 83^{60}) = £1410.81$
Weekly: $PV_{5,52} = 2000/(1.001\ 35^{260}) = £1409.70$
Daily: $PV_{5,365} = 2000/(1.000\ 19^{1825}) = £1409.42$

As was the case with compounding, the effect of increasing the frequency with which interest is discounted is at first quite dramatic but eventually exercises an almost negligible additional effect. Clearly the expression for the present value is approaching some limit as the frequency of discounting increases.

Now it should be remembered that as compounding became effectively continuous (i.e. as the number of compounding periods, m, tended to infinity), the expression $A_t = P(1 + i/m)^{mt}$ tended towards $P(e^{it})$. By a similar logic we would therefore expect that the equivalent discounting expression, $PV(t) = A/(1 + i/m)^{mt}$, would tend towards A/e^{it}.

This is indeed correct, and is the discounting equivalent of continuous compounding. That is, if an interest rate of i is discounted m times per annum, then the present value of an amount of £A to be received t years from now is given by:

$$PV_t = A/(1 + i/m)^{mt}$$

which tends towards A/e^{it} as m tends to infinity.

Using the figures from our last illustration, then with continuous discounting we would obtain

$$PV_{5,\text{Continuous}} = 2000/e^{0.35} = £1409.37$$

This figure is, of course, almost identical to the one we obtained on the basis of daily discounting (£1409.42).

Lotus can confirm these calculations for you if you prepare Worksheet 4.5.

As whatever entry you make in B4 gets larger and larger, you will find that the entries in B5 and B6 get closer and closer to one another.

WORKSHEET 4.5

```
         A                                B
1   Receipt                           2000.00
2   Number of Years from now             5.00
3   Annual Interest Rate                 0.07
4   Number of Compounding Periods      365.00
5   Present Value                 +B1/((1+B3/B4)^(B2*B4))
6   Exponential Discounting       +B1*@EXP(-B3*B2)
7
```

EXAMPLE 4.6

Find the present value of an amount of £3500 to be received in 10 years time if the interest rate is 16 per cent per annum compounded: (a) quarterly, (b) monthly, (c) continuously.

SOLUTION 4.6

All you have to do is make the appropriate entries in Worksheet 4.5 and the correct results will be obtained. These are: (a) £729.01, (b) £714.15, (c) £706.64.

Now in just the same way as continuous compounding was used to model growth processes that did not fall into a discrete accounting pattern (population growth, etc.), continuous discounting should be used to calculate the present value of such processes.

EXAMPLE 4.7

A forestry commission has planted an area of young trees, which is expected to have a value of £10 million in 15 years' time. If the value of usable wood is believed to grow at a continuous exponential rate of 4 per cent per annum, calculate the present value of the tree plantation.

SOLUTION 4.7

Since growth is taken to be at an exponential rate of 4 per cent per annum we have:

$$PV_{15} = 10/e^{(0.04)(15)} = 10/e^{0.6} = £5.48 \text{ million}$$

4.4 Asset depreciation

One of the commonest applications of discounting ideas comes from an area that we have already encountered – the depreciation of physical and financial assets. For example, suppose a company purchased an item of equipment for £1 million and estimated that after ten years it would provide no further services apart from a scrap value of £10 000. Derive an expression that will estimate the value of the asset after four years and confirm that the expression produces a scrap value of £10 000 after ten years.

We have already seen that if straight-line depreciation is employed, then the annual rate of depreciation of the asset would be calculated as

$$(1 \text{ million} - 10\,000)/10 = £99\,000$$

Consequently the value (V) of the asset after t years (V_t) can be written as

$$V_t = 1\,000\,000 - 99\,000t$$

From this it follows that when $t = 4$ and $t = 10$ respectively, we have

$$V_4 = 1\,000\,000 - (4)(99\,000) = £604\,000$$
$$V_{10} = 1\,000\,000 - (10)(99\,000) = £10\,000$$

As we have already suggested, however, assets typically do not depreciate in a simple linear manner. In practice, much of the depreciation takes place in the first two or three years, implying that the annual depreciation is not constant over the asset's life.

Consequently, if we employ a discrete annual discounting approach we would require that our expression for V_t adopts a value of 1 000 000 when $t = 0$ and a value of 10 000 after ten years. This can be provided by an expression such as

$$V_t = 1\,000\,000/(1 + i)^t$$

Notice that when $t = 0$, $V_t = 1\,000\,000$ [since $(1 + i)^0 = 1$]. Furthermore, since we know that when $t = 10$, V_t must equal 10 000, we can write

$$V_{10} = 10\,000 = 1\,000\,000/(1 + i)^{10}$$

Therefore

$$(1 + i)^{10} = 100$$

implying that $(1 + i) = 1.5848$

For this problem we can then write

$$V_t = 1\,000\,000/(1.5848^t)$$

This means that the annual *depreciation quotient* is given by 1.5848^t, which, since it contains a term in t, satisfies our basic requirement that the annual depreciation varies over the life of the asset.

Once again we can calculate V_4 and V_{10} to be

$$V_4 = 1\ 000\ 000/(1.5848^4) = £158\ 489.32$$
$$V_{10} = 1\ 000\ 000/(1.5848^{10}) = 10\ 000$$

Compare these two figures with those that we obtained for the linear depreciation model and notice that in the linear case 39.6 per cent of the asset's original value had been depreciated in the first four years, whereas in our last case the equivalent figure is 84.15 per cent. In both cases, however, the scrap value after ten years is £10 000.

Taking the argument one stage further, we could argue that depreciation is in fact a continuous process, and that we should model it with an appropriate exponential function.

This being the case, we then require an expression such as

$$V_t = 1\ 000\ 000/e^{it}$$

Once again, this expression means that when $t = 0$, $e^{it} = 1$ and so $V_0 = 1\ 000\ 000$. And using the same method as before, we have

$$V_{10} = 10\ 000 = 1\ 000\ 000/e^{10i}$$

Therefore

$$e^{10i} = 100$$

and

$$i = \ln 100/10 = 0.4605$$

WORKSHEET 4.6

	A	B
1	Initial Value	1000000
2	Scrap Value	10000
3	Life of Asset	10
4	Year for Required Asset Value	10
5		
6		
7	Linear Depreciation:	
8	Asset Value	10000
9		
10	Annual Discounting:	
11	Depreciation Quotient	1.5848931925
12	Asset value	10000
13		
14	Continuous Depreciation:	
15	Depreciation Quotient	0.4605170186
16	Asset Value	10000
17		

The denominator of our expression for V_t, i.e. $e^{0.4605t}$, can be thought of as the continuous depreciation quotient.

Once again it is now a straightforward matter to obtain V_4 and V_{10} for this specification of the depreciation process as

$$V_4 = 1\,000\,000/e^{(4)(0.4604)} = £158\,500.00$$
$$V_{10} = 1\,000\,000/e^{(10)(0.4604)} = 10\,000$$

As you can see, these figures are almost identical to those obtained on the basis of annual discounting.

Lotus can perform any of these calculations for you as shown in Worksheet 4.6. Once you have prepared this worksheet, you should find that our previous results are reproduced, and you can use it to experiment with different values for the required asset value year.

EXAMPLE 4.8

Calculate the value at the end of 1988 of an asset that was purchased at the end of 1984 for £250 000 and will be written off for a scrap value of £1000 at the end of 1999. Depreciation is to be calculated using each of the following methods: (a) straight line; (b) annual discounting; and (c) continuous discounting.

SOLUTION 4.8

The solutions can be obtained directly from Worksheet 4.6 if you enter the appropriate amounts. (Remember that the asset's life is 15 years and that you require the value of the asset four years after its purchase.) These solutions are: (a) £183 600; (b) £57 344.179; and (c) £57 344.18.

4.5 Investment appraisal

The techniques illustrated above have important applications in any attempt to evaluate the relative merits of financial projects that yield differing returns at different points in time.

For example, consider a firm that is trying to decide whether to purchase a new machine with an initial cost of £10 000. Suppose also that this machine is expected to provide revenue of £6000 at the end of both its first and second year of use. Thereafter the machine is scrapped without any scrap value.

If the market interest rate is 12 per cent per annum, compounded annually, does this machine represent a viable investment?

It should be clear that the stream of income furnished by the machine must be brought back to the present so that it can be compared with the current cost of

£10 000. Consequently, we must evaluate

$$PV_2 = 6000/(1.12) + 6000/(1.12^2) = £10\ 140.30$$

This figure, representing as it does the value just now of the future stream of income from the machine, must be compared with the cost of £10 000 which must be laid out in order to produce the income stream. Consequently we can form the difference between the present value of the income stream, and the initial cost, to obtain a figure that is known as the net present value (NPV). That is

$$NPV = PV - C$$

where C represents the initial cost of the machine.

In our example, the NPV is £140.30 (£10 140.30 − £10 000) and since this figure is *positive* we would recommend that the machine is purchased in preference to the alternative available: that alternative being to place the funds on deposit at the going market rate of interest of 12 per cent.

This means that the implication of a positive (negative) NPV is that the project being appraised provides an implied rate of return that is greater (less) than the currently available market rate of return.

To see this, imagine that the funds had been placed on deposit for two years at the prevailing rate of 12 per cent per annum (compounded annually). The amount after two years is easily calculated as

$$10\ 000(1.12)^2 = £12\ 544.00$$

This raises an apparent difficulty in the light of our declared preference for the project, since simple arithmetic suggest that the machine will provide a terminal sum of £6000 + £6000 = £12 000; which is *less* than the £12 544 that could have been obtained from the bank.

However, this is to forget that the first return of £6000 from the machine occurs *after one year* and is therefore available to be placed on deposit at the going market rate.

When this is done the terminal value of the returns from the machine are calculated to be

$$£6000(1.12) + £6000 = £12\ 720.00$$

This figure exceeds the terminal value that would have been obtained from the bank by £176.00, thereby confirming our conclusion that purchasing the machine is a superior financial project to the alternative use of the funds.

A problem arises, however, when we attempt to measure this superiority. This is because we have two apparently conflicting measures. On the one hand, on the basis of the NPV calculation, the machine appears to be £140.30 superior to a 12 per cent of return. Whereas on the other hand, this superiority has also been calculated to be £176.00.

In fact, there is no conflict here, since you should be able to see that a *terminal* superiority of £176.00 is identical to a *current* superiority of £140.30 if the current market rate of interest is 12 per cent. This is because the present value of £176.00, discounted at 12 per cent for 2 years, is £140.32.

The net result of this discussion is twofold. First, the NPV technique assumes that the incoming funds are placed on deposit at the going market rate *immediately* they become available.

Secondly, the NPV figure gives the current net superiority of the project being appraised in comparison with the rate of return available from the alternative uses of the funds. This last rate of return is the figure to be used as the discount rate in the NPV calculations, and will usually be taken as the current market rate of interest.

You can save calculational time in many of these problems if you familiarize yourself with the Lotus Net Present Value function, @(NPV), which is constructed as follows:

```
@NPV(Discount Rate, Range of Receipts)
```

Definition The Lotus @NPV function @NPV(i, Receipt Range) calculates the NPV of the stream of returns entered in the range specified in the second argument. The first element in this range should always be the receipt that is received after one year, and the last element in the range should always be the last receipt. All cost items should be entered as negative terms, but initial costs (i.e. year 0, as opposed to recurring costs) should not be entered in the second argument of the function.

You can see how this function works if you reconsider our last illustration about the machine, as shown in Worksheet 4.7. Notice how we have forced Lotus to obtain the present value of the receipts and then added on the (negative) initial cost at its nominal value. This is necessary because the @NPV function will perform incorrectly if the initial cost is included in the argument range. What you must do is specify the range so that the first cell reference represents the cost or return to be received after one year and the last cell reference represents the final element in the income stream.

As you can confirm, Lotus will evaluate the contents of the B5 cell to be £140.32.

At this stage you can also use the @NPV function to rework Example 4.5 and confirm the results for that problem that you obtained manually (see Worksheet 4.8). As you can see, we have applied the @NPV formula in B6 to the range of

```
WORKSHEET 4.7
              A                        B
  1   Initial Cost              -10000
  2     1st Return                6000
  3     2nd Return                6000
  4   Discount Rate                 0.12
  5   Net Present Value   @NPV(B4,B2..B3)+B1
  6
```

WORKSHEET 4.8

B6: @NPV(B9,B2..B5)

	A	B
1	Initial Cost/Revenue	1000
2	Year 1 Income	2000
3	Year 2 Income	2500
4	Year 3 Income	1500
5	Year 4 Income	1000
6	Present Value	5380.672
7	Net Present Value	6380.672
8		
9	Discount Rate	0.13
10		

WORKSHEET 4.9

B8: @NPV(A8,B$2..B$5)+B$1

	A	B
1	Initial Cost/Revenue	-10000
2	Year 1 Income	6000
3	Year 2 Income	6000
4	Year 3 Income	0
5	Year 4 Income	0
6		
7	Discount Rate	Net Present Value
8	0	2000
9	0.01	1822.370
10	0.02	1649.365
11	0.03	1480.818
12	0.04	1316.568
13	0.05	1156.462
14	0.06	1000.355
15	0.07	848.1090
16	0.08	699.5884
17	0.09	554.6671
18	0.1	413.2231
19	0.11	275.1400
20	0.12	140.3061
21	0.13	8.614613
22	0.14	-120.036
23	0.15	-245.746
24	0.16	-368.608
25	0.17	-488.713
26	0.18	-606.147
27	0.19	-720.994
28	0.2	-833.333
29	0.21	-943.241
30	0.22	-1050.79
31	0.23	-1156.05
32	0.24	-1259.10
33	0.25	-1360

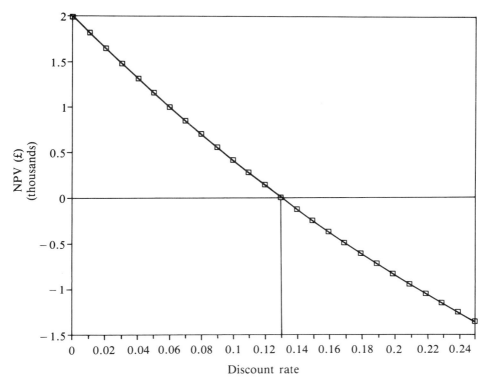

Figure 4.2 NPV as a function of time

receipts in B2..B5, and then added the initial cost to this figure to obtain the NPV in B7.

As you might imagine, the NPV figure obtained for any problem is highly dependent upon the discount rate that is used. We can see this more clearly in Worksheet 4.9 where the @NPV function for the data of the machine illustration (Worksheet 4.7) has been calculated for a number of discount rates. These are then graphed in Figure 4.2.

As you can see, the value of @NPV declines steadily as the discount rate increases, and becomes negative for rates in excess of 13 per cent. This is an important point, since it indicates the *threshold* value of the discount rate that will make viable projects non-viable. In this sense, as we will see in the next section, the value of the discount rate that makes the value of @NPV = 0 can be interpreted as a measure of the rate of return being supplied by the project.

EXAMPLE 4.9

A power station is to be constructed at the start of 1990 at a capital cost of £100 million. Its expected useful lifetime is 18 years, and during this time is expected to produce an average of 1 million megawatt hours (MWh) per annum. The operational costs of the power station are estimated to be £10 million per annum in its first year of operation, and these are expected to increase at an average rate of 6 per cent over the power station's operational life.

The electricity produced is sold at a price of £25 per MWh in its first year of operation, but the price will be raised at an annual rate of 4 per cent per annum.

Assuming that all costs and revenues accrue at the end of each operational year and that the company employs a discount rate of 15 per cent calculate the NPV of the project and comment on its financial viability.

SOLUTION 4.9

Worksheet 4.10 shows the solution.

Three formulae have been used to generate the cost, revenue and net income entries:

in B4	+B3*(1.06)	which is then copied into the cells B5..B20.
in C4	+C3*(1.04)	which is then copied into the range C4..C20.
in D2	+C2−B2	which is then copied to the relevant range.

Finally, the NPV is calculated from the formula (in E2) as @NPV(0.15, D3..D20)+D2.

WORKSHEET 4.10

```
E2: @NPV(0.15,D3..D20)+D2
```

	A	B	C	D	E
1	Year	Costs	Revenues	Net Income	Net Present Value
2	1990	100.00		-100.00	4.59
3	1991	10.00	25.00	15.00	
4	1992	10.60	26.00	15.40	
5	1993	11.24	27.04	15.80	
6	1994	11.91	28.12	16.21	
7	1995	12.62	29.25	16.62	
8	1996	13.38	30.42	17.03	
9	1997	14.19	31.63	17.45	
10	1998	15.04	32.90	17.86	
11	1999	15.94	34.21	18.28	
12	2000	16.89	35.58	18.69	
13	2001	17.91	37.01	19.10	
14	2002	18.98	38.49	19.50	
15	2003	20.12	40.03	19.90	
16	2004	21.33	41.63	20.30	
17	2005	22.61	43.29	20.68	
18	2006	23.97	45.02	21.06	
19	2007	25.40	46.82	21.42	
20	2008	26.93	48.70	21.77	

4.6 The internal rate of return

If we now reconsider our machine example of the previous section, it will be remembered that it was shown that with a discount rate of 12 per cent the NPV of the project was £140.32. Now this must surely mean that the implied rate of return on this project was somewhat in excess of 12 per cent, otherwise the NPV would be zero.

Nevertheless, 'somewhat in excess of 12 per cent' is not a sufficiently exact statement for our purposes, so the question arises of how to obtain an exact figure for the implied rate of return yielded by the project.

The answer to this question is supplied by a concept known as the internal rate of return (IRR), and is defined as follows:

> The IRR is that rate of return, which, if used as the discount rate would make the NPV of the project exactly equal to 0.

In other words

$$IRR = i \text{ such that } PV - C = 0$$

If we apply this idea to our machine illustration, then we are required to find i such that

$$6000/(1+i) + 6000/(1+i)^2 - 10\,000 = 0$$

This should be recognized as a quadratic equation, which, if we let $x = (1+i)$ can be rewritten and solved as follows:

$$6000/x + 6000/x^2 - 10\,000 = 0$$

Multiply all terms by x^2 to produce

$$6000x + 6000 - 10\,000x^2 = 0$$

Divide through by 1000 and rearrange to obtain

$$-10x^2 + 6x + 6 = 0$$

Solve by the quadratic formula, and obtain

$$x = 1.1306 \quad \text{or} \quad x = -0.5306$$

Now since $x = (1+i)$ this means that $i = 0.1306$ or -1.5306, and when we ignore the meaningless negative root we have

$$IRR = i = 0.1306 \text{ (i.e. 13.06 per cent)}$$

This confirms our earlier statement that the IRR would be 'somewhat in excess of 12 per cent'.

You can also confirm that this is indeed the IRR by substituting a value of $i = 0.1306$ into the NPV expression, whereupon you will find that the NPV does in fact become zero. This will only be the case for the data in our example if

$i = 0.1306$. That is

$$6000/(1.1306) + 6000/(1.1306^2) - 10\,000 = 0$$

As a further illustration of this concept consider the following example.

EXAMPLE 4.10

Find the IRR of the following cost and income stream.

An initial expenditure of £12 000, followed by revenue of £8000 after one year and revenue of £6000 after two years.

SOLUTION 4.10

We require i such that

$$PV - C = 8000/(1 + i) + 6000/(1 + i)^2 - 12\,000 = 0$$

Using the same method as before, this can be reduced to the following quadratic equation:

$$-12x^2 + 8x + 6 = 0$$

which has the positive solution $x = 1.115\,06$, implying that $i = 0.115\,06 = 11.506$ per cent.

There are, however, a number of difficulties with the IRR technique when more difficult problems are considered. In particular, where the costs and/or revenues are spread over more than two years, then solving for i involves the solution to high-order polynomial equations.

Fortunately, Lotus has a dedicated internal rate of return function, @IRR, which *provided we recognize its limitations* can eliminate these computational difficulties.

The structure of the @IRR function is

@IRR(Guess, Range)

Definition On the basis of a (preferably realistic) guess of the IRR, the Lotus @IRR function will calculate the internal rate of return of the costs and revenues entered in the second argument range. This range should be constructed so that initial costs precede first-year costs and revenues, which in turn should precede second-year costs and revenues, etc.

You can confirm the results for Example 4.10 above if you prepare Worksheet 4.11. You will find that the correct result (0.11506) is contained in B4.

Now use the IRR function to find the internal rate of return of the stream of costs and revenues associated with Example 4.9. You can use Worksheet 4.10 and

```
WORKSHEET 4.11
  B4: @IRR(0.1,B1..B3)
                       A                      B
         1    Initial Cost/Revenue        -12000
         2    Year 1 Income                 8000
         3    Year 2 Income                 6000
         4    Internal Rate of Return      0.115069
         5
```

add the following two entries:

in E3   internal rate of return
in E4   @IRR(0.2, D2..D20)

You should obtain a result of 0.15797.

You can also confirm that this is indeed the IRR if you use this figure as the discount rate in the @NPV formula contained in E2. The resulting value for the NPV will become 0 if 0.157 97 is the IRR.

As was hinted at earlier however, there are limitations upon the validity of the IRR under certain patterns of cash flows. In particular, an unambiguous result will only be obtained from any Lotus IRR calculation if the signs of the net cash flows correspond to one of the following patterns:

− + + + +   Costs just now, revenues later.
− − + + + +   Costs just now and after one period, revenues thereafter.
− + + + + + −   Costs just now and at the end of the project, revenues in between.

If the actual pattern of net cash flows does not correspond to one of these patterns, then the IRR as calculated can often be ambiguous and even misleading.

4.7 The annual percentage rate

The notion of the annual percentage rate (APR) as frequently seen in advertisements stems from the idea that if the stream of repayments needed to repay a given debt is *not* on the same time basis as quoted in the nominal rate of interest, then the effective rate of interest will differ from this nominal rate.

As we will see, the APR is very closely related to the IRR and EAR concepts, but before we make this association explicit consider the following illustration.

A lender quotes a flat rate of 10 per cent per annum, and requires that a debt of £5000 is to be repaid in two equal annual instalments.

The fact that it is a flat rate which has been quoted has two important implications. First, it means that the repayments are *not* made on a reducing balance basis. Secondly, it means that interest is calculated on a simple rather than a compound basis.

This means that the total interest on the debt is calculated to be $(0.1)(5000) = £500$ for each of the two years for which the debt is outstanding. This gives a total interest requirement of £1000 and a total debt to be repaid of £6000.

From this it is easys see that two annual instalments of £3000 are needed to repay the debt plus interest.

Now if the first repayment is to be made in one year's time, and if the second is to be made in two years' time, then we can calculate the annual percentage rate of interest that will make the present value of this stream of repayments exactly equal to the sum that was borrowed. In other words, we can solve for i in the following expression:

$$3000/(1+i) + 3000/(1+i)^2 = 5000$$

Now you should see the similarity with the IRR concept, since this last expression is similar to the ones we used in explaining the idea of the IRR.

When you solve for i in this expression (either on Lotus or manually) you will obtain a value of 0.1306. This figure is called the APR, and in our illustration indicates that the quoted flat rate of 10 per cent is in fact equivalent to an effective rate that is slightly in excess of 13 per cent.

Several points are worth noting about the APR.

1. Like the IRR it is frequently difficult to calculate, and subject to the same reservations.
2. If annual repayments on the debt are made on an annually reducing balance basis, then the APR and the nominal rate are the same.

To see this, suppose that a debt of £5000 is to be repaid in two equal annual instalments on a reducing balance basis. If the nominal interest rate is 10 per cent compounded annually, then, as you can easily confirm, the Lotus @PMT function will calculate the required repayments to be

$$@PMT(5000, 0.1, 2) = £2880.95$$

Now since these repayments are on a reducing balance basis, and since it is assumed that the first payment will be made after one year, the APR on this debt can be found from calculating the value of i such that

$$2880.95/(1+i) + 2880.95/(1+i)^2 = 5000$$

Clearly we can obtain the required value of i in the same way as before. This is done in Worksheet 4.12.

When you evaluate the contents of B4 you should find that a value of 0.1 (10 per cent) is returned. In other words, annual repayments on a reducing balance basis at a nominal annual interest rate of i represent the only situation in which the calculated APR is the same as the quoted nominal rate.

Of course very few debts are actually repaid on an annual basis, as anyone who

WORKSHEET 4.12

```
B4: (F3) @IRR(0.1,B1..B3)
```

	A	B
1	Initial Cost/Revenue	-5000
2	Year 1 Income	2880.95
3	Year 2 Income	2880.95
4	Internal Rate of Return	0.100
5		

has a mortgage or a bank loan will appreciate. In these cases monthly repayments tend to be the norm, and this means that any quoted annual rate (even if repayments are on a reducing balance basis) will not represent the APR unless the repayments are also annual. You can see this quite easily in the following two examples.

EXAMPLE 4.11

The following credit terms are offered by a car manufacturer for one of its cheaper models.

Special credit offer 3% interest	(APR = 5.80%)
List price	£3637.82
List price less 25% deposit	£2728.37
First year's interest (3% flat)	£81.85
Second year's interest (3% flat)	£81.85
Total debt plus interest	£2892.07
Number of monthly instalments	24
Monthly repayments (2892.07/24)	£120.50
APR	0.0580

The question we require to address is how a flat rate of 3 per cent becomes equivalent to an APR of 5.80 per cent. The answer derives from finding the value of i such that

$$2728.37 = 120.5/(1+i) + 120.5/(1+i)^2 + \cdots + 120.5/(1+i)^{24}$$

If you use the Lotus @IRR function as illustrated above, then you will obtain a result of 0.004 712 (i.e. 0.4712 per cent). Now since the repayments are monthly, this last figure is the monthly rate and so to obtain the APR we must calculate the EAR $(1.004\,712^{12} - 1)$ to obtain 0.0580 (i.e. 5.80 per cent per annum).

Remember to include the sum borrowed as a positive item (in B1 say), and the 24 monthly repayments as negative entries (in B2..B25 say). You can then obtain the IRR of this debt repayment stream in C1 from @IRR(0.1, B1..B25), and the APR in D1 from $(1 + C1)^{12} - 1$.

EXAMPLE 4.12

A £30 000 mortgage is taken out over 25 years at a guaranteed nominal rate of 13 per cent per annum. The repayments on this debt are made monthly but the debt is serviced on an annual reducing balance basis. Calculate the size of the monthly repayments and the APR on this debt.

SOLUTION 4.12

The annual repayments on the debt are calculated from the Lotus @PMT function to be

$$@PMT(30\,000, 0.13, 25) = £4092.77 \text{ per annum}$$

Consequently, the monthly repayments are

$$4092.77/12 = £341.06$$

The APR on this debt is i such that

$$30\,000 = 341.06/(1 + i) + 341.06/(1 + i)^2 + \cdots + 341.06/(1 + i)^{300}$$

On some versions of Lotus this problem is a bit too large for the @IRR function to handle; however, you can confirm that a monthly rate of 0.010 933 makes the present value of the 300 monthly payments of £341.06 exactly equal to £30 000. The APR (EAR) on this debt is therefore 13.94 per cent ($1.0109^{12} - 1$) per annum, and exceeds the nominal rate (13 per cent) *for no other reason* than the fact that the repayments are made monthly while the balance of the debt is only reduced annually.

4.8 Financial security appraisal

There is one crucial difference between compounding and discounting that has not yet been considered. This derives from the notion that while the terminal value of an annuity of n payments can be obtained from the sum to n terms of the appropriate geometric progression; the fact that the common factor $[m = (1 + i)]$ of this series is greater than 1 means that the sum to infinity does not exist. In other words the series does not reach a definite limit.

In discounting, on the other hand, the common factor is given by $m = 1/(1 + i)$, which, being less than 1, means that an appropriate sum to infinity can be obtained.

Consider, for example, an annuity of £100 per annum in perpetuity (i.e. forever).

If the interest rate is represented by i and is compounded annually, then this has a present value given by

$$PV = 100 + 100/(1 + i) + 100/(1 + i)^2 + \cdots + 100/(1 + i)^n$$

Now as n tends to infinity this expression has a sum to infinity (S_∞) given by

$$PV = S_\infty = a/(1 - m)$$

where a is the first term and m is the common factor. Furthermore, since we know that $m = 1/(1 + i)$ this means that

$$PV = S_\infty = 100/[1 - 1/(1 + i)]$$

which, after some algebra, reduces to

$$PV = S_\infty = 100(1 + i)/i$$

Hence if $i = 0.1$ we have

$$PV = 100(1.1)/0.1 = £1100$$

This may seem, at first sight, both perplexing and irrelevant since perpetual annuities are uncommon securities and would surely have a present value that is considerably more than indicated above. However, this is a mistaken view on two counts.

First, many government bonds (such as Consols) are undated securities which promise to pay a fixed interest coupon in perpetuity and can properly be regarded as perpetual annuities.

Secondly, the fact that some of the income elements are received so far in the future means that when these are discounted (i.e. divided) by $(1 + i)$ raised to a very large power they become insignificant. For this reason, most of the numerical worth of the PV figure is obtained from the terms in the earlier years, with subsequent terms becoming increasingly insignificant.

This can be appreciated if we consider a fixed interest security that is purchased for £100 and promises to bear 8 per cent per annum in perpetuity. This means that there is an infinite stream of payments of $(0.08)(10) = £8$ and if we use a discount rate of 8 per cent per annum to bring this stream back to the present, we obtain

$$PV = 8 + 8/1.08 + 8/1.08^2 + \cdots + 8/1.08^n$$

Then, as n tends to infinity the value of PV tends to S_∞ and we have

$$S_\infty = (8)(1.08)/0.08 = £108$$

It is, however, slightly unrealistic to assume that the purchased security provides its first £8 interest coupon immediately it is bought, and consequently we must modify the stream accordingly.

Assuming that the first interest coupon is received 1 year after the purchase of the bond, the stream of interest payments becomes

$$8/1.08 + 8/1.08^2 + \cdots + 8/1.08^n$$

which is an infinite geometric progression in which the first term is 8/1.08 and the common factor is 1/1.08.

The sum to infinity is therefore given by

$$S_\infty = (8/1.08)/(1 - 1/1.08) = 8/0.08 = £100$$

In general, then, if an undated security promises to bear a fixed interest coupon of £R per annum in perpetuity, and if the first coupon is to be received one year from now, the present value of that perpetual stream of income is given by

$$PV = R/i$$

where i is the current market discount rate.

If the purchase price of the security is denoted by £M and if the fixed interest rate on the bond is i per annum it follows that $R = iM$, and the present value becomes

$$PV = R/i = iM/i = M$$

This is an important result, since it implies that when a new undated bond is issued, the purchase price (M) must be the same as the infinite sum of the discounted values of its fixed interest coupons.

Suppose, however, that after this security is issued (bearing what will then be the current market rate of interest), this market rate falls. What will happen to the price that could be obtained for the original security if it was offered for sale?

You should be able to see that if new bonds bear less than old bonds, then the old ones are relatively more attractive, and consequently one would expect their *market* price to rise above their *nominal* price. This is indeed the case as the following illustration will indicate:

Nominal purchase price = £100
Fixed interest rate = 0.1
Fixed interest coupon = £10
Present value of coupons = 10/0.1 = £100

Now assume that the market rate falls to 8 per cent. New bonds with a nominal purchase price of £100 now bear a coupon of £8. That is

Nominal purchase price = £100
Fixed interest rate = 0.08
Fixed interest coupon = £8
Present value of coupons = 8/0.08 = £100

However, if we apply the new (lower) interest rate as the discount rate for the appraisal of the old bond (with the £10 coupon) then we obtain

$$10/0.08 = £125.00$$

This figure represents the maximum price that the old bond with the £10 coupon could be sold for. This is because if £125 is paid for a bond with a £10 coupon,

```
WORKSHEET 4.13
  B5: +B3/B4

                      A                              B
       1   Price of Bond                            100
       2   Guaranteed Nominal Interest Rate         0.1
       3   Interest Coupon                          +B1*B2
       4   Current Market Interest Rate             0.080
       5   Market Price of Bond                     125
       6
```

this will produce an annual stream of income that represents the same annual percentage return (10/125 = 8 per cent), as that from a bond with an £8 coupon for which £100 was paid.

If the interest rate subsequently rises to 12 per cent, for example, then the 10 per cent bond has a PV of 10/0.12 = £85, while the 8 per cent bonds have a PV of 8/0.12 = £67.50.

These points are shown more clearly in Worksheet 4.13 where all bonds have a nominal purchase price of £100, but where their current market price is calculated on the basis of any difference between their nominal guaranteed rate and the current market rate. As you can confirm for yourself, Lotus will evaluate the contents of B5 to be 125.00, but you can enter any other figures that you want and obtain the correct market price.

There is a final point to be drawn from this analysis, which you can see if you consider the following illustration.

Suppose that the current market rate of interest is 8 per cent. Then all bonds previously issued at rates less than 8 per cent have a market value less than their nominal price. Any investor who is forced to sell one of these bonds will therefore take a capital loss.

Conversely, any securities issued at the current rate of interest or previously issued at rates in excess of this current rate have a market value that is at least equal to their nominal price and could therefore be sold without capital loss and often with capital gain.

This principle explains why all financial newspapers find it necessary to quote the going market prices for a wide range of undated securities.

4.9 The financial arithmetic of inflation

In this section we will consider the idea of using an economy's annual inflation rate as the discount rate in the process of converting monetary sums into real amounts.

For example, consider an economy in which the inflation rate is 10 per cent per annum, and in which an individual receives a fixed income of £100 each year.

Imagine also, for the sake of simplicity, that there is only one product on which she can spend this income and that in the current year the price of this product is £5.

Common sense suggests that the £100 can purchase a maximum of 20 products and consequently we can calculate her real income as

$$100/5 = 20 \text{ (products)}$$

In general, then, we have the definition of real income (Y) as money income (M) divided by an index of the level of prices (P). That is

$$Y = M/P$$

Now consider the same individual a year later. Her nominal income is still £100, but because of the inflation rate of 10 per cent per annum, the price of the product has risen to £5.50 and consequently her real income has fallen to

$$100/5(1.1) = 18.18 \text{ (products)}$$

Similarly, after two years her real income will be

$$100/(5)(1.1)^2 = 16.529 \text{ (products)}$$

This idea can be generalized to a situation in which the inflation rate (expressed as a decimal) is m per annum, the price level in the current period is P and the level of nominal income for the whole period is constant and equal to M. We then have Y equal to the real current income given by

$$Y = M/P(1+m)^t$$

Of course it is highly unlikely that the individual's nominal income is fixed throughout the whole period and consequently we can denote its value in any time period by M_t.

Our last expression above then becomes

$$Y = M_t/P(1+m)^t$$

If, in addition, M_t behaves in a systematic manner (increasing at a rate of w per annum, for example) the last expression above becomes

$$Y = M(1+w)^t/P(1+m)^t$$

As you can see, when $t = 0$ (i.e. in the current time period) we have

$$Y = M/P$$

which is the simple case that we started from.

Now consider a situation in which an individual is guaranteed £100 just now, and at the end of each of the next four years (i.e. five payments in total). Suppose also that the annual inflation and interest rates are expected to be m and i respectively for the whole period. The problem is to calculate the real present value of this income stream, and we can proceed as follows.

The nominal stream of income is given by
$$M = 100 + 100 + 100 + 100 + 100$$
The real income stream (Y) is therefore
$$Y = 100/P + 100/P(1+m) + 100/P(1+m)^2 + 100/P(1+m)^3 + 100/P(1+m)^4$$
The present value of this real income stream, i.e. real present value (RPV) is
$$\text{RPV} = 100/P + 100/P(1+m)(1+i) + 100/P(1+m)^2(1+i)^2 \\ + 100/P(1+m)^3(1+i)^3 + 100/P(1+m)^4(1+i)^4$$

In general, then, if the level of prices in the current period is P, if a nominal amount of M_t is to be received t periods from now, and if the annual inflation and interest rates for the period are m and i respectively, then the RPV of a nominal payment received t years from now is given by
$$\text{RPV} = M_t/P(1+m)^t(1+i)^t$$
Furthermore, if the amount M^t is part of a stream of payments then the RPV of that stream is given by
$$\text{RPV} = M_0/P + M_1/P(1+m)(1+i) + \cdots + M_t/P(1+m)^t(1+i)^t$$

EXAMPLE 4.13

Find the RPV of a stream of four payments of $M_0 = 10$, $M_1 = 12$, $M_2 = 15$ and $M_3 = 15$, when the current level of prices is 100 and the expected annual interest and inflation rates for the period are 11 and 15 per cent respectively.

SOLUTION 4.13

The RPV is given by
$$\text{RPV} = 10 + 12/(1.15)(1.11) + 15/(1.15^2)(1.11^2) + 15(1.15^3)(1.11^3) \\ = 10 + 9.4 + 9.20 + 7.21$$
Therefore
$$\text{RPV} = 36.81 \text{ (real income units)}$$

4.10 Exercises

4.1

A building society offers potential clients two different savings schemes: A and B. Scheme A guarantees an interest rate of 9.25 per cent per annum compounded annually, while scheme B offers an interest rate of 9 per cent per annum compounded quarterly.

(a) Which of the two schemes is to be preferred if a saver wishes to obtain the greatest increase in the value, after 4 years, of a given deposit made just now?
(b) The building society now decides that the annual interest rate on scheme A should be adjusted so that a given deposited sum will yield the same amount after a whole number (n) of years ($n > 1$), as it would if placed in scheme B (which still offers 9 per cent per annum compounded quarterly). What should the annual interest rate on scheme A now be?
(c) A rival insurance company decides to offer the following alternative savings plan. For an initial deposit, now, of £1000 the company guarantees a lump sum of £800 after two years, a further lump sum of £500 two years later (i.e. four years after the initial deposit), and nothing thereafter.

Should a saver accept this scheme in preference to either of the schemes offered by the building society in part (b) above?

4.2

A firm is considering the purchase of a new computer that is expected to produce annual net savings in labour costs of £8000 in each of the six years of its operational life.

The computer has an initial cost of £30 000, and maintenance costs of £1000 and all savings and maintenance costs accrue at the *end* of each relevant year.

The company has access to funds at the current market interest rate of 14 per cent per annum, compounded annually, and wishes to decide whether the purchase of the computer is a worthwhile investment.

(a) Explain how such a decision can be aided by discounting methods, and provide a recommendation to the potential purchaser on the basis of such an analysis.
(b) If the market rate of interest fell to 8.5 per cent per annum, would the decision reached in (a) above be altered?
(c) In an attempt to finalize the sale, the computer salesperson offers the firm a 'trade-in' after six years, the terms of which guarantee a £7500 reduction in the price of a replacement computer. Would such an offer alter the decision reached in (a) above (at the 14 per cent interest rate)?

4.3

A firm wishes to acquire a new company car, but has to decide whether it should purchase the vehicle outright or lease one from a leasing company. It intends to keep the car for three years and employs a 12 per cent discount rate in all its investment projects. The relevant expenditures for the alternative acquisition schemes are given below.

Purchase of car
Purchase price = £5000
Service contract for maintenance, service, repair, etc. (payable at the start of years 1 and 2) = £200
Resale value of the car after 3 years = £3500

Leasing scheme
Annual lease (payable at the start of each year for a minimum of three payments) = £1000
Maintenance costs and resale value = 0

(a) Which of the two schemes should the firm choose?
(b) Because of the cashflow situation, the £5000 for the purchase of the car would have to be borrowed from the bank at an interest rate of 12 per cent and repaid in equal annual instalments at the end of each of the three years. What difference does this make to the choice of schemes?
(c) If the borrowing rate demanded by the bank is increased to 18 per cent and the repayment method is as in (b), what difference does this make to the choice of schemes?

4.4

A whisky manufacturer has just completed a production run of 10 000 barrels of whisky at a unit production cost of £400 per barrel. The whisky must be matured for five years before it can be sold and this will impose storage costs of £10 per barrel per annum.

Bottling and labelling a *mature* barrel of whisky will cost £4 per barrel.

The current selling price of a barrel of this whisky is £500, but this is expected to increase by an average of 10 per cent per annum in each of the next five years.

If the current market rate of interest is 11 per cent per annum, design a spreadsheet that will calculate the net present value of the manufacturer's 10 000 barrels of whisky.

How does this net present value change if the interest rate falls to 9 per cent two years after the production run is completed?

4.5

A forestry commission has just planted an area of land with 10 000 saplings at a cost of £11 per tree, £1 of which was planting costs (the remainder being purchase cost).

The trees will be ready for cutting after 10 years at the earliest, and during the maturing period grow at an annual compound rate such that the value of usable wood increases each year by 20 per cent of the initial purchase cost of each tree.

During the maturing period the annual cost of tending the plantation is expected to be equal to 1.5 per cent of the value of the plantation at the start of that year, payable at the start of the *second* and all subsequent years. (The first year's tending costs are included in the planting cost at the start of the first year.)

If the forestry commission employs a discount rate of 10 per cent per annum for the whole period, prepare a spreadsheet that will calculate the net present value of the plantation on the assumption that all of the trees are felled as soon as they mature and that the cost of this felling is 5 per cent of the value of trees felled.

4.6

The forestry commissioners of the previous exercise know that once the trees are mature, then by expert management of the forest they can increase the annual rate of growth of usable wood by *0.5 per cent of its previous growth rate* for every 1 per cent reduction in the value of trees per acre. Accordingly, the following felling strategy is operated.

Fell 50 per cent of the forest value after 10 years, then fell 50 per cent of the remaining value after 11 years, and then fell all of the remaining value after 12 years.

Prepare a spreadsheet that will model this new strategy and then decide whether the net present value of the plantation has increased (as compared to the result of Exercise 4.5).

Assuming that all of the felling must take place at or within two years from maturity, can you suggest a felling strategy that would improve upon the result above?

4.7

The fixed and annual running costs of operating three different types of factory, and their expected useful lives, are given below.

	Factory A	*Factory B*	*Factory C*
Capital cost (£m)	100	90	95
Labour cost (£m)	0.2	0.6	0.3
Fuel cost (£m)	0.6	0.8	0.2
Life-span (years)	5	8	9

Assuming that all three factories produce the same product, that a discount rate of 11 per cent is employed, and that the running costs occur at the end of each year of operation, rank the three factories in terms of their present costs.

4.8

Reconsider Exercise 3.8 of the previous chapter, and suppose in addition that the shipyard offered the shipping company a deal whereby (after the initial 25 per cent payment) no interest was charged and no further payments were due until 2 years after the ship was delivered, would this make any difference to the decision reached in part (b) of the original exercise?

4.11 Solutions to the exercises

4.1

(a) Letting the initial sum deposited be denoted by P we have the following:

Scheme A
$$A_4 = P(1.0925)^4 = 1.42457P$$

Scheme B
$$A_{4,4} = P(1 + 0.09/4)^{16} = 1.4276P$$

Scheme B is slightly preferable to Scheme A.

(b) The required rate to be offered by Scheme A must be the equivalent annual rate of Scheme B. Therefore
$$\text{EAR}(B) = (1 + i/m)^m - 1$$

Since interest is compounded on a quarterly basis, we have $m = 4$ and with $i = 0.09$, the expression above becomes
$$\text{EAR}(B) = (1 + 0.09/4)^4 - 1 = 0.0930833$$

If this interest rate is offered by Scheme A, then the value of any deposit after four years will be given by
$$P(1.0930833)^4 = 1.4276P$$

i.e. the same as Scheme B.

(c) The insurance policy yields the IRR of the following stream of incomings and outgoings
$$-1000 + 800/(1 + i)^2 + 500/(1 + i)^4$$

Lotus can easily find the IRR of this stream, as Worksheet 4.14 indicates. The entry in B6 is @IRR(0.1, B1..B5).

```
WORKSHEET 4.14
                    A                    B
        1   Initial Cost         -1000
        2   First Income             0
        3   Second Income         800
        4   Third Income            0
        5   Fourth Income         500
        6   Rate of Return        0.101092
        7
```

Since the *best* annual rate that either of the building society schemes offers is 9.308 33 per cent the insurance company offer of 10.109 per cent per annum is to be preferred.

4.2

(a) The relevant costs and returns are illustrated in Worksheet 4.15. The entry in D12 is @NPV(D11, E4..E9) + E3.

Being negative, the NPV figure of −2779.33 indicates that the project is not viable at the discount rate employed. (This is also indicated by the fact that the IRR (in D13) is less than the discount rate.)

(b) If you change the discount rate (in D11) to 0.085, then you will find that the NPV rises to £1875.11. The project has become viable as a result of the reduction in the implied cost of credit. (Positive NPV; IRR > discount rate.)

(c) The £7500 'trade in' means that an extra income item after six years is to be received. You can add this to the existing entry in B6 (so that it becomes 14 500), and then notice that even with a 14 per cent discount rate the effect of the 'trade in' has been to make the NPV on the project positive (£637.58 to be exact). The project is now viable, but only because of the 'trade in'. Notice also that the IRR has risen above the discount rate.

WORKSHEET 4.15

	A	B	C	D	E
1		Labour Cost	Maintenance	Purchase Cost	Net Revenue
2	Year	Savings	Costs		
3	0			−30000	−30000
4	1	8000	−1000	0	7000
5	2	8000	−1000	0	7000
6	3	8000	−1000	0	7000
7	4	8000	−1000	0	7000
8	5	8000	−1000	0	7000
9	6	8000	−1000	0	7000
10					
11		Discount Rate		0.14	
12		Net Present Value		−2779.3273842	
13		IRR		0.1055190382	

4.3

(a) Worksheet 4.16 tabulates the relevant costs and revenues for both the purchase and the leasing scheme. As you can see, the leasing scheme has a less negative NPV and is therefore to be preferred.

(b) The three equal annual payments to repay the loan of £5000 can be obtained

WORKSHEET 4.16

	A	B	C	D	E	F	G
1		Resale	Service	Purchase	Net Revenue		Lease
2	Year	Value	Contract	Price			
3	0			-5000	-5000		-1000
4	1		-200	0	-200		-1000
5	2		-200	0	-200		-1000
6	3	3500	0	0	3500		
7							
8							
9							
10							
11			Discount Rate	0.12			
12			NPV purchase	-2846.779	←@NPV(D11,E4..E6)+E3		
13			NPV lease	-2690.051	←@NPV(D11,G4..G5)+G3		

from

$$@PMT(5000, 0.12, 3) = £2081.74$$

These are included in Worksheet 4.17.

Clearly the situation is unchanged as a result of the new arrangements. You should have expected this to be the case since if the firm employs a discount rate of 12 per cent to the project, then this is effectively *charging itself* an interest rate of 12 per cent for the use of the funds. Since this charge is the same as that made by the bank there will be no change in the NPV of the project.

(c) You can go through the arithmetic if you like, but really there is no need, since we can reason as follows. The increased bank lending rate means the annual repayments on the loan will be higher, which, with a 12 per cent discount rate

WORKSHEET 4.17

	A	B	C	D	E	F	G
1		Resale	Service	Loan Re-	Net Revenue		Lease
2	Year	Value	Contract	payment			
3	0			0	0		-1000
4	1		-200	-2081.74	-2281.74		-1000
5	2		-200	-2081.74	-2281.74		-1000
6	3	3500	0	-2081.74	1418.26		
7							
8							
9							
10							
11			Discount Rate	0.12			
12			NPV loan	-2846.779	←@NPV(D11,E4..E6)+E3		
13			NPV lease	-2690.051	←@NPV(D11,G4..G5)+G3		

means that the NPV of the loan scheme will become more negative. Now since the leasing scheme was preferable before the NPV of the purchase scheme became more negative, it follows that it must be even more preferable now. Consequently, there will be no change in the choice of schemes.

4.4

(a) The selling price (P) of a barrel of whisky in five years' time will be

$$P = 500(1.01)^5 = £805.25$$

(b) The storage, production and bottling costs per barrel, and the eventual income, give rise to the stream of outgoings and incomings shown in Worksheet 4.18. As you can see, with a discount rate of 11 per cent, the NPV per barrel is £38.54, and the NPV of the production run is this last figure times 10 000.

```
WORKSHEET 4.18
   D12: @NPV(D11,F4..F8)+F3

              A        B          C         D         E          F
    1                Storage   Production Bottling  Income    Net Revenue
    2        Year    Cost      Cost       Cost
    3        0                 -400       0         0         -400
    4        1       -10       0          0         0         -10
    5        2       -10       0          0         0         -10
    6        3       -10       0          0         0         -10
    7        4       -10       0          0         0         -10
    8        5       -10       0          -4        805.25    791.25
    9
   10
   11               Discount Rate         0.11
   12               NPV per barrel        38.543906
   13               NPV of Prod Run       385439.06
```

4.5

The value (V) of an average tree on maturity will be given by

$$V_{10} = 10(1.2)^{10} = £61.92$$

The associated costs and revenues give rise to the stream shown in Worksheet 4.19. Notice that the tending costs have been calculated from the formula in D4. This is

$$0.015*(1.2^{\wedge}A4)*B\$3$$

i.e. 1.5 per cent of the plantation value after one year and would be evaluated as $0.015(1.2^1) \times (-10) = -0.18$.

When you copy this formula into the range D5..D13, then the A4 cell becomes

WORKSHEET 4.19

	A	B	C	D	E	F	G
1		Purchase	Planting	Tending	Felling	Income	Net Revenue
2	Year	Cost	Cost	Cost	Cost		
3	0	-10	-1	0.00	0.00	0.00	-11.00
4	1	0	0	-0.18	0.00	0.00	-0.18
5	2	0	0	-0.22	0.00	0.00	-0.22
6	3	0	0	-0.26	0.00	0.00	-0.26
7	4	0	0	-0.31	0.00	0.00	-0.31
8	5	0	0	-0.37	0.00	0.00	-0.37
9	6	0	0	-0.45	0.00	0.00	-0.45
10	7	0	0	-0.54	0.00	0.00	-0.54
11	8	0	0	-0.64	0.00	0.00	-0.64
12	9	0	0	-0.77	0.00	0.00	-0.77
13	10	0	0	-0.93	-3.10	61.92	57.89
14							
15		Discount Rate		0.1			
16		NPV per tree		9.1813046			
17		NPV of forest		91813.046			
18		IRR		0.1650092			

A5 (i.e. after two years), the value of the plantation has increased and as a result so too have the tending costs. This process continues for all the cells in column D that are copied to. (Remember that the tending costs are first calculated at the start of the second year since they are included in the planting cost at the start of the first year.)

The NPV of the average tree is £9.181 and is calculated by the formula in D16, which is

$$@NPV(D15, G4..G13) + G3$$

and so the current value of the forest is given by

$$10\,000(9.181) = £0.091\,81 \text{ million}$$

As you can see the IRR has also been calculated (in D18) from the formula

$$@IRR(0.1, G3..G13)$$

4.6

This is a complicated problem, since we must take careful account of the increased growth in the value of usable wood that takes place in the remainder of the plantation after the first 50 per cent has been felled.

Worksheet 4.20 has been constructed with a view to the second part of the question where variations in the felling rate are to be considered. For this reason it is extremely flexible, and will allow unlimited variation in any of the parameters of the problem.

The top section of Worksheet 4.20 contains the parameters of the problem. They are all self-explanatory except, perhaps, for the entry in B23. This is the 0.5 per cent

WORKSHEET 4.20

	A	B	C	D	E
1	Number of trees at start	10000.00			
2					
3	Value of each tree	10.00			
4					
5	Growth rate during				
6	maturing period	0.20			
7					
8	Number of years until				
9	maturity	10.00			
10					
11	Felling cost per value				
12	of tree felled	0.05			
13					
14	Felling rate at maturity	0.50			
15					
16	Felling rate 1 year				
17	after maturity	0.50			
18					
19	Felling rate 2 years				
20	after maturity	1.00			
21					
22	Growth factor as result				
23	of felling 1%	0.50			
24					
25	Tending Costs as % of				
26	forest value	0.015			
27					
28	Year	10.00	11.00	12.00	13.00
29					
30	Value of trees	619173.64	386983.53	253957.94	0.00
31					
32	Value Felled	309586.82	193491.76	253957.94	
33					
34	Felling Cost	-15479.34	-9674.59	-12697.90	
35					
36	Tending Costs	-9287.60	-5804.75	-3809.37	
37					
38	Net Revenue	284819.88	178012.42	237450.67	
39					
40	Remaining Value	309586.82	193491.76	0.00	
41					
42	Growth Rate of Remainder	0.25	0.31	0.47	
43					
44		Year	Net Revenue		
45		0.00	-110000.00		
46		1.00	-1800.00		
47		2.00	-2200.00		
48		3.00	-2600.00		
49		4.00	-3100.00		
50		5.00	-3700.00		
51		6.00	-4500.00		
52		7.00	-5400.00		
53		8.00	-6400.00		
54		9.00	-7700.00		
55		10.00	284819.88		
56		11.00	178012.42		

```
57                      12.00    237450.67
58
59      NPV                      116476.66
60      IRR                        0.17149
```

figure quoted as the effect upon the rate of growth of usable wood as a result of a 1 per cent reduction in the number of trees per acre.

B30: the value of the trees at maturity is calculated from

$$10\ 000(10)(1.2)^{\wedge}10$$

Given the structure of our worksheet, this translates to

$$+B1*B3*(1+B6)^{\wedge}B9$$

Clearly this gives the same answer as in the previous exercise.

B32: the value felled in this year is 50 per cent of the value at maturity, i.e.

$$+B30*B14$$

B34: the felling cost is 5 per cent of the value of trees felled, i.e.

$$-B12*B32$$

B36: the tending costs are 1.5 per cent of the plantation's current value, i.e.

$$-B26*B30$$

B38: the net revenue is the value felled less tending and felling costs, i.e.

$$+B32+B34+B36$$

(Remember that B34 and B36 will both be negative.)

B40: the remaining plantation value is the difference between its value at maturity and the value felled, i.e.

$$+B30-B32$$

This is the figure to which the growth rate for the next year is to be applied.

B42: the growth rate in the next year changes from its value of 20 per cent as a result of any felling that has taken place. To be exact it increases by 0.5 per cent of its previous value for every 1 per cent of the forest that is felled. So if 50 per cent of the forest is felled, the growth rate of the remainder will increase by 25 per cent of its previous value. This previous value was 20 per cent, so the new value is 20% + 25%(20%) = 25%. The growth factor for the next year is therefore 1.25, and this is to be applied to the remaining forest value.

In general, if we let the growth rate in any year be represented by g_t, and in the previous year by g_{t-1}, then we can write:

$$g_t = g_{t-1}(1 + 0.5 f_{t-1})$$

where f_{t-1} is the felling rate in the previous year.

This means that for year 11 we have

$$g_{11} = 0.2[1 + (0.5)(0.5)] = 0.25$$

This confirms our previous calculation.

For the 12th year we have

$$g_{12} = g_{11}[1 + (0.5)(0.5)] = 0.25(1.25) = 0.3125$$

In terms of the formulae in our worksheet we can translate these ideas as

$$+ B6*(1 + B23*B14)$$

which will be the entry in B42.

C30: the value at the end of the 11th year will be the value of the remainder times the growth factor for the 11th year, i.e.

$$+ B40*(1 + B42)$$

The subsequent entries in this column have the same logic as explained above, until the C42 entry is reached. This entry calculates the growth rate for the next year from the formulae

$$+ B42(1 + B23*B17)$$

i.e. previous growth rate times the increase in the growth rate as a result of the felling that has taken place one year after maturity.

This new growth rate is then applied to the remaining value at the end of the 11th year to give the value at the end of the next year, where since 100 per cent of the plantation is felled the process ends.

When all of these ideas are put together it is found that the new strategy has increased the NPV (and the IRR) of the forest considerably. You can see this in the range B45..B60 where the costs during the maturing period have been included as they were calculated in Exercise 4.5. In fact, using Worksheet 4.20, you can reproduce the results of Exercise 4.5 if you simply make the felling rate at maturity equal to 1. Try it.

But you can also try different felling rates in each of the years in an attempt to improve the NPV. In doing this bear the following two ideas in mind.

1. Since the value of the forest (even during the maturing period) is growing at a rate that exceeds the discount rate (20 per cent exceeds 10 per cent), it follows that the 'cost of waiting' is less than the 'cost of not waiting'. Theoretically this would mean that the forest should never be felled, although in practice the growth rate could not continue to remain positive indefinitely since eventually there would be no space left.
2. In addition to this last point, there is the added complication that felling some of the forest allows the remainder to grow more rapidly. This is clearly an argument that increases the 'cost of waiting' and reduces the 'cost of not waiting'. Obviously these points are operating in different directions since point

WORKSHEET 4.21

	A	B	C	D
27				
28	Year	10	11	12
29				
30	Value of trees	+B1*B3*(1+B6)^B9	+B40*(1+B42)	+C40*(1+C42)
31				
32	Value Felled	+B14*B30	+B17*C30	+B20*D30
33				
34	Felling Cost	-B12*B32	-B12*C32	-B12*D32
35				
36	Tending costs	-B26*B30	-B26*C30	-B26*D30
37				
38	Net Revenue	+B32+B34+B36	+C32+C34+C36	+D32+D34+D36
39				
40	Remaining Value	+B30-B32	+C30-C32	+D30-D32
41				
42	Growth Rate of	+B6*(1+B23*B14)	+B42*(1+B23*B17)	+C42*(1+B23*B20)
43	Remainder			

1 favours waiting, while point 2 favours not waiting, and so the issue revolves around which of these two effects is the greater.

The answer is that for the parameters of this particular model, delaying exercises a slightly stronger effect, but not to the extent of waiting until year 12 before felling any of the trees. A strategy of felling 15 per cent both at maturity and one year after maturity will be found to improve the NPV in comparison to any of the strategies outlined, but you may be able to make further improvements for yourself.

It must be stressed however, that these last observations would not necessarily continue to be the case if, for example, the discount rate rose and/or the effect upon the growth rate of the remainder, of every 1 per cent of forest felled increased (from 0.5 to 1 per cent say).

If you are still finding it hard to visualise the problem, then reread the explanatory notes above and at the same time study the formulae 'dump' contained in Worksheet 4.21.

Because of the flexibility of this worksheet, you can use it to experiment with the ideas contained in this exercise. Change the values of the parameters of the problem (systematically if you can) and then note the effects. It should also constitute a valuable lesson in worksheet design since it is this structure that allows easy variation of the parameter values.

4.7

The costs are tabulated in Worksheet 4.22. Notice that the NPV for each of the

WORKSHEET 4.22

	A	B	C	D
1	Year	Factory A	Factory B	Factory C
2	0	-100	-90	-95
3	1	-0.8	-1.4	-0.5
4	2	-0.8	-1.4	-0.5
5	3	-0.8	-1.4	-0.5
6	4	-0.8	-1.4	-0.5
7	5	-0.8	-1.4	-0.5
8	6		-1.4	-0.5
9	7		-1.4	-0.5
10	8		-1.4	-0.5
11	9			-0.5
12				
13				
14	NPV (A) -102.95671761			
15	NPV (B) -97.204571865			
16	NPV (C) -97.768523766			
17				
18	PV-C (A)-102.95671761			
19	PV-C (B) -97.204571865			
20	PV-C (C) -97.768523766			

Solutions to the exercises 225

three factories is calculated both by the @NPV function and (since the running costs are equal for each factory) by the @PV function.

This means that the entry in B14 is

@NPV(0.11, B3..B7) + B2

while the entry in B18 is

−(@PV(0.8, 0.11, 5) + B2)

(The minus sign at the start of the formula is to compensate for the fact that @PV 'does not like' negative returns as its first argument.)

As you can see, the same result is obtained by either method, and remembering that we are dealing with costs the factory rankings would be B, C, A.

4.8

Now that we are familiar with the concept of the APR we can use this knowledge to approach this problem as shown in Worksheet 4.23.

The APR of the the builder's first scheme is calculated in B5 [from @IRR(0.1, B1..G1)], and the equivalent annual rate of the bank loan is calculated in B6 [from $(1 + 0.105/2)^2 - 1$]. Since the latter is clearly less than the former, this confirms the conclusion that we reached in Chapter 3 that the bank loan is a superior prospect.

The effect of the moratorium on the repayments to the builders is displayed in the second row of the worksheet, and the APR of this scheme is calculated in B7 (from @IRR(0.1, B2..H2).

Clearly the effect of the moratorium has been to reduce the APR on the debt to the builders but not quite by enough to make it preferable to the bank loan. However, it is an easy matter to confirm that if an extra year's moratorium was offered, then the APR would fall by enough to alter the decision as to which scheme should be chosen. The calculations for this have been entered into row 3 of the worksheet, and the new APR calculated in B8 from @IRR (0.1, B3..I3).

```
WORKSHEET 4.23
      A          B          C     D     E     F     G     H     I
 1    Scheme 1   -6         1.8   1.8   1.8   1.8   1.8   0     0
 2    Scheme 2   -6         0     1.8   1.8   1.8   1.8   1.8   0
 3    Scheme 3   -6         0     0     1.8   1.8   1.8   1.8   1.8
 4
 5    APR 1      0.152382
 5    EAR Bank   0.107756
 7    APR 2      0.109675
 8    APR 3      0.085945
```

5
Linear Programming I

5.1 Principles of linear programming

Linear programming is an area of applied mathematics that concerns itself with the process of optimization. By this, we mean the procedure of obtaining the best possible outcome from a number of available alternatives.

In some circumstances this may mean a *maximization* process (the greatest profit from a particular activity, for example), but in other cases we may be required to *minimize* the cost of performing some business activity.

In either case, optimization is to be viewed in terms of the eternal business problem of choosing the best way to achieve a given objective in the face of limitations upon the resources available to be used, and in the light of a number of different ways in which these resources can be employed.

The word 'linear' is also crucial to the argument, since in the context of linear programming this means that a linear function of two or more variables is to be used as a mathematical representation of the *objectives* to be achieved by the business activity being undertaken. Accordingly, this function is always referred to as the *objective function* and will usually be a mathematical representation of variables such as output, revenue, cost or profit.

However, since we have already seen that the objective function will always be linear, it follows that there will be no finite maximum or minimum value that it can adopt unless we introduce some modification to the analysis which *constrains* the function to values which are less than plus or minus infinity.

To see this point, suppose we ask the following question:

'What is the greatest sum of two positive numbers?'

Clearly there is no sensible answer to be obtained unless we introduce some added information such as 'the sum of the first number and twice the second number must never exceed 20.' This added restriction means that the maximum value that the first number can adopt is 20 (when the second number is 0), while the maximum value that the second number can adopt is 10 (when the first number is 0). In between these two extremes there are a large number of combinations of values that the two numbers can adopt, but which all satisfy the requirement that the sum of the first and twice the second never exceeds 20.

However, although a combination such as 4 for the first number and 8 for the second number does not violate the restriction, it should be clear that the resulting sum (12) is not as large as it could be. Intuition would suggest that we should let the first number be as large as possible (20) and let the second number be as small as possible (0), and then we will obtain the greatest sum (20) without disobeying the restriction [since 20 + 2(0) does not exceed 20].

What this simple illustration shows is that the process of optimizing linear functions cannot take place unless there is at least one constraint upon the values that the variables of the function can adopt.

In the context of business analysis you can see another version of this idea more clearly if you try to answer the following question:

'What is the minimum cost of production?'

On the face of it this would appear to be a reasonable question, until it is remembered that production costs will be zero when nothing is produced. Consequently, the answer to this question will always be 'zero'.

On the other hand, if the question was rephrased as:

'What is the minimum cost of producing 500 units of output?'

then the requirement that 500 units be produced has turned this into a meaningful question. The introduction of a constraint has brought substance and definition to the problem.

Bearing this in mind means that in the context of linear programming the constraints will also be linear functions of the same variables as are included in the objective function, and will always represent the physical and/or financial restrictions imposed upon the optimization process.

In summary, we can state that linear programming is fundamentally concerned with optimizing a linear objective function (representing the target to be achieved) subject to the restrictions imposed by a set of linear constraints (representing the limited availability of the resources needed to achieve the specified target).

Viewed in this manner, many of the fundamental allocation problems of elementary business economics can be written in terms of a linear program, provided, of course, that the objective function and the relevant constraints can reasonably be modelled by linear relationships.

In respect of this modelling process, it should be stressed at the outset that one of the fundamental difficulties encountered by students in the formulation of linear programming exercises stems from the failure to distinguish between variables and variable names.

For example, in an exercise that refers to the production of nuts and bolts, statements such as 'let x = nuts' and 'let y = bolts' are frequently made. Such statements, when carefully inspected, are seen to be almost meaningless since the *feature* of nuts and bolts that is supposed to be measured by the x and y variables is not defined. Hence x could be the weight of nuts, the diameter, the steel content or any other of a number of characteristics that nuts possess. As a result, the statement 'let $x =$ nuts' is so vague as to be effectively useless in helping us to model the problem. This is because x should be a numerical variable — capable of adopting specific numerical values, whereas 'nuts' is a variable name that is quantitatively unspecified in terms of the feature of nuts to be measured.

In the light of this discussion we must recognize that the choice of what to let the variables represent must be conditioned by the objective of the linear program, since x, y (and any other variables) will always be the unknowns of the problem. Hence if nuts and bolts are produced and sold, and if the objective of the program is to make the greatest profit from this process, then the variables should be defined as the *production levels* of nuts and bolts and the linear program should be employed to find those values of the variables which, when sold, produce the greatest profit.

That is

Let $x =$ the production of nuts per time period
Let $y =$ the production of bolts per time period

We could then use these carefully defined variables to write the linear program that will find those values of x and y that maximize profit.

As a more concrete example, consider a firm that uses three inputs (labour, capital and steel) to produce two outputs (steel girders and steel casings).

The labour input will usually be specified in terms of man hours while the capital input (following the economic definition of capital) will be defined in terms of machine time. The input of steel will, of course, be specified in physical units as kilos or tonnes per time period.

Suppose, in addition, that the technical relationship between inputs and outputs (frequently called the production function) is known to the firm, and is specified in terms of the minimum necessary amounts of each of the three inputs required for the production of a unit of the respective outputs. Hence we might know, for example, that each girder requires 2 units of labour time, 1 unit of machine time and 5 units of steel, while each casing requires 2 units of labour time, 5 units of machine time and 2 units of steel.

In addition, the overall availability of the three inputs must also be known, and for the immediate future at least, must be regarded as fixed. (This last assumption stems from the fact that the need to allocate resources between competing ends is only pressing if such resources are limited in availability.)

For the purposes of this illustration we will take these overall availabilities to be the following:

Labour 24 man hours per day
Capital 44 machine hours per day
Steel 60 tonnes per day

These technical requirements form the basis of the constraints of the linear program, since the combined usage of each input in the production of girders and/or casings cannot exceed the availability of that input. Hence, if it was decided to produce 10 girders and 20 casings, then the total labour usage would be $10 \times 2 = 20$ man hours (for girders) plus $20 \times 2 = 40$ man hours (for casings) giving an overall usage of 60 man hours, which exceeds the available amount by 36 hours. The constraint upon labour availability is therefore violated and such an output combination (10 girders and 20 casings) is said to be non-feasible (i.e. unattainable given the constraint upon labour availability).

It should be recognized, however, that the purpose of the linear program is to *determine* the production levels of girders and/or casings rather than assume them to be 10 and 20 or any other combination. Towards this end we require to formulate the constraints in terms of *unknown variables* which represent the respective outputs of girders and casings. To do this, we will denote the daily production of girders by x and the daily output of casings by y. It should now be clear that we can write the following linear expression as a representation of the total labour usage resulting from producing x girders and y casings per day.

$$2x + 2y = \text{total labour usage per day}$$

(Remember that each girder uses 2 units of labour and each casing also uses 2 units of labour. Consequently, x girders will use $2x$ units of labour and y casings will use $2y$ units of labour.)

The expression above has to be related in some way to the total daily labour hours available, and we do this by noting that the total daily labour usage cannot exceed (i.e. must be less than or equal to) the total daily labour availability. We therefore have a general expression for our first constraint as

$$2x + 2y \leqslant 24$$

Notice that this expression is a linear *inequality* rather than an equality since it allows for the possibility that all the available labour hours will not be used, in which case the constraint is said to be *non-binding*. Alternatively, when the values of x and y are such that the inequality becomes an equality, then the constraint is said to be *binding*.

The constraints that refer to the usage of machine time and steel can be developed by a similar logic.

Hence, if x girders and y casings are produced each day they will require

$(x)(1) + (y)(5)$ hours of machine time per day, and
$(x)(6) + (y)(2)$ tonnes of steel per day

As before, these requirements must be related to the total machine time and steel that the firm has available, and when this is done we obtain the complete set of constraints governing this allocation problem:

$$
\begin{aligned}
2x + 2y &\leqslant 24 & &\text{labour time constraint} \\
1x + 5y &\leqslant 44 & &\text{machine time constraint} \\
6x + 2y &\leqslant 60 & &\text{steel constraint} \\
x &\geqslant 0 \\
y &\geqslant 0
\end{aligned}
$$

You will notice that we have added two further constraints (x and y both ≥ 0). The reason for this is that we must preclude negative (but not zero) valued output levels from our model. From now on these restrictions will be presumed to be present without actually being presented in the program.

Having derived mathematical expressions for the constraints of this problem, we must now perform a similar exercise for the objective function. As with the constraints, this must always be expressed in terms of the unknown variables x and y, and will reflect the behavioural motivation of the firm.

In the simplest case, an objective of maximizing the combined daily output of girders and casings would be written as

$$\text{Maximize} \quad (1)(x) + (1)(y) = Q$$

where Q represents the combined daily output objective function for girders and casings.

Although simple, such an objective function is perfectly reasonable if, for example, the two products were completely complementary in the sense that they *had* to be sold together (such as nuts and bolts). In this case there is effectively only one product (nuts *and* bolts) and the objective function would have to address itself to the question of how many nuts and bolts should be produced per day.

But in most cases the firm will attach a higher priority to one product than to the other, since the products will usually not be sold at the same price and will not be completely complementary. This complication means that the objective function will usually be denominated in monetary as opposed to physical units with the respective selling prices of the products being used to 'weight' their outputs, and the resulting expression having a monetary dimension defined as total revenue (R).

So, for example, if the firm was able to sell girders at £15 each and casings at £16 each, then its total daily revenue would be given by

$$15x + 16y = R$$

Our complete linear program therefore becomes

$$\begin{aligned} \text{Maximize} \quad & 15x + 16y = R \\ \text{Subject to} \quad & 2x + 2y \leq 24 \\ & x + 5y \leq 44 \\ & 6x + 2y \leq 60 \end{aligned}$$

The next task is to derive a method of solving for the optimal values of x and y (i.e. those unique values that satisfy the desired objective of maximizing total daily revenue subject to the relevant constraints). In this respect it is important to recognize the crucial function performed by the constraints in obtaining a determinate finite solution, since on its own the expression

$$15x + 16y = R$$

has no finite maximum value and no finite optimal values for x and y. Only when the constraints are introduced is a 'boundary' created within which a finite solution can be obtained.

Graphical solution methods 231

Now you should realize that solution methods can be divided into two forms: graphical and algebraic, and although each of these will be dealt with in turn, it should be stressed that most realistic linear programming problems are solved by computer packages. Consequently, once the student has grasped how simple linear programs can be solved, it becomes much more important to understand the issues involved in formulating the model and in interpreting solutions produced in the form of computer output.

5.2 Graphical solution methods

Provided there are no more than two variables, graphical methods can be used to provide a simple visual solution method to any linear programming problem. Initially, the procedure is simply to treat the constraints as strict equalities and then plot them as accurately as possible on a sheet of graph paper. For each constraint this is done by first of all letting the variable in x equal zero, solving for y and plotting the obtained coordinate; and then reversing the procedure (i.e. letting $y = 0$) to obtain the coordinate in x. These two coordinates are then joined by a straight line to provide the loci of all x and y values that satisfy the constraint. This procedure is then repeated for all of the constraints in the program, and when completed can be used to produce what is known as the *feasibility polygon*. This is defined as the loci of all x and y values that *simultaneously* satisfy *all* relevant constraints.

Using the example from the previous section we get the following graphical construction.

Labour constraint:

$$2x + 2y \leqslant 24$$
when $x = 0$ $2y = 24$ therefore $y = 12$
when $y = 0$ $2x = 24$ therefore $x = 12$

Machine constraint:

$$x + 5y \leqslant 44$$
when $x = 0$ $5y = 44$ therefore $y = 8.8$
when $y = 0$ $x = 44$ therefore $x = 44$

Steel constraint:

$$6x + 2y \leqslant 60$$
when $x = 0$ $2y = 60$ therefore $y = 30$
when $y = 0$ $6x = 60$ therefore $x = 10$

When these three constraints are plotted on the same axes we obtain the graph shown in Figure 5.1. It will be noticed that although each of the constraints was represented in terms of an *inequality*, the plotted coordinates were obtained by using an *equality* relationship.

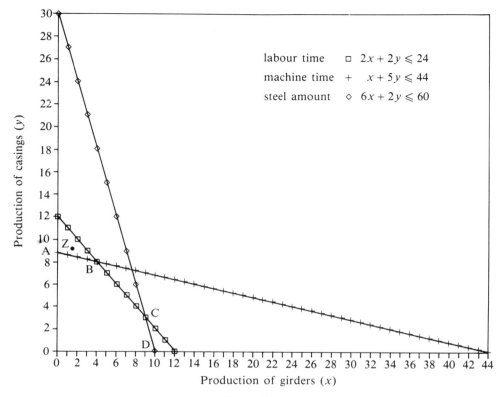

Figure 5.1

This is justified by recognizing that the lines themselves represent the equality, and that coordinates to the left of the lines represent the inequality, while coordinates to the right represent the violation of the inequality constraints.

These latter coordinates are therefore said to be nonfeasible and represent the outer limit of the feasibility polygon (the permissible x, y combinations). This means that in Figure 5.1, the points A–B–C–D define this feasible region.

It should also be noticed that feasibility is defined in terms of satisfying the most *restrictive constraint*, since feasible x, y combinations must satisfy *all* constraints. This means that although a point such as Z satisfies both the labour and the steel constraints, it fails to satisfy the machine time constraint, which exercises an overriding effect to make Z *nonfeasible*.

We can focus attention more closely on this crucial area if we magnify it in our diagrams by excluding those sections of the constraints that do not form part of the feasibility polygon. This is done in Figure 5.2

The effect of these ideas is to allow us to view the feasibility polygon as an *option set* in the sense that it delineates the technical options or possibilities available to the firm. On its own, however, it does not allow the firm to choose between the

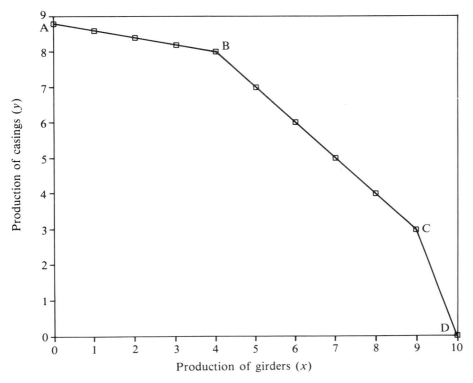

Figure 5.2 The feasibility polygon

numerous options available, since to do this requires reference to the objective function. Only if the firm has a realistic valuation of the relative benefits of producing x as opposed to y can it make a rational decision as to the optimal x, y combination.

To see this, consider as an extreme case this firm's likely response to a reduction in the price of Y to 0. Under such circumstances it makes no rational economic sense to devote any scarce resources *at all* to the production of Y, and consequently production of X should be maximized. The optimal solution will therefore be at the corner D (with $x = 10$). Extreme as this example may be, it nevertheless illustrates the logic involved in choosing the optimal solution from the options available.

When we consider the actual example with the prices of X and Y being £15 and £16 respectively, it should be apparent that the search for the optimal solution is effectively reduced to an evaluation of the intersection points A, B, C and D.

This can be done as follows:

point A $x = 0$, $y = 8.8$, $R = (15)(0) + (16)(8.8) = £140.8$
point B $x = 4$, $y = 8$, $R = (15)(4) + (16)(8) \; = £188$
point C $x = 9$, $y = 3$, $R = (15)(9) + (16)(3) \; = £183$
point D $x = 10$, $y = 0$, $R = (15)(10) + (10)(6) = £150$

Since point B unambiguously has the highest value of R it is deemed to be the optimal solution to this particular linear programming problem.

An alternative way of obtaining the optimal solution is to graph the objective function itself on top of the feasibility polygon. This immediately presents an apparent problem since the expression

$$15x + 16y = R$$

cannot be graphed uniquely without knowing the value of R. The answer is to notice that changes in the value of R merely change the position of the line (the intercept terms) but do not change its unique gradient. Hence by choosing arithmetically convenient values of R (such as 480, 240 and 120, for example) the expression can be graphed and its unique gradient obtained. This is done for these selected values of F in Figure 5.3.

It should also be noted that the gradient of the objective function can always be obtained directly from the x and y coefficients. Hence, if $R = 240$, then when $y = 0$, $x = 16$, while when $x = 0$, $y = 15$.

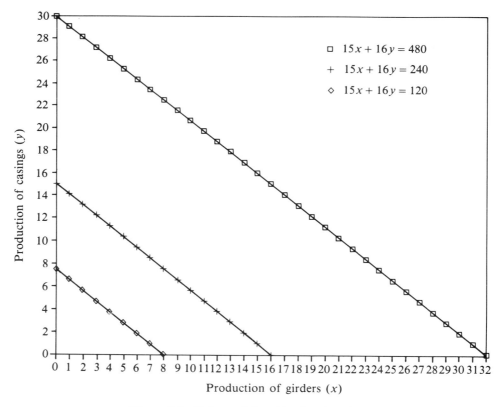

Figure 5.3 Values of the objective function

The ratio 15/16 therefore defines the gradient of the objective function, and this ratio is simply the ratio of the *x coefficient* to the *y coefficient* of the objective function.

But if the gradient does not change as R changes, this means that the expression $15x + 16y = R$ is simply a continuous family of parallel lines, which each have a higher value of R as the distance from the origin is increased. Any number of such lines could have been plotted, but in fact there is never any need to plot more than one, since once the unique gradient has been obtained, maximization is essentially the same as taking any *one* line representing the gradient of the objective function and sliding it away from the origin in a parallel fashion until no more feasible region is left. This will occur when the line representing the objective function is tangent to the feasibility region, and can be seen to be at point B in Figure 5.4. This merely confirms what has been deduced already, and indicates that the solution values of $x = 4$ and $y = 8$ are those that maximize the value of R (£188 in this case).

It should be stressed that given the particular set of constraints (defining the technical options available) the maximum value of R is completely determined by the values contained in the objective function. Changes in the prices obtained for

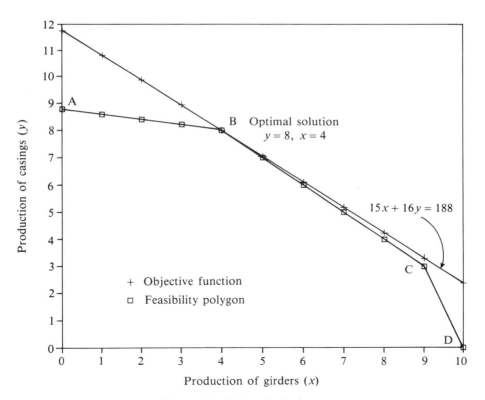

Figure 5.4 Optimal solution

the products can eventually cause changes in the optimal solution, in the sense that the optimal values of x and y will change. This is a reflection of the fact that a reallocation of resources is now justified, since revenue will no longer be maximized at the old solution values of x and y. This will obviously have implications for the utilization rates of the inputs, within, of course, the overall constraint restriction.

5.3 Using Lotus to solve linear programs

As you might imagine, the calculational and graphing processes outlined in the previous section are ideal tasks for the Lotus spreadsheet. To see how this can be done examine Worksheet 5.1a. All we have done in this worksheet is to include the coefficients of the constraints of the problem in the range B2..D5, and the coefficients of the objective function in the range B6..C6. (Space has been left for a fourth constraint if required, but in the absence of one, the entries in B5..D5 have been left blank.)

The entries in columns E and F are simply obtained by dividing the constant term by the coefficient values of x and y respectively. This means that the formulae in E2 and F2 are +D2/B2 and +D2/C2, which are then copied into the E3..F5 range.

These formulae give the maximum values of x and y associated with each constraint, and since we have already seen that it is the most restrictive of these that prevails, we can ask Lotus to take the minimum value from each of the ranges and place them in B8 and B9 respectively.

The formulae are

in B8   @MIN(E2..E5)
in B9   @MIN(F2..F5)

The entry in B7 is simply the maximum value in the E2..E5 range, i.e. the biggest value of x. This can be useful for setting the range of x values to be graphed.

Once this initial section of the worksheet has been prepared, the next task is to ask Lotus to calculate the y values associated with each x value and each constraint.

WORKSHEET 5.1a

	A	B	C	D	E	F
1		x coeff.	y coeff.	constant	Max x	Max y
2	Constraint 1	2	2	24	12	12
3	Constraint 2	1	5	44	44	8.8
4	Constraint 3	6	2	60	10	30
5	Constraint 4					
6	Object. Funct.	15	16			
7	Max (Max x)	44				
8	Max allowed x	10				
9	Max allowed y	8.8				

WORKSHEET 5.1b

	A	B	C	D	E	F
1		x coeff	y coeff.	constant	Max x	Max y
2	Constraint 1	2	2	24	12	12
3	Constraint 2	1	5	44	44	8.8
4	Constraint 3	6	2	60	10	30
5	Constraint 4					
6	Object. Funct.	15	16			
7	Max (Max x)	44				
8	Max allowed x	10				
9	Max allowed y	8.8				
10						
11						
12		x value	y (const 1)	y (const 2)	y (const 3)	
13		0	12	8.8	30	
14		1	11	8.6	27	
15		2	10	8.4	24	
16		3	9	8.2	21	
17		4	8	8	18	
18		5	7	7.8	15	
19		6	6	7.6	12	
20		7	5	7.4	9	
21		8	4	7.2	6	
22		9	3	7	3	
23		10	2	6.8	0	
24		11	1	6.6	-3	
25		12	0	6.4	-6	
26		13	-1	6.2	-9	
27		14	-2	6	-12	
28		15	-3	5.8	-15	
29		16	-4	5.6	-18	
30		17	-5	5.4	-21	
31		18	-6	5.2	-24	
32		19	-7	5	-27	
33		20	-8	4.8	-30	
34		21	-9	4.6	-33	
35		22	-10	4.4	-36	
36		23	-11	4.2	-39	
37		24	-12	4	-42	
38		25	-13	3.8	-45	
39		26	-14	3.6	-48	
40		27	-15	3.4	-51	

Some of these are shown in Worksheet 5.1b where the Data Fill command has been used to enter a range of x values in A13..A40.

The associated y values for each constraint are calculated by solving for y in the general expression

$$ax + by = c$$

implying that

$$y = (c - ax)/b$$

This means that the formulae in B13, C13 and D13 are the Lotus equivalents of this expression, i.e.

in B13   (D$2 − B$2*A13)/C$2
in C13   (D$3 − B$3*A13)/C$3
in D13   (D$4 − B$4*A13)/C$4

Because of the dollar signs, which fix the row references in these formulae, they can then be copied into the range B14..D40. This means that only the rows in the A column (representing the value of x) will update, which is exactly what we require.

As you can see, some of the constraints produce negative values of y for certain values of x. This is really not desirable for a number of reasons, so, provided that we only want to produce a graph of the feasible region, we can eliminate this problem by limiting the values of x to be plotted to those that are less than or equal to the maximum permitted value of x (which we have calculated in B8). For this illustration this means that we can confine the value of x to be plotted to the range 0–10 inclusive. This modification is shown in Worksheet 5.2. You will also notice that in column E we have added the feasible y values. Remembering that the most restrictive constraint dominates, these are calculated by asking Lotus to select the minimum value from the three constraint values of y for each value of x. The formula in E13 is therefore

$$@MIN(B13..D13)$$

and this has been copied into the range E14..23.

Clearly the feasible region is determined by constraint 2 for x values between 0 and 4, by constraint 1 for x values between 5 and 8, and by constraint 3 for x values between 9 and 10.

Now you can graph A13..A23 as the X range, against E13..E23 as the 'A' range, and you will obtain a replica of Figure 5.2 above.

Finally, since you have produced the feasible combinations of x and y in your worksheet, it is an easy matter to calculate the value of the objective function associated with each of these combinations. The formula to do this is entered in F13 and is then copied into F14..F23.

This formula is

in F13   +A13*B$6+E13*C$6

i.e. (x value times price of x) + (y value times price of y)

When these formulae are evaluated by Lotus, you will obtain the value of the objective function for each of the specified feasible x, y combinations.

As you can see our previous conclusions that revenue is maximized (at £188) when $x = 4$ and $y = 8$ is reconfirmed in the worksheet.

However, the real advantage of this approach lies in its ability to respond instantly to variations in the values of any of the parameters of the problem. This will be displayed extensively in the next section, but before you proceed to this, you

WORKSHEET 5.2

	A	B	C	D	E	F
10						Value of
11						Objective
12	x value	y (const 1)	y (const 2)	y (const 3)	Feasible y	Function
13	0				8.8	140.8
14	1	12	8.8	30	8.6	152.6
15	2	11	8.6	27	8.4	164.4
16	3	10	8.4	24	8.2	176.2
17	4	9	8.2	21	8	**188**
18	5	8	8	18	7	187
19	6	7	7.8	15	6	186
20	7	6	7.6	12	5	185
21	8	5	7.4	9	4	184
22	9	4	7.2	6	3	183
23	10	3	7	3	0	150
24		2	6.8	0		

should test your understanding of this worksheet by changing the values of x to be evaluated from 0–10 in steps of 1 to 0–10 in steps of 0.25.

The same formulae will apply as in Worksheet 5.2, but clearly you will have to extend the ranges into which they are copied.

You may not see much point to this exercise, but in fact it is the only way of dealing with a difficulty that we have conveniently avoided up until now. This stems from the fact that there is no necessity that the solution values of x and y will always be whole numbers, and as a result you will have to make a decision as to the step in which the value of x is to increase. Given the power of both Lotus's copying and graphing facilities, there is no real cost in making this increase in x as small as the eventual manageability of the worksheet dictates.

5.4 Changes in the coefficients of the objective function

As has been mentioned on several occasions already, a crucial function of the linear programming technique relates to analyzing the effects of changes in the parameters of the program.

To see this point more clearly, we must recognize that the feasibility polygon for our illustrative example can be viewed as comprising seven distinct sections. These can be seen by referring back to Figure 5.4. Clearly we can identify the points A, B, C and D, and the sections AB, BC and CD as representing all possible x, y combinations.

These points and sections will only represent the optimal allocation if they have the same gradient as the objective function, and consequently an analysis of the sensitivity of the optimal solution to changes in the coefficients of the objective function can be reduced to determining the gradients of the sections AB, BC and CD.

Furthermore, since AB is a section of the line representing the first constraint, it follows that its gradient is given by

$$\text{gradient AB} = 8.8/44 = 0.2$$

A similar logic would calculate the gradients of BC and CD to be

$$\text{gradient BC} = 12/12 = 1$$
$$\text{gradient CD} = 30/10 = 3$$

Notice that the negativity of these gradients has been ignored as it does not influence the argument in any way.

It should now be clear that if the objective function has a gradient that is exactly equal to any of the above values, then the optimal solution is indeterminate in the sense that it can be any x, y combination lying along the appropriate section (AB, BC or CD).

However, a slight improvement in the price of girders (represented by the coefficient of the x variable) would cause the optimal solution to change from anywhere along BC, for example, to the point B; while a slight deterioration in the price of girders would cause an opposite movement in the optimal solution (i.e. towards C).

It is an easy matter to use the relevant section from Worksheet 5.2 to enforce any of these changes and then examine the consequences. For example, if the price of girders increased from 15 to 24, then Worksheet 5.3 indicates the relevant changes. As you can see, the optimal solution is now to produce nine girders and three casings (as opposed to four and eight previously) and the new maximum revenue is £264 as opposed to £188.

Returning to Figure 5.4 you should be able to see that points such as B or C can remain optimal until the ratio of prices reaches an absolute value of 0.2 or 3, in which case the sections AB or CD now become optimal.

Applying this logic to all three sections and all four points allows us to summarize the sensitivity of the optimal solution to changes in the coefficient values of the objective function as follows:

let p_x = the x coefficient in the objective function
let p_y = the y coefficient in the objective function

Then if

$p_x/p_y < 0.2$ the optimal solution is at A
$p_x/p_y = 0.2$ the optimal solution is *along* AB
$0.2 < p_x/p_y < 1$ the optimal solution is at *B*
$p_x/p_y = 1$ the optimal solution is *along* BC
$1 < p_x/p_y < 3$ the optimal solution is at *C*
$p_x/p_y = 3$ the optimal solution is *along* CD
$3 < p_x/p_y$ the optimal solution is at D

It is also worth noting that if the coefficients of the objective function change, then the actual arithmetic amount of the maximum daily revenue attainable will also change (you saw this in Worksheet 5.3). It will still be the maximum attainable given these coefficients and the set of constraints, but it must be realized that any such maximum is neither unique nor global. Rather, it is entirely determined by the fundamental economic conditions that govern the process of price determination. In our discussion so far, the firm has been viewed as a passive reactor to changes in prices which are determined by factors beyond its control, and linear programming in this context is therefore to be regarded as providing the rules of optimal response to any externally generated changes in economic conditions.

Furthermore, it is equally important to note that in the short-term at least there is no requirement that all of the constraints are binding. In fact, the technical conditions of production may be such that some resources will *have* to remain unused. Provided the inputs can be bought and sold in unit amounts, these unused resources (known as slack) can be sold (or not purchased) in the next period, but in the immediate term they are not required. Hence, in our example when the

WORKSHEET 5.3

	A	B	C	D	E	F
6	Object. Funct.	24	16			
7	Max (Max x)	44				
8	Max allowed x	10				
9	Max allowed y	8.8				
10						Value of
11						Objective
12	x value	y (const 1)	y (const 2)	y (const 3)	Feasible y	Function
13	0	12	8.8	30	8.8	140.8
14	1	11	8.6	27	8.6	161.6
15	2	10	8.4	24	8.4	182.4
16	3	9	8.2	21	8.2	203.2
17	4	8	8	18	8	224
18	5	7	7.8	15	7	232
19	6	6	7.6	12	6	240
20	7	5	7.4	9	5	248
21	8	4	7.2	6	4	256
22	9	3	7	3	**3**	**264**
23	10	2	6.8	0	0	240

Changes in Coefficients of the objective function

optimal solution of four girders and eight casings are produced, this uses a total of

$$(4)(2) + (8)(2) = 24 \text{ man hours}$$
$$(4)(1) + (8)(5) = 44 \text{ machine hours}$$
$$(4)(6) + (8)(2) = 40 \text{ tonnes of steel}$$

There are therefore 0 units of labour time, 0 units of machine time and 20 tonnes of steel unused. If conditions remain unchanged in the next period and if unit adjustment of input purchases is possible, then there will be an incentive for the firm to purchase 20 tonnes less of steel.

However, it must also be the case that these surplus availabilities will be sensitive to changes in the optimal solution induced by changes in the coefficients of the objective function, and you can easily modify Worksheet 5.3 to calculate these changes. This is done in Worksheet 5.4 where the tabulated values of x have been copied from the A column to the F column (and also labelled in terms of the points A, B, C and D from Figure 5.4), so that you can see what is going on.

The surplus labour time is calculated in H13 from the formula

$$+ D\$2 - F13*B\$2 - E13*C\$2$$

This represents: total resource availability minus (output of x times labour usage per unit of x) minus (output of y times labour usage per unit of y).

A similar logic for the other two resources produces the formulae for the I13 and J13 cells. These are

in I13 $+ D\$3 - F13*B\$3 - E13*C\$3$
in J13 $+ D\$4 - F13*B\$4 - E13*C\$4$

Once again, the dollar signs fix the addresses containing the coefficient value so that these formulae can then be copied into the range H14..J23.

As Worksheet 5.4 indicates, some combinations of x and y are much more wasteful of resources than others, yet any attempt to evaluate the relative *costs* of such waste is severely hindered by the fact that the foregoing discussion has been one-dimensional.

By this, we mean that the objective function required the maximization of revenue, rather than profit, thereby implying that although the firm used resources to obtain revenue, it appeared to obtain them free of charge. The missing link with regard to both of these objections is of course the concept of cost, which is apparently absent from the foregoing analysis. In fact this absence is apparent rather than real since resource costs (although not monetary costs) are an integral part of the linear programming technique, and are an implicit basis of the optimizing procedure.

Nevertheless, these resource costs (the output foregone if a unit less of any one of the resources were available) are specific to the particular firm and therefore reflect the availability to it of the resources used. This need not provide an accurate reflection of the scarcity of these resources to society as a whole, and consequently

WORKSHEET 5.4

	E	F	G	H	I	J
	Feasible y	Feasible x	Value of Objective Function	Surplus Labour Time	Surplus Machine Time	Surplus Steel
	8.8	0 A	140.8	6.4	0	42.4
	8.6	1	152.6	4.8	0	36.8
	8.4	2	164.4	3.2	0	31.2
	8.2	3	176.2	1.6	0	25.6
	8	4 B	188	0	0	20
	7	5	187	0	4	16
	6	6	186	0	8	12
	5	7	185	0	12	8
	4	8	184	0	16	4
	3	9 C	183	0	20	0
	0	10 D	150	4	34	0

it is advisable to extend our simple model to take explicit account of resource prices and the cost relationships derived from them.

If we continue with the data of the previous example, and in addition introduce the unit prices of labour, capital and steel as £1.25, £0.5 and £1 respectively, then an objective function with regard to profit is easily established. We know from the original data that each girder requires 2 units of labour, 1 unit of machine time and 6 units of steel. Consequently the cost of a girder can be written as

$$(2)(1.25) + (1)(0.5) + (6)(1) = £9$$

Using the same logic with regard to the production of casings, we obtain the unit cost per casing to be

$$(2)(1.25) + (5)(0.5) + (2)(1) = £7$$

It follows that the total costs (C) of producing the (as yet unknown) amounts of girders and casings can be written as

$$C = 9x + 7y$$

and, given the definition of profit (P) as total revenue (R) minus total cost (C) we can derive the following objective function:

$$\text{Maximize} \quad \underset{R}{(15x + 16y)} - \underset{C}{(9x + 7y)} = P$$

In this case, however, the x and y terms can be collected together to give

$$\begin{aligned} \text{Maximize} \quad & 6x + 9y = P \\ \text{Subject to} \quad & 2x + 2y \leq 24 \\ & x + 5y \leq 44 \\ & 6x + 2y \leq 60 \end{aligned}$$

This is a slightly different problem from the one outlined before, in the sense that the revenue per unit of X and Y has now been 'weighted' by the unit costs of the resources needed to produce the desired output levels.

As it turns out, however, even with this new objective function, the optimal solution remains the same as for the case of simple revenue maximization. This is because with the objective function of

$$6x + 9y = P$$

the ratio of the x coefficient to the y coefficient is 6/9, which implies no change in the optimal solution (i.e. at B with $x = 4$ and $y = 8$ and a profit of £96) as opposed to a revenue of £188.

If, however, the cost of a unit of steel to the firm fell to £0.1, then the cost per girder would become

$$2(1.25) + 1(0.5) + 6(0.1) = 3.6$$

The cost per casing would become

$$2(1.25) + 5(0.5) + 2(0.1) = 5.2$$

and the objective function would become

$$(15x + 16y) - (3.6x + 5.2y) = 11.4x + 10.8y = P$$

The ratio of the x coefficient to the y coefficient is now $11.4/10.8 = 1.055$ and our previous analysis indicates that the optimal solution would now be at C as opposed to B with $x = 9$ and $y = 3$.

Worksheet 5.3 can, of course, be used to confirm this result.

The effect of changing the costs of the inputs has been to force a reallocation that would *not* have been observed if the objective function had been specified in terms of revenue alone.

We conclude, therefore, that although the linear program technique does take account of the *physical* use of resources, it cannot consider the *monetary* cost of such usage unless it is specifically told to do so via the introduction of a cost function, which, in conjunction with the revenue function, defines the usual objective function of profit.

5.5 Minimization

Up until now we have concentrated on the maximization aspects of linear programming, but we can still use the methods outlined to deal with minimization problems. There will, however, be two slight modifications to the technique required.

First, since the minimum positive value of any linear function is zero (when $x = y = 0$), at least one, and usually several of the constraints must be of a 'greater than or equal to' nature. In this way the values of x and/or y are constrained to be greater than zero, implying that we are not so much concerned with the minimum cost of doing nothing, but rather with minimizing the cost of carrying out some specified activity.

Secondly, since the objective function is to be minimized, we require its position in our graph to be as *close* to the origin as possible (as opposed to as far away as possible in maximization.) Furthermore, the 'greater than or equal to' nature of the constraints implies that the feasibility region is the area *outside* each of the constraints (as opposed to the area inside for maximization).

Minimization therefore requires that the objective function be moved *towards* the origin until no more feasible region remains.

The points can be seen in operation in the context of the following worked example.

EXAMPLE 5.1

A farmer wishes to provide three vitamin additives (A, B and C) to supplement the diet of his stock. These additives are supplied by two different brands of feed (Moonosh and Cowgrub) as follows (where the entries in the table are the grams of additive per kilo of feed).

	Additive A	Additive B	Additive C
Moonosh	3	6	14
Cowgrub	10	8	7

The farmer also wishes to ensure that a mixture of the two feed brands will contain *at least* 30 g of additive A, *at least* 48 g of additive B and *at least* 56 g of additive C.

The costs per kilo of Moonosh and Cowgrub are £4 and £2.50 respectively, and the farmer wishes to minimize the total cost of producing a mixture that will contain the minimum additive requirements.

SOLUTION 5.1

Let x = the number of kilos of Moonosh used in the mixture, and let y = the number of kilos of Cowgrub used in the mixture.

The objective function will then be given by

$$\text{Minimize} \quad 4x + 2.5y = \text{cost}$$

Since we know that at least 30 g of additive A are to be supplied, and since this additive is provided by Moonosh and Cowgrub in respective amounts of 3 g and 10 g per kilo, the first constraint will be given by:

$$3x + 10y \geqslant 30 \quad \text{(additive A requirement)}$$

By a similar logic we have, for the other two additives

$$6x + 8y \geqslant 48 \quad \text{(additive B requirement)}$$
$$14x + 7y \geqslant 56 \quad \text{(additive C requirement)}$$

Having identified and formulated the relevant linear program, you can still use a Lotus worksheet such as the one developed in Worksheet 5.2 to obtain the solution, but you will have to make some changes to it.

1. The entries in E2..E5 should now be called 'Min x', since in the context of this minimization problem they represent the minimum amounts of Moonosh required to supply each required additive amount. In a similar way, the entries in F2..F5 should be entitled 'Min y', since they represent the minimum amounts of Cowgrub required to supply each required additive amount.

WORKSHEET 5.5

	A	B	C	D	E	F
1		x coeff	y coeff	constant	Min x	Min y
2	Constraint 1	3	10	30	10	3
3	Constraint 2	6	8	48	8	6
4	Constraint 3	14	7	56	4	8
5	Constraint 4					
6	Object. Funct	4	2.5			
7	Max (Min x)	10				
8	Min required x	10				
9	Min required y	3				
10						Value of
11						Objective
12	x value	y (const 1)	y (const 2)	y (const 3)	Feasible y	Function
13	0	3	6	8	8	20
14	0.5	2.85	5.625	7	7	19.5
15	1	2.7	5.25	6	6	19
16	1.5	2.55	4.875	5	5	**18.5**
17	2	2.4	4.5	4	4.5	19.25
18	2.5	2.25	4.125	3	4.125	20.3125
19	3	2.1	3.75	2	3.75	21.375
20	3.5	1.95	3.375	1	3.375	22.4375
21	4	1.8	3	0	3	23.5
22	4.5	1.65	2.625	-1	2.625	24.5625
23	5	1.5	2.25	-2	2.25	25.625
24	5.5	1.35	1.875	-3	1.875	26.6875
25	6	1.2	1.5	-4	1.5	27.75
26	6.5	1.05	1.125	-5	1.125	28.8125
27	7	0.9	0.75	-6	0.9	30.25
28	7.5	0.75	0.375	-7	0.75	31.875
29	8	0.6	0	-8	0.6	33.5
30	8.5	0.45	-0.375	-9	0.45	35.125
31	9	0.3	-0.75	-10	0.3	36.75
32	9.5	0.15	-1.125	-11	0.15	38.375
33	10	0	-1.5	-12	0	40

	E	F	G	H	I	J
	Feasible y	Value of Objective Function	Feasible x	Surplus Addit. A	Surplus Addit. B	Surplus Addit. C
10						
11						
12						
13	8	20	0	50	16	0
14	7	19.5	0.5	41.5	11	0
15	6	19	1	33	6	0
16	5	**18.5**	1.5	24.5	1	0
17	4.5	19.25	2	21	0	3.5
18	4.125	20.3125	2.5	18.8	0	7.9
19	3.75	21.375	3	16.5	0	12.3
20	3.375	22.4375	3.5	14.3	0	16.6
21	3	23.5	4	12	0	21
22	2.625	24.5625	4.5	9.8	0	25.4
23	2.25	25.625	5	7.5	0	29.8
24	1.875	26.6875	5.5	5.3	0	34.1
25	1.5	27.75	6	3	0	38.5
26	1.125	28.8125	6.5	0.8	0	42.9
27	0.9	30.25	7	0	1.2	48.3
28	0.75	31.875	7.5	0	3	54.3
29	0.6	33.5	8	0	4.8	60.2
30	0.45	35.125	8.5	0	6.6	66.2
31	0.3	36.75	9	0	8.4	72.1
32	0.15	38.375	9.5	0	10.2	78.1
33	0	40	10	0	12	84

If any of these minimum amounts are exceeded the constraint is not violated (as in maximization), but one or more of the constraint requirements will be *overfulfilled*. (More than the required minimum amount of an additive will be supplied.) This means that constraint violation in minimization problems will occur when a value of x or y is less than the minimum required amount.

2. The entry in B7 should now be entitled Max (Min x), but the formula will remain the same. Once again the purpose of this entry is merely to indicate the range of x values that need to be plotted.
3. The entries in B8 and B9 should now be entitled 'Minimum required x' and 'Minimum required y', and since, as always, the most restrictive constraint dominates, these entries should now be the *maximum* values in the ranges E2..E5 and F2..F5. This will ensure that all constraints are at least satisfied.
4. The entries in E13..E23 must now select, for each value of x, the *maximum* value from each of the constraints. This will produce the feasibility region for the minimization problem.
5. Since we need to minimize the value of the objective function, the optimal solution will be the values of x and y associated with the lowest value in the range F13..F23.
6. The entries H13..J23 must have their algebraic signs reversed, since they no longer represent the extent to which each resource is *underused*, but now indicate the extent to which each requirement is *overfulfilled*.

If you do not want to have to make all these changes each time the type of linear program problem changes, then make a copy of the original (maximization) worksheet (File, Combine, Copy, Entire File is the command sequence), and then make the changes to the copied file. You will then have one file for maximization and another for minimization.

Whatever way you do it, when these changes are made something like Worksheet 5.5 should be produced. As you can see from this worksheet, the optimal solution is to mix 1.5 kg of Moonosh with 5 kg of Cowgrub at a total (minimum) cost of £18.40.

However, as was the case with maximization, this optimal solution will remain optimal only as long as the costs of the two feeds remain within certain limits. It is left as an exercise for you to confirm that these limits can be represented by the following statements.

If the ratio of the cost per kilo of Moonosh to the cost per kilo of Cowgrub exceeds 2.0, then the optimal solution becomes $x = 0$, $y = 8$.

If the ratio of the cost per kilo of Moonosh to the cost per kilo of Cowgrub is less than 0.75, then the optimal solution becomes $x = 6.666$, $y = 1$.

5.6 Duality

We are now in a position to examine an important property, known as duality, which is possessed by all linear programs, and which has the effect of creating two different, but logically equivalent ways of expressing any linear program.

Consider the following information.

A firm uses two inputs (labour and capital) to produce two outputs (product X and product Y).

Each unit of X requires 3 units of labour and 5 units of capital, while each unit of Y requires 6 units of labour and 2 units of capital.

There are a total of 90 units of labour and 60 units of capital available to the firm, and it can sell all of the output produced at prices of £40 and £100 for units of X and Y respectively.

Now if we

$$\text{let } x = \text{the output of product X}$$
$$\text{let } y = \text{the output of product Y}$$

and assume that the firm wishes to maximize revenue (R), then we can write what is known as the primal linear program for this problem as follows:

Primal program.

$$\begin{aligned} \text{Maximize} \quad & 60x + 100y = R \\ \text{Subject to} \quad & 3x + 6y \leqslant 90 \\ & 5x + 2y \leqslant 60 \end{aligned}$$

You are left to confirm that a solution to this problem would produce optimal solution values of $x = 7.5$, $y = 11.25$ and a maximum revenue of £1575.

However, suppose that instead of the information provided above, we were told the following.

A firm employs 90 units of labour and 60 units of capital and wishes to know what value should be assigned by its accounting system to these resources. That is, it wishes to know the *maximum* amount it should be prepared to pay for an extra unit of each resource.

The senior accountant argues that if an (as yet undetermined) value of £a is assigned to each unit of labour, and a value of £b to each unit of capital, then she can write a linear program that will solve for the values of a and b that will minimize the total cost (C) to the firm of using the two resources.

She proceeds to identify this implied objective function as

$$\text{Minimize} \quad 90a + 60b = C$$

This reflects her view that the values of a and b should be such that the total cost to the firm of using the 90 units of labour and the 60 units of capital should be minimized.

She is, however, immediately confronted with the objection that such an objective function is obviously minimized when the values of a and b are both zero. But she counters this objection by pointing out that such values would not represent the implied worth to the firm of the inputs used. This follows from the fact that the resources are used to produce two outputs (call them products X and Y), and that these products are sold at prices of £60 and £100 respectively.

It must be the case, therefore, that the total assigned value of the inputs used in the production of a unit of X be *at least* equal to £60; while, by the same logic, those inputs used in the production of a unit of Y must have a value to the firm that is *at least* equal to £100.

Now, it is also known that each unit of X requires 3 units of labour and 5 units of capital, while each unit of Y requires 6 units of labour and 2 units of capital.

Using this knowledge, the accountant argues that the following linear program will accurately reflect the firm's identified situation:

Dual program.

$$\begin{align} \text{Minimize} \quad & 90a + 60b = C \\ \text{Subject to} \quad & 3a + 5b \geq 60 \\ & 6a + 2b \geq 100 \end{align}$$

If this program is solved graphically for the *minimum* value, then it is found that the optimal values of a and b are £15.833 and £2.5 respectively, while the minimum cost is calculated to be £1575.

It is no coincidence that this last figure is identical to the maximum revenue attainable in the primal problem, since there is an intimate relationship between the primal and the dual programs.

Neither is it coincidence that only when the inputs are assigned values of £15.833 per unit of labour and £2.5 per unit of capital do the primal solution values of $x = 7.5$ and $y = 11.25$ generate exactly the same total revenue as the total assigned cost. That is

(units of product X)(price of X) + (units of product Y)(Price of Y)

must equal

(units of labour)(unit cost of labour) + (units of capital)(unit cost of capital)

In other words

$$(x)(60) + (y)(100) = (a)(90) + (b)(60)$$

Implying that

$$(7.5)(60) + (11.25)(100) = (15.833)(90) + (2.5)(60) = £1575$$

The firm's profit, *if* the actual costs per unit of input were as assigned, would obviously be zero, but this of course does not imply that a zero profit will *actually* be made. The correct implication to be drawn from the analysis is that the firm could pay *up to* £15.833 per unit of labour and *up to* £2.5 per unit of capital and still not make a loss. These two figures are known as the *shadow costs* of the two inputs, and can be viewed as 'threshold' values for the prices of the two inputs. This means that if the price that has to be paid for an input exceeds its shadow cost, then such a purchase would not represent a positive contribution to the profit made by the operation.

It is not necessary, however, to go through this entire reasoning every time the dual program is to be derived from the primal. This is because a general relationship can always be derived as follows

Primal program.

$$\text{Maximize} \quad ax + by = R$$
$$\text{Subject to} \quad cx + dy \leqslant e$$
$$fx + gy \leqslant h$$
$$ix + jy \leqslant k$$

It will be found that a systematic transposition of the terms in this primal program will produce the dual.

Dual program.

$$\text{Minimize} \quad kq + hr + es = R^*$$
$$\text{Subject to} \quad jq + gr + ds \geqslant b$$
$$iq + fr + cs \geqslant a$$

The effect of this transposition can be seen to mean that the primal problem contains two variables (x and y) and three constraints, while the dual problem contains three variables (q, r and s) and two constraints. Furthermore, the direction of the inequalities in the constraints has been reversed (i.e. from $\leqslant$ to $\geqslant$).

This systematic transposition is symptomatic of the general relationship between primal and dual programs, since it will also be observed that the coefficients associated with any one *variable* in the primal become the coefficients associated with any one *constraint* in the dual.

In this sense the dual can be viewed as a systematic transposition of the primal in which 'variables become constraints' and 'constraints become variables', while the optimal value of the objective function remains unchanged even though it is a maximum value for one formulation (R) and a minimum value (R^*) for the other.

This concludes our present discussion of duality although further reference is made to the concept in Chapter 7 where it will be shown that a simultaneous solution to both the primal and dual programs is provided by the method outlined there.

5.7 Linear programming with a choice of production techniques

In all of the foregoing analysis it has been assumed that the input coefficients relating the output of products to the usage of resources are fixed. This implies that there is only one production technique available to the firm and that this technique is uniquely specified in terms of its input requirements. However, it is possible that there is a *choice* of techniques available, and as a result the linear program technique should be able to incorporate such a possibility into the formulation.

To see the issues involved, consider the following example.

EXAMPLE 5.2

A firm uses two inputs (input A and input B) to produce two outputs (product X and product Y). These inputs can be used with either of two production techniques (T1 and T2).

Using T1, each unit of product X requires 2 units of input A and 6 units of input B, while each unit of product Y requires 4 units of input A and 3 units of input B.

Using T2, each unit of product X requires 3 units of input A and 2 units of input B, while each unit of product Y requires 2 units of input A and 7.5 units of input B.

A total of 120 units of input A and 150 units of input B is available to the firm, and the products are sold at prices of £55 and £100 for X and Y respectively.

Using which technique, what outputs of products X and Y should be produced if the greatest daily revenue is to be made, and assuming that it is not possible to operate the two techniques simultaneously?

SOLUTION 5.2

To formulate the linear program we can proceed as follows:

let $x =$ the daily production level of product X
let $y =$ the daily production level of product Y

Now examine each technique in turn.

Under T1, the objective function is easily seen to be

$$\text{Maximize} \quad 55x + 100y = \text{revenue}$$

The production conditions for this technique imply that the following constraints apply.

$$2x + 4y \leq 120 \text{ (input A restriction)}$$

and that

$$6x + 3y \leq 150 \text{ (input B restriction)}$$

This is the linear program for T1, and by a similar logic for T2 we have, *under T2*

$$\text{Maximize} \quad 55x + 100y = \text{revenue}$$
$$\text{Subject to} \quad 3x + 2y \leq 120 \text{ (input A restriction)}$$
$$2x + 7.5y \leq 150 \text{ (input B restriction)}$$

You can now use a worksheet such as the one created in Worksheet 5.2 to analyze each of the techniques separately and then compare them in terms of their optimality.

The results are shown in Worksheets 5.6 and 5.7, where, since there are only two constraints, the redundant range of cells in column D of the original exhibit have been erased.

As you can see, with these particular product prices, the optimal solution is to use T1 to produce 13.00 units of product X and 23.5 units of product Y (producing a revenue of £3065. (In fact the true solution is $x = 13.66$ and $y = 23.33$, but your scale probably will not show this.) Therein lies the real problem of the graphical method.

Furthermore, there is no combination of x and y values using T2 which can produce a revenue in excess of £2906.66. The second technique is clearly inferior at this set of product prices.

However, it is an easy matter to confirm that if the price of product X rises above £63 (with the price of product Y remaining unchanged), then not only is it preferable to produce a different output combination, but also to do so using T2. To be exact, with an objective function such as

$$80x + 100y = \text{revenue}$$

then the optimal solution is to use T2 to produce 32 units of product X and 11.46 units of product Y (producing a revenue of £3706.66). Try it.

Finally, you should also confirm for yourself that if the ratio between the product prices is exactly equal to 0.627, then the two techniques are 'equally optimal' in the sense that 12 units of X and 24 units of Y should now be produced under T1, or 32 units of X and 11.466 units of Y under T2, but that it makes no difference to revenue as to which technique is used. The maximum revenue is (approximately) £3153 in both cases.

The approach illustrated above can, of course, be extended to a situation in which there is a choice of more than two techniques and indeed to the extreme implication of such extension, where there is perfect substitution between both inputs within certain limits. Under such circumstances the firm can choose, within certain overriding technical constraints, which combination of resources is best suited to the composition of output that is desired. The simplest form of such flexible substitution between inputs can be represented by

$$x = aL_x + bK_x$$
$$y = cL_y + dK_y$$

where a, b, c and d represent the technical constraints of the production process, x and y are the physical output levels of products X and Y respectively, L and K are the inputs of labour and capital, and the subscripted terms refer to the amount of that resource used in the production of that output.

This means that L_x represents the amount of labour allocated to the production of product X, while K_x represents the amount of capital allocated to the production of X. The maximum output (x) obtainable from this allocation is then given by

$$x = aL_x + bK_x$$

For example, if $a = 0.2$ and $b = 0.5$, and if 100 units of labour and 200 units of capital are devoted to the production of product X, then the output obtainable is

WORKSHEET 5.6

Technique 1

	A	B	C	D	E	F
1		x coeff.	y coeff.	constant	Max	Max y
2	Constraint 1	2	4	120	60	30
3	Constraint 2	6	3	150	25	50
4	Constraint 3					
5	Constraint 4					
6	Object. funct.	55	100			
7	Max (Max x)	60				
8	Max allowed x	25				
9	Max allowed y	30				
10						Value of
11						Objective
12	x value	y (const 1)	y (const 2)	y (const 3)	Feasible y	Function
13	0	30	50		30	3000
14	1	29.5	48		29.5	3005
15	2	29	46		29	3010
16	3	28.5	44		28.5	3015
17	4	28	42		28	3020
18	5	27.5	40		27.5	3025
19	6	27	38		27	3030

7	26.5			
8	26			
9	25.5			
10	25			
11	24.5			
12	24			
13	23.5			
14	23			
15	22.5			
16	22			
17	21.5			
18	21			
19	20.5			
20	20	36	26.5	3035
21	19.5	34	26	3040
22	19	32	25.5	3045
23	18.5	30	25	3050
24	18	28	24.5	3055
25	17.5	26	24	3060
26		24	23.5	**3065**
27		22	22	2970
28		20	20	2825
29		18	18	2680
30		16	16	2535
31		14	14	2390
32		12	12	2245
33		10	10	2100
34		8	8	1955
35		6	6	1810
36		4	4	1665
37		2	2	1520
38		0	0	1375
39				
40				

WORKSHEET 5.7

Technique 2

	A	B	C	D	E	F
1		x coeff.	y coeff.	constant	Max	Max y
2	Constraint 1	3	2	120	40	60
3	Constraint 2	2	7.5	150	75	20
4	Constraint 3					
5	Constraint 4					
6	Object. Funct.	55	100			
7	Max (Max x)	75				
8	Max allowed x	40				
9	Max allowed y	20				
10						
11						Value of
12	x value	y (const 1)	y (const 2)	y (const 3)	Feasible y	Objective Function
13	0	60	20		20	2000
14	1	58.5	19.7333333		19.7333333	2028.333333
15	2	57	19.4666666		19.4666666	2056.666666
16	3	55.5	19.2		19.2	2085
17	4	54	18.9333333		18.9333333	2113.333333
18	5	52.5	18.6666666		18.6666666	2141.666666
19	6	51	18.4		18.4	2170
20	7	49.5	18.1333333		18.1333333	2198.333333
21	8	48	17.8666666		17.8666666	2226.666666
22	9	46.5	17.6		17.6	2255
23	10	45	17.3333333		17.3333333	2283.333333
24	11	43.5	17.0666666		17.0666666	2311.666666
25	12	42	16.8		16.8	2340

13	40.5	16.5333333	16.5333333	2368.333333
14	39	16.2666666	16.2666666	2396.666666
15	37.5	16	16	2425
16	36	15.7333333	15.7333333	2453.333333
17	34.5	15.4666666	15.4666666	2481.666666
18	33	15.2	15.2	2510
19	31.5	14.9333333	14.9333333	2538.333333
20	30	14.6666666	14.6666666	2566.666666
21	28.5	14.4	14.4	2595
22	27	14.1333333	14.1333333	2623.333333
23	25.5	13.8666666	13.8666666	2651.666666
24	24	13.6	13.6	2680
25	22.5	13.3333333	13.3333333	2708.333333
26	21	13.0666666	13.0666666	2736.666666
27	19.5	12.8	12.8	2765
28	18	12.5333333	12.5333333	2793.333333
29	16.5	12.2666666	12.2666666	2821.666666
30	15	12	12	2850
31	13.5	11.7333333	11.7333333	2878.333333
32	12	11.4666666	11.4666666	2906.666666
33	10.5	11.2	10.5	2865
34	9	10.9333333	9	2770
35	7.5	10.666666	7.5	2675
36	6	10.4	6	2580
37	4.5	10.1333333	4.5	2485
38	3	9.8666666	3	2390
39	1.5	9.6	1.5	2295
40	0	9.33333333	0	2200

given by

$$x = 0.2(100) + 0.5(200) = 120$$

However, an *identical* output level could also have been obtained from a large number of alternative allocations (such as using 200 units of labour and 160 units of capital). This is the basic implication of perfectly flexible input substitution.

The equations presented above define what is often referred to as the production functions of the products X and Y since they define the way in which the production process transforms inputs into outputs. Furthermore, the form of these two equations implies perfect linear substitution between labour and capital in the production of both products X and Y.

However, perfect linear substitution between labour and capital for all values of L_x, L_y, K_x and K_y is an extremely unrealistic assumption, since at least *some* of both inputs will usually be required. Accordingly the equations could be modified to

$$x = aL_x + bK_x \quad L_x \geqslant e \quad K_x \geqslant f$$
$$y = cL_y + dK_y \quad L_y \geqslant g \quad K_y \geqslant h$$

where e, f, g and h are constants that represent the *limits* within which the process of linear substitution is technically permissible.

To illustrate these points, consider a firm that produces two products (X and Y) under production conditions given by

$$x = 2L_x + 4K_x \quad L_x \geqslant 10 \quad K_x \geqslant 5$$
$$y = L_y + 6K_y \quad L_y \geqslant 4 \quad K_y \geqslant 12$$

The firm pays £2 per unit of labour employed, of which there are 100 units available per time period, and £5 per unit of capital employed, of which there are 90 units available per time period.

If, in addition, it can sell units of X for £10 each and units of Y for £15 each, then the linear program that maximizes profit can be written as

$$\begin{aligned}
\text{Maximize} \quad & 10x + 15y - 2(L_x + L_y) - 5(K_x + K_y) = \text{profit} \\
\text{Subject to} \quad & L_x + L_y \leqslant 100 \\
& K_x + K_y \leqslant 90 \\
& L_x \geqslant 10 \\
& K_x \geqslant 5 \\
& L_y \geqslant 4 \\
& K_y \geqslant 12
\end{aligned}$$

It will be noticed that the formulation above has a 'mixture' of variables (i.e. x, y, L_x, L_y, K_x and K_y) but this complication can easily be remedied by remembering that

$$x = 2L_x + 4K_x$$
$$y = L_y + 6K_y$$

Now we can substitute these expressions in the objective function to obtain

$$10(2L_x + 4K_x) + 15(L_y + 6K_y) - 2(L_x + L_y) - 5(K_x + K_y) = P$$

which, after collecting terms becomes

Maximize $\quad 18L_x + 35K_x + 13L_y + 85K_y = P$
Subject to
$$\begin{aligned} L_x + L_y &\leq 100 \\ K_x + K_y &\leq 90 \\ L_x &\geq 10 \\ K_x &\geq 5 \\ L_y &\geq 4 \\ K_y &\geq 12 \end{aligned}$$

Two things will be noted about the linear program above. First, the inequalities are 'mixed' in the sense that some are of a 'greater than or equal to' nature while others are of a 'less than or equal to' form.

Secondly, there are four variables in the final formulation (L_x, L_y, K_x and K_y), and consequently it cannot be represented in two-dimensional geometry. This highlights the fundamental limitation of the graphical method, namely that while it is a useful method of understanding the issues involved in simple two-dimensional problems, it cannot be extended to consider programs that involve three or more variables.

To deal with this limitation requires converting the linear program solution technique from graphical to algebraic form, and the result of doing this is the so-called *simplex* method of Chapter 7.

5.8 Exercises

5.1

Find the values of x and y that

Maximize $\quad 2x + 6y$
Subject to
$$\begin{aligned} 2x + 4y &\leq 100 \\ x + 6y &\leq 1200 \\ 5x + 2y &\leq 130 \end{aligned}$$

5.2

Find the values of x and y that

Minimize $\quad 10x + 6y$
Subject to
$$\begin{aligned} 10x + 4y &\geq 10 \\ 8x + 6y &\geq 12 \\ 6x + 12y &\geq 18 \end{aligned}$$

5.3

A firm produces two products (X and Y) which both use three inputs (A, B and C). Each unit of X requires 12 units of A, 6 units of B, and 3 units of C, while each unit of Y requires 3 units of A, 3 units of B, and 3 units of C.

The firm has access to a total of 270 units of A, 150 units of B, and 120 units of C per time period, and sells products X and Y at prices of £6 and £4 respectively.

(a) Determine the sales of X and Y that maximize revenue.
(b) Within what range of prices for the two products will the sales of X and Y which maximize revenue remain unchanged?
(c) If the firm has to pay £0.1, £0.5 and £0.3 for units of A, B and C respectively, find the sales of X and Y that will maximize profit.

5.4

A chemical production process consists of mixing two compounds (A and B) to produce a blend that must contain at least 15 per cent phosphorous, at least 12 per cent potassium, and at least 25 per cent iodine.

Each kilo of compound A costs £25 and contains 20 per cent phosphorous, 15 per cent potassium and 50 per cent iodine. Each kilo of compound B costs £10 and contains 10 per cent phosphorous, 30 per cent potassium and 5 per cent iodine.

Write and solve a linear program that will fulfil the manufacturer's objective of supplying *at least* 1 kg of the blend at the minimum cost.

5.5

A firm operates two production processes (process 1 and process 2), which are each capable of producing its best-selling product (P), which the firm sells for a price of £800.

Each unit of product P requires 1 hour's production time on one or other of two production processes.

On process 1, each unit of P requires 40 units of input A and 60 units of input B. On process 2 each unit of P requires 60 units of input A and 80 units of input B.

The firm has access to a total of 1200 units of input A and 2400 units of input B per day, and can operate *either* production process for a maximum of 24 hours per day.

It is estimated that the hourly energy and maintenance costs of the two processes are £20 for process 1 and £10 for process 2.

Inputs A and B can be obtained at respective unit costs of £5 and £4.

(a) Define two variables that represent the firm's *hourly* usage of the two processes in the production of P.
(b) Considering both processes, formulate and solve the linear program that will determine the number of hours that should be used on each of the two processes, if the firm's objective is to maximize the daily profit obtainable from the production of P.

(c) If the price of input B fell to £0.50 per unit, what changes would this cause in the optimum usage levels of the two processes?
(d) Explain why the solution to (b) above is not really affected by any changes in the prices of inputs A and B.
(e) If, by paying £4.1 per unit for input A and £5.1 per unit for input B, the firm could guarantee an unlimited daily supply of those two inputs, would such a strategy be justified in comparison with the profit situation in (b) above?

5.6

A house-building company has purchased 250 000 square metres of land, for which it paid £1 million, and on which it proposes to build two types of dwelling (terraced and semi-detached).

Each terraced block consists of five individual units, each requiring 200 sq m of land (including garden space). Each semi-detached block consists of two individual units, each requiring 400 sq m of land (also including garden space).

It is proposed to sell terraced units at £48 000 each and semi-detached units at £64 000 each, while the estimated construction costs are £40 000 and £52 000 for terraced and semi-detached houses respectively.

The planning authorities will not allow the total number of blocks on the site to exceed 260.

The building company estimates that a total of 10 000 sq m of land must be used for access facilities and communal play areas, while the availability of mortgage funds suggests that the total expenditure on houses of either type will not exceed £48 million.

(a) Formulate and solve a linear programme to determine the optimum number of houses of each type that should be built to maximize the company's profits. What is the maximum possible profit?
(b) If it was discovered that 100 000 sq m of land was unsuitable for building purposes, what changes would this imply for the optimal solution in (a) above?
(c) If the firm received a discount of 10 per cent on the price it paid for the land, what difference would this imply for the optimal solution?

5.9 Solutions to the exercises

5.1

You can use Worksheet 5.2 to solve this problem as long as you remember to alter the range of x values to be evaluated. A summary of what you should obtain is shown in Worksheet 5.8.

The optimal solution is when $x = 15$ and $y = 17.5$, giving the objective function a maximum value of 135.

WORKSHEET 5.8

	A	B	C	D	E	F
1		x coeff.	y coeff.	constant	Max x	Max y
2	Constraint 1	2	4	100	50	25
3	Constraint 2	1	6	120	120	20
4	Constraint 3	5	2	130	26	65
5	Constraint 4					
6	Object. Funct.	2	6			
7	Max (Max x)	120				
8	Max allowed x	26				
9	Max allowed y	20				
10						
11						Value of
12	x value	y(const 1)	y(const 2)	y(const 3)	Feasible y	Objective Function
13	0	25	20	65	20	120
14	1	24.5	19.8333333	62.5	19.8333333	121
15	2	24	19.6666666	60	19.6666666	122
16	3	23.5	19.5	57.5	19.5	123
17	4	23	19.3333333	55	19.3333333	124
18	5	22.5	19.1666666	52.5	19.1666666	125
19	6	22	19	50	19	126
20	7	21.5	18.8333333	47.5	18.8333333	126
21	8	21	18.6666666	45	18.6666666	128
22	9	20.5	18.5	42.5	18.5	129
23	10	20	18.3333333	40	18.3333333	130
24	11	19.5	18.1666666	37.5	18.1666666	131
25	12	19	18	35	18	132
26	13	18.5	17.8333333	32.5	17.8333333	133
27	14	18	17.6666666	30	17.6666666	134
28	15	17.5	17.5	27.5	17.5	**135**
29	16	17	17.3333333	25	17	134
30	17	16.5	17.1666666	22.5	16.5	133
31	18	16	17	20	16	132
32	19	15.5	16.8333333	17.5	15.5	131
33	20	15	16.6666666	15	15	130
34	21	14.5	16.5	12.5	12.5	117
35	22	14	16.3333333	10	10	104
36	23	13.5	16.1666666	7.5	7.5	91
37	24	13	16	5	5	78

5.2

Being a minimization problem, you should adapt Worksheet 5.5 to obtain Worksheet 5.9.

The optimal solution is when $x = 0.5$ and $y = 1.3333$, giving the objective function a minimum value of 13.00.

5.3

(a) The objective function will be given as

$$\text{Maximize} \quad 6x + 4y = \text{revenue}$$

where $x =$ the production of product X per time period, and $y =$ the production of product Y per time period.

The limitations upon resource availability produce the following constraints:

$$12x + 3y \leqslant 270 \quad \text{(input A restriction)}$$
$$6x + 3y \leqslant 150 \quad \text{(input B restriction)}$$
$$3x + 3y \leqslant 120 \quad \text{(input C restriction)}$$

This program can then be solved by adapting Worksheet 5.2 to give Worksheet 5.10.

The optimal solution is to produce 10 units of product X and 30 units of product Y. This will produce the maximum revenue of £180.

(b) The gradients of the constraints are 4, 2 and 1 for constraints 1, 2 and 3 respectively, while the gradient of the objective function is 1.5. Consequently, since the current optimal solution has the gradient of the objective function lying between the gradients of the second and third constraints, it follows that this solution will remain optimal as long as the gradient of the objective function lies between 1 and 2.

This is easily confirmed if you 'run' your worksheet first of all with an objective function of

$$3x + 4y = \text{revenue} \quad \text{(gradient less than 1)}$$

and then with an objective function of

$$9x + 4y = \text{revenue} \quad \text{(gradient greater than 2)}$$

You will find that the optimal solution changes to $x = 0$ and $y = 40$ (when the objective function gradient is less than 1), but to $x = 20$ and $y = 10$ (when the objective function gradient exceeds 2).

(c) The introduction of input costs means that we need to calculate the unit costs of each of the outputs.

Since each unit of product X uses 12 units of input A, 6 units of input B, and 3 units of input C, and since these inputs have unit costs of £0.1, £0.5 and £0.3 respectively, we can write

$$\text{unit cost of } X = 0.1(12) + 0.5(6) + 0.3(3) = £5.1$$

WORKSHEET 5.9

	A	B	C	D	E	F
10						Value of
11						Objective
12	x value	y (const 1)	y (const 2)	y (const 3)	Feasible y	Function
13	0.0000	2.5000	2.0000	1.5000	2.5000	15.0000
14	0.1667	2.0833	1.7778	1.4167	2.0833	14.1667
15	0.3333	1.6667	1.5556	1.3333	1.6667	13.3333
16	0.5000	1.2500	1.3333	1.2500	1.3333	**13.0000**
17	0.6667	0.8333	1.1111	1.1667	1.1667	13.6667
18	0.8333	0.4167	0.8889	1.0833	1.0833	14.8333
19	1.0000	0.0000	0.6667	1.0000	1.0000	16.0000
20	1.1667	-0.4167	0.4444	0.9167	0.9167	17.1667
21	1.3333	-0.8333	0.2222	0.8333	0.8333	18.3333
22	1.5000	-1.2500	0.0000	0.7500	0.7500	19.5000
23	1.6667	-1.6667	-0.2222	0.6667	0.6667	20.6667
24	1.8333	-2.0833	-0.4444	0.5833	0.5833	21.8333
25	2.0000	-2.5000	-0.6667	0.5000	0.5000	23.0000
26	2.1667	-2.9167	-0.8889	0.4167	0.4167	24.1667
27	2.3333	-3.3333	-1.1111	0.3333	0.3333	25.3333
28	2.5000	-3.7500	-1.3333	0.2500	0.2500	26.5000
29	2.6667	-4.1667	-1.5556	0.1667	0.1667	27.6667

WORKSHEET 5.10

	A	B	C	D	E	F
1		x coeff.	y coeff.	constant	Max	Max y
2	Constraint 1	12	3	270	22.5	90
3	Constraint 2	6	3	150	25	50
4	Constraint 3	3	3	120	40	40
5	Constraint 4					
6	Object. Funct.	6	4			
7	Max (Max x)	40				
8	Max allowed x	22.5				
9	Max allowed y	40				
10						Value of
11						Objective
12	x value	y (const 1)	y (const 2)	y (const 3)	Feasible y	Function
13	0	90	50	40	40	160
14	1	86	48	39	39	162
15	2	82	46	38	38	164
16	3	78	44	37	37	166
17	4	74	42	36	36	168
18	5	70	40	35	35	170
19	6	66	38	34	34	172
20	7	62	36	33	33	174
21	8	58	34	32	32	176
22	9	54	32	31	31	178
23	10	50	30	30	30	**180**
24	11	46	28	29	28	178
25	12	42	26	28	26	176
26	13	38	24	27	24	174
27	14	34	22	26	22	172
28	15	30	20	25	20	170
29	16	26	18	24	18	168
30	17	22	16	23	16	166
31	18	18	14	22	14	164
32	19	14	12	21	12	162
33	20	10	10	20	10	160
34	21	6	8	19	6	150
35	22	2	6	18	2	140
36	22.5	0	5	17.5	0	135

Applying the same logic to product Y produces

$$\text{unit cost of } Y = 0.1(3) + 0.5(3) + 0.3(3) = £2.7$$

The profit function therefore becomes

$$(6 - 5.1)x + (4 - 2.7)y = 0.9x + 1.3y = \text{profit}$$

The gradient of this new objective function is less than 1, so as we saw above, the optimal solution will be when $x = 0$ and $y = 40$, with a maximum profit of £52 [i.e. $0(0.9) + 40(1.3)$].

5.4

The variables of this problem should be defined as

x = the amount of compound A used in the blend
y = the amount of compound B used in the blend

This allows us to identify the objective function as

$$\text{Minimize} \quad 25x + 10y = \text{cost}$$

Since at least 1 kg of the blend must be supplied, our first constraint is

$$x + y \geqslant 1$$

The requirement that the blend of the two compounds should contain at least 15 per cent phosphorous means that the supply of the blend $(x + y)$ must contain at least $0.15(x + y)$ of phosphorous.

Compound A supplies 0.2 kg of phosphorous per kilo, while compound B supplies 0.1 kg of phosphorous per kilo. So it follows that a blend of x kg of compound A with y kg of compound B will supply $0.2x + 0.1y$ kg of phosphorous. This produces our second constraint, since we know that the supply of phosphorous from the blend must be at least 0.15 times the combined supply. We therefore have

$$0.2x + 0.1y \geqslant 0.15(x + y)$$

Therefore

$$0.05x - 0.05y \geqslant 0$$

By the same logic we can identify the potassium and iodine constraints as

$$0.15x + 0.3y \geqslant 0.12(x + y)$$

implying that

$$0.03x + 0.18y \geqslant 0$$

and

$$0.5x + 0.05y \geqslant 0.25(x + y)$$

WORKSHEET 5.11

	A	B	C	D	E	F	G
1		x coeff.	y coeff.	constant	Min x	Min y	gradient
2	Constraint 1	0.05	-0.05	0	0	0	1
3	Constraint 2	0.03	0.18	0	0	0	0.16666666
4	Constraint 3	0.25	0.2	0	0	0	1.25
5	Constraint 4	1	1	1			1
6	Object. Funct.	25	10				2.5
7	Max (min x)	0					
8	Min required x	0					
9	Min required y	0					
10							
11							Value of
12							Objective
13	x value	y (const 1)	y (const 2)	y (const 3)	y (const 4)	Feasible y	Function
14	0.0000	0.0000	0.0000	0.0000	1.0000	0.0000	0.0000
15	0.0500	0.0500	-0.0083	-0.0625	0.9500	0.0500	1.7500
16	0.1000	0.1000	-0.0167	-0.1250	0.9000	0.1000	3.5000
17	0.1500	0.1500	-0.0250	-0.1875	0.8500	0.1500	5.2500
18	0.2000	0.2000	-0.0333	-0.2500	0.8000	0.2000	7.0000
19	0.2500	0.2500	-0.0417	-0.3125	0.7500	0.2500	8.7500
20	0.3000	0.3000	-0.0500	-0.3750	0.7000	0.3000	10.5000
21	0.3500	0.3500	-0.0583	-0.4375	0.6500	0.3500	12.2500
22	0.4000	0.4000	-0.0667	-0.5000	0.6000	0.4000	14.0000
23	0.4500	0.4500	-0.0750	-0.5625	0.5500	0.4500	15.7500
24	**0.5000**	0.5000	-0.0833	-0.6250	0.5000	**0.5000**	17.5000
25	0.5500	0.5500	-0.0917	-0.6875	0.4500	0.5500	19.2500
26	0.6000	0.6000	-0.1000	-0.7500	0.4000	0.6000	21.0000
27	0.6500	0.6500	-0.1083	-0.8125	0.3500	0.6500	22.7500
28	0.7000	0.7000	-0.1167	-0.8750	0.3000	0.7000	24.5000
29	0.7500	0.7500	-0.1250	-0.9375	0.2500	0.7500	26.2500
30	0.8000	0.8000	-0.1333	-1.0000	0.2000	0.8000	28.0000
31	0.8500	0.8500	-0.1417	-1.0625	0.1500	0.8500	29.7500
32	0.9000	0.9000	-0.1500	-1.1250	0.1000	0.9000	31.5000
33	0.9500	0.9500	-0.1583	-1.1875	0.0500	0.9500	33.2500
34	1.0000	1.0000	-0.1667	-1.2500	0.0000	1.0000	35.0000

implying that
$$0.25x - 0.2y \geq 0$$

Remembering that there are now four constraints, you can enter these values into Worksheet 5.5 (after inserting a new column before column E). This will produce the results shown in Worksheet 5.11.

As you can see from the worksheet, the optimal solution is to blend 0.5 kg of compound A with 0.5 kg of compound B at a cost of £17.50. This will supply

$$0.2(0.45) + 0.1(0.6) = 0.15 \text{ kg of phosphorous}$$
$$0.15(0.45) + 0.3(0.6) = 0.2475 \text{ kg of potassium}$$
$$0.5(0.45) + 0.05(0.6) = 0.255 \text{ kg of iodine}$$

The potassium and iodine requirements are seen to be overfulfilled.

Although this is in fact the optimal solution, this method has the disadvantage that it only performs a limited evaluation of x (so that combinations such as 0.49 kg of compound A and 0.51 kg of compound B have not been considered). You can rectify this by respecifying the worksheet so that it focuses more closely on the optimal solution. To do this you could allow the optimal value of x to increase and decrease by some small amount (0.01 say), and then see whether the value of the objective function decreases in either case. If it does, then that value of x was not optimal. You can then respecify the range of x values to be evaluated with a smaller increment than before and target the analysis on those values of x that are close to what you previously believed the optimal solution to be.

If you do this for this problem, then you will find that a solution of $x = 0.5$ and $y = 0.5$ is in fact optimal.

Alternatively, you could graph the feasibility polygon and then examine the optimal point visually, but you will still encounter the problem that your observed solution is only as accurate as the scale that is used by your graph.

Clearly these considerations provide a strong argument for an algebraic approach to problems such as these, but you will have to wait until Chapter 7 when such an algebraic technique is explained.

Finally, it should be noted that the considerable oversupply of both potassium and iodine may constitute a problem in certain circumstances (since too much of a 'good thing' can often be as bad as too little). In such circumstances it may be necessary to introduce strict *equalities* to some or all of the constraints, or at least redefine the requirements in terms of 'at least this much, but no more than that much'. Once again, however, you will have to wait until Chapter 7 until you find out how to do this.

5.5

(a) Let $x =$ the number of hours operating process 1, and let $y =$ the number of hours operating process 2.

(b) Since each unit of the product requires 1 hour of production time on one or other of the processes, we can define the output of the product *in terms of process hours*. That is

$$x + y = \text{the output of product P}$$

This means that the revenue from producing P can also be defined in terms of process hours as

$$800x + 800y = \text{revenue}$$

Furthermore, since each unit of P produced on process 1 requires 40 units of input A and 60 units of input B, we can deduce the hourly production costs of operating process 1 to be

$$40(5) + 60(4) = £440$$

When the hourly energy and maintenance costs are included, then the hourly operational costs for process 1 (C1) are given by

$$C1 = 440 + 20 = £460$$

Consequently, the profit per hour of operating process 1 is £340, i.e. (£800 − £460).

Using the same logic with reference to process 2 we can calculate the hourly operating costs (C2) to be

$$C2 = 60(5) + 80(4) + 10 = £630$$

The profit per operating hour on process 2 is therefore £170.

Our objective function can now be written as

$$\text{Maximize} \quad 340x + 170y = \text{profit}$$

To obtain the constraints for the problem we can note that since there are only 24 hours available in any one day for each process, and since they cannot be operated *simultaneously*, we have

$$x + y \leqslant 24$$

Furthermore, the limited availability of the two inputs means that

$$40x + 60y \leqslant 1200 \quad \text{(input A availability)}$$
$$60x + 80y \leqslant 2400 \quad \text{(input B availability)}$$

These last two constraints complete our program and produce (using Worksheet 5.2) the solution shown in Worksheet 5.12.

As you can see, the optimal solution is to operate process 1 for 24 hours per day and not to operate process 2 at all. This will produce the greatest profit of £8160.

(c) If the price of input B fell to £0.5 per unit then the objective function would become

$$[800 - 40(5) - 60(0.5) - 20]x + [800 - 60(5) - 80(0.5) - 10]y$$

When identical terms are collected this becomes

$$550x + 450y = P$$

WORKSHEET 5.12

	A	B	C	D	E	F
1		x coeff.	y coeff.	constant	Max	Max y
2	Constraint 1	1	1	24	24	24
3	Constraint 2	40	60	1200	30	20
4	Constraint 3	60	80	2400	40	30
5	Constraint 4					
6	Object. Funct.	340	170			
7	Max (Max x)	40				
8	Max allowed x	24				
9	Max allowed y	20				
10						Value of
11						Objective
12	x value	y (const 1)	y (const 2)	y (const 3)	Feasible y	Function
13	0	24	20	30	20	3400
14	1	23	19.3333333	29.25	19.3333333	3626.666666
15	2	22	18.6666666	28.5	18.6666666	3853.333333
16	3	21	18	27.75	18	4080
17	4	20	17.3333333	27	17.3333333	4306.666666
18	5	19	16.6666666	26.25	16.6666666	4533.333333
19	6	18	16	25.5	16	4760
20	7	17	15.3333333	24.75	15.3333333	4986.666666

21	8	14.6666666	16	24	5213.333333
22	9	14	15	23.25	5440
23	10	13.3333333	14	22.5	5666.666666
24	11	12.6666666	13	21.75	5893.333333
25	12	12	12	21	6120
26	13	11.3333333	11	20.25	6290
27	14	10.6666666	10	19.5	6460
28	15	10	9	18.75	6630
29	16	9.3333333	8	18	6800
30	17	8.6666666	7	17.25	6970
31	18	8	6	16.5	7140
32	19	7.3333333	5	15.75	7310
33	20	6.6666666	4	15	7480
34	21	6	3	14.25	7650
35	22	5.3333333	2	13.5	7820
36	23	4.6666666	1	12.75	7990
37	24	4	0	12	**8160**
38					
39					
40					

WORKSHEET 5.13

	A	B	C	D	E	F
1		x coeff.	y coeff.	constant	Max	Max y
2	Constraint 1	1000	800	240000	240	300
3	Constraint 2	1	1	260	260	260
4	Constraint 3	240000	128000	48000000	200	375
5	Constraint 4					
6	Object. Funct.	40000	24000			
7	Max (Max x)	260				
8	Max allowed x	200				
9	Max allowed y	260				
10						Value of
11						Objective
12	x value	y (const 1)	y (const 2)	y (const 3)	Feasible y	Function
13	0	300	260	375	260	6240000
14	10	287.5	250	356.25	250	6400000
15	20	275	240	337.5	240	6560000
16	30	262.5	230	318.75	230	6720000
17	40	250	220	300	220	6880000
18	50	237.5	210	281.25	210	7040000
19	60	225	200	262.5	200	7200000
20	70	212.5	190	243.75	190	7360000

21	80	200	180	225	180	7520000
22	90	187.5	170	206.25	170	7680000
23	100	175	160	187.5	160	7840000
24	110	162.5	150	168.75	150	8000000
25	120	150	140	150	140	8160000
26	130	137.5	130	131.25	130	**8320000**
27	140	125	120	112.5	112.5	8300000
28	150	112.5	110	93.75	93.75	8250000
29	160	100	100	75	75	8200000
30	170	87.5	90	56.25	56.25	8150000
31	180	75	80	37.5	37.5	8100000
32	190	62.5	70	18.75	18.75	8050000
33	200	50	60	0	0	8000000
34		273.75	239	335.625	239	
35		272.5	238	333.75	238	
36		271.25	237	331.875	237	
37		270	236	330	236	
38						
39						
40						

When you replace the old objective function with this new one in the worksheet, you will find that it makes no difference to the optimal allocation, although the profit from the existing allocation increases to £13 200.

(d) The simple reason for this is that the most binding constraint is the availability of process hours, and even running process 1 for 24 hours still leaves surplus amounts of inputs A and B. Process 2, however, *could* use up all the available quantity of input A (but not of input B) if it was operated for 24 hours. Nevertheless, the fact that process 1 uses less of *both* inputs than process 2 means that no matter what happened to the prices of these inputs, process 1 would always be preferred to process 2. This means that since there are surpluses of both inputs when process 1 is operated for 24 hours, and since process 1 is always to be preferred to process 2, the inputs are not truly scarce resources and unlimited variation in their prices would not cause the optimal allocation to change.

The only exception to this would be if the prices of the inputs rose to such an extent that losses were made. However, all this would do is to make it no longer worthwhile to operate process 1 at all. It would not make process 2 *any more* viable, and the optimal allocation would then be to close down the operation entirely.

(e) From what has been said in (d) above, it should be clear that the availability of inputs A and B is not a binding constraint, and so an unlimited supply of them would not alter the optimal allocation. It is hours on process 1 that is the scarce resource, and it would seem to be the case that this firm should scrap process 2 and replace it with an additional process 1.

5.6

(a) A great deal of confusion can be avoided if the variables are correctly defined at the outset, and in this respect it is the number of *blocks* of each type which are the crucial variables. Consequently

$$\text{let } x = \text{the number of terraced blocks}$$
$$\text{let } y = \text{the number of semi-detached blocks}$$

Now since the profit on a terraced unit is £8000, it follows that the profit on a terraced block (containing five units) will be £40 000. In a similar way, the profit on a semi-detached block will be £24 000.

The objective function is therefore given by

$$\text{Maximize} \quad 40\,000x + 24\,000y = \text{profit}$$

Notice that the £1 million that the company paid for the land has not been included in this equation. This is because it represents a fixed cost that is *not attributable* to any *variable* in the program. In other words it is not a cost that can be avoided by any decision as to the relative numbers of each type of block which should be constructed.

The availability of building land produces the following constraint (remembering that it is housing blocks that concern us):

$$1000x + 800y \leqslant (250\,000 - 10\,000)$$

(Remember that 10 000 sq m of land must be set aside for access and play areas.)

The planning authority's restrictions on the number of blocks that can be built mean that

$$x + y \leqslant 260$$

while the mortgage restriction that the total expenditure should not exceed £48 million means that

$$5(48\,000)x + 2(64\,000)y \leqslant 48\,000\,000$$

That is

$$240\,000x + 128\,000y \leqslant 48\,000\,000$$

Taking all of these arguments together means that we can write the final program as

$$\begin{aligned}
\text{Maximize} \quad & 40\,000x + 24\,000y = \text{profit} \\
\text{Subject to} \quad & 1000x + 800y \leqslant 240\,000 \\
& x + y \leqslant 260 \\
& 240\,000x + 128\,000y \leqslant 48\,000\,000
\end{aligned}$$

Worksheet 5.2 can be used to find the optimal solution as shown in Worksheet 5.13. The building company should build 130 terraced blocks and 130 semi-detached blocks, and this will produce a profit of £7.32 million (i.e. £8.32 million − £1 million).

(b) The effect of this alteration will be to change the land availability constraint to

$$1000x + 800y \leqslant (240\,000 - 100\,000)$$

You can make this alteration to the worksheet and then 'run' it again. You should find that it is now better to build 140 terraced blocks and no semi-detached blocks, and that the maximum profit that can be made has fallen to £4.6 million (£5.6 million − £1 million).

(c) As has already been suggested, the fact that this discount has been obtained from fixed costs means that there will be no change to the optimal allocation (i.e. in the values of x and y). The amount of profit actually made will, however, rise by the amount of the discount (£100 000), but this has *not resulted* from any change in the number of houses built.

6
Matrix Algebra

6.1 Preliminaries

We are all familiar with the idea of using a table to present numerical data items in summary form. Furthermore, we all recognize that provided these data items are of a conventional mathematical form, then each individual item can be subject to normal arithmetic or algebraic operations. However, the question arises of whether the items that comprise the table can be manipulated *collectively* (i.e. as a unit as opposed to individually), and to answer this question we must refer to the concept of a matrix.

In its simplest form a matrix is merely a table (or rectangular array) of data elements, in which each element is uniquely identified by means of two numerical subscripts (denoted by i and j). The first subscript (i) always refers to the row of the matrix in which the element is located, while the second subscript (j) identifies the column location of the element.

Clearly this notation is very similar to that which we have been using when referring to a cell of the Lotus worksheet, with the exception that instead of using a letter to identify a column, another number is used. (There is also another slight difference as Lotus employs the convention 'column letter, row number' to identify a cell address, while matrix algebra reverses this convention and uses 'row number, column number'). Apart from these two points you can effectively think of your Lotus worksheet as an exceptionally large matrix.

Conventionally we use uppercase letters to symbolize the whole matrix (i.e. the collection of elements), and lower case *subscripted* letters to symbolize individual elements.

This means that we can define a_{ij} as the element in the ith row of the jth column of the matrix A.

In this notation, the largest values adopted by i and j define what is known as the dimension (or order) of the matrix, so if we denote these largest values by m and n respectively, the dimension is said to be $m \times n$ (read as m by n). For example, a matrix with 5 rows and 3 columns would be said to be of dimension 5×3.

EXAMPLE 6.1

In the first six months of a given year a firm produces three different products at three different factories. Form a matrix to represent the outputs (measured in thousands) of the three products from each of the factories.

SOLUTION 6.1

$$\text{Factory} \begin{array}{c} \\ 1 \\ 2 \\ 3 \end{array} \begin{array}{c} \text{Product} \\ \begin{array}{ccc} 1 & 2 & 3 \end{array} \\ \begin{array}{c} \text{output of product} \\ \text{type at factory} \\ \text{location} \end{array} \end{array} = \begin{bmatrix} a_{11} & a_{12} & a_{13} \\ a_{21} & a_{22} & a_{23} \\ a_{31} & a_{32} & a_{33} \end{bmatrix} = [A] = (3 \times 3)$$

If we know the actual outputs, then we could rewrite this matrix as (for example)

$$A = \begin{bmatrix} 100 & 50 & 90 \\ 65 & 34 & 72 \\ 80 & 43 & 96 \end{bmatrix}$$

As you can see, the matrix A contains nine ordered elements which each identify the output of product i from factory j. Hence $a_{23} = 72$ represents the output from the second factory of the third product, while a_{31} represents the output from the third factory of the first product.

Since the definition of a matrix simply specifies a rectangular array of elements, there is no need for the largest values of m and n to be equal, but if they are, then this produces what is known as a square matrix. As we shall see later on, square matrices possess particular properties that are of considerable value in mathematical modelling, but at the moment it is sufficient to note that there is no necessity for a matrix to be square.

In fact, there are two other dimensions that are of considerable use in the modelling process, and neither of them is square. These are defined by either m or n being equal to 1, in which case, if $m = 1$ a row *vector* is obtained, while if $n = 1$ a column vector results. Conventionally vectors are represented by lowercase letters, while matrices are represented by uppercase letters, and both are sometimes enclosed in square brackets.

Finally, if both m and n are equal to 1, then this defines a *scalar number*, and illustrates the point that all conventional numbers can be regarded as special cases of $m \times n$ matrices in which $m = n = 1$.

These points can be seen more clearly as follows:

$$a = [a_{11} \quad a_{12} \quad \ldots \quad a_{1n}]$$

is a row vector of dimension $1 \times n$.

$$a = \begin{bmatrix} a_{11} \\ a_{21} \\ \ldots \\ \ldots \\ a_{m1} \end{bmatrix}$$

is a column vector of dimension $m \times 1$.

$$a = [a_{11}]$$

is a scalar number of dimension 1×1.

6.2 Special types of matrix

Before proceeding to the formal rules of matrix algebra, it will be useful to identify a few special matrix types and clarify their function.

6.2.1 The identity matrix

The identity matrix is a *square* matrix of *of any dimension* which acts as the matrix algebra equivalent of the scalar number 1 in conventional algebra. It is characterized by being composed entirely of ones and zeros in the following way:

$$I = [1] = \begin{bmatrix} 1 & 0 \\ 0 & 1 \end{bmatrix} = \begin{bmatrix} 1 & 0 & 0 \\ 0 & 1 & 0 \\ 0 & 0 & 1 \end{bmatrix}$$

The terms that comprise what is called the principal diagonal of the matrix (top left to bottom right) are always equal to 1, while zeros appear elsewhere.

It will also be noted that the identity matrix can be of any dimension as long as it is square. This means that an appropriate identity matrix can always be found for certain specific algebraic operations. This is important, since as you will see later any square matrix remains unchanged after being multiplied by an identity matrix of appropriate dimension, thereby confirming our earlier statement about I performing the matrix algebra equivalent of 1 in scalar algebra.

6.2.2 The null matrix

This matrix is the equivalent of zero in scalar algebra, and is characterized by being comprised entirely of zero elements.

It can be of any dimension (i.e. not necessarily square) and has the feature that when multiplied by any matrix of appropriate dimension it reproduces the null matrix (i.e. itself) as the product.

It also has the feature that if the null matrix is added to, or subtracted from any other matrix of appropriate dimension, then the latter remains unchanged in value.

Now you should have noticed that the preceding discussion has placed much emphasis on the phrase 'of appropriate dimension'. This is because the algebraic operations of addition, subtraction, multiplication and division are only defined in matrix algebra under certain circumstances. This means that we can only perform *collective* arithmetic operations on sets of matrices if certain conditions are met.

These conditions relate entirely to the dimensions of the matrices that are the subjects of the proposed operations, and for this reason we must always be clear as to when certain processes can be carried out and when they cannot.

6.3 Matrix addition and subtraction

As we have just said, unlike conventional algebra you will find that there are a number of conditions that govern whether particular arithmetic operations can be performed on any two or more matrices.

As regards addition and subtraction of matrices, this can only be done if the matrices to be added or subtracted are of the same dimension. This being the case, then the sum or difference is obtained by adding or subtracting the terms in the same relative location. For example:

$$\text{if } A = [a_{11} \ a_{12}] \text{ and } B = [b_{11} \ b_{12}]$$
$$\text{then } A + B = [a_{11} + b_{11} \ a_{12} + b_{12}]$$

Furthermore, it should also be noted that any two or more matrices are regarded as equal to one another if and only if they are of the same dimension *and* all their elements are equal and identically located. For example:

$$\text{if } A = \begin{bmatrix} 1 & 2 \\ 3 & 4 \end{bmatrix} \text{ and } B = \begin{bmatrix} 1 & 2 \\ 3 & 4 \end{bmatrix} \text{ and } C = \begin{bmatrix} 1 & 2 \\ 4 & 3 \end{bmatrix}$$

then A equals B but neither A nor B equals C (because the elements in row 2 of C, although numerically the same as those in row 2 of A and B, are in different locations).

It is also the case that if $A = B$, then $A + B = 2A = 2B$. You can see this in the following illustration:

$$\text{if } A = \begin{bmatrix} 1 & 2 \\ 3 & 4 \end{bmatrix} \text{ and } B = \begin{bmatrix} 1 & 2 \\ 3 & 4 \end{bmatrix}$$

$$\text{then } A + B = \begin{bmatrix} 2 & 4 \\ 6 & 8 \end{bmatrix} = 2 \begin{bmatrix} 1 & 2 \\ 3 & 4 \end{bmatrix} = 2A = 2B$$

This last result stems from the fact that any matrix multiplied by a scalar number

WORKSHEET 6.1

	A	B	C	D	E	F	G	H
1	1	2	+	8	9	=	9	11
2	3	4		12	8		15	12

produces a new matrix in which every element is multiplied by that scalar. (Notice that this is a very special case of matrix multiplication. Normally it is not as simple as this.)

At this stage we should be thinking that Lotus could help us to perform these matrix operations. This is indeed the case, but only once you have appreciated the basic rules of matrix algebra. In fact, Lotus has an exceptionally powerful matrix handling facility in the Matrix option of the Data menu, but as you will see it is reserved for more complicated processes than simple addition or subtraction.

However, if repeated addition and subtraction of large matrices is to be carried out, then it is a simple matter to write the formulae that will do this for you. You can see this in Worksheet 6.1. The formula in G1 is +A1 + D1 and this has been copied into G2 and then into H1..H2.

EXAMPLE 6.2

In addition to the information from Example 6.1, the outputs of the products from the three factories in the second six months of the year was given by the matrix B, where

$$B = \begin{bmatrix} 67 & 39 & 50 \\ 45 & 23 & 90 \\ 82 & 56 & 40 \end{bmatrix}$$

Form a matrix that will indicate the total annual output of all three products from all three factories.

SOLUTION 6.2

If we represent the required matrix by D, then clearly we have

$$D = A + B = \begin{bmatrix} 100 & 50 & 90 \\ 65 & 34 & 72 \\ 80 & 43 & 96 \end{bmatrix} + \begin{bmatrix} 67 & 39 & 50 \\ 45 & 23 & 90 \\ 82 & 56 & 40 \end{bmatrix} = \begin{bmatrix} 167 & 89 & 140 \\ 109 & 57 & 162 \\ 162 & 99 & 136 \end{bmatrix}$$

EXAMPLE 6.3

Suppose, in addition, that the firm in Example 6.2 has annual sales that were given by the matrix S, where

$$S = \begin{bmatrix} 150 & 80 & 125 \\ 99 & 50 & 162 \\ 143 & 89 & 121 \end{bmatrix}$$

Form a matrix E that will represent the firm's annual excess production of each of the products at each of the factories.

SOLUTION 6.3

Clearly

$$E = D - S = A + B - S$$

Therefore

$$E = \begin{bmatrix} 167 & 89 & 140 \\ 109 & 57 & 162 \\ 162 & 99 & 136 \end{bmatrix} - \begin{bmatrix} 150 & 80 & 125 \\ 99 & 50 & 162 \\ 143 & 89 & 121 \end{bmatrix} = \begin{bmatrix} 17 & 9 & 15 \\ 10 & 7 & 0 \\ 19 & 10 & 15 \end{bmatrix}$$

6.4 Matrix multiplication

Unless (as we saw earlier) one of the matrices is in fact a scalar, matrix multiplication is only possible when the matrices that are to form the product are what is known as *conformable*. This will be the case if, *and only if*, the number of columns in the first matrix of the product is equal to the number of rows in the second matrix of the product.

A little reflection will confirm that this requirement means that the order in which a particular multiplicative operation is to be carried out is of considerable importance, since if A is a 3×2 matrix and B is a 2×4 matrix, then the product AB is conformable, but the product BA is not.

The implications of conformability are considerable and create a number of possibilities as regards any matrix product. These can be understood as follows:

1. Neither of the products AB nor BA exist (both are nonconformable). For example, if A has dimension 3×2 and B has dimension 4×5, then neither product exists.
2. AB exists but BA does not. For example, if A has dimension 3×2 and B has dimension 2×4, then AB can be formed but BA cannot.

3. BA exists but AB does not. For example, if A has dimension 2×4 and B has dimension 3×2, then BA can be formed but AB cannot.
4. Both AB and BA exist but will not be equal except in very special circumstances.

To appreciate the significance of these statements we need further understanding of how a matrix product is created from two or more conformable matrices. If we look at the two matrices

$$A = \begin{bmatrix} 3 & 1 \\ 5 & 2 \end{bmatrix} \quad B = \begin{bmatrix} 4 & 6 \\ 3 & 5 \end{bmatrix}$$

we immediately notice that since both of the matrices are square, the conformability requirements are met for both the product AB and the product BA.

Now, to obtain the product AB we must multiply each element in the first row of A by the corresponding element in the first column of B, and then take the sum of these products. This produces the first element (row 1, column 1) of the product matrix.

We then multiply each element in the first row of A by the corresponding element in the second column of B and then take the sum of these individual elements. This produces the next element (row 1, column 2) of the product matrix.

To obtain the remaining elements in the product we repeat the last procedure, but this time using the second row of A with initially the first, and then the second column of B.

These operations produce the following product for our illustrative matrices.

$$AB = \begin{bmatrix} 3 & 1 \\ 5 & 2 \end{bmatrix} \begin{bmatrix} 4 & 6 \\ 3 & 5 \end{bmatrix} = \begin{bmatrix} (3)(4) + (1)(3) & (3)(6) + (1)(5) \\ (5)(4) + (2)(3) & (5)(6) + (2)(5) \end{bmatrix}$$

Therefore

$$AB = \begin{bmatrix} 15 & 23 \\ 26 & 40 \end{bmatrix}$$

As another example, if

$$M = \begin{bmatrix} 2 & 4 & 9 \\ 1 & 0 & 5 \end{bmatrix} \quad N = \begin{bmatrix} 1 & 3 \\ 0 & 6 \\ 7 & 8 \end{bmatrix}$$

Then

$$MN = \begin{bmatrix} (2)(1) + (4)(0) + (9)(7) & (2)(3) + (4)(6) + (9)(8) \\ (1)(1) + (0)(0) + (5)(7) & (1)(3) + (0)(6) + (5)(8) \end{bmatrix}$$

$$= \begin{bmatrix} 65 & 102 \\ 36 & 43 \end{bmatrix}$$

It should be clear from this last illustration that the processes involved in matrix multiplication necessarily mean that a matrix of dimension $n \times m$ multiplied by a matrix of dimension $m \times p$ will produce a new matrix of dimension $n \times p$. (In effect what happens is that the dimension of the product is determined by the nonconformable row and column dimensions of the two matrices, with the conformable dimension disappearing). In other words, M, which is 2×3, times N, which is 3×2, produces MN, which is 2×2.

Now that we know how to perform matrix multiplication we can confirm our earlier statement that even if both products exist they will not *usually* be identical. To do this all we have to do is form the product BA from our two earlier matrices. This produces

$$BA = \begin{bmatrix} 4 & 6 \\ 3 & 5 \end{bmatrix} \begin{bmatrix} 3 & 1 \\ 5 & 2 \end{bmatrix} = \begin{bmatrix} (4)(3)+(6)(2) & (4)(1)+(6)(2) \\ (3)(3)+(5)(5) & (3)(1)+(5)(2) \end{bmatrix}$$

Therefore

$$BA = \begin{bmatrix} 42 & 16 \\ 34 & 13 \end{bmatrix}$$

which does not equal

$$AB = \begin{bmatrix} 15 & 23 \\ 26 & 40 \end{bmatrix}$$

The results of this discussion clearly suggest that unlike scalar algebra where it is always true that $ab = ba$, in matrix algebra there is a difference between premultiplication by A (AB) and postmultiplication by A (BA), and that care must always be taken to ensure that the correct product is being evaluated.

You may now be thinking that the arithmetic operations involved in matrix multiplication could become extremely tedious if large matrices are involved. This is entirely true, but fortunately we can use the Lotus Data Matrix command to relieve much of this tedium.

Consider the two matrices A and B which we multiplied above. The first task will be to enter them alongside one another in the worksheet. This has been done in A1..B2 and D1..E2 of Worksheet 6.2.

Since both matrices are square, they are automatically conformable and so we can proceed by selecting Data, then Matrix and then Multiply.

Now you are prompted for the first range to multiply, and so respond with A1..B2.

Next Lotus wants to know the range containing the second matrix, so respond with D1..E2.

WORKSHEET 6.2

	A	B	C	D	E	F	G	H
1	3	1	×	4	6	=	15	23
2	5	2		3	5		26	40

Finally you are required to specify the output range (i.e. where Lotus is to place the product of the two matrices), so respond with G1. (Lotus knows that the matrix product of appropriate dimension is to be placed in the block of cells commencing at G1.)

As you can see, the product that we obtained manually has been reproduced in the output area.

You should now use this Data Matrix Multiply command to confirm our earlier observation that AB does not generally equal BA. In other words, form the product BA in the worksheet.

EXAMPLE 6.4

Referring back to Example 6.2, suppose that in addition to the matrix D representing the three factories' production of the three products, we also had information on the usage of three fuel inputs (C, E and G), per unit of each of the three products. Letting this latter matrix be represented by U, form a matrix product that will represent the total usage of each of the three fuel inputs at each of the three factories for all three products.

SOLUTION 6.4

Clearly we require some data for the U matrix, so take it as

$$U = \text{Product} \begin{array}{c} 1 \\ 2 \\ 3 \end{array} \begin{array}{c} \text{usage of fuel} \\ \text{type per unit} \\ \text{of product} \end{array} = \begin{bmatrix} 3 & 6 & 2 \\ 1 & 5 & 7 \\ 4 & 2 & 3 \end{bmatrix}$$

with Input columns C, E, G.

Furthermore, it will be remembered that the matrix D could be viewed as

$$D = \text{factory} \begin{array}{c} 1 \\ 2 \\ 3 \end{array} \begin{array}{c} \text{output of product} \\ \text{type at factory} \\ \text{location} \end{array} = \begin{bmatrix} 167 & 89 & 140 \\ 109 & 57 & 162 \\ 162 & 99 & 136 \end{bmatrix}$$

with Product columns 1, 2, 3.

Now we can form the matrix product

$$DU = \begin{bmatrix} 167 & 89 & 140 \\ 109 & 57 & 162 \\ 162 & 99 & 136 \end{bmatrix} \times \begin{bmatrix} 3 & 6 & 2 \\ 1 & 5 & 7 \\ 4 & 2 & 3 \end{bmatrix}$$

Notice that this product has been carefully formed to achieve our declared purpose.

This is particularly important since the product *UD* also exists but is of limited practical meaning in this example. (Can you see why?)

However, *DU* will have as its first element:

$$(167)(3) + (89)(1) + (140)(4)$$

Clearly this represents, for the first factory, the output of the first product times its usage of C per unit, plus the output of the second product times its usage of C per unit, plus the output of the third product times its usage of C per unit. Added together this gives the first factory's total usage of the C input.

A similar logic applies to the other factories and the other products, so that the product *DU* can be viewed as

$$DU = \text{Factory} \begin{array}{c} \\ 1 \\ 2 \\ 3 \end{array} \begin{array}{ccc} \multicolumn{3}{c}{\text{Input}} \\ \text{C} & \text{E} & \text{G} \\ \multicolumn{3}{c}{\text{units of input}} \\ \multicolumn{3}{c}{\text{used at factory}} \\ \multicolumn{3}{c}{\text{location}} \end{array}$$

If you ask Lotus to form this product (or do it manually), then you will obtain

$$DU = \begin{bmatrix} 1150 & 1727 & 1377 \\ 1032 & 1263 & 1103 \\ 1129 & 1739 & 1425 \end{bmatrix}$$

EXAMPLE 6.5

Using the matrix *DU* from Example 6.4, calculate the firm's total fuel costs at each of the factories, if it is known that the unit costs of C, E and G are £5, £4 and £6 respectively.

SOLUTION 6.5

All you have to do is form the following matrix product (*R*) where *M* is a column vector of the unit costs:

$$DUM = R = \begin{bmatrix} 1150 & 1727 & 1377 \\ 1032 & 1263 & 1103 \\ 1129 & 1739 & 1425 \end{bmatrix} \times \begin{bmatrix} 5 \\ 4 \\ 6 \end{bmatrix} = \begin{bmatrix} 20\,920 \\ 16\,830 \\ 21\,151 \end{bmatrix}$$

The resulting column vector now has a monetary dimension and measures the *total* input costs at each of the three factories as a result of producing the specified outputs of all three products with the specified input requirements per unit of each product.

6.5 Inverting a matrix

You may have noticed that we have studiously avoided the process of matrix division in the discussion so far. This is because matrix division is far from straightforward and needs to be handled with extreme care.

Basically the principle is the same as in scalar algebra, but the process of doing it is considerably different. For example, suppose that we had the following scalar algebra equation:

$$ax = b$$

If we multiply both sides of the equation by the inverse of a $(1/a)$, then we obtain

$$(1/a)ax = (1/a)b$$

implying that

$$x = b/a$$

(when the terms in a are 'cancelled').

Clearly, the process of multiplying any expression by an inverted term is equivalent to dividing that expression by the term. Equally clearly, the product $a(1/a) = 1$, and so we might try to apply this idea to matrices.

For example, consider the following matrix:

$$A = \begin{bmatrix} 3 & 1 \\ 5 & 2 \end{bmatrix}$$

What we require is to find a second matrix (A inverse = A^{-1}) such that if we multiply A by this matrix then we obtain the identity matrix (I). In other words we require

$$A^{-1} \text{ such that } A(A^{-1}) = I$$

All we have to do is find this inverse matrix and we can proceed to perform the matrix equivalent of division.

However, it is not quite as simple as this. First, finding the inverse of a matrix is arithmetically complex (although Lotus can help). Secondly, the inverse only exists for square matrices, and so there may be division operations that cannot be carried out. Thirdly, even if the matrix to be inverted *is* square, this is no guarantee that an inverse exists. In particular, if one or more columns or rows is a constant multiple of any other column or row, then the inverse cannot be calculated.

However, provided these restrictions are observed we can use Lotus to find the inverse of the matrix A as follows.

First of all place a 2×2 matrix to be inverted in the range A1..B2. Now select Invert from the Data Matrix command and respond to the first prompt (Range to invert:) with A1..B2.

Once again, an output range must be specified so choose a convenient area such as D1..E2. The result should resemble Worksheet 6.3.

WORKSHEET 6.3

	A	B	C	D	E	F	G	H
1	3	1	×	2.00	-1.00	=	1.00	0.00
2	5	2		-5.00	3.00		0.00	1.00
3	A		×	A^-1		=	I	
	Matrix	Times		Matrix			Matrix	

If the inverse of the specified matrix exists, Lotus immediately places it in the output range, as you can confirm if you ask it to multiply the first matrix by its inverse and place the resulting product in G4..H5. Try it for yourself and you will find that, as anticipated, an identity matrix is produced in G4..H5.

Now, finding the inverse of a matrix is an extremely useful process, as you will soon see.

6.6 Using matrix algebra to solve sets of linear equations

The primary purpose of inverting a matrix is to allow computers to solve sets of simultaneous linear equations.

For example, in order to solve the following set of equations

$$2x + 5y + 3z = 28$$
$$x - y + z = 5$$
$$3x + 2y - z = 9$$

we can proceed as follows.

Rewrite the equations in matrix form as

$$As = b$$

where A is the matrix of variable coefficients, s is the column vector of unknown solution values for x, y and z, and b is the column vector of constant terms. That is

$$\begin{bmatrix} 2 & 5 & 3 \\ 1 & -1 & 1 \\ 3 & 2 & -1 \end{bmatrix} \begin{bmatrix} x \\ y \\ z \end{bmatrix} = \begin{bmatrix} 28 \\ 5 \\ 9 \end{bmatrix}$$
$$\quad A \qquad\quad s \;=\; b$$

Now, if we *premultiply* both sides by A^{-1} we obtain

$$(A^{-1})(A)(s) = (A^{-1})(b)$$

Then, since $(A^{-1})(A) = I$, we have

$$Is = (A^{-1})(b)$$

WORKSHEET 6.4

	A	B	C	D	E
1	2	5	3		28
2	1	-1	1		5
3	3	2	-1		9
4		A			b
5					
6	-0.03030	0.333333	0.242424		3
7	0.121212	-0.33333	0.030303		2
8	0.151515	0.333333	-0.21212		4
9		A^-1			s

Therefore

$$s = (A^{-1})(b)$$

Enter the A matrix in the A1..C3 cells of your worksheet and the b vector in E1..E3. Now invert A and place the inverse in A6..C8.

To obtain the solution vector (s) all you have to do now is ask Lotus to multiply the matrix in A6..C8 (the inverse of A) by the b vector in E1..E3, and place the output in E6..E8. As you can see in Worksheet 6.4, the solutions are contained in this row vector and produce the result that $x = 3$, $y = 2$ and $z = 4$.

6.7 Input–output analysis

Input–output analysis, like linear programming, is one of the prime examples of a mathematical technique that has been developed for the specific purpose of modelling the relationships that constitute business and economic systems.

The essential idea of the input–output technique is a recognition of the fact that many products not only represent finished marketable output, but are also used as inputs in the production of other products and in the production of that product itself.

The simplest example of such relationships would be in a basic agricultural system that produces only wheat and cattle. Under such circumstances, the production of wheat must satisfy the following:

1. Final consumer demand for wheat (to make bread).
2. The food requirements of the cattle.
3. The seed requirements for the next year's harvest.

The effect of these requirements is that wheat is not only a final product (flour) but also an input in the production of cattle, and an input in the production of itself (seed).

Input-output analysis

By a similar logic the production of cattle must satisfy the following:

1. Final consumer demand for meat and milk.
2. The fertilizer requirements of wheat production.
3. The requirements to breed more cattle.

Once again, cattle are not only a final product, but also an input in the production of wheat and an input in the production of themselves.

Viewed in this way the task of input-output analysis is to find those production levels of both cattle and wheat that meet *all* requirements from *all* sources.

As a more concrete example consider the following.

EXAMPLE 6.6

A simple economic system produces only three products, coal, electricity and steel. Each product is used as an input in the production of not only itself, but also the other two products as well, in such a way that: each unit of coal requires 0.2 units of coal itself, 0.15 units of electricity and 0.12 units of steel; each unit of electricity requires 0.2 units of coal, 0.16 units of electricity itself and 0.15 units of steel; and each unit of steel requires 0.3 units of coal, 0.40 units of electricity and 0.22 units of steel itself.

The final consumer demands for the three products are 100 units of coal, 250 units of electricity and 200 units of steel.

Calculate the required output levels of all three products if all demands are to be met exactly.

SOLUTION 6.6

Let c = the required output of coal, e = the required output of electricity and s = the required output of steel.

Clearly the value of c must be such that it meets its own input requirements, the requirements of the other two products and the requirements of final consumption. Now its own requirements depend upon its *own* production (c), while the requirements of the other two products depend upon *their* respective outputs (e and s). Consequently, the value of c must be such that

$$c = 0.2c + 0.2e + 0.3s + 100$$

Study this equation carefully since you *might* have thought that it should have been

$$c = 0.2c + 0.15e + 0.12s + 100$$

This is not correct, however, since the logic must be:

output of coal = (requirement of coal by coal) + (requirement of coal by electricity)
  + (requirement of coal by steel) + (final consumer demand)
  = (0.2 units per unit of coal) + (0.2 units per unit of electricity)
  + (0.3 units per unit of steel) + 100
  = $0.2c + 0.2e + 0.3s + 100$

This can be written as

$$c = 0.2c + 0.2e + 0.3s + 100$$

By a similar logic we can also write

$$e = 0.15c + 0.16e + 0.4s + 250$$
$$s = 0.12c + 0.15e + 0.22s + 200$$

If we let x be the column vector of unknowns

$$x = \begin{bmatrix} c \\ e \\ s \end{bmatrix}$$

then in matrix terms the three equations above can be written as

$$x = Ax + b$$

where

$$A = \begin{bmatrix} 0.2 & 0.2 & 0.3 \\ 0.15 & 0.16 & 0.4 \\ 0.12 & 0.15 & 0.22 \end{bmatrix} \quad \text{and} \quad b = \begin{bmatrix} 100 \\ 250 \\ 200 \end{bmatrix}$$

Therefore

$$x - Ax = b$$

and, taking care to ensure conformability

$$(I - A)x = b$$

(Notice that $x(I - A)$ is nonconformable.)

Now premultiply both sides by the inverse of $(I - A)$ to obtain

$$[(I - A)^{-1}](I - A)x = [(I - A)^{-1}]b$$

Therefore

$$x = [(I - A)^{-1}]b$$

To solve this matrix equation on Lotus the first thing to do is enter the matrix of technical coefficients (A) in A1..C3, and the final demand vector (b) in I1..I3. Now you will have to write formulae in E1..G3 to calculate the $(I - A)$ matrix.

So, in E1, F2 and G3 enter

$$1 - A1, \ 1 - B2 \text{ and } 1 - C3$$

In the remaining cells (E2, E3, F1, F3, G1 and G2), enter

$$0 - A2, \ 0 - A3, \ 0 - B1, \ 0 - B3, \ 0 - C1 \text{ and } 0 - C2$$

This will produce the $(I - A)$ matrix in E1..G3, and now all you have to do is proceed as before when you solved for the solution vector in a set of linear equations.

Place the inverse of $(I - A)$ in A6..C8, then multiply this inverse by the final demand vector (in I1..I3), and then output the solution vector to E6..E8.

This has been done in Worksheet 6.5. From this you can see that 433.735 units of coal should be produced, 582.269 units of electricity and 435.113 units of steel.

You can confirm that these are the correct outputs if you multiply A by x to obtain the vector of input requirements and then add the final demand vector (b) to this product. As you can see, the result ($Ax + b$) is the x vector, indicating that the outputs of the three products are exactly sufficient to meet all input requirements from all sources (Ax) plus final demand (b).

At this stage it is appropriate to point out that the matrix containing the technical coefficients (A) in the above example was carefully chosen to avoid a potential difficulty that can arise.

To see this, we must remember that negative outputs are not acceptable solutions to our equation system, and so the structure of A must be such that these are avoided. But under what circumstances will A only produce positive solutions?

WORKSHEET 6.5

	A	B	C	D	E	F	G	H	I
1	0.20	0.20	0.30		0.80	-0.20	-0.30		100.00
2	0.15	0.16	0.40		-0.15	0.84	-0.40		250.00
3	0.12	0.15	0.22		-0.12	-0.15	0.78		200.00
4		A				(I-A)			b
5									
6	1.465	0.495	0.817		433.735				
7	0.406	1.448	0.899		582.269				
8	0.304	0.355	1.581		435.113				
9		(I-A)^-1			x				
10									
11									
12	0.20	0.20	0.30		433.735		333.73		
13	0.15	0.16	0.40	×	582.269	=	332.27		
14	0.12	0.15	0.22		435.113		235.11		
15		A			x		Ax		
16									
17	333.73				100.00		433.735		
18	332.27		+		250.00	=	582.269		
19	235.11				200.00		435.113		
20	Ax				b		x		

294   *Matrix Algebra*

First of all, it should be clear that no product can use more than 100 per cent of its own output as an input. This means that all of the elements on the principal diagonal of A must be less than or equal to 1 (but ≥ 0).

Furthermore, if other products also use this product as an input, it follows that the combined input requirements for this product must be less than 100 per cent of its output. This means that the sum of the elements along each and every row of A must be less than or equal to 1 (but ≥ 0).

Clearly, the first requirement is included in the second and so we can conclude that it represents the necessary circumstances for a positive set of solutions.

That is, the sum of the elements along each and every row of A must be less than or equal to 1.

6.8 Exercises

6.1

A transport company has four lorries, which in a particular week travel distances of 2000, 1800, 1890 and 2080 miles. The respective fuel consumption rates (in *gallons per mile*) for each of the lorries are 0.3, 0.25, 0.4 and 0.35.

(a) Form a matrix product that will give the firm's total weekly fuel consumption.
(b) Form another matrix product that will give the firm's weekly fuel consumption by each of the lorries.
(c) Form another matrix product that will give the fuel consumption of each of the lorries and the fuel consumption that *would* result if each of the lorries also travelled each of the other lorries' distances at each of the other lorries' fuel consumption rates.

6.2

A firm sells each of its three products (X, Y and Z) in each of three distinct markets (A, B and C). The prices (in £'s) that it charges for each product, in each market, are given in the following table:

		Market		
		A	B	C
	X	8	7	6
Product	Y	15	18	16
	Z	25	29	27

The total sales (in 000s of units) of the products to each of the markets are given

Exercises

in the following table:

		Market		
		A	B	C
	X	2.1	3.4	7.1
Product	Y	8.2	5.5	6.0
	Z	3.9	7.6	4.2

Form a matrix product that will give the revenue in each market from the sales of all products.

6.3

A firm uses three inputs (L, K and R) to produce three products (U, V and W).

Each unit of product U requires 2 units of L, 4 units of K and 3 units of R. Each unit of product V requires 5 units of L, 2.5 units of K and 6 units of R. Each unit of product W requires 1 unit of L, 5.5 units of K and 3.5 units of R.

Over a particular period the firm used a total of 1000 units of L, 2500 units of K and 2000 units of R.

(a) What was the output of the three products over this period?
(b) In the next period the firm's usage of the three inputs was 1100, 2400, and 2100 of L, K and R respectively. Calculate the new output levels of the three products.

6.4

A simple economic system involves the production of 2 products (X and Y).

The conditions of production are such that each unit of X requires 0.2 units of X and 0.6 units of Y, while each unit of Y requires 0.4 units of X and 0.3 units of Y.

The final demand for the two products is 32 units and 64 units for X and Y respectively.

(a) Calculate the outputs of the two products necessary to satisfy all the demands of the system.
(b) As a result of a change in the conditions of production, it is now the case that each unit of X requires 0.3 units of X and 0.4 units of Y, while each unit of Y requires 0.8 units of X and 0.7 units of Y. Calculate the new outputs of the three products.

6.5

The process of making a particular dietary supplement involves combining three compounds (X, Y and Z) into a 100 gram capsule.

The supplement must contain exactly 22 per cent vitamin A and 24 per cent vitamin B, while the vitamin contents of the compounds to be combined are as follows:

	Compound					
		X	Y	Z	X	Y	Z
A	vitamin content				0.2	0.3	0.1
Vitamin B	(grams) per gram of compound				0.3	0.12	0.4

Form a matrix equation that will allow you to solve for the required amounts of each compound that should be used in the blend.

6.9 Solutions to the exercises

6.1

(a) If you let the distances be contained in a row vector (d) and the gallons per mile in a column vector (g) then the product dg will give

$$dg = [2000 \quad 1800 \quad 1890 \quad 2080] \times \begin{bmatrix} 0.30 \\ 0.25 \\ 0.40 \\ 0.35 \end{bmatrix} = [2534]$$

(b) To do this we can form the matrix D as follows:

$$D = \begin{bmatrix} 2000 & 0 & 0 & 0 \\ 0 & 1800 & 0 & 0 \\ 0 & 0 & 1890 & 0 \\ 0 & 0 & 0 & 2080 \end{bmatrix}$$

Notice how the 'active' numbers have been placed on the principal diagonal, with zeros everywhere else. This allows us to postmultiply D by g to produce a 4×1 column vector containing the fuel usages for each of the lorries. That is

$$Dg = \begin{bmatrix} 2000 & 0 & 0 & 0 \\ 0 & 1800 & 0 & 0 \\ 0 & 0 & 1890 & 0 \\ 0 & 0 & 0 & 2080 \end{bmatrix} \times \begin{bmatrix} 0.30 \\ 0.25 \\ 0.40 \\ 0.35 \end{bmatrix} = \begin{bmatrix} 600 \\ 450 \\ 756 \\ 728 \end{bmatrix} \text{gallons}$$

(c) In this case, if we form the product gd, we obtain

$$gd = \begin{bmatrix} 0.30 \\ 0.25 \\ 0.40 \\ 0.35 \end{bmatrix} \times [2000 \quad 1800 \quad 1890 \quad 2080]$$

```
WORKSHEET 6.6
         A            B            C            D            E            F
  1     0.3           x           2000         1800         1890         2080
  2     0.25                                    d
  3     0.4
  4     0.35
  5     g
  6
  7     600          540          567          624
  8     500          450          472.5        520
  9     800          720          756          832
 10     700          630          661.5        728
 11                               gd
```

You might as well ask Lotus to do the calculations for you, in which case Worksheet 6.6 will be produced. This shows a 4×4 matrix in which the first element is the actual fuel usage of lorry 1. However, the second element in the first row will contain the fuel usage that lorry 2's distance *would have used* if it had travelled its distance at lorry 1's fuel consumption rate.

In other words, the elements 'off' the principal diagonal give hypothetical usage rates that can be used to answer questions such as 'what if lorry j travelled its distance at lorry i's fuel consumption rate?'

Questions such as these can often provide useful management information, since it should be clear that if the firm wanted to reduce its total fuel usage, then a reallocation of the lorry distances could do this.

To be exact, lorry 2 should take over lorry 4's route, lorry 4 should take over lorry 3's route, and lorry 3 should take over lorry 2's route. Now the lorries with the best fuel consumption rates are travelling the longest distances and the vector g could be rewritten as

$$g = \begin{bmatrix} 0.30 \\ 0.40 \\ 0.35 \\ 0.25 \end{bmatrix}$$

The product dg would become

$$dg = [2000 \quad 1800 \quad 1890 \quad 2080] \times \begin{bmatrix} 0.30 \\ 0.40 \\ 0.35 \\ 0.25 \end{bmatrix} = [2501.5]$$

As anticipated, the total fuel consumption has been reduced.

6.2

You will have to be careful here, since both matrices are conformable, and if you simply form the product randomly, then you will never be sure that the result is the required one.

Bearing this in mind we can let the matrix of prices be denoted by P and the matrix of sales be denoted by S. If we form the product PS, then the first element will be calculated as

$$(8)(2.1) + (7)(8.2) + (6)(3.9)$$

Clearly this gives the price of X in A times the sales of X in A, plus the price of X in B times the sales of Y in A, plus the price of X in C times the sales of Z in A. Equally clearly, some of the terms are 'mixed' in the sense that the prices and sales refer to different products, and so we conclude that PS is not an appropriate product.

If we form SP, on the other hand, then the first element is calculated as

$$(2.1)(8) + (3.4)(15) + (7.1)(25)$$

This represents the sales of X in A times the price of X in A, plus the sales of X in B times the price of Y in A, plus the sales of X in C times the price of Z in A. Once again the terms are 'mixed' and so this product is also inappropriate.

However, if you perform an operation known as *transposition*, then progress can be made. Basically the transpose of a matrix is obtained by exchanging each row with each column of the matrix (so that row 1 becomes column 1, row 2 becomes column 2 and so on). Conventionally the transpose of a matrix is symbolized by adding the $'$ symbol to its letter (or ^{T}, i.e. S^T), so we would write

$$S' = \begin{bmatrix} 2.1 & 8.2 & 3.9 \\ 3.4 & 5.5 & 7.6 \\ 7.1 & 6.0 & 4.2 \end{bmatrix}$$

If we now form the product PS', then the first element will be calculated as

$$(8)(2.1) + (15)(8.2) + (25)(3.9)$$

This represents the price of X in A times the sales of X in A, plus the price of Y in A times the sales of Y in A, plus the price of Z in A times the sales of Z in A. Now you should be able to see that this is the product that the question calls for, since it clearly represents the total revenue from the sales of each of the products in market A.

Now that we know the exact nature of the product that we are forming we can ask Lotus to do it for us. This would produce Worksheet 6.7. The elements on the principal diagonal give the revenue in each market, and the elements 'off' this diagonal give the hypothetical revenues that would result if the prices of product i were applied to the sales of product j.

You might also note that the product $S'P$ also exists and would have as its

WORKSHEET 6.7

	A	B	C	D	E	F	G
1	8	7	6	x	2.1	8.2	3.9
2	15	18	16		3.4	5.6	7.6
3	25	29	27		7.1	6	4.2
4		P				S'	
5							
6	83.2	140.1	109.6				
7	206.3	318	262.5				
8	342.8	526.5	431.3				
9		PS'					

principal diagonal elements the revenue resulting from the sale of each product in all markets (i.e. revenue from the sale of X in A, B and C, etc.).

6.3

(a) If we let u, v and w represent the (unknown) output levels of the three products, then the total usage of input L will be given by

$$2u + 5v + w = \text{usage of L}$$

Similarly, the usage levels of K and R would be given by

$$4u + 2.5v + 5.5w = \text{usage of K}$$
$$3u + 6v + 3.5w = \text{usage of R}$$

In matrix terms this can be written as

$$Ax = \begin{bmatrix} 2 & 5 & 1 \\ 4 & 2.5 & 5.5 \\ 3 & 6 & 3.5 \end{bmatrix} \times \begin{bmatrix} u \\ v \\ w \end{bmatrix}$$

Since we know the total usages of the three inputs for the period we can form the following matrix equation:

$$Ax = b$$

where b is the column vector of total usages.

By the method explained earlier we can write

$$x = (A^{-1})b$$

and you can use Worksheet 6.4 to find the inverse of A and then multiply it by b. This would produce Worksheet 6.8.

The outputs of u, v and w are 158.29, 75.37 and 306.53 respectively.

(b) All you have to do is replace the original total usage levels with the new ones in the b vector and then perform a remultiplication of $(A^{-1})b$. (Notice that the

WORKSHEET 6.8

	A	B	C	D	E
1	2.00	5.00	1.00		1000.00
2	4.00	2.40	5.50		2500.00
3	3.00	6.00	3.50		2000.00
4		A			b
5					
6	1.236	0.578	-1.261		158.291
7	-0.126	-0.201	0.352		75.377
8	-0.844	-0.151	0.764		306.633
9		A^-1			x

inverse of A is unaffected by the change in total usage levels and therefore does not need to be recalculated.)

The new values of u, v and w will be

$$u = 97.99$$
$$v = 118.09$$
$$w = 313.56$$

6.4

(a) The input–output equations are

$$x = 0.2x + 0.4y + 32$$
$$y = 0.6x + 0.3y + 64$$

implying that

$$z = Az + b$$

Collecting terms produces

$$0.8x - 0.4y = 32$$
$$-0.6x + 0.7y = 64$$

In matrix terms this becomes

$$(I - A)z = b$$

Therefore

$$z = ((I - A)^{-1})b$$

The solution is obtained by the now familiar method and is reproduced as Worksheet 6.9 (using a modified version of Worksheet 6.5).

The requisite outputs are 150 units of X and 220 units of Y.

(b) You can repeat the above procedure if you want, but you will find that negative output is produced. This is because the sum of the coefficients of A is greater than 1 for both rows of the matrix. There is no positive solution.

WORKSHEET 6.9

	A	B	C	D	E	F	G	H	I
1	0.20	0.40			0.80	-0.40			32.00
2	0.60	0.30			-0.60	0.70			64.00
3		A				(I-A)			b
4									
5	2.188	1.250			150.000				
6	1.875	2.500			220.000				
7		(I-A)^-1			z				

6.5

You might be tempted to argue that since 100 grams of the supplement must be produced, the relevant equations would be

$$0.2x + 0.3y + 0.1z = 0.22(100)$$

and

$$0.3x + 0.12y + 0.4z = 0.24(100)$$

However, as you can see, there are more variables than equations in this formulation, and as a result a definite solution cannot be obtained.

Consequently, we should formulate the problem as follows.

$$\begin{aligned} x + y + z &= 100 \\ 0.2x + 0.3y + 0.1z &= 0.22(x + y + z) \\ 0.3x + 0.12y + 0.4z &= 0.24(x + y + z) \end{aligned}$$

To formulate this in matrix terms we must first of all collect all terms in x, y and z on the lefthand side of the equations. This produces

$$\begin{aligned} x + y + z &= 100 \\ -0.02x + 0.08y - 0.12z &= 0 \\ 0.06x - 0.12y + 0.16z &= 0 \end{aligned}$$

and implies the following matrix equation:

$$Av = b$$

where

$$A = \begin{bmatrix} 1 & 1 & 1 \\ -0.02 & 0.08 & -0.12 \\ 0.06 & -0.12 & 0.16 \end{bmatrix} \quad v = \begin{bmatrix} x \\ y \\ z \end{bmatrix} \quad \text{and} \quad b = \begin{bmatrix} 100 \\ 0 \\ 0 \end{bmatrix}$$

The solution is now straightforward and would produce Worksheet 6.10.

Therefore 20 grams of compound X should be mixed with 50 grams of compound Y and 30 grams of compound Z.

WORKSHEET 6.10

	A	B	C	D	E
1	1.00	1.00	1.00		100.00
2	-0.02	0.08	-0.12		0.00
3	0.06	-0.12	0.16		0.00
4		A			b
5					
6	0.200	35.000	25.000		20.000
7	0.500	-12.500	-12.500		50.000
8	0.300	-22.500	-12.500		30.000
9		A^-1			v

7
Linear Programming II

7.1 The simplex algorithm

An algorithm is simply a step-by-step routine for performing a particular task. Consequently, the simplex algorithm is merely an algebraic method of allowing computers to perform the routine calculations involved in any linear programming problem.

To illustrate the nature and appreciate the algorithm, reconsider the linear programme that we solved in Section 4 of Chapter 5.

$$\begin{aligned}
&\text{Maximize} && 6x + 9y = \text{profit} \\
&\text{Subject to} && 2x + 2y \leqslant 24 && \text{(labour constraint)} \\
&\text{And} && x + 5y \leqslant 44 && \text{(machine time constraint)} \\
&\text{And} && 6x + 2y \leqslant 60 && \text{(steel constraint)}
\end{aligned}$$

As in our original example the constraints are in the form of inequalities, but to permit algebraic solution we must convert each *inequality* to an *equality* by introducing what is known as a *slack variable* to each of the constraints. These slack variables (S_1, S_2 and S_3) make no contribution to the profit of the undertaking, since their function is simply to allow the inequalities of the constraints to be expressed as equalities.

When the slack variables are introduced to the constraints they mean the following:

$$\begin{aligned}
2x + 2y \leqslant 24 \quad &\text{becomes} \quad 2x + 2y + S_1 = 24 \\
1x + 5y \leqslant 44 \quad &\text{becomes} \quad 1x + 5y + S_2 = 44 \\
6x + 2y \leqslant 60 \quad &\text{becomes} \quad 6x + 2y + S_3 = 60
\end{aligned}$$

Notice that if we set $x = y = 0$ (i.e. produce neither product) then $S_1 = 24$, $S_2 = 44$ and $S_3 = 60$. This implies that the firm is not using *any* of its resources to produce output and that the values of the slack variables are therefore maximal.

A situation such as this (in which $x = y = 0$) is called the *basic solution* (or the *basis*), and is the starting point for the simplex algorithm, since *any* reallocation *must* represent an improvement upon the basic solution, in which nothing is produced and no profit is made. What the simplex algorithm does is to provide a

Table 7.1

B	x	y	S_1	S_2	S_3	A
S_1	2	2	1	0	0	24
S_2	1	5	0	1	0	44
S_3	6	2	0	0	1	60
P	6	9	0	0	0	0

systematic method of improving the situation until no further improvement can be obtained.

The first step is to write the problem including the slack variables in matrix form (called a simplex tableau) as shown in Table 7.1.

This is seen to be a matrix representation of the equations that constitute the basic solution with the values of the relevant variables being found under the appropriate headings.

These headings are contained in the top row of the tableau, and identify the variables represented in the column directly below. Consequently, the entries in the column headed 'x' are the coefficients of the x variable in each of the constraints (in the first three rows); and in the objective function (in the last row).

The column headed 'A' contains the constants on the righthand side of each of the constraints of the program in the first three rows, and in its last row, the value of the objective function when $x = y = 0$. This will always be 0 in the basic solution.

The column headed 'B' is merely a column of labels, the first three of which contain the names of those variables that are *nonzero* in the basic solution. Initially, these will always be the slack variables, and the entries therefore indicate that in the basic solution with $x = y = 0$ the values adopted by S_1, S_2 and S_3 are 24, 44 and 60 respectively.

The final entry in column B contains the label 'P' and identifies the coefficients of the objective function (6 and 9 for x and y, 0 for each of S_1, S_2 and S_3). The value of the objective function in the basic solution is contained in column A of this last row, and as we have seen will always be 0.

In short, column A always gives the values adopted by the variables identified in the corresponding row of column B. This is a good way to view the tableau, since what the simplex method does is to alter some of the variables identified in column B and alter the values adopted by these variables as the algorithm searches for the optimal solution. Once it has found it, the solution values of each variable (identified in column B) will be contained in column A. This is known as the final tableau.

For the problem in our example, a lot of arithmetic and a knowledge of the algorithm, eventually produces the final tableau shown in Table 7.2. This final tableau can be seen to confirm the results that we obtained in Chapter 5, since it is to be interpreted as follows:

Table 7.2

B	x	y	S_1	S_2	S_3	A
x	1	0	0.625	−0.25	0	4
y	0	1	−0.125	0.25	0	8
S_3	0	0	−3.5	1	1	20
P	0	0	2.625	0.75	0	96

The optimal value of x (identified in the first row of column B) is 4 (and is contained in the first row of column A).

The optimal value of y (identified in the second row of column B) is 8 (and is contained in the second row of column A).

The optimal (maximum) value of P (identified in the last row of column B) is 96 (and is contained in the last row of column A).

In this optimal solution, the value of S_3 is 20, and this tells us that there are 20 units of this resource (steel) unused.

You will have noticed that the final tableau contains a number of entries that have not been explained. As you will see, some of these can be very useful, but before they are explained we will show you how the final tableau can be obtained.

Basically, there are two methods of performing the simplex algorithm: manually or by computer package. Only the latter will be illustrated in this text, and the specific program that we will use is known as LINPRO. This is by far the most widely available linear programming package, so you should have no difficulty gaining access to it.

7.2 The LINPRO program

The LINPRO program is written in BASIC language and can maximize or minimize an objective function of up to 30 variables subject to a maximum of 18 constraints. All it requires is that you enter the data for your linear program in a specific format, and then the package will do the rest. Although there are many versions of LINPRO (available both on mainframe and personal computers), most versions are constructed in such a way that their format consists of four main features. These will be explained with reference to the last linear program above, i.e.

$$\begin{aligned}
\text{Maximize} \quad & 6x + 9y = \text{profit} \\
\text{Subject to} \quad & 2x + 2y \leqslant 24 \quad \text{(labour constraint)} \\
\text{And} \quad & x + 5y \leqslant 44 \quad \text{(machine time constraint)} \\
\text{And} \quad & 6x + 2y \leqslant 60 \quad \text{(steel constraint)}
\end{aligned}$$

1. The first task is to arrange the constraints of your problem in such a way that any 'less than' constraints precede any strict equalities, which in turn precede

any 'greater than' constraints. For our illustration all of the constraints are of a 'less than or equal to' nature, and so the existing order satisfies this requirement.

2. Once this arrangement has been made, you must keep this order intact and then enter the coefficients of the variables on the lefthand side of the constraints anywhere in lines 1–99 of the program. You must give the coefficients of each constraint its own line number, but you *do not* enter the coefficients of any slack variables. For our example this produces

$$1 \text{ DATA } 2,2$$
$$2 \text{ DATA } 1,5$$
$$3 \text{ DATA } 6,2$$

Notice that the spaces between the line numbers and the 'D' of DATA, and between the 'A' of DATA and the first coefficient value are essential. There is, however, no space (but a comma) between coefficient values, and no comma after the last coefficient value in any line. (You press the Enter key after this last value has been typed.)

3. Next, on a new line, you should enter the constant terms from the righthand side of the program. These must never be negative. This produces

$$4 \text{ DATA } 24,44,60$$

4. Finally you must enter the coefficients from the objective function of the linear program. For a maximization problem these are to be entered as they appear in the program, but for a minimization problem the algebraic signs of the coefficients are reversed. For our maximization problem this produces

$$5 \text{ DATA } 6,9$$

All the required information has now been entered, although you must remember that if a variable does not appear in every constraint, then its coefficient is zero and *must be entered as such*.

After entering the data in this format you are now ready to run the program, which is done by typing RUN

You will now have to respond to three prompts.

```
TYPE '2' FOR OUTPUT OF TABLEAUX AND BASIS AT EACH ITERATION.
TYPE '1' FOR THE BASIS ONLY.
TYPE '0' FOR JUST THE SOLUTION.
WHICH?
```

Usually you will respond with '2' or '0' (although you *must not* actually type the inverted commas), and thereby obtain either the step by step 'journey' that the computer makes through the tableaux of the problem, or simply the final solution. We will assume that you respond with '2', but any legal response will produce the second prompt.

The LINPRO program

```
WHAT ARE M (THE NUMBER OF RESTRICTIONS) AND N (THE NUMBER OF
VARIABLES) OF THE DATA MATRIX?
```

Clearly our problem has three constraints and two variables, so we should respond with

$$3,2$$

(The commas are essential.) This will produce the third prompt.

```
HOW  MANY  'LESS  THANS',  'EQUALS',  'GREATER  THANS'?
```

Our problem only has three constraints and they are all 'less thans', so we respond with

$$3,0,0$$

(Once again the commas are essential, and you must actually supply zeros if appropriate, rather than *imply* them.)

Although the syntax of data entry and prompt response in LINPRO is fairly simple, it is still easy to make typing mistakes and/or illegal responses. If you do this in responding to the prompts, then the program will 'hang up' and prompt you with something like 'redo from start?' In this case you must press the Ctrl and C keys simultaneously and then you will be able to repeat your responses.

Once all the prompts have been satisfactorily answered the program will proceed to find the solution values of the problem (if they exist) and will then produce the following output for our example problem:

```
YOUR VARIABLES    1 THROUGH 2
SLACK VARIABLES   3 THROUGH 5
```

(Each tableau for each stage of the solution process is then displayed on the screen.)
Finally, you obtain

```
ANSWERS:
        VARIABLE              VALUE
           1                    4
           2                    8
           5                    20
   OBJECTIVE FUNCTION VALUE    96

   DUAL VARIABLES
        COLUMN                VALUE
           3                   2.525
           4                   0.75
           5                   0.00
```

```
           TABLEAU AFTER TWO ITERATIONS
       1        0       0.625      -0.25       0
       4
       0        1      -0.125       0.25       0
       8
       0        0       -3.5         1         1
      20
       0        0       2.625       0.75       0
      96
```

As you can see, although the numbers are the same as in Table 7.2, it is not immediately obvious that the actual tableau is the same, since because of the limited width of the screen LINPRO frequently uses two or more lines to display any one row of the tableau. Furthermore, the variable identification labels are absent.

However, this is easily rectified by noting that variable 1 in LINPRO is what we have called x (since its coefficient was entered first in each data line), variable 2 is what we have called y and variables 3, 4 and 5 are the slack variables from the first, second and third constraints (S_1, S_2 and S_3).

Also, since LINPRO has identified the values of these variables as 4 for x, 8 for y, 20 for S_3 and (by implication) 0 for both S_1 and S_2, it is an easy matter to label the final LINPRO tableau appropriately if necessary (see Table 7.3). You can see that the solution tableau is identical to the one produced earlier in Table 7.2.

Notice also that LINPRO has produced the solution values of the dual variables as well as the primal solution values. We will find a use for these in the next section.

Table 7.3 Tableau after two iterations

B	x	y	S_1	S_2	S_3
x	1	0	0.625	−0.25	0
x	4 ← column A				
y	0	1	−0.125	0.25	0
y	8 ← column A				
S_3	0	0	−3.5	1	1
S_3	20 ← column A				
P	0	0	2.625	0.75	0
P	96 ← column A				

EXAMPLE 7.1

Use LINPRO to repeat the solution of Exercise 5.1.

SOLUTION 7.1

The problem was to find the values of x and y that

$$\begin{aligned} \text{Maximize} \quad & 2x + 6y \\ \text{Subject to} \quad & 2x + 4y \leqslant 100 \\ & x + 6y \leqslant 120 \\ & 5x + 2y \leqslant 130 \end{aligned}$$

And so we enter the data to LINPRO as

```
1 DATA 2,4
2 DATA 1,6
3 DATA 5,2
4 DATA 100,120,130
5 DATA 2,6
```

The responses to the three prompts will be

```
2
3,2
3,0,0
```

When you type RUN you receive the following (edited) output:

```
YOUR VARIABLES     1 THROUGH 2
SLACK VARIABLES    3 THROUGH 5
```

ANSWERS:

	VARIABLE	VALUE
	1	15
	2	17.5
	5	20

OBJECTIVE FUNCTION VALUE   135

DUAL VARIABLES

COLUMN	VALUE
3	0.75
4	0.5
5	0.00

TABLEAU AFTER 2 ITERATIONS

1	0	.750000	-.5000001	0
15				
0	1	-.125	.25	0
17.5				
0	0	-3.5	2	1
20				
0	0	.7500001	.5	0
135				

EXAMPLE 7.2

Use LINPRO to repeat the solution to Exercise 5.2.

SOLUTION 7.2

The problem was to find the values of x and y that

$$\begin{aligned}
\text{Minimize} \quad & 10x + 6y \\
\text{Subject to} \quad & 10x + 4y \geqslant 10 \\
& 8x + 6y \geqslant 12 \\
& 6x + 12y \geqslant 18
\end{aligned}$$

And so we enter the data to LINPRO as

```
1 DATA 10,4
2 DATA 8,6
3 DATA 6,12
4 DATA 10,12,13
5 DATA -10,-6
```

The responses to the three prompts will be

```
   2
   3,2
   0,0,3
```

In this case you will find that on many versions of LINPRO a problem arises, and that the error message 'SOLUTION UNBOUNDED' appears. If this happens, then this is where our knowledge of how to form the dual of any linear program comes in useful, since we can rewrite the program in its *dual form* and run it again. For this problem the dual is

$$\begin{aligned}
\text{Maximize} \quad & 18a + 12b + 10c \\
\text{Subject to} \quad & 6a + 8b + 10c \leqslant 10 \\
\text{And} \quad & 12a + 6b + 4c \leqslant 6
\end{aligned}$$

Now LINPRO can find a solution as follows:

```
YOUR VARIABLES    1 THROUGH 3
SLACK VARIABLES   4 THROUGH 5
```

ANSWERS:

VARIABLE	VALUE
3	.4285715
2	.7142857
OBJECTIVE FUNCTION VALUE	12.85714

The final tableau used for sensitivity analysis

```
                    DUAL VARIABLES:
                    COLUMN          VALUE
                       4           .4285715
                       5          1.428572

                    TABLEAU AFTER 3 ITERATIONS
    a           b       c       S<1>        S<2>          A
-2.142857       0       1      .2142857    -.2857143    .4285715
 3.428572       1       0     -.1428572     .3571429    .7142857
 1.714286       0       0      .4285715    1.428572   12.85714
                                   x            y
```

Because we have solved the *dual* of the program, it will be necessary to convert our solution back to the original variables (x and y). This is done by noting that in the dual program the first constraint contained the slack variable in column 4 of our solution (the S_1 column above). Now since this constraint in the dual was derived from the coefficients of the x variable (6, 8, 10) it follows that this dual variable solution value is the solution value for x (0.428 5715) and that the dual variable value for column 5 (1.428 572) is the solution value for y.

Notice that these final solution values are slightly different from those obtained by the graphical method, but this is entirely due to the fact that we did not allow the value of x to vary in sufficiently small amounts in the graphical solution.

7.3 The final tableau used for sensitivity analysis

As if the information already identified in the final tableau was not enough, there is more to be obtained if required.

Returning to Table 7.3, the solution values in row P of the S_1, S_2 and S_3 columns are the shadow costs of the resources that we explained in Section 6 of Chapter 5.

These values (2.625, 0.75 and 0) represent the maximum amount that the firm would be prepared to pay for an extra unit of the resource associated with that shadow cost. Hence, since S_1 is derived from, and therefore refers to the labour constraint, the firm would be prepared to pay up to £2.625 for an extra unit of labour. This is because with that extra unit of labour it could reallocate production of products X and Y in such a way that the total profit would increase by £2.625. Consequently, it would be prepared to pay *up to* this amount for the opportunity to do so. The shadow cost is therefore the *additional* profit contribution of an extra unit of the resource with which it is associated.

In the same way, the firm would be prepared to pay up to £0.75 for an extra unit of the resource associated with the S_2 variable (machine time), but would pay £0 for the resource associated with the S_3 variable (steel). This latter conclusion has a common-sense interpretation when it is remembered that in the optimal solution there are 20 units of steel left over. Therefore, it is not a scarce resource and the simplex tableau indicates this fact by assigning it a zero shadow cost.

Clearly, the shadow costs are the values of the dual variables that LINPRO has produced as part of its output.

Now, we have said that if extra units of labour and/or capital are available, then the firm will reallocate its production of the two products to take advantage of the new availabilities. But what will be the exact nature of this reallocation?

To work this out suppose that an extra unit of labour becomes available with the other two resources maintaining their original availabilities. We *could* repeat the linear program with the only difference being that the labour availability is now (24 + 1) instead of 24. That is, we could

$$
\begin{aligned}
&\text{Maximize} && 6x + 9y = \text{profit} \\
&\text{Subject to} && 2x + 2y \leqslant 25 && \text{(labour constraint)} \\
&\text{And} && x + 5y \leqslant 44 && \text{(machine time constraint)} \\
&\text{And} && 6x + 2y \leqslant 60 && \text{(steel constraint)}
\end{aligned}
$$

But such a repetition is completely unnecessary, since all we have to do is extract, *from the optimal solution tableau*, the column vector with which we are concerned.

In this case we wish to consider the effect of an extra unit of labour being available and consequently we extract the column vector that refers to the S_1 variable (since this derives from the labour constraint). When we extract this vector (call it $[S_1]$), and add the variable labels from the final solution we get

$$[S_1] = \begin{array}{c} x \\ y \\ S_3 \\ P \end{array} \begin{bmatrix} 0.625 \\ -0.125 \\ -3.5 \\ 2.625 \end{bmatrix} \begin{array}{c} S_1 \\ \end{array}$$

This vector must then be multiplied by the change in the availability of the resource, so we will denote these changes in availabilities by ΔR_1, ΔR_2 and ΔR_3 for resources 1, 2 and 3 (labour, machine time and steel in this case). This means that if an extra unit of labour became available, then it can be represented by the scalar $[\Delta R_1] = [1]$.

When $[S_1]$ is multiplied by the (scalar) vector $[\Delta R_1]$ this will give us a new vector which measures the change in the optimal values of the solution variables implied by the change in the availability of the resource. We will call this new vector $[\Delta U]$. This means that we can write

$$[\Delta U] = [S_1][\Delta R_1]$$

Since this vector gives the *change* in the optimal values of the solution variables, the new values will be given by the old values plus these changes. This means that since the old values were contained in the column that was headed 'A' in the final tableau, we can define the vector $[A]$ to be:

$$[A] = \begin{bmatrix} 4 \\ 8 \\ 20 \\ 96 \end{bmatrix}$$

The new solution vector (which we will call $[AN]$) will therefore be given by:

$$[AN] = [\Delta U] + [A] = [S_1][\Delta R_1] + [A]$$

When these vectors are evaluated for our example we obtain

$$[AN] = \begin{matrix} x \\ y \\ S_3 \\ P \end{matrix} \begin{bmatrix} 0.625 \\ -0.125 \\ -3.5 \\ 2.625 \end{bmatrix} [1] + \begin{bmatrix} 4 \\ 8 \\ 20 \\ 96 \end{bmatrix} = \begin{bmatrix} 4.625 \\ 7.875 \\ 16.5 \\ 98.625 \end{bmatrix}$$

We conclude that an extra unit of labour will cause the output of product X to increase by 0.625 units (to $x = 4.625$); the output of product Y to decrease by 0.125 units (to $y = 7.875$); the amount of unused steel to decrease by 3.5 units (to $S_3 = 16.5$); and the profit to increase by 2.625 units (to $P = 98.625$).

By a similar logic, if an extra unit of machine time was available (i.e. $[\Delta R_2] = [1]$), then we would extract the S_2 vector and obtain

$$[AN] = [S_2][\Delta R_2] + [A]$$

That is

$$[AN] = \begin{matrix} x \\ y \\ S_3 \\ P \end{matrix} \begin{bmatrix} -0.25 \\ 0.25 \\ 1 \\ 0.75 \end{bmatrix} [1] + \begin{bmatrix} 4 \\ 8 \\ 20 \\ 96 \end{bmatrix} = \begin{bmatrix} 3.75 \\ 8.25 \\ 21 \\ 96.75 \end{bmatrix}$$

Finally, if an extra unit of steel was available, then we should expect that since there are 20 units left over in the optimal solution anyway, an extra unit is unlikely to be used and consequently will instigate no reallocation except to add *another* unused unit to the existing stock of unused units.

This is confirmed by extracting the S_3 vector and proceeding as before

$$[AN] = [S_3][\Delta R_3] + [A]$$

That is

$$[AN] = \begin{matrix} x \\ y \\ S_3 \\ P \end{matrix} \begin{bmatrix} 0.00 \\ 0.00 \\ 1 \\ 0.00 \end{bmatrix} [1] + \begin{bmatrix} 4 \\ 8 \\ 20 \\ 96 \end{bmatrix} = \begin{bmatrix} 4.00 \\ 8.00 \\ 21.00 \\ 96.00 \end{bmatrix}$$

This incremental approach to the changes in resource availabilities can be extended to changes in resource availabilities that are greater than 1, but we must be careful not to impinge upon constraints that are at first *not binding* for small changes in resource availabilities but *eventually become so* as the size of these changes increases.

For example, suppose an extra 5 units of labour were available to the firm. You can see that a reallocation could be made to take advantage of such a change since

$$[AN] = \begin{matrix} x \\ y \\ S_3 \\ P \end{matrix} \underset{\begin{bmatrix} 0.625 \\ -0.125 \\ -3.5 \\ 2.625 \end{bmatrix}}{[S_1]} \underset{[5]}{[\Delta R_1]} + \underset{\begin{bmatrix} 4 \\ 8 \\ 20 \\ 2.625 \end{bmatrix}}{[A]} = \underset{\begin{bmatrix} 7.125 \\ 7.375 \\ 2.5 \\ 109.125 \end{bmatrix}}{[AN]}$$

However, the effect of an extra 6 units of labour becoming available would not produce a continuation of this reallocation process. This is because steel is not a scarce resource with an extra 5 units of labour being available, but becomes scarce when an extra 6 are available. You can see this below:

$$[AN] = \begin{matrix} x \\ y \\ S_3 \\ P \end{matrix} \underset{\begin{bmatrix} 0.625 \\ -0.125 \\ -3.5 \\ 2.625 \end{bmatrix}}{[S_1]} \underset{[5]}{[\Delta R_1]} + \underset{\begin{bmatrix} 4 \\ 8 \\ 20 \\ 2.625 \end{bmatrix}}{[A]} = \underset{\begin{bmatrix} 7.75 \\ 7.25 \\ -1.00 \\ 111.75 \end{bmatrix}}{[AN]}$$

The fact that a constraint would be violated is indicated by the negative sign in front of the S_3 variable, and tells us that such a reallocation cannot take place unless more steel is available.

This means that the maximum amount of extra labour that can actually be utilized is given by the absolute value of the ratio between the surplus steel in the final solution (20) and the usage of steel implied by the reallocation of production in response to more labour becoming available (-3.5). That is

$$\text{ABS}(20/-3.5) = 5.714$$

By a similar logic the maximum amount of extra capital which can be taken advantage of is given by

$$\text{ABS}(4/-0.25) = 16$$

Though in this case you should note that it is the production of X (rather than the surplus steel) that would become negative if the change in capital availability exceeded 16.

In general, the constraint upon the ability to take advantage of changes in resource availability is determined by the relationship between the values in the A column of the optimal solution and the *negative* values in the extracted vector, since these indicate the rate at which resources are used up by the production process.

7.4 Changes in the coefficients of the objective function

The simplex final tableau provides another piece of important information which was obtained much less easily by the graphical method. To see this reconsider the

Table 7.4

B	x	y	S_1	S_2	S_3	A
x	1	0	0.625	−0.25	0	4
y	0	1	−0.125	0.25	0	8
S_3	0	0	−3.5	1	1	20
R	0	0	2.625	0.75	0	188

example of Section 2 in Chapter 5:

$$\text{Maximize} \quad 15x + 16y = \text{revenue}$$
$$\text{Subject to} \quad 2x + 2y \leqslant 24$$
$$\text{And} \quad x + 5y \leqslant 44$$
$$\text{And} \quad 6x + 2y \leqslant 60$$

It should be remembered that in Section 4 of Chapter 5 we showed that the optimal solution of $x = 4$, $y = 8$ and $R = £188$ remained optimal only as long as the absolute ratio between the price of product X and the price of product Y lay within the range

$$0.2 < p_x/p_y < 1$$

Price ratios outside this range were seen to cause the optimal solution to change.

Now the question arises of whether the final simplex tableau contains this information, and to answer this we produce the final tableau for this (revenue maximization) problem in Table 7.4.

Observe that the elements in the y and x rows of the S_1 column (−0.125 and 0.625) are in proportion to one another in an absolute ratio of $0.125/0.625 = 0.2$.

Similarly, the elements in the y and x rows of the S_2 column (0.25 and −0.250 are in proportion to one another in an absolute ratio of $0.25/0.25 = 1$.

Clearly, the simplex method has automatically generated the necessary information to determine the range within which the optimal solution remains unchanged. That is

$$0.2 < p_x/p_y < 1$$

For different problems it will, of course, not always be the columns S_1 and S_2 which contain these ratios, but it will always be those columns associated with variables with *positive shadow costs*, and those rows associated with the solution values of the operational variables of the problem (i.e. x and y, etc.).

EXAMPLE 7.3

Use LINPRO to repeat the solution to Exercise 5.3.

SOLUTION 7.3

(a) The linear program was

$$\begin{align}
\text{Maximize} \quad & 6x + 4y = \text{revenue} \\
& 12x + 3y \leqslant 270 \quad \text{(input A restriction)} \\
& 6x + 3y \leqslant 150 \quad \text{(input B restriction)} \\
& 3x + 3y \leqslant 120 \quad \text{(input C restriction)}
\end{align}$$

where x = the production of product X per time period and y = the production of product Y per time period.

```
              YOUR VARIABLES    1 THROUGH 3
              SLACK VARIABLES   4 THROUGH 6
              ANSWERS
                                VARIABLE         VALUE
                                   1              10
                                   2              30
                                   3              60
              OBJECTIVE FUNCTION VALUE           180
              DUAL VARIABLES
                                COLUMN           VALUE
                                   3             0.000
                                   4             0.6667
                                   5             0.6667
```

TABLEAU AFTER 3 ITERATIONS

B	x	y	S<1>	S<2>	S<3>	A
x	1	0	0.00	0.3333	-0.33333	10
y	0	1	0.00	-0.3333	0.66667	30
S<1>	0	0	1.00	-3	2	60
R	0	0	0	0.6666	0.66666	180

(b) We can identify the elements in the y and x rows of the S_2 column to be in an absolute ratio of $0.3333/0.3333 = 1$, while the same row elements in the S_3 column are in an absolute ratio of $0.6667/0.3333 = 2$.

This confirms our previous conclusion that the optimal solution is unchanged for objective function coefficients whose absolute ratios (x coefficient/y coefficient) lie in the range 1–2.

7.5 Exercises

7.1

A building company has acquired 250 000 square metres of land, for which it paid £2 000 000 and on which it plans to build three types of dwelling: terraced, semi-detached and detached.

Each terraced block consists of four individual units which each require 180 square metres of land and which will be sold for £40 000 per unit.

Each semi-detached block consists of two individual units which each require 250 square metres of land and which will be sold for £50 000 per unit.

Each detached block consists of one individual unit which requires 400 square metres of land and which will be sold for £62 000 per unit.

The construction costs for the three types of unit are £34 000, £42 000 and £52 000 for terraced, semi-detached and detached units respectively.

A total of 25 000 square metres will have to be earmarked for access and recreational facilities.

The planning authorities will not allow the total number of blocks on the site to exceed 300, nor the number of terraced blocks to exceed 150, while the mortgage situation is such that it is felt that the number of detached blocks should not exceed 50.

(a) Formulate and solve the linear program that will maximize the building company's profit.
(b) What difference would be implied for the optimal solution if the firm had received a 10 per cent discount on the price it paid for the land?
(c) Obtain a measure of the opportunity cost to the firm of the planning authority's restrictions that:
   (i) the total number of blocks must not exceed 300
   (ii) the number of terraced blocks must not exceed 150
(d) If it were later discovered that 15 000 sq m of the land was unsuitable for building purposes, what difference would this imply for the optimal solution?

7.2

An oil-fired power station burns three grades of oil: grades A, B and C.

The efficiency with which electricity can be produced from the burning of these oils depends upon the presence of three ingredients (X, Y and Z) which are known to be present *in each tonne* of the three grades as follows:

	Tonnes of ingredient per tonne of oil		
	X	Y	Z
Grade A	0.2	0.4	0.3
Grade B	0.1	0.3	0.2
Grade C	0.3	0.2	0.4

Maximum efficiency in the burning process requires the presence of at least 200 tonnes of ingredient X, at least 175 tonnes of ingredient Y and at least 300 tonnes of ingredient Z, *in one hour* of continuous electricity production.

The power station purchases the oil at prices of £60, £80 and £70 per tonne for grades A, B and C respectively, and is required to operate for 12 hours per day.

(a) Formulate the linear program that will minimize the total daily cost of electricity production.
(b) Obtain the optimal utilization rates of the three grades of oil.
(c) If a new burning process became available which meant that the minimum necessary amount of ingredient X was reduced to 150 tonnes per hour, what changes would this induce in the optimal solution in (b) above?
(d) If a new grade of oil were to become available at the same price as grade A, but which contained 0.2, 0.41 and 0.31 tonnes of ingredients X, Y and Z respectively, should the new grade of oil be used in preference to grade A?

7.3

A publishing company sells its major textbook at home, in the United States and in Australasia. The production costs per textbook are £8 regardless of the book's market destination, but transport costs per textbook are £0.5, £1.00 and £1.50 for books distributed to the home, US and Australasian markets respectively. The selling prices for the textbook are £10, £12 and £14 in the respective markets (home, US and Australasian), while demand conditions are such that at these prices, annual sales in each of the markets cannot exceed 12 000, 4000 and 8000 respectively.

(a) The publisher has just completed a production run of 20 000 copies, and requires you to write and solve a linear program that will determine the sales volumes which should be allocated to each of the three markets if profits are to be maximized.
(b) On completion of this task you discover that as a result of import controls introduced by the US government the maximum volume of sales in that market has been reduced by 5 per cent. Indicate the effect upon the optimal solution of such a change.
(c) How would the company's profits have been affected if it had been the Australasian market in which the maximum sales volume had been reduced by 5 per cent?
(d) On the basis of your analysis can you recommend an increase in the production run?
(e) You are also asked to consider the following suggestion for an alteration in the company's pricing policy:

$$\text{Selling price per unit} = 1.15 \text{ (unit production costs)} + \text{(unit transport costs)}$$

and are told that for every 1 per cent reduction in selling price, maximum sales in each of the markets will increase by 0.25 per cent of their previous value.
Rewrite and solve the linear program to take account of this proposal.

7.4

A firm operates two factories A and B which are *each* capable of producing the firm's main product (X). Factory A, however, is also capable of producing another product (Y). Each product requires two inputs (I and II) and the table below gives for each factory and each product the requirements (in units per hour) of the two inputs.

Product	Requirements per hour			
	Factory A		Factory B	
	Input I	Input II	Input I	Input II
X	20	30	30	40
Y	40	50	–	–

The firm has access to a total of 900 units of input I and 1200 units of input II per day; while factories A and B can be operated for a maximum of 12 hours and 15 hours respectively, in any one day. Each unit of each product requires one hour's production time at either factory.

Products X and Y have selling prices of £900 and £1000 respectively and demand for each product exceeds the maximum production level.

(a) Considering both factories, how many hours should be used in the production of X and/or Y if the firm's objective is to maximize daily sales revenue?
(b) Which of the inputs can properly be regarded as a 'scarce' resource?
(c) If *either* factory A or factory B could be operated for an extra hour per day, what would happen to the firm's daily sales revenue and its utilization of inputs? Explain how any implied reallocation could be implemented.

7.5

A profit maximizing firm uses labour, capital and raw materials to produce three commodities, X, Y and Z.

Each unit of X requires 3 units of labour, 2 units of capital, and 4 units of raw material. Each unit of Y requires 2 units of labour, 1 unit of capital and 2 units of raw material. Each unit of Z requires 4 units of labour, 2 units of capital and 4 units of raw material.

In addition, each unit of capital requires half a unit of labour for maintenance purposes, while the ordering, purchasing and storing of each unit of raw material requires a quarter of a unit of Labour.

Units of X, Y and Z sell at prices of £25, £18 and £26 respectively, while units of labour, capital and raw materials cost £2, £3 and £1 respectively.

There are totals of 420 units of labour, 120 units of capital and 600 units of raw material available to the firm.

(a) Show that the firm's objective may be modelled by the following linear program:

$$\begin{aligned} \text{Maximize} \quad & 5x + 7y + 7z = \text{profit} \\ \text{Subject to} \quad & 5x + 3y + 6z \leq 420 \\ \text{And} \quad & 2x + y + 2z \leq 120 \\ \text{And} \quad & 4x + 2y + 4z \leq 600 \end{aligned}$$

where x, y and z are the production levels of X, Y and Z respectively.

(b) Find the production levels of X, Y and Z that maximize profit.
(c) Which input(s) can be properly regarded as 'scarce' resources?
(d) If an extra 2 units of capital were available, how would the optimal solution change?
(e) If, in addition to the above requirements, each unit of Y required a quarter of a unit of X, formulate and solve the new linear program that incorporates these extra requirements (still maximizing profits).

7.6

A firm can allocate its output among three different markets (A, B and C). The following table gives the relevant market and production conditions facing the firm:

	Market		
	A	B	C
Unit production costs (£)	0.4	0.4	0.4
Unit transport costs (£)	0.1	0.16	0.05
Unit sales price (£)	0.6	0.64	0.5
Maximum sales penetration at this price	2000	4000	6000

Under its present production conditions the firm's maximum output is 10 000 units.

(a) Determine the sales to each of the three markets that will maximize total profit.
(b) Which constraints are binding, and which would the firm most like to be relaxed?
(c) The firm is also considering an alteration in its pricing policy:

unit price = (unit production costs) plus a 10 per cent mark up on unit production costs plus unit transport costs

It estimates that a 1 per cent reduction in unit price will produce a 1 per cent increase in maximum sales penetration in each of the markets.
Rewrite and solve the linear program to take account of this proposal.

7.7

A production process consists of making three different products (A, B and C) by assembling different amounts of two basic components (X and Y).

Each unit of A requires 9 units of component X, 13 units of component Y and 5 minutes of assembly time. Each unit of B requires 6 units of component X, 3 units of component Y and 10 minutes of assembly time. Each unit of C requires 9 units of component X, 6 units of component Y and 20 minutes of assembly time.

The firm currently obtains from its supplier a daily delivery of 8100 units of component X and 5700 units of component Y for which it pays £2 and £3 per unit respectively.

A daily workforce of 15 assembly workers is employed on an 8 hour shift basis for which the hourly wage rate is £12.

The products are sold at prices of £63, £29, and £47 for A, B and C respectively.

(a) Formulate a linear program that will maximize the firm's daily profit, and thereby determine the optimal production levels of the three products.
(b) Indicate the effect upon all relevant variables of the following separate changes in resource availabilities:
  (i) a 10 per cent increase in the daily delivery of component X;
  (ii) a 10 per cent increase in the daily delivery of component Y;
  (iii) an extra 2 hours assembly time being available at the going wage rate of £12 per hour;
  (iv) an extra 2 hours assembly time being available but only at the overtime rate of £18 per hour.
(c) What is the maximum hourly overtime rate that the firm would be prepared to pay?
(d) Reformulate, and solve, the linear program in (a) above to take account of the following changes:
  (i) The introduction of a bonus scheme that increases the hourly wage rate by 25 per cent in exchange for a 20 per cent reduction in the assembly time of each of the three products.
  (ii) Using the new labour availabilities from (i) above, a fall in demand for product A, which reduces daily sales to a maximum of 250 units, and reduces the selling price to £60.

7.6 Solutions to the exercises

7.1

(a) Reconsideration of Exercise 5.6 will show that the structure of these two problems is very similar, although there are three types of dwelling in this case.

Consequently

let T = the number of terraced blocks constructed
let S = the number of semi-detached blocks constructed
let D = the number of detached blocks constructed

The objective function of maximizing profit (P) can then be identified as

Maximize $4(40\,000 - 34\,000)T + 2(50\,000 - 42\,000)S + 1(62\,000 - 52\,000)D = P$
Subject to $\quad 4(180)T \;+\; 2(250)S \;+\; 1(400)D \;\leqslant 225\,000$
And $\quad\quad\quad\; T \;+\;\quad\;\; S \;+\;\quad\;\; D \;\leqslant 300$
And $\quad\quad\quad\; T \quad\quad\quad\quad\quad\quad\quad\quad\quad\;\; \leqslant 150$
And $\quad\quad\quad\quad\quad\quad\quad\quad\quad\quad\quad\;\; D \;\leqslant 50$

If you run this program through LINPRO, then the following answers and final tableau are obtained:

```
             YOUR VARIABLES    1 THROUGH 3
             SLACK VARIABLES   4 THROUGH 7

             ANSWERS:
                         VARIABLE      VALUE
                            4          42000
                            2            150
                            1            150
                            7             50
             OBJECTIVE FUNCTION VALUE 6000000

             DUAL VARIABLES:
                         COLUMN        VALUE
                            4              0
                            5          16000
                            6           8000
                            7              0
                  TABLEAU AFTER 2 ITERATIONS
```

S<4>	0	0	-100	1	-500
S<4>	-220	0	42000		
T	0	1	1	0	1
T	-1	0	150		
S	1	0	0	0	0
S	1	0	150		
S<4>	0	0	1	0	0
S<4>	0	1	50		
P	0	0	6000	0	16000
P	8000	0	6000000		

The optimal solution is to build 150 terraced blocks and 150 semi-detached blocks. This will leave 42 000 square metres of land unused, and the restriction on

Solutions to the exercises 323

the number of detached blocks does not operate as an effective constraint at all.

When the £2.5 million that was paid for the land is subtracted this leaves a net profit of £4.5 million.

(b) As you saw in Chapter 5 the fact that this reduction applies to a fixed cost makes no difference to the optimal allocation, although the profit will increase by £0.25 million to £4.75 million.

(c)

(i) Given the ordering of our constraints the restriction on the total number of blocks contains the second slack variable, and so we are concerned with the shadow cost of the resource represented by S_2. This is seen to be 16 000 (column 5 Dual variable) and therefore indicates that the opportunity cost to the company of this particular restriction is £16 000. That is, profit would increase by £16 000 if the restriction on the total number of blocks was relaxed by 1.

(ii) By a similar logic, the shadow cost associated with the restriction upon the number of terraced blocks is 8000 (column 6 Dual variable) and provides the measure of the opportunity cost of this constraint.

(d) The land constraint contains the S_1 slack variable but since 42 000 square metres of land are left over in the optimal solution, all that will happen is that this surplus will be reduced by 15 000 (to 27 000 square metres). You can confirm this by extracting the S_1 vector (column 4) and noting that its first element is 1 and all other elements are 0.

7.2

(a) The objective function is easily identified as

$$\text{Minimize} \quad 60a + 80b + 70c = \text{cost}$$

where

a = the number of tonnes of grade A coal burned per day
b = the number of tonnes of grade B coal burned per day
c = the number of tonnes of grade C coal burned per day

These tonnages must supply at least 200, 175 and 300 tonnes of ingredients X, Y and Z in one hour of continuous electricity production. Therefore the requirement that the power station operate for 12 hours per day means that at least 12(200) = 2400 tonnes of X must be supplied, at least 12(175) = 2100 tonnes of Y must be supplied, and at least 12(300) = 3600 tonnes of Z must be supplied.

The ingredients are present in the various grades of oil as indicated, so that burning c tonnes of grade C oil, for example, will supply $0.3c$ tonnes of ingredient X and $0.2c$ tonnes of ingredient Y, and so on. We therefore have the following three constraints:

$$0.2a + 0.1b + 0.3c \geqslant 2400$$

i.e. (ingredient X supply) $\geqslant$ (ingredient X requirement)

And $\quad 0.4a + 0.3b + 0.2c \geqslant 2100$

i.e. (ingredient Y supply) $\geqslant$ (ingredient Y requirement)

And $\quad 0.3a + 0.2b + 0.4c \geqslant 3600$

i.e. (ingredient Z supply) $\geqslant$ (ingredient Z requirement)

When you run this through LINPRO the solution may be found to be unbounded, confirming our previous observation that certain types of minimization problems can frequently cause difficulties on some versions of LINPRO. In particular, this tends to happen when the constraints are all of a 'greater than or equal' to nature.

As a result of these difficulties it is often better to use the dual formulation of the primal program (although you can only do this if the nature of the constraints is not mixed). For this exercise the Dual would be

Maximize $\quad 3600u + 2100v + 2400w = C^*$
Subject to $\quad 0.3u + 0.4v + 0.2w \leqslant 60$
And $\quad 0.2u + 0.3v + 0.1w \leqslant 80$
And $\quad 0.4u + 0.2v + 0.3w \leqslant 70$

When you run this through LINPRO you will find that a bounded solution is obtained.

```
YOUR VARIABLES    1 THROUGH 3
SLACK VARIABLES   4 THROUGH 6

ANSWERS:
               VARIABLE          VALUE
                  2                30
                  5                39
                  1               160
OBJECTIVE FUNCTION VALUE         639000

DUAL VARIABLES:
               COLUMN            VALUE
                  4              1200
                  5                 0
                  6              8100
```

TABLEAU AFTER 2 ITERATIONS

v	0	1	-.1	4	0
v	-3	30			
S<1>	0	0	-.03	-.8000001	1
S<1>	.1	39			
u	1	0	.8	-2	0
u	4	160			
C*	0	0	270	1200	0
C*	8100	639000	extra	a	b
	c	cost	ingredient X		

(b) As in our previous minimization problem the solution values of our primal variables (a, b and c) are provided as the dual variable solution values. Identification is done by remembering that columns 4, 5 and 6 of the tableau relate to the three slack variables in the constraints, and that these constraints derived from the coefficients of the primal variables a, b and c respectively. This means that the dual variable in column 4 gives the value of a, column 5 gives the value of b and column 6 gives the value of c. The power station should therefore burn 1200 tonnes of grade A oil and 8100 tonnes of grade B oil at a cost per 12 hours of £639 000. This will exactly fulfil the requirements of ingredients Y and Z, and will overfulfil the ingredient X requirement by 270 tonnes per 12 hour shift.

(c) Since the supply of ingredient X is already excess to requirements, the introduction of the new process will simply mean that the excess supply will increase from 270 to 570 tonnes (since the minimum requirement is now 1800 tonnes per 12 hour shift as opposed to 2100 previously).

(d) Since the new grade of oil contains the *same* amount of ingredient X and *more* of both ingredients Y and Z than grade A oil, it follows that burning the same tonnage of the new grade will supply more of ingredients Y and Z than would grade A oil. Furthermore, since the constraints upon ingredients Y and Z are binding in the optimal solution, (and since ingredient X is oversupplied) it also follows that the required supply of all ingredients could be provided by burning *less* of the new grade of oil. Since this new grade is available at the same price as grade A oil it also follows that the total cost would be reduced.

You could confirm this by reworking the program with the new constraints

$$0.2a + 0.1b + 0.3c \geqslant 2400$$
And $$0.41a + 0.3b + 0.2c \geqslant 2100$$
And $$0.31a + 0.2b + 0.4c \geqslant 3600$$

7.3

(a) Let h = sales to the home market, u = sales to the US market and a = sales to the Australasian market.

Then

profit per book sold in the home market $= 10 - 8 - 0.5 = £1.50$
profit per book sold in the US market $= 12 - 8 - 1 = £3.00$
profit per book sold in the Australasian market $= 14 - 8 - 1.50 = £4.50$

The objective function representing total profit is therefore given by

Maximize $\quad 1.5h + 3u + 4.5a = $ profit

This function is subject to the following constraints:

$$h + u + a \leqslant 20\,000$$

That is, total sales to all three markets cannot exceed the production run of 20 000 copies.

$$\text{And} \quad h \quad \leqslant 12000$$
$$\text{And} \quad u \quad \leqslant 4000$$
$$\text{And} \quad a \leqslant 8000$$

That is, the demand restrictions mean that sales to each of the markets are confined as above.

The optimal solution tableau is produced below, although you might note that a 'common-sense' strategy of *sequentially* satisfying the demand in the most profitable markets produces the same result.

```
YOUR VARIABLES    1 THROUGH 3
SLACK VARIABLES   4 THROUGH 7

ANSWERS:
              VARIABLE       VALUE
                 1           8000
                 5           4000
                 2           4000
                 3           8000
OBJECTIVE FUNCTION VALUE    60000


DUAL VARIABLES:
              COLUMN         VALUE
                 4           1.5
                 5           0
                 6           1.5
                 7           3
```

TABLEAU AFTER 3 ITERATIONS

B	h	u	a	S<1>	S<2>	S<3>	S<4>	A
h	1	0	0	1	0	-1	-1	8000
S<2>	0	0	0	-1	1	1	1	4000
u	0	1	0	0	0	1	0	4000
a	0	0	1	0	0	0	1	8000
P	0	0	0	1.5	0	1.5	3	60000

(b) Since the maximum volume of sales in the US market has fallen by 5 per cent, this means that u must now be less than or equal to 3800. The change in the constraint value is therefore -200 and since this constraint contains the S_3 slack variable we extract that vector to obtain

$$[AN] = \begin{matrix} h \\ S_2 \\ u \\ a \\ P \end{matrix} \begin{bmatrix} -1.00 \\ 0.00 \\ 0.00 \\ 0.00 \\ 1.50 \end{bmatrix} \begin{matrix} [S_3] \\ \\ [-200] \end{matrix} + \begin{matrix} [\Delta R_3] + \\ \\ \\ \\ \end{matrix} \begin{bmatrix} 8000 \\ 4000 \\ 4000 \\ 8000 \\ 60000 \end{bmatrix} = \begin{bmatrix} 8200 \\ 3800 \\ 3800 \\ 8000 \\ 59700 \end{bmatrix}$$

As you can see, 200 copies have been diverted from the US market to the home market, and as a result the profit has fallen by £300.

(c) A similar analysis (extracting the S_4 vector this time), would show that 400 copies (5 per cent of 8000) would have to be diverted from the Australasian market to the home market, and that the profit would fall by £600.

(d) Since there is demand unsatisfied in the home market (indicated by the shadow cost of 1.5 in the S_1 column), an increase in production would be justified, provided that the cost per copy did not increase by more than £1.50.

(e) Under this new pricing policy the prices in the three markets would become

home market price $1.15(8) + 0.5 = £9.70$
US market price $1.15(8) + 1.00 = £10.20$
Australasian market price $1.15(8) + 1.50 = £10.70$

The price in the home market has fallen by $(10 - 9.7)/10 = 3$ per cent and so maximum sales in that market will increase by $3(0.25)$ per cent of $12\,000 = 90$ (i.e. to 12 090).

By a similar logic you should find that sales in the US market will increase by $15(0.25)$ per cent of $4000 = 150$ (i.e. to 4150), and that sales in the Australasian market will increase by $23.57(0.25)$ per cent of $8000 = 471$ (i.e. to 8471).

The profit per copy is now £1.20 in all three markets so the new program becomes

Maximize $1.2h + 1.2u + 1.2a = $ profit
Subject to $h + u + a \leqslant 20\,000$
And $h \leqslant 12\,090$
And $u \leqslant 4150$
And $a \leqslant 8471$

This has the following final solution:

```
ANSWERS:
         VARIABLE    VALUE
            1         7379
            5         4711
            2         4150
            3         8471
OBJECTIVE FUNCTION VALUE 24000
```

```
DUAL VARIABLES:
    COLUMN        VALUE
       4           1.2
       5            0
       6            0
       7            0
```

The result of this new pricing strategy has been to reduce the profit by £36 000. Furthermore, since sales are now equally profitable in any of the markets, the shadow costs of the demand restrictions have all become zero. The only real constraint is the size of the production run (shadow cost = 1.2), and this indicates that if production could be increased it would be profitable to do so, but that it would not matter *from the point of view of profit alone*, which market it was sold in.

7.4

(a) Let H_{ax} = the number of hours operating factory A in the production of X, let H_{ay} = the number of hours operating factory A in the production of Y and let H_{bx} = the number of hours operating factory B in the production of X.

Since 1 unit of each product *always* requires 1 hour of production time at either factory, we can express the output of the products in terms of factory process hours as

$$\text{output of } X = H_{ax} + H_{bx}$$
$$\text{output of } Y = H_{ay}$$

Therefore, the objective function is

$$\text{Maximize} \quad 900H_{ax} + 1000H_{ay} + 900H_{bx} = \text{revenue}$$

The restrictions upon the availability of resources means that

$$20H_{ax} + 40H_{ay} + 30H_{bx} \leq 900$$
$$30H_{ax} + 50H_{ay} + 40H_{bx} \leq 1200$$

Finally, the restrictions upon the maximum number of hours for which each factory can be used mean that

$$H_{ax} + H_{ay} \leq 12$$
$$H_{bx} \leq 15$$

When you run this through LINPRO the following solution is obtained:

```
YOUR VARIABLES     1 THROUGH 3
SLACK VARIABLES    4 THROUGH 7
```

```
                ANSWERS:
                    VARIABLE              VALUE
                       3                   15
                       5                   30
                       2                   10.5
                       1                    1.5
                OBJECTIVE FUNCTION VALUE    25350


                DUAL VARIABLES:
                    COLUMN               VALUE
                       4                 5.000002
                       5                 0
                       6                 800
                       7                 750

                  TABLEAU AFTER 3 ITERATIONS
B        H<ax>  H<ay>  H<bx>   S<1>     S<2>   S<3>   S<4>      A
H<bx>      0      0      1       0        0      0      1      15
S<2>       0      0      0      -1        1    -10    -10      30
H<ay>      0      1      0     .05        0     -1   -1.5      10.5
H<ax>      1      0      0    -.05        0      2    1.5       1.5
R          0      0      0   5.000002     0    800    750    25350
```

(b) Inspecting row R we see that the resources associated with constraints 1, 3 and 4 have positive shadow costs. Consequently, input I and the hours available at both factories are scarce resources. Input II (with a zero shadow) cost is not a scarce resource.

(c) If factory A could be operated for an extra hour per day, then we can calculate the effect by extracting the S_3 column vector and letting $[\Delta R_3] = 1$. This produces

$$[AN] = \begin{matrix} H_{bx} \\ S_2 \\ H_{ay} \\ H_{ax} \\ R \end{matrix} \begin{bmatrix} [S_3] \\ 0.00 \\ -10.00 \\ -1.00 \\ 2.00 \\ 800.00 \end{bmatrix} [\Delta R_3] + \begin{bmatrix} [A] \\ 15 \\ 30 \\ 10.5 \\ 1.5 \\ 25\,350 \end{bmatrix} = \begin{bmatrix} [AN] \\ 15 \\ 20 \\ 9.5 \\ 3.5 \\ 26\,150 \end{bmatrix}$$

An extra hour being available at factory A would cause the firm to reduce the processing time devoted to product Y by 1 hour and to increase the processing time devoted to product X by 2 hours (i.e. the extra available hour plus the hour released from producing Y). Revenue would increase by £800.

If, on the other hand it was factory B that was operated for an extra hour, then the effects can be seen by extracting S_4 column vector to produce

$$[AN] = \begin{matrix} H_{bx} \\ S_2 \\ H_{ay} \\ H_{ax} \\ R \end{matrix} \begin{matrix} [S_4] \\ \begin{bmatrix} 1.00 \\ -10.00 \\ -1.50 \\ 1.50 \\ 750.00 \end{bmatrix} \end{matrix} \begin{matrix} [\Delta R_4] + \\ [1] \end{matrix} + \begin{matrix} [A] \\ \begin{bmatrix} 15 \\ 30 \\ 10.5 \\ 1.5 \\ 25\,350 \end{bmatrix} \end{matrix} = \begin{matrix} [AN] \\ \begin{bmatrix} 16 \\ 20 \\ 9 \\ 3 \\ 26\,100 \end{bmatrix} \end{matrix}$$

In this case the extra hour being available at factory B *not only* has an effect there (1 extra hour's operation in the production of X), but *also* causes a reallocation to take place *within* factory A, where 1.5 hours processing time are switched from the production of Y to the production of X. Daily revenue increases by £750.

7.5

(a) Let $x =$ the output of commodity X, let $y =$ the output of commodity Y and let $z =$ the output of commodity Z.
Therefore

$$\text{revenue} = 25x + 18y + 26z$$

Each unit of X requires 3 units of labour, 2 units of capital and 4 units of raw material as direct inputs, and *in addition*, the 2 direct units of capital will require another 1 labour unit indirectly, and the 4 units of raw material will require another 1 indirect labour unit. Therefore, taking indirect and direct labour requirements together, each unit of X will require a total of 5 units of labour.

The cost per unit of X is therefore given by

$$5(2) + 2(3) + 4(1) = 20$$

and the cost of x units will be $20x$.

The profit per unit of X is clearly £5 and so the profit function for X is $5x$.

If we use the same logic for the other two products, then it will be found that the cost per unit of Y is £11 and the cost per unit of Z is £22.

The objective function is therefore

$$\text{Maximize} \quad 5x + 7y + 4z = \text{profit}$$

Furthermore, the availability of the resources means that the following constraints apply:

$$\begin{aligned} (3+2)x + (2+1)y + (4+2)z &\leqslant 420 \\ 2x + 1y + 2z &\leqslant 120 \\ 4x + 2y + 4z &\leqslant 600 \end{aligned}$$

(b) The solution to this program is

```
YOUR VARIABLES    1 THROUGH 3
SLACK VARIABLES   4 THROUGH 6

ANSWERS:
              VARIABLE        VALUE
                 4             60
                 2            120
                 6            360
OBJECTIVE FUNCTION VALUE      840

DUAL VARIABLES:
              COLUMN          VALUE
                 4              0
                 5              7
                 6              0
```

TABLEAU AFTER 1 ITERATION

B	x	y	z	S<1>	S<2>	S<3>	A
S<1>	-1	0	0	1	-3	0	60
y	2	1	2	0	1	0	120
S<3>	0	0	0	0	-2	1	360
P	9	0	10	0	7	0	840

(c) The resource associated with the second slack variable (capital) is the only one to have positive shadow cost (7), so we conclude that it is the only scarce resource. There are 60 units of labour and 360 units of raw material left over.

(d) Extract the S_2 column vector and multiply by 2 to obtain

$$[S_2] \quad [\Delta R_2] + \quad [A] \quad = [AN]$$

$$\begin{matrix} S_1 \\ y \\ S_3 \\ P \end{matrix} \begin{bmatrix} -3 \\ 1 \\ -2 \\ 7 \end{bmatrix} [2] \; + \; \begin{bmatrix} 60 \\ 120 \\ 360 \\ 840 \end{bmatrix} = \begin{bmatrix} 54 \\ 122 \\ 356 \\ 854 \end{bmatrix}$$

(e) If each unit of Y also required 0.25 units of commodity X, then the cost per unit of Y would increase to $11 + 0.25(20) = £15$, and so the profit per unit of Y would fall to £3.

We also need to introduce the additional constraint that the output of X must be at least equal to 25 per cent of the output of commodity Y. This means that $x \geqslant 0.25y$, which should be rewritten and entered to LINPRO as

$$x - 0.25y \geqslant 0$$

When you alter the objective function to accommodate the lower profit margin on Y and add this new constraint as the last constraint of the program, the following solution is obtained from LINPRO. Notice that the slack variables are now contained in columns 5, 6 and 7 of the output, since LINPRO has introduced what is known as a surplus variable in column 4, and what is known as an artificial variable in column 8. The latter is merely a computational aid and has little significance for sensitivity analysis, while the former indicates the extent to which any greater than or equal to constraint is exceeded. The full solution is

```
YOUR VARIABLES          1 THROUGH 3
SURPLUS VARIABLES       4 THROUGH 4
SLACK VARIABLES         5 THROUGH 7
ARTIFICIAL VARIABLES    8 THROUGH 8

ANSWERS:
            VARIABLE            VALUE
               5                 80
               2                 80
               7                360
               1                 20
OBJECTIVE FUNCTION VALUE        340

DUAL VARIABLES:
            COLUMN              VALUE
               4               .6666667
               5                  0
               6               2.833333
               7                  0
```

As you can see, the result of these amendments has been to reduce the profit to £340 and to force a reallocation such that 80 units of product Y and 20 units of product X are now produced. Also, the shadow costs representing the relative scarcity of the resources have also changed. In particular, the dual variable in column 4 indicates that the requirement that some X must be produced (in order to produce Y) is a real resource cost (£0.666 6667 per unit). Furthermore, there are now 80 units of labour left over (variable 5) as opposed to 60 before, but the surplus raw material remains unchanged at 360 units.

7.6

(a) Let x = sales to market A, let y = sales to market B and let z = sales to market C.
    Therefore

$$\text{revenue} = 0.6x + 0.64y + 0.5z$$
$$\text{costs} = 0.5x + 0.56y + 0.45z$$
$$\text{profit} = 0.1x + 0.08y + 0.05z$$

This profit function has to be maximized subject to

$$x + y + z \leq 10\,000$$
$$x \leq 2000$$
$$y \leq 4000$$
$$z \leq 6000$$

The following answers are produced:

```
YOUR VARIABLES   1 THROUGH 3
SLACK VARIABLES  4 THROUGH 7

ANSWERS:
              VARIABLE       VALUE
                 3           4000
                 1           2000
                 2           4000
                 7           2000
        OBJECTIVE FUNCTION VALUE      720

DUAL VARIABLES:
              COLUMN         VALUE
                 4            .05
                 5            .05
                 6            .03
                 7             0
```

(b) Constraints 1, 2 and 3 (slack variables 1, 2 and 3) have positive shadow costs and therefore are binding constraints (dual variables in columns 4, 5 and 6). The final constraint (slack variable 4, dual variable in column 7) is not binding and has a 0 shadow cost.

Constraints 1 and 2 have the same (highest) shadow cost and therefore are the ones that should be relaxed first if possible.

(c) The price of X becomes $0.4 + 0.1(0.4) + 0.1 = £0.54$; the price reduction in $X = (0.6 - 0.54)/0.6 = 10$ per cent; the increase in sales to $A = 0.1(2000) = 200$.

The price of Y becomes $0.4 + 0.1(0.4) + 0.16 = £0.60$; the price reduction in $Y = (0.64 - 0.60)/0.64 = 6.25$ per cent; the increase in sales to $B = 0.0625(4000) = 250$.

The price of Z becomes $0.4 + 0.1(0.4) + 0.05 = £0.49$; the price reduction in $Z = (0.50 - 0.49)/0.50 = 2$ per cent; the increase in sales to $C = 0.02(6000) = 120$.

The new program becomes

Maximize $0.04x + 0.04y + 0.04z$
Subject to $x + y + z \leq 10\,000$
             $x \leq 2200$
             $y \leq 4250$
             $z \leq 6120$

The solution is

```
ANSWERS:
        VARIABLE        VALUE
            2           3880
            5           2200
            6            370
            3           6120
    OBJECTIVE FUNCTION VALUE    400

DUAL VARIABLES:
        COLUMN          VALUE
            4           .04
            5            0
            6            0
            7            0
```

The effect of this alteration to the program is to show that the only scarce resource is the size of the production run.

7.7

(a) Let a = the output of product A, let b = the output of product B and let c = the output of product C.

Therefore

$$\text{revenue} = 63a + 29b + 47c$$
$$\text{unit costs of product A} = 9(2) + 13(3) + 5/60(12) = £58$$
$$\text{unit costs of product B} = 6(2) + 3(3) + 10/60(12) = £23$$
$$\text{unit costs of product C} = 9(2) + 6(3) + 20/60(12) = £40$$

Therefore the objective function is

Maximize $\quad 5a + 6b + 7c = \text{profit}$
Subject to $\quad 9a + 6b + 9c \leqslant 8100$
And $\quad 13a + 3b + 6c \leqslant 5700$
And $\quad 5a + 10b + 20c \leqslant (15)(8)(60)$ (minutes)

The solution is

```
YOUR VARIABLES    1 THROUGH 3
SLACK VARIABLES   4 THROUGH 6

ANSWERS:
        VARIABLE        VALUE
            4           1933.044
            1            307.8261
            2            566.087
    OBJECTIVE FUNCTION VALUE         4935.653
```

Solutions to the exercises

```
                DUAL VARIABLES:
                        COLUMN              VALUE
                           4                  0
                           5                  .173913
                           6                  .5478261

                TABLEAU AFTER 3 ITERATIONS
    0               0           -3         1       -.5217392
 -.4434783       1933.044
    1               0            0         0        8.695652E-02
-2.608696E-02    307.8261
    0               1            2         0       -4.347826E-02
   .1130435      566.087
    0               0            5         0        .173913
   .5478261     4935.653
```

The optimal solution is to produce 307.8261 units of product A and 566.087 units of product B. This produces the maximum revenue of 4935.653 and leaves 1933.044 units of component X unused.

(b) (i) Extract the fourth column (S_1) and multiply by 810. (ii) Extract the fifth column (S_2) and multiply by 570. (iii) Extract the sixth column (S_3) and multiply by 120. (iv) Extract the sixth column (S_3) and multiply by 120, but in this case profit will not increase by this amount since the extra overtime payment will have to be subtracted. This would produce a reduction in profit equivalent to $120(0.547\,8261) - 120(18 - 12) = -654.26$.

(c) The maximum hourly overtime rate is given by the shadow cost of the labour input plus the existing wage rate, i.e. £12 + £0.547 8261 = £12.55.

(d) (i) The wage rate increases to $12 + 0.25(12) = £15$. The assembly times are reduced to 4 minutes for A, 8 minutes for B and 16 minutes for C. However, because of the increased wage rate you will find that the unit cost of the three products remains unchanged. So the profit function remains as

$$5a + 6b + 7c = \text{profit}$$

However, these reduced assembly times do have to be incorporated into the overall labour time constraint as

$$4a + 8b + 16c \leqslant 7200$$

When you alter this constraint, the following solution is obtained:

```
                ANSWERS:
                    VARIABLE             VALUE
                        4              1134.783
                        1               260.8696
                        2               769.5652
                OBJECTIVE FUNCTION VALUE        5921.74
```

DUAL VARIABLES:
```
COLUMN      VALUE
   4          0
   5        .173913
   6        .6847826
```

The fact that less assembly time (albeit at a higher wage rate) is now required has raised the profit to £5921.74. This has been effected by increasing the output of product A relative to that of product B, and makes sense because product B uses less labour than product A. So although the monetary profit margins on A and B have remained the same, the relative labour resource costs of product A have been reduced by the improved assembly times.

This is also indicated by the fact that labour now has a higher shadow cost in the optimal solution (£0.684 as opposed to £0.547) and has therefore become more scarce (so much so that the overtime rate could now increase to £12.68 per hour.)

(ii) The reduction in the price of A alters the profit function to

$$2a + 6b + 7c = \text{profit}$$

Also, the limitation upon the demand for A means that the following additional constraint must be used:

$$a \leqslant 250$$

Introducing this restriction as the last constraint, the new program has the following solution:

```
YOUR VARIABLES  1 THROUGH 3
SLACK VARIABLES 1 THROUGH 7

ANSWERS:
   VARIABLE      VALUE
      4          2700
      5          3000
      2           900
      7           250
   OBJECTIVE FUNCTION VALUE   5400

DUAL VARIABLES:
   COLUMN       VALUE
      4           0
      5           0
      6          .75
      7           0
```

As you can see, the profit has been reduced because, although product A uses more labour than product B, the firm still wanted to produce 260 units of A prior to the new circumstances. However, when the demand restrictions are introduced (along with the reduced profitability of A), it no longer finds product A sufficiently attractive, and as a result switches to producing nothing but product B.

Furthermore, the third constraint (labour time) is now the only one with a positive shadow cost (£0.75). This may puzzle you, but it simply indicates that the reduced profit on A has more influence on the allocation decision than the demand restriction. This follows because if it was not the case, then the dual variable in column 7 (representing the demand restriction) would be positive. It is primarily the reduced profit margin on A that has stimulated the reallocation decision.

8
Principles of Differential Calculus

8.1 Differential rates of change

Although few of us formally recognize it, we are all familiar to some extent or another with the basic concept of differential calculus. This is because in our daily lives we frequently use phrases such as miles per hour, or miles per gallon, without necessarily realizing that these concepts are simply verbal statements of what calculus calls a *differential rate of change* or a *derivative*.

By this, it means the *instantaneous* rate of change of one variable with respect to another. Viewed in these terms, it should be clear that when we quote a speed such as 40 miles per hour, we are in fact computing the rate of change of *distance* with respect to *time* (i.e. miles *per* hour).

If you keep this simple idea in mind, then you should be able to see that a rate of change must always be quoted in terms of at least *two* units of measurement, and that these units identify which variable is changing with respect to which. In our example of speed, this means that miles per hour measures the rate of change of distance (measured in miles) with respect to time (measured in hours).

Now if differential calculus was simply concerned with calculating arithmetic rates of change, then there would be little more to explain. However, you may have noticed that we have said that the differential rate of change (derivative) is the *instantaneous* rate of change of one variable with respect to another, and it is the word 'instantaneous' that can cause difficulties.

The reason for this is that in order to calculate a simple rate of change we have to let one variable (the independent one) change by some measurable amount and then calculate the change in the second (the dependent one), that has resulted from the change in the first. However, if we can count and measure the change in the independent variable, then we are not really observing instantaneous change, but rather an *average* change as the variable moves from one value to another.

Instantaneous change, on the other hand, implies that the change in the value of the independent variable is so small as to be negligible, and as a result, unmeasurable. But if this is the case, how can we then calculate the rate of change

Differential rates of change

on the basis of an unmeasurable change in the value of the independent variable?

This is the fundamental dilemma of differential calculus and requires that we approach the problem from the perspective of some *limiting* value which the rate of change *approaches* but never *quite reaches*.

To see this idea in more concrete terms consider a train which is travelling at a speed such that the distance travelled (y) is given in terms of the elapsed time (x) by

$$y = 3x^2$$

where y is measured in metres and x is measured in seconds.

What we are going to do is try to derive a method of calculating the train's speed in metres per second (m.p.s.) at various *instants* in time, and to do this we can construct Worksheet 8.1.

As you can see, we have entered four values for x in A2..A5, and then calculated the distance travelled (y) in B2..B5 from the formula in B2

$$3 * A2^2 \quad \text{(copied into B3..B5)}$$

The change in the value of x (Δx) and the associated change in the value of y (Δy) are then calculated in C3..C5 and D3..D5 from the following formulae:

$$\text{in C3} \quad + A3 - A2$$
$$\text{in D3} \quad + B3 - B2$$

which were then copied into the remainder of the range.

Finally, in E3, the change in *y per unit of change* in x ($\Delta y / \Delta x$) is taken as our measure of the rate of change of y with respect to x, and is calculated from

$$+ D3/C3 \quad \text{(copied into E4..E5)}$$

From these calculations we can argue that between $x = 0$ and $x = 1$ the train's speed was 3 m.p.s., between $x = 1$ and $x = 2$ it was 9 m.p.s., and between $x = 2$ and $x = 3$ it was 15 m.p.s.

Although this is perfectly valid reasoning, it does not actually answer the question that we originally posed, since that required that we calculate the speed *at* $x = 1$ or *at* $x = 2$, etc., rather than *between* $x = 1$ and $x = 2$. Nevertheless, for the moment, our best estimate of the speed *at* $x = 2$ would be 9 m.p.s.

WORKSHEET 8.1

	A	B	C	D	E
1	x	y	$\tilde{x}$	$\tilde{y}$	$\tilde{y}/\tilde{x}$
2	0	0			
3	1	3	1	3	3
4	2	12	1	9	9
5	3	27	1	15	15

In the worksheets in this chapter $\tilde{x}$ represents Δx and $\tilde{y}$ represents Δy.

WORKSHEET 8.2

	A	B	C	D	E
1	x	y	x̃	ỹ	ỹ/x̃
2	0	0			
3	0.5	0.75	0.5	0.75	1.5
4	1	3	0.5	2.25	4.5
5	1.5	6.75	0.5	3.75	7.5
6	2	12	0.5	5.25	10.5
7	2.5	18.75	0.5	6.75	13.5
8	3	27	0.5	8.25	16.5

But by now it should be clear that if we want to improve this estimate, then we must make the change in the value of x become smaller (i.e. consider smaller time intervals). This has been done in Worksheet 8.2 where the time intervals for which the changes are evaluated are now in units of 0.5 second as opposed to 1 second previously.

As you can see, our estimates of the speeds at various values of x have changed as a result of this alteration, and we would now argue that the train's speed at $x = 2$ is 10.5 m.p.s. as opposed to 9 m.p.s. previously.

Nevertheless, this estimate is still based upon the average change in distance between $x = 1.5$ and $x = 2$ (i.e. a time interval of 0.5 seconds), and though it is more accurate than the previous estimate it can still be improved by considering even smaller time intervals.

This has been done in Worksheet 8.3 where for reasons of space we have concentrated the analysis on values of $x = 1$, 2 and 3. The logic of this worksheet's structure is as follows.

The first thing to do is to enter the values of x with which we are concerned in the cells A3, A6 and A9.

WORKSHEET 8.3

	A	B	C	D	E
1	x	y	x̃	ỹ	ỹ/x̃
2	0.9	2.43	0.1		
3	1	3	0.1	0.57	5.7
4	1.1	3.63	0.1	0.63	6.3
5	1.9	10.83			
6	2	12	0.1	1.17	11.7
7	2.1	13.23	0.1	1.23	12.3
8	2.9	25.23			
9	3	27	0.1	1.77	17.7
10	3.1	28.83	0.1	1.83	18.3

Now enter the Lotus formula for the function in B2, and copy this into the range B3..B10. This means that, for this example, the entry in B2 would be

$$3*A2^2$$

(Do not worry if a lot of zeros appear at this stage; you have not completed the values of x in column A yet.)

Now enter the change in x (Δx) that is to be considered in the C2 cell (use 0.1 to start with), and in C3 enter +C2. You should then copy the contents of C3 into the range C4..C10, and note that this procedure will automatically reproduce whatever value you enter in C2 for the change in x into all other relevant cells of this column. (The entries in C5 and C8 are redundant and should be erased.)

This procedure makes the worksheet extremely flexible and will allow you to examine the effect of smaller and smaller changes in the value of x without having to engage in extensive copying.

What we require now is that values within plus or minus Δx of each chosen value of x are also evaluated. So, in A2 enter

$$+A3-C3$$

This will produce $1-\Delta x$ in the A2 cell, and to produce $1+\Delta x$ in the A4 cell you should enter

$$+A3+C3$$

in A4. Now you will have to repeat this process for each of the selected values of x, so you should enter

+A6−C6	in A5
+A6+C6	in A7
+A9−C9	in A8
+A9+C9	in A10

This will produce values of x in the vicinity of $x = 1$, 2 and 3, with the proximity being determined by the value that was entered in C2 for the change in x.

Finally, you can complete columns D and E in the same way as in the last worksheet, so enter

+B3−B2	in D3
+D3/C3	in E3

Now copy these formulae into the D4..E12 range, and your worksheet is nearly complete. You will, however, have to erase the contents of D5..E5 and D8..E8, since these calculations refer to changes in the value of x that exceed 0.1 (1.1 to 1.9, 2.1 to 2.9).

Notice how adaptable this worksheet is, since if you want to alter the change in x that is to be considered, then all you have to do is enter the new value for Δx in C2, and all consequent changes to the worksheet will be made for you.

Furthermore, if you want to change the values of x to be considered, then you simply have to alter the values in A3 and/or A7 and/or A11, and the new calculations will be performed automatically.

Even if you want to change the function being analyzed, then you can do this by typing the new Lotus formula in B2 and then copying it into B3..B12.

Make sure that you prepare this worksheet properly since we shall be using it again.

Now that we are measuring the elapsed time in tenths of seconds ($\Delta x = 0.1$) we would estimate the speed at $x = 2$ to be 11.7 m.p.s.

Clearly, we can keep on considering smaller and smaller time intervals until we run out of computational accuracy, but if you modify the last worksheet so that time intervals of a thousandth of a second ($\Delta x = 0.001$) are considered, then you will find that the estimated speed at $x = 2$ becomes 11.997 m.p.s. Furthermore, if you use time intervals of a millionth of a second ($\Delta x = 0.000\ 001$), then you will find that the speed at $x = 2$ becomes indistinguishable from 12 m.p.s. (11.999 999).

Although it is the accuracy of our calculational techniques that is responsible for our inability to distinguish between 12 and 11.999 999, you should be able to see that as the size of the time intervals are reduced, then the estimated speeds get closer and closer to their limiting values.

This process is summarized in Worksheet 8.4 for time intervals (Δx) of 0.1, 0.01, 0.001, 0.0001 and 0.000 01 seconds and for time values (x) of 1, 2, and 3. From this worksheet we would argue that after 1 second has elapsed the speed has approached a value of 6 m.p.s., that after 2 seconds have elapsed the speed has approached 12 m.p.s., and that after 3 seconds it has approached 18 m.p.s.

These limiting values are what differential calculus defines as the derivative of y with respect to x (given the symbol dy/dx), and are to be thought of as the limiting value of the ratio $\Delta y/\Delta x$ as Δx becomes infinitesimally small.

In symbols we can write

$$dy/dx = \text{limit of } \Delta y/\Delta x \text{ as } \Delta x \text{ tends to } 0$$

At this stage, however, you should be thinking that there must be an easier way of calculating the derivative than the one we have employed. The answer is that there is, and to see how, look carefully at Worksheet 8.5, which has been derived from the previous discussion. Even the most casual inspection would suggest that

WORKSHEET 8.4

	A	B	C	D	E	F
1	x	0.1	0.01	0.001	0.0001	0.000 01
2	x					
3	1	5.7	5.97	5.997	5.9997	5.9997
4	2	11.7	11.97	11.997	11.9997	11.9997
5	3	17.7	17.97	17.997	17.9997	17.9997
6						

WORKSHEET 8.5

```
      A      B         C
1     x      y=3x^2    dy/dx
2     1      3(1)^2    6
3     2      3(2)^2    12
4     3      3(3)^2    18
5
```

the value of dy/dx is given by 6 times the value of x. That is

$$dy/dx = 6x$$

However, although it is an easy matter to deduce this from the information above, we still had to know the limiting values of dy/dx *before* we could make this deduction. Clearly it would be preferable if we could derive an expression for dy/dx *directly* from the original function without having to perform the limiting calculations every time.

To do this we could reason as follows. The function is $y = 3x^2$, and its derivative is $6x$. Careful inspection of these two relationships reveals that the derivative can be obtained by multiplying the function by 2 and then dividing this product by x. That is

$$\text{derivative} = dy/dx = 2(\text{function})/x = 2(3x^2)/x = 6x$$

Although this is clearly valid in this case, we really must ask whether it can be taken as a *general* rule, and to answer this we must ask where the figure of '2' came from.

One answer would be 'from the exponent (power) of the term in x in the original function', and so perhaps we could change our rule to

'Multiply the function to be differentiated by the exponent (power) of the term in x and then divide by x.'

For our illustration this would still produce $dy/dx = 6x$, but for *different* functions with *different* values for the exponent of x, then different expressions for the derivative would be obtained.

For example, if we were required to find the derivative of the function

$$y = 5x^3$$

then we would multiply the function by 3 and then divide the result by x to obtain

$$dy/dx = 3(5x^3)/x = 15x^2$$

This simple rule can be extended quite easily to accommodate the general class of polynomial functions as follows:

if $y = ax^n$
then $dy/dx = n(ax^n)/x = nax^{n-1}$

This procedure for obtaining the derivative from the original function without having to engage in the arithmetic calculations associated with the limiting process is the most basic rule of differential calculus, so make sure you appreciate it fully before proceeding.

EXAMPLE 8.1

A firm's profits (y) are given in terms of sales (x) by

$$y = 0.1x^2$$

(a) Calculate the instantaneous rate of change of profits with respect to sales when 10 units are sold.
(b) Is it worthwhile for the firm to sell more than 10 units?

SOLUTION 8.1

(a) We have

$$y = 0.1x^2$$

Therefore

$$dy/dx = 2(0.1)x^{2-1} = 0 \cdot 2x \text{ (£ per unit of sales)}$$

When $x = 10$ we have

$$dy/dx = 0.2(10) = 2 \text{ (£ per unit of sales)}$$

(b) Since the rate of change of profits with respect to sales is positive for all positive values of sales, this implies that profits are persistently increasing as sales increase. Consequently as many sales as possible should be made, and expansion beyond 10 units would be justified.

EXAMPLE 8.2

The output (y) obtainable from the value (x) of a firm's fixed capital assets is given by

$$y = 10x^{0.5}$$

(a) Obtain an expression for the rate of change of output with respect to asset value.
(b) Obtain an expression for the proportional rate of change of output with respect to asset value.
(c) What are the measurement units of this last expression?

SOLUTION 8.2

(a) $dy/dx = 0.5(10x^{0.5-1}) = 5x^{-0.5} = 5/x^{0.5}$. So

$$dy/dx = 5/x^{0.5} \text{ (output units per £ of asset value)}$$

In this case, it should be clear that although output always rises as asset value rises, the rate of change of output with respect to asset value declines as x increases. This means that the *additional* contribution to output of each *extra* unit of asset value is becoming less.

(b) The proportional rate of change of output with respect to x will be given by:

$$(dy/dx)/y = 5x^{-0.5}/10x^{0.5} = 0.5x^{-1} = 0.5/x$$

You can interpret this as meaning that the instantaneous rate of change of the function with respect to x, as a proportion of the value of the function, is decreasing as x increases (since $0.5/x$ falls with increases in x).

(c) The measurement units are output units per unit of asset value, per unit of output.

EXAMPLE 8.3

A firm's annual rent on its factory is £c million.

(a) Ignoring all other costs, obtain an expression for the average cost of producing x units of output.
(b) Derive an expression for the instantaneous rate of change of average cost when x units of output are produced.
(c) Obtain an expression for the proportional rate of change of average cost with respect to its own value.
(d) Derive an expression for the proportional change in average cost which results from a given proportional change in output.

SOLUTION 8.3

(a) Let average cost $= y$. Therefore

$$y = c/x \text{ (£ million per unit of output)}$$

(b) Rewrite $y = c/x$ as $y = cx^{-1}$. Then

$$\begin{aligned} dy/dx &= -1cx^{-1-1} \\ &= -1cx^{-2} \\ &= -c/x^2 \text{ (£ million per unit of output, per unit of output)} \end{aligned}$$

Since this expression is unambiguously negative for all positive output levels, we can conclude that as output increases average cost declines at a rate given by c over the square of x.

Since c/x^2 gets closer and closer to zero as x increases, this implies that the greatest reduction in average costs, when output increases, takes place when output is relatively small, and that subsequent reductions become smaller and smaller. Nevertheless, as long as dy/dx remains negative (as it will for all finite values of x), then average cost will continue to decline as output increases.

(c) Expressing dy/dx as a proportion of y produces

$$(dy/dx)/y = (-c/x^2)/(c/x) = -cx^{-2}/cx^{-1}$$
$$= -1x^{-1} = -1/x$$

This means that the rate of change of average costs with respect to output at any given output level, when expressed as a proportion of the average costs associated with that output level, is always decreasing (since $(dy/dx)/y < 0$) and given by -1 over the output level. Now since the expression $-1/x$ gets closer and closer to zero as x increases, this means that the proportional rate of change of average costs with respect to output tends towards zero as output increases.

(d) The change in $y = \Delta y$; the proportional change in $y = \Delta y/y$; the change in $x = \Delta x$; the proportional change in $x = \Delta x/x$. Consequently

The *proportional* change in y per unit of *proportional* change in $x(p) = (\Delta y/y)/\Delta x/x)$

Rearrangement produces

$$p = (\Delta y/\Delta x)(x/y)$$

Then taking the limit of $\Delta y/\Delta x$ as Δx tends to zero, gives

$$p = (dy/dx)(x/y)$$

We already have $dy/dx = -c/x^2$. Therefore

$$p = (-c/x^2)(x/y)$$

But $y = c/x$, and, therefore

$$p = (-c/x^2)[x/(c/x)] = (-c/x^2)(x^2/c) = -1$$

In its simplest terms this can be interpreted as meaning that an increase in output of a per cent (for example) will lead to a proportionate change in average costs of -1 times a (i.e. an a per cent reduction). (Students of economics will recognize this as an elasticity calculation.)

8.2. The derivative as a measure of the gradient of a function

Although we have been at pains to stress that the derivative measures the instantaneous rate of change of y with respect to x, there is another way in which it can be interpreted.

The derivative as a measure of gradient

This is to recognize that the instantaneous rate of change of y with respect to x is simply another way of referring to what is more commonly known as the gradient of the function at a specified value of x.

You can see this more clearly in Worksheet 8.6 and Figure 8.1 where the function

$$y = 0.01x^2$$

and its derivative

$$dy/dx = 0.02x$$

have been evaluated and then graphed for selected values of x.

At the same time the straight line that is tangential to the function at an x value of 10 has also been included in the graph. The fact that this line *just* touches the function when $x = 10$ means that the gradient of this line also measures the gradient of the function at $x = 10$.

Simple trigonometry tells us that the gradient of any straight line is given by the ratio between sides that are opposite and adjacent to the angle being measured.

Accordingly, if we form the triangle that has the line that is tangential to the function at $x = 10$ as its hypotenuse, then we can calculate the gradient of this hypotenuse.

This has been done in the diagram (A/B) and can be seen to produce a ratio of $(2.6)/13 = 0.2$. We conclude that the gradient of the function $y = 0.01x^2$ when

WORKSHEET 8.6

	A	B	C
	x	y=0.01x^2	dy/dx=0.02x
1			
2	0	0	0
3	1	0.01	0.02
4	2	0.04	0.04
5	3	0.09	0.06
6	4	0.16	0.08
7	5	0.25	0.1
8	6	0.36	0.12
9	7	0.49	0.14
10	8	0.64	0.16
11	9	0.81	0.18
12	10	1	0.2
13	11	1.21	0.22
14	12	1.44	0.24
15	13	1.69	0.26
16	14	1.96	0.28
17	15	2.25	0.3
18	16	2.56	0.32
19	17	2.89	0.34
20	18	3.24	0.36

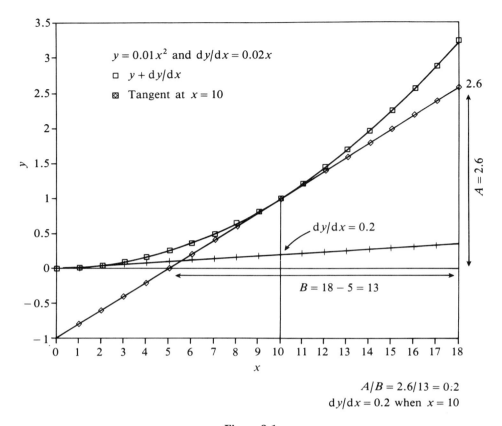

Figure 8.1

$x = 10$ is 0.2. Now observe the calculated value of the derivative when $x = 10$ and you will see that it is identical.

In short, the value of the derivative of any function for any chosen value of x measures the gradient of the function at that chosen value of x.

In our case it is clear that the function $y = 0.1x^2$ gets steeper as the value of x increases, and this is reflected in the fact that the value of the derivative also increases as x increases.

This last result derives from the fact that the derivative contained a term in x, but you may be wondering what happens if this is not the case.

The answer is that *it always will*, except in two special cases of the form of the function to be differentiated.

Case 1 $y = c$ (a constant).   In this case the value of y is completely unrelated to the value of x (since no term in x appears in the function), and so as far as x is concerned, the value of y is constant. Now it is by definition true that the value of a constant does not change, and so we conclude that its rate of change and hence its derivative with respect to x is zero.

That is

$$\text{if } y = c \quad \text{then} \quad dy/dx = 0$$

Graphically the function would be represented by a horizontal straight line, which consequently has a gradient of zero.

Case 2 $y = c + mx$ (where c and m are constants)   As you will remember, this expression defines the equation of a straight line with an intercept of c and a gradient of m.

Since we have seen that the derivative of a constant is 0, and since the derivative of the term mx is m, it follows that the derivative of the equation

$$y = c + mx$$

is given by

$$dy/dx = 0 + m$$

thereby confirming our prior knowledge that the gradient of any straight line is constant and generally given by m.

In all circumstances other than these two special cases, the derivative will contain at least one term in x, indicating that the gradient of the function *depends* upon the value of x being considered.

You may have noticed that with the exception of Case 2 above, all the functions differentiated so far have been single term. But how should we proceed if the function is of a form such as

$$y = ax^n + bx^m - cx^p$$

The answer is quite simply to regard the derivative of the whole function as the sum of the derivatives of its component *additive* parts. In other words

$$dy/dx = nax^{n-1} + mbx^{m-1} - pcx^{p-1}$$

EXAMPLE 8.4

A firm's profit (y) is given in terms of its sales (x) by

$$y = x^{1.5} - 2x^{0.5}$$

Calculate the rate of change of profits with respect to sales when 100 units of output are sold.

SOLUTION 8.4

$$dy/dx = 1.5x^{0.5} - x^{-0.5}$$

and when $x = 100$

$$dy/dx = 15 - 0.1 = 14.9 \text{ (£s per unit of output)}$$

8.3 Identifying stationary points in a function

To understand the role of calculus in clarifying the behaviour of different types of function, consider the following example.

EXAMPLE 8.5

The price (p) of a firm's product is known to depend upon the quantity demanded (x) as follows:

$$p = 200 - 4x$$

Over what range of x values is the firm's total revenue: (a) rising; (b) falling; (c) unchanging?

SOLUTION 8.5

The demand relationship suggests that in order to increase sales the price will have to fall. As a result, the firm's revenue is being simultaneously *decreased* by the fact that a lower price is charged, but *increased* by the fact that more units are sold (albeit at this lower price).

To examine the *net* result of these two effects more closely we require to form a revenue function (R) from the following general relationship:

$$R = (\text{price})(\text{quantity demanded})$$

When we remember that the price is given in terms of x by $p = 200 - 4x$, we can then write

$$R = (200 - 4x)(x) = 200x - 4x^2$$

This is immediately recognizable as a quadratic equation, and as a result, we should suspect that it neither rises continually nor falls continually, but rather *changes direction* at some (as yet undetermined) value of x.

To investigate this suspicion we can differentiate R with respect to x and then examine the sign of the resulting derivative.

Accordingly

$$dR/dx = 200 - 8x$$

You can now enter both R and dR/dx as separate columns in a worksheet (and then graph them if you want). The calculations have been done in Worksheet 8.7.

WORKSHEET 8.7

	A	B	C
1	x	R=200x-4x^2	dR/dx=200-8x
2	0	0	200
3	2.5	475	180
4	5	900	160
5	7.5	1275	140
6	10	1600	120
7	12.5	1875	100
8	15	2100	80
9	17.5	2275	60
10	20	2400	40
11	22.5	2475	20
12	25	2500	0
13	27.5	2475	-20
14	30	2400	-40
15	32.5	2275	-60
16	35	2100	-80
17	37.5	1875	-100
18	40	1600	-120
19	42.5	1275	-140
20	45	900	-160

The formula in B2 is 200*A2 − 4*A2^2 (copied into B3..B20), and the formula in C2 is 200 − 8*A2 (copied into C3..C20).

Clearly, revenue is rising (since $dR/dx > 0$) for x values that are less than 25, and declining for x values that exceed 25. However, when $x = 25$ you can see that $dR/dx = 0$, and that R is neither rising nor falling. In this last case we say that the revenue function is *stationary*, and that this is a consequence of the fact that the gradient of R is zero when $x = 25$.

This logic allows us to devise a simple rule for identifying the value of x at which a stationary value of the function occurs.

This would be to *set* the derivative of the function equal to zero and then solve for the implied value of x.

In our example this would produce

$$dR/dx = 200 - 8x = 0$$

implying that

$$8x = 200 \quad \text{and} \quad x = 25$$

This confirms that, as we saw in the worksheet, the derivative of this particular function has a value of zero when $x = 25$, and so the stationary value of R is given by

$$\text{stationary } R = 200(25) - 4(25^2) = 2500$$

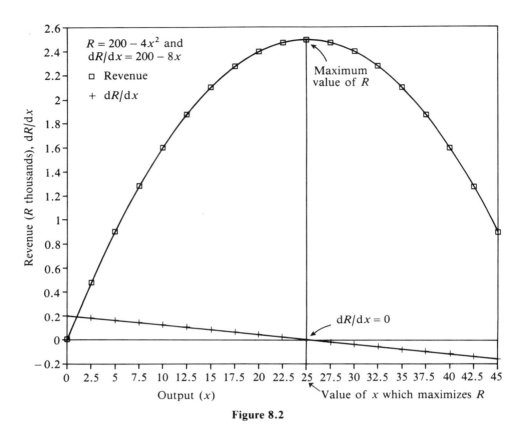

Figure 8.2

This conclusion can also be seen in Figure 8.2 where R and dR/dx have both been plotted.

Although we have said that the revenue function has a stationary value when $x = 25$, you might be thinking that it would be more informative if we stated what is apparent from Figure 8.2: that this is a maximum value of R.

Indeed it would, but the problem is that although it is true in the case of this particular function, it will not *necessarily* be true in all circumstances.

To see why this is, consider the following example.

EXAMPLE 8.6

A firm's average cost of production (C) is given in terms of its output (x) by

$$C = x^2 - 10x + 50$$

If we differentiate this function with respect to x and set it equal to zero, then

Identifying stationary points in a function

we obtain

$$dC/dx = 2x - 10 = 0$$

implying that $x = 5$.

Although it will still be valid to claim that the function has a stationary point at $x = 5$ (when $C = 25 - 50 + 1000 = 1025$), it is not valid to argue that this is a maximum value of the function. The reason for this should be obvious from Worksheet 8.8 and Figure 8.3.

Clearly, when $x = 5$ the value of C is at its *minimum* (rather than its maximum) value in the case of this function.

Apparently our rule of equating the derivative to zero and solving for x is ambiguous, since all it does is to tell us *where* that function changes direction, and not *which way* it changes.

In other words, finding the value of x at which the derivative is zero identifies a stationary point, but does not identify the *nature* (maximum or minimum) of this stationary point.

To determine this requires that we investigate the function more closely in the vicinity of the stationary point, and so you should now refer back to Worksheets 8.7 and 8.8.

If you compare them carefully, then you will see that in the case of the revenue

---

WORKSHEET 8.8

B2: [W22] +A2^2-10*A2+50

	A	B	C
1	x	C=x^2-10x+50	dC/dx=2x-10
2	0	50	-10
3	1	41	-8
4	2	34	-6
5	3	29	-4
6	4	26	-2
7	5	25	0
8	6	26	2
9	7	29	4
10	8	34	6
11	9	41	8
12	10	50	10
13	11	61	12
14	12	74	14
15	13	89	16
16	14	106	18
17	15	125	20
18	16	146	22
19	17	169	24
20	18	194	26

354 *Principles of Differential Calculus*

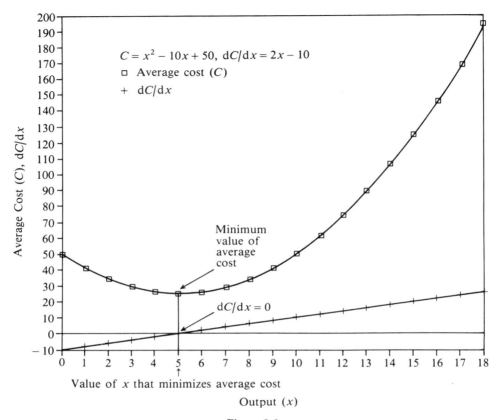

Figure 8.3

function, the derivative is positive before the stationary point, and negative afterwards, while in the case of the cost function the opposite is the case (negative before and positive afterwards).

So, if we evaluate the gradient for a value of x slightly less than that associated with the stationary point, and then for a value of x that is slightly more than the stationary point value, we should be able to tell whether the stationary point is a maximum or a minimum value.

This logic implies that a decision rule would be as follows:

	Before stationary point value	At stationary point value	After stationary point value	Nature of stationary point
Sign of derivative	+	0	−	maximum
	−	0	+	minimum

However, there is an alternative (and more efficient) way of reaching the same conclusion if we argue as follows.

If the stationary point is a maximum, then the gradient of the function will be positive before this point and negative after it. Therefore, the gradient is decreasing (i.e. going from positive through zero to negative). Now if the gradient is decreasing, then *its rate of change* must be negative. But the rate of change of the gradient is the derivative of the function representing the gradient (i.e. the derivative of the derivative), and known as the *second* derivative. From now on this second derivative will be represented symbolically as $d(dy/dx)/dx$ (i.e. the derivative of dy/dx with respect to x). (This is also known as d^2y/dx^2 and pronounced 'd squared y by dx squared'.)

So, if the second derivative is negative (when evaluated at the stationary point value of x), then the function will have attained a maximum value.

In short, a maximum turning point requires that for the stationary point value of x, the derivative of the function is zero and the second derivative is negative.

A converse logic applies to the identification of a minimum turning point, and would result in the conclusion that a minimum turning point requires that for the stationary point value of x, the derivative of the function is zero and the second derivative is positive.

If we apply this logic to our two functions then we obtain

$$R = 200x - 4x^2$$

So

$$dR/dx = 200 - 8x$$

and

$$d(dR/dx)/dx = -8$$

which is unambiguously negative for all values of x, and therefore implies a maximum turning point.

On the other hand, with

$$C = x^2 - 10x + 50$$

then

$$dC/dx = 2x - 10$$

and

$$d(dC/dx)/dx = 2$$

which is unambiguously positive for all values of x, and therefore implies a minimum turning point.

These two sets of calculations clearly confirm our decision rule.

But you may have noticed that all of the functions considered so far have had only one stationary point, yet it is not difficult to construct functions that have more than one.

EXAMPLE 8.7

Over an eight year period a firm's profits (W) were given by the following function of time (t):

$$w = t^3 - 15t^2 + 63t + 10\,000$$

Calculate the maximum and minimum profits made by the firm during this period.

SOLUTION 8.7

We can start by differentiating the profit function with respect to t and then setting this derivative equal to zero. That is

$$dW/dt = 3t^2 - 30t + 63 = 0$$

Clearly this is a quadratic equation that will have two solution values, obtainable by using the quadratic formula to solve for t_1 and t_2.

Therefore

$$t_1, t_2 = \{30 \pm [(30^2 - 4(3)(63)]^{0.5})\}/(2)(3)$$
$$= [30 \pm (144)^{0.5}]/6$$
$$t_1 = (30 + 12)/6 = 7$$
$$t_2 = (30 - 12)/6 = 3$$

It should now be clear that the function has two stationary points when $t = 3$ and when $t = 7$, and to determine their nature we should calculate the second derivative and evaluate it for each value of t.

Therefore

$$d(dW/dt)/dt = 6t - 30$$

Obviously you cannot say whether this expression is positive or negative unless you evaluate it for a given value of t. However, since we know that the two values of t with which we are concerned are $t = 3$ and $t = 7$, we have, when $t = 3$

$$6t - 30 = -12$$

which is unambiguously negative, and indicates a (local) maximum value of $w = 10\,081$.

On the other hand, when $t = 7$

$$6t - 30 = 12$$

which is unambiguously positive, and indicates a (local) minimum value of $w = 10\,049$.

Notice that we have used the term 'local' maximum and minimum values. The reason for this is that we are only investigating the function over an eight year period, and therefore are not concerned with what happens after more than eight years have passed. In fact, after $t = 7$ the function starts to rise continually, so that eventually the local maximum value of 10 081 will inevitably be exceeded. However, since in this case the function never turns back down after $t = 7$, we are justified in arguing that when $t = 3$, a local maximum is attained. Of course for different functions there may be more than one local maximum, in which case they have to be compared in order to determine which is the greatest (i.e. the *global* maximum).

You will obtain a visual impression of this relationship if you look at the solution to Exercise 8.10.

EXAMPLE 8.8

A firm has the demand function of Example 8.5 and the average cost function of Example 8.6. At what level of output is the greatest profit made?

SOLUTION 8.8

The key to a correct solution is to recognize that in its simplest form profit (W) is defined as the difference between total revenue and total costs.

So, remembering that our information pertains to average costs, we can write:

$$\text{total costs } (TC) = (\text{average costs})(\text{output})$$

Therefore

$$TC = (x^2 - 10x + 50)(x) = x^3 - 10x^2 + 50x$$

Since we already have an expression for total revenue (R) we can therefore write

$$W = (200x - 4x^2) - (x^3 - 10x^2 + 50x)$$

Collecting terms (and taking care with the signs) produces

$$W = -x^3 + 6x^2 + 150x$$

Now we can differentiate W with respect to x, set this derivative equal to zero and solve for x.

$$dW/dx = -3x^2 + 12x + 150 = 0$$

Once again, the quadratic formula is required and produces $x = 9.34$ (when the meaningless negative root is ignored).

The second derivative is

$$\begin{aligned} d(dW/dx)/dx &= -6x + 12 \\ &= -6(9.34) + 12 \\ &= -44.04 \quad \text{when } x = 9.34 \end{aligned}$$

and indicates that this is, in fact, a maximum turning point.

We can conclude that the greatest profit is made when an output of 9.34 units is produced and sold.

The price charged will be
$$200 - 4(9.34) = £162.64$$

The total revenue will be
$$9.34(162.64) = £1519.06$$

The total cost will be
$$9.34^3 - 10(9.34^2) + 50(9.34) = £409.42$$

Consequently the profit will be
$$1519.06 - 409.42 = £1109.64$$

Finally, the average cost per unit of production will be
$$409.42/9.34 = £43.83$$

Clearly this is *not* the minimum average cost of production (which we have seen is £25 when $x = 5$), and neither is the revenue the maximum revenue (which is £2500 when $x = 25$). But it is nonetheless the greatest *profit* when the behaviour of *both* costs and revenue is taken into account.

EXAMPLE 8.9

A firm's demand function (q) is given in terms of price (p) by

$$q = a - bp \text{ (where } a \text{ and } b \text{ are constants)}$$

Obtain an expression for the price elasticity of demand (e_p).

SOLUTION 8.9

The first task is to obtain a clear definition of what is meant by the price elasticity of demand.

You can take it to mean the *proportional* change in the quantity demanded which results from a given *proportional* change in price.

In symbols we can let Δq = the absolute change in quantity demanded, and Δp = the absolute change in price. Therefore

$\Delta q/q$ = the proportional change in quantity demanded
$\Delta p/p$ = the proportional change in price

It follows therefore that

$$e_p = \text{price elasticity of demand} = (\Delta q/q)/\Delta p/p)$$

which can be rearranged to
$$e_p = (\Delta q/\Delta p)(p/q)$$

If we let Δp tend to zero, then $\Delta q/\Delta p$ tends to dq/dp and the last expression becomes
$$e_p = (dq/dp)(p/q)$$

This is a completely general mathematical definition of the price elasticity concept, but if, as is true in this case, a specific form of the demand function is known, then we can proceed as follows:
$$q = a - bp$$

Therefore
$$dq/dp = -b$$
$$e_p = (-b)(p/q) = (-b)[p/(a-bp)]$$

So if, for example, the demand function was given by
$$q = 200 - 5p$$

then
$$e_p = (-5)[p/(200 - 5p)]$$

and, when a price of £25 is charged, the price elasticity is
$$e_p = (-5)(25/75) = -1.333$$

This is to be interpreted as meaning that when a price of £25 is charged, then a 1 per cent *increase* in price would cause the quantity demanded to *fall* by 1.333 per cent.

Now calculate the percentage increase in the quantity demanded if, from an original price of £30, the price was *reduced* by 1 per cent.

You should find that the answer is 3 per cent, i.e. $-1\%[-5(30/50)] = 3$ per cent.

EXAMPLE 8.10

Calculate the price elasticity of demand for the following demand function:
$$q = 1000/p \text{ where } p = \text{price and } q = \text{quantity demanded}$$

SOLUTION 8.10

It is probably more helpful to write the function as
$$q = 1000p^{-1}$$

In which case

$$dq/dp = -1000p^{-2}$$

Therefore

$$e_p = (-1000p^{-2})(p/q) = (-1000p^{-2})(p/(1000p^{-1}))]$$
$$e_p = (-1000p^{-2})[p(p/1000)] = -1$$

As you can see, this particular demand function has the peculiar property that the price elasticity of demand is always equal to -1 regardless of the price being charged.

At this stage you should also appreciate that the second derivative can also provide useful information even if the function under consideration does not possess any stationary values.

For example, suppose you were asked to model a firm's total cost of production (C) in such a way that as output (x) increased, so too did the value of C.

Obviously, this is not a difficult task, but the fact that you can perform it in a number of ways does bring a degree of ambiguity to the process.

You can see this in Worksheets 8.9(a), (b) and (c) and Figure 8.4, where each of the functions graphed satisfy our basic requirement that C increases as x increases. However, you should also be able to see that they satisfy the requirement in significantly different ways.

WORKSHEET 8.9a

B2: (F3) [W15] +A2^1.1

	A	B	C	D
1	x	C1=x^1.1	dC1/dx=1.1x^0.1	d^2C1/dx^2=0.11x^(-0.9)
2	0	0.000	0.000	0.000
3	3	3.348	1.228	0.041
4	6	7.177	1.316	0.022
5	9	11.212	1.370	0.015
6	12	15.385	1.410	0.012
7	15	19.665	1.442	0.010
8	18	24.033	1.469	0.008
9	21	28.474	1.491	0.007
10	24	32.979	1.512	0.006
11	27	37.541	1.529	0.006
12	30	42.153	1.546	0.005
13	33	46.813	1.560	0.005
14	36	51.515	1.574	0.004
15	39	56.256	1.587	0.004
16	42	61.034	1.599	0.004
17	45	65.847	1.610	0.004
18	48	70.691	1.620	0.003
19	51	75.566	1.630	0.003
20	54	80.470	1.639	0.003

WORKSHEET 8.9b

```
B21: [W15] ' C2=x
```

	A	B	C	D
21	x	C2=x	dC2/dx=1	d^2C2/dx^2=0
22	0	0	1	0
23	3	3	1	0
24	6	6	1	0
25	9	9	1	0
26	12	12	1	0
27	15	15	1	0
28	18	18	1	0
29	21	21	1	0
30	24	24	1	0
31	27	27	1	0
32	30	30	1	0
33	33	33	1	0
34	36	36	1	0
35	39	39	1	0
36	42	42	1	0
37	45	45	1	0
38	48	48	1	0
39	51	51	1	0
40	54	54	1	0

WORKSHEET 8.9c

```
B42: (F3) [W15] +A42^0.95
```

	A	B	C	D
41	x	C3=x^0.95	dC3/dx=0.95x^(-0.05)	d^2C3/dx^2=-0.0475x^(-1.05)
42	0	0.000	0.000	0.000
43	3	2.840	0.899	-0.015
44	6	5.486	0.869	-0.007
45	9	8.064	0.851	-0.005
46	12	10.598	0.839	-0.003
47	15	13.100	0.830	-0.003
48	18	15.578	0.822	-0.002
49	21	18.035	0.816	-0.002
50	24	20.474	0.810	-0.002
51	27	22.898	0.806	-0.001
52	30	25.308	0.801	-0.001
53	33	27.707	0.798	-0.001
54	36	30.095	0.794	-0.001
55	39	32.472	0.791	-0.001
56	42	34.841	0.788	-0.001
57	45	37.201	0.785	-0.001
58	48	39.553	0.783	-0.001
59	51	41.898	0.780	-0.001
60	54	44.236	0.778	-0.001

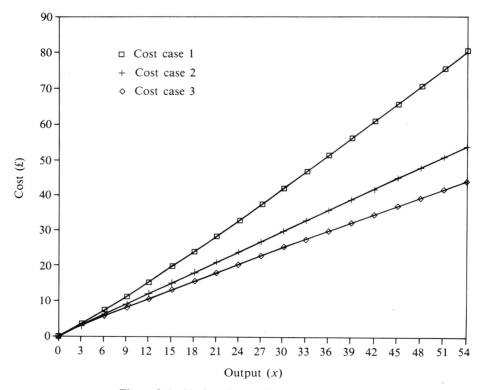

Figure 8.4 Various increasing cost functions

Case 1, for example, has C increasing at an increasing rate (since the gradient is clearly getting larger). Case 2 on the other hand, has C increasing at a constant rate (since it is a linear function and has a constant gradient), while case 3 has C increasing at a decreasing rate.

As you can also see from Worksheet 8.9, the derivatives of each of the functions are unambiguously positive for all positive values of x, as must be the case if C is to increase as x increases.

However, a different picture emerges if we examine the second derivatives of each function. As you might have anticipated, case 1 has a second derivative that is always $\geqslant 0$, case 2 has a second derivative that is always 0, and case 3 has a second derivative that is always $\leqslant 0$.

The signs of these second derivatives are the clue to a more precise description of each function's behaviour, since it should be clear that Table 8.1 can be constructed.

Since there is often confusion about what is meant by decreasing at an increasing or decreasing rate, examples of the last three cases have been produced in Figure 8.5.

Table 8.1

Sign of first derivative	Sign of second derivative	Behaviour of function
Positive	Positive	Increasing at an increasing rate
Positive	0	Increasing at a constant rate
Positive	Negative	Increasing at a decreasing rate
Negative	Positive	Decreasing at an increasing rate (case 4 below)
Negative	0	Decreasing at a constant rate (case 5 below)
Negative	Negative	Decreasing at a decreasing rate (case 6 below)

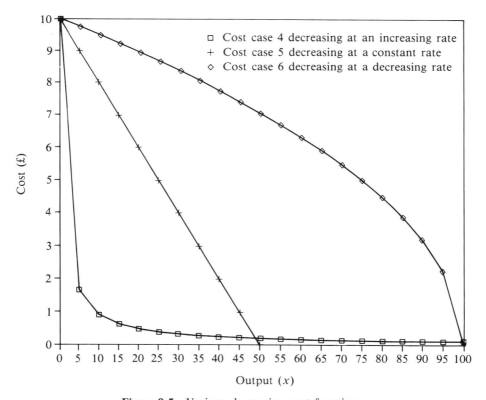

Figure 8.5 Various decreasing cost functions

As you can see, decreasing at an increasing rate means that the negatively sloped curve is becoming flatter, and that its gradient is getting closer to zero. However, since this is happening from a *negative* value of the gradient, it means that the gradient is in fact increasing (i.e. becoming less negative).

On the other hand, a function that decreases at a decreasing rate has its gradient becoming *more* negative, which is therefore decreasing.

8.4 Some further rules of differentiation

You will almost certainly have noticed that up until now, the functions that we have differentiated have all been additive forms of the standard polynomial function (ax^n).

But you will also appreciate that the process of modelling various business and economic phenomena cannot restrict itself to this limited class of functions.

A good example of this is found if we are required to model the depreciation that takes place over time in a firm's assets. This is to be done in such a way that the value of the assets just now is £1 million (say) but that this value declines in a *nonlinear* manner as time passes.

Clearly, since a linear function is precluded from our options we would be forced to try and model the asset value (v) in terms of time (t) by functions such as $v = 1/t$, or $v = 1/t^2$, or $v = 1/t^3$, etc.

The problem with this, however, is that in each of the above cases the value of v when $t = 0$ is undefined (since anything divided by zero is infinite), and our first requirement, that when $t = 0$, $v = £1$ million, is obviously not satisfied.

There are a number of ways in which this problem can be overcome, but they all produce functions that are not of the standard polynomial form, and therefore require *special* rules for differentiating them.

For example, the functions
$$v = 1/(x + 1)$$
$$v = 1/(x^2 + 1)$$
$$v = e^{-x}$$

all satisfy our requirements, but cannot be subjected to the single 'standard' rule of differentiation that we possess at the moment.

To deal with this we must develop new rules for new functions, and although it is beyond the scope of this text to consider every rule of differentiation, there are two that will pay handsome dividends.

8.4.1 The chain rule

As the name suggests, the chain rule applies to circumstances in which the dependent variable (y) is linked to the independent variable (x) via some *intermediate* variable (u), rather than being *directly* dependent upon the value of x.

Under such circumstances, any change in the value of x affects u in the first instance, but then, via the chain relationship, eventually affects the value of y.

This idea can be represented more clearly in terms of the following two functional statements:

$$y = f(u)$$
$$u = g(x)$$

If this is the case, then the chain rule states that the rate of change of y with respect to x is given by the rate of change of y with respect to u times the rate of change of u with respect to x. That is

$$dy/dx = (dy/du)(du/dx)$$

EXAMPLE 8.11

The level of investment (y) is known to depend upon the level of interest rates (u) as follows:

$$y = 10 - 10u$$

where y is measured in £ millions and u is measured as a decimal.

Also, the level of interest rates is known to depend upon the money supply (x) as follows:

$$u = 1 - 0.01x$$

where x is also measured in £ millions.

Obtain an expression for the rate of change of investment with respect to the money supply.

SOLUTION 8.11

We have

$$y = 10 - 10u$$
$$u = 1 - 0.01x$$

Therefore

$$dy/du = -10$$
$$du/dx = -0.01$$

Applying the chain rule then produces

$$dy/dx = (dy/du)(du/dx) = (-10)(-0.01) = 0.1$$

implying that investment is a direct linear function of the money supply, and that a given increase in the money supply will cause the level of investment to increase by an amount equal to 10 per cent of the given increase.

EXAMPLE 8.12

The public sector borrowing requirement (P) depends upon the level of government expenditure (G) as follows:

$$P = 4 + G$$

where P and G are both measured in £ billions.

In addition, the level of government expenditure depends upon the level of unemployment (U) as follows:

$$G = 2 + U^2$$

where U is measured as a percentage of the working population.

Obtain an expression for the rate of change of the public sector borrowing requirement with respect to the level of unemployment.

SOLUTION 8.12

We have

$$P = 4 + G$$
$$G = 2 + U^2$$

Therefore

$$dP/dG = 1$$
$$dG/dU = 2U$$

Consequently

$$dP/dU = (dP/dG)(dG/dU) = (1)(2U) = 2U$$

The implication of this is that a given increase in unemployment will have an effect upon the public sector borrowing requirement that is not only double this increase in unemployment, but also depends upon the level from which unemployment increased. This means that the *higher* the level of unemployment the *greater* is the effect upon P.

EXAMPLE 8.13

A firm's total costs of production (C) are given in terms of its level of production

(x) by
$$C = 5(x + 1)^{0.5}$$
where x is measured in 000s of units and C is measured in £000s.

Obtain an expression for the rate of change of total costs with respect to output.

SOLUTION 8.13

You may be thinking that this problem has got no relevance to the chain rule, since there is no chain specified in the problem.

However, if you recall our opening remarks in this section about 'standard' functions and their derivatives, then you should see that this function is not of a standard form. Consequently, we should approach it from the point of view of trying to *turn it into* our standard form, and it is here that the chain rule can help.

This is because even though a chain does not exist in the problem, there is nothing to stop us from creating one, *if it will serve our purpose*. The trick is to appreciate how to do this, and how it can create a standard function which we can differentiate.

So, if we let
$$u = (x + 1)$$
then the function
$$y = 5(x + 1)^{0.5}$$
can be rewritten as
$$y = 5u^{0.5}$$

Now, *viewed in terms of u*, this function is in a form that we can differentiate as
$$dy/du = 2.5u^{-0.5}$$

However, since it is the rate of change of y with respect to x that is required, and *not* the rate of change of y with respect to u, we must apply the chain rule to the artificial chain that we have created. Therefore
$$dy/dx = (dy/du)(du/dx) = (2.5u^{-0.5})(du/dx)$$

But what is du/dx? Well, since we have let
$$u = (x + 1)$$
it follows that
$$du/dx = 1$$
Therefore
$$dy/dx = (2.5u^{-0.5})(1)$$

which, when we replace u with $(x+1)$ becomes

$$dy/dx = 2.5(x+1)^{-0.5} = 2.5/(x+1)^{0.5}$$

As you can see, this method of creating a chain to turn 'difficult' functions into standard forms can be extremely useful, and allows us to differentiate a wide range of functions that are otherwise unapproachable.

EXAMPLE 8.14

Now consider the problem that we stated at the start of this section. That was to model the depreciation which takes place over time in a firm's assets, in such a way that the value of the assets just now is £1 million, but that this value declines in a nonlinear manner as time passes.

Obtain an expression for the rate of change of asset value (v) with respect to time (x) for the function that has been chosen.

SOLUTION 8.14

We suggested earlier that functions such as $v = 1/(x+1)$, or $1/(x^2+1)$, or $v = e^{-x}$ would achieve our objective, but that they could not at that time be differentiated. Well, now the first two or these can (and you will be able to differentiate the third by the time you have read the next section).

So, if we use

$$v = 1/(x^2+1)$$

to model our problem, then we can rewrite this as

$$v = (x^2+1)^{-1}$$

Once again, this is not in a standard form, but if we let

$$u = (x^2+1)$$

then

$$du/dx = 2x$$

Now we can write

$$v = u^{-1}$$

Therefore

$$du/du = -u^{-2}$$
$$dv/dx = (dv/du)(du/dx) = (-u^{-2})(2x)$$

which, when u is replaced with $(x^2 + 1)$, becomes

$$dv/dx = [-(x^2 + 1)^{-2}](2x) = -2x/(x^2 + 1)$$

For all positive values of x this derivative is clearly negative, and implies that as x increases the rate of depreciation (dv/dx) declines (rather than being constant as would be the case in straight-line depreciation). Notice also that $v(0) = 1/(0 + 1) = 1$, thereby satisfying our initial requirement.

8.4.2 The product rule

Sometimes it will be the case that the function to be differentiated is in fact a *product* of two separate functions of x [such as $(x + 1)$ and $(x - 1)$]. In this case, the first bracketed term $(x + 1)$ is to be regarded as the first function of the product, and the second bracketed term $(x - 1)$ as the second function of the product.

Under such circumstances, the rate of change of y with respect to x is composed of the *sum* of two elements: the first function times the derivative of the second function, plus the second function times the derivative of the first function.

In more formal terms this means that if

$$y = [f(x)][g(x)]$$

and if we let

$$u = f(x)$$
$$v = g(x)$$

then y can be written as

$$y = uv$$

and dy/dx is calculated from the product rule to be

$$dy/dx = u(dv/dx) + v(du/dx)$$

To see why this is the case, consider the following function:

$$y = x(x + 1)$$

Simple expansion of this expression would allow us to rewrite it as

$$y = x^2 + x$$

of which the derivative is

$$dy/dx = 2x + 1$$

So now we know that the derivative of the function is $2x + 1$, but does the product rule produce the same result?

To answer this we can proceed as follows:

$$y = x(x + 1)$$

So, let
$$u = x \quad \text{and} \quad v = x + 1$$

Therefore
$$du/dx = 1 \quad \text{and} \quad dv/dx = 1$$

Applying these expressions to the product rule gives
$$\begin{aligned}dy/dx &= u(dv/dx) + v(du/dx) \\ &= x(1) + (x+1)(1) \\ &= 2x + 1\end{aligned}$$

As anticipated, the same result has been produced as above.

However, the real value of the product rule is to be appreciated when the two functions adopt forms such that the sort of algebraic simplification which we did above in order to produce a standard form is either impossible or extremely tedious. You can see two examples of cases such as this now.

EXAMPLE 8.15

A firm's total costs of production (C) are given in terms of its level of production (x) by
$$C = 5x(x+1)^{0.5}$$

where x is measured in 000s of units and C is measured in £000s.

SOLUTION 8.15

This problem is very similar to Example 8.13 above, with the exception that there is an additional multiplicative term in x included in the function. However, even such a minor modification as this requires that we use the product rule as no amount of algebraic manipulation can turn the function into a standard differentiable form.

So, let
$$u = 5x \quad \text{and} \quad v = (x+1)^{0.5}$$

Then by the chain rule
$$du/dx = 5 \quad \text{and} \quad dv/dx = 0.5(x+1)^{-0.5}$$

Therefore
$$dy/dx = \underbrace{(5x)}_{u}\underbrace{[0.5(x+1)^{-0.5}]}_{dv/dx} + \underbrace{[(x+1)^{0.5}}_{v}\underbrace{(5)]}_{du/dx}$$

After simplification this becomes
$$dy/dx = 2.5x[(x+1)^{-0.5} + (x+1)^{0.5}]$$

As you can see, this is quite a complicated expression, and as such may not convey much to you. However, suppose that we also knew that each unit of output is sold at a constant price of £100. Is it worthwhile in terms of profit for the firm to expand its output beyond a level of (a) 99 units or (b) 224 units? To answer this, we can reason as follows.

The derivative of y with respect to x measures how total costs change as output changes, so if any increase in output adds more to the firm's costs than it does to its revenue, then such an increase in output is not justified.

The increase in revenue for any extra unit of output is clearly given by £100, so to answer our question we simply have to evaluate the derivative for each of the specified output levels and then compare it with £100. If the value of the derivative is less than £100, then output should be expanded until the derivative equals £100, but otherwise it should be reduced.

So, when $x = 99$, $dy/dx = 74.75$, which is less than 100 and indicates that output should be expanded.

On the other hand, when $x = 224$, $dy/dx = 112.3$, which indicates that output is too high.

(You can confirm for yourself that if an output of 177.44 units is produced, then this creates the greatest profit since the addition to costs will be exactly 100 at this level of production.)

EXAMPLE 8.16

The quantity demanded (q) of a firm's product is given in terms of the price charged (p) by
$$q = 100/(p+1)$$
where q is measured in 000s and p is measured in £s.

Obtain an expression for the firm's total revenue and for the rate of change of revenue with respect to price.

SOLUTION 8.16

The expression for total revenue (R) will be
$$R = pq = 100p/(p+1) = 100p[(p+1)^{-1}]$$
Therefore, if we let $u = 100p$ and let $v = (p+1)^{-1}$, then
$$du/dp = 100$$
$$dv/dp = -(p+1)^{-2}$$

Applying the product rule then produces

$$dR/dp = 100p[-1(p+1)^{-2}] + [(p+1)^{-1}][100]$$
$$u \quad\quad dv/dp \quad\quad + \quad v \quad\quad du/dp$$

which, upon simplification becomes

$$dR/dp = -100[p(p+1)^{-2} - (p+1)^{-1}]$$

Once again, this is not a simple expression, but suppose that in this case we know that each unit of output costs the firm a constant £5 to produce. Should the firm raise its price above a level of (a) £3 or (b) £4?

The same logic applies to this question as to the previous example with the exception that in this case it is the price charged that is being varied. So, when $p = 3$, $dR/dp = 6.25$, indicating that the increased revenue (£6.25) exceeds the increased cost (£5) and that the price should be raised if more profits are to be made.

On the other hand, when $p = 4$, $dR/dp = 4$, which means that the increased revenue is less than the increased cost, and that the price should be lowered.

(Once again, you can confirm that if a price of £3.47 is charged, then the increase in revenue is identical to the increase in cost and that profits are maximized.)

8.5 The derivative of the exponential function

Although you have already encountered the exponential function (e^x) in previous chapters of this text, it is only with an understanding of basic calculus that its full significance can be appreciated.

This is because the most important property of this class of function stems from the behaviour of its derivative.

In its simplest form, the exponential function has the unique feature that its instantaneous rate of change at any chosen value of x is always the *same* as the value of the function at that chosen value of x. In other words, the function is its *own* derivative.

You can confirm this statement if you modify Worksheet 8.3 to give Worksheet 8.10.

The formula in B2 is now @EXP(A2) (e to the power of the contents of A2) and this has been copied into B3..B12.

As you can see, even with $\Delta x = 0.0001$, the value of $\Delta y/\Delta x$ is very close to the value of y (e^x).

From this we can conclude that if

$$y = e^x$$

then

$$dy/dx = e^x$$

WORKSHEET 8.10

	A	B	C	D	E
1	x	y=e^x	x̃	ỹ	ỹ/x̃
2	0.9999	2.718010	0.0001		
3	1	2.718281	0.0001	0.000271	2.718145
4	1.0001	2.718553	0.0001	0.000271	2.718417
5	1.9999	7.388317			
6	2	7.389056	0.0001	0.000738	7.388686
7	2.0001	7.389795	0.0001	0.000738	7.389425
8	2.9999	20.08352			
9	3	20.08553	0.0001	0.002008	20.08453
10	3.0001	20.08754	0.0001	0.002008	20.08654

This is a crucial result, since it implies that if the value of some variable is given by the expression e^x, then it is growing at a rate such that its rate of change is always *100 per cent* of whatever its value happens to be. You can see this more clearly as follows.

If $y = e^x$, then $dy/dx = e^x$, and

$(dy/dx)/y$ = the rate of growth of y as a proportion of the value of $y = e^x/e^x = 1$

Now suppose that we wanted y to grow at a rate that was always 10 per cent of its value (rather than 100 per cent). What modification should we make to the function e^x in order to achieve this objective?

We could first of all try

$$y = 0.1e^x$$

but if you enter this expression into the B2 cell of the last worksheet [0.1*@EXP(A2)], then after copying you would obtain Worksheet 8.11

As you can see, dy/dx would appear to be given by $0.1e^x$ and so the proportional rate of growth remains at 100 per cent [since $(dy/dx)/y = 0.1e^x/0.1e^x = 1$].

WORKSHEET 8.11

	A	B	C	D	E
1	x	y=0.1e^x	x̃	ỹ	ỹ/x̃
2	0.9999	0.271801	0.0001		
3	1	0.271828	0.0001	0.000027	0.271814
4	1.0001	0.271855	0.0001	0.000027	0.271841
5	1.9999	0.738831			
6	2	0.738905	0.0001	0.000073	0.738868
7	2.0001	0.738979	0.0001	0.000073	0.738942
8	2.9999	2.008352			
9	3	2.008553	0.0001	0.000200	2.008453
10	3.0001	2.008754	0.0001	0.000200	2.008654

WORKSHEET 8.12

	A	B	C	D	E
1	x	y=e^0.1x	$\bar{x}$	$\bar{y}$	$\bar{y}/\bar{x}$
2	0.9999	1.105159	0.0001		
3	1	1.105170	0.0001	0.000011	0.110516
4	1.0001	1.105181	0.0001	0.000011	0.110517
5	1.9999	1.221390			
6	2	1.221402	0.0001	0.000012	0.122139
7	2.0001	1.221414	0.0001	0.000012	0.122140
8	2.9999	1.349845			
9	3	1.349858	0.0001	0.000013	0.134985
10	3.0001	1.349872	0.0001	0.000013	0.134986

Perhaps we should try multiplying *only the term in x* (rather than the whole function) by 0.1, and see what happens to dy/dx. This has been done in Worksheet 8.12 where the formula in B2 is now @EXP(0.1∗A2).

It would appear from these calculations that if

$$y = e^{0.1x}$$

then

$$dy/dx = 0.1e^{0.1x}$$

and that

$$(dy/dx)/y = 0.1e^{0.1x}/e^{0.1x} = 0.1$$

This is indeed correct and allows us to generalize to the following statement. If

$$y = e^{rx}$$

then

$$dy/dx = re^{rx}$$

and

$$(dy/dx)/y = re^{rx}/e^{rx} = r$$

In words, this means that the rate of change of the function e^{rx} is always equal to r per cent of whatever the value of the function is. This is often referred to as constant *exponential* growth at a rate of r per cent.

Now suppose that instead of requiring that the value of y increases at a constant rate of r per cent of whatever its value happens to be, we require that it decreases (i.e. depreciates) at a constant exponential rate of r per cent. How can we modify the exponential function to achieve this objective?

In fact it is quite easy, since all we have to do is change the sign of r from positive

WORKSHEET 8.13

	A	B	C	D	E
1	x	y=e^-0.2x	x̄	ȳ	ȳ/x̄
2	0.9999	0.818747	0.0001		
3	1	0.818730	0.0001	-0.00001	-0.16374
4	1.0001	0.818714	0.0001	-0.00001	-0.16374
5	1.9999	0.670333			
6	2	0.670320	0.0001	-0.00001	-0.13406
7	2.0001	0.670306	0.0001	-0.00001	-0.13406
8	2.9999	0.548822			
9	3	0.548811	0.0001	-0.00001	-0.10976
10	3.0001	0.548800	0.0001	-0.00001	-0.10976

to negative so that the function becomes

$$y = e^{-rx}$$

You can see this for $r = -0.2$ if you make this change to your worksheet [enter @EXP(−0.2∗A2) in B2]. You should then obtain Worksheet 8.13.

Clearly, we would now estimate that dy/dx is given by $-0.2e^{-0.2x}$, and that the proportional rate of growth is now −20 per cent.

In general, then, if

$$y = e^{-rx}$$

then the function has a negative gradient given by

$$dy/dx = -re^{-rx}$$

and the proportional rate of growth is $-r$ per cent.

The function e^{-rx} is often known as a negative exponential function and is frequently used for modelling asset depreciation (when x represents time) or demand functions (when x represents price).

EXAMPLE 8.17

The value (v) of a firm's assets are depreciating over time (t) in accordance with

$$v = 2e^{-0.2t}$$

where v is measured in millions of £s and t is measured in years.

(a) Calculate the value of the firm's assets after four years.
(b) Calculate the *rate* of depreciation after four years.
(c) Calculate the proportional rate of depreciation in the firm's assets.
(d) Calculate the length of time it takes for the value of the firm's assets to be halved.

SOLUTION 8.17

(a) Since $v = 2e^{-0.2t}$, then when $t = 4$
$$v = 2e^{-0.8} = £0.8986 \text{ million}$$

(b) $dv/dt = -0.4e^{-0.2t}$, so when $t = 4$
$$dv/dt = -0.4e^{-0.8} = -£0.1797 \text{ million}$$

(c) $(dv/dt)/v = -0.4e^{-0.2t}/2e^{-0.2t} = -£0.2$ million per £1 million of value.

(d) Since the original value of the assets was £2 million (when $t = 0$), we require to find the value of t such that
$$v = 2e^{-0.2t} = 0.5(2)$$

Therefore
$$e^{-0.2t} = 0.5$$

and
$$-0.2t(\ln e) = \ln 0.5$$

implying that
$$t = -5(\ln 0.5) = 3.465 \text{ years}$$

The value of the firm's assets will have depreciated by 50 per cent of their original value after 3.465 years.

EXAMPLE 8.18

The demand (q) for a firm's product is known to depend upon the price charged (p) as follows:
$$q = e^{-0.4p}$$
where q is measured in millions of units and p is measured in £s.

Obtain an expression for total revenue, and determine the price that should be charged if revenue is to be maximized.

SOLUTION 8.18

Since revenue (R) is defined as price times quantity demanded, we have
$$R = pq = pe^{-0.4p}$$

Clearly this product contains two *separate* functions of p (p and $e^{-0.4p}$), and so we should employ the product rule as follows.

Let $u = p$, therefore $du/dp = 1$. Let $v = e^{-0.4p}$, therefore $dv/dp = -0.4e^{-0.4p}$.

Accordingly
$$dR/dp = (p)[-0.4e^{-0.4p}] + (e^{-0.4p})(1)$$
which can be simplified to
$$dR/dp = -e^{-0.4p}(0.4p - 1)$$

To determine the value of p associated with a stationary value of R we must set this derivative equal to zero and solve for p.

The last expression for dR/dp will equal zero if *either* of its component products are equal to zero, but $e^{-0.4p}$ has a value of zero *only* if p is infinitely large. So, a determinate solution can only be obtained from $(0.4p - 1)$ being equal to zero. Therefore

$$0.4p - 1 = 0, \text{ implies that } p = 2.5$$

In consequence, we conclude that if a price of £2.50 is charged, then the value of R will be stationary.

But is this stationary value a maximum or a minimum value?

To determine this we must differentiate dR/dp again with respect to p and evaluate the sign of this second derivative when $p = 2.5$.

Consequently, since $dR/dp = -e^{-0.4p}(0.4p - 1)$ is also a product of two separate functions of p, we should apply the product rule again.

Let $u = -e^{-0.4p}$, therefore $du/dp = 0.4e^{-0.4p}$. Let $v = (0.4p - 1)$, therefore $dv/dp = 0.4$.

As a result
$$d(dR/dp)/dp = [-e^{-0.4p}(0.4)] + (0.4p - 1)(0.4e^{-0.4p})$$
which can be simplified to
$$d(dR/dp)/dp = -0.4e^{-0.4p}[1 - (0.4p - 1)]$$
$$= -0.4e^{-0.4p}(2 - 0.4p)$$

When $p = 2.5$ this evaluates to
$$-0.4e^{-1}(1) = -0.1471$$
which is clearly negative, and allows us to conclude that when $p = £2.50$ the firm's revenue is *maximized* at a value of
$$R = 2.5(e^{-1}) = £0.919\,69 \text{ million}$$

EXAMPLE 8.19

A firm's market share (y) is known to depend upon its level of advertising expenditure (x) as follows:
$$y = (1 - e^{-0.01x})$$
where y is measured as a *decimal* percentage, and x is measured in £000s.

The product being advertised is sold at a price of £10 and is produced at a constant unit cost of £5.

Calculate the optimal amount of advertising expenditure that should be undertaken if the firm is to make the greatest profit, and if the total size of the market is currently constant, and equal to 100 thousand units of output.

SOLUTION 8.19

The firm's total revenue (R) will be given by its market share (y), times the size of the market (100 thousand units), times the price charged (£10). That is

$$R = (1 - e^{-0.01x})(100)(10) \text{ (£ thousand)}$$

On the other hand, the firm's total costs (C) will be given by its share of the market (y), times the size of the market (100 thousand units), times the unit cost of production (£5), plus the advertising expenditure undertaken (x). That is

$$C = (1 - e^{-0.01x})(100)(5) + x \text{ (£ thousand)}$$

Therefore, the profit made (W) will be given by

$$W = R - C = 500(1 - e^{-0.01x}) - x$$

Differentiating with respect to x and setting this derivative equal to zero produces

$$dW/dx = 5e^{-0.01x} - 1 = 0$$

implying that

$$e^{-0.01x} = 0.2$$

and (after taking natural logarithms of both sides), that

$$-0.01x = \ln 0.2$$

Therefore

$$x = -100(\ln 0.2) = 160.944 \text{ (£ thousand)}$$

The market share will be

$$y = [1 - e^{(-0.01)(160.944)}] = 0.8$$

The sales will be

$$0.8(100) = 80 \text{ (thousand units)}$$

The revenue will be

$$80(10) = 800 \text{ (£ thousand)}$$

The total costs will be

$$80(5) + 160.944 = 560.944 \text{ (£ thousand)}$$

and the profit will be

$$800 - 560.944 = 239.944 \text{ (£ thousand)}$$

We should of course, check that this value of x does in fact produce a maximum turning point, so

$$d(dW/dx)/dx = -0.05e^{-0.01x}$$

which is clearly negative for all positive values of x.

You might like to note that the function we have used to model the market share is one of a class of exponential functions that are known as *logistic* functions and have the general form

$$y = a(1 - e^{-rx})$$

where a and r are constants.

All of these functions have the characteristic that as the value of x increases, so too does the value of y, but in such a way that it gets closer and closer to a limiting value that is given by the value of a. This is because when $x \to \infty$, $e^{-rx} \to 0$ and $y = a(1 - 0) = a$. You can see this in Worksheet 8.14 and Figure 8.6 where the function

$$y = 10(1 - e^{-0.5x})$$

WORKSHEET 8.14

	A	B
1	x	y=10(1-e^(-0.5x))
2	0	0
3	1	3.934693
4	2	6.321205
5	3	7.768698
6	4	8.646647
7	5	9.179150
8	6	9.502129
9	7	9.698026
10	8	9.816843
11	9	9.888910
12	10	9.932620
13	11	9.959132
14	12	9.975212
15	13	9.984965
16	14	9.990881
17	15	9.994469
18	16	9.996645
19	17	9.997965
20	18	9.998765

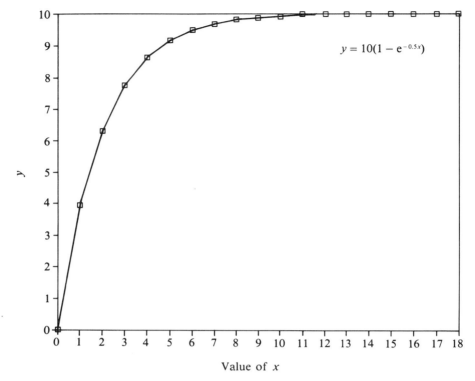

Figure 8.6 A logistic function

has been evaluated and then graphed for various values of x from the Lotus formula in B2, i.e. 10*(1 − @EXP(−A2*0.5)) copied into B3..B20.

As predicted, the value of y is steadily approaching a value of 10 in this case, but you should also be able to see that if we employed a value of $a = 1$, then this would be one way of modelling a situation in which the value of y approached some maximum value of 100 per cent, but did so in such a way that the effort (in terms of the necessary increase in x) of increasing y from a value of 90 per cent (say) to 91 per cent and then from 91 to 92 per cent becomes increasingly large. Clearly there is a process of *saturation* taking place, with the value of y being increasingly unable to absorb or respond to the effect of a given increase in x. This is typical of the effect of advertising expenditure on such variables as revenue or market share.

8.6 Inventory control

An important application of some of the ideas explained in this chapter is to be found in an area known as inventory (or stock) control.

In its simplest form, the notion to be grasped is that of a firm that uses up an item of stock in its production process at some constant rate per time period. Allied to this is the idea that the items of stock will have to be ordered by the firm, and then delivered by the supplier in such a way that the user's requirements are met. These requirements will always involve three factors:

1. There must never be a 'stock-out' (i.e. no stock in hand). (Or if there is, the cost of such an eventuality must be known.)
2. The cost of holding an item of stock for a given length of time must be taken into account. This cost will involve both storage costs and the lost interest on the funds used to buy the stock. Clearly both of these factors will depend upon the average length of time for which an item of stock is held.
3. The cost of ordering a new batch of stock must be considered. This cost will clearly depend upon the production, stockholding and transportation circumstances of the supplier, as well as those of the firms that supply the supplier.

It should be evident that factor 2 above argues in favour of holding as little stock as possible, while factors 1 and 3 suggest that more stock should be held than would be the case in the absence of ordering and 'stock-out' costs. There is clearly a trade-off between these different costs, and it is the purpose of inventory control to determine the optimal amount of stock that should be ordered if these *combined* costs are to be minimized.

To see how this can be done we can proceed by defining some useful terms.

The order quantity (Q).
The optimum order quantity (OQ).
The annual usage of the stock item (U).
The cost of one order (C).
The stockholding costs as a proportion of the average stock value, i.e. the stock holding costs per unit (H).
The average stock in hand (S^*).

Using these definitions it should be clear that the number of orders per annum (N) will be given by $N = U/Q$, i.e. the annual usage divided by the order quantity. Furthermore, the *annual* ordering costs (OC) will be given by $OC = NC = CU/Q$, i.e. the annual number of orders times the cost of one order.

When we consider the holding costs, then we must remember that these will depend upon the average stock in hand, which, with a constant usage rate, will be given by

$$S^* = Q/2$$

If you find this hard to understand, think of it this way. Suppose that the firm orders Q units at the start of the year and uses it up at a rate of b units per month.

Clearly, the firm's stock level (S) will be given by

$$S = Q - bt$$

where t is measured in months.

This simple linear equation means that when $t = 0$ (i.e. before any stock is used), $S = Q$, while when $t = 12$ all the stock will have been used up and so $S = 0$. This means that $Q - 12b = 0$, implying that $Q = 12b$.

The equation for S can therefore be rewritten as

$$S = 12b - bt$$

The average stock in hand will be that amount of stock which is held for half of the period, i.e. when $t = 6$. Therefore

$$S^* = S \text{ when } t = 6 = 12b - 6b = 6b$$

Since we have already seen that $Q = 12b$, it follows that

$$S^* = 6b = 12b/2 = Q/2$$

From this, it is now an easy matter to derive an expression for the total holding costs (TH) as

$$TH = (S^*)H = QH/2$$

Clearly the firms total costs (T) will be the sum of the annual ordering costs and the total holding costs, giving us

$$T = CU/Q + QH/2$$

and we need to minimize this expression with respect to Q.

Consequently $dT/dQ = -CU/Q^2 + H/2$ must be equal to zero, implying that

$$Q^2 = 2CU/H$$
$$Q = (2CU/H)^{0.5}$$

This value of Q is the optimum order quantity (OQ) and so we have

$$OQ = (2CU/H)^{0.5}$$

EXAMPLE 8.20

A small manufacturing firm uses 200 000 units of a particular item at a constant annual rate. The item costs £10 per unit, the cost of making a single order is £125, and the holding costs are 0.5 per cent of the average stock value.

Calculate the optimum order quantity, and from this, the optimum number of orders per annum.

SOLUTION 8.20

Clearly we have

$$U = 200\,000$$
$$C = £125$$
$$H = 0.05(10) = £0.5$$

Consequently

$$OQ = [(2)(125)(200\,000)/0.5]^{0.5} = 10\,000 \text{ units}$$

Since the optimum order quantity is 10 000 units, it clearly follows that 200 000/10 000 = 20 orders should be made each year if the total ordering and holding costs are to be minimized at a value of £5000.

You can use Lotus to confirm this result if you prepare Worksheet 8.15. What you should find is that if you choose any value for the Order Quantity other than the optimum one calculated in B11, then the total cost will rise above its minimum value (for this example) of £5000.

WORKSHEET 8.15

	A	B
1	Order Quantity Q	11000
2	Annual Usage of item U	200000
3	Ordering Cost C	125
4	Price of Product	10
5	Holding Cost per unit H	0.5
6	Average Stock S*	+B1/2
7	Number of Orders	+B2/B1
8	Ordering Cost	+B7*B3
9	Holding Cost	+B5*B6
10	Total cost	+B8+B9
11	Optimum Order Quantity	(2*B3*B2/B5)^0.5

8.7 Exercises

8.1

A country's population (p) was estimated to be given in terms of time (t) by the following expression:

$$p = 0.1t^{0.5} + 1$$

where p is measured in millions and t is measured in years.

The country's economists have argued that serious food shortages will result if the rate of growth of the population was not quartered between years 1 and 4.

(a) Did this happen?
(b) If the economists had actually meant that the *proportional* rate of growth would have to be halved, did this happen between years 1 and 4?

8.2

A farmer produces wheat under the following conditions of production:

$$y = -x^3 + 5x^2 + 10x$$

where y = total yield in tons, and x = the number of labour units employed (measured in man hours per day).

The rent on the farmer's land was £1000 per annum and the cost of seed was £500. The farmer pays his workforce a wage of £40 per labour unit, and knows that he can sell his entire crop for a fixed price of £100 per ton.

Calculate the number of labour units that should be employed if the greatest profit is to be made.

8.3

For a particular firm, the total cost (c) of producing q units of output is given by

$$c = 1000 + 5q + 10q^2$$

where c is measured in £s and q is measured in 000s of units.

(a) At what value of q is the average cost of production minimized?
(b) Show that if average cost is at its minimum value, then average cost and marginal cost are equal.

The output produced is sold under the following demand conditions

$$p = 5400 - 2q^2$$

where p represents the selling price in £s.

(c) At what level of sales is the firm's profit maximized?
(d) Obtain an expression for the price elasticity of demand and evaluate this expression when the profit maximizing price is charged.
(e) What is the price elasticity of demand when the price which maximizes revenue is charged?

8.4

The total cost (cg) of gathering information depends upon the number of clients interviewed (x) in the following manner

$$cg = 10x^{1.1}$$

The total cost (cp) of processing and collating the information gathered also depends upon the number of interviews, but as follows:

$$cp = 200x^{0.6}$$

(a) How many interviews should be carried out if the average cost of gathering and processing the information is to be minimized?
(b) What is this minimum average cost? The effect upon revenue (r) of the information obtained depends upon the number of interviews as follows:

$$r = 1500x^{0.6}$$

(c) How many interviews should be carried out if the organization's profit from the information is to be maximized?

8.5

What is the greatest rectangular area of ground that can be enclosed by 5000 metres of fencing, if any two opposite sides of the rectangle must have double thicknesses of fencing material?

8.6

A firm's profit (w) is known to depend upon its sales (x units) in the following way:

$$p = 400x + 21x^2 - (x^3)/3$$

(a) What is the maximum profit obtainable?
(b) For an outlay of £100 000 on advertising the firm believes it can change the profit function to

$$p = 4[400x + 21x^2 - (x^3)/3]$$

Would such an outlay be justified in terms of the new profit made?

8.7

A firm sells its product under market conditions such that the price (p) it receives for selling q units is given by

$$p = 10 + 100/(q + 5)$$

where p is measured in £s and q is measured in millions of units.
The firm's total costs (c) of producing q units are given by

$$c = 10.2q$$

Find the profit maximizing output level.

8.8

The relationship between a firm's output (Q) and its usage of labour (L) is known

to be
$$Q = 0.5L$$

The output produced is sold in accordance with the following demand function where P represents the selling price:
$$P = 100 - (Q^2)/3$$

The firm's total costs of production (C) are as follows:
$$C = 6Q^2 + 7.5Q + 96$$

Determine the quantity of labour that should be employed if profits are to be maximized.

8.9

The proportion (p) of potential customers who will have responded to the advance notice of a new product after it has been advertised for x days is estimated to be
$$p = 1 - e^{-0.45x}$$

The marketing area contains 12 million potential customers, and it is believed that each response to the advance notice will result in the sale of one unit of the product at a price of £1.

The cost of producing the advance notice is £100 000, and it costs £60 000 for each day that the notice appears in a newspaper.

Calculate the length of time for which the notice should be advertised if the greatest profit is to be made.

8.10

Prepare a worksheet and a diagram that will display the behaviour of the profit function in Example 8.7, i.e.
$$\text{profit } (W) = t^3 - 15t^2 + 63t + 10\,000$$

8.8 Solutions to the exercises

8.1

(a) Since $p = 0.1t^{0.5} + 1$, we have
$$dp/dt = 0.05t^{-0.5}$$

So, when $t = 1$, $dp/dt = 0.05(1)^{-0.5} = 0.05$ million people per annum.
But when $t = 4$, $dp/dt = 0.05(4)^{-0.5} = 0.025$ million people per annum.
Clearly the rate of growth has only been halved and not quartered.

(b) The proportional rate of growth will be given by

$$(dp/dt)/p = 0.05t^{-0.5}/(0.1t^{0.5} + 1)$$

Therefore when $t = 1$

$$(dp/dt)/p = 0.05/(0.1 + 1)$$
$$= 0.04545 \text{ million people per annum, per head of population}$$

While when $t = 4$

$$(dp/dt)/p = 0.025/(0.2 + 1)$$
$$= 0.0208 \text{ million people per annum, per head of population}$$

The reduction in the proportional rate of growth is therefore

$$0.0208/0.045\,45 = 45.83 \text{ per cent}$$

Clearly this reduction is closer to the required 25 per cent reduction than when the simple growth rates were used, but even so, the requirement has still not been fulfilled.

8.2

The revenue function (r) will be

$$r = 100(-x^3 + 5x^2 + 10x)$$

The cost function (c) will be

$$c = 1000 + 500 + 40x$$

Therefore profit (w) will be given by

$$w = -100x^3 + 500x^2 + 1000x - 40x - 1500$$

Differentiating with respect to x, and setting this derivative equal to zero, produces

$$dw/dx = -300x^2 + 1000x + 1000 - 40 = 0$$

Solution by the quadratic formula gives

$$x_1 = 4.111, \quad x_2 = -0.778$$

implying that $x = 4.111$ when the negative root is ignored.

The farmer should therefore employ 4.111 man hours per day, which will produce a harvest of 56.134 tons.

The second derivative is given by

$$d(dw/dx)/dx = -600x + 1000$$

which is less than zero when $x = 4.111$ and implies a maximum value of the profit function (of £3948.99).

8.3

(a) The average cost of production (a) will be given by

$$\text{(total cost)/output} = (1000 + 5q + 10q^2)/q$$

Therefore

$$a = 1000/q + 5 + 10q$$

To find this function's stationary value we should differentiate with respect to q and set the resulting derivative equal to zero. Therefore

$$da/dq = -1000q^{-2} + 10 = 0$$

implying that

$$10 = 1000/q^2$$

and that

$$10q^2 = 1000$$

whereby

$$q = 10$$

Differentiation with respect to q again produces

$$d(da/dq)/dq = 2000q^{-3} = 2 \text{ when } q = 10$$

The positive value for the second derivative indicates that we have located a minimum turning point when $q = 10$.

(b) Since marginal cost (m) is defined as the rate of change of total costs with respect to output, we have

$$m = dc/dq = 5 + 20q$$

We have seen that average costs are minimized when $q = 10$, so the value of m at this output level will be

$$m = 5 + 20(10) = 205$$

At the same time, the value of average costs will be

$$a = 1000/10 + 5 + 10(10) = 205$$

We conclude that average and marginal costs will be equal when average costs are at their minimum value.

(c) The firm's revenue (r) will be given by

$$r = (5400 - 2q^2)q = 5400q - 2q^3$$

Therefore profit (w) will be given by

$$w = 5400q - 2q^3 - 1000 - 5q - 10q^2$$

which, after collecting terms becomes
$$w = 5395q - 2q^3 - 1000 - 10q^2$$

Differentiating with respect to q and setting the result equal to zero produces
$$dw/dq = 5395 - 6q^2 - 20q = 0$$

This can now be solved by the quadratic formula, and produces a positive solution of
$$q = 31.7 \text{ (thousand units)}$$

The second derivative is
$$d(dw/dq)/dq = -12q - 20$$

which is obviously negative for all positive values of q, and therefore confirms that a maximum turning point has been located.

The selling price will be
$$5400 - 2(31.7)^2 = £3390.34$$

and the maximum profit that can be made will be
$$w = £96\,262\,000$$

when the profit function (w) is evaluated for $q = 31.7$.

(d) the price elasticity of demand (e_p) will be given by
$$e_p = (dq/dp)(p/q)$$

So, since
$$p = 5400 - 2q^2$$

it follows that
$$q^2 = (2700 - 0.5p)$$

and that
$$q = (2700 - 0.5p)^{0.5}$$

Therefore, employing the chain rule with $u = (2700 - 0.5p)$, we have
$$dq/dp = 0.5(-0.5)(2700 - 0.5p)^{-0.5}$$

which can be rewritten as
$$dq/dp = -0.25/(2700 - 0.5p)^{0.5}$$

This expression can now be substituted into our expression for e_p to produce
$$e_p = -0.25/(2700 - 0.5p)^{0.5}] \, [p/(2700 - 0.5p)^{0.5})]$$

which reduces to $-0.25p/(2700 - 0.5p)$

So, since we have already seen that profits are maximized when $q = 31.7$, and $p = £3390.34$, the value of e_p is then -0.84, implying that a 1 per cent increase in price would cause a 0.84 per cent reduction in the quantity demanded.

(e) The revenue function (r) will be given by

$$r = (5400 - 2q^2)(q) = 5400q - 2q^3$$

and will be maximized when

$$dr/dq = 5400 - 6q^2 = 0$$

This implies that $q = 30$ and that $p = 5400 - 2(30^2) = 3600$. Therefore

$$e_p = -0.25(3600)/(2700 - 0.5(3600)) = -1$$

This is no coincidence, since it is a general tenet of elementary economic analysis that the price elasticity of demand will always be equal to -1 when the price charged and the quantity sold are such that revenue is maximized.

8.4

(a) the average cost (c) of gathering and processing the information will be given by

$$(cg + cp)/x = (10x^{1.1} + 200x^{0.6})/x$$

implying that

$$c = 10x^{0.1} + 200x^{-0.4}$$

The minimum average cost is therefore given by the value of x such that

$$dc/dx = x^{-0.9} - 80x^{-1.4} = 0$$

implying that

$$1 - 80x^{-0.5} = 0$$

when all terms are multiplied by $x^{0.9}$.

So

$$80x^{-0.5} = 1$$

and (after rearranging)

$$x^{0.5} = 80$$

Therefore

$$x = 80^2 = 6400 \text{ interviews}$$

The second derivative is

$$d(dc/dx)/dx = -0.9x^{-1.9} + 112x^{-2.4}$$

which, when $x = 6400$ evaluates to 0.000 000 0293, which being positive, indicates that a minimum value has been attained by the function.

(b) The actual average cost is given by
$$c = 10(6400^{0.1}) + 200(6400^{-0.4})$$
$$= £30.03 \text{ per interview gathered and processed}$$

(c) The profit (w) will be given by
$$w = 1500x^{0.6} - 10x^{1.1} - 200x^{0.6}$$

So
$$dw/dx = 900x^{-0.4} - 11x^{0.1} - 120x^{-0.4}$$

Collecting terms and then equating this derivative to zero then produces
$$dw/dx = 780x^{-0.4} - 11x^{0.1} = 0$$

Therefore, if we multiply throughout by $x^{0.4}$, we obtain
$$dw/dx = 780 - 11x^{0.5} = 0$$

implying that
$$x^{0.5} = 70.90$$

and that

$x = 5028$ (to the nearest interview).

Once again, we should check that this is in fact a maximum value for w, so
$$d(dw/dx)/dx = -320x^{-1.4} - 1.1x^{-0.9}$$

which is clearly negative for all positive values of x (including 5028) and therefore indicates a maximum turning point.

8.5

Let the length of the rectangle $= x$ and the breadth $= y$. Make the sides constituting the breadth be of double thicknesses of fencing material.

Therefore the perimeter (p) to be fenced is given by
$$p = 2x + 4y$$

Since there are only 5000 metres of fencing material available, we can write
$$2x + 4y = 5000$$

implying that
$$2x = 5000 - 4y$$

and that
$$x = 2500 - 2y$$

The area (a) enclosed by the fence will be given by

$$a = xy$$

and we require that this be maximized.

However, this expression contains two variables (x and y) and so to determine its maximum value we require to employ our previous conclusion that

$$x = 2500 - 2y$$

When this is substituted into our expression for area we obtain

$$a = (2500 - 2y)(y) = 2500y - 2y^2$$

Therefore

$$da/dy = 2500 - 4y$$

and when this is set equal to 0, we obtain

$$y = 625 \text{ metres}$$

implying that $x = 1250$ metres.

The area enclosed will be $625(1250) = 781\,250$ square metres and this is the maximum area that can be enclosed since

$$d(da/dy)\, dy = -4 \text{ is clearly negative}$$

8.6

(a) We have

$$p = 400x + 21x^2 - (x^3)/3$$

Therefore the stationary points can be determined from

$$dp/dx = 400 + 42x - x^2 = 0$$

Solution by the quadratic formula then produces

$$x_1 = -8, \quad x_2 = 50$$

and we can ignore the negative solution.

To determine the nature of the stationary point, we have

$$d(dp/dx)/dx = 42 - 2x$$

which when $x = 50$ has a value of -58, implying a maximum profit of

$$400(50) + 42(50^2) + (50^3)/3 = £30\,833.33$$

(b) The effect of the advertising campaign is to increase the profit function by a factor of 4, but the profit maximizing output level will be unchanged at $x = 50$.

Therefore, an *extra* $3(30\,833.33) = £92\,500$ of profit will be made, for an extra outlay of £100 000, which is clearly not justifiable.

8.7

As usual we must identify the revenue (r) and cost (c) functions, and then form a function representing profit (w).

Accordingly
$$r = pq = 10q + 100q/(q+5)$$
$$c = 10.2q$$

Therefore
$$w = 10q + 100q[(q+5)^{-1}] - 10.2q$$

Remembering that the middle term in this expression is a product of two separate functions of q, we have
$$dw/dq = 10 + 100q[-(q+5)^{-2}] + 100[(q+5)^{-1}] - 10.2$$

Collecting terms, and equating to zero produces
$$100/(q+5) - 100q/[(q+5)^2] - 0.2 = 0$$

Now multiply throughout by $(q+5)^2$ to obtain
$$100(q+5) - 100q - 0.2[(q+5)^2] = 0$$

implying that
$$100q + 500 - 100q - 0.2[(q+5)^2] = 0$$

Therefore
$$0.2[(q+5)^2] = 500$$
$$(q+5)^2 = 2500$$
$$q + 5 = 50 \quad \text{and} \quad q = 45$$

Since the first derivative contains two terms that are quite complicated (and one of which is a product), we have to differentiate very carefully to obtain the second derivative. So, letting
$$x = -100q[(q+5)^{-2}]$$
$$y = 100[(q+5^{-1}]$$

we have
$$d(dw/dq)/dq = dx/dq + dy/dq$$

Now applying the product rule to x, we obtain
$$dx/dq = -100q[-2(q+5)^{-3}] + [(q+5)^{-2}](-100)$$

and
$$dy/dq = -100[(q+5)^{-2}]$$

Therefore, after substituting these expressions for dx/dq and dy/dq, and collecting terms, we obtain

$$d(dw/dq)/dq = 100q[2(q+5)^{-3}] - 200[(q+5)^{-2}]$$

which when $q = 45$ has a value of -0.008 and implies a maximum value for the profit function.

8.8

Since $Q = 0.5L$, and since we are required to find the value of L that maximizes profit, we should write the revenue (r) and cost (c) functions in terms of L as

$$r = \{100 - [(0.5L)^2]/3\}(0.5L)$$
$$r = 50L - 0.041\,666L^3$$

and

$$c = 6(0.5L)^2 + 7.5(0.5L) + 96$$
$$c = 1.5L^2 + 3.75L + 96$$

Therefore profit (w) is given by

$$w = -(0.041\,666)L^3 - 1.5L^2 + 46.25L - 96$$

and

$$dw/dL = -(0.125)L^2 - 3L + 46.25 = 0$$

implying that the positive solution is

$$L = 10.67 \text{ labour units.}$$

The second derivative is

$$d(dw/dL)/dL = -0.25L - 3$$

which is negative for all positive values of L and implies a maximum value for profit when 10.67 labour units are employed. This will produce an output of 5.335 units, a revenue of £482.88, a total cost of £306.78, and a (maximum) profit of £176.1.

8.9

The revenue function (r) will be given as

$$p(12)(1) = 12(1 - e^{-0.45x}) \text{ (£ million)}$$

The cost function (expressed in £ millions) will be given by

$$0.1 + 0.06x \text{ (£ millions)}$$

Therefore profit (w) is given by

$$w = 12(1 - e^{-0.45x}) - 0.1 - 0.06x$$

So

$$dw/dx = 5.4e^{-0.45x} - 0.06$$

Solutions to the exercises

implying that

$$e^{-0.45x} = 0.011\ 1111$$

and, taking natural logarithms, that

$$-0.45x = \ln 0.011\ 1111$$

Therefore

$$x = 9.9999 = 10 \text{ to the nearest day.}$$

The proportion of the market area contacted will be 98.88 per cent = 11.8666 million potential customers, and the revenue will be £11.8666 million, for an expenditure of £0.16 million.

The second derivative is

$$d(dw/dx)/dx = -2.43e^{-0.45x}$$

which is negative for all positive values of x, and so we have a maximum value of the profit function.

8.10

You should obtain something similar to Worksheet 8.16 and Figure 8.7.

WORKSHEET 8.16

	A	B
1	Year	Profit (w)
2	0	10000
3	0.5	10027.87
4	1	10049
5	1.5	10064.12
6	2	10074
7	2.5	10079.37
8	3	10081
9	3.5	10079.62
10	4	10076
11	4.5	10070.87
12	5	10065
13	5.5	10059.12
14	6	10054
15	6.5	10050.37
16	7	10049
17	7.5	10050.62
18	8	10056
19	8.5	10065.87
20	9	10081
21	9.5	10102.12
22	10	10130
23	10.5	10165.37
24	11	10209
25	11.5	10261.62
26	12	10324

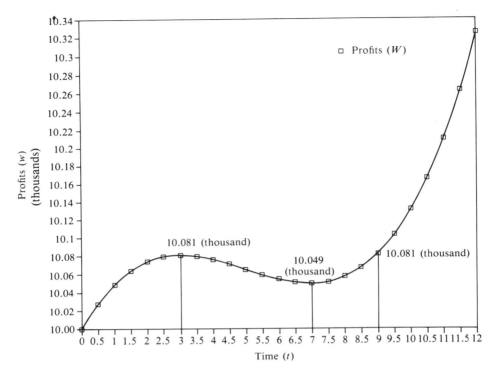

Figure 8.7 Profits over time

In order to provide a clear impression of the relationship we have tabulated t from 0 to 12 in steps of 0.5 in A2..A26.

Alongside, the value of W is calculated from the formula in B2:

$$-A2^3 - 15*A2^2 + 63*t + 10000$$

which was then copied into B3..B26.

With A2..A26 defined as the X range, and B2..B26 as the A range, Figure 8.7 is easily obtained. As you can see, the *global* minimum value of W is 10 000 when $t = 0$, but the local minimum is attained when $t = 7$ and $W = 10\,049$.

On the other hand, a *local* maximum is attained when $t = 3$ and $W = 10\,081$, but there is no finite global maximum, since once t exceeds 7 the value of W rises continually with increases in t, and exceeds the local maximum for any value of t in excess of 9.

It is left as an exercise for you to enter formulae for the first and second derivatives of the profit function and thereby confirm our previous remarks about their values and algebraic signs.

9
Introductory Statistical Analysis

9.1 Preliminaries

Whether you realize it or not, at some time or another you will almost certainly have performed some kind of elementary statistical analysis. This is because, in essence, statistics is concerned with the process of making sense from, and bringing order to, collections of data observations.

Your monthly bank statement, your end-of-term assessment marks, or your quarterly telephone bill, are all examples of data observations that can be collected together (over several months, terms or quarters) to form what is known as a *data set*, thereby creating the basic unit of statistical analysis.

Given this basic unit, the purpose of elementary statistical analysis can be summarized in terms of five fundamental objectives:

1. Data collection.
2. Data collation.
3. Visual portrayal of the data's properties.
4. Summary measures of the data's characteristics.
5. Drawing conclusion on the basis of the foregoing analysis.

Taking each of these objectives in turn, we must consider a number of issues.

9.1.1 Data collection

In many cases the nature of the problem to be investigated will be such that there is little or no relevant information available. In this case the investigator will have to use interview and/or postal questionnaire techniques to extract the raw data from a group or groups of identified respondents.

In other cases, however, it may be possible to use (and amend if necessary), data that have already been collected and made accessible in one or more of the numerous statistical data banks now available.

9.1.2 Data collation

Once collected (from whatever source), the data will then have to be brought together and presented in some manageable form. This is known as *collation*, and will frequently involve summarizing and tabulating the information so that it can be interpreted and analyzed more efficiently.

9.1.3 Visual portrayal of the data

After collation, it will often be desirable to produce a pictorial display of the data's features. As you have already seen, Lotus supports a number of graphic techniques, and the primary task in this regard will always be to choose the most appropriate graph so that a clear visual impression of the data's properties is produced. This will obviously be conditioned by the nature of the data themselves, and by the purposes to which they are to be put.

9.1.4 Summary characterizations

Particularly in the case of large data sets, it will usually be necessary to obtain one or more summary statistics which measure certain characteristics of the data set.

As far as elementary statistical analysis is concerned, there are two basic features that must be measured:

1. Measurement of the data's *central* or 'average' value.
2. Measurement of the extent to which the data is *dispersed* around its central value.

As we will see, there are in fact a number of measures of central tendency, and as a consequence, a number of measures of dispersion, each related to the particular measure of centralization that has been employed.

9.1.5 Drawing conclusions

Once the previous four objectives have been achieved, the data can then be used as part of the decision-making process.

This will always involve the task of drawing conclusions on the basis of the information that has been provided by the data, and in some cases can be a straightforward matter.

In many cases, however, the old adage that there are 'lies, damned lies and statistics' will be particularly apposite, and will mean that conclusive interpretation of the data will have to be subject to a number of reservations.

9.2 Collating the data

One of the most effective ways of collating data is to create what is known as a *frequency distribution*. To see how this works consider the following example.

EXAMPLE 9.1

A survey was made of the various types of car that arrived at a petrol station over a period of 30 minutes. The results were as follows: Ford, Ford, Vauxhall, Renault, Vauxhall, Ford, Vauxhall, Volvo, Ford, Vauxhall, Ford, Saab, Ford, Leyland, Leyland, Fiat, Renault, Leyland, Ford, Vauxhall.

SOLUTION 9.1

Clearly we can summarize this data by counting the number of cars of each type and then classifying them as shown in Table 9.1.

The summarizing device constructed above is known as a *frequency distribution* as it indicates the frequency of occurrence of each value of the variable being measured (car manufacturer).

It would obviously be convenient if we could get Lotus to do this collation for us, but before this can be done we will have to devise a numerical code for the different data observations upon the variable. This is because we are going to use the Lotus Data Distribution command, which requires that the variable observations be of a *numeric* as opposed to *textual* nature.

However, it is a simple matter to code the different manufacturers as shown in Table 9.2.

We can now convert our observed manufacturer names to their appropriate code and enter the codes for the raw data in A2..A21 of our worksheet. In addition, we

Table 9.1

Manufacturer	Frequency
Ford	7
Vauxhall	5
Renault	2
Volvo	1
Saab	1
Fiat	1
Leyland	3
Other	0

Table 9.2

Manufacturer	Code
Ford	1
Vauxhall	2
Renault	3
Volvo	4
Saab	5
Fiat	6
Leyland	7
Other	8

should enter the eight *different* possible codes in B2..B9. This is done in Worksheet 9.1, where the *uncollated* values of the variable are denoted by 'x code' and the *different* values that the code can adopt are denoted by 'X code'.

As you can see, the Worksheet also contains the frequency distribution for X in column C, but how did we get Lotus to do this?

The answer is that we used the Data Distribution command (/, Data, Distribution), which first of all produces a prompt to 'enter values range'. In our case the raw data is contained in A2..A21, so this should be your first response.

Next you will be prompted to 'enter bin range'. This is where Lotus will place the collated values of x code, and the frequencies associated with each different

WORKSHEET 9.1

	A	B	C	D
1	x code	X code	frequency	Model
2	1	1	7	Ford
3	1	2	5	Vauxhall
4	2	3	1	Renault
5	3	4	2	Volvo
6	2	5	1	Saab
7	1	6	1	Fiat
8	2	7	3	Leyland
9	4	8	0	Other
10	1		0	
11	2			
12	1			
13	5			
14	1			
15	7			
16	7			
17	6			
18	3			
19	7			
20	1			

value of the variable, so now you see why we placed these different values of x (X code) in B2..B9. This will form the first column of our bin range, and since we would like the associated frequencies placed alongside, we should respond to the second prompt with B2..C9.

After you have returned this response, Lotus will proceed to analyze the information in the data range (column A), and will collate it in terms of the specified X values and associated frequencies in the range B2..C9. The additional entry in C10 tells you the number of observations that lie outside the range of X values specified in the bin. In this case there are none.

Furthermore, if you want a reminder of the codes employed, it is an easy matter to place these in column D (for example) as has been done in Worksheet 9.1.

Finally, although the principles involved in pictorial representation of data sets have still to be discussed, the fact that you have been using line graphs since Chapter 2, means that it will still be instructive at this stage to ask Lotus to produce such a graph of the data. Taking D2..D8 as the X range and C2..C8 as the A range would produce Figure 9.1. For reasons which should now be apparent it is called a *frequency polygon*.

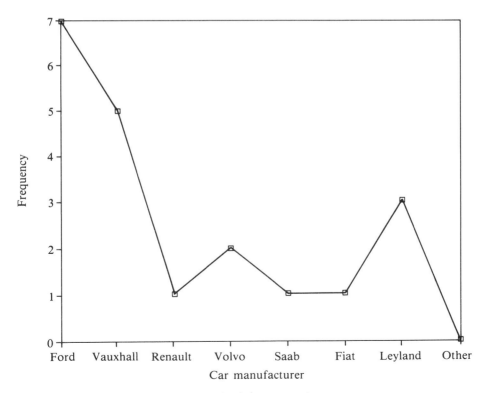

Figure 9.1 The frequency polygon

Introductory Statistical Analysis

As you can imagine, the Data Distribution command is an exceptionally powerful device, but you may be wondering if it can still be used when the variable being measured is of a more complicated nature.

The answer is that it can, as the following example indicates.

EXAMPLE 9.2

The following data refer to the age of onset of asthma gathered from a survey of 30 asthma sufferers:

X (age of onset in years) 3.23, 10.53, 10.76, 6.14, 10.13, 6.19, 10.38, 12.53, 5.46, 3.76, 4.47, 1.37, 8.29, 2.08, 11.05, 0.42, 8.96, 1.23, 13.10, 2.97, 9.03, 5.37, 9.44, 6.33, 2.42, 9.19, 3.99, 5.61, 5.75, 6.95.

Collate this data into an appropriate frequency distribution.

SOLUTION 9.2

To do this we must first of all recognize that since age is a *continuous* variable (i.e. capable of being measured to as many decimal places as we like), it makes little sense to construct a frequency distribution in which X is allowed to adopt *every conceivable* value. Even in our example where age has only been measured to two decimal places such a procedure would simple produce an enormous list of X values with frequencies of zero associated with most of them.

For this reason it is much more sensible to employ a device known as a *class interval*, in which a number of value ranges of the variable are constructed. The choice of the width of each class interval will obviously be conditioned by the range of values that the data adopts, and by the desired number of class intervals. This latter choice must take account of the fact that with too many class intervals the abbreviating purpose of collation will be defeated, while with two few class intervals much of the information will be obscured. For this reason it will usually be advisable to limit the number of class intervals to a maximum of about 16 and a minimum of about 6.

Once the number of class intervals has been chosen, then in conjunction with the range of values adopted by the data, the width of each class interval is determined.

The data in our example span a range of 0.42 to 13.1 years, and so we could employ seven class intervals, each with a width of 1.99 years. This would be done as follows:

X (age of onset in years)
greater than or equal to 0 but less than 2
greater than or equal to 2 but less than 4
greater than or equal to 4 but less than 6

greater than or equal to 6 but less than 8
greater than or equal to 8 but less than 10
greater than or equal to 10 but less than 12
greater than or equal to 12 but less than 14

You can get Lotus to do the frequency collation for you in the same way as before, but in this case you will have to be careful how you specify the X values for the bin range. This is because the continuous nature of the data creates a slight problem in defining the upper end of one class interval in relation to the bottom end of the next one.

The easiest way to deal with this problem is to think of each class interval as spanning a range of 1.99 years and to use values of 1.99, 3.99, 5.99 and so on, as the X values in the bin range. This means that a value of 1.98 or 1.99 would be

WORKSHEET 9.2

	A	B	C	D
1	x	X	f	cf
2	3.23	1.99	3	3
3	10.53	3.99	6	9
4	10.76	5.99	5	14
5	6.14	7.99	4	18
6	10.13	9.99	5	23
7	6.19	11.99	5	28
8	10.38	13.99	2	30
9	12.53		0	
10	5.46			
11	3.76			
12	4.47			
13	1.37			
14	8.29			
15	2.08			
16	11.05			
17	0.42			
18	8.96			
19	1.23			
20	13.10			
21	2.97			
22	9.03			
23	5.37			
24	9.44			
25	6.33			
26	2.42			
27	9.19			
28	3.99			
29	5.61			
30	5.75			
31	6.95			

included in the first class interval, but that a value of 2.00 or 2.01 would be included in the second interval.

If you use these values for the class interval then Worksheet 9.2 is obtained. Once again it is an easy matter to get Lotus to produce the frequency polygon associated with this data set, and this is done for you in Figure 9.2.

At this stage it will be instructive to appreciate an important adjunct to the process of constructing frequency distributions. This is known as a *cumulative frequency distribution* and can be thought of as the answer to the question: 'how many values of X are less than or equal to the upper limit of each class interval?'

Clearly, since there are seven class intervals in our example, there are seven upper limits (1.99, 3.99, ..., 13.99), and so there are in fact seven answers to this question, with each one constituting a value in the cumulative frequency distribution.

Referring once again to Worksheet 9.2 you should be able to see that there are three observations on X that are less than or equal to 1.99, and six observations that lie between 2 and 3.99 inclusive. Consequently, there must be $3 + 6 = 9$ observations that are less than or equal to 3.99 (i.e. the three that lie between 0 and 1.99 inclusive, plus the six that lie between 2 and 3.99 inclusive.

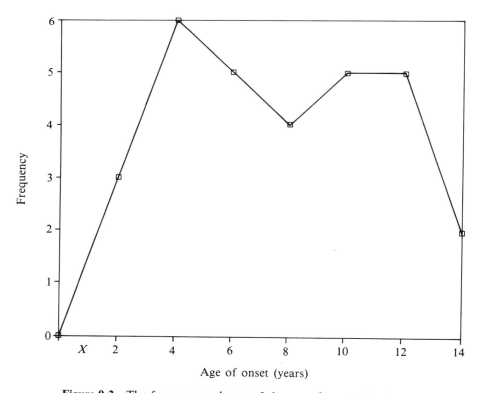

Figure 9.2 The frequency polygon of the age of onset of asthma

An extension of this logic would deduce that there are a total of 14 observations that are less than or equal to 5.99, 18 less than or equal to 7.99, 23 less than or equal to 9.99, 28 less than or equal to 11.99, and 30 (i.e. all of them) less than or equal to 13.99.

You can get Lotus to do these calculations for you in column D (under the heading 'cf') by entering the following formula in D2:

$$@SUM(C\$2..C2)$$

This should then be copied into the range D3..D8, where, since the last cell reference in the range to be summed is not fixed, it will update for each row that is copied to and produce a running total of the frequencies for each of the class intervals. (This is an important mechanism for creating running totals so make sure you understand it.)

This running total is the cumulative frequency distribution, and we will discover an important use for it shortly, but at the moment it will be enough to ask Lotus to produce a line graph of the distribution. This is reproduced in Figure 9.3.

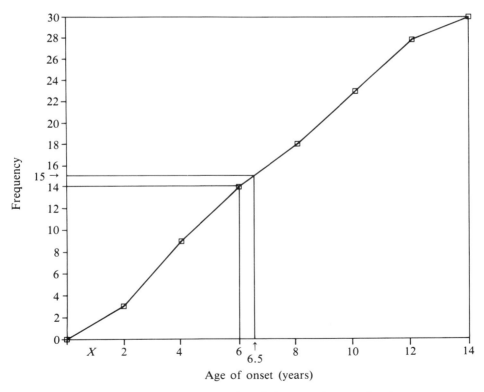

Figure 9.3 Cumulative frequencies of the age of onset of asthma

You can then use this graph to consider the following question: 'what proportion of respondents in the survey first experienced the onset of asthma at an age that was six or less?'

The answer can be read directly from the graph where it is clear that a total of 14 respondents suffered asthmatic onset at an age that was less than six, and consequently that $14/30 = 46.66$ per cent of the survey met this criterion.

Alternatively, you could consider a slightly different question: 'at less than what age did 50 per cent of the respondents in the survey experience their first asthma attack?'

The answer can be obtained by reasoning that since there are 30 individuals in the survey we are looking for the age associated with the 15th (50 per cent of 30) cumulative frequency. This can easily be read from the graph and is seen to be 6.5 years. This means that half of the individuals in the survey experienced the onset of asthma at an age that was 6.5 years or less.

As a final point in this section, we should consider how the frequency distribution could be constructed for data that is neither textual nor continuous. This will mean that the data set consists of a number of *discrete* or integer valued observations. To see the issues involved consider the following example.

EXAMPLE 9.3

The following data refer to a survey of the number of accidents per week on a particular section of motorway over a period of 30 weeks. The results were as follows:

x (number of accidents per week) 9, 7, 1, 0, 10, 5, 11, 12, 1, 2, 11, 10, 1, 7, 4, 5, 11, 0, 15, 3, 5, 5, 5, 7, 5, 12, 13, 7, 10, 1.

SOLUTION 9.3

In this case the problem is caused by the fact that the data is not continuous, since it is impossible to have a fractional number of accidents. This will mean that the Lotus Data Distribution command will find it difficult to distinguish between the bottom end of one class interval and the upper end of the previous one. However, the problem is easily dealt with if we regard each class interval as overlapping half way into the next one.

For our data this would mean that the class intervals should be as follows:

greater than or equal to 0 but less than or equal to 2.5
greater than 2.5 but less than or equal to 5.5
greater than 5.5 but less than or equal to 8.5
greater than 8.5 but less than or equal to 11.5
greater than 11.5 but less than or equal to 14.5

Collating the data

greater than 14.5 but less than or equal to 17.5
greater than 17.5 but less than or equal to 20.5

Now you can use the *upper ends* of each of these intervals as the values for X in the Lotus bin range, secure in the knowledge that since noninteger values cannot be observed, the calculated frequencies will be unaffected, but that any graph of the data will be effectively continuous.

If you do this, Worksheet 9.3 and Figure 9.4 can be obtained. Once again, you can use the cumulative frequency distribution in this diagram to answer questions such as: 'on how many weeks were there 8 or less accidents?' or 'what was the highest number of accidents that occurred on 50 per cent of the weeks?'

You should be able to see that the answers are 19 weeks, when the cumulative frequency associated with 8.5 accidents is read from the graph, and 5.5 (treated as

WORKSHEET 9.3

	A	B	C	D
1	x	X	f	cf
2	9	2.5	7	7
3	7	5.5	8	15
4	1	8.5	4	19
5	0	11.5	7	26
6	10	14.5	3	29
7	5	17.5	1	30
8	11	20.5	0	30
9	12		0	
10	1			
11	2			
12	11			
13	10			
14	1			
15	7			
16	4			
17	5			
18	11			
19	0			
20	15			
21	3			
22	5			
23	5			
24	5			
25	7			
26	5			
27	12			
28	13			
29	7			
30	10			
31	1			

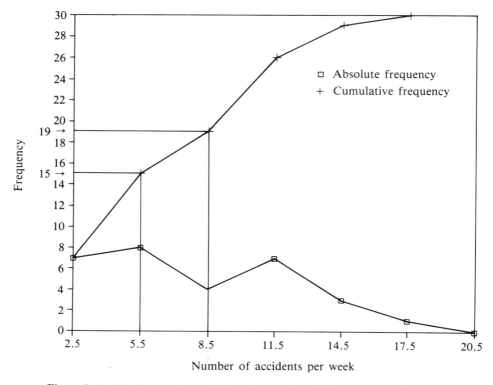

Figure 9.4 Absolute and cumulative frequencies of the number of accidents

5) accidents when the number of accidents associated with a cumulative frequency of 15 is read from the graph. This last result stems from the fact that on 15 weeks there were at most five accidents, and on the remaining 15 weeks there were at least six accidents.

9.3 Pictorial representation of data sets

You have already seen how the line graph can be used to display frequency distributions, but Lotus also supports a number of other pictorial displays.

To see how these can be used consider Worksheet 9.4 where the data refer to a daily breakdown of five constituent cost elements at each of three factories.

The first decision to be made in terms of the most appropriate way to display this data is whether you wish to gain a visual impression of the following:

1. Each cost element at all factories.
2. All cost elements at each factory.
3. All cost elements at all factories.

WORKSHEET 9.4

	A	B	C	D
1		Factory 1	Factory 2	Factory 3
2	Cost element			
3	Labour	1200	1450	1140
4	Raw materials	930	780	1020
5	Fuel	340	250	400
6	Interest	90	75	95
7	Other	110	100	120

Taking each of these objectives in turn we can proceed as follows:

1. In this case you should use either a bar chart or a stacked bar chart with the X range being defined as B1..D1 and the A, B, C, D and E ranges being defined as B3..D3, B4..D4, B5..D5, B6..D6, and B7..D7 respectively. This would produce Figures 9.5 and 9.6.
2. In this case you should transpose the table so that the X range is A3..A7, and the A, B, and C ranges contain the data for each factory (B3..B7, C3..C7, and D3..D7). Remembering to cancel the D and E graph ranges from the previous display, this would produce Figures 9.7 and 9.8

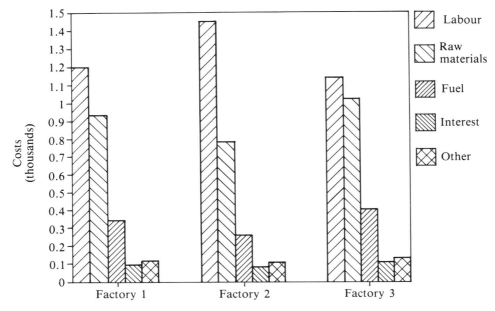

Figure 9.5 Cost component per factory

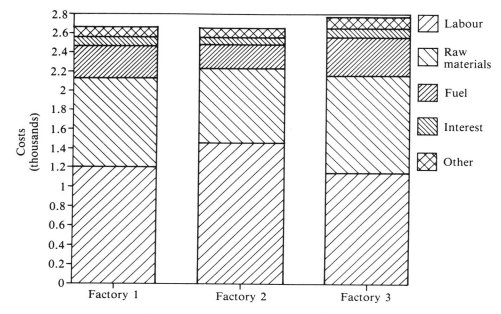

Figure 9.6 Cost component per factory

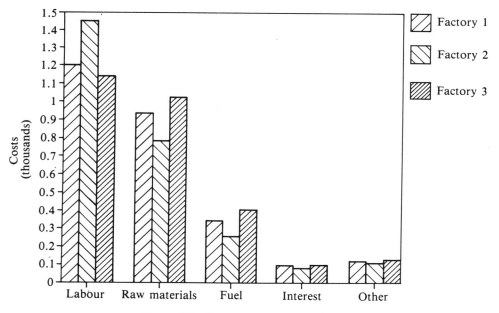

Figure 9.7 Factory component of costs

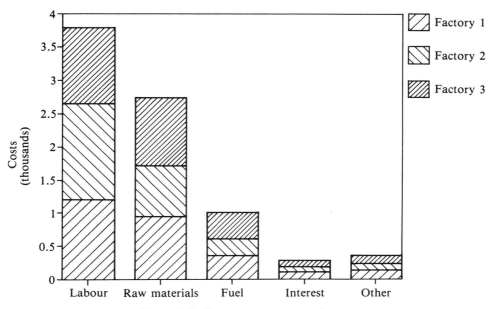

Figure 9.8 Factory component of costs

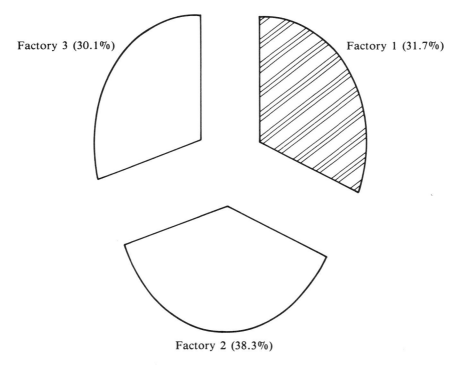

Figure 9.9 Factory component of all costs

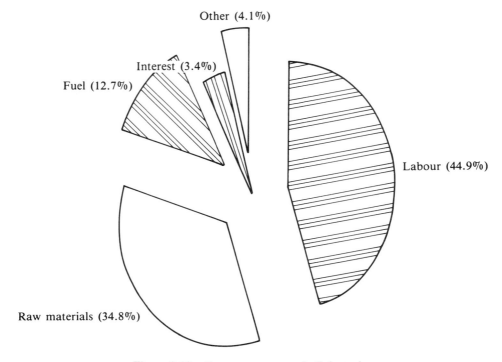

Figure 9.10 Cost component of all factories

3. In this case we could employ a pie chart which can either display the 'all' factory component of each of the five cost elements, or the 'all' cost component of each of the three factories.

To obtain the first of these charts, the X range must be defined as B1..D1, and the A, B, C, D and E ranges will be B3..D3, B4..D4, B5..D5, B6..D6 and B7..D7; while to obtain the second chart the X range will be A3..A7 and the A, B and C ranges as B3..B7, C3..C7 and D3..D7.

Defined in either of these ways, Figures 9.9 and 9.10 can be produced.

9.4 Measures of central tendency in simple data sets

As there will usually be several values of the observed variable, it will frequently be instructive to calculate some single value that measures the central or 'average' value of the data set. This measure of *central tendency* may well be the same as one of the observed data elements, but there is no necessity that this be the case, since the averaging process is capable of calculating a central value that is not the same as any one of the observed data items. Furthermore, even in the case of discrete data sets, there is no requirement that the central value is also integer valued. This means that the central value could be one that is actually incapable of being observed (such as 2.5 accidents per week, for example).

Bearing these ideas in mind, we can proceed by explaining the five most common measures of central tendency that statistics employs.

9.4.1 The arithmetic mean

The *arithmetic mean* is the name that statistics uses for what we more commonly refer to as 'the average'. To see how it can be calculated, consider the following example.

EXAMPLE 9.4

The following data refer to the daily number of clients placed by an employment agency over a period of seven working days.

x (number of clients placed) 15, 28, 21, 13, 19, 23, 21

Calculate the arithmetic mean of the data set.

SOLUTION 9.4

For any data set the arithmetic mean is calculated by obtaining the total arithmetic worth of all the observations and then dividing this total by the number of observations. For our data this would produce

$$(15 + 28 + 21 + 13 + 19 + 23 + 21)/7 = 140.00/7$$
$$= 20.00$$

This means that 'on average' 20 clients were placed per day, and although this happens to be an integer value, you can see that there was no occasion over the seven-day period when 20 clients were actually placed.

More generally, we can use the following notational conventions to define the arithmetic mean for any simple data set:

let n = the total number of observations in the data set
let x_i = the ith observation in the data set where i can be any integer value in the range 1 to n (we say $i = 1, ..., n$)
let Σx_i = the sum of the n observations, i.e. $(x_1 + x_2 + \cdots + x_n)$
let $\bar{x}$ = the arithmetic mean of the data set

Then
$$\bar{x} = (\Sigma x_i)/n$$

If you now apply this formula to the data in Example 9.4, then you will find that

$$\Sigma x_i = 140.00$$
$$n = 7$$

Therefore

$$\bar{x} = 140.00/7 = 20.00$$

Lotus can also perform these calculations with its @AVG function, which has the following syntax:

@AVG(DATA RANGE)

Thus, if you enter the seven data observations in the range A2..A8, then the formula

@AVG(A2..A8)

will calculate the arithmetic mean of the data. Try it for yourself in your own worksheet.

9.4.2 The mode

The second measure of central tendency is known as the *mode* and is quite simply defined as that value of the variable which occurs most often. For our data set there is only one value of x that occurs more than once (21) and so we conclude that this is the modal value of the data set.

Clearly, calculation of the mode requires that you make reference to the frequency distribution of x, so we will return to this topic in the next section when measures of central tendency are calculated for collated data sets. At this stage it will be enough to note that there may be no unique value for the mode if more than one value of x occurs with equal frequency. In this case the distribution could be bimodal, trimodal or even multimodal.

9.4.3 The median

For simple data sets you can think of the median as representing the 'middle' value of the variable when these values have been placed in order of magnitude. This is because the exact definition of the median is:

> that value of x above and below which 50 per cent of the observations lie.

Now since the data in our example contain seven observations, all we have to do is order the observations and then select the value of x associated with the fourth (middle) observation. This would produce:

x (number of clients placed)   13,   15,   19,   21,   21,   23,   28
observation number   1   2   3   4   5   6   7

The median is clearly seen to be 21 and in this case is equal to the mode.

You should note that calculation of the median was straightforward in this case because of the fact that there was an odd number of observations, and the 'middle' one was clearly the fourth. If, however, there was an even number of observations, then the middle two observations must be selected and then averaged (i.e. divided by 2) to produce an estimate of the median value.

At this stage you may be wondering which of these three measures of central tendency is the 'best'. The answer is that 'best' is not really the correct word since we are more concerned with appropriateness. This means that the alternative measures should be viewed as being complementary rather than competitive, with the most appropriate being dependent upon the nature of the data to be investigated.

To see this consider the following example.

EXAMPLE 9.5

The following data refer to the daily output of a particular component produced by each of five machines in a factory's production system.

x (output)   490,   510,   495,   490,   1000

Calculate the most appropriate measure of central tendency that will allow you to advise the management on its policy of scrapping the whole system if the output per machine is less than 550 units per day, or if more than 50 per cent of the machines have a daily output of less than 500 units.

SOLUTION 9.5

The arithmetic mean output is 597 units per day, so on the first criterion the system should not be scrapped, but since the median daily output is 495 units, on the second criterion it should be. (It should be clear, in fact, that 60 per cent of the machines will have an output that is less than 500 units per day.) You would have to ask the management to give you more information on which of the two criteria is to be given more weight, since the single extreme observation of 1000 is exercising a disproportionate effect on the value of the arithmetic mean.

In short, it is generally true that the arithmetic mean is much more sensitive to extreme observations than the median, but that the median gives no indication of the *arithmetic extent* to which each of the upper and lower 50 per cent of observations differ from the middle value.

9.4.4 The geometric mean

The geometric mean is a measure of central tendency that takes account of the fact that for certain types of data the arithmetic mean is not the most appropriate measure of central tendency. To see what is meant by this consider the following example.

EXAMPLE 9.6

An individual's salary was £10 000 in 1983, but was increased by 10 per cent in 1984, by 15 per cent in 1985, by 25 per cent in 1986 and by 30 per cent in 1987. What is the 'average' rate of growth of the individual's salary for these five years?

SOLUTION 9.6

Your first instinct will probably be to calculate the arithmetic mean of 10, 15, 25 and 30 per cent, and obtain

$$(10 + 15 + 25 + 30)/4 = 20 \text{ per cent}$$

However, if this *is* an appropriate measure of central tendency, then it should, *when applied to the £10 000 initial salary*, produce the same figure for 1987 as was actually earned.

To see whether this is indeed the case, study the calculations performed in Worksheet 9.5. As you can see, the growth rates for each of the years have been entered in C2..F2, and the associated growth *factors* (1 + the growth rate) immediately below.

These growth factors have been used to calculate the actual salary earned over

WORKSHEET 9.5

	A	B	C	D	E	F
1	Year	1983	1984	1985	1986	1987
2	Growth rate		0.1	0.15	0.25	0.3
3	Growth factor		1.1	1.15	1.25	1.3
4	Actual salary	10000	11000	12650	15812.5	20556.25
5	Arithmetic mean					
6	growth rate	0.2				
7	Arithmetic mean					
8	growth factor	1.2				
9	Estimated salary					
10	on basis of					
11	arithmetic mean					
12	growth factor	10000	12000	14400	17280	20736
13	Error in estimate	0	-1000	-1750	-1467.5	-179.75

the period in the range B4..F4, where the entry in C4 is +B4*C3 and this has been copied into the D4..F4 range.

The arithmetic mean growth rate is calculated in B6 from the formula @AVG(C2..F2), and the arithmetic mean growth factor is calculated in B8 from the formula 1+B6.

This allows us to estimate the salary for each year (in B12..F12) on the basis of the arithmetic mean growth factor. (The entry in C12 is +B12*$B8, and this has been copied into D12..F12.)

Finally, the difference between the actual salary and the salary estimated on the basis of the arithmetic mean growth factor is calculated in B13..F13 from the formula +B4−B13, which was then copied into C13..F13.

As you can see, the actual salary in 1987 is £179.75 less than that estimated on the basis of the arithmetic mean growth rate. It would therefore appear that the arithmetic mean is an inappropriate measure of 'average' growth in this case.

The reason for this is immediately obvious when we recognize that although the actual salaries are not in a strict geometric progression, they do behave in a similar manner.

Consequently, the appropriate measure of central tendency should be calculated from what is known as the *geometric mean*.

For a data set in which there are n observations, this is generally defined as the nth root of the product of all the observations. That is

geometric mean = $(x_1 \times x_2 \times \cdots \times x_n)^{1/n}$
(where all values of x must be greater than zero)

Accordingly, if we calculate the geometric mean of the four *growth factors* we should obtain an appropriate measure of central tendency. This has been done for our data in Worksheet 9.6 with the geometric mean being calculated in B15 from the formula (C3*D3*E3*F3)^0.25. Lotus will then evaluate this to be

$$(1.1 * 1.15 * 1.25 * 1.3)\hat{\ }0.25 = 1.197\ 39$$

The implication of this is that the behaviour of the salaries in question is best represented by a geometric progression in which there is a common ratio of 1.197 39 (i.e. the geometric mean).

If this common ratio is then applied to the initial salary of £10 000, then although the calculated figures for the years *in between* 1983 and 1987 will not be equal to the salaries actually earned, the final figure (for 1987) will be the same.

This is confirmed in Worksheet 9.6 where the formula in C19 (+B19*$B15) has been copied into the range D19..F19.

The common ratio of 1.197 39 implies that the average growth rate for the period is 0.197 39 = 19.739 per cent and it is this figure that should be used as the measure of central tendency.

This discussion allows us to conclude that when percentage rates of growth are the variables to be averaged, then the procedure of taking the geometric mean of the growth factors is the one to be preferred.

WORKSHEET 9.6

	A	B	C	D	E	F
1	Year	1983	1984	1985	1986	1987
2	Growth rate		0.1	0.15	0.25	0.3
3	Growth factor		1.1	1.15	1.25	1.3
4	Actual salary	10000	11000	12650	15812.5	20556.25
5	Arithmetic mean					
6	growth rate	0.2				
7	Arithmetic mean					
8	growth factor	1.2				
9	Estimated salary					
10	on basis of					
11	arithmetic mean					
12	growth factor	10000	12000	14400	17280	20736
13	Error in estimate	0	-1000	-1750	-1467.5	-179.75
14	Geometric mean					
15	growth factor	1.197390				
16	Estimated salary					
17	on basis of					
18	geometric mean					
19	growth factor	10000	11973.90	14337.45	17167.53	20556.25
20	Error in estimate	0	-973.909	-1687.45	-1355.03	0.00

9.4.5 The harmonic mean

The harmonic mean is another statistic that can be used in circumstances where the nature of the data is such that the simple arithmetic mean does not produce a satisfactory measure of central tendency.

To see some of the issues involved, consider the following example.

EXAMPLE 9.7

A van driver has to make three deliveries to three different shops on a particular morning, with a schedule that is outlined below.

Journey	Distance (miles)	Speed (m.p.h.)
Base to shop 1	20	25
Shop 1 to shop 2	20	30
Shop 2 to shop 3	20	20
Shop 3 to base	20	40

Calculate the 'average' speed of the driver over all four journeys.

SOLUTION 9.7

Once again, you might be tempted to calculate the arithmetic mean of the four speeds and obtain a value of

$$(25 + 30 + 20 + 40)/4 = 115/4 = 29.25 \text{ m.p.h.}$$

However, this method would only give an accurate estimate if the speeds of each journey were all the same. Clearly this is not the case, and so we should approach the problem from first principles as follows.

The first journey will take the driver $20/25 = 0.8$ hours, the second journey will take $20/30 = 0.6666$ hours, the third journey will take $20/20 = 1$ hour, and the fourth journey will take $20/40 = 0.5$ hours.

Consequently, the total driving time is 2.9666 hours, and in that time a total distance of 80 miles has been travelled. The average speed for all four journeys is therefore given by

$$80/2.9996 = 26.9668 \text{ m.p.h.}$$

Having solved the problem from first principles, you can now note that the 'average' speed is in fact measured by what is known as the *harmonic mean* of the four speeds. This is defined as the number of observations divided by the sum of the reciprocals of the x values. That is

$$\text{harmonic mean} = n / [\Sigma (1/x_i)] \quad (i = 1, \ldots, n)$$

For our data this would produce

$$4 / (1/25 + 1/30 + 1/20 + 1/40) = 4/0.148\ 333 = 26.966 \text{ m.p.h.}$$

In conclusion, you should now realize that as a general rule the harmonic mean is frequently the most appropriate measure of central tendency for data sets in which the variable is measured in terms of units of one variable *per* unit of another (miles per hour, miles per gallon, etc.).

9.5 Measures of central tendency in collated data sets

Having seen how to calculate the various measures of central tendency in simple data sets, we should now consider how this can be done for data that have been collated into a frequency distribution.

To see the issues involved refer to the data from Example 9.3 which have been reproduced with a few additions in Worksheet 9.7.

The first addition is in column E where the values of X have simply been reproduced for a reason that will soon become clear.

The next addition is in column F where the midpoints of the class intervals have been entered under the heading X'. The reason for this is that the collation procedure inevitably means that instead of having 30 definite values of x, we now have the class interval values of X with each actual value of x having been placed in its appropriate class. This not only means that we have 'lost' some information (as the 'price' of collation) but also that there is now an upper and a lower value for the variable in each class interval.

To deal with this we must take the midpoint of each class interval as the 'representative' value of the variable, and then recognize that any resulting calculations based upon these midpoints will only be *estimates* of the actual statistic being computed. This loss of accuracy is the other price that must be paid for the convenience of collation, but as long as our class intervals have been chosen sensibly the cost should be fairly small. Consequently, the first midpoint is calculated as $(2.5 - 0)/2 = 1.25$, the second as $2.5 + (5.5 - 2.5)/2 = 4$, and so on.

Remembering that what we require is an estimate of each measure of central tendency *on the basis of the frequency distribution*, we can estimate the arithmetic mean by recalling that it is most generally defined as the total arithmetic worth of all the observations divided by the number of observations. Using our midpoint values of X, this means that since there are seven observations with a value of 1.25, these have a total arithmetic worth of $7(1.25) = 8.75$. By the same logic the eight observations with a midpoint value of 4 will have a total arithmetic worth of $8(4) = 32$.

Clearly we can calculate the arithmetic worth of the observations in each class

WORKSHEET 9.7

	A	B	C	D	E	F	G	H	I
1	x	X	f	cf	X	X'	fX'	Actual	x
2	9	2.5	7	7	2.5	1.25	8.75	Arithmetic Mean	0
3	7	5.5	8	15	5.5	4	32	6.5	0
4	1	8.5	4	19	8.5	7	28		1
5	0	11.5	7	26	11.5	10	70	Estimated	1
6	10	14.5	3	29	14.5	13	39	Arithmetic Mean	1
7	5	17.5	1	30	17.5	16	16	6.4583333333	1
8	11	20.5	0	30	20.5	19	0		2
9	12							Modal Class	3
10	1							5.5	4
11	2								5
12	11							Actual Median	5
13	9							6	5
14	1								5
15	7							Estimated	5
16	4							Median Class	5
17	5							5.5	7
18	11								7
19	0								7
20	15								7
21	3								9
22	5								10
23	5								10
24	5								10
25	7								11
26	5								11
27	12								11
28	13								12
29	7								12
30	10								13
31	1								15

interval by forming the product of the relevant frequency and its associated midpoint. This has been done in column G under the heading fX' (i.e. frequency times midpoint).

All we have to do now is ask Lotus to sum each of these products to provide us with the total arithmetic worth of the observations, and then divide this total by the number of observations.

Remembering that the total number of observations will be the sum of the frequencies in each class interval, this means that we can calculate the arithmetic mean from the frequency distribution by the following Lotus formula:

$$@SUM(G2..G8)/@SUM(C2..C8)$$

This formula has been entered into the H7 cell of the worksheet and, as you can see, returns a value of 6.458 33.

At the same time, the arithmetic mean of the original uncollated data has been calculated in H3 from the formula

@AVG(A2..A31)

This returns a value of 6.5, which is very close to our estimate on the basis of the frequency distribution.

Our next objective will be to calculate the modal class interval on the basis of the frequency distribution. Since this is such a small data set you can immediately see that the class interval 2.5–5.5 has got the highest frequency (eight observations).

However, for larger data sets it might be useful if we could get Lotus to calculate this value for us. Since the mode is the most frequently occurring value of the variable we are obviously looking for the value of X' associated with the maximum value in the frequency distribution range @MAX(C2..C8).

You should be able to see, however, that all this last formula will do is to return the maximum value of the *frequency*, and *not* the value of X' associated with that frequency.

To get Lotus to do what we want requires that we have an understanding of the LOOKUP function. This function can either search a range of columns (@VLOOKUP) or a range of rows (@HLOOKUP), but in either case the syntax of the function is the same. Since our data is constructed in columns we will use the @VLOOKUP function which has the following syntax:

@VLOOKUP (Value to be looked up, Range of cells in which to look,
  Column offset to determine the looked up value to be
  returned)

For example, suppose that from the data in Worksheet 9.7 we wanted Lotus to return the value of X associated with a frequency of 3. Clearly the answer is 14.5, but to obtain this from the @VLOOKUP function we should write

@VLOOKUP(3,C2..E8,2)

This means 'look up the value of 3 in the *first* column of the lookup range (column C) and then return the associated value from the column that is 2 columns removed (offset) from the first column (i.e. column E)'.

If you try this for yourself, then you should find that a value of 14.5 is returned. (Now you should appreciate why we reproduced the values of X in column E, since the @VLOOKUP function cannot work 'backwards' by having a negative value for the offset. The value to be returned must *always* be to the right of the value to be looked up.)

Bearing these ideas in mind, you can obtain an estimate of the modal class by entering the following formula in H10:

@VLOOKUP(@MAX(C2..C8),C2..E8,2)

A value of 5.5 will be returned, indicating that the 3.5–5.5 interval is the modal class. (Notice how the @MAX function has been 'nested' in the @VLOOKUP function.)

You can also use the @VLOOKUP function to calculate the median class interval if you remember that the median is defined as that value of the variable above and below which 50 per cent of the observations lie.

This means that in this example we are seeking the value of X associated with the 30th/2 = 15th *cumulative* frequency. This is easily calculated from the following formula:

$$@VLOOKUP(D8/2, D2..E8, 1)$$

Remember that *for this data set* D8 will always contain the total number of observations, so D8/2 will calculate the middle observation. Furthermore, since the cumulative frequencies are contained in column D and the values of X in column

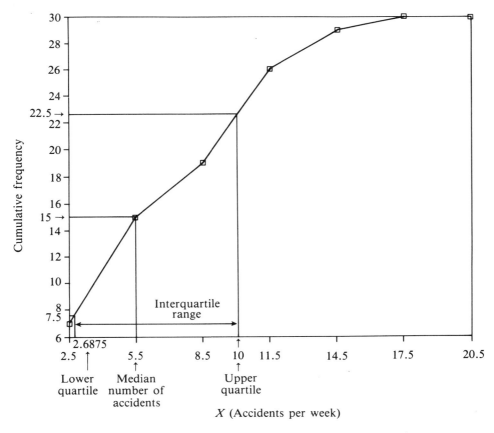

Figure 9.11 Cumulative frequencies of accidents per week

E, this defines our lookup range, while the offset of 1 ensures that it is the associated value of X that is returned.

This formula has been entered to the H17 cell, and returns a value of 5.5, indicating that the median class is 2.5–5.5. If you now examine the *ordered* raw data (which have been placed in column I) you will see that 15 observations have a value of 5 or less, while the remaining 15 have a value of 7 or more. The median is therefore $(5 + 7)/2 = 6$.

Furthermore, since the cumulative frequency associated with the upper end of the class interval is actually the middle one (the 15th), this means that the estimated value of the median can be taken as 5.5.

However, this piece of good fortune cannot always be guaranteed, and you should appreciate that it is quite possible for the middle observation to lie between the upper and lower limits of the class interval. In this case the median itself must also be located within this interval, and the easiest way of determining its exact location is to use the cumulative frequency distribution graph that we constructed earlier. All you have to do is read off the value of X associated with the middle cumulative frequency. This has been done in Figure 9.11, where our conclusion that the median was 5.5 is confirmed. However, with different data sets and different frequencies, the graph is quite capable of indicating that the median can lie at some intermediate point in the class interval. The graph also indicates some other features which will soon be explained.

9.6 Measures of dispersion in simple data sets

Much of the purpose of calculating the various measures of central tendency is so that they can be used as benchmarks in the process of calculating the extent to which the data are dispersed. This is because dispersion is not really an absolute concept, but rather a relative one, in which the arithmetic spread of the data elements is related to one or other of their central values.

For this reason, although the difference between the maximum and the minimum value of x (known as *the range*) is the simplest and most obvious measure of dispersion, it is of limited analytical value. This is because two different data sets are capable of having the same values for the range, yet are equally capable of displaying completely different patterns of dispersion in between their two identical polar values. You can see this quite clearly in the following two data sets (*a* and *b*):

a 10, 48, 49, 50, 51, 52, 100
b 10, 100, 100, 100, 100, 100

Clearly there is only one extreme observation in the second data set (10), as opposed to a much wider spread in the first, and for this reason we would feel intuitively justified in arguing that the first set was more dispersed than the second. Yet their range values are the same.

To deal with this deficiency we should think in terms of measuring the difference (or deviation) of each individual x value from its central (arithmetic mean) value, and then using the sum of these deviations as our measure of dispersion. That is, we define the deviation (d_i) of each individual x value (x_i) from its arithmetic mean value ($\bar{x}$) as

$$d_i = x_i - \bar{x} \qquad (i = 1, ..., n)$$

and the sum of these deviations as

$$\Sigma d_i = \Sigma (x_i - \bar{x}) \qquad (i = 1, ..., n)$$

You can see how this can be done in Worksheet 9.8, where the data (in column A) refer to output of a particular factory over a period of seven days.

The arithmetic mean of the data set has been calculated in A10 [@AVG(A2..A8)], and then, in column B, this mean value has been subtracted from each value of x (to produce d). The formula in B2 is therefore

$$+A2 - A\$10$$

and this has been copied into B3..B8.

Finally, in B10, the sum of these deviations has been calculated from the formula

@SUM(B2..B8)

As you can see, this sum turns out to be zero for this data set, and therein lies the fundamental problem with this approach. By this we mean that it is not coincidence in this data set that the sum of deviations is zero, it will *always* be the case for *all* data sets, since the process of subtracting the arithmetic mean from

---

WORKSHEET 9.8

	A	B	C
1	x	d	d^2
2	45	-0.71428	0.510204
3	56	10.28571	105.7959
4	23	-22.7142	515.9387
5	48	2.285714	5.224489
6	50	4.285714	18.36734
7	46	0.285714	0.081632
8	52	6.285714	39.51020
9	Arithmetic Mean		
10	45.71428	0.00	685.4285
11			
12			variance
13	97.91836		97.91836
14			
15			standard
16			deviation
17	9.895371		9.895371

each observation inevitably produces positive and negative deviations, which collectively sum to zero. In short, this means it is always the case that

$$\Sigma d_i \quad (i = 1, \ldots, n) = 0$$

This creates a serious problem in our attempt to devise an accurate measure of dispersion, since the clear implication is that as measured by the summed deviations from the arithmetic mean, all data sets will have the *same index of dispersion*, and that this index will be zero. As a method of distinguishing between different degrees of dispersion in various data sets, such an index is obviously useless.

However, the principle involved in our definition of dispersion remains sound, and if we could only devise some way of preventing the positive and negative deviations from cancelling one another out, then the method could be retained.

This is easily done by *squaring* each deviation and then calculating the associated *sum of squared deviations*. This means that we calculate

$$(d_i)^2 = (x_i - \bar{x})^2$$

and then sum each of these squared deviations to obtain

$$\Sigma (d_i)^2 = \Sigma (x_i - \bar{x})^2$$

This has been done in column C of Worksheet 9.8 from the formula (in C2)

$$+ B2\char`\^2 \quad \text{(copied into C3..C8)}$$

The sum of these squared deviations is calculated in the usual manner in C10, and as you can see returns a value of 685.4285. In other words

$$\Sigma (d_i)^2 = 685.4285$$

This statistic is (nearly) our best measure of dispersion in relation to the arithmetic mean, but if you think about it, then you will realize that it is inevitably sensitive to the *total number of observations*. This would mean that a widely dispersed data set with only a few observations could have a lower value for the sum of squared deviations than a concentrated data set in which there were a large number of observations. In other words, more observations means more deviations, and this means that there is a greater chance of there being a high value for the sum of squared deviations.

To deal with this we must *standardize* the index of dispersion (as measured by the sum of squared deviations) by the total number of observations (n). This produces the following statistic, which is known as the *variance* of x:

$$\text{variance of } x = [\Sigma (d_i)^2]/n$$

Finally, to compensate for having squared the deviations earlier we can take the square root of the variance to produce a statistic known as the *standard deviation*:

$$\text{standard deviation of } x = [\Sigma (d_i)^2]^{0.5}$$

Both the variance and the standard deviation of x have been calculated in

Worksheet 9.8 from the following formulae:

in C13   +C10/7
in C17   +C13^0.5

As you can see, values of 97.91 and 9.895 are returned.

Now that you have learnt the logic on which the variance and the standard deviation are founded, you can ask Lotus to save you some time by using its dedicated variance and standard deviation functions. These have the following syntax:

@VAR(DATA RANGE)
@STD(DATA RANGE)

For our illustration the data range is A2..A8, and so you can enter the appropriate function in the A13 and A17 cells. You should find that the same results as were calculated earlier are returned.

The variance and the standard deviation are by far the most frequently used measures of dispersion, and are to be interpreted as meaning that the *higher* is the arithmetic value of either of these statistics, then the *greater* is the degree of dispersion displayed by the data set from which they were calculated.

Although this conclusion is generally valid, a slight problem arises when, instead of just measuring dispersion within a data set, we attempt to *compare* the dispersion between two data sets that are measured in different units. To understand this point more clearly consider the following example.

EXAMPLE 9.8

The following two data sets refer to the weekly take-home pay of seven British and seven French employees.

British pay (£)   140.23, 156.50, 123.21, 99.99, 178.87, 147.67, 161.25.

French pay (francs)   1500.56, 1410.76, 1300.00, 1000.78, 1850.56, 1450.80, 1670.90.

Which of the two data sets has the greatest degree of dispersion?

SOLUTION 9.8

The two data sets have been entered into columns A and B of Worksheet 9.9 and the arithmetic mean and standard deviation of both data sets calculated in rows 11 and 15.

As you can see, both the arithmetic mean and the standard deviation take-home pay for the French employees is considerably higher than for their British counterparts, but we should immediately suspect such a simple conclusion on the

WORKSHEET 9.9

	A	B	C
1	x (£)	y (francs)	y/10
2	140.23	1500.56	150.056
3	156.5	1410.76	141.076
4	123.21	1300	130
5	99.99	1000.78	100.078
6	178.87	1850.56	185.056
7	147.67	1450.8	145.08
8	161.25	1670.9	167.09
9			
10	mean	mean	mean
11	143.96	1454.9085714	145.49085714
12			
13	standard	standard	standard
14	deviation	deviation	deviation
15	24.10247	249.99194407	24.999194407
16			
17	coeff. of	coeff. of	
18	variation	variation	
19	16.74%	17.18%	

grounds that the units in which the variables are measured are also different. To be exact, since a pound sterling is approximately equivalent to 10 French francs, we really should adjust one or other of the data sets to take account of this fact.

This is done in column C of the worksheet where the French pays have been divided by 10.

When you calculate the arithmetic mean and standard deviation of this adjusted data set, then you can see that the differences in central tendency and dispersion that were previously observed have now almost disappeared.

In this case, we were able to use our knowledge of the exchange rate to convert one of the data sets to the same units as the other, but what should we do if such a conversion factor is not readily available?

The answer is that we can form a statistic known as the *coefficient of variation* (cv), which is defined for each data set as

$$cv = 100(\text{standard deviation}/\text{arithmetic mean}) \text{ per cent}$$

What this statistic does is to provide a *relative* measure of dispersion in the sense that the dispersion in the data set (as measured by the standard deviation) is related to the arithmetic mean value, thereby compensating for any overestimation that may have occurred as a result of differences in measurement units. Of course it will also compensate for any differences in the magnitude of the observations in the two data sets that *are not due* to different measurement units, but if there is no difference apart from this, then the coefficient of variation will return an equal value for both data sets.

Z scores   429

When this statistic is calculated for each of the original two data sets (in A19 and B19) then you can see that the relative dispersion in the two data sets is approximately the same. The formulae in A19 and B19 are (A15/A11) and (B15/B11) and these have been formatted to show percentages (/DFP).

9.7 Z scores

The last example has indicated some of the difficulties that can be encountered when data sets need to be compared. To see another illustration of this and an important remedy, consider the following example.

EXAMPLE 9.9 ══

Two groups (A and B) of five trainees were assessed by two different training officers (X and Y). Group A was assessed by officer X and group B was assessed by officer Y, and the following percentage marks awarded:

group A % mark   40, 45, 50, 55, 60
group B % mark   60, 80, 80, 95, 100

Can you conclude on the basis of this data that group B contains a better set of trainees than group A?

SOLUTION 9.9 ═══

The problem here lies in trying to decide whether it is differences in the capabilities of the trainees that has been measured, or differences in the expectations and marking practices of the two assessors.

To help us to do this we can first of all calculate the arithmetic mean and standard deviation mark of both groups. This is done in Worksheet 9.10.

You can easily see that group B has got both the highest arithmetic mean and standard deviation mark, but as the coefficient of variation indicates, the relative difference in dispersion between the two groups is not as wide as casual inspection suggests.

Nevertheless, the coefficient of variation does not allow us to devise a *standardized mark* for each of the trainees that can then be used to compensate for any differences in the severity of assessment that may exist between the two assessors.

To do this we must employ a statistic known as the Z score, which is defined as the difference between the raw score and the arithmetic mean score of the group, divided by the standard deviation score of the group. That is, for each group

$$Z = (\text{raw score} - \text{mean score})/\text{standard deviation score}$$

WORKSHEET 9.10

E2: (F4)[W16](B2-B$11)/B$15

	A	B	C	D	E	F
1	Trainee	Group A	Trainee	Group B	Z score A	Z score B
2	V	40	P	60	-1.4142	-1.6429
3	W	45	Q	80	-0.7071	-0.2143
4	X	50	R	80	-0.0000	-0.2143
5	Y	55	S	95	0.7071	0.8571
6	Z	60	T	100	1.4142	1.2143
7						
8						
9						
10		mean A		mean B	mean Z score A	mean Z score B
11		50		83	0.00	0.00
12						
13		standard		standard	standard	standard
14		deviation A		deviation B	deviation Z	deviation Z
15		7.07106781		14	score A	score B
16		Coeff. of		Coeff. of	1.00	1.00
17		Variation A		Variation B		
18		14.14%		16.87%		
19						
20						

	A	B	C	D
	Raw	Raw	Z score	Z score
	Order	Score	Order	
21				
22	V	40	Z	1.4142
23	W	45	T	1.2143
24	X	50	S	0.8571
25	Y	55	Y	0.7071
26	Z	60	X	0.0000
27	P	60	R	-0.2143
28	Q	80	Q	-0.2143
29	R	80	W	-0.7071
30	S	95	V	-1.4142
31	T	100	P	-1.6429

These Z scores (Z_A and Z_B) have been calculated in columns E and F of the worksheet from the following formulae:

in E2   (B2 − B$11)/B$15
in F2   (D2 − D$11)/D$15

which were then copied into the range E3..F6.

As should be clear from the rankings in A23..D32, calculating the Z score for each of the trainees has had the effect of altering the rankings that would have been made on the basis of the original raw scores. In particular, on the basis of the raw scores the worst trainee in group B would have been ranked equally with the best trainee in group A. However, on the basis of the Z scores this ranking has been altered, with the best trainee in group A now being ranked best overall, and the worst trainee in group B achieving a lower Z score than the worst in A. The new rankings have been calculated in the range D23..D32 of the worksheet.

This reordering of the ranks has been entirely due to the fact that the Z score takes account of relative as opposed to absolute performance, in the sense that each individual's mark is related to the mean performance of his or her group and the dispersion of marks within that group.

You should also note that each set of Z scores possesses the useful property that the arithmetic mean is zero, and the standard deviation is 1. You can confirm this in your worksheet by asking Lotus to calculate these statistics for each of the Z score ranges (E2..E6, and F2..F6).

Now, if we argue that passing the assessment should be a relative criterion rather than an absolute one, then you should be able to see that we can define the relative pass mark as greater than or equal to zero. This will ensure that only those trainees who perform at least as well as the mean performance of their group will be deemed to have passed the assessment. The disadvantage of this approach is, of course, that in an exceptionally poor group of trainees some will still pass, while in an outstanding group some will have to fail. This may well be what is required by the assessors (if, for example, only a fixed percentage of the trainees out of each intake are to be offered permanent positions), but it is cold comfort for those able trainees who happen to be part of an extremely able group but will nevertheless be rejected.

Another illustration of this problem can be found in competitions where four heats of say five contestants are examined (quizzed) and the winners of each heat plus 'the best runner-up' proceed to the final.

However, in the light of the previous discussion it should be clear that identifying the best runner-up is not as straightforward as it sounds. Most competitions of this sort define it as the second placed competitor with the highest absolute score. Yet if there is a fixed number of points to be gained (meaning that points are gained at the expense of other competitors in the heat), then relative performance should be considered.

For example, in a heat in which two contestants score all the points (the other three scoring zero), the runner-up's absolute score is likely to be higher than in a heat where the points are more evenly distributed.

In other words, it is easier to obtain a high score in a non-competitive heat than in a competitive one.

For this reason the 'best' runner up really should be defined as the one with the highest Z score. This will mean that since the mean score will be the same for all heats (there is a fixed number of points and competitors), the highest Z score will tend to be produced by heats in which the standard deviation number of points is low (i.e. with a narrow competitive spread of points).

9.8 Measures of dispersion in collated data sets

When the data have been collated into a frequency distribution, then although you can still use the Lotus @VAR and @STDVN functions to calculate the variance and standard deviation from the raw data, they cannot be used to extract these statistics from the frequency distribution.

To do this requires that we proceed in a manner similar to that which was explained in relation to the calculation of the arithmetic mean for grouped data.

By way of explanation, reconsider the data from Example 9.3 which have been reproduced from the first seven columns of Worksheet 9.7 in Worksheet 9.11.

As in the case of calculating the arithmetic mean, our first approach must recognize that since there are several observations associated with each midpoint value of X, then there must be an associated number of deviations for each of these values. In other words, since there are eight observations with a midpoint value of 4, then there must also be eight deviations and eight squared deviations of this midpoint value from the arithmetic mean value.

The arithmetic worth of all eight of these squared deviations is therefore given by

$$8[(4 - \bar{x})^2]$$

More generally, we can calculate the arithmetic worth of the squared deviations for each class interval by forming the product of the relevant frequency and the associated squared deviation of the midpoint value of X from the arithmetic mean value. This has been done in column H of the worksheet under the heading f(d^2) (i.e. each frequency times its squared deviation). Notice, of course, that each deviation is now defined as the difference between the midpoint value of X and the arithmetic mean value. That is

$$d_i = (X_i' - \bar{x})$$

Accordingly, and noticing that the estimated arithmetic mean value of x has been calculated in G12, the formula in H2 is

$$+\text{C2}*((\text{F2} - \text{G\$12})\char`\^2)$$

This has then been copied into the H3..H8 range.

Finally, the estimated variance and the standard deviation of the frequency distribution have been calculated in the H12 and H16 cells from the following

WORKSHEET 9.11

	A	B	C	D	E	F	G	H
	x	X	f	cf	X	X'	fX'	f(d^2)
1								
2	9	2.5	7	7	2.5	1.25	8.75	189.8871
3	7	5.5	8	15	5.5	4	32	48.34722
4	1	8.5	4	19	8.5	7	28	1.173611
5	0	11.5	7	26	11.5	10	70	87.80381
6	10	14.5	3	29	14.5	13	39	128.3802
7	5	17.5	1	30	17.5	16	16	91.04340
8	11	20.5	0	30	20.5	19	0	0
9	12							
10	1		actual				est.	est.
11	2		mean				mean	var
12	11		6.5				6.458	18.22118
13	10		actual					
14	1		var					est.
15	7		17.91					st. dev.
16	4		actual					4.268627
17	5		st. dev.					
18	11		4.015					
19	0							
20	15							
21	3							
22	5							
23	5							
24	5							
25	7							
26	5							
27	12							
28	13							
29	7							
30	10							
31	1							

formulae:

in H12 @SUM(H2..H8)/@SUM(C2..C8)
in H16 +H12^0.5

Notice that these estimates are quite close to the true values that we have calculated in B15 and B18 from the dedicated Lotus variance and standard deviation formulae — @VAR(A2..A31) and @STD(A2..A31).

Although the variance and the standard deviation are the most common measures of dispersion, you may be wondering what should be done if it has been decided that the median is the most appropriate measure of central tendency for this particular data set.

The answer is that we can employ a statistic known as the *interquartile range* to measure the range within which the middle 50 per cent of the data observations lie.

Index numbers

To understand how this is constructed, remember that the median was defined as that value of x above and below which 50 per cent of the observations lie.

In a similar way, the upper quartile value of x is defined as that value of x above which 25 per cent of the observations lie, and the lower quartile value of x as that value of x below which 25 per cent of the observations lie. Clearly then, 50 per cent of the observations will lie between the upper and lower quartiles, and the lower the range of x values that include these 50 per cent of observations, then the less is the dispersion of the data in relation to its median value.

You can read the upper and lower quartile values for the data in Worksheet 9.11 from the cumulative frequency graph produced earlier in Figure 9.11, where, since 25 per cent of the observations will be less than the 7.5th cumulative frequency, and 25 per cent of the observations will be greater than the 22.5th cumulative frequency, we obtain a value of 2.6875 for the lower quartile, and a value of 10 for the upper quartile. The interquartile range is therefore $10 - 2.6875 = 7.2125$.

9.9 Index numbers

An index number is simple a statistical method of measuring the change in one or more data items between two different time periods. Conventionally the earlier time period is known as the base period and identified by the subscript 'b', while the later one is referred to as the current period and identified by the subscript 'c'.

Also by convention, the calculation of the index number is such that the value of the index in the base period is denoted by 100. This means that any change in the value of the index (to 114 for example) can immediately be expressed in percentage terms as 14 per cent.

You will almost certainly have encountered some type of index number at some time or another, since they are regularly used to make time period comparisons of a number of business and economic variables. The index of retail prices is perhaps the most famous, but you may have heard of the sterling exchange rate index, the Dow-Jones stock market index, the index of consumer expenditure, or the index of industrial production. In all of these cases, the fundamental point to remember is that they are all simply statistical measures of the average percentage change in the quantity, price or value of a data set of related items between some chosen base period and the current period.

To see some of the issues involved in the construction of index numbers consider the following example.

EXAMPLE 9.10

The following data refer to the annual purchase quantities of three different types of electronic equipment from a large retail outlet in 1980 and 1990.

	Purchase quantity (000s)	
Item	1980	1990
Televisions	15.62	17.45
Video recorders	10.67	15.90
Stereo systems	17.90	18.78

Calculate an index number that will measure the change in the purchase quantities of all three items between the two years.

SOLUTION 9.10

Our first step is to denote the purchase quantity in 1980 as Q_b, and the equivalent value in 1990 as Q_c, and then form the following ratio:

$$\Sigma Q_c / \Sigma Q_b = (17.45 + 15.90 + 18.78)/(15.62 + 10.67 + 17.90)$$
$$= 52.13/44.19 = 1.1797$$

This ratio is then multiplied by 100 to give a value of 117.97, which is our index number for the change in purchase quantities between 1980 and 1990, and indicates that there has been a 17.97 per cent increase in purchases.

In this simple form the index number has supplied us with some useful information, but you should be able to see that it is deficient in the sense that only physical quantities have been measured, and no account has been taken of the prices at which these items of electronic equipment were sold. This is an important omission since a 10 per cent increase in an item that sells for £100 is less significant in monetary terms than a 2 per cent increase in an item that sells for £1000.

To take account of this deficiency we must introduce the prices of the items in both the current period (P_c) and in the base period (P_b).

This has been done in Worksheet 9.12, along with a few additional calculations that will soon be explained.

The entries in rows 6 and 7 calculate expenditure on each of the three items in

WORKSHEET 9.12

	A	B	C	D	E	F
1		Televisions	Videos	Stereos		
2	Q<b> (1980)	15.62	10.67	17.9		
3	P<b> (1980)	260	340	180		
4	Q<c> (1990)	17.45	15.9	18.78		
5	P<c> (1990)	230	299	210		
6	Q<b>P<b>	4061.2	3627.8	3222	10911	Exp Index
7	Q<c>P<c>	4013.5	4754.1	3943.8	12711	116.50

each of the two years from the following products:

$$\text{base period expenditure} = Q_b P_b$$

(The Lotus formulae in B6..D6 are +B2*B3, +C2*C3 and +D2*D3).

$$\text{current period expenditure} = Q_c P_c$$

(The Lotus formulae in B7..D7 are +B4*B5, +C4*C5 and +D4*D5).

The total expenditure on all three items for each of the years is then obtained by summing the individual expenditure items ($\Sigma Q_b P_b$ and $\Sigma Q_c P_c$), so the Lotus formulae in E6 and E7 are @SUM(B6..D6) and @SUM(B7..D7).

On the basis of these calculations you can now calculate an expenditure index number by forming the ratio between the current period's total expenditure (in E7) and the base period's total expenditure (in E6), and then multiplying this ratio by 100. This has been done in the F7 cell and returns a value of 116.50.

Although the expenditure index can be a useful statistic, there is more than this to be obtained from the information provided.

In particular, there will be circumstances in which we want to compare the quantities between the two periods rather than the expenditure. To do this we must weight each quantity by an appropriate price, but this raises the apparent difficulty that using the appropriate price would simply produce the expenditure index ($\Sigma Q_c P_c / \Sigma Q_b P_b$).

However, we can deal with this problem if we think in terms of weighting the two different period quantities by either the base period's prices or the current period's prices. This would mean that we could value the base period's quantities as if the current period's prices had prevailed at that time (current weighting), or alternatively, value the current period's quantities as if the base period's prices still prevailed (base weighting).

These ideas can be summarized in the following two expressions:

$$\text{base weighted quantity index number} = \Sigma Q_c P_b / \Sigma Q_b P_b$$

As you can see, the subscripts for the quantities are different in the numerator and the denominator (meaning that quantities are being compared), but the subscripts for the prices are the same (meaning that the quantities are both being valued at base period prices).

By a similar logic we have:

$$\text{current weighted quantity index number} = \Sigma Q_c P_c / \Sigma Q_b P_c$$

In this case, it should be clear that the quantities in both periods are being valued at current period prices.

Lotus can perform these calculations for you, as Worksheet 9.13 indicates. The entries in row 8 are simply the current quantities valued at base period prices (+B4*B3, +C4*C3, etc.), while those in row 9 are the base quantities valued at current period prices (+B2*B5, +C2*C5, etc.).

This allows us to calculate the base weighted quantity index number in F10 from

WORKSHEET 9.13

	A	B	C	D	E	F
1		Televisions	Videos	Stereos		
2	Q<b> (1980)	15.62	10.67	17.9		
3	P<b> (1980)	260	340	180		
4	Q<c> (1990)	17.45	15.9	18.78		
5	P<c> (1990)	230	299	210		
6	Q<b>P<b>	4061.2	3627.8	3222	10911	Exp Index
7	Q<c>P<c>	4013.5	4754.1	3943.8	12711	116.50
8	Q<c>P<b>	4537	5406	3380.4	13323	base weighted quantity index
9	Q<b>P<c>	3592.6	3190.33	3759	10541	122.11
10						
11						current weighted quantity index
12						
13						104.92
14						base weighted price index
15						
16						96.62
17						current weighted price index
18						
19						95.41

the Lotus formula 100*E8/E6, and the current weighted quantity index number in F13 from 100*D7/D9.

As you can see, both index numbers indicate that there has been a significant increase in the volume of sales of electronic equipment.

If we can use this technique to calculate quantity index numbers, then it should be an easy matter to reverse the logic to calculate base weighted and current weighted price index numbers.

This has been done in Worksheet 9.13, where the index numbers in F17 and F20 have been calculated from the following two expressions:

base weighted price index number = $\Sigma Q_b P_c / \Sigma Q_b P_b$
(in F17   100*E9/E6)

Once again the weights have the same subscripts on the top and bottom of the expression (base period quantities), while the feature being compared (prices) has different subscripts.

By a similar logic:

current weighted price index number = $\Sigma Q_c P_c / \Sigma Q_c P_b$
(in F20: 100*E7/E8)

Clearly the decade has displayed a decline in the overall price of electronic equipment, regardless of whether these prices are base weighted or current weighted by the quantities sold.

Now that you are familiar with the principles involved in calculating index numbers you should realize that the choice of whether to use base weights or current weights is never an easy one.

However, the fact that using current weights means that the index numbers have to be recalculated each period, and that comparison is only possible between the current and the base period, has had the effect of making base weighted index numbers more popular.

On the other hand, using base weights is clearly only justified for as long as those weights remain generally relevant to the current period and to the variable being compared. Nevertheless, as long as a sensible approach is adopted to the process of updating the weights (by choosing a new base period and/or including new products to the 'basket' of items), then the fact that period on period series of base weighted index numbers can easily be calculated and used for purposes of comparison is a major advantage of this method.

9.10 Exercises

9.1

Collate the following data set into a frequency distribution, and from this distribution estimate the arithmetic mean and the median of the data:

x 9, 7, 8, 9, 6, 6, 4, 2, 1, 0, 4, 2, 2, 9, 6, 5, 4, 8, 7, 7, 8, 1, 0, 2, 4,
9, 7, 6, 6, 1, 1, 0, 2, 1, 4, 3, 1, 7, 8

9.2

To what extent does the data set given in Table 9.3 justify the conclusion that 'country A has a higher level of family income than country B, but country B has a more equal distribution of that income'?

Table 9.3

Family income (£000s)	% of A families	% of B families
< 5	16.0	0.5
≥ 5 but < 10	13.0	1.0
≥ 10 but < 15	9.0	22.0
≥ 15 but < 20	5.0	25.0
≥ 20 but < 25	4.5	24.0
≥ 25 but < 30	3.5	7.0
≥ 30 but < 35	3.0	4.5
≥ 35 but < 40	3.0	4.5
≥ 40 but < 45	4.0	4.0
≥ 45 but < 50	4.5	2.5
≥ 50 but < 55	3.5	2.0
≥ 55 but < 60	5.0	1.5
≥ 60 but < 65	8.0	1.0
≥ 65 but < 70	10.0	0.5
≥ 70	8.0	0.0

9.3

The data in Table 9.4 refer to the sales volumes (Q), selling prices (P), and unit production costs (C) of a firm's three products (X, Y and Z) over the last four years.

Calculate four base weighted price index numbers and four base weighted cost index numbers for each of the four years, and display them in an appropriate chart.

9.4

The data in Table 9.5 refer to the marks obtained by two groups of students in a final examination in quantitative methods.

Calculate each student's Z score in the examination, and then taking both groups together, rank their relative performances.

Table 9.4

	Year			
	1987	1988	1989	1990
X sales (000s)	12.90	13.20	14.00	14.50
X price (£s)	0.40	0.45	0.50	0.59
X costs (£s)	0.35	0.39	0.42	0.49
Y sales (000s)	2.80	3.70	4.60	4.80
Y price (£s)	0.95	1.25	1.50	1.99
Y costs (£s)	0.78	1.02	1.25	1.75
Z sales (000s)	7.45	8.35	9.78	10.50
Z price (£s)	1.25	1.78	1.99	2.30
Z costs (£s)	1.00	1.23	1.65	1.95

Table 9.5

Student identification number	Group A % mark	Student identification number	Group % mark
001	42	008	56
002	43	009	60
003	47	010	59
004	50	011	65
005	44	012	68
006	42	013	70
007	46	014	65

9.5

Over a period of nine months a small business carried out 100 insulation projects. A scheduled completion time was calculated for each project at the time of tender, and after completion, the number of days above ($+$) or below ($-$) schedule was recorded (to the nearest half day). The results were as shown in Table 9.6.

(a) Calculate the arithmetic mean, the median and the mode for these data.
(b) Calculate the standard deviation and the interquartile range for these data.
(c) A project that is completed on or before schedule produces a net profit of £500, whereas a project that is late produces a penalty payment of 2 per cent of the net profit per half day that completion is above schedule.
    Calculate the average net profit to the business from these 100 projects.

Table 9.6

x (days)	Number of projects
−1.5	10
−1.0	5
−0.5	17
0.0	40
0.5	18
1.0	5
1.5	3
2.0	2

9.6

The data in Table 9.7 refer to the annual percentage increase in the price of a company's ordinary shares over the period 1984–1989.

Calculate the most appropriate measure of the average increase in share price over the period.

Table 9.7

Year	% increase in share price
1984	7
1985	8
1986	10
1987	12
1988	15
1989	18

9.7

A transport firm owns a fleet of six lorries which, on a particular week, recorded the distance and fuel consumption figures shown in Table 9.8.

Calculate the most appropriate measure of the average miles per gallon of the fleet.

Table 9.8

Lorry number	Distance (miles)	Miles per gallon
1	2200	25
2	1889	28
3	2111	30
4	1656	27
5	1798	24
6	1846	20

9.8

The data in Table 9.9 refer to the annual profits (in millions of £s) from four supermarket chains (Adsa, Cesto, Po-oc and Strepo) in each of three regions of the country.

Prepare two appropriate charts that will display the relative performance of each supermarket chain in all regions, and of all supermarket chains in each region of the country.

Table 9.9

Region	Adsa	Cesto	Po-oc	Strepo
Scotland	0.61	0.45	0.71	0.56
England	5.78	6.98	7.56	8.42
Wales	0.34	0.42	0.61	0.51

9.11 Solutions to the exercises

9.1

Worksheet 9.14 provides the solution. The data distribution command was used on the data range A2..A40, with a bin range of B2..C12 (remember to enter the values of X in B2..B12 before you specify the bin range).

The raw data have been replicated and ordered in column D, where you can see that the middle (20th) observation is the (last) x value of 4.

The cumulative frequencies are calculated in column E in the same way as was done in Worksheet 9.2 (@SUM(C$2..C2), entered in E2 and then copied into E3..E12.)

Finally, the estimated arithmetic mean is calculated from @SUM(G2..G12)/@SUM(C2..C12). Notice that since class intervals were not required, the estimated mean is the same as the true mean (@AVG(A2..A40)).

9.2

You can set the data up as has been done in Worksheet 9.15.

Clearly the first contention would appear to be justified both in terms of the arithmetic mean and in terms of the median which has been calculated from the cumulative frequency diagram of Figure 9.12.

On the other hand, the modal income class for country B is between £15 000 and £20 000, whereas for country A it is less than £5000. On this measure of central tendency, the claim is not justified.

The second contention requires that we consider the dispersion of the two data sets, both absolutely and relatively. Clearly the standard deviation family income

WORKSHEET 9.14

	A	B	C	D	E	F	G
	x	X	f	x order	cf		fX
1							
2	9	0	3	0	3		0
3	7	1	6	0	9		6
4	8	2	5	0	14		10
5	9	3	1	1	15	are <=3	3
6	6	4	5	1	20	are <=4	20
7	6	5	1	1	21	est. median	5
8	4	6	5	1	26	4	30
9	2	7	5	1	31		35
10	1	8	4	1	35		32
11	0	9	4	2	39		36
12	4	10	0	2	39		0
13	2		0	2			
14	2			2			
15	9			2	true mean		est. mean
16	6			3	4.538461		4.538461
17	5			4			
18	4			4	true		
19	8			4	median		
20	7			4	4		
21	7			4			
22	8			5			
23	1			6			
24	0			6			
25	2			6			
26	4			6			
27	9			6			
28	7			7			
29	6			7			
30	6			7			
31	1			7			
32	1			7			
33	0			8			
34	2			8			
35	1			8			
36	4			8			
37	3			9			
38	1			9			
39	7			9			
40	8			9			

WORKSHEET 9.15

	A	B	C	D	E	F	G	H	I	J
	X	A	B	X'	AX'	BX'	A(d^2)	B(d^2)	cf A	cf B
1										
2	4.99999	16	0.5	2.4999	39.999	1.2499	16435.235	219.45114	16	0.5
3	9.99999	13	1	7.4999	97.499	7.4999	9512.1330	254.40250	29	1.5
4	14.99999	9	22	12.499	112.49	274.99	4375.8228	2637.8550	38	23.5
5	19.99999	5	25	17.499	87.499	437.49	1453.5126	885.06250	43	48.5
6	24.99999	4.5	24	22.499	101.24	539.99	653.41133	21.660001	47.5	72.5
7	29.99999	3.5	7	27.499	96.249	192.49	173.95878	114.81749	51	79.5
8	34.99999	3	4.5	32.499	97.499	146.24	12.607509	368.56124	54	84
9	39.99999	3	4.5	37.499	112.49	168.74	26.107485	888.31124	57	88.5
10	44.99999	4	4	42.499	169.99	169.99	252.80994	1451.6099	61	92.5
11	49.99999	4.5	2.5	47.499	213.74	118.74	754.66115	1446.0062	65.5	95
12	54.99999	3.5	2	52.499	183.74	104.99	1127.7086	1687.8049	69	97
13	59.99999	5	1.5	57.499	287.49	86.249	2633.5123	1739.1037	74	98.5
14	64.99999	8	1	62.499	499.99	62.499	6249.6196	1524.9024	82	99.5
15	69.99999	10	0.5	67.499	674.99	33.749	10857.024	970.20124	92	100
16	99.99999	8	0	84.999	679.99	0	20361.619	0	100	100

mean A	mean B	st. dev A	st. dev B
34.549	23.449	27.364163	11.920465

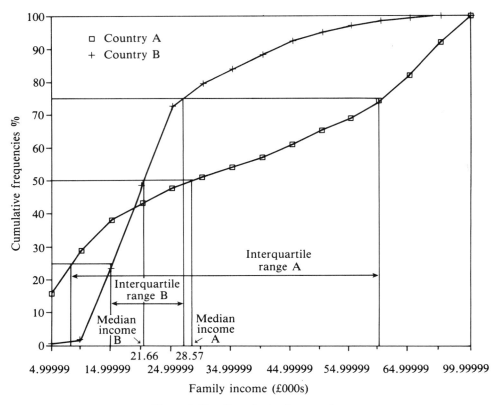

Figure 9.12 Cumulative frequencies

in A is more than twice that in B, indicating that there is a higher degree of dispersion of family incomes in A (resulting from the extremes of wealth and poverty). This justifies the second contention, which is corroborated by the fact that the middle 50 per cent of incomes in B span a range that is less than a quarter of the equivalent range for A. You can see this quite clearly from the cumulative frequency diagram where the upper and lower quartiles have been indicated for both countries.

9.3

Since a price and a cost index number is required for each year, we should regard 1987 as the base period and then view 1988, 1989 and 1990 *in turn* as the current periods.

This has been done in Worksheet 9.16.
The entry in B11 is

$$+ B3*\$B2 + B6*\$B5 + B9*\$B8$$

WORKSHEET 9.16

	A	B	C	D	E
1	Year	1987	1988	1989	1990
2	X Sales	12.9	13.2	14	14.5
3	X Price	0.4	0.45	0.5	0.59
4	X Cost	0.35	0.39	0.42	0.49
5	Y Sales	2.8	3.7	4.6	4.8
6	Y Price	0.95	1.25	1.5	1.99
7	Y Cost	0.78	1.02	1.25	1.75
8	Z Sales	7.45	8.35	9.78	10.5
9	Z Price	1.25	1.78	1.99	2.3
10	Z Cost	1	1.23	1.65	1.95
11	P<c>Q<b>	17.1325	22.566	25.4755	30.318
12	P<b>Q<b>	17.1325			
13	C<c>Q<b>	14.149	17.0505	21.2105	25.7485
14	C<b>Q<b>	14.149			
15	Price				
16	Index numbers	100	131.7145	148.6969	176.9619
17	Cost				
18	Index numbers	100	120.5067	149.9081	181.9810

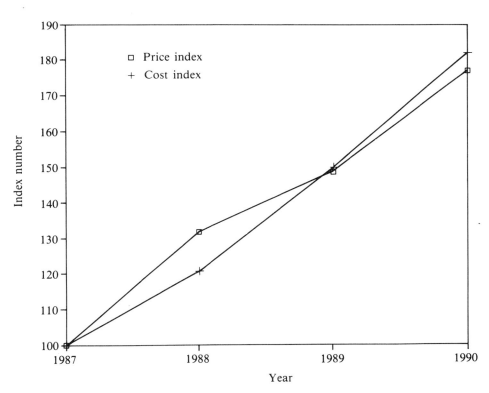

Figure 9.13 Price and cost index numbers

i.e. price times sales for each product, and this has been copied into C11..E11, where the dollar signs ensure that the price in each new year is multiplied by the sales in the base year.

Notice that although the label in A11 says Q⟨c⟩P⟨b⟩, the fact that 1987 is both the current and the base year for the purposes of calculating the first index number means that the same value will always be returned in B11 as in B12. This allows us to calculate the index number for 1987 as 100 times the ratio between B11 and B12 and ensures that this ratio will always be 100 for the base year.

The remaining price index numbers can now be calculated in C16..E16 from 100*C11/B12, 100*D11/B12 and 100*E11/B12.

A similar logic allows us to calculate the cost index numbers from the entry in B13, which is

$$+ B4*\$B2 + B7*\$B5 + B10*\$B8 \quad \text{(copied into C13..E13)}$$

In this case the cost index numbers are calculated in B18..E18 from 100*B13/B14, 100*C13/B14, 100*D13/B14 and 100*E13/B14.

A bar chart or a line chart would be an acceptable visual presentation of the two index number series and the latter of these is produced in Figure 9.13.

9.4

You can modify Worksheet 9.10 to calculate and then order the Z scores for each of the students. This would produce Worksheet 9.17.

The implication of the Z scores is that student number 4's raw score of 50 is a better *relative* performance than student number 13's raw score of 70.

9.5

The solution can be obtained from Worksheet 9.18, where the arithmetic mean and the standard deviation are calculated by the now familiar method.

By inspection, the mode is clearly 0 days, and the 50th observation also has a value of 0 days (identifying the median). The 25th cumulative frequency identifies the lower quartile to be -0.5 days, and the 75th cumulative frequency isolates the upper quartile as a value of 0.5 days. This means that the interquartile range is $0.5 - (-0.5) = 1$ day, and implies that the middle 50 per cent of projects are completed within plus or minus half a day of the median number of days. Since the median is 0 days (i.e. on schedule), we can conclude that the middle 50 per cent of projects are completed either on schedule or half a day early or half a day late.

The effect upon the profits from the number of projects undertaken for each value of X is calculated in column E by multiplying each frequency (in column B) by the following conditional expression:

$$@IF(A3<=0,500,500-500*0.02*A3*2)$$

This means return a profit of £500 if the value of X is on or ahead of time,

WORKSHEET 9.17

	A	B	C	D	E	F
1	Student	Group A	Student	Group B	Z score A	Z score B
2	001	42	008	56	-1.0397504898	-1.5461646096
3	002	43	009	60	-0.6758378184	-0.697289922
4	003	47	010	59	0.7798128674	-0.9095085939
5	004	50	011	65	1.8715508817	0.3638034376
6	005	44	012	68	-0.3119251469	1.0004594533
7	006	42	013	70	-1.0397504898	1.4248967971
8	007	46	014	65	0.4159001959	0.363803476
9						
10		mean A		mean B	mean Z score A	mean Z score B
11		44.85714		63.2857142	0.00	0.00
12						
13		standard		standard	standard	standard
14		deviation A		deviation B	deviation Z	deviation Z
15		2.747912		4.71212071	score A	score B
16					1	1
17	Raw	Raw	Z Score		Z score	
18	Order	score	Order			
19						
20	001	42	004		1.87155088	
21	002	43	013		1.42489679	
22	003	47	012		1.00045945	
23	004	50	003		0.77981286	
24	005	44	007		0.41590019	
25	006	42	014		0.36380343	
26	007	46	011		0.36380343	
27	008	56	005		-0.3119251	
28	009	60	002		-0.6758378	
29	010	59	009		-0.6972899	
30	011	65	010		-0.9095085	
31	012	68	001		-1.0397504	
32	013	70	006		-1.0397504	
33	014	65	008		-1.5461646	

WORKSHEET 9.18

```
          A         B         C        D        E         F         G
 1   X (days)  Number of     fX     f(d^2)    profit
 2             Projects
 3    -1.5        10        -15     2.0736    5000
 4    -1          5          -5     0.8836    2500
 5    -0.5       17         -8.5    0.1936    8500
 6     0         40          0      0.0036   20000
 7     0.5       18          9      0.3136    8820
 8     1          5          5      1.1236    2400
 9     1.5        3          4.5    2.4336    1410
10     2          2          4      4.2436     920
11
12
13                         mean    st dev   upper      inter       profit
14                         -0.06   0.335690 quartile   quartile    per project
15                         median                0.5  range                495.5
16                          0               lower                 1
17                         mode             quartile
18                          0                        -0.5
```

otherwise reduce the profit per project by 2 per cent of £500 per half day that it is late.

This logic means that the formula in E3 is

$$+B3*(@IF(A3<=0, 500, 500-500*0.02*A3*2))$$

and when this is copied into the range E4..E10 the profit is calculated in accordance with the number of days that each project was late.

The average profit per project is then calculated in G15 from the formula

$$@SUM(E3..E10)/@SUM(B3..B10)$$

WORKSHEET 9.19

```
           A            B                 C
 1        Year       % increase in      growth
 2                   share price        factor
 3        1984            7              1.07
 4        1985            8              1.08
 5        1986           10              1.1
 6        1987           12              1.12
 7        1988           15              1.15
 8        1989           18              1.18
 9
10                  geometric mean
11                    1.1160055339
```

WORKSHEET 9.20

	A	B	C	D	E	F
1	Lorry	distance	miles per	fuel use	1/mpg	distance*1/mpg
2	Number	(miles)	gallon	(gallons)		
3						
4	1	2200	25	88	0.04	88
5	2	1889	28	67.4642857	0.03571428	67.464285714
6	3	2111	30	70.3666666	0.03333333	70.366666667
7	4	1656	27	61.3333333	0.03703703	61.333333333
8	5	1798	24	74.9166666	0.04166666	74.916666667
9	6	1846	20	92.3	0.05	92.3
10		total		total		
11		distance		fuel use		harmonic mean
12		11500		454.380952		25.309159505
13			Average			
14			mpg.			
15			25.3091595			

452   *Introductory Statistical Analysis*

9.6

Because the data are expressed as percentage rates of increase, the most appropriate measure of central tendency is the geometric mean.

Remembering to express these as *growth factors* (1 + growth rate/100) you can use Worksheet 9.19 to perform the calculations.

If you apply the calculated geometric mean as the growth factor to any chosen share price (P), then you will find that the eventual price is the same as would have been calculated from applying each of the individual growth factors. In other words

$$P(1.116)^6 = P(1.07)(1.08)(1.1)(1.12)(1.15)(1.18)$$

9.7

In this case the fact that the data are expressed as miles *per* gallon, means that we should calculate the harmonic mean as our measure of central tendency.

You can do this either from first principles, or, remembering that the distances travelled by each lorry are not the same, from the formula

$$\Sigma f / \Sigma f(1/x)$$

In either case the results are displayed in Worksheet 9.20.

The entry in D3 is simply +B3/C3 and this has been copied into D4..D8. This allows you to calculate the total fuel use by all the lorries and then find the average miles per gallon by dividing the total distance travelled by the total fuel used.

Alternatively you can calculate the harmonic mean by making the entry (+B2*1/C3) in F3, and then copying it into F4..F8. This then allows you to write the harmonic mean formula in F11 as

$$@SUM(B3..B8)/@SUM(F3..F8)$$

9.8

First of all, you should enter the data into a worksheet, and then recognize that for simultaneous presentation the stacked bar chart should be used.

Worksheet 9.21 can then be used to produce the Figures 9.14 and 9.15.

```
WORKSHEET 9.21
            A           B        C        D        E
       1               Adsa     Cesto    Po-oc    Strepo
       2   Region
       3   Scotland    0.61     0.45     0.71     0.56
       4   England     5.78     6.98     7.56     8.42
       5   Wales       0.34     0.42     0.61     0.51
```

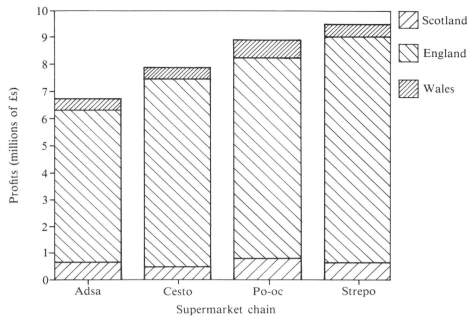

Figure 9.14 Profits of supermarkets by region

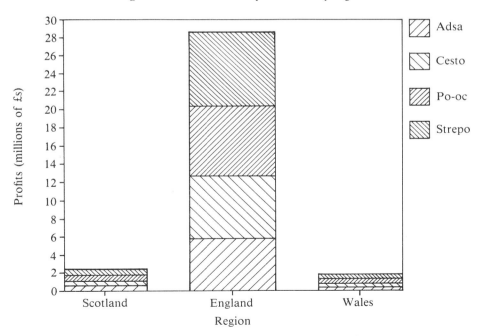

Figure 9.15 Profits of regions by supermarket

WORKSHEET 9.22

	A	B	C	D	E
1		Adsa	Cesto	Po-oc	Strepo
2	Region				
3	Scotland	0.61	0.45	0.71	0.56
4	England	5.78	6.98	7.56	8.42
5	Wales	0.34	0.42	0.61	0.51
6					
7		Adsa	Cesto	Po-oc	Strepo
8	Region				
9	Scotland	26.18	19.31	30.47	24.03
10	England	20.11	24.29	26.30	29.30
11	Wales	18.09	22.34	32.45	27.13
12					
13		Adsa	Cesto	Po-oc	Strepo
14	Region				
15	Scotland	9.06	5.73	8.00	5.90
16	England	85.88	88.92	85.13	88.72
17	Wales	5.05	5.35	6.87	5.37

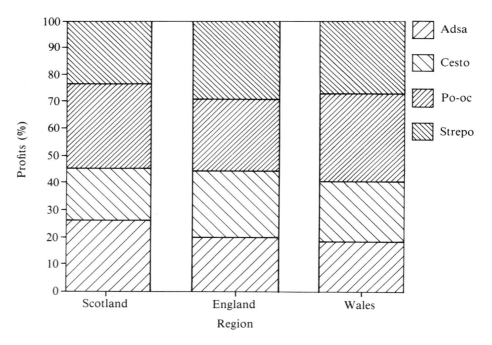

Figure 9.16 Percent component bar chart

In Figure 9.14 the X range was defined as B1..E1 and the A, B and C ranges as B3..E3, B4..E4, and B5..E5.

To obtain the graph shown in Figure 9.15, the X range was defined as A3..A5, and the A, B, C and D ranges as B3..B5, C3..C5, D3..D5 and E3..E5.

As you can see, the fact that profits for England are so much higher than for the other two regions means that the components in the Welsh and Scottish bars are swamped by the need for the scale to accommodate the English data.

You can deal with this by creating what is known as a percentage component bar chart.

To do this for each region (with the supermarkets as components) you must convert each value in the worksheet to a percentage of its row total, and then graph these new values in the same way as before.

(To obtain a percentage component bar chart for each supermarket – with the regions as components – each value in the worksheet must be expressed as a percentage of its column total.)

The necessary calculations have been done for you in Worksheet 9.22 and the resulting percentage component bar chart for each region (with supermarkets as components) has been produced in Figure 9.16.

As you can see, for the data in question it is a much more efficient visual display than the simple stacked bar chart, as long as it is acceptable to display the *relative* (as opposed to absolute) composition of profits in each region.

10
Linear Regression and Business Forecasting

10.1 Introduction

Linear regression is the process of fitting a linear relationship of the form $y = a + bx$ to a set of data observations on the variables x and y. The word regression literally means 'moving backwards', but as used in statistics it is probably more helpful to think of it as meaning 'moving towards', or 'fitting'.

Viewed in this way, linear regression can be construed as meaning the process of finding the equation of the straight line that has moved towards (i.e. fits) the observed data to the greatest extent.

It is of course possible that the observed data possess x and y coordinates that of their own accord (i.e. quite naturally) correspond exactly to the coordinates of a single straight line. This being the case, a plot of the data would produce something like Figure 10.1.

It is much more likely, however, that there will be one or more *outlying* observations whose coordinates are not consistent with those of a single unique straight line. This is shown in Figure 10.2.

In this case the regression technique can be thought of as an averaging process whereby the 'best' straight line through the data is extracted.

To understand this more clearly we will construct an example that will allow us to develop and follow the regression technique to its logical conclusion.

10.2 The problem

Suppose you have been asked by a client to determine the effect of different application levels of a new brand of fertilizer upon crop yield; and then recommend the most efficient application level. Obviously the first step must be to try and extract whatever relationship exists between crop yield and fertilizer application, and to do this we must first of all define our model and its variables.

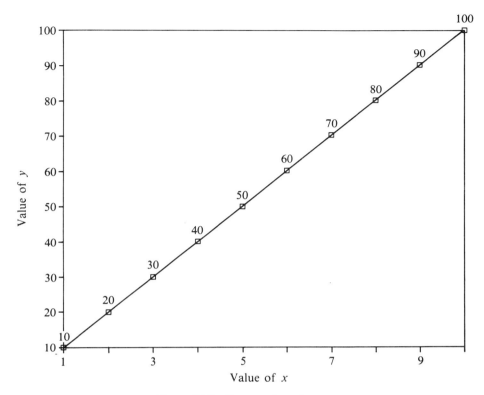

Figure 10.1 Scatter plot of y on x

10.3 The model

As you might expect, the model to be used is a linear one (since at this stage we know of no other). This is a perfectly valid first approach since linear regression can be performed easily and quickly within the Lotus 1-2-3 package or on a calculator. However, it is as well to bear in mind from the outset that there is no necessary presumption in business or anywhere else that relationships must be linear. Indeed, as we will see later, the linear model is often not justified in terms of the data, and may therefore have to be abandoned in favour of some alternative (nonlinear) model. At this stage, however, it is the logical first step, and provided we have some mechanism for identifying its limitations, it will get us started.

The presumed model is therefore linear and of the form

$$y = a + bx$$

where a is the intercept term and b is the gradient term of the presumed line.

But what are the x and y terms of this equation?

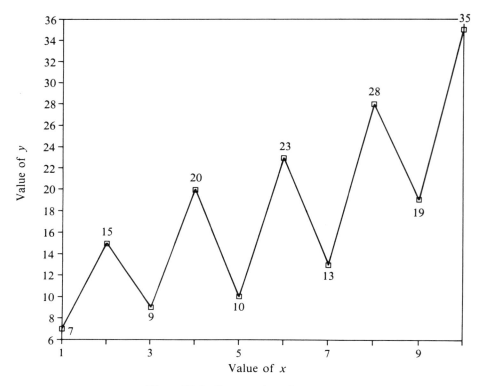

Figure 10.2 Scatter plot of y on x

In this case it is intuitively apparent that it is fertilizer application that influences crop yield rather than vice versa, and as a consequence we can identify crop yield as the dependent variable (y) and fertilizer application as the independent variable (x). Our model can therefore be verbally stated as:

crop yield is a linear function of fertilizer application.

The task of linear regression is to determine the precise nature of this relationship by finding the implied values of the intercept and gradient terms, so that an equation such as $y = 5 + 0.9x$ can be obtained.

Once again, it is as well to note at this stage that it will not always be as easy to identify the dependent and independent variables as was done above. In many real-life applications, the direction of causation (i.e. which variable influences which) will be far from clear, and this can cause untold difficulties. But in our example, as is explained in the next section, we can be fairly sure that the relationship is properly defined in terms of causation.

10.4 The data

Having defined our model, the next task is to put some 'meat on its bones' by collecting data on the relationship between crop yield and fertilizer application.

The standard approach is to perform a *controlled* experiment in which different chosen amounts of fertilizer are applied to a set of plants and their yields subsequently recorded after a given time period.

Although this is easy enough to describe, there are a number of potential difficulties that have to be considered. The most important of these are as follows:

1. The values of x (fertilizer application) chosen by the experimenter must include zero. This acts as a 'control' in the sense that it provides us with information on what yield is to be expected in the *absence* of any fertilizer application.
2. Those nonzero values of x should span a reasonable range, and should not increase in large jumps. This of course begs the question of what is 'reasonable' and what is 'large', and so the experimenter will have to be guided by prior knowledge and a realization that it will usually be impossible to perform the experiment in such a way that *continuous* application levels can be obtained.
3. The application levels must be entirely under the experimenter's control. This may seem to be the case in our example until it is remembered that measurement error is an unavoidable fact of experimental life. In most cases it will have to be accepted that data is always subject to measurement error even in the controlled laboratory (let alone in the volatile business world), and that the experimental results will inevitably reflect this error. All that can be done is to make the greatest effort to ensure that it is kept to a minimum.
4. The conditions under which the experiment is carried out must be fully controlled in terms of all the other factors that influence plant growth (such as water received, soil conditions and light exposure). Only if this can be achieved is it possible to identify the *single* effect of fertilizer application on yield, as opposed to the *combined* effect of these other factors.

This last point is important since while it may be possible to control these other factors within the confines of the laboratory, it is a different matter in real life where many business variables are subject to influence by other variables entirely beyond the company's control. You only have to think of the effect that an increase in interest rates, or a decline in the exchange rate has upon a firm's profitability to realize that these 'external' factors are uncontrollable from the firm's viewpoint, yet nevertheless exercise a crucial influence.

As if this were not enough, there is the further problem created by the fact that if you do not already know which variables influence our dependent variable, how can you control them?

For example, we would all accept that water, light and soil conditions influence plant growth, and would recognize the need to control these, but what if it were to become known that magnetic variation also exercises an effect and that this varies within the laboratory. Previous experiments that did not have a control for this effect would now be partially invalidated by such a discovery, yet were carried out in good faith by controlling for those factors known about *at the time*. The fact that our knowledge is continually increasing is little comfort to the experimenter who is trying to control factors whose effects have not been discovered.

For this reason the relationship to be investigated should always reflect the logical reasons for expecting there to be a relationship to be discovered. It is not acceptable to carry out a 'blanket' approach, whereby every independent variable that you can think of is tried in a regression model until one that 'fits' is discovered, regardless of any apparent reason for expecting there to be a relationship.

Provided these four points are fully accommodated in the experimental design, the designated independent variable (x) can truly be regarded as independent. This is important since without this knowledge it is much more difficult to identify the direction of the causal relationship between x and y. Only if the independent variable is *completely* under the experimenter's control can it be *absolutely* clear that it is x that is causing y to change rather than the other way around.

Bearing these points in mind we might proceed to establish our application levels as

$$x \quad 0, 1, 2, 3, 4, 5, 6, 7, 8, 9, 10$$

where x is measured in grams of fertilizer application per day.

Once we have decided upon our application levels, the next problem is to decide what to apply them to. Ideally we should obtain a set of *absolutely* identical plants and then apply the chosen levels to each of them (i.e. the first plant receives 0 grams, the second plant receives 1 gram, and so on). The problem with this is that it is very difficult to be sure that the plants were truly identical even in terms of their physical characteristics, let alone in terms of their genetic make-up. We have to accept that apparently identical plants differ in their inherent vigour and that this will exercise an effect upon their yield that is *not related* to the amount of fertilizer they receive.

To deal with this problem we should apply *each* application level to 11 sets of (say) 30 or so *apparently* identical plants and then record the average yield over the experimental period. This would mean that the first set of 30 plants would each receive 0 grams of fertilizer, the second set of 30 would each receive 1 gram and so on; and that the mean crop yield would be calculated and recorded as the y values corresponding to 0 grams of application, 1 gram, etc.

Suppose, now, that this is what we have done and that we obtain the results shown in Table 10.1 for y (recorded in kilos).

Even a cursory examination of the results suggests that fertilizer application has a marked effect upon yield at low application levels, but that this effect diminishes quite quickly (as saturation sets in) and eventually displays an adverse effect as the plants are being overwhelmed (poisoned) by fertilizer. This immediately casts doubt upon our linearity assumption, but we will conveniently overlook this for the

Table 10.1

x (fertilizer application, g)	y (yield, kg)
0	0.21
1	0.35
2	0.41
3	0.46
4	0.50
5	0.52
6	0.53
7	0.53
8	0.53
9	0.51
10	0.49

moment until we have seen how to perform a regression on the data we have obtained. We will, however, return to this problem at a later stage.

10.5 The scatter diagram

Our first step should always be to create a scatter diagram of the results obtained. This is shown in Figure 10.3

As you can see, there is no perfect linear pattern immediately observable, but the line that has been inserted in Figure 10.3 is not a bad 'average'. The intercept term (a) is 0.3 and the gradient term (b) is 0.025, therefore implying that the equation of our regression line is

$$y = 0.3 + 0.025x$$

But how was this line obtained?

The answer is that it was drawn in by eye, thereby raising the obvious problem that not all eyes are the same in terms of what they see. This approach would produce a myriad of different regression equations all from the same data, depending upon who was performing the experiment and how they perceived the data. Obviously this is unsatisfactory if (as should be the case) we require an objective statement of the relationship that produces the same results from a given data set *regardless* of who is performing the regression.

To obtain this we must employ an algebraic approach that is known (for reasons which will become apparent) as 'least squares'.

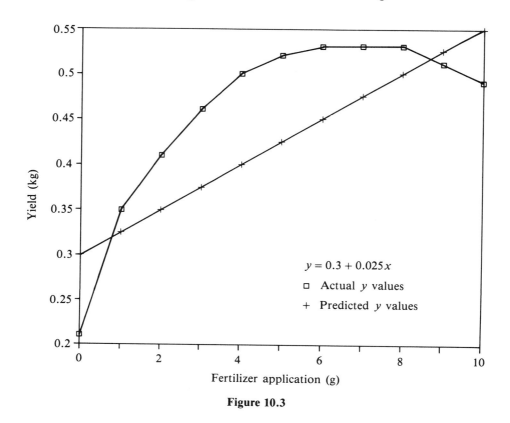

Figure 10.3

10.6 The 'least squares' regression equation

If we consider carefully what we are attempting to do with our data, then it should be apparent that we are trying to fit the 'best' straight line to the data set. This is what would have been hoped for when fitting by eye, since certain lines would be excluded on the basis that 'they don't look right'. But whereas the eye has an intuitive (albeit subjective) grasp of what looks best, how can inanimate algebra select the best line?

The answer is to ask what we really mean by 'best' and then define it in terms that algebra can understand. To do this, it would seem logical to define best as involving the *least error*; but then we encounter the problem of what is meant by error. To answer this, look at Figure 10.4, which is simply Figure 10.3 reproduced with a few amendments. These amendments take account of the fact that we are liable to become confused between the actually observed x, y coordinates and those coordinates predicted by the regression line. For this reason we refer to the observed values as

$$x_i, y_i \quad \text{where } i = 1, 2, 3, \ldots, 11$$

The 'least squares' regression equation

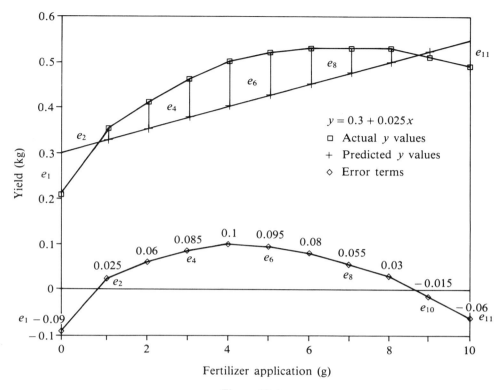

Figure 10.4

and we refer to the regression line as

$$\hat{y} = a + b(x)$$

where the 'hat' above the y term indicates that it is a *predicted value* (i.e. predicted on the basis of the regression equation).

By using this notation, we can see that for any observed value of x ($x_2 = 1$, for example) there are two associated values of y: the observed value ($y_2 = 0.35$), and the predicted value

$$\hat{y}_2 = a + b(x_2) = 0.3 + 0.025(1) = 0.325$$

This being the case, we can surely define the difference between the observed value of y when $x = x_2$, and the predicted value of y when $x = x_2$ as the second error term: e_2. Furthermore, since there are 11 pairs of x, y observations, it follows that there will be 11 error terms: $e_1, e_2, \ldots, e_{11}$, each one associated with the vertical difference between each observed y value and its associated predicted value. Each of these error terms is indicated in the lower section of the diagram above.

We can therefore define any error term as e_i and write

$$e_i = (y_i - \hat{y}_i)$$

This is a crucial definition, so make sure you understand it.

Since there are 11 error terms, it surely makes sense to define the total error as the sum of the individual errors, i.e.

$$\text{total error} = \Sigma e_i = \Sigma (y_i - \hat{y}_i)$$

Phrased in these terms, we can now see that a reasonable algebraic definition of the 'best' straight line would be:

that line which has the least total error: Σe_i

This would be perfectly valid were it not for the fact that as you can see from Figure 10.4, some of the error terms will be positive (such as e_2 and e_3), while others will be negative (such as e_1 and e_{11}). This means that the positive and negative errors will tend to cancel one another out in the addition process, with the result that under certain circumstances the total error *could* be calculated as *zero* when in fact there was not a single observation actually lying on the line.

Clearly this is unsatisfactory, since an error is an error regardless of whether it is positive or negative, and it is only an algebraic peculiarity that is masking this fact.

To deal with this problem we must employ the same device as we used with the variance in the last chapter; namely to square each error term and then use the sum of these squared errors as our measure of total (squared) error.

When we do this we obtain

$$\text{total squared error} = \Sigma(e_i^2) = \Sigma[(y_i - \hat{y})^2]$$

This statistic is often referred to as the sum of squared errors (SSE), and it is this that is to be made as small as possible. We therefore wish to find the values of a and b that define the straight line that: *minimizes the sum of squared errors*.

The technique for doing this is beyond the scope of this text, so it is enough to understand that after a lot of calculus and a lot of messy algebra two equations are produced which will allow calculation of the values of a and b that minimize the sum of squared errors:

$$b = [\Sigma(xy) - (\Sigma x)(\Sigma y/n)] / [\Sigma(x^2) - (\Sigma x)(\Sigma x/n)]$$
$$a = \bar{y} - b(\bar{x})$$

where n = the number of *pairs* of observations, and where $\bar{x}$ and $\bar{y}$ represent the arithmetic mean values of x and y respectively.

These two equations calculate the unique values of the gradient and the intercept that define the unique straight line that minimizes the sum of squared errors. This does not mean that the total squared error will be zero, simply that it is as low as is possible in a linear model, and lower than any other straight line would produce.

Whether it is good *enough* is a question we will shortly address, but for the moment it is the best that we have.

When the two equations above are evaluated for our example data set we obtain

$$b = [27.77 - (55)(5.0402/11)]/[385 - (55)(55/11)] = 0.0234$$
$$a = 0.4582 - 0.0234(5) = 0.3414$$

The predicted equation of the regression line is therefore

$$\hat{y} = 0.3414 + 0.0234x$$

An important point to notice is that this equation is defined for any finite value of x, and not just for those values of x that were applied in our experiment. This means that we can make predictions about the yield that would result from fertilizer application levels that were *not* actually applied.

When these predictions are made on the basis of values of x that lie within the observed experimental range, then this process is known as *interpolation*.

On the other hand, when the prediction uses a value of x that is outside the observed range, then this is known as *extrapolation*.

As you might imagine, extrapolation is much less accurate then interpolation for the simple reason that while a relationship may be perfectly linear within its observed range of x values, there is no mechanism for determining how it behaves beyond these x values. It *might* remain linear, but the only way to be sure about this is to extend the range of x values employed.

As you will certainly have noticed, the calculations involved in linear regression can be quite tedious even with a calculator, and so you will be pleased to know that Lotus 1-2-3 can perform them for you. To see how this works bring an empty worksheet up onto the screen and read on.

10.7 Linear regression using Lotus 1-2-3

The Lotus regression facility is a submenu of the Data command, and so to access it you must select Data from the main menu and then Regression from the menu that then appears. To see how it works it will be best to have some data in our worksheet, so enter the data from the fertilizer example into your blank worksheet. The data for x (fertilizer application) should be placed in the range A2..A12, and the data for y (yield) should be placed alongside in the range B2..B12.

Now select the Regression option and you will see that a new menu appears:

X Range Y Range Output Range Intercept Reset Go Quit

First of all, we need to define the X Range for the regression, so select X Range and then respond with A2..A12. Then do the same for the Y Range, except define it as B2..B12.

The next thing that Lotus requires is instructions on where the regression calculations are to be placed. This will require a block of cells, but you need only tell Lotus the top lefthand cell in the block. So, choose an empty cell that is close to the data (such as A14) and press the return key.

The worksheet is now ready to perform the regression and when you select 'Go' the results of the regression will be returned to the range A14..D22. You should obtain something like Worksheet 10.1.

There are several things to notice about this output. First, the intercept and gradient terms are located in D15 and C21 respectively. This means that the regression equation is

$$\hat{y} = 0.341\,363 + 0.023\,363x$$
$$= 0.34 + 0.0234x \text{ (after rounding)}$$

These figures confirm our previous result.

Secondly, there are a number of terms that have not yet been explained. Don't worry, they will be dealt with soon.

Thirdly, you will notice that the values of y predicted by the regression equation, and the associated error terms have not been produced. You may think that this is not important, but you would be mistaken. However, you can rectify this omission quite easily as shown in Worksheet 10.2.

The entry in C2 is obtained by adding the constant term from the regression output (D15) to the gradient term (C21) multiplied by the value of x (A2). But so that this can be copied into C3..C12, the row references of the cells containing the regression coefficients are fixed. This gives (in C2)

$$+ D\$15 + C\$21*A2$$

Once these terms have been evaluated, we can then ask Lotus to graph the predicted values from the regression equation and compare them with the actual values. This would produce something like Figure 10.5.

The entry in D2 is simply the difference between the actual value of y (B2) and the value of y predicted by the regression equation for the first value of x (C2). This

---

WORKSHEET 10.1

	A	B	C	D
14		Regression Output:		
15	Constant			0.341363
16	Std Err of Y Est			0.066932
17	R Squared			0.598269
18	No. of Observations			11
19	Degrees of Freedom			9
20				
21	X Coefficient(s)		0.023363	
22	Std Err of Coef.		0.006381	

$y = a + bx$

WORKSHEET 10.2

	A	B	C	D	E
1	x	y	pred y	error	squared error
2	0.00	0.21	0.341364	-0.131364	0.017256
3	1.00	0.35	0.364727	-0.014727	0.000217
4	2.00	0.41	0.388091	0.021909	0.000480
5	3.00	0.46	0.411455	0.048545	0.002357
6	4.00	0.50	0.434818	0.065182	0.004249
7	5.00	0.52	0.458182	0.061818	0.003821
8	6.00	0.53	0.481545	0.048455	0.002348
9	7.00	0.53	0.504909	0.025091	0.000630
10	8.00	0.53	0.528273	0.001727	0.000003
11	9.00	0.51	0.551636	-0.041636	0.001734
12	10.00	0.49	0.575000	-0.085000	0.007225
13				Sum of Squ Errs	0.040319

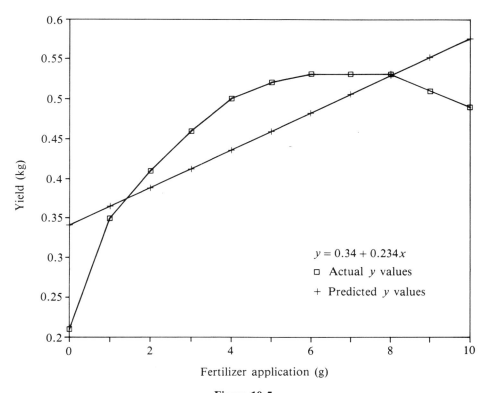

Figure 10.5

is the error term associated with the first x, y observation (e_1), i.e. $+B2-C2$. This entry has then been copied into the range D3..D12.

The entry in E2 is the square of the first x, y observation's error term, i.e. $+D2^2$. This, too, has been copied into the range E3..E12.

Finally, the last entry in column E (E13) is the sum of the squared error terms, i.e. @SUM(E2..E12). This last figure (0.040 319) measures the total sum of squared errors (SSE) in the regression equation, and for any given regression equation will clearly be greater the larger is the number of x, y observations. For this reason, if we divide the sum of squared errors by the number of paired observations (11), then we will obtain a measure of the 'average' squared error of the regression equation.

When this is done we obtain

$$0.040\ 319/11 = 0.003\ 66$$

We have averaged this figure by the number of pairs of observations (11), but what we really require is that it be averaged by the number of *independent* pairs of observations. The reason for this is that the regression process uses up information from the data set as it performs its calculations. What this means is that since two statistics (the intercept and the gradient) have been calculated from the data set, there are two pairs of observations that are no longer free to adopt any value other than that which is consistent with the regression equation. This means that instead of 11 independent x, y values, there are only nine. We say that two degrees of freedom have been lost, and that as a result only nine degrees of freedom remain. As you can see in the Lotus Regression Output in Worksheet 10.1, the available degrees of freedom are produced in the D19 cell.

If we now average the sum of squared errors by the available degrees of freedom, we obtain

$$0.040\ 319/9 = 0.004\ 48$$

Finally, if we take the square root of this figure (to compensate for having squared the error terms earlier), then we obtain a statistic that is known as the standard error of the y estimate and is denoted by se_y. This would be calculated for our data as 0.066 932.

This is the figure that Lotus has placed in the D16 cell of Worksheet 10.1, and, as the name implies, is a measure of the amount of 'average' error in the estimate of y that the regression equation contains. You will immediately notice that it is difficult to say whether this average error is large or small, since at the moment there is no known standard of measurement. But this will soon be rectified.

10.8 Understanding the results

As we have already suggested, the output section of the Lotus Regression facility contains a number of terms that are not familiar. In particular, the entry identified as R Squared requires some explanation.

To understand this term, recall that, as we have already suggested, the linear regression technique will fit the best *straight line* to the data regardless of whether a linear function is the most appropriate in terms of its 'goodness of fit'. You will also recall that in our current example, the fact that the effect of fertilizer application diminished as the level of application increased has already caused us to question whether the linear model was the best one to use.

In this context, the value of R Squared (R^2) provides a measure of the extent to which the observed data correspond to a linear function. In other words, it takes the best straight line, examines it, and then awards it a 'mark' on the basis of the degree of correspondence between the data and that best straight line. This mark can then be looked up in a table of 'pass marks' to see whether the particular line under consideration 'passes the examination'. (You may well wonder at this stage what the 'pass mark' is – more on this shortly.)

To see how R Squared performs this testing, think of the problem as follows.

We already know that the least squares regression line will minimize the sum of squared errors, but how large is this minimum? To answer this we can note that once we have obtained the fitted regression equation, it is an easy matter to calculate these (squared) error terms and sum them to produce the sum of squared errors.

Since we know this statistic to be the sum of the squared error terms, it would seem logical to regard it as a measure of the *unexplained variation* in the y variable, (i.e. unexplained by the regression equation). This is exactly what we do.

But now we must face the question of whether these sum of squared errors are 'large' or 'small'; and as we have seen already, this is complicated by the fact that we do not possess a known scale of measurement or a known range of values within which the summed errors are likely to fall.

We can partially deal with this if we employ the notion of the *proportion* of the *total variation* in the y variable which is unexplained, since then we will obtain a statistic that is placed on a scale between 0 and 1.

But how do we calculate the total variation in the y variable?

The answer is quite simply to define it as the sum of squared deviations of each observed y value from its mean value, i.e.

$$\Sigma[(y_i - \bar{y})^2]$$

where, as usual, $\bar{y}$ denotes the mean value of y.

You will notice that this is simply the numerator in the formula for the variance of y which was explained in the previous chapter, and as we saw there, represents the total variation of each y value around its mean value. It is often referred to as the *total sum of squares* (TSS).

To summarize then, we have

SSE = unexplained variation = $\Sigma(e_i^2) = \Sigma[(y_i - \hat{y})^2]$
TSS = total sum of squares = $\Sigma[(y_i - \bar{y})^2]$

From these two definitions it follows that the *proportional unexplained variation*

(PUV) can be written as

$$PUV = SSE/TSS$$

That is

$$PUV = \Sigma(e_i^2)/\Sigma[(y_i - \bar{y})^2]$$

If this statistic measures the proportional unexplained variation, and if, as it does, it lies between 0 and 1, then it surely follows that the *proportional explained variation* (PEV) must be given by

$$PEV = 1 - PUV = 1 - \Sigma(e_i^2)/\Sigma[(y_i - \bar{y})^2]$$

This is indeed the case, and produces the statistic known as R Squared. It is an extremely important statistic as it gives us the proportion of the total variation in the y value that is explained by the regression equation of y on x. In this sense it is the regression equation's 'examination' mark, with the 'examination' being the question:

'How well do the observed data correspond to a linear function?'

For the data in our example we have

$$SSE = 0.040\ 319$$

Furthermore, you can easily confirm that the TSS in y will be computed to be

$$TSS = 0.100\ 36$$

Therefore

$$PUV = 0.040\ 319/0.100\ 36 = 0.401\ 74$$

and

$$PEV = R\ Squared = 1 - PUV = 1 - 0.401\ 74 = 0.598\ 26$$

This is precisely the result contained in cell D17 of the Lotus Regression output in Worksheet 10.1.

The calculations above may seem needlessly complicated in order to obtain a statistic that Lotus produces automatically, but it must be remembered that any statistic is meaningless unless the principles upon which it is founded are fully appreciated. Besides, as you can now see it takes longer to describe the calculations than it does for Lotus to do them.

There is another important statistic which can easily be calculated by taking the square root of R Squared. This is known as the correlation coefficient and is also a measure of linear association. Although Lotus does not produce the correlation coefficient automatically in its regression output, it is an easy matter to calculate it by entering the following formula in any vacant cell of Worksheet 10.1:

$$@IF(C21>0, D17^{\wedge}0.5, -(D17^{\wedge}0.5))$$

Notice that this will take the positive square root of R Squared if *b* is positive and the negative square root otherwise.

Clearly the correlation coefficient indicates not only the extent of association, but also the nature of this association (direct if positive, indirect if negative). Furthermore, a (maximum) value of 1 indicates a perfect direct linear association, a (minimum) value of -1 indicates a perfect indirect linear association, while a value of zero indicates that no linear association between the variables has been found.

Once you have calculated the value of the correlation coefficient and/or R Squared, the next question that arises is whether it is large enough to allow you to conclude that there is 'a strong linear association' between the x and y variables. The methods for doing this rigorously exceed the scope of this text, but we can obtain a working rule of thumb as follows.

What we are looking for is some measure of what we have previously called the 'pass mark'. Unfortunately, however, like many types of examination the pass mark in this subject is not fixed (at 40 or 50 per cent, for example), but varies. In this case it depends both upon the number of degrees of freedom, and upon how *sure* we require to be that we do not draw an incorrect conclusion.

This reflects the intuitive idea that with only a few observations (say five or six) it is more likely that a 'good linear fit' could have occurred *by chance* than if there were 29 or 30 observations. This means that in the latter case the pass mark for R Squared and the correlation coefficient should be lower than in the former case.

As regards the possibility of drawing a mistaken conclusion, statistical tables usually allow us to choose between risk factors of 10, 5, 1 and 0.1 per cent. This is to be interpreted as meaning that we are prepared to accept one or other of these risk factors as the 'price' of drawing a conclusion from the data. What this means is that although, for example, a given calculated value of R Squared 'passes' the examination if we are prepared to accept a 10 per cent risk of being wrong, it might 'fail' if we were only prepared to accept a 5 per cent risk of being mistaken.

Taking these two ideas together, we should be able to see that the 'pass' mark is in fact a table of pass marks with the number of degrees of freedom forming one side of the table and the risk of error (expressed as a decimal) forming the other. Since our example has 11 pairs of observations there are nine degrees of freedom, and the relevant row of the table could be found from any set of statistical tables as:

	Risk of error			
Degrees of freedom	0.1	0.05	0.01	0.001
9	0.2718	0.3845	0.4573	0.7346

What this means is that with 11 pairs of observations, and with a willingness to accept a 5 per cent chance of error, the pass mark for R Squared is 0.3845 or more.

Any calculated value of R Squared that is less than 0.3845 is not sufficiently high to allow us to be *acceptably* sure that there is a linear association between the two variables. If, however, we had employed 15 pairs of observations, then we would find that, keeping the same risk factor of 5 per cent, the required value of R Squared produced by the tables would now only be 0.2641.

Using our actual calculated value of R Squared (0.5983) you can see that it passes the test if we are willing to accept a 1 per cent risk, but fails it if we are only willing to endure a 0.1 per cent risk.

You may well still be puzzled about this risk of error idea, since you might argue that R Squared reflects the association between an observed set of data values. Surely this is an objective 'fact'?

Unfortunately, the answer is 'not really', since if you recall our opening remarks on this topic, you will remember that measurement error was emphasized as a potential source of difficulty. In the context of our recent remarks, what this means is that if, for example, you perform the experiment once and find that the sum of squared errors is zero (i.e. every point lies on the line), there is no guarantee that if you were to perform the experiment again (with a different set of measurement errors), that you would obtain the same set of results. Therefore the question raised is: 'which of the two sets of results (if either) is correct?'

Furthermore, even if you repeated the experiment a large number of times and took a 'consensus', all this would do is 'average' the measurement error of the experiment. It would do nothing to deal with the fact that many experiments are subject to a further source of variation, which stems from the inability to exercise absolute control over all external factors at all times. This produces the added complication that each time the experiment is performed it is almost impossible to distinguish between measurement error and lack of control error, with the result that there is little alternative but to accept the fact that any regression equation, and any associated R Squared value are not 'objective facts', but rather only one of a large number of equations and coefficients that could have been calculated from different observed data sets.

In short, the correlation coefficient and R Squared are *random* variables that are capable of variation in such a way that it is not a simple matter to claim that any one experimental value is any more 'correct' than any other.

10.9 Sampling variation in the values of the regression coefficients

As the previous section has suggested, if we repeated the fertilizer experiment 10 or 15 times, it would be unlikely that we should obtain the same regression equation on each occasion. Since these equations are entirely defined in terms of their a and b values, this means that there is not *one* unique value of a and *one* unique value of b, but rather a range or *distribution* of these values. Furthermore, any of the values in this distribution are capable of being calculated, depending upon the actual data of the experiment. This means that it is quite possible to obtain a different regression equation each time the experiment is carried out.

This poses a serious problem for the investigator, since he or she can never be sure whether the calculated values of a and b are typical or atypical of the 'true' relationship unless the resources are available to permit repeated experimentation. This is the difficulty created by *sampling variation* in the values of a and b.

Concentrating on the value of the gradient for the moment, you can appreciate the difficulty if you imagine 15 runs of the fertilizer experiment which produce the following distribution of b values:

Value of b	Frequency
−0.08 to −0.02	1
−0.0199 to 0.0199	2
0.02 to 0.0799	3
0.08 to 0.1199	6
0.12 to 0.1799	2
0.18 to 0.1999	1

Clearly we could graph this distribution and obtain the diagram shown in Figure 10.6.

The immediate impression is that some b values are more likely to occur than others, but that if we were forced to hazard a guess at the 'true' value, then we would probably choose the peak of the distribution and the estimate that b lay between 0.08 and 0.119 99.

Nevertheless, other values of b are clearly possible, and if the experiment was performed another 15 times, then additional values could be encountered, and, as a result, the peak of the distribution might move. This would cause us to choose a different value for our guess.

Yet repeated experimentation can be a costly and time-consuming business, so it would clearly be much better if, *on the basis of one experiment alone*, we could obtain some measure of the variation in b that is likely to occur.

Fortunately, such a measure has already been produced in the Lotus regression output, and is known as the standard error of the coefficient. Although this is called a standard error, this phrase is merely used to indicate that it relates to the estimation procedure that the regression is performing. In its most basic form the standard error of the coefficient is simply the standard deviation of all possible sample values of the x coefficient (i.e. what we have called b). It therefore measures the statistical variation that can take place in the value of b as a result of sampling variation. It will be referred to from now on as the standard error of b, and given the symbol se_b.

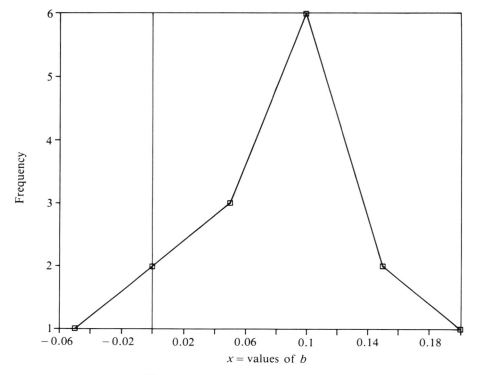

Figure 10.6 Distribution of b values

To understand the significance of the standard error of b, you should appreciate that it is composed of two elements:

1. The 'average' error of the regression equation, which we have already encountered as the standard error of the y estimate.
2. The variation that has taken place in the independent variable (x) in relation to its mean value. That is

$$\Sigma[(x_i - \bar{x})^2]$$

The exact relationship between these two components (remembering that it is a standard deviation rather than a variance) is

$$se_b = [se_y]/\{[\Sigma(x_i - \bar{x})^2]^{0.5}\}$$

For our illustration we already have the standard error of y estimated to be 0.066 932, and if you calculate the denominator for yourself you will find that it comes to 10.488. Therefore

$$se_b = 0.066\ 932/10.488 = 0.006\ 381$$

This is precisely the entry that Lotus has made in the C22 cell of its regression output.

There is an intuitive meaning to this statistic. First, as we have already seen, the numerator represents the 'average' error of the regression equation. It would therefore seem plausible to expect that the greater is this error, then the greater is the ability of the calculated value of b to vary from experiment to experiment.

Secondly, the denominator is the square root of the summed deviations of the independent variable from its mean value. This measures the variation in x around its mean value. If the x values chosen by the experimenter are highly concentrated, this variation will be small, and as a consequence, for any given numerator the value of se_b will be large. This is because the experimental values of x have been so limited that it makes little sense to try and understand the nature of the relationship outside this limited range. The standard error of b indicates this fact by adopting a higher value (implying a greater degree of sampling variation in b) than it would have adopted if the x values had been more dispersed.

In summary, if the 'average' error of the regression equation is large, and if it has been obtained on the basis of limited experimental data for x, then the standard error of b will be large.

On the other hand, if the 'average' error of the regression equation is small, and if it has been obtained on the basis of a wide range of experimental data for x, then the standard error of b will be small. This last case is what the investigator requires, since it means that the potential variation in the values of b that *could* be calculated will be relatively small.

Once we know how to estimate the potential variation in the values of b, we still have to know what to do with this statistic. In fact, this is quite simple, since our knowledge of the meaning and value of se_b allows us to derive what is known as a confidence range for the values of b that are likely to occur. This is done by multiplying se_b by 1.96 and then adding and subtracting this product from the calculated value of b. That is

$$\text{actual } b \pm 1.96(se_b)$$

For our illustration this would produce

$$0.023\,363 \pm 1.96(0.006\,381) = 0.023\,363 \pm 0.0125$$

Consequently, the sampling variation that can take place in b means that it is most likely to vary between 0.0359 and 0.0109.

At this stage you may well be wondering where the figure of 1.96 came from. The answer is that it represents an important value in a function known as the normal distribution. Without going into the details of this distribution, you will have to take it on trust that 95 per cent of all possible values that the distribution's variable can adopt will lie in the range given by

$$\text{variable mean} \pm 1.96 \text{ (variable standard deviation)}$$

This allows us to identify a known scale against which any value of the variable can be measured and its *relative* magnitude determined.

It so happens that if the number of observations in our experiment exceeds 30 (as it usually will in most real cases), then the distribution of the b values in all possible experimental regression equations is approximately normal.

So if we take our calculated b value as an estimate of the variable mean, and se_b as the variable's standard deviation, then the last expression above becomes

$$\text{actual } b \pm 1.96(se_b)$$

This is the confidence range for b and tells us the limits within which 95 per cent of all possible b values will lie. It follows, of course, that 5 per cent will lie outside this range, but this is the risk factor that we emphasized in the previous section.

We can now repeat one of the most important results in regression theory:

> If the number of pairs of observations exceeds 30, then 95 per cent of all possible b values that could be calculated will lie in the range that is given by the actual value of b plus or minus 1.96 times the standard error of b.

(If the number of pairs of observations does not exceed 30, then the distribution of all possible b values is only approximately normal and a rigorous approach would have to modify the value of 1.96 in accordance with what is known as the t distribution. At our level of analysis, however, the difference that this makes is moderately small and we will overlook this complication and use the normal value of 1.96 regardless of the number of pairs of observations. In practice, however, the appropriate t statistic would have to be used.)

However, you may still not appreciate the significance of this result for the simple reason that knowledge of the confidence range for b does not immediately tell us what we want to know, i.e. how reliable our experimental b value is as an estimate of the 'true' b value that would only emerge after repeated experimentation.

But if we rephrase the question as 'what is the "worst" value of b that could be encountered?', then it should be clear that the answer would be a gradient value of zero. This would imply that there was no association between y and x, since the regression equation would be represented by a horizontal line in which the value of y was the same, regardless of the value of x. In this case the value of x is clearly exercising *no influence* at all upon the value of y and consequently there is no functional relationship to be discovered.

If we apply this idea to our confidence range for b, then it surely follows that if this range includes a value of $b = 0$ then our 'worst' outcome is included in the range of likely outcomes, and cannot be excluded from the experimental results that could have been produced.

On the other hand, if a value of $b = 0$ is *not* included in the confidence range, then this implies that the 'worst' outcome is unlikely to be encountered. In this case we would feel 95 per cent confident of any inference that the value of b is significantly different from zero (i.e. different from the situation in which there is no linear relationship between y and x).

It should now be clear that the implication of this discussion is to suggest that instead of there being one unique regression equation (defined by single values of a and b), there is a range of regression equations and associated regression lines. This follows from the fact that if, as we have seen, the value of the gradient term is subject to sampling variation, then so too will be the value of the intercept term. Taken together, the sampling variation that can take place in both parameters of the regression equation means that we must view the predicted value of y as being more accurately reflected by a plane than by a single line.

This plane will be defined by upper and lower confidence limits placed around the calculated regression equation, and although it is beyond the scope of this text to derive the formula for these limits rigorously, you can obtain a reasonable estimate of the 95 per cent limits by taking the predicted value of y for any given value of x and then adding and subtracting 1.96 times the standard error of the y estimate. That is

$$\hat{y} = a + bx \pm 1.96 se_y$$

To do this on Lotus requires that we modify the worksheet models produced in Worksheets 10.1 and 10.2 as shown in Worksheet 10.3. As you can see, the data, the regression output and the predicted values of y are still located in the same cells as in Worksheets 10.1 and 10.2. However, we have added an expression in C23 which can be used to calculate the upper and lower values of the predicted value of y. This formula reflects the discussion above and is given by 1.96*D16. This is then used to calculate two new predicted values of y (pred y U using the upper limit and pred y L using the lower limit).

The calculation method is the same as for the predicted value of y since the formula in D2 is +D$15+C$21*A2+C$23. Similarly the formula in E2 is +D$15+C$21*A2−C$23. These formulae are then copied into the D3..D12 and E3..E12 cells below.

We can now ask Lotus to graph

y   against x
pred y   against x
pred y U   against x
pred y L   against x

This will produce the diagram shown in Figure 10.7 in which the scatter plot, the fitted regression equation, and its upper and lower 95 per cent confidence limits are clearly displayed.

As we have said before, these confidence limits reflect the fact that there is sampling variation in both the value of b and in the value of a. We have also seen that this former variation is measured by se_b, but what about the equivalent standard error for a: se_a? Unfortunately, the Lotus regression output does not

WORKSHEET 10.3

	A	B	C	D	E
1	x	y	pred y	pred y U	pred y L
2	0.00	0.21	0.341364	0.472550	0.210177
3	1.00	0.35	0.364727	0.495914	0.233540
4	2.00	0.41	0.388091	0.519278	0.256904
5	3.00	0.46	0.411455	0.542641	0.280268
6	4.00	0.50	0.434818	0.566005	0.303631
7	5.00	0.52	0.458182	0.589369	0.326995
8	6.00	0.53	0.481545	0.612732	0.350359
9	7.00	0.53	0.504909	0.636096	0.373722
10	8.00	0.53	0.528273	0.659460	0.397086
11	9.00	0.51	0.551636	0.682823	0.420450
12	10.00	0.49	0.575000	0.706187	0.443813
13					
14			Regression Output: y=a+bx		
15	Constant			0.34136	
16	Std Err of Y Est			0.06693	
17	R Squared			0.59827	
18	No. of Observations			11.00000	
19	Degrees of Freedom			9.00000	
20					
21	X Coefficient(s)		0.02336		
22	Std Err of Coef.		0.00638		
23	Sampling Variation	0.1312			

produce this statistic but you can calculate it for yourself from the following equation:

$$se_a = (se_b)\{[(\Sigma(x^2)/n]^{0.5}\}$$

It is left as an exercise for you to write an appropriate Lotus formula for this expression and place it in C25. You should find that

$$se_a = 0.03774$$

Then, by the same logic as we used with b we can deduce that the 95 per cent confidence interval for the intercept will be given by

$$\text{upper value of } a = \text{actual value} + 1.96(se_a)$$

and

$$\text{lower value of } a = \text{actual value} - 1.96(se_a)$$

Once again, we will frequently be concerned with whether this range includes a value of zero, since if it does then this would mean that the intercept term was not significantly different from zero, and that the implied regression line could well emanate from the origin.

For the data in our illustration this means that 95 per cent of all possible values of a will lie in the range 0.341 46 ± 1.96(0.037 74), i.e. from 0.4155 to 0.2676.

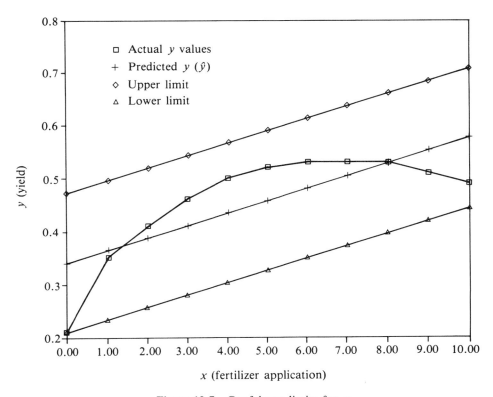

Figure 10.7 Confidence limits for y

As a final point in this section, it will have been noticed that 95 per cent confidence limits (with a normal value of 1.96) are the only ones that have been calculated. But what if we prefer to use some other degree of confidence, such as 90 or 99 per cent?

You can deal with this quite easily by noting that the most frequently used normal values, and their associated confidence levels are as follows:

1.64	90 per cent confidence
1.96	95 per cent confidence
2.32	98 per cent confidence
2.58	99 per cent confidence

Clearly the greater is the degree of confidence required, the greater is the normal value. This means that the absolute width of any calculated confidence interval will also be greater, reflecting the intuitive idea that we can only be 'more sure' by accepting a wider range of possible values in which our statistic can lie.

10.10 Association versus causation

What the analysis above has done is to allow you to determine the extent (if any) of the statistical linear associations between y and x. Assuming that this is satisfactorily established, the next question is whether we can conclude from this that we have identified a *causal* relationship between the independent variable and the dependent one. To answer this you must be absolutely clear on the distinction between association and causation.

To appreciate this you only have to think of an experiment that records a student's age against the number of examinations that he or she has passed at college or university. Without doubt we would find a high degree of statistical association between these two variables (even allowing for mature students and child prodigies), but the direction of causation (if any) is far from clear.

It is certainly not tenable to contend that the number of examinations passed determines a student's age, but could the student's age be determining the number of examinations passed?

Obviously there is a sense in which the latter hypothesis is valid, since if examinations are passed, then students tend to get older in the process. But although this is a necessary condition it is hardly sufficient; otherwise age alone would be the only requirement in passing examinations.

Clearly there is at least one other variable exercising an influence 'behind the scenes' upon both age and the number of examinations passed, and we might suspect that the student's IQ, or the number of school qualifications obtained, or even the year of study should be investigated.

What these reservations mean is that although statistical association can perhaps be established, the crucial step involved in turning this association into a causal relationship is fraught with danger. This is particularly so in those areas (common in business) where one variable not only influences a second variable but where the resulting value of this second variable then exercises a secondary influence upon the value of the first variable. For example, it will usually be the case that increased investment will lead to increased profits, but it is also the case that these increased profits provide the funds to finance further investment. Such a situation is known as 'feedback' and is a statistical nightmare for even the most experienced analyst, since it will never be clear as to which variable is influencing the other one. Clearly the direction of causation has been obscured by the feedback.

10.11 Nonlinear models transformed into linear ones

As was observed earlier, and as is clear from Figure 10.3, the data for our fertilizer example does not lend itself easily to linear interpretation. So the question arises of whether, given our suspicions of nonlinearity, we can modify our analysis *within the confines* of the linear regression model.

The answer is that we can; under certain circumstances.

For example, suppose that instead of hypothesizing a linear relationship, we suspected that y and x were related as follows:

$$y = a(x^b)$$

Clearly (since this equation describes a polynomial function), y and x will not be related in a linear fashion unless $b = 1$. However, if we perform a logarithmic transformation of both sides of the equation, then we will obtain

$$\log y = \log a + b(\log x)$$

At first sight, the effect of this transformation may not be obvious. However, closer inspection of the expression should reveal that this is a linear equation of the standard form, *provided that we recognize* that the variables are *log y* and *log x*, rather than y and x. In other words, the intercept of the line is log a, the gradient is b (as before), and the variables are log y and log x.

Now all we have to do is to force Lotus to perform the regression analysis on the logarithmically transformed variables rather than upon y and x. That is, the independent variable is now log x (C2..C12) and the dependent variable is now log y (D2..D12).

However, a problem arises when we ask Lotus to calculate the value of log 0 since, as we saw in Chapter 2, this is not defined. For this reason we must redefine the regression range as C3..C12 for the independent variable and D3..D12 for the dependent variable. This will exclude the x value of 0 from the regression analysis.

The calculations are performed in Worksheet 10.4. As you can see from the worksheet the logarithmic regression equation is

$$\log y = -0.429\,58 + 0.1678(\log x)$$

This is the linear version of the assumed polynomial expression, but the latter can be identified by noting that since

$$\log a = -0.429\,58$$

it follows that

$$a = 10^{-0.429\,58} = 0.3718$$

Furthermore, since b is *not* in a logarithmic form, it is a simple matter to identify the implied polynomial expression as

$$y = 0.3718(x^{0.1678})$$

As you can also see, the value of R Squared has increased from its original value of 0.5983 for the assumed linear equation, to 0.810 79 for the logarithmic equation (representing the assumed polynomial function). On the basis of this we can conclude that the polynomial function is a better 'fit' to the data than the simple linear function.

Although you could graph the regression equation in its logarithmic form, it will usually be more instructive to graph the implied polynomial form. Worksheet 10.4

```
WORKSHEET 10.4

        A              B           C              D           E           F
  1     x              y         log x          log y       pred y      error
  2   0.00           0.21         ERR         -0.677781    0.000000    0.21000
  3   1.00           0.35       0.000000      -0.455932    0.371892   -0.02189
  4   2.00           0.41       0.301030      -0.387216    0.417775   -0.00778
  5   3.00           0.46       0.477121      -0.337242    0.447196    0.01280
  6   4.00           0.50       0.602060      -0.301030    0.469319    0.03068
  7   5.00           0.52       0.698970      -0.283997    0.487230    0.03277
  8   6.00           0.53       0.778151      -0.275724    0.502370    0.02763
  9   7.00           0.53       0.845098      -0.275724    0.515537    0.01446
 10   8.00           0.53       0.903090      -0.275724    0.527222    0.00278
 11   9.00           0.51       0.954243      -0.292430    0.537749   -0.02775
 12  10.00           0.49       1.000000      -0.309804    0.547343   -0.05734
 13
 14              Regression Output: log y=log a+b log x
 15   Constant                               -0.42958
 16   Std Err of Y Est                        0.02738
 17   R Squared                               0.81079
 18   No. of Observations                    10.00000
 19   Degrees of Freedom                      8.00000
 20
 21   X Coefficient(s)    0.16784
 22   Std Err of Coef.    0.02867
 23   Upper Value of b    0.22403
 24   Lower Value of b    0.11166
```

performs the required calculations in columns E and F. The entry in E2 is

$$(10 \char`\^ D\$15)*(A2 \char`\^ C\$21)$$

and this is copied into the E3..E12 cells.

The error terms in column F are simply the difference between the actual y values and the predicted values on the basis of the polynomial equation. Notice the size of the error term for $x = 0$.

You can gain a visual impression of this if you ask Lotus to graph y against x, and then superimpose the predicted values and the associated error terms for the polynomial regression equation. This would produce Figure 10.8.

Finally, you may well be wondering what should be done if neither the linear nor the polynomial functions provide a satisfactory 'fit' to the data. The answer is that provided we are determined to remain within the confines of the linear regression model, then as another alternative we could hypothesize an exponential function of the form

$$y = a(b^x)$$

If we perform a logarithmic transformation of both sides of this equation we obtain

$$\log y = \log a + x(\log b)$$

This is known as a semi-log transformation, since although y is in logarithmic

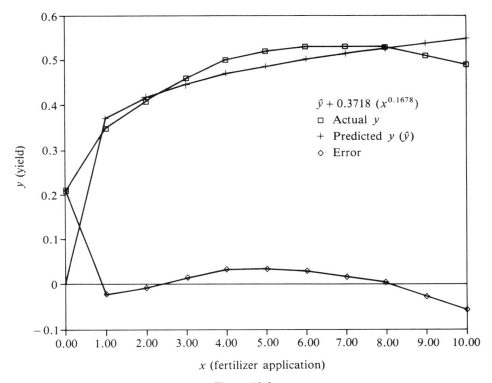

Figure 10.8

form, x has remained in its original (nonlogarithmic) form. Nevertheless, this is still a linear equation with log y being a linear function of x. The intercept will be log a and the gradient will be log b.

Worksheet 10.4 can perform the regression for you without major modification. All you have to do is tell Lotus that the independent variable is x (A2..A12), and that the dependent variable is log y (D2..D12) (Notice that the problem of taking the logarithm of zero does not arise in this formulation.) You will, of course, have to adjust the formula for the predicted value of y, since this will now require that the coefficients of the derived exponential equation are used.

These are obtained by converting the logarithmic values of a and b back to their natural form. That is

$$\log a = -0.487\ 36 \quad \text{therefore } a = 10^{-0.487\ 36} = 0.3255$$
$$\log b = 0.027\ 06 \quad \text{therefore } b = 10^{0.027\ 06} = 1.064$$

Consequently

$$y = 0.3255(1.064^x)$$

When these changes are made you should obtain something like Worksheet 10.5,

WORKSHEET 10.5

```
        A              B              C              D              E              F
 1      x              y              log x          log y          pred y         error
 2      0.00           0.21                          -0.677781      0.325567       -1.00335
                                      ERR
 3      1.00           0.35           0.000000       -0.455932      0.346498       -0.80243
 4      2.00           0.41           0.301030       -0.387216      0.368776       -0.75599
 5      3.00           0.46           0.477121       -0.337242      0.392485       -0.72973
 6      4.00           0.50           0.602060       -0.301030      0.417719       -0.71875
 7      5.00           0.52           0.698970       -0.283997      0.444575       -0.72857
 8      6.00           0.53           0.778151       -0.275724      0.473158       -0.74888
 9      7.00           0.53           0.845098       -0.275724      0.503578       -0.77930
10      8.00           0.53           0.903090       -0.275724      0.535955       -0.81168
11      9.00           0.51           0.954243       -0.292430      0.570413       -0.86284
12     10.00           0.49           1.000000       -0.309804      0.607086       -0.91689
13
14              Regression Output: log y=log a+x(log b)
15     Constant                                      -0.48736
16     Std Err of Y Est                               0.08682
17     R Squared                                      0.54281
18     No. of Observations                           11.00000
19     Degrees of Freedom                             9.00000
20
21     X Coefficient(s)    0.02706
22     Std Err of Coef.    0.00828
23     Upper Value of b    0.04329
24     Lower Value of b    0.01084
```

where the entry in E2 is now

(10^D$15)*((10^C$21)^A2)   (copied into E3..E12)

The results of this regression show that R Squared has fallen to 0.5428 and that as a consequence the semi-log transformation has not improved the strength of association in comparison with the double-log transformation (or even in comparison with the simple linear model).

The preceding analysis has done enough to suggest that there are a number of ways in which the raw data can be transformed so that the linear regression model can still be applied. It is beyond the scope of this text to explain further types of transformation, but a few more ideas will be found in the exercises at the end of this chapter.

As a final point in this section, if neither of the methods outlined above produce satisfactory values of R Squared, then you may just have to accept that the linear regression model is incapable of modelling your data set. Other methods are available (such as quadratic, or multiple term polynomial regression), but these are not supported by Lotus. You could write the formulae to perform these types of regression yourself, but it has to be said that they become increasingly complex and difficult to manage. It would be much more sensible to look for a dedicated regression package such as 'Statgraphics' or 'Minitab' which will perform these advanced regressions as a standard routine.

10.12 Rank correlation

In all of the previous discussion the variables have always been capable of being measured on the standard cardinal measurement scale. However, there may be circumstances in which our data represent subjective evaluations of various alternatives that cannot be measured in the same way. For example, it is an easy matter to say that £3 exceeds £1 by an amount of £2 (cardinal measurement), but it is not so easy to say *by how much* tea is preferred to coffee. Even if we know that we do prefer tea to coffee, the extent of this preference cannot be measured in consistent units.

We can, of course, ask individuals to rank their likings of various drinks, but all this will do is to reveal their preferences in numerical terms rather than allow us to calculate the *extent* of these preferences. For example, a market survey might produce something like Worksheet 10.6. From this we can see that the first individual prefers coffee (ranked 1) to beer (ranked 2). But we cannot assume that the extent of this preference is measured by the difference in these ranks. This is because the implication of such a calculation would be that the first individual prefers coffee to beer by exactly the same amount as he or she prefers beer to milk, and that the extent of this preference is exactly the same as the amount of the second individual's preference of milk to whisky. Clearly such calculations make a nonsense of what our common sense tells us. The problem is that preferences can only be measured on an *ordinal* scale which allows us to know that one value is greater than another value but not *by how much* it is greater.

However, provided we accept the limitations imposed by ordinal measurement scales we can still carry out meaningful analysis.

To do this we will develop a concept known as the *rank correlation coefficient* (rcc), which, like the ordinary correlation coefficient, lies between -1 and $+1$. What this statistic does is to calculate the degree of association between any two sets of ranked data, measured in terms of the extent to which the preferences revealed by the ranks agree or disagree. Since Lotus does not possess an inbuilt rank correlation coefficient function, we will have to write the formulae for ourselves. Using Worksheet 10.6, the first step is to ensure that at least one of the columns contains the ranks in ascending order. This is already the case for the first individual's ranks, but if it was not then you could use the Data Sort command to achieve this objective.

The next step is to form a new column (D) which calculates squared difference in the rankings of the two individuals (call this d^2). The formula (in D3) would be

$$(B3 - C3)^2$$

which should then be copied into the range D4..D8.

In D9 you should sum these squared rank differences and then multiply them by 6, i.e.

$$6*(@SUM(D3..D8))$$

WORKSHEET 10.6

```
              A                  B                C
1                          Ranked by        Ranked by
2        Drink:            Individual 1     Individual 2
3        Coffee                 1                6
4        Beer                   2                3
5        Milk                   3                1
6        Whisky                 4                2
7        Tea                    5                4
8        Fruit Juice            6                6
```

Note: the value of 6 is *always* used, and does not derive from any aspect of the data set being used.

Then, in D10 enter the formula for the rank correlation coefficient. This is

$$rcc = 1 - \{[6\Sigma(d^2)] / [n(n^2 - 1)]\}$$

where n = the number of *pairs* of ranks.

Lotus can calculate the value of n with its @COUNT function, since @COUNT(B3..B8) would return a value of 6. This means that the Lotus formula for the rank correlation coefficient (in D10) would be

1 − (D9/(@COUNT(B3..B8)*(@COUNT(B3..B8)^2) − 1)).

When Lotus evaluates this expression, you should find that a value of −0.0285 is returned (see Worksheet 10.7).

At this stage you might be thinking that the formula in D10 is needlessly messy, and this would be true if it was always the case that there were only six observations. However, given that this will not always be the case, the purpose of

WORKSHEET 10.7

```
    D10: [W15] 1-(D9/(@COUNT(B3..B8)*(@COUNT(B3..B8)^2-1)))

             A              B              C              D
    1                    Ranked by      Ranked by      Squared
    2    Drink:          Individual 1   Individual 2   Difference
    3    Coffee               1              6            25
    4    Beer                 2              3             1
    5    Milk                 3              1             4
    6    Whisky               4              2             4
    7    Tea                  5              4             1
    8    Fruit Juice          6              5             1
    9                                   6Σ d^2           216
   10                                   rcc          -0.0285714286
```

this formulation is to allow you to make up a dedicated Lotus rank correlation worksheet.

Assuming that you will never have more than 100 rankings, which you will always place in B3..B102 and C3..C102, then you can place the squared rank differences in D3..D102, and 6 times the sum of these squared differences in D101, i.e.

$$6*(@SUM(D3..D102))$$

Now you can write the rank correlation coefficient formula in D104 as

$$1 - (D103/(@COUNT(B3..B102)*(@COUNT(B3..B102)^2) - 1))$$

The reason that this works is that the @COUNT function, when applied to a range of cells, only counts those cells that are not blank (as opposed to containing a zero entry). This means that you can enter as many ranks as your problem requires and then erase those cells that are not required. The @COUNT function will return the number of pairs of ranks that have been entered.

However, the entries in column D, which attempt to subtract one blank entry from another, will return ERR to these cells and this will prevent Lotus from summing the non blank cells in the D column. For this reason you should edit the 6*(@SUM(D3..D102)) formula in D103 to 6*(@SUM(D1..D?)), where the question mark represents the row number of the last entered rank. This will then produce the required value for the rank correlation coefficient in D104.

As regards the interpretation of this statistic, then it should be clear that a value of -1 indicates that the two sets of rankings are in complete disagreement (i.e. one set of rankings is the perfect reverse of the other set). You can confirm for yourself that if this is the case, then it will produce a value of -1.

Conversely, if the two sets of rankings are in perfect agreement, then the coefficient will be evaluated to $+1$.

But what about values in between these two polar cases? Clearly, the higher is the absolute value of the coefficient, the greater is the degree of agreement (if the coefficient is positive) or disagreement (if the coefficient is negative). Furthermore, it would seem logical to conclude that a value of zero implies neither agreement nor disagreement, and this is indeed the case. As you can see, our illustrative example has a value that appears to be quite close to zero, but how do we define 'close' if we have no information about the scale of measurement.

To be more precise than this requires that we know more about the likely values that the coefficient can adopt (in the same way as we did for the intercept and gradient terms of the regression equation). In other words, we require some measure of the sampling variation that can take place in this statistic. As before, the measure of this sampling variation is known as the standard error of the statistic and would be denoted as se_{rcc}.

It is beyond the scope of this text to explain how this can be derived, but you can still look up the value of *rcc* in statistical tables and see whether it satisfies your required risk criterion.

For our example, with only four $(n-2)$ degrees of freedom the relevant row of the statistical table is as follows:

v risk	0.1	0.05	0.01	0.001
4 required rcc	0.7293	0.8114	0.9172	0.9741

As you can see, even accepting a 10 per cent risk of being wrong, our calculated value of the rcc (-0.0285) is nowhere near high enough to allow us to conclude that there is a significant association between the two sets of rankings.

10.13 Time series analysis

An important application of the regression techniques developed in this chapter lies in an area known as time series analysis. What this means is that the independent variable is taken to be the passage of time, and that the linear regression equation is used to extract the *trend* that the dependent variable adopts as time passes.

Unfortunately, however, when time is used as the independent variable there are a number of additional complications introduced to the regression technique. These stem from the fact that the dependent variable will be subject to a number of influences that are highly sensitive to the units of which the passage of time are measured (months, quarters, years, etc.).

For example, if only annual data have been observed, then it will be impossible to identify any seasonal influence (such as more fuel consumed in winter) that acts upon the data.

However, as long as we recognize these difficulties, then we can accommodate them in our model and thereby develop a technique for splitting the raw time series data in to its various component parts. This is the basic objective of time series analysis.

As a simple starting point, let us presume that any set of quarterly time series data is composed of three elements: a trend value (t), a seasonal element (s) and a residual component (r).

Having defined the components of our model, we now have to decide upon the form that the model should take. In this simple context there are two basic choices: additive or multiplicative.

In the first case the model would assume the following form:

$$y = t + s + r$$

while in the second case it would be

$$y = tsr$$

In either of these cases, however, the first step will always be to establish the trend on the basis of the least squares regression equation.

To see how this is done examine Worksheet 10.8a, where a data set consisting of quarterly observations over a five-year period has been entered in columns A and

WORKSHEET 10.8a

	A	B	C	D
1	time	series	linear	
2			trend	
3	(x)	(y)	(t)	
4	1.00	20.00	15.371429	
5	2.00	15.00	16.163910	
6	3.00	10.00	16.956391	
7	4.00	18.00	17.748872	
8	5.00	24.00	18.541353	
9	6.00	18.00	19.333835	
10	7.00	13.00	20.126316	
11	8.00	21.00	20.918797	
12	9.00	28.00	21.711278	
13	10.00	22.00	22.503759	
14	11.00	19.00	23.296241	
15	12.00	25.00	24.088722	
16	13.00	32.00	24.881203	
17	14.00	26.00	25.673684	
18	15.00	21.00	26.466165	
19	16.00	29.00	27.258647	
20	17.00	35.00	28.051128	
21	18.00	28.00	28.843609	
22	19.00	22.00	29.636090	
23	20.00	32.00	30.428571	
24				
25				
26		Regression Output: y=a+bx		
27	Contant		14.57895	
28	Std Err of Y Est		4.75022	
29	R Squared		0.50696	
30	No. of Observations		20.00000	
31	Degrees of Freedom		18.00000	
32				
33	X Coefficient(s)	0.79248		
34	Std Err of Coef.	0.18421		

B under the headings x and y. Notice that x has been defined in terms of the quarter number (1–20). The Lotus regression output has been placed in the block of cells commencing in A26, and the calculated values of a and b have been used to generate the linear trend entries in column C. Consequently, the formula in C4 is

$$+D\$27 + C\$38*A4$$

which has been copied into the range C5..C23.

This column provides us with the linear trend values predicted by the regression equation of y on x ($14.578\,95 + 0.792\,48x$).

The next task is to calculate the de-trended series, but how this is done will

WORKSHEET 10.8b

D4: (F6) [W10] +B4-C4

	A	B	C	D	E
1	time	series	linear	de-trended	
2			trend	series	
3	(x)	(y)	(t)	(y-t)	
4	1.00	20.00	15.371429	4.628571	
5	2.00	15.00	16.163910	-1.163910	
6	3.00	10.00	16.956391	-6.956391	
7	4.00	18.00	17.748872	0.251128	
8	5.00	24.00	18.541353	5.458647	
9	6.00	18.00	19.333835	-1.333835	
10	7.00	13.00	20.126316	-7.126316	
11	8.00	21.00	20.918797	0.081203	
12	9.00	28.00	21.711278	6.288722	
13	10.00	22.00	22.503759	-0.503759	
14	11.00	19.00	23.296241	-4.296241	
15	12.00	25.00	24.088722	0.911278	
16	13.00	32.00	24.881203	7.118797	
17	14.00	26.00	25.673684	0.326316	
18	15.00	21.00	26.466165	-5.466165	
19	16.00	29.00	27.258647	1.741353	
20	17.00	35.00	28.051128	6.948872	
21	18.00	28.00	28.843609	-0.843609	
22	19.00	22.00	29.636090	-7.636090	
23	20.00	32.00	30.428571	1.571429	
24					
35					
36		1st qu.	2nd qu.	3rd qu.	4th qu.
37	year 1	4.62857	-1.16391	-6.95639	0.25113
38	year 2	5.45865	-1.33383	-7.12632	0.08120
39	year 3	6.28872	-0.50376	-4.29624	0.91128
40	year 4	7.11880	0.32632	-5.46617	1.74135
41	year 5	6.94887	-0.84361	-7.63609	1.57143
42	Sum	30.4436	-3.5188	-31.4812	4.5564
43	Avg	6.08872	-0.70376	-6.29624	0.91128
44					
45					
46					
47					
48					
49					
50					

WORKSHEET 10.8c

	A time (x)	B series (y)	C linear trend (t)	D de-trend series (y−t)	E seasonal variation (s)	F seasonal adjusted (y−s)	G residual variation (y−t−s)
1							
2							
3							
4	1.00	20.00	15.371429	4.628571	6.088722	13.91128	−1.46015
5	2.00	15.00	16.163910	−1.163910	−0.703759	15.70376	−0.46015
6	3.00	10.00	16.956391	−6.956391	−6.296241	16.29624	−0.66015
7	4.00	18.00	17.748872	0.251128	0.911278	17.08872	−0.66015
8	5.00	24.00	18.541353	5.458647	6.088722	17.91128	−0.63008
9	6.00	18.00	19.333835	−1.333835	−0.703759	18.70376	−0.63008
10	7.00	13.00	20.126316	−7.126316	−6.296241	19.29624	−0.83008
11	8.00	21.00	20.918797	0.081203	0.911278	20.08872	−0.83008
12	9.00	28.00	21.711278	6.288722	6.088722	21.91128	0.20000
13	10.00	22.00	22.503759	−0.503759	−0.703759	22.70376	0.20000
14	11.00	19.00	23.296241	−4.296241	−6.296241	25.29624	2.00000
15	12.00	25.00	24.088722	0.911278	0.911278	24.08872	0.00000
16	13.00	32.00	24.881203	7.118797	6.088722	25.91128	1.03008
17	14.00	26.00	25.673684	0.326316	−0.703759	26.70376	1.03008
18	15.00	21.00	26.466165	−5.466165	−6.296241	27.29624	0.83008
19	16.00	29.00	27.258647	1.741353	0.911278	28.08872	0.83008
20	17.00	35.00	28.051128	6.948872	6.088722	28.91128	0.86015
21	18.00	28.00	28.843609	−0.843609	−0.703759	28.70376	−0.13985
22	19.00	22.00	29.636090	−7.636090	−6.296241	28.29624	−1.33985
23	20.00	32.00	30.428571	1.571429	0.911278	31.08872	0.66015

depend on the nature of the presumed time series model. In the additive case the de-trended series will be given by

$$\text{de-trended series} = y - t$$

but in the multiplicative model it will be obtained from

$$\text{de-trended series} = y/t$$

Dealing with the additive case first of all, this means that the entries in column D should be obtained by subtracting the entries in column C from those in column B.

The next task is to try and identify the seasonal component (if any) contained in the de-trended series. To do this we must collect together all the de-trended values that pertain to the same quarter of the year (i.e. quarters 1, 5, 9, 13, 17; 2, 6, 10, 14, 18, etc.).

Consequently, for the first quarter of year 1 the difference between the actual value of y (20.00) and the trend value (15.371 429) is 4.628 57.

These 'equivalent quarter' values have been placed in the block of cells commencing in A37, then summed and averaged to produce an average value for the season that they represent. They are displayed in Worksheet 10.8b.

You should be able to see that the four entries in the 'Avg' row represent an estimate of the seasonal variation of the series, so the next step will be to place them in column E (against their appropriate quarter) and then subtract them from the actual series values to produce what is known as the seasonally adjusted series. This should be done in column F of the worksheet.

Finally, the residual elements will be defined by

$$r = y - s - t$$

and these should be placed in column G of your worksheet.

When all these calculations have been completed the final result should look something like Worksheet 10.8c.

Clearly the seasonally adjusted series is one of the most important results of this analysis, since it is almost impossible to encounter any set of published statistics without finding that they have been seasonally adjusted. In its basic form, what the seasonally adjusted series does is to indicate what the behaviour of the dependent variable would have been like *had it not been subject to seasonal variation*.

If you graph the actual series, the trend and the seasonally adjusted series on the same axes, then you will obtain a more obvious indication of what has been done. This is illustrated in Figure 10.9.

The principles of extracting the seasonal and residual variations from a presumed multiplicative model are exactly the same as in the additive case, with the obvious exception that to 'de-trend' the series the value of y is divided by the value of t. This will mean that the de-trended series is in proportion to the actual series. The same procedure of collecting equivalent quarter de-trended ratios is still employed and this will produce the seasonal variation *factor*. The actual series is then divided

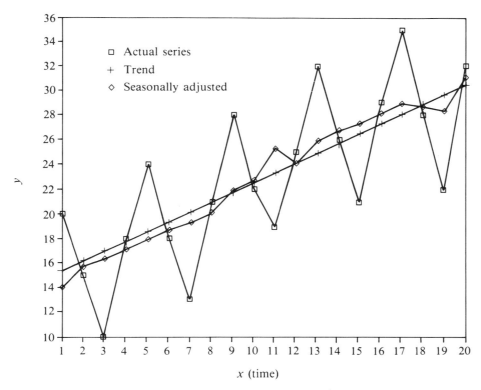

Figure 10.9 Time series analysis

by this seasonal factor to obtain the seasonally adjusted series. Finally, the residual elements are obtained by dividing the actual series (y) by the product of the de-trended series and the seasonal factor (*ts*). Using the same data as before, these calculations are performed in Worksheet 10.9.

As you can see, the resulting seasonally adjusted series for the multiplicative model is slightly different from that obtained by the additive model. Nevertheless, they still display a broad concordance as is indicated in Worksheet 10.10 and Figure 10.10.

As a final consideration in this section, you should realize that the analysis of time series is an extremely complex undertaking. This stems from the fact that the passage of time is the 'universal variable', i.e. just about everything changes with the advance of time. But whether it is the passage of time *per se* that is causing the dependent variable to change, or the influence of another variable or variables, is difficult to determine. This will often be of minor importance if all we are trying to do is describe and analyze the past behaviour of the dependent variable, but if, as is often the case we are going to make *predictions* about the future on the basis of past experience, the the influence of other variables cannot be ignored so easily.

WORKSHEET 10.9

	A time (x)	B series (y)	C linear trend (t)	D de-trend series (y/t)	E seasonal variation (s)	F seasonal adjusted (y/s)	G residual variation (y/ts)
1							
2							
3							
4	1.00	20.00	15.371429	1.301115	1.283801	15.57874	1.01349
5	2.00	15.00	16.163910	0.927993	0.964016	15.55991	0.96263
6	3.00	10.00	16.956391	0.589748	0.717411	13.93901	0.82205
7	4.00	18.00	17.748872	1.014149	1.034277	17.40346	0.98054
8	5.00	24.00	18.541353	1.294404	1.283801	18.69449	1.00826
9	6.00	18.00	19.333835	0.931010	0.964016	18.67189	0.96576
10	7.00	13.00	20.126316	0.645921	0.717411	18.12072	0.90035
11	8.00	21.00	20.918797	1.003882	1.034277	20.30403	0.97061
12	9.00	28.00	21.711278	1.289652	1.283801	21.81024	1.00456
13	10.00	22.00	22.503759	0.977614	0.964016	22.82120	1.01411
14	11.00	19.00	23.296241	0.815582	0.717411	26.48412	1.13684
15	12.00	25.00	24.088722	1.037830	1.034277	24.17147	1.00344
16	13.00	32.00	24.881203	1.286111	1.283801	24.92598	1.00180
17	14.00	26.00	25.673684	1.012710	0.964016	26.97050	1.05051
18	15.00	21.00	26.466165	0.793466	0.717411	29.27192	1.10601
19	16.00	29.00	27.258647	1.063883	1.034277	28.03890	1.02862
20	17.00	35.00	28.051128	1.247722	1.283801	27.26279	0.97190
21	18.00	28.00	28.843609	0.970752	0.964016	29.04516	1.00699

| | | 19.00 | 22.00 | 29.636090 | 0.742338 | 0.717411 | 30.66583 | 1.03475 |
| | | 20.00 | 32.00 | 30.428571 | 1.051643 | 1.034277 | 30.93948 | 1.01679 |

Regression Output:

Constant	14.57895
Std Err of Y Est	4.75022
R Squared	0.50696
No. of Observations	20.00000
Degrees of Freedom	18.00000

X Coefficient(s)	0.79248	
Std Err of Coef.	0.18421	

	1st qu.	2nd qu.	3rd qu.	4th qu.
year 1	1.30112	0.92799	0.58975	1.01415
year 2	1.29440	0.93101	0.64592	1.00388
year 3	1.28965	0.97761	0.81558	1.03783
year 4	1.28611	1.01271	0.79347	1.06388
year 5	1.24772	0.97075	0.74234	1.05164
Sum	6.4190	4.8201	3.5871	5.1714
Avg	1.28380	0.96402	0.71741	1.03428

WORKSHEET 10.10

	A time	B series	C linear trend	D seasonally adjusted	E seasonally adjusted
1					
2					
3	(x)	(y)	(t)	(y-s) Add.	(y/s) Mult.
4	1.00	20.00	15.371429	13.911278195	15.578739526
5	2.00	15.00	16.163910	15.703759398	15.559906060
6	3.00	10.00	16.956391	16.296240602	13.939011554
7	4.00	18.00	17.748872	17.088721805	17.403456027
8	5.00	24.00	18.541353	17.911278195	18.694487432
9	6.00	18.00	19.333835	18.703759398	18.671887272
10	7.00	13.00	20.126316	19.296240602	18.120715021
11	8.00	21.00	20.918797	20.088721805	20.304032032
12	9.00	28.00	21.711278	21.911278195	21.810235337
13	10.00	22.00	22.503759	22.703759398	22.821195555
14	11.00	19.00	23.296241	25.296240602	26.484121954
15	12.00	25.00	24.088722	24.088721805	24.171466704
16	13.00	32.00	24.881203	25.911278195	24.925983243
17	14.00	26.00	25.673684	26.703759398	26.970503837
18	15.00	21.00	26.466165	27.296240602	29.271924265
19	16.00	29.00	27.258647	28.088721805	28.038901377
20	17.00	35.00	28.051128	28.911278195	27.262794171
21	18.00	28.00	28.843609	28.703759398	29.045157979
22	19.00	22.00	29.636090	28.296240602	30.665825421
23	20.00	32.00	30.428571	31.088721805	30.939477382

This forecasting approach is clearly fraught with danger, but as long as we remember that a successful forecast can be thought of as one that performs better than a guess, then we can continue to make predictions and feel at least partially confident that our decision making is more informed than would have been the case if we decided everything on the toss of a coin.

10.14 A case example

The following data were collected in an attempt to investigate the relationship between an 'all electric' office's average daily consumption of electricity and the mean daily outside temperature. The results are shown in Worksheet 10.11.

1. Obtain the equation of the best linear relationship between electricity consumption and outside temperature, and use this equation to predict the mean daily electricity consumption on a day when the average outside temperature was: (a) $-10°C$, (b) $30°C$, (c) $15.5°C$.
2. What factors should you consider in any attempt to improve the accuracy of your regression model?

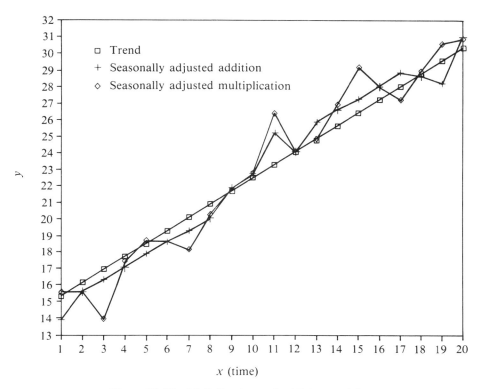

Figure 10.10 Muliplicative and additive models

3. A parallel study in which the mean daily electricity consumption (y kWh) was regressed on the average daily inside temperature ($x°C$) produced the Lotus regression output shown in Worksheet 10.12.

10.15 Discussion and solutions

1. A scatter plot of the data immediately suggests that the relationship is nonlinear as Figure 10.11 indicates.

Given this, we should expect that the simple linear regression model might not perform well. However, this is not confirmed by the regression output in Worksheet 10.13.

As you can see, the R Squared value is in excess of 0.8 and is significantly different from zero, as is the gradient of the regression equation. Our linear model is therefore

$$y = 275.1827 - 8.076x$$

WORKSHEET 10.11

	A	B
1	Mean Outside	Daily Electricity
2	Temp C	Usage KWH
3	x	y
4	-8.00	350.00
5	-7.00	350.00
6	-6.00	340.00
7	-5.00	325.00
8	-4.00	320.00
9	-3.00	317.00
10	-2.00	310.00
11	-1.00	302.00
12	0.00	299.00
13	1.00	280.00
14	2.00	267.00
15	3.00	254.00
16	4.00	243.00
17	5.00	235.00
18	6.00	220.00
19	7.00	205.00
20	8.00	199.00
21	9.00	187.00
22	10.00	159.00
23	11.00	132.00
24	12.00	114.00
25	13.00	100.00
26	14.00	102.00
27	15.00	109.00
28	16.00	114.00
29	17.00	119.00
30	18.00	124.00
31	19.00	129.00
32	20.00	135.00
33	21.00	141.00
34	22.00	148.00
35	23.00	156.00
36	24.00	164.00

The implied line is superimposed on the actual data in Figure 10.12. Nevertheless we should consider some form of logarithmic transformation of the data before accepting the simple linear model as being the best fit.

But as we have already seen, the double logarithmic transformation encounters difficulties when an x value of zero is included in the data range (and also when negative values of x have been observed). Since we cannot discard such a large

WORKSHEET 10.12

```
                A              B              C              D
41                     Regression Output:
42   Constant                                             2588.475
43   Std Err of Y Est                                     41.12092
44   R Squared                                            0.776373
45   No. of Observations                                  33
46   Degrees of Freedom                                   31
47
48   X Coefficient(s)              -141.6055359
49   Std Err of Coef.              13.649761725
```

Mean daily electricity consumption (y kWh) regressed on average daily inside temperature (x°C)

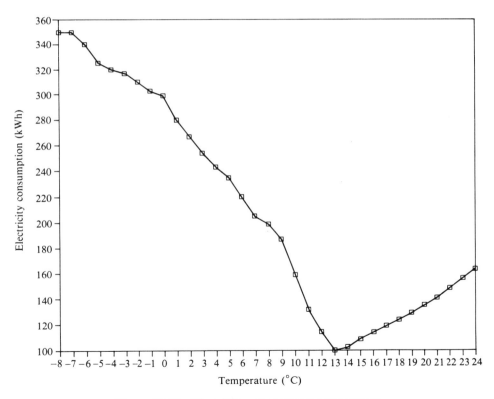

Figure 10.11 Electricity usage versus temperature

WORKSHEET 10.13

	A	B	C	D
41		Regression Output:		
42	Constant			275.1827
43	Std Err of Y Est			35.59033
44	R Squared			0.832482
45	No. of Observations			33
46	Degrees of Freedom			31
47				
48	X Coefficient(s)		−8.075868984	
49	Std Err of Coef.		0.6506558304	

y (kWh) regressed on x (outside temperature, °C)

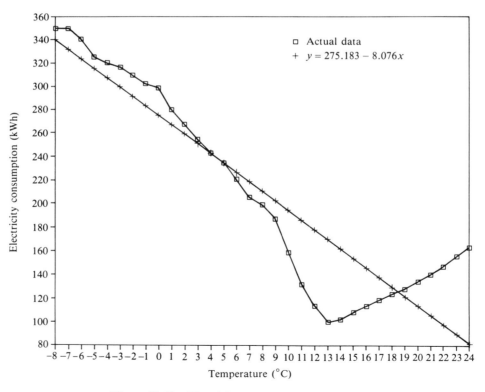

Figure 10.12 Electricity usage versus temperature

portion of our data set, we could try to deal with this by presuming a model of the form

$$y = a[(x+c)^b]$$

where c is a constant that can be selected to ensure that the independent variable does not adopt a value of zero. In this case, with a minimum temperature of $-8°C$ we can let $c = 9$, and then regress y on $(x + 9)$, which will always be positive and greater than zero. Our presumed polynomial model is then

$$y = a[(x+9)^b]$$

This is equivalent to the linear equation

$$\log y = \log a + b[\log(x+9)]$$

Since the data show a marked inverse relationship over much of its range, we should expect that b will be negative and this is confirmed in the Lotus regression output produced in Worksheet 10.14

As you can see, the value of R Squared has not increased as a result of the transformation and so we cannot conclude that the double log transformation has improved the properties of our model.

Furthermore, the technique employed is not entirely satisfactory, since we would obtain different regression output if we had used $(x + 12)$ or $(x + 15)$ as our independent variable.

This problem does not arise if we use a semi-logarithmic transformation, but it seems unlikely that it will improve matters since it should be clear that the data is adopting a form that is best modelled by a quadratic equation.

Nevertheless, in the absence of quadratic regression techniques, we can see what the semi-log transformation produces. This is done in Worksheet 10.15. As we suspected, there is no improvement upon the simple linear model, and so we conclude that this latter version is the best we can do with the regression techniques available to us.

WORKSHEET 10.14

	A	B	C	D
41		Regression Output:		
42	Constant			2.749198
43	Std Err of Y Est			0.101441
44	R Squared			0.704061
45	No. of Observations			33
46	Degrees of Freedom			31
47				
48	X Coefficient(s)		−0.413106071	
49	Std Err of Coef.		0.0481034645	

$\log y = \log a + b \ [\log(x + 9)]$

WORKSHEET 10.15

	A	B	C	D
41		Regression Output:		
42	Constant			2.420085
43	Std Err of Y Est			0.089305
44	R Squared			0.770633
45	No. of Observations			33
46	Degrees of Freedom			31
47				
48	X Coefficient(s)		-0.016662450	
49	Std Err of Coef.		0.001632671	

$\log y = \log a + \log b \, (x)$

The predicted values of y when $x = -10$, when $x = 30$ and when $x = 15.5$ are obtained from the following equations:

$$y = 275.138 - 8.076(-10) = 355.94$$
$$y = 275.183 - 8.076(30) \;\; = 32.90$$
$$y = 275.183 - 8.076(15.5) = 150.05$$

Bearing the scatter diagram in mind, the last result seems to be quite reasonable, but we should have serious reservations about the second one given the behaviour of the data for x values in excess of $13\,°C$. Even the first one might be a bit suspect if there is an upper limit to the output, and hence the electricity consumption, of the heating system.

We can partially solve these difficulties if we partition the data around a value of $x = 13$, and argue that there is one regression equation for x values that are 13 or less, and another one for x values of 14 or more. If we do this then we obtain the two regression outputs shown in Worksheet 10.16.

This allows to argue that

$$y = 279.655 - 11.7165x \quad \text{if } x \leqslant 13$$
$$y = 17.864 + 5.9545x \quad \text{if } x \geqslant 14$$

Taking these two equations together, we can write a Lotus conditional formula that will allow us to predict the value of y depending upon the value of x. For the data set and the regression output ranges that we have been using such a statement would be

@IF(X<=13,D$42+C$48*A4,D$53+C$59*A4)

This means that if x is less than or equal to 13, then predict the value of y on the basis of the top regression output, otherwise use the lower regression output figures. The formula can then be copied into all relevant cells.

WORKSHEET 10.16

```
               A             B             C                 D
41                    Regression Output: y=a+bx (X<=13)
42    Constant                                       279.6549
43    Std Err of Y Est                               14.88614
44    R Squared                                      0.964823
45    No. of Observations                            22
46    Degrees of Freedom                             20
47
48    X Coefficient(s)           -11.71654432
49    Std Err of Coef.            0.5002508425
50
51
52                    Regression Output: y=a+bx (x>14)
53    Constant                                       17.86363
54    Std Err of Y Est                               1.818813
55    R Squared                                      0.992424
56    No. of Observations                            11
57    Degrees of Freedom                             9
58
59    X Coefficient(s)            5.9545454545
60    Std Err of Coef.            0.1734170173
```

When this is done it can be graphed to produce something like Figure 10.13. Clearly this is a better estimate of the relationship than that provided by the simple linear model.

If we use this to revise our predictions for $x = -10$, $x = 30$ and $x = 15.5$ we obtain the following results:

$$y = 279.655 - 11.7165(-10) = 396.82$$
$$y = 17.863 + 5.954(30) \quad = 196.48$$
$$y = 17.863 + 5.954(15.5) \quad = 110.15$$

However, even with this modification, we might still be concerned about our prediction for $x = -10$. Can you work out why? Think about it and then read on.

2. There are a number of factors to be considered in the construction of the experiment which will impinge upon its accuracy.

(a) We should suspect that the apparently quadratic nature of the data stems from the fact that electricity is used not only to heat, but also to cool (via air-conditioning and refrigeration). This means that we should try to separate these two effects in our experimental data – a task that may not be easy without some more sophisticated method of monitoring electricity usage. An added complication is that electricity will also be used for lighting, and that this usage will vary over the year roughly in line with the outside temperature (dark, cold

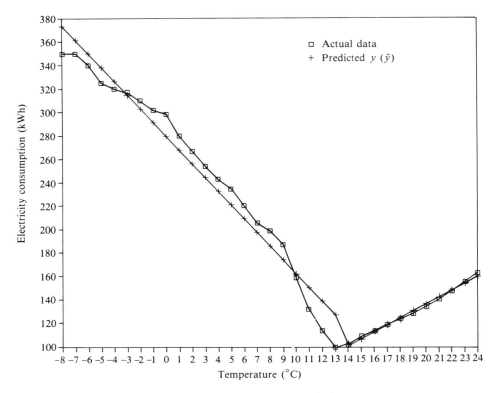

Figure 10.13 Conditional prediction

winter days, light, warm summer ones). This association is unlikely to be perfect, however, and once again we would really like to extract its effect from the total electricity usage.

(b) The independent variable is clearly not under the experimenter's control, and so it will be necessary to monitor a large number of days to obtain a sufficient range of different x values. This is complicated by the fact that it is more likely to be the average temperature during the working day that we are concerned with (although some heating during the night will usually be required in winter). Even then, it does not necessarily follow that two or more days with the same mean temperature will require the same amount of heating. It is also the distribution of temperature around this mean that is important, especially during working hours.

(c) If the building is thermostatically controlled, then the electricity consumption for heating purposes is bound to mirror the outside temperature. The issue becomes whether the settings of the thermostats are exercising an added unseen effect upon electricity consumption.

(d) The nature of the heating system will create an upper limit to electricity consumption, since no matter how cold it becomes the system can only work to its limitations and the associated maximum electricity consumption. This is why we might have reservations about the predicted fuel consumption when $x = -10°C$.

3. It is not surprising that the data display a high degree of correlation since the purpose of using electricity is to create a difference between the inside and the outside temperatures. In this respect the nature of the relationship has been complicated by the fact that the inside temperature (IT) depends upon the outside temperature (OT) *and* the effect of electricity used for heating purposes (EC).

We could try to model this in the following way:

$$IT = OT + a + b(EC)$$

This means, for example, that if no electricity was used for heating purposes ($EC = 0$), then the inside temperature would equal the outside temperature plus a (where a is a constant representing the insulation of the building). However, as some electricity is used, this causes the difference between the inside and outside temperatures to rise, and so the b coefficient can be viewed as an indicator of the efficiency of the heating system.

This, of course, is not a simple linear model, since now there are *two* independent variables (OT and EC), which requires that we use a technique known as multiple regression. Lotus can do this for you, but the statistics involved in understanding what is happening exceed the scope of this text.

10.16 Exercises

10.1

The data in Worksheet 10.17 refer to an investigation of the relationship between the retail price of a firm's product and the average weekly sales of that product. The data was collected on a weekly basis over a period of 10 years.

(a) Produce a graph of the relationship between weekly sales and price.
(b) Obtain the least squares regression equation of weekly sales on price.
(c) Does the value of R Squared indicate a strong linear association between the variables?
(d) Are you confident that the gradient of the regression equation is significantly different from zero?
(e) Elementary economic theory suggests that if the price of a product rises, the sales of that product will fall. Your regression equation would seem to refute this theory. Why?
(f) How might you modify your analysis to accommodate the previous difficulty?

WORKSHEET 10.17

	A	B
1	Price (£)	Weekly
2		Sales
3	0.45	1412
4	0.48	1509
5	0.5	1599
6	0.53	1659
7	0.61	1679
8	0.63	1757
9	0.7	1799
10	0.75	1840
11	0.81	1891
12	0.9	1967
13	0.95	1989
14	0.99	2080
15	1.04	2123
16	1.11	2250
17	1.17	2367
18	1.21	2450
19	1.25	2568
20	1.3	2678

10.2

(a) Calculate the trend and the seasonally adjusted series for the monthly data shown in Worksheet 10.18.
(b) Plot the actual series, the trend and the seasonally adjusted series on the same axes.
(c) What conclusions can you draw from your analysis?

10.3

An economist performed a linear regression of the monthly index of the value of manufacturing output, upon the monthly index of the value of fixed capital investment. The following Lotus regression output was obtained:

Regression output constant	68.866
Std Err of Y Est	3.3200
R Squared	0.7071
No. of observations	12
Degrees of freedom	10
X Coefficient(s)	2.3961
Std Err of Coef.	0.4976

(a) What conclusions can be drawn from the results?
(b) State any reservations you have about the validity of the method employed.

WORKSHEET 10.18

	A Time (months)	B Monthly Sales of Turkeys 000's
1		
2		
3		
4	1	3.21
5	2	2.7
6	3	3
7	4	4.25
8	5	2.8
9	6	2.5
10	7	2.4
11	8	2.5
12	9	2.8
13	10	2.4
14	11	3
15	12	8.9
16	13	3.4
17	14	2.9
18	15	3.1
19	16	4.8
20	17	3.2
21	18	3.13
22	19	2.99
23	20	2.76
24	21	3.5
25	22	3.7
26	23	3.52
27	24	7.67
28	25	3.7
29	26	2.98
30	27	3.33
31	28	4.9
32	29	2.98
33	30	2.79
34	31	3.04
35	32	3.15
36	33	3.26
37	34	3.47
38	35	3.02
39	36	7.58

10.4

The data in Worksheet 10.19 refer to an accountant's estimate of the book value of an item of capital equipment at various points in time.

(a) Calculate the least squares regression equation of book value on time.
(b) Perform the most appropriate logarithmic transformation of the data and then recalculate the regression equation.

WORKSHEET 10.19

	A	B
1	Time	Book Value
2	(years)	y (£000's)
3	0	1000
4	0.5	6666.6666667
5	1	5000
6	1.5	4000
7	2	3333.3333333
8	2.5	2857.1428571
9	3	2500
10	3.5	2222.2222222
11	4	2000
12	4.5	1818.1818182
13	5	1666.6666667
14	5.5	1538.4615385
15	6	1428.5714286
16	6.5	1333.3333333
17	7	1250
18	7.5	1176.4705882
19	8	1111.1111111
20	8.5	1052.6315789
21	9	1000
22	9.5	952.38095238
23	10	909.09090909
24	10.5	869.56521739
25	11	833.33333333
26	11.5	800
27	12	769.23076923
28	12.5	740.74074074
29	13	714.28571429
30	13.5	689.65517241
31	14	666.66666667
32	14.5	645.16129032
33	15	625
34	15.5	606.06060606
35	16	588.23529412
36	16.5	571.42857143
37	17	555.55555556
38	17.5	540.54054054
39	18	526.31578947
40		

(c) What is your best estimate of the book value of this item of equipment after 25 years?

10.5

The following study was carried out in an attempt to investigate the beer-drinking habits of young people (under 30). Groups of 40 individuals for each given age were

WORKSHEET 10.20

	A	B
1	Age (years)	Mean weekly beer
2	x	consumption (pints) y
3	15	3.5
4	16	4.8
5	17	5.9
6	18	6.6
7	19	7.3
8	20	7.7
9	21	8.1
10	22	8.2
11	23	8.2
12	24	7.9
13	25	7.8
14	26	7.6
15	27	7.8
16	28	7.7
17	29	7.75

interviewed and asked to estimate their average weekly consumption of beer. The results were as shown in Worksheet 10.20.

(a) Estimate the least squares regression equation of beer consumption upon age, and comment on your results.

(b) Estimate the mean weekly beer consumption of: (i) a new-born baby; (ii) a centenarian.

(c) In the light of your answer to part (b) what modifications should you make to your regression model?

(d) State any reservations you have about the methods employed by the investigation team.

10.17 Solutions to the exercises

10.1

(a) The graph of the data is produced in Figure 10.14.

(b) The Lotus regression output is as shown in Worksheet 10.21.

(c) The value of R Squared is exceptionally high, although with only 16 degrees of freedom it needs to be. Tables will show that it is significantly different from zero with a risk factor of less than 0.1 per cent.

(d) The same comment as in (c) above applies to the gradient of the regression equation. Approximately 95 per cent of all possible gradient values lie in the range 1262.79 ± 118.16. This range does not include zero.

Linear Regression and Business Forecasting

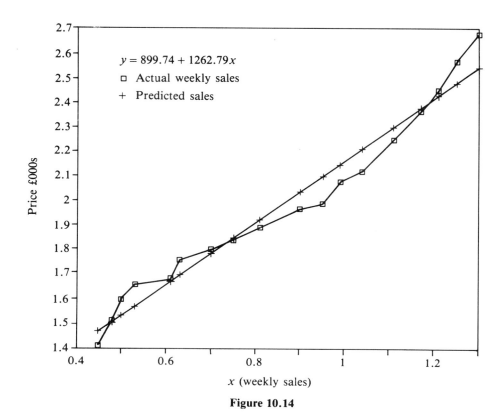

Figure 10.14

```
WORKSHEET 10.21
                A              B         C              D
    21                      Regression Output:
    22   Constant                                    899.7352
    23   Std Err of Y Est                             71.13551
    24   R Squared                                     0.964805
    25   No. of Observations                         18
    26   Degrees of Freedom                          16
    27
    28   X Coefficient(s)             1262.793
    29   Std Err of Coef.               60.29636
```

(e) There are a number of other factors that influence the quantity demanded. In particular, since the study covers a period of 10 years, there will have been income increases, which would appear to have exercised a considerable effect.

(f) You can improve the accuracy of your model by attempting to control the other factors which influence the quantity demanded. This is never easy in this sort of investigation, but we could start by expressing the data on price as a proportion of mean weekly income. Then, over the period, we would probably find that this 'real price' has declined, thereby re-establishing the inverse relationship between price and sales that was expected.

10.2

(a) The calculations are contained in Worksheet 10.22 where the 'seasonal' variation has been calculated on a monthly basis.

It will be noticed that R Squared is very low, indicating that the trend equation is a poor representation of the actual data. This is hardly surprising when you look at the graph of the data.

(b) These calculations produce the graph shown in Figure 10.15.

(c) Clearly there are monthly peaks at Christmas and at Easter, nevertheless the overall trend is of slowly increasing turkey consumption.

When the seasonally adjusted data is examined, it would seem to suggest that although turkey consumption is still a seasonal event, it is becoming less so. This could be partly because people are consuming other types of meat on the festive occasions, but also because they are consuming relatively more turkey at other times. This is indicated by the fact that for the first year the seasonally adjusted figure at Christmas exceeds the trend value, whereas for the second and third years the opposite is true.

10.3

(a) The R Squared value is reasonably high but there are only 10 degrees of freedom. The gradient is likely to vary by an amount of almost ± 1, which, given its value of 2.39 is quite a significant variation. It would appear, however, to be significantly different from zero.

(b) There are a number of reservations.

(i) Why were so few observations taken?
(ii) Do we really believe that if investment fell to zero, then output would remain at an index value of 68.866? This partly depends upon the values that the index can adopt but also upon the length of time before a reduction in investment affects production.
(iii) In the light of this last point some kind of time lag should have been incorporated into the model.
(iv) Even if this had been done, it would still remain unclear whether the dependent and independent variables have been specified correctly. Clearly output does

WORKSHEET 10.22

	A Time (months)	B Monthly Sales of Turkeys 000's	C Trend	D de-trend series	E seasonal variation	F seasonally adjusted
1						
2						
3						
4	1	3.21	3.079054	0.130945	0.00553539	3.204464607
5	2	2.7	3.108393	-0.40839	-0.6004710	3.300471042
6	3	3	3.137733	-0.13773	-0.3464774	3.346477477
7	4	4.25	3.167073	1.082926	1.13084942	3.119150579
8	5	2.8	3.196413	-0.39641	-0.5551570	3.355157014
9	6	2.5	3.225752	-0.72575	-0.7711634	3.271163449
10	7	2.4	3.255092	-0.85509	-0.7971698	3.197169884
11	8	2.5	3.284432	-0.78443	-0.8331763	3.333176319
12	9	2.8	3.313772	-0.51377	-0.4791827	3.279182754
13	10	2.4	3.343111	-0.94311	-0.5051891	2.905189189
14	11	3	3.372451	-0.37245	-0.5445289	3.544528957
15	12	8.9	3.401791	5.498208	4.29613127	4.603868725
16	13	3.4	3.431131	-0.03113	0.00553539	3.394464607
17	14	2.9	3.460471	-0.56047	-0.6004710	3.500471042
18	15	3.1	3.489810	-0.38981	-0.3464774	3.446477477
19	16	4.8	3.519150	1.280849	1.13084942	3.669150579
20	17	3.2	3.548490	-0.34849	-0.5551570	3.755157014
21	18	3.13	3.577830	-0.44783	-0.7711634	3.901163449
22	19	2.99	3.607169	-0.61716	-0.7971698	3.787169884
23	20	2.76	3.636509	-0.87650	-0.8331763	3.593176319
24	21	3.5	3.665849	-0.16584	-0.4791827	3.979182754
25	22	3.7	3.695189	0.004810	-0.5051891	4.205189189
26	23	3.52	3.724528	-0.20452	-0.5445289	4.064528957
27	24	7.67	3.753868	3.916131	4.29613127	3.373868725
28	25	3.7	3.783208	-0.08320	0.00553539	3.694464607
29	26	2.98	3.812548	-0.83254	-0.6004710	3.580471042
30	27	3.33	3.841888	-0.51188	-0.3464774	3.676477477
31	28	4.9	3.871227	1.028772	1.13084942	3.769150579
32	29	2.98	3.900567	-0.92056	-0.5551570	3.535157014

	A	B	C	D	E	F
33	30	2.79	3.929907	-1.13990	-0.7711634	3.561163449
34	31	3.04	3.959247	-0.91924	-0.7971698	3.8371698884
35	32	3.15	3.988586	-0.83858	-0.8331763	3.9831763319
36	33	3.26	4.017926	-0.75792	-0.4791827	3.7391782754
37	34	3.47	4.047266	-0.57726	-0.5051891	3.9751891189
38	35	3.02	4.076606	-1.05660	-0.5445289	3.5645289957
39	36	7.58	4.105945	3.474054	4.29613127	3.2838687255
40						
41		Regression Output:				
42	Constant			3.049714		
43	Std Err of Y Est			1.472506		
44	R Squared			0.043395		
45	No. of Observations			36		
46	Degrees of Freedom			34		
47						
48	X Coefficient(s)		0.029339			
49	Std Err of Coef.		0.023624			
50						
51	Year	1	2	3	Average	
52	Month					
53	1	0.13095	-0.03113	-0.08320	0.00553539	
54	2	-0.40839	-0.56047	-0.83254	-0.6004710	
55	3	-0.13773	-0.38981	-0.51188	-0.3464774	
56	4	1.08293	1.280849	1.028772	1.13084942	
57	5	-0.39641	-0.34849	-0.92056	-0.5551570	
58	6	-0.72575	-0.44783	-1.13990	-0.7711634	
59	7	-0.85509	-0.61716	-0.91924	-0.7971698	
60	8	-0.78443	-0.87650	-0.83858	-0.8331763	
61	9	-0.51377	-0.16584	-0.75792	-0.4791827	
62	10	-0.94311	0.004810	-0.57726	-0.5051891	
63	11	-0.37245	-0.20452	-1.05660	-0.5445289	
64	12	5.49821	3.916131	3.474054	4.29613127	

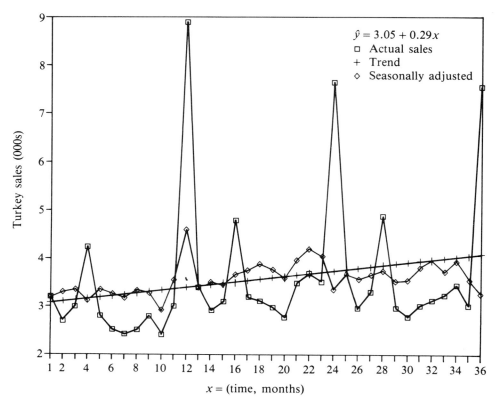

Figure 10.15 Time series of turkey sales

depend upon investment, but it can equally well be argued that output influences investment (since if high output leads to high profits, then this will provide both the motivation and the wherewithal to undertake more investment).

(v) Since the data consist of value indices, we will have to be sure that the influence of inflation has been accommodated by the model. In this sense it is a slight blessing that so few periods have been used, but even then, we still do not know what total time period they span.

In short, this represents a good example of *how not* to carry out and present a regression analysis.

10.4

The regression outputs for parts (a) and (b) of the problem are produced in Worksheet 10.23. Notice the last one where an R Squared value of 1 has been

Solutions to the exercises 515

obtained for the regression equation

$$\log y = 4 - \log(x + 1)$$

This was a bit of a 'cheat' since the data were constructed to correspond exactly to the polynomial equation implied by this logarithmic expression. That is

$$y = 10^4 [(x + 1)^{-1}] = 10\,000/(x + 1)$$

WORKSHEET 10.23

		A	B	C	D
(a)	41	Regression Output: y on x			
	42	Constant			4096.849
	43	Std Err of Y Est			1340.825
	44	R Squared			0.533703
	45	No. of Observations			37
	46	Degrees of Freedom			35
	47				
	48	X Coefficient(s)		−261.337	
	49	Std Err of Coef.		41.29039	
	50				
(b,i)	51	Regression Output: log y on x			
	52	Constant			3.603268
	53	Std Err of Y Est			0.114222
	54	R Squared			0.881516
	55	No. of Observations			37
	56	Degrees of Freedom			35
	57				
	58	X Coefficient(s)		−0.05676	
	59	Std Err of Coef.		0.003517	
	60				
(b,ii)	61	Regression Output: log y on log x excluding x=0			
	62	Constant			3.728630
	63	Std Err of Y Est			0.034407
	64	R Squared			0.986615
	65	No. of Observations			36
	66	Degrees of Freedom			34
	67				
	68	X Coefficient(s)		−0.77476	
	69	Std Err of Coef.		0.015475	
	70				
(b,iii)	71	Regression Output: log y on log(x+1)			
	72	Constant			4
	73	Std Err of Y Est			0
	74	R Squared			1
	75	No. of Observations			37
	76	Degrees of Freedom			35
	77				
	78	X Coefficient(s)		−1	
	79	Std Err of Coef.		0	

As we have said before, you will not always be able to see that the data fit $(x + 1)$ rather than x or $(x + 2)$, etc., but you can take heart from the fact that the simple double log transformation (excluding $x = 0$ from the calculations) performs almost as well. The implied polynomial equation is

$$y = 10^{3.728}(x^{-0.774\,76}) = 5353.4/(x^{0.774\,76})$$

So, for part (c), using this last equation we would estimate that after 25 years the value of the item of equipment would be

$$5353.4/(25^{0.77\,476}) = 442.14$$

The actual value (given our 'cheated' knowledge) would be

$$10\,000/(25 + 1) = 384.61$$

Furthermore, the predicted value on the basis of the simple linear equation would be

$$4096.85 - 261.337(25) = -2435.57$$

This confirms that the relationship is not linear and that the moderately high value of R Squared (0.5337) is quite misleading if estimates are to be made outside the range of the observed data set.

10.5

(a) The regression output is produced in Worksheet 10.24. As you can see, the R Squared value is not very high, due mainly to the fact that the data start to 'turn down' for ages in excess of 21.

(b) When $x = 0$, $y = 2.200$, implying that newborn babies consume 2.2 pints of beer per week!

When $x = 100$, $y = 24.57$, and it is difficult to say whether this is a reasonable estimate. It would appear to be rather high, however.

WORKSHEET 10.24

	A	B	C	D
21		Regression Output:		
22	Constant			2.200833
23	Std Err of Y Est			0.976114
24	R Squared			0.530895
25	No. of Observations		15	
26	Degrees of Freedom		13	
27				
28	X Coefficient(s)		0.22375	
29	Std Err of Coef.		0.058334	

y (pints) = $a + bx$ (age)

(c) Surely we require that the function that is to model the data behaves in such a way that there is no beer consumption up to age 14 or so, that consumption increases for ages between 15 and 21, but eventually approaches some upper limit or even declines as age increases. Such an elongated S-shaped function is known as a logistic curve, but it is not easily produced within the confines of our linear regression model (even with logarithmic transformations).

(d) We can express a number of reservations.

(i) The sampling technique should differentiate between men and women, and between those individuals who do not drink any form of alcohol at all.

(ii) The effect of increasing income has not been considered, and since this will usually also increase with age, it is a serious omission. We should suspect that there are a number of effects operating here. Increasing income enhances the capability to indulge in alcohol consumption, while increasing responsibility and recognition of the potential dangers reduce the inclination to indulge this capability. Both of these factors are of course related to age.

(iii) There should be some form of control for the social class and/or socializing habits of the respondents.

(iv) We should be suspicious about the accuracy of the data since it requires an estimate to be supplied by the respondent which may (either inadvertently or deliberately) be incorrect.

11
Principles of Probability and Decision Making

11.1 Uncertainty and probability

In most of our previous analysis the decision-making process has been largely based upon the search for well-defined, definite solutions, since only in a few cases have we used Lotus conditional statements to allow for the possibility of more than one answer to the question posed.

In practice, however, the fact that many processes can produce any one of several different eventual outcomes means that we require some method of assessing the likelihood of different outcomes occurring, and that the effects of uncertainty must be considered.

If this can be done, then these likelihoods (or probabilities) can then be used to guide the decision-making process in such a way that the full implications of alternative strategies and decisions in the face of uncertainty can be considered and analyzed.

You will probably have noticed that we have already used words such as 'outcomes', 'likelihood' and 'probability', so it should come as no surprise to learn that decision making in an uncertain environment is fundamentally based upon the mathematical principles that govern the analysis of random events.

These principles are known as probability analysis, and without an understanding of their implications little progress in the decision-making field can be made.

11.2 Principles of probability analysis

The starting point for probability analysis is the notion of a *random trial* in which a particular process or activity is carried out a certain number of times. This activity must be capable of producing two or more different outcomes, and there must be uncertainty as to which of the possible outcomes will actually occur.

For example, tossing a coin, or drawing a card from a standard pack of playing cards, or rolling a die, can all be thought of as instances of random trials.

If a given random trial is carried out one or more times, then this creates what is known as an *experiment*, so that tossing a coin six times, or rolling a pair of dice would constitute experiments in which the number of random trials is six and two respectively.

As we have said, however, for any given random trial, there must be at least two different possible outcomes, and these are called the *basic outcomes* of the trial.

For example, in the process of tossing a coin once, there are two basic outcomes: heads or tails, while in the process of rolling a die there are six basic outcomes: 1, 2, 3, 4, 5, or 6.

If we consider all possible basic outcomes that can result from a given random trial, and collect them together, then this defines what is known as the *sample space* of the trial.

Consequently, for the process of tossing a coin once, the sample space consists of two elements, while there will be six elements in the sample space associated with the random trial of rolling a die once.

The purpose of the random trial will usually be to record whether certain particular outcomes in which we are interested have occurred. These will usually have been defined by the experimenter in such a way that they represent outcomes that are subsets of the sample space, and are known as random events.

Accordingly, the event 'heads', and the event '6' are both examples of particular outcomes that can be generated from the sample spaces associated with the coin-tossing and die-rolling trials.

Clearly, the greater is the number of basic outcomes that can occur, the greater too is the number of events that can be defined. In the coin-tossing trial, for example, there are really only two events that can be defined:

event 1   the coin turns up heads
event 2   the coin turns up tails

In the case of rolling a die, however, there are a number of events that the experimenter could define. For example

event 1   a '6' is obtained
event 2   a '3' is obtained
event 3   an even number is obtained
event 4   an odd number is obtained
event 5   a number less than 3 is obtained

and so on.

Furthermore, as the number of random trials being carried out increases, so too will the number and complexity of the events that can be defined from the sample space. But before we can consider such complications, we require a few more definitions.

Associated with the idea of a random event is the notion of a *random variable*.

This can be thought of as a variable that can adopt a range of values depending upon the outcomes generated from a given series of random trials.

For example, in our coin-tossing experiment, if we define the event $E1$ as

$E1$: the coin turns up heads

and if we define the variable X as

$X =$ the number of heads obtained on the trial

then there are clearly only two values that X can adopt

$X = 0$ or 1

But if we tossed the coin twice, then X could adopt values of

$X = 0$ or 1 or 2

While if we tossed the coin three times, then X could be

$X = 0$ or 1 or 2 or 3

In all of these cases, however, X is to be regarded as a random variable, and the purpose of probability analysis is to derive figures that represent the relative likelihood, or probability, of each value that the random variable can adopt. Before we can do this, however, we require a definition of the notion of *probability*.

In its simplest form a probability is no more than a number, lying between 0 and 1 inclusive, which represents the likelihood of a particular event occurring. The probability of any event E is given the symbol $P(E)$ and can be calculated from the following ratio:

$$P(E) = \frac{\text{the number of outcomes that satisfy the event}}{\text{the total number of possible outcomes}}$$

For example, if a die is rolled once, and if the event $E1$ is defined as:

$E1$: the number obtained is less than 5

then since the outcomes 1 or 2 or 3 or 4 will each satisfy the event requirement, and since there are six basic outcomes, we can conclude that

$P(E1) = 4/6 = 0.6666$

By a similar logic, if the event $E2$ is defined as the number obtained being even, then we would argue that

$P(E2) = 3/6 = 0.5$

From this you should be able to see that a probability value of 1 implies that the event is certain to occur, while a probability value of zero implies that the event is incapable of occurring. Clearly, the higher the probability value, then the greater is the likelihood that the defined event will occur.

These simple ideas form the cornerstone of all probability analysis, so make sure you have understood them.

11.3 Probabilities for more complex events

The difficulties frequently encountered by the student in probability analysis usually stem from two developments that add complexity to the simple ideas outlined so far.

1. Different types of events.
2. Increases in the number of trials.

To understand the issue involved, you must appreciate that in probability analysis events can first of all be classified by whether or not they are *mutually exclusive*.

By this we mean that two or more events are to be regarded as mutually exclusive if they *cannot occur together* in any one trial, and are to be regarded as non-mutually exclusive if they are capable of *simultaneous occurrence*.

For example, consider a set of playing cards that has been curtailed in such a way that it contains only the face cards (king, queen, jack) of each suit (hearts, clubs diamonds and spades). Clearly there are a total of 12 cards in our sample space, and on the basis of one card drawn at random, now suppose we define the following events:

$E$1   the card is a heart
$E$2   the card is a club
$E$3   the card is a king

What can we say about each of these events?

Obviously $E$1 and $E$2 are mutually exclusive since any one card cannot *simultaneously* be both a heart *and* a club.

However, you should be able to see that the events

$$E1 \text{ and } E3$$
$$E2 \text{ and } E3$$

are not mutually exclusive, since the king of hearts and the king of clubs satisfy *both* criteria (i.e. a king and a heart, a king and a club).

In this case the events $E$1 and $E$3, and $E$2 and $E$3, are said to be *joint events*, in the sense that they are capable of occurring together (i.e. jointly).

If this is the case, then we can argue that if the events are not mutually exclusive, then the probability of the joint event must be greater than zero, but if they are mutually exclusive then the probability of the joint event will be zero. This is an important point, as you will see shortly.

But at this stage you may be wondering how to calculate the probability of a joint event. The principles involved can be appreciated if you look at Worksheet 11.1. All we have done here is to construct a matrix of all possible suit/denomination combinations.

Clearly there is only one cell out of the 12 (B2) which satisfies the joint event:

$$E1 \text{ and } E3$$

WORKSHEET 11.1

	A	B	C	D	E	F	G
1		Heart	Club	Diamond	Spade		Total
2	King	1	1	1	1		4
3	Queen	1	1	1	1		4
4	Jack	1	1	1	1		4
5							
6	Total	3	3	3	3		

(i.e. a heart *and* a king) and so we conclude that the probability of $E1$ and $E2$ occurring simultaneously is 1/12.

In symbols we say that

$$P(E1 \text{ and } E3) = 1/12$$

Although this is a perfectly valid way of reaching this conclusion, you should appreciate that it would be extremely tedious to construct tables such as the one above every time we were required to calculate the probability of a joint event.

However, suppose we reason as follows:

$P(E1) = 1/4$ (since there are four suits and only one of them is hearts)
$P(E3) = 1/3$ (since there are three denominations and only one of them is a king)

Given these two pieces of information, how do we extract our known probability of 1/12 for the joint event?

The answer is clearly to multiply the two probabilities together. That is

$$P(E1 \text{ and } E3) = [P(E1)][P(E3)] = (1/4)(1/3) = 1/12$$

This is a crucial result, since it clearly implies that in order to obtain the probability of the simultaneous occurrence of two events, we should *multiply* the probabilities of the individual events.

This rule is, of course, only valid if the events are actually capable of joint occurrence; nonsense will result if the rule is simply applied mechanically.

For example, on any one toss of a coin

let $E1$ = the coin turns up heads
let $E2$ = the coin turns up tails

Therefore

$$P(E1) = 0.5$$
$$P(E2) = 0.5$$

and

$$P(E1 \text{ and } E2) = (0.5)(0.5) = 0.25$$

WORKSHEET 11.2

	A	B
1	Probability of 1st event	0.4
2	Probability of 2nd event	0.3
3	Are they mutually exclusive?	1
4	P(1st event and 2nd event)	0

Apparently, the probability that the coin will turn up *both* heads *and* tails is 0.25. Clearly this is nonsense, or else some very strange coins are being used.

This illustration brings us back to the point that we made earlier: that if the events are mutually exclusive, then the probability of the joint event is zero.

Lotus can be made to understand this, as you can see in Worksheet 11.2.

In B3 you must tell Lotus whether the events are mutually exclusive or not (enter 1 if they are, or 0 if they are not).

On the basis of this information, Lotus then calculates the probability of the joint event in B4 from the conditional formula

$$@IF(B3=1,0,B1*B2)$$

Try a few examples for yourself.

Although we have concentrated our attention on the joint event, you may be wondering what happens to our probability calculations if instead of trying to calculate the probability of $E1$ *and* $E2$, we want the probability of $E1$ *or* $E2$.

Returning to our card example, you should be able to see that if we require

$$P(E1 \text{ or } E2)$$

then we are asking for the probability that the card is *either* a heart *or* a spade.

Clearly, there are three hearts available, and three spades, so there are six cards in total that satisfy our requirement, and the probability is therefore $6/12 = 0.5$. Therefore

$$P(E1 \text{ or } E2) = P(E1) + P(E2) = 3/12 + 3/12 = 0.5$$

As a general rule, however, this formulation is deficient in the sense that it is *only* valid if the events are mutually exclusive (as hearts and spades are).

To see this, suppose that we were required to calculate the probability of

$$E1 \text{ or } E3$$

i.e. a heart or a king.

If we simply apply this last rule, then we would obtain

$$P(E1 \text{ or } E3) = P(E1) + P(E3) = 1/4 + 1/3 = 7/12$$

Yet careful inspection of the matrix of outcomes would reveal that if we count the number of cells in Worksheet 11.1 that satisfy *either* outcome, then we obtain a

WORKSHEET 11.3

	A	B
1	Probability of 1st event	0.25
2	Probability of 2nd event	0.3333
3	Are they mutually exclusive?	0
4	P(1st event and 2nd event)	0.083325
5	P(1st event or 2nd event)	0.499975

total of 6 and not 7. That is

$$B2, C2, D2, E2, B3 \text{ and } B4$$

Clearly the probability of obtaining a heart or a king is 6/12 and not 7/12 as our simple rule has suggested.

However, we can salvage this rule if we recognize that the problem has stemmed from the fact that the simple expression has *double counted* the joint event: heart and king (in B2). In other words, the king of hearts has been counted as *both* a king *and* a heart instead of just the king of hearts.

To salvage our basic rule we must *subtract* the probability of the joint event from our previous calculation to obtain

$$P(E1 \text{ or } E3) = P(E1) + P(E3) - P(E1 \text{ and } E3)$$
$$= 1/4 + 1/3 - (1/4)(1/3) = 6/12$$

Of course, if the events are mutually exclusive, then as we have already seen, the probability of the joint event is zero, and so the last expression reduces to the simple rule.

These ideas allow us to modify the last worksheet as shown in Worksheet 11.3. The entry in B5 is +B1+B2−B4. As you can see, if the events are mutually exclusive, then the entry in B4 will be zero and so the formula B5 is equivalent to +B1+B2.

Otherwise, however, the joint probability will be subtracted from the sum of the two individual probabilities.

EXAMPLE 11.1

A card is drawn at random from a standard pack of 52 playing cards. Calculate the probability that it is either a spade or a denomination that is less than 5 (ace counts high).

SOLUTION 11.1

Let $E1$ = the card is a spade. Therefore

$$P(E1) = 13/52 = 1/4 = 0.25$$

Let $E2$ = the card is less than 5. Therefore

$$P(E2) = 12/52 = 0.230\ 7692$$

(remember that the ace counts high). Accordingly

$$P(E1 \text{ or } E2) = 0.25 + 0.230\ 769\ 2 - (0.25)(0.230\ 7692)$$

Using the last worksheet (with the events being non-mutually exclusive) you should find that this evaluates to

$$P(E1 \text{ or } E2) = 0.4231$$

Try it.

Now that we have established the difference between mutually exclusive and non-mutually exclusive events, we should consider another distinction that influences the the calculation of probabilities, namely that between *independent* and *dependent* events.

As an example, consider the following experiment. A card is drawn at random from a pack of 52 playing cards. The suit and denomination are noted, and then it is replaced. The pack is shuffled, another card is drawn, and its suit and denomination noted.

Calculate the probability that the cards are both hearts.

The crucial statement in the context of this problem is the fact that the card has been replaced in the pack after the first draw. This means that the possible outcomes on the second trial are *not influenced* in any way by whatever the outcome was on the first trial. The events $E1$ (the first card is a heart) and $E2$ (the second card is a heart) are said to be *independent*.

Furthermore, since we are considering more than one trial, there is an added degree of complexity that is best dealt with by constructing what is known as a *probability tree*.

So, on the first trial the card can either be a heart (H) or not a heart (H^*), and on the second trial the same outcomes are possible.

Diagrammatically, all possible combinations of outcomes can be displayed in the probability tree shown in Table 11.1.

As you can see, each branch of the tree represents the outcomes after each trial, and combines them with the possible outcomes on the previous trial. Clearly, as the

Table 11.1

1st trial	2nd trial	Number of hearts (X)	Probability P(X)
$H(1/4)$	$H(1/4)$	2	$(1/4)(1/4) = 1/16$
	$H^*(3/4)$	1	$(1/4)(3/4) = 3/16$
$H^*(3/4)$	$H(1/4)$	1	$(3/4)(1/4) = 3/16$
	$H^*(3/4)$	0	$(3/4)(3/4) = 9/16$

number of trials increases, the number of branches in the tree multiply in accordance.

At the end of each branch of the tree, the overall outcome in terms of the number of hearts obtained can be entered, and, alongside, the probability of that overall outcome. These have been calculated from the multiplicative probability rule, since an outcome such as two hearts can only occur if the first card is a heart *and* if the second card is a heart. Notice also that since there are two trials this implies that the events heart on the first draw and heart on the second draw are not mutually exclusive, and thanks to replacement are independent.

Suppose we define the random variable X to be

$X =$ the number of hearts obtained

We can use the calculations contained in the probability tree to construct what is known as the *probability distribution* of the random variable, in which each value that X can adopt is associated with its respective probability: $P(X)$.

This would be done as follows

X	0	1	2
$P(X)$	9/16	6/16	1/16

The probabilities of zero hearts and of two hearts are read directly from the probability tree, but how did we obtain a figure of 6/16 for the probability of exactly one heart?

The answer is to note that the outcome of exactly one heart can occur in either of two ways. Namely

$(H$ and $H^*)$ or $(H^*$ and $H)$

So

$$P(X = 1) = P(H \text{ and } H^*) + P(H^* \text{ and } H)$$
$$= (1/4)(3/4) + (3/4)(1/4) = 6/16$$

Notice that since $(H$ and $H^*)$ and $(H^*$ and $H)$ are mutually exclusive, their joint probability is zero, thereby leaving the actual probability unaffected when subtracted.

Also notice that

$$P(H \text{ and } H^*) = P(H^* \text{ and } H) = 3/16$$

This is an important point as it implies that if an event (such as exactly one heart) can occur in more than one way, then the probability of that event occurring can be calculated by evaluating the probability of it occurring *any one way* and then multiplying this probability by the *number of ways that the event can occur*. That is

$$P(X = 1) = 2[P(H \text{ and } H^*)] = 2[P(H^* \text{ and } H)]$$

As a final point, observe that the sum of the probabilities in the probability distribution of X is 1. This is because the probability distribution must contain *every* possible outcome, and so the probability that any one or other of these possible outcomes actually prevails must be certainty.

EXAMPLE 11.2

For the experiment defined above, construct the probability distribution for the random variable

$$X = \text{the number of face cards obtained}$$

(Assume that ace is counted as a face card along with the jack, queen and king of each suit.)

SOLUTION 11.2

The probability tree would be as shown in Table 11.2, where F and F^* represent a face card and 'not a face card' respectively.
Therefore

X	0	1	2
$P(X)$	16/169	72/169	81/169

Of course, you can get Lotus to evaluate the probabilities for you, if you prepare a worksheet similar to Worksheet 11.4. The entry in F3 is +B3∗D3 and this has been copied into F5, F7, and F9.

At this stage it is important to stress that the results above derive entirely from our specification that the first card was replaced in the pack before the second card was drawn.

However, if this is not the case, then the analysis will have to be modified to take account of the fact that whatever card is obtained on the first draw will *influence* the outcomes, and therefore the probabilities, that can be obtained on the second draw.

Table 11.2

1st trial	2nd trial	Number of face cards (X)	Probability P(X)
$F(16/52)$	$F(16/52)$	2	$(4/13)(4/13) = 16/169$
	$F^*(36/52)$	1	$(4/13)(9/13) = 36/169$
$F^*(36/52)$	$F(16/52)$	1	$(9/13)(4/13) = 36/169$
	$F^*(36/52)$	0	$(9/13)(9/13) = 81/169$

```
WORKSHEET 11.4
       A              B              C              D              E              F
  1  Trial 1                      Trial 2                        X=No. of        P(X)
  2                                                              Hearts
  3    F          0.30769230       F          0.30769230           2          0.09467455
  4
  5    F          0.30769230       NF         0.69230769           1          0.21301775
  6
  7    NF         0.69230769       F          0.30769230           1          0.21301775
  8
  9    NF         0.69230769       NF         0.69230769           0          0.47928994

F = face card; NF, not a face card.
```

Under these circumstances (without replacement), the probabilities from one trial to the next are said to be *conditional* or *dependent*.

To see this, we can construct the probability tree shown in Table 11.3 and then evaluate the probability distribution associated with the random variable

X = the number of hearts obtained (without replacement)

As you can see, the probability that the second card is a heart depends upon what the first card was. If this was a heart, then there are only 12 Hearts left and 51 cards in total, so the probability that the second card is a heart is 12/51.

On the other hand, if the first card was not a heart, then there are still 13 Hearts left out of a remaining total of 51, and so the probability that the second card is a heart is 13/51.

This logic means that the probability distribution for X will given by

X	2	1	0
$P(X)$	(13/52)(12/51)	2(13/52)(39/51)	(39/52)(38/51)
$P(X)$	156/2652	1014/2652	1482/2652

Once again, the probabilities of the individual events still add up to 1, but in this

Table 11.3

1st trial	2nd trial	Number of hearts (X)	Probability P(X)
H(13/52)	H(12/51)	2	(13/52)(12/51)
	H^*(39/51)	1	(13/52)(39/51)
H^*(39/52)	H(13/51)	1	(39/52)(13/51)
	H^*(38/51)	0	(39/52)(38/51)

case the probability distribution is clearly different from the one produced when the card was replaced.

The result of our discussion to date means that any random event can be classified in any of four ways, as Worksheet 11.5 illustrates.

Work through each of the classifications and make sure that you understand how the probabilities were obtained.

EXAMPLE 11.3

A firm sells 75 per cent of its output in region A and 25 per cent in region B.

In region A, 60 per cent of the output is distributed from supermarket chains where the average selling time of an item is six days. The remainder is distributed from small retailers where the average selling time is ten days.

In region B, 70 per cent of the output is sold from supermarkets with an average selling time of seven days, and the remainder from small retail outlets with an average selling time of nine days.

Calculate the probability that a randomly selected item will be sold within an average of

(a) 6 days.
(b) 9 days.
(c) Between 7 and 10 days.

SOLUTION 11.3

We can identify the possibilities shown in Table 11.4.
On the basis of this we would conclude that

(a) P(sold in six days) = P(A and S) = 0.45.
(b) P(sold in nine days) = P(B and SR) = 0.075.
(c) P(Sold between seven and nine days) = P(B and S) + P(B and SR) = 0.175 + 0.075 = 0.25.

Table 11.4

Region	Outlet	Outcome	Probability	Selling time
A (0.75)	S (0.6)	A & S	0.450	6
A (0.75)	SR (0.4)	A & SR	0.300	10
B (0.25)	S (0.7)	B & S	0.175	7
B (0.25)	SR (0.3)	B & SR	0.075	9

WORKSHEET 11.5

	A	B	C
		Non Mutually Exclusive Events	Mutually Exclusive Events
		a) 1 card drawn at random from standard pack.	b) 1 card drawn at random from standard pack.
	Independent Events	E1: Card is a King	E1: Card is a King
		E2: Card is a Heart	E2: Card is a Spade
		P(E1)=1/13	P(E1)=1/4
		P(E2)=1/4	P(E2)=1/4
		P(E1 and E2)=(1/13)(1/4)=1/52	P(E1 and E2)=0
		P(E1 or E2)=4/52+13/52−1/52	P(E1 or E2)=1/4+1/4−0
		=16/52	=0.5
		c) 2 cards drawn from pack without replacement.	d) 2 cards drawn from pack without replacement.
		E1: 1st card is a Heart	E1: 1st card is the Ace of Hearts
	Dependent Events	E2: 2nd card is a Heart	E2: 2nd card is the Ace of Hearts
		P(E1)=13/52=0.25	P(E1)=1/52
		P(E2)=12/51=0.2353 if E1 has occurred.	P(E2)=0 if E1 has occurred.
		P(E2)=13/51 if E1 has not occurred.	P(E2)=1/51 if E1 has not occurred.
		P(E1 and E2)=(0.25)(0.2353) = 0.0588	P(E1 and E2)=0

Note.
You may be suspecting that there is a slight problem with the terminology "E1 or E2" that we have been employing. To be exact, it is not entirely clear whether the "or" conjunction in P(Heart or Heart) is to be interpreted as meaning:
"exactly one Heart" or "at least one Heart".
In the former case we would require:
P[(H and H*) or (H* and H)]
whereas in the latter case we need:
P[(H and H*) or (H* and H) or (H and H)]
The answer is that "or" is usually interpreted to mean the joint event is included once, but not double counted.
For example, in one roll of a pair of dice, we would argue that the probability of getting a six [P(6)] would be:
P(6)=1/6+1/6-1/36=11/36
Clearly this counts the 'double six' once, since the satisfying set of outcomes is:
16, 26, 36, 46, 56, 66, 65, 64, 63, 62, 61.
On the other hand however, if we require the probability of exactly one six being obtained, then we need:
P(six on the first or six on the second)=(1/6)(5/6)+(5/6)(1/6)
That is: 10/36, which clearly does not count the double six.
This ambiguity is the reason that we have not calculated P(W1 or E2) in cases c) and d) above although you could argue that:
c) P(E1 or E2)=(13/52)(39/51)+(39/52)(12/51)
d) P(E1 or E2)=1/52+1/51

EXAMPLE 11.4

In a manufacturing process, 40 per cent of all the output produced is inspected for defects. Any item that is found to be defective is rejected and *not* marketed.

If the process consistently produces 10 per cent of its output with defects, calculate the probability that

(a) a randomly selected item will be defective;
(b) a randomly selected *marketed* item will be defective;
(c) the company feels that the proportion of defective marketed output should never exceed 5 per cent. What proportion of output must be inspected if this is to be achieved?

SOLUTION 11.4

The probabilities are outlined in Table 11.5.
Consequently

(a) P(defective item) $= P$(I and D) $+ P$(NI and D) $= 0.040 + 0.060 = 0.1$; which is what we would have expected from common sense.
(b) Since any items that are inspected and found to be defective are not marketed, this means that only 96 per cent of the total output will be marketed. Of this 96 per cent, it should be clear that 6 per cent will be defective (since it was not inspected) and so the probability that a marketed item will be defective is given by $0.06/0.96 = 0.0625$.
(c) Let the proportion of output that is inspected be x. Therefore $(1 - x)$ is not inspected.
   The marketed output will be

$$x(0.9) + (1 - x)(1) = 0.9x + 1 - x = 1 - 0.1x$$

and of this output

$$(1 - x)(0.1) = 0.1 - 0.1x$$

Table 11.5

Inspected/not inspected	Defective/not defective	Outcome	Probability
I (0.40)	D (0.1)	I & D	0.040
I (0.40)	ND (0.9)	I & ND	0.360
NI (0.60)	D (0.1)	NI & D	0.060
NI (0.60)	ND (0.9)	NI & ND	0.540

will be defective *and* marketed. Consequently the proportion of marketed output that is defective will be

$$(0.1 - 0.1x)/(1 - 0.1x)$$

Since the company requires that this ratio must not exceed 5 per cent, we can write and solve the following equation:

$$(0.1 - 0.1x)/(1 - 0.1x) = 0.05$$

implying that

$$0.095x = 0.05$$
$$x = 0.5263$$

This means that 52.63 per cent of the output should be inspected if the proportion of marketed output that is defective is not to exceed 5 per cent.

11.4 Expected values

Closely associated with the idea of a random variable is the notion of the expected value of that random variable: $E(X)$.

In simple terms this is no more than the arithmetic mean value of the probability distribution associated with the random variable.

For example, in the previous section we saw that the probability distribution associated with X = the number of hearts in the replacement experiment (with two cards being drawn) was given by

X	0	1	2
$P(X)$	9/16	6/16	1/16

Consequently

$$E(X) = (0)(9/16) + (1)(6/16) + (2)(1/16) = 0.5 \text{ hearts}$$

What this means is that, on average, if the experiment was repeated a large number of times, then each trial would produce an average of 0.5 hearts.

Of course on any one trial such an outcome is clearly impossible, but if, for example, two cards were drawn 100 times then we would expect that the total number of hearts obtained would be

$$100(0.5) = 50$$

Clearly this is only an expectation, since other outcomes are possible, but it is the most likely outcome in comparison with the alternative number of hearts that could be obtained. (Of course, if two trials produce the expectation of 0.5 hearts, then it must follow that the expected number of 'not hearts' will be 1.5).

EXAMPLE 11.5

The information in Table 11.6 refers to the number of occupants per household who are eligible to pay the community charge in a particular local authority area.

If the local authority need to raise £10 million from the 10 000 households that form its tax base, calculate the necessary size of the community charge.

Table 11.6

Number of occupants	% of households
1	0.08
2	0.39
3	0.24
4	0.18
5	0.06
6	0.04
7	0.01

SOLUTION 11.5

If the community charge is set at £x, then the expected revenue [$E(R)$] will be given by

$$E(R) = [0.08(1)(x) + 0.39(2)(x) + 0.24(3)(x) + \cdots + 0.01(7)(x)]\,10\,000$$

Therefore

$$E(R) = (2.91x)(10\,000) = 29\,100x$$

Consequently, since this must raise £10 million, the value of x is:

$$x = 10\,000\,000/29\,100 = £343.64$$

(We have conveniently ignored the possibility that some households might have more than seven eligible payees.)

EXAMPLE 11.6

Sixty per cent of a firm's investment projects are in region A, and the remainder in region B.

Of the projects in region A, 70 per cent make a profit of £10 million, and 30 per cent make a loss of £2 million. Of the projects in region B, 50 per cent make a profit of £8 million, and 50 per cent make a loss of £1 million.

1. Calculate the probability that a randomly selected project will make a loss.
2. Calculate the expected profit from a randomly selected project.

SOLUTION 11.6

You can visualize the problem as shown in Table 11.7.

1. The probability that a loss will be made is given by

$$P(L) = P(A \text{ and } L) + P(B \text{ and } L) = 0.18 + 0.2 = 0.38$$

2. We can calculate the expected profit from:

$$E(\text{profit}) = 4.2 - 0.36 + 1.6 - 0.2 = £5.24 \text{ million}$$

Alternatively, you could modify Worksheet 11.4 as shown in Worksheet 11.6 to solve this problem.

Table 11.7

Region	Profit/loss	Outcome	Probability of outcome	Profit	E (profit) (probability × profit)
A (0.60)	P (0.7)	A & P	0.420	10	4.2
A (0.60)	L (0.3)	A & L	0.180	−2	−0.36
B (0.40)	P (0.5)	B & P	0.200	8	1.6
B (0.40)	L (0.5)	B & L	0.200	−1	−0.2

WORKSHEET 11.6

	A	B	C	D	E	F	G
1	Region	Prob	Outcome	Prob	Profit/	P(X)	E(X)
2					Loss (X)		
3							
4		A	0.6	Profit	0.7	10	0.42	4.2
5							
6		A	0.6	Loss	0.3	−2	0.18	−0.36
7							
8		B	0.4	Profit	0.5	8	0.2	1.6
9							
10		B	0.4	Loss	0.5	−1	0.2	−0.2
							Total E(X) 5.24

EXAMPLE 11.7

Eighty per cent of a company's employees are 'contracted in' to the company's pension scheme. Of these employees, 30 per cent take early retirement with an average pension of £12 000 per annum, while the remainder retire at age 65 with a pension of £15 000 per annum.

Twenty per cent of the employees are 'contracted out' of the pension scheme, and of these, 15 per cent take early retirement with an average pension of £8500 per annum. The remainder retire at age 65 with an average pension of £12 500 per annum.

Calculate the expected pension of a randomly selected employee.

SOLUTION 11.7

Once again Worksheet 11.4 could be modified to provide the answer, as shown in Worksheet 11.7.

WORKSHEET 11.7

	A	B	C	D	E	F	G
1	Contract	Prob	Outcome	Prob	Pension	P(X)	E(X)
2	in/out				(X)		
3							
4	CI	0.8	ER	0.3	12	0.24	2.88
5							
6	CI	0.8	R 65	0.7	15	0.56	8.4
7							
8	CO	0.2	ER	0.15	8.5	0.03	0.255
9							
10	CO	0.2	R 65	0.85	12.5	0.17	2.125
11							
12						Total E(X)	13.66

CI = contracted in; CO, contracted out; ER, early retirement; R, retire at 65.

WORKSHEET 11.8

	A	B	C	D	E	F	G
1	Region	Prob	Outlet	Prob	Selling	P(X)	E(X)
2			Type		Time (X)		
3							
4	A	0.75	S	0.6	6	0.45	2.7
5							
6	A	0.75	SR	0.4	10	0.3	3
7							
8	B	0.25	S	0.7	7	0.175	1.225
9							
10	B	0.25	SR	0.3	9	0.075	0.675
11							
12						Total E(X)	7.6 (days)

S = supermarket; SR, small retailer.

EXAMPLE 11.8

In Example 11.3 of the previous section, calculate the expected selling time of a randomly selected product item.

SOLUTION 11.8

Modify Worksheet 11.4 as shown in Worksheet 11.8.

11.5 Conditional probabilities

So far, we have only given conditional probability a cursory examination, yet it constitutes an important part of the decision-making process.

To see the issues involved consider the following example.

EXAMPLE 11.9

In a particular company, 60 per cent of the employees are male and 40 per cent are female.

Of the males, 25 per cent are graduates, while 30 per cent of the females are graduates.

1. Calculate the probability that a randomly selected individual is: (a) a male graduate; (b) a female graduate; (c) a male non-graduate; (d) a female non-graduate.
2. Given that a randomly selected individual is female, calculate the probability that she is a graduate.
3. Given that a randomly selected individual is a graduate, calculate the probability that she is female.

SOLUTION 11.9

1. The probability tree provides a straightforward solution to this part of the question. So, using a modification of Worksheet 11.4 we obtain Worksheet 11.9. Consequently

$$P(M \text{ and } G) = 0.15$$
$$P(F \text{ and } G) = 0.12$$
$$P(M \text{ and } NG) = 0.45$$
$$P(F \text{ and } NG) = 0.28$$

WORKSHEET 11.9

	A Sex	B Prob	C Grad/ non Grad	D Prob	E P(X)
1					
2					
3					
4	M	0.6	G	0.25	0.15
5					
6	M	0.6	NG	0.75	0.45
7					
8	F	0.4	G	0.3	0.12
9					
10	F	0.4	NG	0.7	0.28

2. Since we know that the individual in question is female and that 40 per cent of these are graduates, it follows that the probability that an individual is a graduate given that she is female is 0.4. We say that

$$P(G/F) = P(\text{graduate given female}) = 0.4$$

3. This is the more complicated part of the question as it requires that we incorporate the fact that we are told that the individual is a graduate into the calculation.

However, we can start by asking what proportion of the total sample space are graduates.

Clearly:

$(0.6)(0.25) = 0.15 = 15$ per cent are male graduates
$(0.4)(0.3) = 0.12 = 12$ per cent are female graduates

So

$0.15 + 0.12 = 0.27$ are graduates of one kind or another (male or female)

It is these individuals who now constitute our sample space, since we are told that the individual in question is a graduate.

Consequently, our sample space is now the 27 per cent of employees who are graduates, and since 12 per cent of these are female graduates, we can conclude that 12 per cent of the 27 per cent = 44.4444 per cent will be female.

More generally, if $E1$ and $E2$ are any two non-mutually exclusive events, then

$$P(E1/E2) = P(E1 \text{ and } E2)/P(E2)$$

For example, in our last example let

$E1 = $ the individual is female
$E2 = $ the individual is a graduate

Conditional probabilities   539

Then

$$P(E1/E2) = (0.4)(0.3)/[(0.4)(0.3) + (0.6)(0.25)] = 0.4444$$

This expression represents what is known as Bayes' theorem and in words states that:

> The probability of the event A occurring given that the event B has occurred is equal to the probability that A and B both occur, divided by the probability that B will occur.

This last probability must be clearly understood to mean the probability that A and B will occur plus the probability that 'not A' and B will occur.

EXAMPLE 11.10

The manager of a drug company's project to find an effective treatment for migraine obtained the following information as the results of clinical trials on their latest preparation.

Forty per cent of those migraine sufferers tested showed an improvement in their condition, 50 per cent showed no improvement, while 10 per cent experienced a worsening of their condition.

Unfortunately a range of side-effects was also observed. These were experienced by 15 per cent of those whose condition improved, 35 per cent of those whose condition was unchanged, and 50 per cent of those whose condition deteriorated.

1. Given that a randomly selected migraine sufferer experienced side-effects, what is the probability that his or her condition worsened?

    The expected revenues over the next 10 years from sales of the drug to a migraine sufferer are estimated to be

    | £5000 | if the individual's condition improves |
    | £500 | if the individual's condition is unchanged |
    | £50 | if the individual's condition worsens |

    However, it is also estimated that the cost of compensating a migraine sufferer for any side-effects is £2000.

2. What is the expected net of compensation revenue from the sale of the preparation to a randomly selected migraine sufferer?

    Detecting the true extent of any side-effects is not an easy task, and as a consequence it is assumed by the company that of those migraine sufferers who experience side-effects, 30 per cent will make no claim for compensation, while 20 per cent of those who experience no side-effects will make a false compensation claim.

3. How does this information alter the expected net revenue calculated above?

SOLUTION 11.10

The decision tree for the first part of this question is provided in Worksheet 11.10.
  1. We require:

$$P(\text{condition worsened}/\text{experienced side effects}) = P(W/S)$$

Using Bayes' theorem we have

$$\begin{aligned}P(W/S) &= P(W \text{ and } S)/P(S) \\ &= 0.05/(0.06 + 0.175 + 0.05) \\ &= 0.17543\end{aligned}$$

2. From the worksheet you can see that the expected net revenue, $E(\text{revenue} - \text{compensation})$ is given by

$$E(R - C) = 0.06(3000) + 0.34(5000) + \cdots + 0.05(50) = £1685$$

3. You can expand the last worksheet to include whether a compensation claim is presented as shown in Worksheet 11.11.

As you can see, the expected net of compensation revenue is reduced to £1570. This results from the fact that the effect of the false claimants has exceeded the effect of the justified non-claimants.

WORKSHEET 11.10

	A	B	C	D	E	F	G	H
1	Cond-	Prob	Side	Prob	P(X)	REV	COMP	E(NET R)
2	ition		effects					
3								
4	I	0.4	S	0.15	0.06	5000	2000	180
5								
6	I	0.4	NS	0.85	0.34	5000	0	1700
7								
8	NI	0.5	S	0.35	0.175	500	2000	-262.5
9								
10	NI	0.5	NS	0.65	0.325	500	0	162.5
11								
12	W	0.1	S	0.5	0.05	50	2000	-97.5
13								
14	W	0.1	NS	0.5	0.05	50	0	2.5
15								
16							Total E(NET R)	1685

I = condition improved; NI, condition not improved; W, condition worse; S, side effects; NS, no side effects.

WORKSHEET 11.11

	A	B	C	D	E	F	G	H	I	J
1	Cond-	Prob	Side	Prob	Claim	Prob	P(X)	REV	COMP	E(NET R)
2	ition		effects							
3										
4	I	0.4	S	0.15	C	0.7	0.042	5000	2000	126
5										
6	I	0.4	S	0.15	NC	0.3	0.018	5000	0	90
7										
8	I	0.4	NS	0.85	C	0.2	0.068	5000	2000	204
9										
10	I	0.4	NS	0.85	NC	0.8	0.272	5000	0	1360
11										
12	NI	0.5	S	0.35	C	0.7	0.1225	500	2000	-183.7
13										
14	NI	0.5	S	0.35	NC	0.3	0.0525	500	0	26.25
15										
16	NI	0.5	NS	0.65	C	0.2	0.065	500	2000	-97.5
17										
18	NI	0.5	NS	0.65	NC	0.8	0.26	500	0	130
19										
20	W	0.1	S	0.5	C	0.7	0.035	50	2000	-68.25
21										
22	W	0.1	S	0.5	NC	0.3	0.015	50	0	0.75
23										
24	W	0.1	NS	0.5	C	0.2	0.01	50	2000	-19.5
25										
26	W	0.1	NS	0.5	NC	0.8	0.04	50	0	2
27										
28								Total E(NET R)		1570

C = compensation claim; NC, no compensation claim.

EXAMPLE 11.11

A firm is considering a type of project that has typically yielded a gross profit of £3 million on 60 per cent of occasions, and a loss of £4 million on the remainder.

1. What is the expected profit from a randomly selected project of this type?

To help them in their decision making, they employ a team of consultants who are paid 20 per cent of any profit made, but who must pay 10 per cent of any loss incurred if they recommend a loss-making project. The consultants feel that they can successfully predict a profit-making project 90 per cent of the time and a loss-making project 70 per cent of the time.

2. If the consultants predict that a randomly selected projected will make a profit, what is the probability that a loss will actually be made?
3. If the firm follows the consultants' advice and only undertakes those projects that are recommended as profit making, calculate the expected net revenue on

a randomly selected project. What is the value to the firm of the consultants' advice?
4. If the consultants shared equally in profits and losses, what is the largest percentage commission that makes their advice worthwhile?

SOLUTION 11.11

1. Without any advice from the consultants the firm's expected profit from carrying the projects out randomly, will be given by

$$0.6(3) + 0.4(-4) = £0.2 \text{ million}$$

The probability tree and the profit and loss outcomes are contained in Worksheet 11.12.

2. We require

$$P(\text{loss/profit predicted}) = 0.12/(0.12 + 0.54) = 0.1818$$

3. The expected profit from only carrying out those projects that the consultants recommend as profitable means that no profit/loss will be obtained on projects that would have made a profit but were predicted to be loss making, and on projects that would have made a loss and were predicted correctly. Consequently the expected profit will be given by

$$E(\text{profit}) = 0.54(3 - 0.6) + 0.12(-4 + 0.4) = £0.864 \text{ million}$$

(Remember the 20 per cent commission (£0.6 million) on a profit-making project, and the 10 per cent refund (£0.4 million) on a loss-making project which the consultants recommended as profitable.)

WORKSHEET 11.12

	A	B	C	D	E	F	G	H	I
1	Profit/	Prob	Pred-	Prob	P(X)	Profit/	Fee/	Net Prof/	E(P)
2	Loss		iction			Loss (X)	Refund	loss (P)	
3									
4	P	0.6	PP	0.9	0.54	3	0.6	2.4	1.296
5									
6	P	0.6	PL	0.1	0.06	0	0	0.0	0
7									
8	L	0.4	PP	0.3	0.12	-4	-0.4	-3.6	-0.432
9									
10	L	0.4	PL	0.7	0.28	0	0	0	0
11									
12								Total E(P)	0.864

P = profit; L, loss; PP, predict profit; PL, predict loss.

The consultants' advice has clearly been worth

$$£0.864 - £0.2 = £0.664 \text{ million}$$

4. Let the consultants' commission/refund = x (on both profits and losses). We therefore require

$$(3 - 3x)(0.54) + (-4 + 4x)(0.12) = 0.2$$

That is, the expected profit is the same as would be obtained by carrying the projects out randomly.

Solving for x produces

$$x = 0.824$$

implying that if the consultants share in both profits and losses up to an extent of 82.4 per cent, then their advice is still worthwhile to the firm.

EXAMPLE 11.12

An estate agent's property list only contains houses in each of three areas: Arlington, Brumford and Chisingham. Twenty-five per cent of the property list is in Arlington, 40 per cent is in Brumford and 35 per cent is in Chisingham.

In Arlington 60 per cent of the housing on the list is terraced, 30 per cent is semi-detached and 10 per cent is detached. In Brumford 40 per cent of the housing is terraced, 25 per cent is semi-detached and 35 per cent is detached. In Chisingham 20 per cent of the housing is terraced, 60 per cent is semi-detached and 20 per cent is detached.

The estate agent takes a 10 per cent commission on the value of all houses sold, and the average price (in £000s) of each of the three types of house in each of the three areas is as follows:

	Arlington	*Brumford*	*Chisingham*
Terraced	32	40	30
Semi-detached	60	80	70
Detached	85	100	90

1. Calculate the probability that a randomly selected house from the estate agent's list is terraced.
2. Calculate the probability that a randomly selected house from the list is not detached.
3. Given that a randomly selected house from the list is in Arlington, calculate the probability that it is detached.

4. Given that a randomly selected house is detached, calculate the probability that it is in Brumford.
5. What is the expected commission to the estate agent from the sale of a randomly selected property from the list?

By reducing his commission to 8 per cent the estate agent can increase his share of detached property in each area by an amount of 5 per cent (at the expense of terraced property).

6. Is such a reduced rate of commission justified in terms of the increase in the expected commission from a randomly selected property from the list?

SOLUTION 11.12

The probability tree is produced in Worksheet 11.13.

1. $P(\text{terraced}) = (0.25)(0.6) + (0.4)(0.4) + (0.35)(0.2)$
   $= 0.38$
2. $P(\text{detached}) = (0.25)(0.1) + (0.4)(0.35) + (0.35)(0.2)$
   $= 0.235$

WORKSHEET 11.13

G4: 0.1*F4

	A	B	C	D	E	F	G	H
1	Area	Prob	House Type	Prob	P(X)	House Price	Commiss	E(commiss)
2								
3								
4	A	0.25	T	0.6	0.15	32	3.2	0.48 ← E4*G4
5								
6	A	0.25	SD	0.3	0.075	60	6	0.45
7								
8	A	0.25	D	0.1	0.025	85	8.5	0.2125
9								
10	B	0.4	T	0.4	0.16	40	4	0.64
11								
12	B	0.4	SD	0.25	0.1	80	8	0.8
13								
14	B	0.4	D	0.35	0.14	100	10	1.4
15								
16	C	0.35	T	0.2	0.07	30	3	0.21
17								
18	C	0.35	SD	0.6	0.21	70	7	1.47
19								
20	C	0.35	D	0.2	0.07	90	9	0.63
21								
22							E(commission)=6.2925	

A = Arlington; B, Brumford; C, Chisingham; T, terraced; SD, semi-detached; D, detached.

Therefore
$$P(\text{not detached}) = 1 - 0.235 = 0.765$$

3. We require $P(\text{detached/in Arlington})$, which is directly seen to be 0.1.
4. $P(\text{in Brumford/detached}) = P(B \text{ and } D)/P(D)$
$$= (0.4)(0.35)/0.235$$
$$= 0.14/0.235$$
$$= 0.59574$$

5. Worksheet 11.13 shows that the expected commission from a randomly selected house is
$$E(\text{commission}) = 0.1\,[0.15(32) + 0.075(60) + 0.025(85) + \cdots + 0.07(90)]$$
$$= £6.2925 \text{ thousand}$$

6. You can modify the last worksheet by entering the new proportions of house types in column D (terraced down by 0.05 detached up by 0.05). Also remember to alter the commission from 0.1 to 0.08 in column G. These changes produce Worksheet 11.14.

As you can see, the expected commission has fallen to £5.267 thousand, and so the reduced commission rate was not justified in terms of the extra expected income that is generated.

WORKSHEET 11.14

G4: 0.08*F4

	A Area	B Prob	C House Type	D Prob	E P(X)	F House Price	G Commiss	H E(commiss)
1								
2								
3								
4	A	0.25	T	0.55	0.1375	32	2.56	0.352 ← E4*G4
5								
6	A	0.25	SD	0.3	0.075	60	4.8	0.36
7								
8	A	0.25	D	0.15	0.0375	85	6.8	0.255
9								
10	B	0.4	T	0.35	0.14	40	3.2	0.448
11								
12	B	0.4	SD	0.25	0.1	80	6.4	0.64
13								
14	B	0.4	D	0.4	0.16	100	8	1.28
15								
16	C	0.35	T	0.15	0.0525	30	2.4	0.126
17								
18	C	0.35	SD	0.6	0.21	70	5.6	1.176
19								
20	C	0.35	D	0.25	0.0875	90	7.2	0.63
21								
22							E(commission)=5.267	

11.6 Simulating random behaviour on Lotus

Now that you are familiar with the ideas of random variables, you should appreciate that Lotus supports a function that can generate a series of random values within any desired range. This function is called

@RAND

and each time it is evaluated, it will generate a random number between 0 and 1 in the cell containing it.

Actually, there is a slight problem with @RAND under certain circumstances, since the value that Lotus returns changes every time an entry is made in any cell of the worksheet. This is because, by default, Lotus is programmed to recalculate all expressions *automatically* whenever an entry is made. (This is known as automatic recalculation, but as you will see this status can be changed.)

Any 'normal' formulae that are unaffected by a new entry will clearly retain their original value (though Lotus recalculates them anyway), but @RAND is not like this. It will be re-evaluated every time an entry is made to the worksheet, unless you switch automatic recalculation off and replace it with manual recalculation.

This is done from the Worksheet menu where you should then select Global, then Recalculation and then Manual.

If you do this, then in order to evaluate the worksheet after any alteration you must press F9 (Calculate) each time you want Lotus to perform a recalculation. The point is, however, that any @RAND entries will retain their values until F9 is pressed.

To see how @RAND works, prepare Worksheet 11.15. In A2 the entry is @RAND and this has been copied into A3..A20.

You will now have 19 random numbers in this range which can each vary between 0 and 1, but if you want them to vary between 0 and 100, say, then all you have to do is change the entries to

100*@RAND

This has been done in column B.

Alternatively, if the random number must be a whole number (integer) then the entries would be

@INT(100*@RAND)

You can see this working in column C of the worksheet.

Now try to generate 19 integer random numbers in the range 100 to 1000. The formula would be

@INT(900*@RAND)+100

(i.e. 100 plus 900 times whatever value between 0 and 1 that @RAND has generated). Clearly this produces a minimum value of 100 (if @RAND = 0), and a maximum value of 1000 (if @RAND = 1).

WORKSHEET 11.15

	A Rand. no.	B Rand. No.	C Integer	D Rand. No.	E Integer	F Rand. No.	G 100-1000
1	0.0830923	52.9855443	66		378		
2	0.2371883	58.7627835	9		185		
3	0.7481256	58.5938486	93		846		
4	0.8333011	48.8106313	40		771		
5	0.9382300	60.9833148	83		363		
6	0.9886417	76.8973100	2		578		
7	0.5683690	46.0677529	6		356		
8	0.4298445	90.9105232	70		506		
9	0.0932751	92.6420088	79		254		
10	0.4532635	86.5347249	85		859		
11	0.1640493	2.2638232	28		767		
12	0.1914268	6.7397588	87		741		
13	0.4539040	80.4921965	37		362		
14	0.1524560	15.1907020	33		420		
15	0.4380831	87.4876313	49		538		
16	0.2427768	35.5588924	1		211		
17	0.4803778	65.1397803	62		223		
18	0.9141131	16.3899023	81		681		
19	0.7007242	95.6419318	31		476		

548   *Principles of Probability and Decision Making*

As you will see, random numbers can be very useful as a method of modelling processes that display random variation.

Accordingly, imagine a situation in which a variable such as sales or income was subject to periodic random variation above or below some known average value. For example, suppose that sales were on average equal to 100 units per day, but that values within ±5 per cent of this figure were all capable of occurring (i.e. between 95 and 105 in steps of 1).

The task is to develop a worksheet that will get Lotus to generate the random pattern of sales over (say) the next 19 days.

To do this, it should be clear that we must employ an expression of the form

$$0.05*@RAND$$

However, although this will produce a random number between 0 and 0.05, it will always be positive, yet the variation that we want to model can be ±5 per cent. Clearly we must find some method of generating negative random variation.

Once this has been done, the variation in the value adopted by the variable can be calculated from

$$0.05*@RAND*(\text{variable average value})$$

and the actual value of the variable will be obtained by adding the variation in average value to the variable's average value, i.e.

$$\text{actual value} = \text{average value} + 0.05*@RAND*(\text{average value})$$

Remember that since we are going to force 0.1*@RAND to adopt positive or negative values, the expression above will generate values that can be greater than, or less than the variable's average value (in the range ±5 per cent).

Of course, if only integer output levels can be produced, then we will have to rewrite the righthand side of this last expression as

$$\text{average value} + @INT(0.05*@RAND*(\text{average value}))$$

Bearing this in mind, the negative random variation we require can be achieved in either of two ways.

First, we could use a second random number to generate another sequence and then force Lotus to add the variation to the average value if the second random number is greater than 0.5 but to subtract the variation if the second random number is less that 0.5. (If the random number is exactly equal to 0.5, then we should really require the number to be re-evaluated, but we will ignore this difficulty for the moment.)

Obviously this requires a conditional statement, so we could proceed as shown in Worksheet 11.16.

The entry in B6 simply forces Lotus to add the variation to the average value if the second random number (in B5) is greater than 0.5, but subtract it otherwise.

This worksheet will produce a series of integer random values in the range 95–105 in the B6 cell, each time F9 is pressed. Try it.

WORKSHEET 11.16

	A	B
1	Variable Average Value	100
2	Required Proportionate Variation	0.05
3	Random Proportionate Variation	+B2*@RAND
4	Variation in Variable Value	@INT(B1*B3)
5	Second Random Number	@RAND
6	Actual Variable Value	@IF(B5>0.5,B1+B4,B1-B4)

In order to produce a forecast for 19 days, we will have to use these ideas in a worksheet similar to Worksheet 11.17. Columns A and B are simply two columns of random numbers generated from @RAND. Next, we have included the average value (100) and the required proportionate variation (5 per cent) in their own cells (D2 and E2) and then referred to these cell references thereafter, so that the model can easily accommodate different percentage variations and/or different variable average values.

The crucial entry is in C2 and is

@IF(A2 > 0.5,D$2 + @INT(B2*D$2*E$2),D$2 − @INT(B2*D$2*E$2))

Although this looks complicated, it is simply a modification of the ideas in the last worksheet. All it does is to check whether the first random number exceeds 0.5, and

WORKSHEET 11.17

	A	B	C	D	E
1	rand 1	rand 2	Forecast	Av. value	Variation
2	0.190239	0.611043	100	100	0.05
3	0.455123	0.974679	98		
4	0.374063	0.192853	99		
5	0.452507	0.514007	98		
6	0.903266	0.144053	104		
7	0.081950	0.658209	100		
8	0.194136	0.462471	100		
9	0.220947	0.276271	99		
10	0.487215	0.464347	98		
11	0.922412	0.894427	104		
12	0.901434	0.150723	104		
13	0.162663	0.203661	100		
14	0.747045	0.336534	103		
15	0.746634	0.072102	103		
16	0.956709	0.339266	104		
17	0.854693	0.984170	104		
18	0.744127	0.274063	103		
19	0.965427	0.078356	104		
20	0.849583	0.252150	104		

thereby decides whether the variation is to be added to, or subtracted from, the average value. Once this has been determined, then the integer value of the proportional variation (E2) times the average value (D2) times the second random number (B2) is calculated and added to, or subtracted from, the average value. The dollar signs attached to the D2 and E2 cell references are used to ensure that this formula can be copied consistently into C3..C20 (or as many cells as you require).

If you prepare this worksheet then you will find that a new sequence can be generated each time you press F9. Try it.

The second way of generating negative variations from positive random numbers is to force Lotus to take the difference between two random numbers, i.e.

$$@RAND - @RAND$$

This will produce a positive or negative result depending upon whether the second random number is greater or less than the first.

Using this method we could produce Worksheet 11.18.

With this method, the variable value will be produced in B5 every time F9 is pressed.

Although we have suggested that these two methods of creating negative random variation are equivalent, there is actually a difference that is not immediately obvious. This stems from the fact that the two methods generate significantly different predicted patterns for the actual values of the variable.

The reason for this can be understood if we ask the question of whether we require a pattern which implies that values of 95, 96, etc., are *just as likely to occur* as values of 104, 105, etc.; or whether we require a pattern in which values that are close to the average value of 100 are *more likely* to occur than values that are further away.

In other words, if we plot the number of times a particular value occurs against its actual value, which of the frequency distributions shown in Figure 11.1 do we require?

In fact, the first method above generates a frequency distribution similar to distribution A, while the second method produces a graph which is much more akin to distribution B.

To see why this is the case, imagine that @RAND could only adopt values of 0, 0.5 or 1. This means that the only combination of values that @RAND − @RAND can produce are those shown in Table 11.8.

```
WORKSHEET 11.18
                    A                                B
    1  Variable Average Value                      100
    2  Required Proportionate Variation            0.05
    3  Random Proportionate Variation    +B2*(@RAND-@RAND)
    4  Variation in Variable Value             @INT(B1*B3)
    5  Actual Variable Value                       +B1+B4
```

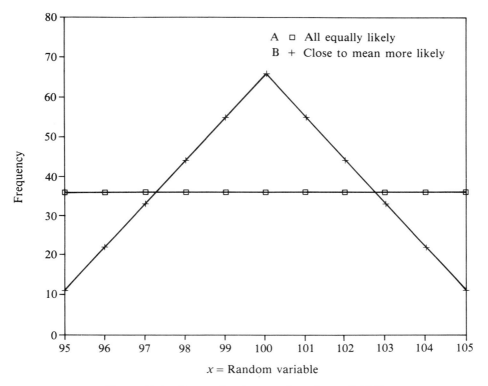

Figure 11.1 Contrasting frequencies using @RAND

From Table 11.8 it is easy to see that the frequencies of different values for our special assumed form of @RAND − @RAND can be summarized as shown in Table 11.9.

Since it is @RAND − @RAND that is used to generate the predicted values in the second method, it seems intuitively reasonable to expect that a graph of the

Table 11.8

@RAND	@RAND	@RAND − @RAND
0	0	0
0	0.5	−0.5
0	1	−1
0.5	0	0.5
0.5	0.5	0
0.5	1	−0.5
1	0	1
1	0.5	0.5
1	1	0

Table 11.9

@RAND − @RAND	Frequency
−1	1
−0.5	2
0	3
0.5	2
1	1

frequencies of the predicted values would follow this basic pattern. Without going into the proof of this, you can obtain confirmation of this statement in Worksheet 11.19. All we have done here is to produce forecasts based upon both methods in columns C and F.

The entries in column C are the same as in Worksheet 11.17, while the entry in F2 is

$$@INT(E\$2*(A2-B2)*D\$2)+D\$2$$

As you can see, different patterns of forecasts are generated by the two methods, but this is not simply due to the fact that they are random forecasts.

To see this, notice that we have calculated the mean and standard deviation of both forecasts in E4..E10. If our statement about the expected shape of the frequency distributions generated by the two methods is correct, then we would expect that while, on average, they both have similar mean values, the standard deviation of forecast A would be consistently (but not always) greater than that of forecast B (since distribution A in Figure 11.1 is clearly more dispersed than distribution B).

If you generate a few forecasts for yourself, then you should find that this is indeed the case.

Now you can use these ideas to consider the following example.

EXAMPLE 11.13

A company's production run of 15 days produces a constant 1000 units of output each day.

The average sales of the product are 970 units per day, but this is subject to 10 per cent variation in such a way that each integer value in the range 873–1063 has an equal probability of occurrence.

Any output that is not sold is added to stock.

Simulate the pattern of the firm's stockholding over a number of 15 day periods.

SOLUTION 11.13

Worksheet 11.20 models this problem

WORKSHEET 11.19

	A	B	C	D	E	F
	rand 1	rand 2	Forecast A	Av. value	Variation	Forecast B
				100	0.05	
1	0.714973	0.888514	103			100
2	0.007906	0.019493	100			100
3	0.984844	0.199194	104	mean A	100.7894736	103
4	0.410573	0.400390	98			100
5	0.528499	0.653797	102	mean B	99.63157894	100
6	0.930601	0.380087	104			102
7	0.806432	0.780696	104	st dev A	2.196698605	100
8	0.694572	0.236517	103			102
9	0.517180	0.668463	102	st dev B	1.337712108	100
10	0.296446	0.873453	99			98
11	0.093350	0.776112	100			97
12	0.436666	0.642963	98			99
13	0.386137	0.404473	99			100
14	0.460664	0.633675	98			100
15	0.522675	0.250573	102			101
16	0.406171	0.971741	98			98
17	0.170632	0.716904	100			98
18	0.418675	0.931373	98			98
19	0.694396	0.897443	103			99

WORKSHEET 11.20

	A	B	C	D	E	F	G
1	Production	rand 1	rand 2	Demand	Excess	Stock	Cum stock
2	1000	0.488558	0.279810	943	-57	57	57
3	1000	0.589241	0.749286	1042	42	0	15
4	1000	0.924437	0.187975	988	-12	12	27
5	1000	0.727518	0.312879	1000	0	0	27
6	1000	0.580880	0.933102	1060	60	0	0
7	1000	0.043836	0.411390	931	-69	69	69
8	1000	0.373414	0.160033	955	-45	45	114
9	1000	0.656795	0.846815	1052	52	0	62
10	1000	0.518839	0.929036	1060	60	0	2
11	1000	0.873813	0.630731	1031	31	0	0
12	1000	0.519544	0.342449	1003	3	0	0
13	1000	0.787252	0.966906	1063	63	0	0
14	1000	0.523793	0.769966	1044	44	0	0
15	1000	0.457466	0.137218	957	-43	43	43
16	1000	0.046373	0.094420	961	-39	39	82
17							
18	Av. demand 970						
19	variation 0.1						

	H	I	J	K	L
	St hold cost	Price	cost/day	lost demand	If no stock
1	2	50			
2			114	0	0
3			30	0	42
4			54	0	0
5			54	0	0
6			0	33	60
7			138	0	0
8			228	0	0
9			124	0	52
10			4	0	60
11			0	29	31
12			0	3	3
13			0	63	63
14			0	44	44
15			86	0	0
16			164	0	0
17		Total stockholding cost=996		Lost profit 8600	Lost profit 17750
18					
19			Benefit 9150		
20			Benefit-cost 8154		

As you can see, we have used the first method of random simulation, since the question tells us that each integer value in the range has an equal probability of occurring. Also notice that we have included the average demand and its variation in B18 and B19.

This means that the random pattern of demand is generated in column D from the entry in D2. This is

$$@IF(B2>0.5, B\$18 + @INT(C2*B\$18*B\$19), B\$18 - @INT(C2*B\$18*B\$19))$$

(copied into D3..D16).

Allowing for the different locations of the average value, the variation and the random numbers, this formula is identical to the one that we used in Worksheet 11.17.

In E2 we have calculated the excess demand from $+D2-E2$ (copied into E3..E16), and in F2 we have calculated the daily addition to stock.

This is done by noting that the daily addition to stock can never be less than zero and will be given by the amount by which production exceeds demand. Consequently, if demand exceeds production, the daily addition to stock will be zero, while if excess demand is negative, the daily addition to stock will be equal to that excess. The formula in F2 is therefore

$$@IF(E2<0, -E2, 0)$$

For example, if E2 = -40, then the daily addition to stock is $-(-40) = 40$. The formula in F2 was then copied into F3..F16.

However, the purpose of holding stock is so that excess demand on one day can be met by the accumulated stock from previous days when there was negative excess demand. Consequently, in G2 we have made the entry $+F2$, which will place the first day's stock in G2.

All we have to do now is write a formula that will allow the cumulative stock to increase from this amount by however much production exceeds demand on the next day, but decrease by however much accumulated stock has to be used to meet any excess demand on that next day. The formula that will do this has been written in G3 as

$$@IF(E3<G2, G2-E3, 0)$$

and then copied into G4..G16.

Notice how this works. As long as the excess demand on the current day (E3) is less than the accumulated stock on the previous day, then the previous day's accumulated stock is reduced by this amount (i.e. G2 − E3). This will actually reduce the accumulated stock if E3 is greater than zero, leave it unchanged if E3 is equal to zero, but increase it if E3 is negative (since negative excess demand means production in excess of demand).

On the other hand, if E3 is greater than or equal to G2 (implying that the current day's excess demand equals or exceeds the accumulated stock), then all the stock is used up and the current day's accumulated stock becomes zero.

Bearing these ideas in mind, suppose that each unit of stock imposes a stockholding cost of £2 per unit, per day that it is held, (including its day of production), and that the product is sold for a profit of £50.

We have entered these values in H2 and I2.

Given any random pattern of the firm's stock over the 15 day period can we develop a method of testing whether the implied stockholding costs are justified in terms of the lost profit that they may prevent?

Clearly, the daily stockholding costs will be given by +G2*H$2, which has been entered in J2 and copied into J3..J16.

The total stockholding costs, for the 15 day period are therefore @SUM(J2..J16), which has been entered in J17.

To calculate the lost profit, we must remember that we are assuming that the demand must be satisfied on the day that it is exercised, and that a 'stock out' means that any day's excess demand can only be satisfied to the extent of the accumulated stock available. Consequently, in K2 we can calculate the unsatisfied demand on the first day from @IF(G2=0,E2,0). This reflects the fact that on the first day any excess of demand over production will necessarily go unsatisfied.

On the second and subsequent days, however, any accumulated stock can be used to satisfy any excess demand up to a level associated with a 'stock out'. The unsatisfied demand will then be the difference between the excess demand and the amount of that excess demand that the accumulated stock could meet. This allows us to write the following formula in K3:

$$@IF(G3=0, E3-G2, 0)$$

and copy it into K4..K16.

For example, on day 4 (G5) the accumulated stock was 27, and on day 5 the excess demand (E6) was 60. Consequently there are 60 − 27 (E6 − G5) = 33 units of demand lost on the fifth day. This is the entry calculated in K6.

The lost profit is therefore the sum of all the unsatisfied demand times the price of the product. This is calculated in K17 from

$$+I\$2*@SUM(K2..K16)$$

This last entry is the potential profit lost as a result of running out of stock, and indicates the extent to which the actual stockholding pattern is deficient in preventing loss of profit. However, before we can evaluate the justification of the stockholding costs incurred, we need to know what the total loss of profit *would have been* had there been no stocks held at all. This is easily calculated by adding up all the positive excess demands and then multiplying by the product price. We have done this in L2 from the formula

$$@IF(E2>0, E2, 0)$$

copied into L3..L16 and then summed and multiplied by I2 in L17.

As you can see in our illustrative worksheet, the total stockholding cost of £996 has failed to prevent a profit loss of £8600, but without any stock the profit loss would have been £17 750. Consequently we conclude that the expenditure of £996 has produced a net benefit of £11 750 − £8600 = £9150, and is clearly justified in this case. Try it for yourself and see, for different patterns of demand, whether these results are consistently repeated.

Once again you must appreciate that these cost and lost profit figures will depend not only upon the random pattern that was generated, but also on the relative magnitude of stockholding costs in relation to the price of the product. This is why these last two figures were placed in their own cells, since you can now use the worksheet to explore different random patterns and different product prices and/or stockholding costs.

You can also use the worksheet to investigate the properties of a stocking policy whereby production is equated with demand in the previous period in an attempt to minimize stockholding costs. As you should expect, this has the effect of increasing the amount of lost profit, as your worksheet should show if you alter it to reflect such a policy by making each day's production equal to the previous day's demand. This means that the entry in A3 would become + D2 and would be copied into A4..A16. (More realistic would be such a policy plus a safety margin of, say, 10 per cent of the previous day's demand.)

Experiment with this as well.

11.7 Markov chains

The ideas of conditional probability outlined earlier have an important application in a method of forecasting which uses the notion of *Markov chains*. In its simplest sense, a Markov chain can be viewed as a sequence of random events in which the probability of each subsequent event is conditioned by the nature of the event that preceded it. Each event is therefore linked to its immediate predecessor as in a chain.

As far as our objectives are concerned, we would like to develop some method of using the observed sequence of events to calculate the probability of a particular outcome on the next and subsequent trials.

By way of illustration, consider a period of 15 days in which a portfolio of shares was observed in terms of whether its financial performance improved or deteriorated. With 1 representing a rise in value and 0 representing a fall in value, suppose the following sequence was observed over the 15 days:

$$1, 0, 0, 1, 0, 0, 0, 1, 1, 0, 0, 1, 0, 1, 0$$

From this sequence, can we estimate the probability that the portfolio rose in value on the 16th day?

A simple approach to the problem would argue that on six occasions out of the 15 days the portfolio rose in value and so

$$P(1) = 6/15, \text{ implying that } P(0) = 9/15$$

However, the problem with such a simple approach is that it takes no account of the pattern of events that was observed.

To do this we could ask the following questions:

1. On how many days out of the 15 did the portfolio rise in value after having:
   (a) Risen on the previous day?
   (b) Fallen on the previous day?
2. On how many days out of the 15 did the portfolio fall in value after having:
   (a) Risen on the previous day?
   (b) Fallen on the previous day?

So, letting 1 1, 1 0, 0 0 and 0 1 represent all possible previous day/current day, combinations of outcomes, we could answer the questions in Table 11.10, where 1 in the body of the table represents these occurrences of a particular sequence.

As you can see from Table 11.10, we have a total of 14 different sequences, but we can now separate these into two distinct classes.

1. Those occasions when the portfolio rose on the previous day (the sequence 1 1, or 1 0). Clearly there were $1 + 5 = 6$ occasions when this happened.
2. Those occasions when the portfolio fell on the previous day (the sequence 0 0, or 0 1). Equally clearly there were $4 + 4 = 8$ occasions when this happened.

This classification then allows us to calculate the probability of each of the possible outcomes and assemble them in the following table (which will soon

Table 11.10

Day	Outcome	1 1	1 0	0 0	0 1
1	1				
2	0		1		
3	0			1	
4	1				1
5	0		1		
6	0			1	
7	0			1	
8	1				1
9	1	1			
10	0		1		
11	0			1	
12	1				1
13	0		1		
14	1				1
15	0		1		
Totals		1	5	4	4

become a matrix):

	Previous day	
	1	0
Current day 1	1	4
0	5	4
Total	6	8

These observed frequencies are easily turned into probabilities as

	Previous day	
	1	0
Current day 1	1/6	4/8
0	5/6	4/8

Remembering that we are looking for the probability that the portfolio will rise on the 16th day, we can use our knowledge that it actually fell on the 15th (previous) day to confine our attention to that column of the table on which the previous day value was zero.

Consequently, we would argue that on the 16th day

$$P(1) = 4/8 \quad P(0) = 4/8$$

On the other hand, had the portfolio risen in value on the previous (15th) day, then we would have estimated the probabilities as

$$P(1) = 1/6 \quad P(0) = 5/6$$

Notice that these probabilities are different from the ones that we calculated earlier, since they take account of the fact that we *know* that a fall in value took place on the 15th day.

But, suppose we now ask what the probability is of a rise in value on the 17th day. Clearly this will depend upon what actually happened on the 16th day, and upon the new probabilities that emerge as a result of whatever this outcome was.

But we know that the probabilities of the previous day/current day sequences are

$$P(1\ 1) = 1/6$$
$$P(1\ 0) = 5/6$$
$$P(0\ 1) = 4/8$$
$$P(0\ 0) = 4/8$$

Table 11.11

16th day	17th day	Outcome	Sequence probability	Probability 16th/17th day
1 (1/2)	1	1 1	(1/6)	(1/2)(1/6) = 1/12
1 (1/2)	0	1 0	(5/6)	(1/2)(5/6) = 5/12
0 (1/2)	1	0 1	(4/8)	(1/2)(4/8) = 1/4
0 (1/2)	0	0 0	(4/8)	(1/2)(4/8) = 1/4

And we also know from our previous calculation that the probability of a rise on the 16th day is 1/2 (given that it fell on the 15th day). We can thus construct Table 11.11.

Lines 1 and 3 of Table 11.11 are the only two that satisfy our requirement that the portfolio rise in value on the 17th day, so

$$P(1) \text{ on the 17th day} = 1/12 + 1/4 = 0.333\,33$$

Meaning that

$$P(0) \text{ on the 17th day} = 5/12 + 1/4 = 0.666\,66$$

As you can see, the situation becomes increasingly complicated as we consider more and more days.

Fortunately, however, this Markov chain can be evaluated by an easier method, especially since it is a matrix technique that can be incorporated into Lotus.

To see how this works, reconsider the table we produced for the probabilities of the various outcomes on the 16th day and express it as a matrix, i.e.

$$\begin{bmatrix} 1/6 & 4/8 \\ 5/6 & 4/8 \end{bmatrix}$$

This is known as the transition matrix (T) and can be used for the repeated evaluation of the probabilities on subsequent days, since it represents all possible previous day/current day sequences.

To do this we require another matrix (actually a column vector we will call s) to represent the status on the previous day. So remembering that there was a fall in value on the 15th day we could write:

$$[s] = \begin{bmatrix} 0 \\ 1 \end{bmatrix} = \begin{matrix} P(1) \\ P(0) \end{matrix}$$

(Remember that since we know the portfolio fell in value on the 15th day, it follows that $P(1) = 0$ and $P(0) = 1$. These are the entries in our status matrix.)

Now premultiply the status vector by the transition matrix to obtain

$$Ts_{16} = \begin{bmatrix} 1/6 & 4/8 \\ 5/6 & 4/8 \end{bmatrix} \begin{bmatrix} 0 \\ 1 \end{bmatrix} = \begin{bmatrix} 0.5 \\ 0.5 \end{bmatrix} = [e]$$

The column vector $[e]$ that results from this multiplication clearly contains the probabilities we obtained earlier for the outcomes on the 16th day. That is

$$\begin{matrix} P(1) & 0.5 \\ P(2) & 0.5 \end{matrix} = [e]$$

But if we now use e as the status matrix for the next (17th) day, then we obtain

$$Ts_{17} = \begin{bmatrix} 1/6 & 4/8 \\ 5/6 & 4/8 \end{bmatrix} \begin{bmatrix} 0.5 \\ 0.5 \end{bmatrix} = \begin{bmatrix} 0.3333 \\ 0.6666 \end{bmatrix}$$

This reproduces the probabilities that we obtained earlier for the 17th day.

By a similar logic the probabilities for the 18th day would be obtained by replacing s with e for the 17th day to obtain

$$Ts_{18} = \begin{bmatrix} 1/6 & 4/8 \\ 5/6 & 4/8 \end{bmatrix} \begin{bmatrix} 0.3333 \\ 0.6666 \end{bmatrix} = \begin{bmatrix} 0.38888 \\ 0.61111 \end{bmatrix} = \begin{matrix} P(1) \\ P(0) \end{matrix}$$

Clearly, there is a sequential process taking place here, and if you were to calculate a sufficient number of links in the chain, then you would find that the probabilities 'settle down' to values of

$$\begin{matrix} P(1) & 0.375 \\ P(0) & 0.625 \end{matrix}$$

But how did we obtain these values?

Quite simply by solving the following matrix equation:

$$\begin{bmatrix} 1/6 & 4/8 \\ 5/6 & 4/8 \end{bmatrix} \begin{bmatrix} x \\ (1-x) \end{bmatrix} = \begin{bmatrix} x \\ (1-x) \end{bmatrix}$$

That is, we require that the unknown probabilities, x and $(1 - x)$, remain the same on the current day as on the previous day. If such a solution can be obtained, then it represents the equilibrium probabilities of the Markov chain.

If we represent the values in the transition matrix by

$$\begin{matrix} a & b \\ m & n \end{matrix}$$

then by matrix multiplication we have

$$ax + b(1 - x) = x \\ mx + n(1 - x) = (1 - x)$$

So, if we multiply the first equation by n/b we obtain

$$(na/b)x + n(1 - x) = (n/b)x$$

Now subtract the second equation from this modified version of the first to obtain

$$(na/b)x - mx = (n/b)x - (1 - x)$$

Collecting terms in x then creates

$$x(na/b - m - n/b - 1) = -1$$

whereby

$$x = -1/(na/b - m - n/b - 1)$$

Now remember that in our illustration $a = 1/6$, $b = 1/2$, $m = 5/6$, $n = 1/2$; and so this last expression evaluates to

$$-1/(1/6 - 5/6 - 1 - 1) = -1/(-16/6) = 6/16 = 3/8 = 0.375$$

This confirms that, as we claimed earlier, this particular Markov chain settles down to equilibrium values of

$$x = P(1) = 3/8 \quad \text{and} \quad (1 - x) = P(0) = 5/8$$

This is an important piece of reasoning since we can use this equilibrium expression as a Lotus formula to allow easy evaluation of the equilibrium probabilities.

To model a Markov chain on Lotus the first thing to do is enter the observed sequence of outcomes (as 1s and 0s) in A2..A16.

Next, we require that Lotus examine the sequence and classify each cell in accordance with whether it was a rise or a fall, and whether the previous day was a rise or a fall.

So, in B3 we should write

$$@IF((A2=1)*(A3=1)1,0)$$

This is a Lotus conditional statement, but it has been modified by being forced to consider the joint event

1 on the current day and 1 on the previous day

This is done by placing each of the joint outcomes in brackets and then connecting them with a multiplication symbol, i.e. $(A2=1)*(A3=1)$.

Incidentally if you wanted Lotus to test for 1 on the current day *or* 1 on the previous day then the expression would be

$$@IF((A3=1)+(A3=1),1,0)$$

This reflects our previous observations that in probability 'and' means multiply whereas 'or' means add, although clearly the actual multiplication or addition is not carried out. The symbols $*$ and $+$ merely act as indicators, which Lotus can understand, of the type of event to be tested for.

You can apply a similar logic to columns C, D and E where the occurrences of the other possible sequences will be calculated. The formulae are

in C3 $@IF((A2=1)*(A3=0),1,0)$
in D3 $@IF((A2=0)*(A3=0),1,0)$
in E3 $@IF((A2=0)*(A3=1),1,0)$

Now all you have to do is tell Lotus to count the occurrences in each outcome column by

in B17 @SUM(B3..B16)
in C17 @SUM(C3..C16)
in D17 @SUM(D3..D16)
in E17 @SUM(E3..E16)

You can now calculate the probabilities and enter them as a matrix in F3..G4 from the following ratios (see Worksheet 11.21):

in F3 +B17/(B17+C17) i.e. P(1/1)
in F4 +C17/(B17+C17) i.e. P(0/1)
in G3 +D17/(E17+D17) i.e. P(1/0)
in G4 +E17/(E17+D17) i.e. P(0/0)

Now that you have your transition matrix (T) in F3..G4, you can then force Lotus to evaluate each subsequent step of the chain. To do this efficiently, however, we must employ a little ingenuity.

To start with, since the portfolio fell in value on the 15th day, you should enter 0 in H3 and 1 in H4. This means that our status vector is located in H3..H4, and is

$$S = \begin{bmatrix} 0 \\ 1 \end{bmatrix} = \begin{matrix} P(1) \\ P(0) \end{matrix}$$

Now tell Lotus to multiply the transition matrix (T) by the status vector (s) and output the resulting vector (e) to F6..F7.

WORKSHEET 11.21

	A	B	C	D	E	F	G	H
1	Outcome	11	10	00	01			
2	1					[T]		[s]
3	0	0	1	0	0	0.166666	0.5	0.376543
4	0	0	0	1	0	0.833333	0.5	0.623456
5	1	0	0	0	1	[e]		[ē]
6	0	0	1	0	0	0.376543		0.375
7	0	0	0	1	0	0.623456		0.625
8	0	0	0	1	0			
9	1	0	0	0	1			
10	1	1	0	0	0			
11	0	0	1	0	0			
12	0	0	0	1	0			
13	1	0	0	0	1			
14	0	0	1	0	0			
15	1	0	0	0	1			
16	0	0	1	0	0			
17	Total	1	5	4	4			

This gives us the solution vector (e) for the 16th day, but for the 17th day we require that the e vector replace the s vector in H3..H4. In other words we require that each solution matrix becomes the status matrix for the next round.

So, with recalculation set to *manual*, make the following entries in H3 and H4:

in H3   +F6
in H4   +F7

With these formulae operational, each solution matrix in the sequence can be obtained from the following Lotus routine:

/Data Matrix Multiply F3..G4 (1st matrix to multiply) H3..H4 (2nd matrix to multiply) F6..F7 (output range)

(You only have to specify the matrix ranges once, since thereafter you can accept the defined matrices and output range by pressing the return key three times.)

Now press F9 to force a manual recalculation and you will find that the current day's solution matrix becomes the status matrix for the next day.

Repeat the matrix multiplication procedure and the next day's value will be output to F6..F7, and when you press F9 again this will be transferred to H3..H4, ready to be used for the next day, and so on.

If you repeat this procedure eight or nine times, then you will find that the probabilities are almost indistinguishable from their equilibrium values of 0.375 and 0.625.

Finally, remembering that we have already derived expressions for calculating these equilibrium values earlier in the discussion, we can rewrite these as the following Lotus formulae:

in H6 $-1/((F3*G4/G3)-F4-(G4/G3)-1)$
in H7 $1-H6$

This is just the Lotus equivalent of the expression we derived earlier, but with the entries in F3, G3, F4 and G4 taking the place of the terms a, b, m and n.

Every time you alter the sequence of events, then the new equilibrium values will be calculated for you, as you can easily confirm if you alter the sequence in your worksheet to

1, 0, 0, 0, 0, 1, 1, 1, 0, 1, 1, 0, 1, 1, 1

You should find that the equilibrium probabilities are

$$P(1) = 0.5714$$
$$P(2) = 0.428$$

Remember that in this case the last day was a value of 1, making $P(1)$ on that day $= 1$ and $P(0) = 0$. The first status vector would therefore be

$$s = \begin{bmatrix} 1 \\ 0 \end{bmatrix} = \begin{matrix} P(1) \\ P(0) \end{matrix}$$

11.8 The binomial distribution

In Section 11.3 we showed how to construct the probability distribution for the random variable $X =$ the number of hearts obtained on two draws with replacement, from a standard pack of playing cards. We found it to be as follows:

$$\begin{array}{cccc} X & 0 & 1 & 2 \\ P(X) & 9/16 & 6/16 & 1/16 \end{array}$$

The question we must now address is whether we can identify a pattern in these probabilities that will allow easier consideration of situations in which a larger number of trials is carried out, thereby making the construction of the probability tree unmanageable. The answer is that the pattern is given by what is known as the *binomial distribution*, which can be appreciated as follows.

Consider a manufacturing process that always produces p per cent defective items in its output (and therefore $(1 - p)$ per cent nondefective items).

A random sample of three items of output is taken and each item inspected for the known defect.

Can we obtain expressions for the random variable

$X =$ the number of defective items discovered?

Clearly, with D representing a defective item and N representing a nondefective item the probability tree would be shown in Table 11.12.

Notice that there is only one way of obtaining exactly zero defective items, and only one way of obtaining exactly three defective items.

On the other hand there are three ways of obtaining exactly one defective item, and each way has a probability of

$$(p)(1 - p)^2$$

Consequently

$$P(1) = 3(p)(1 - p)^2$$

Table 11.12

Item 1	Item 2	Item 3	Number of defective items (X)	Probability P(X)
D(p)	D(p)	D(p)	3	$(p)(p)(p) = p^3$
D(p)	D(p)	N($1-p$)	2	$(p)(p)(1-p) = p^2(1-p)$
D(p)	N($1-p$)	D(p)	2	$(p)(1-p)(p) = p^2(1-p)$
D(p)	N($1-p$)	N($1-p$)	1	$(p)(1-p)(1-p) = p(1-p)^2$
N($1-p$)	D(p)	D(p)	2	$(1-p)(p)(p) = p^2(1-p)$
N($1-p$)	D(p)	N($1-p$)	1	$(1-p)(p)(1-p) = p(1-p)^2$
N($1-p$)	N($1-p$)	D(p)	1	$(1-p)(1-p)(p) = p(1-p)^2$
N($1-p$)	N($1-p$)	N($1-p$)	0	$(1-p)(1-p)(1-p) = (1-p)^3$

Similarly, since there are also three ways of obtaining exactly two defective items, each with a probability of

$$(p^2)(1-p)$$

it follows that

$$P(2) = 3(p^2)(1-p)$$

Consequently, the probability distribution will be given by

X	$P(X)$
0	$(1-p)^3$
1	$3(p)(1-p)^2$
2	$3(p^2)(1-p)$
3	p^3

To identify the pattern that underlies these probabilities, notice four things.

1. The powers of p and $(1-p)$ always add up to the number of trials (which is three in this case but generally represented by n).
2. The power of p is always equal to the value of X and the power of $(1-p)$ must therefore be $3 - X$ (or $n - X$ more generally).
3. As X increases in steps of 1, the powers of p and $(1-p)$ 'swap', also in steps of 1.
4. The polar cases of $X = 0$ and $X = 3$ have coefficients of 1, but the intermediate values ($X = 1$ and $X = 2$) both have coefficients of 3. This reflects the point that we made earlier about having to multiply the probability of an event occurring any one way by the number of ways that it can occur.

These four points are enough to allow us to state that

$$P(X) = \text{(the number of ways that } X \text{ defectives can occur in } n \text{ trials)} \times [p^X][(1-p)^{n-X}]$$

Therefore, since our illustration has three trials:

$$P(X) = \text{(the number of ways that } X \text{ defectives can occur in three trials)} \times (p^3)[(1-p)^{3-X}]$$

Consequently, to find the probability that $X = 2$ we could write

$$P(2) = 3(p^2)[(1-p)^1]$$

which is the result that we obtained earlier from the probability tree.

However, we still have to obtain an efficient way of calculating the number of ways that X defective items can be obtained from n trials.

The answer to this is given by what is known as a *combination*, and can tell us the number of ways that an outcome of X defective items can be obtained on the basis of n trials.

This is given the symbol

$$_nC_X$$

and can be evaluated from

$$_nC_X = n!/[(n-X)!\,X!]$$

where $n!$ (read as n factorial) means

$$(n)(n-1)(n-2)\ldots(3)(2)(1)$$

(Note as a point of definition that $0! = 1$.)

For example:

$$\begin{aligned}_6C_4 &= 6!/[(6-4)!\,4!] \\ &= 6!/(2!)(4!) \\ &= (6)(5)(4)(3)(2)(1)/(2)(1)(4)(3)(2)(1) \\ &= 15\end{aligned}$$

There are therefore 15 different ways of combining four objects out of six objects.

So, since our illustration contains three trials, we have

$$\begin{aligned}_3C_0 &= 1 \\ _3C_1 &= 3 \\ _3C_2 &= 3 \\ _3C_3 &= 1\end{aligned}$$

Now observe that these are precisely the coefficients that have been attached to the associated values of X in our probability distribution with $n = 3$.

What this means is that we can now write

$$P(X) = {}_nC_X[p^X]\,[(1-p)^{n-X}]$$

When $X = 1$ and $n = 3$, we therefore obtain

$$P(1) = {}_3C_1[p]\,[(1-p)^2] = 3p(1-p)^2$$

The last expression for $P(X)$ is known as the binomial distribution and will give, for any specified number of trials (n), and any specified probability of a defined event on any one trial (p), the probability that exactly X defined events will occur.

Notice that the prefix 'Bi' in the word binomial implies that there are only two outcomes, but as we have seen before, the events can be defined in such a way that the binary nature of the distribution is preserved, even if there are more than two outcomes per trial (6, 'not 6'; heart, 'not heart', for example).

Also notice that for once Lotus cannot help us to perform the calculation of binomial probabilities, since it neither possesses a factorial function, nor a dedicated combination function. Most calculators do, however, so you will have to make do with them (or learn how to program Lotus to do it for you).

Finally, as a last point of terminology, notice that if X is distributed as a binomial random variable, then we represent this as

$$X \sim \text{Bi}(n, p)$$

where the '$\sim$' symbol means 'is distributed'.

The expected value of X in a binomial distribution is given by

$$E(X) = np$$

For example, if a coin is tossed 80 times (n), then we would expect there to be $np = 80(0.5) = 40$ heads, and $80 - 40 = 40$ tails.

EXAMPLE 11.14

A small firm employs a work force of 12 full-time employees. On any given day there is a 0.1 probability that an employee will be absent.

1. Calculate the probability that on a randomly selected day there will be: (a) no absentees; (b) two absentees.
2. The firm has to close down if there are less than 10 employees present on any given day. Calculate the probability that the firm will be forced to close on any randomly selected day.

SOLUTION 11.14

1. Let $X =$ the number of absentees. Therefore

$$X \sim \text{Bi}(0.1, 12)$$

As a result

$$P(0) = {}_{12}C_0 (0.1^0)(0.9^{12}) = 0.2824$$

Also

$$P(2) = {}_{12}C_2 (0.1^2)(0.9^{10}) = 66(0.01)(0.3486) = 0.2301$$

2. The firm will close down if the number of *absentees* exceeds two (i.e. three or more) since then there will be less than 10 employees present. Therefore:

$$\begin{aligned} P(X \geqslant 3) &= 1 - P(0) - P(1) - P(2) \\ &= 1 - 0.2824 - 0.3675 - 0.2301 \\ &= 0.1201 \end{aligned}$$

EXAMPLE 11.15

A multiple-choice examination consists of 10 questions that must each be answered from a choice of four answers, only one of which is correct in each case.

1. Calculate the probability that a candidate who guesses all the answers will achieve a mark of 40 per cent or more.
2. The examiner feels that the probability of passing the examination by chance should never exceed 0.02. What pass mark should be set if this is to be the case?

SOLUTION 11.15

1. Let X = the number of correct answers. Then

$$X \sim \text{Bi}(10, 0.25)$$

Therefore

$$P(X \geqslant 4) = 1 - P(0) - P(1) - P(2) - P(3)$$

So

$$P(0) = {}_{10}C_0 (0.25^0)(0.75^{10}) = 0.0563$$
$$P(1) = {}_{10}C_1 (0.25^1)(0.75^9) = 0.1877$$
$$P(2) = {}_{10}C_2 (0.25^2)(0.75^8) = 0.2816$$
$$P(3) = {}_{10}C_3 (0.25^3)(0.75^7) = 0.2503$$
$$\text{Total} = 0.7759$$

Therefore

$$P(X \geqslant 4) = 1 - 0.7759 = 0.2241$$

2. If the pass mark was 40 per cent, then as we have seen above, the candidate will have a 0.2241 probability of passing the examination by chance.

However, if the pass mark was 50 per cent, then

$$P(\text{pass}) = P(x \geqslant 5) = 1 - P(0) - P(1) - P(2) - P(3) - P(4)$$
$$= 1 - 0.7759 - P(4) = 1 - 0.7759 - 0.1460 = 0.0781$$

Even with a pass mark of 50 per cent the required probability has not been achieved.

Consequently, if the pass mark is set at 60 per cent, then

$$P(\text{pass}) = P(x \geqslant 6) = 1 - P(0) - P(1) - P(2) - P(3) - P(4) - P(5)$$
$$= 1 - 0.7759 - 0.1460 - P(5) = 0.0197$$

Since this probability is less than 0.02 we conclude that the pass mark should be set at 60 per cent if the examiner's objective is to be achieved.

11.9 The Poisson distribution

Closely related to the binomial distribution is another probability distribution known as the Poisson distribution.

However, unlike the binomial distribution, where the number of trials (n) *and* the probability of the defined event on any one trial (p), *both* had to be known, the Poisson distribution simply requires that we know the average number of defined events that occurred in some previous time period (i.e. np).

You should be able to see that if we know n and p, then np can be calculated, but that the converse is not true, since knowing the value of np is not enough to allow determinate calculation of n and p.

However, knowledge of np alone is all that is required for evaluation of Poisson probabilities, and this can be very useful in circumstances where we are considering some process in which either p or n is not easily defined. For example, in the process of tossing a coin, we know that the probability that it will turn up tails on any one trial is 0.5, and we can control the experiment in such a way that the number of trials is recorded and therefore known. But now suppose that we were investigating the number of customers who arrive per minute at a supermarket checkout. The number of trials and the probability that a customer will arrive in the given minute are not defined. All we will know is that in the recent past an average number of (say) 3.2 customers arrived per minute. The question that the Poisson distribution can answer is, given this historic arrival rate, what is the probability that exactly 0, or 1, or 2, or x customers will arrive in any randomly selected period of 1 minute?

To see how an appropriate Poisson distribution can be constructed, consider the following example.

EXAMPLE 11.16

The number of accidents per week on a busy stretch of motorway was recorded over a period of 26 weeks and the data shown in Table 11.13 obtained.

Calculate the probabilities that in a randomly selected week, there will be exactly X accidents.

SOLUTION 11.16

The first thing to do is calculate the average number of accidents per week, so prepare the first three columns of Worksheet 11.22. As you can see, the data imply that on average there were 2.846 accidents per week, calculated in B15.

Now if (and this is a 'big' if) the data can in fact be represented by a Poisson

Table 11.13

X (number of accidents per week)	Number of weeks
0	2
1	3
2	8
3	7
4	3
5	1
6	0
7	1
8	0
9	0
10	1
11 or more	0

distribution, then the probability distribution is generally defined by

$$P(X) = (e^{-m})(m^X)/X!$$

where m is the average number of defined events per time period.

In our example, m has been calculated as 2.846, so

$$P(0) = (e^{-2.84})(2.84^0)/0! = e^{-2.8}$$

However, we might as well get Lotus to do these calculations for us, although once again, we will be hampered by the fact that Lotus does not possess a factorial function. Provided we restrict ourselves to a few values of X, however, we can deal with the majority of forms of the distribution.

Therefore (remembering that the mean value is contained in B15 of the last worksheet), make the following entry in D2:

$$(@EXP(-B\$15))*(B\$15^\wedge A2)$$

and copy it into D3..D12.

This is the numerator of the Poisson distribution expression but we still have to obtain $X!$ without a factorial expression. To do this, remember that the product of any set of numbers can be obtained by summing their logarithms and then using this sum as the exponent of the logarithm's base. So (remembering that the logarithm of zero is undefined) enter @LOG(A3) in E3 and copy this into E4..E12.

Now force Lotus to raise 10 to the power of the running total of these logarithms. The formula 10^(@SUM(E$3..E3) is entered in F3 and copied into F4..F12.

This will produce $X!$ in the cells F3..F12, but since $0! = 1$ you should complete the column by entering a value of 1 in F2. With the factorial values calculated, to obtain the Poisson probabilities all you have to do is enter +D2/F2 in G2, and copy this into G3..G12.

WORKSHEET 11.22

	A	B	C	D	E	F	G	H	I
	X	f	fX	numerator	log X	X!	P(X)	P(X<=X)	P(X>=X)
1	0	2	0	0.058067		1	0.0580	0.0581	1.0000
2	1	3	3	0.165268	0	1	0.1652	0.2233	0.9419
3	2	8	16	0.470378	0.301029	2	0.2351	0.4585	0.7767
4	3	7	21	1.338770	0.477121	6	0.2231	0.6817	0.5415
5	4	3	12	3.810347	0.602059	24	0.1587	0.8404	0.3183
6	5	1	5	10.84483	0.698970	120	0.0903	0.9308	0.1596
7	6	0	0	30.86606	0.778151	720	0.0428	0.9737	0.0692
8	7	1	7	87.84958	0.845098	5040	0.0174	0.9911	0.0263
9	8	0	0	250.0334	0.903089	40320	0.0062	0.9973	0.0089
10	9	0	0	711.6335	0.954242	362880	0.0019	0.9993	0.0027
11	10	1	10	2025.418	1	3628800	0.0005	0.9998	0.0007
12	11+	0	0				0.0001	1.0000	0.0002
13		26	74						
14	Mean	2.846							

Finally, in G13 you should enter

$$1 - @SUM(F2..F12)$$

to obtain the probability of 11 or more accidents.

You can see these probabilities in column G of the worksheet, where you should notice that we have also calculated a running total of the probabilities in column H (by the method that is now familiar).

This gives us the probability that there will be *at most* X accidents per week, and we can use this to answer a question such as: what is the probability of there being at most four accidents in a randomly selected week?

The answer is clearly 0.8404, i.e. the entry in H6.

If you want to calculate the probability of there being *at least* four accidents per week, then

$$P(X \geq 4) = 1 - P(x \leq 3)$$

This means that you can make the following entries in column I:

1. Enter 1 in I2 (since it is certain that there must be at least zero or more accidents per week).
2. In I3 enter $1 - H2$ and copy this into I4..I13.

EXAMPLE 11.17

A telephone switchboard can handle a maximum of four calls per minute without having to put customers on 'hold'.

If the number of calls arriving per minute is a Poisson random variable with a mean of three calls per minute, calculate the probability that the switchboard will be overloaded in any randomly selected period of 1 minute.

SOLUTION 11.17

With $m = 3$ per minute, the switchboard will be overloaded if five *or more* calls arrive in any period of 1 minute. So

$$P(X \geq 5) = 1 - P(X \leq 4)$$

in a Poisson Distribution with mean 3. (We say that $X \sim Po(3)$, i.e. X is distributed as a Poisson variable with mean 3.)

You can obtain the answer by entering a value of 3 for the mean value in B15 of the last worksheet and then reading the answer directly from column G ($X \geq 5$) or indirectly (by subtracting $P(X \leq 4)$ from 1) from column F.

In either case you should find the answer to be 0.1847.

EXAMPLE 11.18

A small business stocks 5 units of a particular item at the start of every working week. The demand for the item is a Poisson random variable with mean 4.5 items per working week.

The item sells for £15 per unit.

1. Calculate the probability that the business will run out of stock in any randomly selected week.
2. Calculate the expected revenue per week.
3. If the average weekly stock holding cost of an item is £2.50, would it be worthwhile for the business to stock six items at the start of every working week?

SOLUTION 11.18

1. With $m = 4.5$ per working week, a 'stock out' will occur if X (the number of items demanded per week) exceeds 5 (i.e. 6 or more). From a modified version of your Poisson worksheet (with 4.5 entered in B15) (see Worksheet 11.23) you should find this probability to be

$$P(X \geqslant 6) \text{ if } X \sim \text{Po}(4.5) = 0.2971$$

2. The expected revenue, $E(R)$, can be calculated from the following expression:

$E(R) =$
$\quad £15[P(0)(0) + P(1)(1) + P(2)(2) + P(3)(3) + P(4)(4) + P(5)(5) + P(6+)(5)]$

Notice the last term in this expression which allows for the demand to be 6 or more, in which case all 5 units of stock will be sold.

So, in H2 of your worksheet enter 15*A2*F2, and copy this into H3..H7.

This will give you the expected revenue for each of the X values 0–5 inclusive.

Finally, since the probability of six or more items being demanded is contained in G8, the entry in H8 should be 15*5*G8, giving the expected revenue if six or more items are demanded. Now the total expected revenue can be calculated in H14 from @SUM(H2..H8) to obtain $E(R) = £128.45$.

3. If six items of stock are held per week the *extra* stockholding cost will be £2.50.

The extra unit of stock will only be sold if the demand is at least equal to six items per week, and we have already calculated this probability to be

$$P(X \geqslant 6) = 0.2971$$

So, the extra revenue of £15 has a probability of occurrence of 0.2971, and an expectation of

$$0.2971(15) = £4.4565$$

WORKSHEET 11.23

	A	B	C	D	E	F	G	H
	X	numerator	log X	X!	P(X)	P(X<=X)		E(R)
1	0	0.011108		1	0.0111	0.0111	1.0000	0
2	1	0.049990	0	1	0.0499	0.0611	0.9889	0.916492
3	2	0.224957	0.301029	2	0.1124	0.1736	0.9389	5.207342
4	3	1.012307	0.477121	6	0.1687	0.3423	0.8264	15.40331
5	4	4.555382	0.602059	24	0.1898	0.5321	0.6577	31.92621
6	5	20.49922	0.698970	120	0.1708	0.7029	0.4679	52.71978
7	6	92.24650	0.778151	720	0.1281	0.8311	0.2971	22.28021
8	7	415.1092	0.845098	5040	0.0823	0.9134	0.1689	
9	8	1867.991	0.903089	40320	0.0463	0.9597	0.0866	
10	9	8405.962	0.954242	362880	0.0231	0.9829	0.0403	
11	10	37826.83	1	3628800	0.0104	0.9933	0.0171	
12	11+				0.0066	1.0000	0.0067	
13	Mean	4.5						E(R) 128.45

This clearly exceeds the additional stockholding cost and so it is worthwhile to stock six items.

If you apply a similar logic to a consideration of whether seven items should be stocked, in comparison with six, then you will find that this too is worth the extra stockholding cost, but only just.

This is because with a stock of seven the probability of a stock-out becomes

$$P(X \geq 7) = 0.1689$$

and this implies that the extra unit of stock will have an expected extra revenue of

$$0.1689(15) = £2.5335$$

which is just in excess of the extra stockholding cost of £2.50.

Not surprisingly, if eight items were stocked the extra expected revenue falls to

$$P(X \geq 8)(15) = (0.0866)(15) = £1.299$$

which is less than £2.50 and therefore not worthwhile. The optimum stock level given the average weekly demand, the stockholding cost and the price of the product therefore is 7 units.

You can also see these results in the worksheet if you alter it so that the probabilities of $X = 0, 1, 2, 3, 4, 5, 6$ and 7 or more are used to calculate the expected revenue.

With six items being stocked, the expected revenue increases to £132.91, which represents an increase of £4.46 for a cost of £2.50, and a net gain of £1.9565 (i.e. the difference between the £4.4565 extra revenue, and the £2.50 extra cost that was obtained above).

11.10 The normal distribution

You will probably have noticed that in both the binomial distribution and the Poisson distribution the fact that the random variable is a *number of outcomes* means that the values of X in these distributions must be integer. (For this reason the binomial and the Poisson distributions are said to be *discrete*, and only integer values of the random variable can have their probabilities evaluated.)

Yet many processes we may be required to consider do not lend themselves to discrete analysis, since their random variables are of a *continuous* nature.

This raises the obvious question of whether we can find a continuous probability distribution that will allow investigation of the probabilities associated with continuous random variables.

One answer is given by what is known as the normal distribution, which has an importance stemming from the fact that the random variables associated with a large number of common processes turn out to be normally distributed.

The first thing to recognize is that there is no such thing as 'the' normal distribution, since, like the binomial distribution, any normal distribution is defined in terms of two parameters.

These are the mean value (u) and the standard deviation (σ) of the data set that is assumed to be normally distributed.

Clearly this means that there is a different normal distribution for every possible combination of u and σ, meaning that there is literally an infinite number of normal distributions.

There is, however, one normal distribution known as the standard normal distribution which can be used as a template to analyze any other, nonstandard normal distribution. (An example would be an exchange rate that allows a number of different currencies each to be expressed in pounds or dollars, and then magnitudes compared.)

Even the standard normal distribution is defined by a very complex equation that is difficult to evaluate, so normal tables containing the probabilities of a standard normally distributed random variable have been constructed. (e.g. Appendix I).

But before you look at such a table, there are six points worth noting about the standard normal distribution.

1. It is constructed on the basis of a mean value of 0 and a standard deviation of 1.
   In symbols we say that
   $$X \sim N(0, 1)$$
   In other words, the random variable X is normally distributed with mean zero and unit standard deviation.
2. The standard normal distribution (like all other normal distributions) is perfectly symmetrical about its mean value, and has a characteristic 'bell' shape.
3. The probability distribution is asymptotic to the X axis on both sides of the mean value, so that the value on the Y axis never reaches zero for finite values of X (both positive and negative).
4. The total area underneath the normal distribution is 1. This means that the probability of X lying between ∞ and $-\infty$ is 1 (i.e. certainty).
5. Because of point 4 the probability of any value of X being exceeded is given by the area underneath and to the right of the X value of the normal distribution.
6. A diagram of the curve associated with the standard normal distribution would have the appearance shown in Figure 11.2.

Suppose that X is normally distributed with mean zero and unit standard deviation (i.e. $X \sim N(0, 1)$. What is the probability that X exceeds zero?

In other words, calculate
$$P(X > 0) \text{ if } X \sim N(0, 1)$$

One glance at Figure 11.2 and an appreciation of the implications of symmetry surely suggests that
$$P(X > 0) = 0.5$$

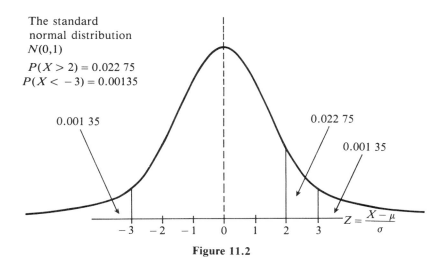

Figure 11.2

Now look at the table in Appendix I and observe that the value in the body of the table associated with a lefthand column value of zero, is 0.5 (The value in the lefthand column is called Z rather than X for reasons that will soon become apparent.)

Symmetry and common sense was all that was required for this last conclusion, but suppose we now ask for

$$P(Z > 1) \text{ if } Z \sim N(0, 1)$$

The table in Appendix I is now essential reference and we would conclude that

$$P(Z > 1) = 0.1587$$

So now let us calculate

$$P(Z > 1.96)$$

The answer is 0.0250.

This gives us an important reference point, since it implies that in a standard normal distribution, 2.5 per cent of all variable values exceed 1.96. (This has already been mentioned in Chapter 10.)

But what would be the following probability?

$$P(Z < -1.96)$$

You do not need to consult the table since symmetry comes to the rescue again to supply the answer as 0.0250.

(In fact, you cannot use the table for negative values of the variable, since the symmetry implications of the probability distribution are used to allow only positive values to be tabulated.)

Now suppose we ask for the probability that X lies *between* 1.96 and -1.96. You should be able to see that since 2.5 per cent of all values exceed 1.96, and 2.5 per cent are less than -1.96, then 95 per cent of all values must lie between 1.96 and -1.96. So

$$P(-1.96 < X < 1.96) = 0.95$$

This is a crucial result, since although we are only dealing with the standard normal distribution at the moment, it happens to be the case that for *any* normal distribution, 95 per cent of all values of the variable will lie in a range that is given by

$$u \pm 1.96(\sigma)$$

Since we happen to be dealing with the standard normal distribution at the moment, then this last expression becomes

$$0 \pm 1.96(1) = 0 \pm 1.96$$

But, provided you accept the general expression, you should be able to see that it provides an important clue as to why the table of the standard normal distribution is the *only* one that we need to evaluate the probabilities in *any* normal distribution.

So, suppose that

$$X \sim N(6, 4)$$

From our most recent discussion we would argue that 95 per cent of all X values will lie in the range

$$6 \pm 1.96(4) = 6 \pm 9.84$$

However, with the same (nonstandard) normal distribution, within what range would 87.4 per cent of all values lie?

This question is not immediately answerable as it stands, but if we refer to the standard normal distribution table, then we will see that 6.3 per cent of all values exceed a Z value of 1.53, and (by symmetry) 6.3 per cent of all values are less than a Z value of -1.53. Consequently $(100 - 6.3 - 6.3) = 87.4$ per cent of all Z values lie between 1.53 and -1.53.

Although this is true for the standard normal distribution, it is an easy matter to use this figure of 1.53 in the context of our *nonstandard distribution*.

Thus, 87.4 per cent of all variable values in a normal distribution which is $N(6, 4)$ will lie in the range

$$6 \pm 1.53(4) = 6 \pm 6.12$$

You should appreciate what we are doing here. Any normal distribution can be converted to a standard normal distribution by the knowledge that

$$u \pm \text{(standard normal distribution value of } Z)(\sigma)$$

will include $100[1 - 2(\text{standard normal distribution table value of } Z]$ per cent of all variable values.

The normal distribution

For example, if $Z = 2.01$, then the range $u \pm 2.01(\sigma)$ will include $100[1 - 2(0.022\,22)] = 95.5556$ per cent of all possible variable values (since the standard normal distribution value of $Z = 2.01$ is $0.022\,22$).

Although this is true, and easily understood, the method is needlessly tedious. We should therefore remember that in Chapter 9 we pointed out that applying the Z transformation (to obtain a Z score) also meant that the data distribution would possess a zero mean and a unit standard deviation.

In other words

$$Z = (X - \mu)/\sigma$$

will always have mean zero and unit standard deviation.

Clearly we can use this knowledge as our exchange rate between any nonstandard normal distribution and the standard one.

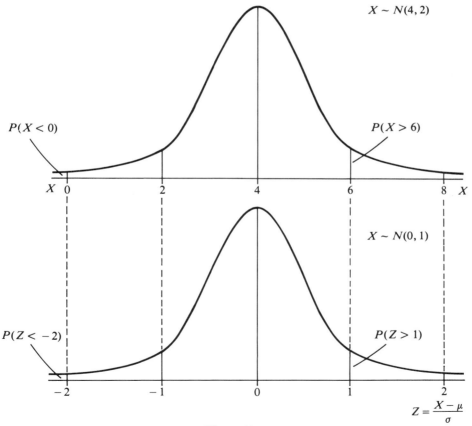

Figure 11.3

Suppose we are required to find

$$P(X > 6) \text{ in a } N(4, 2)$$

All we have to do is convert from $N(4, 2)$ to $N(0, 1)$ by using the Z transformation. Consequently, $P(X > 6)$ in a $N(4, 2)$ is identical to

$$P(Z > [(X - \mu)/\sigma] \text{ in a } N(0, 1)$$

Therefore

$$P(X > 6) = P(Z > [(6 - 4)/2]) \text{ in } N(0, 1)$$
$$= P(Z > 1)$$
$$= 0.1587$$

You can see this in Figure 11.3 where the $N(4, 2)$ distribution and the $N(0, 1)$ have had their correspondence displayed.

EXAMPLE 11.19

A company's current account balance is normally distributed with mean £10 000 and standard deviation £6000.
Calculate the probability that the company's account is overdrawn.

SOLUTION 11.19

Let X = the company's current account balance. Therefore

$$X \sim N(10\,000, 6000)$$

Since the account will be overdrawn if X is less than zero, we require

$$P(X < 0) \text{ in } N(10\,000, 6000) = P(Z < [(0 - 10\,000)/6000]) \text{ in } N(0, 1)$$

Therefore

$$P(X < 0) = P(Z < -1.666) \text{ in } N(0, 1) = P(Z > 1.6666) = 0.0485$$

EXAMPLE 11.20

Over a period of two years the exchange rate between pounds and dollars was normally distributed with mean $1.3 and standard deviation $0.15.
Calculate the probability that the exchange rate on a randomly selected day was:

1. Less than $1.2.
2. Greater than $1.5.
3. Between $1.35 and $1.40.
4. Between $1.25 and $1.40.

SOLUTION 11.20

Let X = the exchange rate. We know that

$$X \sim N(1.3, 0.15)$$

Now consult Figure 11.4. Therefore:

1.
$$P(X < 1.2) \text{ in } N(1.3, 0.15) = P[Z < 1.2 - 1.3)/0.15)] \text{ in } N(0, 1)$$
$$= P(Z < 0.666\,66) \text{ in } N(0, 1)$$

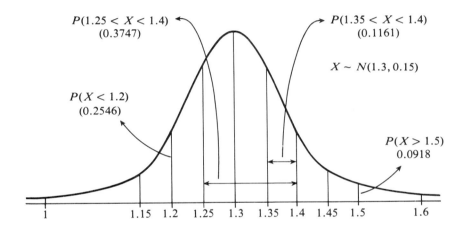

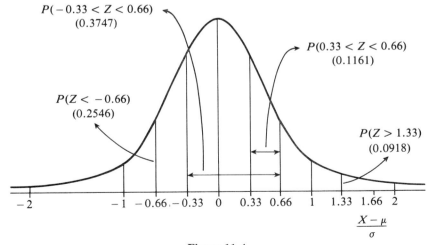

Figure 11.4

From the table in Appendix I and symmetrical logic this is seen to be equivalent to

$$P(Z > 0.666\,666) = 0.2546$$

2. $P(X > 1.5) = P(Z > 1.3333) = 0.0918$.
3. Notice that both 1.35 and 1.4 are above the mean value of the distribution. So

$$P(1.35 < X < 1.4) = P(X > 1.35) - P(X > 1.4)$$

which is equivalent to

$$P(Z > 0.333\,33) - P(Z > 0.666\,66) = 0.3707 - 0.2546 = 0.1161$$

4. In this case the two values of X lie on *opposite* sides of the mean. So

$$P(1.25 \leqslant X < 1.40) = 1 - P(X < 1.25) - P(X > 1.40)$$

which is equivalent to

$$1 - P(Z > 0.33) - P(Z > 0.6666) = 1 - 0.3707 - 0.2546 = 0.3747$$

EXAMPLE 11.21

A company's annual sales revenue is normally distributed with mean £1.8 million and standard deviation £0.4 million.

The company's annual fixed costs are £1 million.

1. Calculate the probability that the company will fail to cover its fixed costs in a randomly selected year.

The company's variable costs are normally distributed with mean £0.5 million and standard deviation £0.3 million.

2. Calculate the probability that the firm will at least break even in a randomly selected year.

SOLUTION 11.21

1. Let $R =$ the firm's annual revenue. Therefore

$$R \sim N(1.8, 0.4)$$

Consequently, the fixed costs will not be covered if

$$R < 1 \text{ in } N(1.8, 0.4)$$

Now

$$P(R < 1) \text{ in } N(1.8, 0.4) = P(Z < [(1 - 1.8)/0.4]) \text{ in } N(0, 1)$$

Therefore
$$P(R < 1) = P(Z < -2) = P(Z > 2) = 0.02275$$

2. This is a more difficult question but we can proceed as follows. Let $C =$ the firm's annual variable costs. Therefore
$$C \sim N(0.5, 0.3)$$

Now, with R still representing revenue, it follows that the variable $(R - C - 1)$ will represent profit (remembering that fixed costs are £1 million).

Consequently, in order to break even $(R - C - 1)$ must at least equal zero. This means that we need to calculate
$$P([R - C - 1] > 0)$$

Before we can do this, however, we need to know how the combined variable $(R - C - 1)$ is distributed.

To determine this we could argue as follows. If $R \sim N(1.8, 0.4)$ and $C \sim N(0.5, 0.3)$, then
$$(R - C) \sim N(1.8 - 0.5, \ [(0.4^2) + (0.3^2)]^{0.5})$$
implying that
$$(R - C) \sim N(1.3, 0.5)$$

This result derives from the following general statistical theorem:
$$\text{If } X \sim N(a, b) \quad \text{and} \quad Y \sim N(c, d)$$
then
$$(X \pm Y) \sim N(a \pm c, \ [(b^2) + (d^2)]^{0.5})$$

Notice that the standard deviation of the difference between any two or more normally distributed variables is the same as the standard deviation of the sum of these two variables, and that this is obtained by summing the individual variances and then taking the square root of this sum.

Now if
$$(R - C) \sim N(1.3, 0.5)$$
then
$$(R - C - 1) \sim N(1.3 - 1, \ 0.5) = N(0.3, 0.5)$$

(Remember that since fixed costs by definition do not vary, their standard deviation is zero.)

To solve our problem we therefore require $P([R - C - 1] > 0$ in a distribution that is $N(0.3, 0.5)$, which is equivalent to

$$P(Z > [(0 - 0.3)/0.5]) = P(Z > -0.6) \text{ in } N(0, 1)$$
$$= 1 - P(Z < 0.6)$$
$$= 1 - P(Z > 0.6)$$
$$= 1 - 0.2743$$
$$= 0.7257$$

11.11 Exercises

11.1

On any given day a stall-holder has a 0.9 probability of earning £100 and a 0.1 probability of losing £100.

Calculate the probability that over a period of three randomly selected days the stall holder will break even.

11.2

In a particular income group, 40 per cent of the individuals are 'reached' by a new advertising campaign.

If they are reached, then the probability that they will buy the product within a year is 70 per cent, while 20 per cent of those who are *not reached* will buy the product within a year *anyway*.

(a) Calculate the probability that a randomly selected individual will buy the product within a year.
(b) If the income group consists of 10 000 individuals, and if the product is sold for £10, calculate the expected annual income to the advertiser.
(c) If the advertising campaign cost a total of £35 000 per annum, was it a worthwhile investment?
(d) With the given response rate, what proportion of the income group would have to be reached if the advertising campaign was to break even in the first year?

11.3

A manufacturing process has produced the following sequence of defective (D) and nondefective (N) batches over its last 13 production runs:

$$D \ N \ N \ N \ D \ N \ N \ N \ D \ N \ N \ D$$

(a) Calculate the probability that the 14th production run will produce a defective batch.
(b) Calculate the equilibrium probability of a defective batch.
(c) A defective batch costs the firm £10 000, but for an expenditure of £1000 per batch the equilibrium probability of producing a defective batch can be reduced to 0.2. Is such an investment worthwhile?

11.4

The probability that a firm will make a profit of £10 million on a particular type of project is 0.8, and the probability that it will make a loss of £2 million is 0.2. Six such projects are carried out.

(a) Calculate the probability that two projects will make a loss.
(b) Calculate the expected profit/loss from the six projects.
(c) Calculate the probability that at least two projects will make a loss.
(d) If the expected profit/loss from undertaking six of these projects had to be at least £50 million, what probability of a loss-making project would have to prevail?

11.5

A car-hire firm owns a fleet of eight cars. The daily demand for these cars is a Poisson random variable with a mean value of five cars per day. The cars are rented for £100 per day.

(a) Calculate the probability that on a randomly selected day there will be a demand for six cars.
(b) Calculate the probability that on a randomly selected day the entire fleet is rented out.
(c) Calculate the firm's expected revenue.

11.6

The stock market price of a firm's shares over a given period is normally distributed with mean £10 and standard deviation £2.50.

If the share price falls below £8 but stays above £5, then there is 0.3 probability of a takeover bid, while if the price falls to or below £5 but stays above £2, then there is a 0.6 probability of a takeover bid.

If the share price falls to or below £2, then a takeover bid is certain.

(a) Calculate the probability that the share price will be: (i) below £8; (ii) below £5; (iii) below £2; (iv) between £8 and £5; (v) between £5 and £2.
(b) Calculate the probability of a takeover bid being made in the given period.

11.7

The production line of a manufacturing firm employs machines of three different ages.

Fifty per cent of its plant is ten years old, 30 per cent is five years old and 20 per cent is two years old.

From past experience it is known that machines that are ten years old have a 0.25 probability of malfunctioning in any given eight-hour shift, while those that are five years old have a 0.1 probability, and those that are two years old have a 0.03 probability.

(a) Calculate the probability that a randomly selected machine will malfunction in any given shift.
(b) Given that a randomly selected machine has malfunctioned, what is the probability that it was ten years old?
(c) Given that a randomly selected machine has malfunctioned, calculate the probability that it was at least five years old.
(d) The malfunction of a machine has the following effect upon maintenance costs and loss of revenue in any shift:

Machine type	Maintenance cost	Lost revenue
10 year old	300	1000
5 year old	150	2000
2 year old	200	3000

A machine is randomly selected from a shift. Calculate the expected cost to the firm from a malfunction in this machine in this shift.

(e) A machine has malfunctioned during a given shift. Calculate the expected cost to the firm in this shift.

11.12 Solutions to the exercises

11.1

Let X = the number of days that a profit of £100 is made. Therefore

$$X \sim Bi(3, 0.9)$$

You can evaluate the probability distribution of X from this expression if you want, but in fact there is no need. This is because if you tabulate all possible outcomes, and the income associated with each outcome, then you will find that a break even outcome cannot occur over the space of two days. You can see this below.

X	Profit	Loss	Net profit
0	0	300	−300
1	100	200	−100
2	200	100	100
3	300	0	300

11.2

The probability tree is shown in Table 11.14.

Table 11.14

Reached/not reached	Buy/not buy	Outcome (X)	P(X)	E(X) £000s
R(0.4)	B	R & B(0.7)	0.28	28
R(0.4)	NB	R & NB(0.3)	0.12	0
NR(0.6)	B	NR & B(0.2)	0.12	12
NR(0.6)	NB	NR & NB(0.8)	0.48	0

(a) $P(\text{buy}) = P(\text{reached and buy}) + P(\text{not reached and buy})$

$$P(\text{buy}) = 0.28 + 0.12 = 0.4$$

(b) $E(\text{income}) = 0.4(10)(10000) = £40\,000$

(c) Without the advertising campaign the expected income would be

$$P(\text{NR \& B})(10)(10\,000) = 0.12(10)(10\,000) = £12\,000$$

From this you can see that the effect of the campaign is to increase the expected income by £28 000. This clearly does not justify the expenditure of £35 000.

(d) Let the proportion of potential buyers reached by the campaign = p.

To have the same net income effect as without any advertising (£12 000) the expected income must equal £47 000. That is

Without advertising:

expected income = 12 000
Outlay   =   0
Net expected income = 12 000

With advertising:

expected income = 40 000
Outlay   = 35 000
Net expected income   = 5000

Only if the expected income is £47 000 will the campaign be justified.

Remembering that more potential buyers being reached means less potential buyers *not being reached* (and therefore less who would have bought the product anyway), we require

$$[p(0.7) + (1-p)(0.2)]\,100\,000 = 47\,000$$

implying that

$$0.5p = 0.27 \quad \text{and that} \quad p = 0.54$$

(You might have thought that a 'reach rate' of 0.5 would have sufficed, since

$$0.7p(100\,000) = 35\,000$$

implies that $p = 0.5$ is sufficient to produce enough income to cover the £35 000 cost of the campaign. But this is to forget the effect of the reduced number of unreached buyers who would have bought anyway. Some of the advertising expenditure is wasted in terms of its net effect.)

11.3

Using the Markov chain worksheet (Worksheet 11.21), with a defective batch being represented by 1 and a nondefective batch by 0, we find that with an initial status vector in H3..H4 of

$$s = \begin{bmatrix} 1 \\ 0 \end{bmatrix} = \begin{matrix} P(1) \\ P(0) \end{matrix}$$

Worksheet 11.24 can be obtained.

(a) P(defective batch on the 14th day) $= 0$. There is an intuitive meaning to this apparently strange result. If you observe the sequence, then you will see that there were no occasions when there were two successive defective batches. Consequently, since the 13th day had a defective batch, the Markov chain technique concludes (somewhat dangerously) that such an eventuality is impossible. This reflects the frequently held, though unsatisfactory, view that because some event has never occurred in the past, it is incapable of occurring in the future.

```
WORKSHEET 11.24
         A      B  C  D  E    F           G              H
  1   Outcome  1  1  1  0  0  0  0  1
  2       1                         [T]            [s]
  3            0  0  1  0  0        0 0.333333    0.259259
  4            0  0  0  1  0        1 0.666666    0.740740
  5            0  0  0  1  0    [e]                  ē
  6            0  0  0  1  0  0.259259               0.25
  7            1  0  0  0  1  0.740740               0.75
  8            0  0  1  0  0
  9            0  0  0  1  0
 10            0  0  0  1  0
 11            1  0  0  0  1
 12            0  0  1  0  0
 13            0  0  0  1  0
 14            1  0  0  1  1
 15   Total       0  3  6  3
```

The entries in F3..G4 represent:
F3: $P(1/1) = P$(defective/previous item defective)
F4: $P(0/1) = P$(nondefective/previous item defective)
G3: $P(1/0) = P$(defective/previous item nondefective)
G4: $P(0/0) = P$(nondefective/previous item nondefective)

(b) $P(\text{defective}) = 0.25$ (from the equilibrium value of $P(1)$ in this Markov chain).

(c) If the equilibrium probability of a defective batch was reduced to 0.2, then the expected net saving per batch would be

$$0.05(10\,000) = £500$$

which is less than the cost of £1000 per batch in achieving this reduction and therefore not worthwhile.

11.4

(a) Let $X =$ the number of loss-making projects. Therefore

$$X \sim \text{Bi}(6, 0.2)$$

Consequently

$$P(2) = {}_6C_2[(0.2^2)(0.8^4)] = 0.245\,76$$

(b) Since $X \sim \text{Bi}(6, 0.2)$ we would expect that $6(0.2) = 1.2$ projects will make a loss, and 4.8 will make a profit.

Therefore, the expected profit from six such projects will be given by

$$E(\text{profit}) = (1.2)(-2) + (4.8)(10) = £45.6 \text{ million}$$

(c) We require

$$\begin{aligned}P(X \geqslant 2) &\text{ in Bi}(6, 0.2) \\ &= 1 - P(0) - P(1) \\ &= 1 - {}_6C_0[(0.2^0)(0.8^6)] - {}_6C_1[(0.2^1)(0.8^5)] \\ &= 1 - 0.2621 - 0.3932 = 0.3446\end{aligned}$$

(d) Let $p =$ the required probability of a loss making project. Therefore

$$6p(-2) + 6(1-p)(10) = 50$$

implying that $p = 0.1388$ at most.

11.5

(a) Let $X =$ the number of cars demanded per day. Therefore

$$X \sim \text{Po}(5)$$
$$P(6) = (e^{-5})(5^6)/6! = 0.1462$$

(b) The entire fleet will be rented out if $X \geqslant 8$. From a modified version of Worksheet 11.23 you should find this probability to be

$$P(X \geqslant 8) = 0.1334$$

(c) The expected revenue values are calculated in column H of Worksheet 11.25, and give a total expected revenue of £1963.84.

WORKSHEET 11.25

	A	B	C	D	E	F	G	H
1	X	numerator	log X	X!	P(X)	P(X<=X)	P(X>=X)	E(R)
2	0	0.006737		1	0.0067	0.0067	1.0000	0
3	1	0.33689	0	1	0.0336	0.0404	0.9933	4.042768
4	2	0.168448	0.301029	2	0.0842	0.1247	0.9596	24.93040
5	3	0.842243	0.477121	6	0.1403	0.2650	0.8753	79.50777
6	4	4.211216	0.602059	24	0.1754	0.4405	0.7350	176.1973
7	5	21.05608	0.698970	120	0.1754	0.6160	0.5595	307.9803
8	6	105.2804	0.778151	720	0.1462	0.7622	0.3840	457.3100
9	7	526.4021	0.845098	5040	0.1044	0.8666	0.2378	606.6398
10	8	2632.010	0.903089	40320	0.0652	0.9319	0.1334	307.2314
11	9	13160.05	0.954242	362880	0.0362	0.9682	0.0681	
12	10	65800.26	1	3628800	0.0181	0.9863	0.0318	
13	11+				0.0136	1.0000	0.0137	
14								
15	Mean	5						1963.839

11.6

(a) Let $X =$ the stock market price of the firm's shares. Therefore

$$X \sim N(10, 2.50)$$

Consequently:

(i) $P(X < 8)$ in $N(10, 2.50) = P(Z < -0.8)$ in $N(0, 1)$ which equals

$$P(Z > 0.8) = 0.2119$$

(ii) $P(X < 5)$ in $N(10, 2.50) = P(Z < -2)$ in $N(0, 1)$, which equals

$$P(Z > 2) = 0.022\,75$$

(iii) $P(X < 2)$ in $N(10, 2.50) = P(Z < -3.2)$ in $N(0, 1)$, which equals

$$P(Z > 3.2) = 0.000\,69$$

(iv) $P(5 < X < 8) = P(X < 8) - P(X < 5) = 0.2119 - 0.022\,75 = 0.189\,15$.

(v) $P(2 < X < 5) = P(X < 5) - P(X < 2) = 0.022\,75 - 0.000\,69 = 0.022\,06$.

(b) the overall probability of a takeover bid being made can be evaluated from the following:

Share price	Takeover	Probability
5 < price < 8 (0.189 15)	T (0.3)	0.056 74
2 < price < 5 (0.022 06)	T (0.6)	0.013 24
price < 2 (0.000 69)	T (1)	0.000 69

Consequently

$$P(\text{takeover}) = 0.056\,74 + 0.013\,24 + 0.000\,69 = 0.070\,67$$

11.7

You can use Worksheet 11.10 to model this problem, as shown in Worksheet 11.26.

(a) $P(\text{malfunction}) = 0.125 + 0.03 + 0.006 = 0.161$.
(b) $P(10 \text{ years old}/\text{malfunction}) = (0.5)(0.25)/0.161 = 0.7764$.
(c) $P(10 \text{ or } 5 \text{ years old}/\text{malfunction}) = (0.125 + 0.03)/0.161 = 0.9627$.
(d) Ten years old: $E(\text{cost per shift}) = 0.125(1300) = £162.5$
     Five years old: $E(\text{cost per shift}) = 0.03(2150) = £64.5$
     Two years old: $E(\text{cost per shift}) = 0.006(3200) = £19.2$

Consequently, the expected cost from a malfunction in a randomly selected machine is

$$£162.5 + £64.5 + £19.2 = £246.20$$

```
WORKSHEET 11.26
       A       B        C         D        E      F        G
   1   Age     Prob     Fault/OK  Prob     P(X)   Cost     E(cost)
   2
   3
   4   10      0.5      M         0.25     0.125  1300     162.5
   5
   6   10      0.5      NM        0.75     0.375  0        0
   7
   8   5       0.3      M         0.1      0.03   2150     64.5
   9
  10   5       0.3      NM        0.9      0.27   0        0
  11
  12   2       0.2      M         0.03     0.006  3200     19.2
  13
  14   2       0.2      NM        0.97     0.194  0        0
  15
  16                                              E(cost per shift) 246.2
```

10 = 10 year old machine; 5, 5 year old machine; 2, 2 year old machine; M, malfunction; NM, no malfunction.

(e) In this case we know that a malfunction has occurred, and so it is the conditional probabilities that should be used in the calculation of the expected cost. Therefore

$$P(10 \text{ year old}/\text{malfunction}) = 0.7764 \text{ (as calculated above)}$$
$$P(5 \text{ year old}/\text{malfunction}) = (0.3)(0.1)/0.161 = 0.1863$$
$$P(2 \text{ year old}/\text{malfunction}) = (0.2)(0.03)/0.161 = 0.0373$$

Consequently

$$\text{expected cost} = 0.7764(1300) + 0.1863(2150) + 0.0373(3200)$$
$$= £1529.23$$

Notice that this expected cost is considerably higher than the one obtained in part (d) above. The simple reason for this is that in the most recent case we know that a machine has malfunctioned and are required to calculate the expected cost of this malfunction. In the previous case, however, the machine that was randomly selected may or may not have broken down in that shift, and so the expected cost takes account of the probability that no malfunction will occur.

Of course, if we take the expected cost of a known malfunction (£1529.23) and multiply it by the probability of a malfunction occurring in any shift (0.161), then we should obtain the expected cost of a malfunction in a randomly selected machine (which may or may not malfunction). That is

$$(0.161)(1529.23) = £246.20$$

Appendix

Appendix: The standard normal distribution

$Z=(x-\mu)/\sigma$	0.00	0.01	0.02	0.03	0.04	0.05	0.06	0.07	0.08	0.09
0.0	0.5000	0.4960	0.4920	0.4880	0.4840	0.4801	0.4761	0.4721	0.4681	0.4641
0.1	0.4602	0.4562	0.4522	0.4483	0.4443	0.4404	0.4364	0.4325	0.4286	0.4247
0.2	0.4207	0.4168	0.4129	0.4090	0.4052	0.4013	0.3974	0.3936	0.3897	0.3859
0.3	0.3821	0.3783	0.3745	0.3707	0.3669	0.3632	0.3594	0.3557	0.3520	0.3483
0.4	0.3446	0.3409	0.3372	0.3336	0.3300	0.3264	0.3228	0.3192	0.3156	0.3121
0.5	0.3085	0.3050	0.3015	0.2981	0.2946	0.2912	0.2877	0.2843	0.2810	0.2776
0.6	0.2743	0.2709	0.2676	0.2643	0.2611	0.2578	0.2546	0.2514	0.2483	0.2451
0.7	0.2420	0.2389	0.2358	0.2327	0.2296	0.2266	0.2236	0.2206	0.2177	0.2148
0.8	0.2119	0.2090	0.2061	0.2033	0.2005	0.1977	0.1949	0.1922	0.1894	0.1867
0.9	0.1841	0.1814	0.1788	0.1762	0.1736	0.1711	0.1685	0.1660	0.1635	0.1611
1.0	0.1587	0.1562	0.1539	0.1515	0.1492	0.1469	0.1446	0.1423	0.1401	0.1379
1.1	0.1357	0.1335	0.1314	0.1292	0.1271	0.1251	0.1230	0.1210	0.1190	0.1170
1.2	0.1151	0.1131	0.1112	0.1093	0.1075	0.1056	0.1038	0.1020	0.1003	0.985
1.3	0.0968	0.0951	0.0934	0.0918	0.0901	0.0885	0.0869	0.0853	0.0838	0.0823
1.4	0.0808	0.0793	0.0778	0.0764	0.0749	0.0735	0.0721	0.0708	0.0694	0.0681

1.5	0.0668	0.0655	0.0643	0.0630	0.0618	0.0606	0.0594	0.0582	0.0571	0.0559
1.6	0.0548	0.0537	0.0526	0.0516	0.0505	0.0495	0.0485	0.0475	0.0465	0.0455
1.7	0.0446	0.0436	0.0427	0.0418	0.0409	0.0401	0.0392	0.0384	0.0375	0.0367
1.8	0.0359	0.0351	0.0344	0.0336	0.0329	0.0322	0.0314	0.0307	0.0301	0.0294
1.9	0.0287	0.0281	0.0274	0.0268	0.0262	0.0256	0.0250	0.0244	0.0239	0.0233
2.0	0.02275	0.02222	0.02169	0.02118	0.02068	0.02018	0.01970	0.01923	0.01876	0.01831
2.1	0.01786	0.01743	0.01700	0.01659	0.01618	0.01578	0.01539	0.01500	0.01463	0.01426
2.2	0.01390	0.01355	0.01321	0.01287	0.01255	0.01222	0.01191	0.01160	0.01130	0.01101
2.3	0.01072	0.01044	0.01017	0.00990	0.00964	0.00939	0.00914	0.00889	0.00866	0.00842
2.4	0.00820	0.00798	0.00776	0.00755	0.00734	0.00714	0.00695	0.00676	0.00657	0.00639
2.5	0.00621	0.00604	0.00587	0.00570	0.00554	0.00539	0.00523	0.00508	0.00494	0.00480
2.6	0.00466	0.00453	0.00440	0.00427	0.00415	0.00402	0.00391	0.00379	0.00368	0.00357
2.7	0.00347	0.00336	0.00326	0.00317	0.00307	0.00298	0.00289	0.00280	0.00272	0.00264
2.8	0.00256	0.00248	0.00240	0.00233	0.00226	0.00219	0.00212	0.00205	0.00199	0.00193
2.9	0.00187	0.00181	0.00175	0.00169	0.00164	0.00159	0.00154	0.00149	0.00144	0.00139
3.0	0.00135									
3.1	0.00097									
3.2	0.00069									
3.3	0.00048									
3.4	0.00034									
3.5	0.00023									
3.6	0.00016									
3.7	0.00011									
3.8	0.00007									
3.9	0.00005									
4.0	0.00003									

Index

@ABS function 21
algebraic modelling 31
  and equations 51
  and flexibility 32
  and functions 46
  and indices 40
  and spreadsheets 32–4
annual percentage rate 203
annuities 144
  definition of 144
  terminal value of 145
arithmetic mean 413
  calculation of 413
  limitations of 415
arithmetic progression 95
argument of Lotus functions 20
asset 167
  appreciation 167
  depreciation 84, 93
  growth rates 167
association 480
asymptote 83
@AVG function 21, 414

bar chart 409
base 86
  of exponential functions 94
  of logarithmic functions 86
  year 435
Bayes' theorem 539

binomial distribution 566

calculus 338
  and derivative 342
  and price elasticity 358
  differential 338
  rules of differentiation 343, 364, 369
causation 48, 480
cell address 3
central tendency 398
  arithmetic mean 413
  geometric mean 416
  harmonic mean 419
  measures of 412, 420, 433
  median 414
  mode 414
charts *see* diagrams
class interval 402
coefficient 428
  of correlation 470
  of rank correlation 485
  of variation 428
combination 568
compounding 136
  and fractional years 142
  continuous 164
  formulae 137
  period 160

conditional
  probabilities 528, 537
  nests 37
  prediction in regression 504
  tests 21, 36
confidence range 475, 476
/Copy command 13
  absolute 15
  dollar fixing 16
  relative 13
conformability 283
constant exponential growth 374
continuous
  compounding 164
  data 402
  depreciation 194
  discounting 191
constraints
  binding 229
  linear 226, 229
  non binding 229
correlation 470
  coefficient 470
  meaning of 471
  rank 485
@COUNT function 21, 486, 487
@CTERM function 140
cumulative frequency 404
  calculation of 404, 405
  diagram of 405
cursor movement 5

data 397
  characteristics 398
  collation 398, 399–401
  collection 397
  continuous 402
  discrete 406
  presentation 398, 408
  set 397
/Data command
  Distribution 400, 406
  Fill 95
  Matrix invert 288

  Matrix multiply 283
  Regression 465
degrees of freedom 468
dependent variables 48, 458
depreciation 84, 193
derivative 342
  and maximization 354
  and minimization 354
  and stationary points 350
  as a function of x 348
  as gradient of function 346
  calculation 343
  definition 342
  second 355
deviation
  mean 425
  standard 426
diagrams
  bar 409
  line 27
  pie 411
  stacked bar 409
differentiation
  basic rules of 343, 349
  of chain of functions 364
  of exponential functions 372
  of product of two functions 369
  principles of 339, 343
discounting
  and annual percentage rate 203
  and depreciation 193
  and financial securities 206
  and inflation 209
  and internal rate of return 201
  and investment appraisal 195
  and multiple income streams 185
  and present value 182
  continuous 191
  formula 183
  period 190
dispersion 398, 424
  in collated data sets 433
  in simple data sets 424
  relative 428

Index 601

distribution
  binomial 566
  frequency 399
  normal 577, 581
  Poisson 571
  probability 526, 577
  standard normal 578
dual program 251, 310

e, the number 94
  and depreciation 375
  and exponential function 94
  and growth 164
  deriviation of 163
elasticity 358
electricity usage model 496–505
endogenous 32
endowment 155
equations
  behavioural 112
  exponential 90
  in modelling 51, 113
  linear 60
  logarithmic 89
  matrix solution method 289
  quadratic 78
  simultaneous 53, 70, 72, 289
  solution methods 51, 78, 94, 289
equilibrium 112
equivalent annual rate 166
ERR message 84
error
  in regression 462
  standard 468
escape key 5, 6
events
  conditional 528
  dependent 528
  exogenous 33
  independent 525
  joint 521
  mutually exclusive 521
@EXP function 94
exponential function 90

and compounding 164
and discounting 194
and growth rates 167, 373
extrapolation 465

factorial 568
feedback 480
/File commands
  List 24
  Retrieve 24
  Save 24
financial security appraisal 206
frequency
  cumulative 404
  distribution 399
  polygon 401
function 46
  and dependence 48
  and modelling
  exponential 372
  general form 46–7
  hyperbolic 81
  linear 60
  logarithmic 86
  logistic 379
  production 228, 260
  quadratic 74
@FV function 146

geometric mean 416
geometric series 100
  definition 100
  infinite 109
gradient 61
/Graph command
  A–F range 25
  Options 26
  Type 25
  View 25
  X range 25

harmonic mean 419
@HLOOKUP function 422
hyperbolic function 81

identity matrix   280
@IF function   21–3, 36, 448
independent
  events   528
  observations   468
  variables   458
index numbers
  base weighted   437, 439
  construction of   435
  current weighted   437, 439
  expenditure   437
  price weighted   437, 439
  quantity weighted   437, 439
  simple   436
indices   40
@INT function   546
intercept   61
interest
  compound   136
  rate   130
  simple   132
interpolation   465
inter-quartile range   423–4
  internal rate of return   201
input-output analysis
  simple model   290
  solution by matrix   292
inventories
  control methods   380
  simulating random patterns of   546–58
inverse matrix   288
@IRR function   202

joint
  event   521
  probability   523

least squares   462
  line   465
  regression   462
  technique   464
linear function   60
  gradient   61

graph of   63–4
  intercept   61
linear programming   226, 303
  and choice of production techniques   253
  and constraints   227
  and definition of variables   228
  duality 250, 310
  formulation   229
  maximization   236
  minimization   246
  on Lotus   236
  sensitivity of solution   240, 311
  simplex method   261, 303
  shadow costs   252, 311
LINPRO   305
logarithm   86
  common   86
  operational rules   88
  natural   94
logarithmic function   86
  in equation solving   94, 126
@LOG function   86
logistic function   379
  equation of   379
  graph of   380
Lotus
  data entry   6
  formulae   9
  function keys   8
  functions   20–3
  menu commands   12

macro economic model   112–16
manual recalculation   546
marginal cost   388
Markov chains   558
matrix
  addition   281
  identity   280
  inversion   288
  multiplication   283
  null   280
  subtraction   281

matrix (*continued*)
  transition   561
  transposition   298
@MAX function   21
maximum
  calculus conditions for   354
mean
  arithmetic   413
  deviation   425
  geometric   416
  harmonic   419
median   414
@MIN function   21
minimum
  calculus conditions for   354
mode   414
mutually exclusive   521

net present value   196
normal distribution   577
@NPV function   190, 197
null matrix   280

parameter   33
pie chart   411
@PMT function   157
Poisson distribution   571
present value   181
  and investment appraisal   195
  calculation of   183
price elasticity   358
primal program   251
probability   520
  and relative frequency   520
  binomial   566
  conditional   528, 537
  joint   521
  Poisson   571
  tree   525
profit maximization
  and differentiation   388
  and linear programming   245
proportional rates of growth   374
@PV function   187

quadratic function   77
  equation of   77
  formula   78
  graphs of   75–9
/Quit command   24

@RAND function   546
random variables   519
  and simulation   546
  expected value of   533
range   424
rank correlation   485
rate of change   339
recursive   133
reducing balance   155
regression   456
  coefficients   464
  confidence range   475
  error terms   463
  equation   465
  formula   464
  least squares method   461–2
  logarithmic transformation   481–2
  proportional unexplained
    variation   469
  simple model   457
  standard error of coefficients   472, 478
  standard error of estimate   468
  total sum of squares   469
  unexplained variation   469

sampling variation   472
scalar number   279
scale
  cardinal   485
  ordinal   485
  normal   579
scatter diagram   461
seasonal adjustment   492
seasonal variation   488
series
  arithmetic   95
  geometric   100

series (*continued*)
  infinite   109
shadow cost   252, 311
  of correlation coefficient   471
  of regression coefficients   475
simplex method   261, 303
simulation   546–58
simultaneous equation system   289
sinking fund
  definition of   148
  terminal value of   149
@SQRT function   21
standard deviation   426
standard error
  of estimate   468
  of regression coefficients   472, 478
standard normal distribution   578
stationary points   350
status indicator   4
@STD function   427
stock accumulation model   552–8
@SUM function   21
sum of squared deviations   426
sum of squared errors   464

tax model   34–8
@TERM function   150
terminal value   149
time series
  additive model   492
  multiplicative model   492–3
  regression trend   488
  residual   488
  seasonal adjustment   492
transition matrix   561
transpose matrix   298

universal constant   31

@VAR function   427
variables
  controlled   50
  dependent   48, 458
  dual   250
  endogenous   32
  exogenous   33
  independent   48, 458
  slack   303
variance   426
vector
  column   279
  row   279
@VLOOKUP function   422

weighted index numbers   437, 439
/Worksheet commands
  Column   18
  Delete   19–20
  Erase   17
  Global   18
  Insert   18–19

Z scores   429